PRACTICAL NUTRITION IN TODAY'S WORLD

A Customized Version of *Nutrition: Real People, Real Choices*, Third Edition, by Clinton D. Allred, Nancy D. Turner and Karen Geismar

Andrea Villarreal
Susan Gaumont

Kendall Hunt
publishing company

Content noted with an asterisk (*) was provided by Andrea Villarreal and Susan Gaumont.

www.kendallhunt.com
Send all inquiries to:
4050 Westmark Drive
Dubuque, IA 52004-1840

PAK ISBN: 978-1-5249-0204-9
Text Alone ISBN: 978-1-5249-0205-6

Printed in the United States of America

Contents

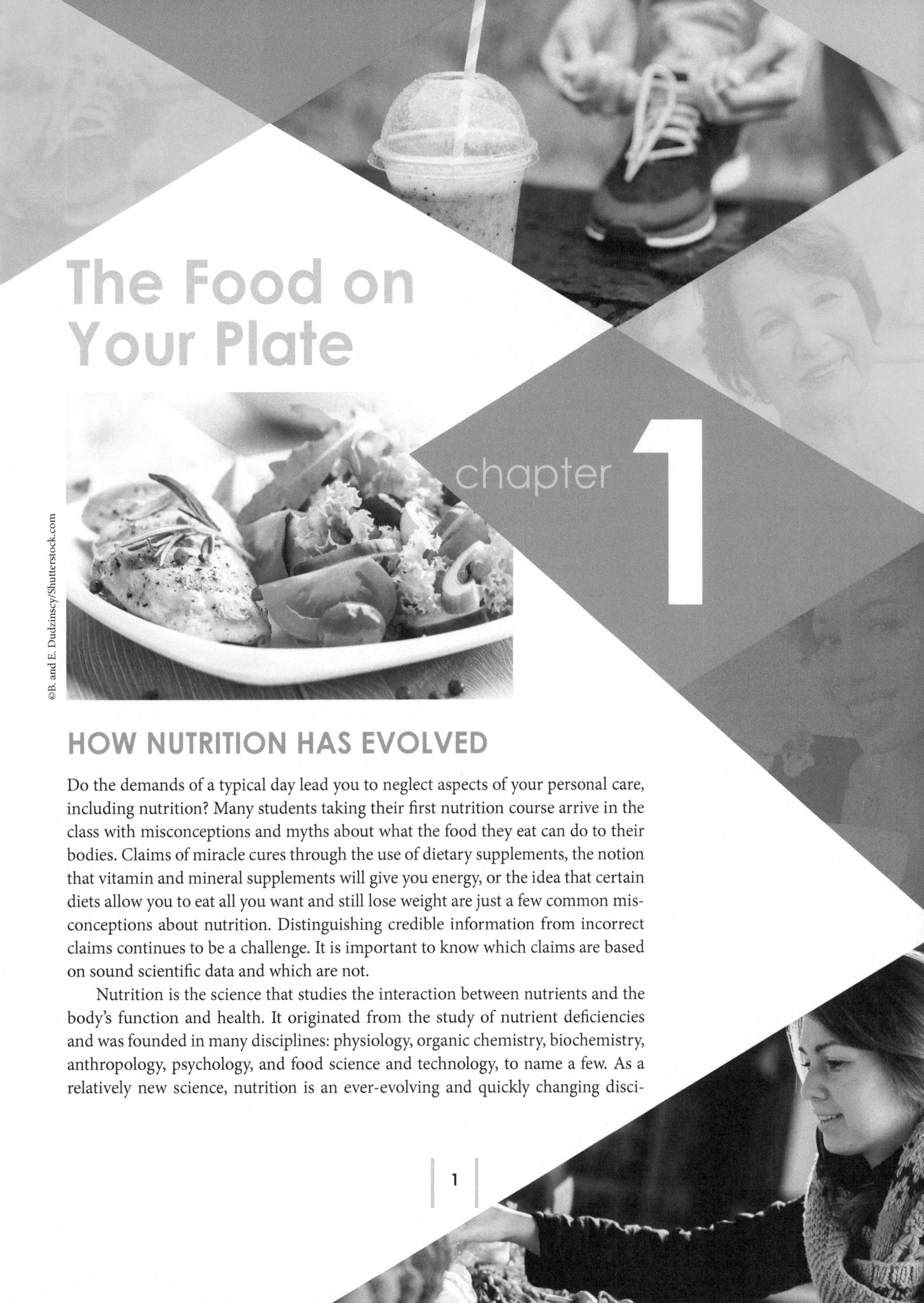

The Food on Your Plate

chapter 1

©B. and E. Dudzinscy/Shutterstock.com

HOW NUTRITION HAS EVOLVED

Do the demands of a typical day lead you to neglect aspects of your personal care, including nutrition? Many students taking their first nutrition course arrive in the class with misconceptions and myths about what the food they eat can do to their bodies. Claims of miracle cures through the use of dietary supplements, the notion that vitamin and mineral supplements will give you energy, or the idea that certain diets allow you to eat all you want and still lose weight are just a few common misconceptions about nutrition. Distinguishing credible information from incorrect claims continues to be a challenge. It is important to know which claims are based on sound scientific data and which are not.

Nutrition is the science that studies the interaction between nutrients and the body's function and health. It originated from the study of nutrient deficiencies and was founded in many disciplines: physiology, organic chemistry, biochemistry, anthropology, psychology, and food science and technology, to name a few. As a relatively new science, nutrition is an ever-evolving and quickly changing disci-

Look familiar? With all the nutrition information available, how do you make good decisions about what to purchase at the grocery store?

pline. Today the field of nutrition has evolved to include various interactions with toxicology, behavioral and sociological influence, chronic disease development, and health promotion. Many of us are interested in how food and nutrients can promote better health and prevent and treat certain diseases. Much of the interest and some of the myths about nutrition stem from the potential role of nutrients as medicine; that is, can certain nutrients cure a particular disease? You will discover in this chapter and throughout this book that much of what we know about nutrition has evolved from studies of disease and it remains an active area of research in order to continue developing new information.

The nutritional concerns of the American public have changed over the years as well. Early in the 20th century, undernutrition or nutritional deficiencies was the primary nutrition problem. This is not necessarily the case now as the types of foods that Americans consume have changed since the early 20th century. Today, many Americans eat more refined foods and participate in less physical activity. The combination of our less-than-ideal nutritional intake, excess Calorie intake, and decreasing physical activity is harmful to our health as a nation.

How Do We Define Nutrition?

nutrient
A substance that the body needs for energy, growth, and development.

Food contains substances that are called *nutrients*. A **nutrient** is a substance that the body requires for energy, regulation of body processes, and structure. Nutrients are often classified as *essential* or *non-essential*. An *essential nutrient* is one that is necessary for life and one that the body cannot make at all or cannot make in sufficient amounts to sustain its functions. Therefore, essential nutrients must be provided by the foods we eat. A *non-essential nutrient* is one that the body can make in sufficient amounts.

An essential nutrient for one organism may not be essential for another. Let's take vitamin C, for example. You have probably heard that vitamin C is good for you and is needed in your diet. This is true; without vitamin C in your diet you would not be able to live. However, did you know that many other animals make their own vitamin C and do not require it in their diets? Cats, dogs, rats, and rabbits all make enough vitamin C for normal health and thus do not need an extra source.

What's so important about nutrition?

Other compounds or chemicals found in food, particularly plant-based foods, are being discovered that appear to provide some health benefit. These compounds are not nutrients and are not essential for life but seem to improve our health if included in the diet regularly. These plant chemicals, known as *phytochemicals*, are being isolated and studied to determine how they may protect against chronic diseases such as heart disease, cancer, and diabetes.

Classifying Nutrients

Nutrients are divided into two broad classes: (1) nutrients that provide energy and (2) nutrients that don't provide energy but do support metabolism or basic bodily functions (Table 1.1). We introduce them as general concepts here, and in subsequent chapters we expand on each.

TABLE 1.1 Summary of Nutrient Classes

Class	Nutrient	Energy (kcal/g)	Function
Nutrients that provide energy	Carbohydrate	4	Provides energy
	Lipids (fats)	9	Provides energy, stores energy
	Protein	4	Promotes growth and maintenance
Nutrients that support metabolism	Vitamins	0	Regulate biochemical reactions, antioxidants
	Minerals	0	Regulate biochemical reactions, provide structure
	Water	0	Regulates temperature, provides lubrication
Alcohol is not a nutrient, but it supplies Calories (Chapter 6).			

Plant foods, such as tea, olives, and tomatoes often have chemicals that improve your health, although they may not be considered essential.

Nutrients That Provide Energy

macronutrients

Nutrients needed in large amounts, such as carbohydrates, proteins, fats, and water.

micronutrients

Nutrients needed in small amounts, such as vitamins and minerals.

The nutrients that provide energy for the body are also referred to as **macronutrients** simply because, relative to other compounds, they are required and consumed in large amounts. This is not to suggest that the **micronutrients** are less important; they are just needed in much smaller quantities. The energy-yielding macronutrients are carbohydrate, fat, and protein. Water is a macronutrient, but it does not yield energy; it is discussed separately.

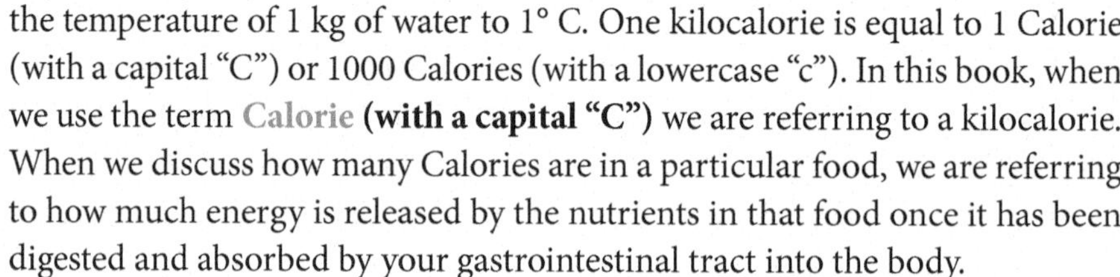

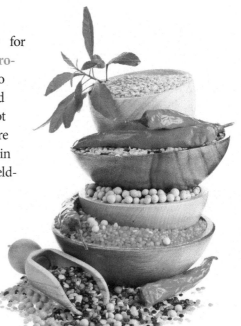

© Snowbelle/Shutterstock.com

A *Calorie* is a scientific unit used to measure energy. The Calories used to measure food energy are actually *kilocalories* (kcal). The definition of a kilocalorie is the amount of energy needed to raise the temperature of 1 kg of water to 1° C. One kilocalorie is equal to 1 Calorie (with a capital "C") or 1000 Calories (with a lowercase "c"). In this book, when we use the term **Calorie (with a capital "C")** we are referring to a kilocalorie. When we discuss how many Calories are in a particular food, we are referring to how much energy is released by the nutrients in that food once it has been digested and absorbed by your gastrointestinal tract into the body.

Calorie

A scientific unit of energy; the calories used to measure food energy are actually kilocalories (kcal). One kilocalorie, or food calorie, equals 1 Calorie or 1,000 calories.

carbohydrate

A category of macronutrients that includes energy-yielding nutrients such as starches and sugars, as well as non-energy-yielding nutrients such as fibers.

fat

An energy-yielding nutrient that is insoluble in water; it provides more than twice as much energy as carbohydrate or protein.

protein

An energy-yielding nutrient that contains nitrogen; its primary purpose is to support growth, maintenance, and repair of tissues.

CARBOHYDRATES. **Carbohydrates** include sugars, starches, and fibers. The primary function of carbohydrates is to provide energy. As a general rule, for every gram of carbohydrate consumed, 4 kcal of energy are released. Carbohydrates are composed of the elements carbon, oxygen, and hydrogen.

LIPIDS. The next class of nutrients is *lipids*, also known as fats. The most commonly consumed type of lipid is *triglyceride*. Foods such as oils and butter are common sources of **fat**. Like carbohydrate, the primary function of fat is to provide energy. Fat provides 9 kcal per gram, more than twice the amount of energy in carbohydrates. Fat, like carbohydrate, is composed of carbon, oxygen, and hydrogen, but contains twice as many hydrogen atoms as a carbohydrate. This property of having lots of hydrogen is one reason why fats yield more energy when broken down. Thus foods that have a much higher fat content deliver more energy. Other types of lipids include sterols, such as cholesterol, and phospholipids.

PROTEIN. *Although **protein** provides 4 kcals/gram, its primary purpose is to support growth, maintenance and repair of tissue. Protein is unique in that it contains nitrogen in addition to the carbon, hydrogen and oxygen found in the other macronutrients.*

How to Calculate Calories in Your Food. Now that you know the energy content of the macronutrients, you can easily calculate the energy content of a food. You need to know the portion size and how many grams of carbohydrate, fat, and/or protein are in the portion. Suppose the label on a food product indicates that it has 15 g of carbohydrate, 5 g of fat, and 8 g of protein.

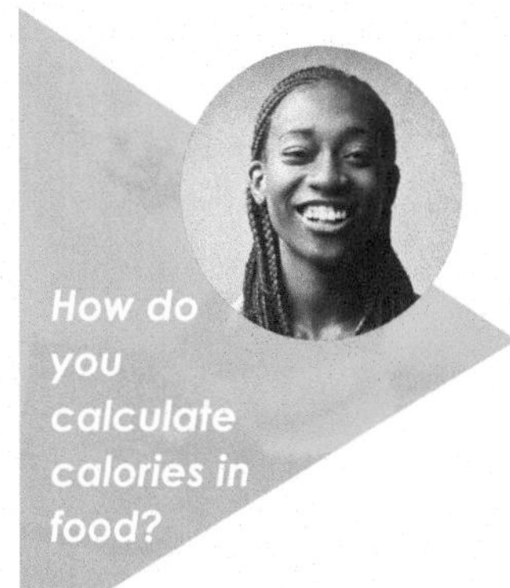

The total energy content of that food is as follows:

$$15 \text{ g carbohydrate} \times 4 \text{ kcal/g} = 60 \text{ kcal}$$
$$5 \text{ g fat} \times 9 \text{ kcal/g} = 45 \text{ kcal}$$
$$8 \text{ g protein} \times 4 \text{ kcal/g} = 32 \text{ kcal}$$
$$\text{Total kcal} = 137 \text{ kcal}$$

metabolism
The biochemical activity that occurs in cells, releasing energy from nutrients or using energy to create other substances such as proteins.

Notice that even though the food contains only 5 g of fat, they contribute more total Calories than the 8 g of protein. Not included in the previous example is **alcohol**. Alcohol contributes 7 kcal per gram consumed. That is for the alcohol alone. Mixed drinks such as a daiquiri or margarita have additional Calories from the mixers combined with the alcohol.

What Substances Are Needed to Support Your Metabolism?

Metabolism is the biochemical activity that occurs in cells, releasing energy from nutrients or using energy to create other substances such as proteins. We have briefly discussed the roles of carbohydrate, fat, and protein in this process; now let's consider the roles of **vitamins**, **minerals**, and water. Many consumers believe that vitamins and minerals will "give you energy" or act as a "pick-me-up." After all, that is how they are marketed. However, what vitamins and minerals do is help the macronutrients, such as carbohydrates, fats, and proteins, release their energy; but vitamins cannot be broken down to provide energy themselves. Some think that if a vitamin or mineral assists in a certain bodily function, consuming more of it may be better for you. For example, many people think that because vitamin C boosts the body's immune function, taking increased amounts of it will help prevent colds. However, consuming vitamins and minerals in excess can actually be harmful to your health, as they may reach a toxic level when consumed in

©MayaTheB/Shutterstock.com

Beware! Many over-the-counter supplement products make false claims regarding their role as an energy source.

large amounts. Vitamins and minerals have many other roles in the body besides supporting metabolism, including providing structure. For example, calcium is needed to build bones. We will now discuss the functions of vitamins and minerals, as well as water.

APPLICATION TIP

Taking a vitamin and mineral supplement does *not* give you any extra energy.

vitamins
A group of nutrients that contain carbon and are required in small amounts to maintain normal body function.

organic
Carbon-containing compound; derived from living matter.

fat-soluble vitamins
Vitamins that are insoluble in water, can be stored in the body for long periods of time, and do not need to be consumed daily.

water-soluble vitamins
Vitamins that dissolve in water, are not stored in the body to any extent, and are excreted mostly through the urine.

VITAMINS. **Vitamins** are a group of nutrients that contain carbon (**organic**) and are required in small amounts to maintain normal body function. Vitamins are classified into two broad categories: (1) fat-soluble and (2) water-soluble (Table 1.2). The **fat-soluble vitamins** are insoluble in water, can be stored in the body for long periods of time, and do not need to be consumed daily. Because they can be stored, they can build up and become toxic if consumed in excess. The **water-soluble vitamins** dissolve in water, are generally not stored in the body to any extent, and are excreted mostly through the urine. These normally must be consumed daily to replenish the lost vitamins. Compared to those that are fat soluble, the risk of toxicity is not as great with the water-soluble vitamins; however, this does not mean that you cannot consume toxic amounts of water-soluble vitamins. Some water-soluble vitamins can be toxic if taken in large amounts, such as vitamin C, which can cause gastrointestinal upset and kidney stones. Both groups of vitamins play significant roles in regulating metabolism and maintaining health. Many of the individual vitamins will be discussed in more detail in Chapter 8.

TABLE 1.2 Vitamins and Minerals in Human Nutrition

Vitamins	Minerals
Fat soluble:	**Major Minerals:**
Vitamin A	Sodium
Vitamin D	Potassium
Vitamin E	Chloride
Vitamin K	Calcium
	Phosphorus
	Magnesium
	Sulfur

Water soluble:	Trace Minerals
Thiamin (vitamin B_1)	Iron
Riboflavin (vitamin B_2)	Zinc
Niacin (vitamin B_3)	Copper
Pyridoxine (vitamin B_6)	Iodine
Cobalamin (vitamin B_{12})	Selenium
Folate	Manganese

minerals
Inorganic compounds required in small amounts for structure and regulating processes in the body.

inorganic
Compound or element not derived from living matter; also, does not contain carbon.

major minerals
A mineral required by the body in excess of 100 mg per day.

trace minerals
A mineral required by the body in an amount less than 100 mg per day; also called a trace element.

electrolytes
Minerals such as sodium, potassium, and chloride that assume a charge when dissolved in water.

Minerals. **Minerals** are **inorganic** compounds necessary for structure and regulating processes in the body. They are classified into two groups: **major minerals** or **trace minerals**. This classification is based on the relative requirements of each mineral. Major minerals are required by the body in amounts equal to or in excess of 100 mg per day and trace minerals are required by the body in an amount less than 100 mg per day.

Major minerals such as sodium, potassium, and chloride are often called **electrolytes**. An **electrolyte** is a mineral that assumes a charge when dissolved in water. Once electrolytes are dissolved, one of their primary roles is to maintain the body's water balance. Water balance is important for many purposes, including controlling temperature and lubricating joints.

Almost all of the minerals can be toxic if consumed in excess. This is particularly true of the trace minerals such as iron, zinc, copper, and selenium. (see Table 1.2 for complete list).

WATER. **Water** is a macronutrient that does not yield energy; however, life as we know cannot exist without water. It is the largest single component of living organisms, making up approximately 50-70 percent of their body by weight. Water balance is important for controlling temperature and lubricating joints, as well as other important functions. We will discuss water more thoroughly in Chapter 7.

APPLICATION TIP

Did you know that alcohol contains almost twice as many Calories as table sugar?

Other Food Components Consumed in the Diet

There are two compounds left that we present separately. Neither is considered a nutrient, but each impacts our health either positively or negatively.

alcohol
A nonnutrient that has 7 kcal per gram.

ALCOHOL. **Alcohol** provides 7 kcal per gram and therefore contributes to energy intake. When metabolized by the body, alcohol yields energy but does not provide vitamins and minerals, and it has other characteristics that can be detrimental to health and well-being when consumed in excess. That being said, moderate intake of alcohol may have some health benefits. Chapter 6 discusses the risks and potential benefits of alcohol use.

phytochemicals
Chemical compounds in plants that have various effects on body functions; they are not nutrients in the classical sense.

PHYTOCHEMICALS. **Phytochemicals**, while not nutrients, are chemical compounds in plants that have various effects on body functions and play an important role in health. We discuss them throughout this book. Many of these compounds have powerful health benefits, with emerging evidence of their roles in combating heart disease, cancer, diabetes, and other serious degenerative diseases.

What's HOT

SUPERFOODS

If you have been searching for the latest information on eating a healthy diet, you have probably heard the term "superfoods." It has become a buzzword in recent popular nutrition information. This term was first introduced by Steven G. Pratt, a medical doctor. He introduced the term and the concept in a popular book he authored called *Superfoods Rx*. According to his website (http://www.superfoodsrx.com/superfoods/), superfoods are referred to as being high in critical nutrients and beneficial phytochemicals, and low in Calories. Foods such as these are often referred to as nutrient dense foods. Dr. Pratt makes the argument that these foods can prevent age-related chronic diseases such as heart-disease, type 2 diabetes, high blood pressure, and certain cancers. Research suggests that there may be some truth to this belief, but just eating one or two of these foods may not offer any health benefit. What is important to remember is that including a variety of nutrient dense foods can be part of healthy diet and, along with exercise and maintaining a healthy weight, may actually help reduce your risk of developing some of the chronic conditions previously mentioned.

Registered Dietitian Nutritionists would call these foods nutrient dense. A list of some of these superfoods follows:

Apples Avocados Beans Blueberries Broccoli	Dark chocolate Dried superfruits Extra virgin olive oil Garlic Kiwi	Low-fat yogurt Oats Onions Oranges Pomegranates Pumpkin	Soy Spinach Tea Tomatoes Turkey Walnuts Wild salmon

BEFORE YOU GO ON...

1. Define *nutrient*.
2. Which substances supply your body with energy?
3. What is the major difference between major minerals and trace minerals?
4. Why are minerals such as sodium and potassium called *electrolytes*?

WHY DO WE MAKE THE FOOD CHOICES WE DO?

Have you ever wondered why you eat the foods you do or why a friend of yours may eat foods that are unfamiliar to you? Think about it for a while and list the reasons why you eat certain foods for breakfast, lunch, dinner, and snacks, or even how often you eat per day. Some of these reasons are as follows:

- Taste
- Environment
- Culture and tradition
- Family
- Finances
- Convenience
- The media
- Age
- Health issues

Taste

Food likes and dislikes are typically based on the sensory attributes of food that influence taste. These can be learned traits, in that, we develop a certain taste for food early in life. For instance, early introduction of salty foods may allow some to develop a taste preference for them. Mouthfeel, texture, smell, and aftertaste are all attributes that affect our likes or dislikes of a food.

©jabiru/Shutterstock.com

Red beans and rice are commonly consumed by some cultures, such as Cajuns in the southern United States. Other cultures also have their favorite dishes.

Environment

The term *environment* as we use it here refers to where one eats food or a meal, who one eats with, how one eats, and other factors that surround them that may influence what and how much they consume. Teenagers may eat differently when they are away from home. Older people living alone and even young college students living on their own and cooking for themselves may not prepare meals that are as healthy as they would be if they cooked for a group. Even the size of the plate or utensils and cookware can have an influence.

Culture and Tradition

Cultural differences within our communities as well as between different parts of the world typically influence what we eat. For example, many Asian communities have a diet high in fish compared to that of the United States. Asian communities consume a lot of rice, and even Asians living in the United States tend to consume more rice than non-Asians.

Some regional dietary differences in the United States originally may have had a cultural basis. For instance, in the South grits and collard greens are regularly found in diets. Seafood gumbo and red beans and rice are dishes found among Cajun communities in Louisiana. Many Hispanics living in the United States and Central America are apt to have greater levels of legumes (beans) and chilies in their diets than people of northern and central European descent. Many of these cultural aspects turn into traditions. In other words, many people eat certain foods because that's the way it has been done for a long time.

Culture & ETHNIC FOOD

WHAT DOES RELIGION HAVE TO DO WITH DIETS?

Culture and religion can have a profound impact on what we eat. We have already briefly discussed the relationship between food choices and cultural influence; religious doctrines may be a determinant as well. For example, Mormons avoid coffee, tea, alcoholic beverages, and tobacco and many Hindus are vegetarian. At one time Catholics could not eat meat on Fridays, and many still refrain from eating meat on Fridays during Lent. Some Jews follow a kosher diet. Kosher laws deal with both foods that can and cannot be eaten and how they are to be prepared. Muslims follow Islamic dietary laws and do not ordinarily consume pork.

Family

Closely linked to culture is family; most families have food preferences based on their cultures. As children, what we eat with our family typically influences us throughout our lives. For instance, as adults we often consume the same foods we did as children because they remind us of a time when we were younger and among family and friends. Many times these foods are referred to as *comfort foods.*

© Monkey Business Images/Shutterstock.com

The family unit typically plays a prominent role in influencing what we eat. The traditional family Thanksgiving meal is a good example of culture and family combining to determine our food choices. Do all Americans eat turkey at Thanksgiving? Why?

Finances

Cost is, of course, a major factor in deciding what we consume. Plant foods, especially grain-based foods such as bread and rice, are most commonly consumed worldwide because of their relatively low cost. Meat and milk are more expensive in most cultures because of the higher costs of raising cattle, hogs, and other livestock. Even in the United States many families cannot afford meat, or they may be able to purchase only smaller and cheaper cuts that have a higher fat content. Fruits and vegetables that are fresh are also typically more expensive compared to canned or frozen.

Convenience

Convenience can also play a large role for everyone, but especially for single consumers who prepare their own food. Two-income households or busy families with hectic lifestyles may want easy-to-prepare foods or frozen meals when their available time for cooking is limited. Eating out at restaurants, particularly fast food restaurants, may be more common for those who are single or with a busy schedule. Convenience may also mean local access to specific foods such as fresh fruit, vegetables, or meat. For example, those living in certain parts of a city may not have a grocery store nearby and may find buying food at convenience stores easier compared to driving or taking public transportation to the closest grocery store. These *food deserts*, urban areas that contain very few grocery stores or resources to purchase healthy, nutritious foods, may encourage residents to purchase sugary or high fat foods as a substitute. In many parts of the world, including the United States, some foods are more convenient and available at certain times of the year; examples include peaches in Michigan and Georgia, strawberries in California, lobster in Maine, and shrimp along the Gulf Coast.

The Media

The media, through advertisements and coverage of nutrition and health topics, certainly play a role in our food selection process. New food items often must be advertised in order to make us aware of their existence. In the past, these advertisements have been in the form of commercials aired during television shows. A relatively recent form of advertising is known as *product placement*, the use of name brand products and restaurant names included in a television show. Young consumers appear to be primarily targeted by this form of advertising and it may be just as effective as television commercials in encouraging them to purchase these items. Increasingly, the Internet has been used as another format for food advertisement. Soft drinks, beers, and snack foods tend to show increased consumption when pushed by aggressive media campaigns.

Age

Our life stage also plays a role in our choice of foods. Older people may consume foods that were available or popular when they were younger and ignore those that are newer or trendy. Older people may lose their sense of taste and smell. Trouble with chewing may lead to eating less meat and fiber. On the other end of the age spectrum, teenagers are likely to consume more food items independent of the family and succumb to peer pressure to eat or not eat certain foods.

Health Issues

People with certain illnesses may choose foods to help alleviate the illness. Those with high cholesterol or a history of heart disease may choose low-fat foods. Postmenopausal women may consume extra calcium to prevent fragile bones. As more nutrition information linking diet with disease becomes available, this factor may become more important in influencing what we eat.

BEFORE YOU GO ON...

1. List at least six factors that can influence what people eat.
2. How might a person's environment affect what he eats?

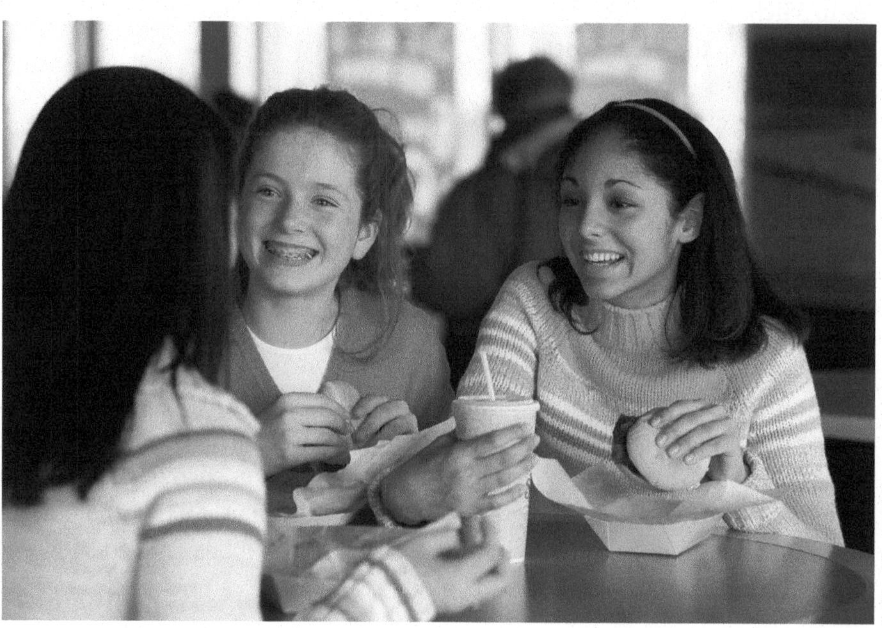

© Blend Images/Shutterstock.com

Fast foods are a reality of our culture. Each year, research shows more people, especially adolescents, are eating a greater number of their meals away from home.

HOW DO THE FOOD CHOICES WE MAKE INFLUENCE OUR HEALTH?

© Valentina Razumova/Shutterstock.com

During the 20th century, the United States and many other Western nations underwent a transformation in the types of diseases that afflict us. We still suffer from **malnutrition**, but a different type. In the strict sense of the word, *mal*, means "bad," so malnutrition refers to bad or poor nutrition status. We can subdivide malnutrition into two categories: **undernutrition**, or inadequate amounts of specific nutrients, and **overnutrition**, or too much of a specific nutrient. Either of these can involve any of the nutrients we have discussed thus far. In general, as a nation we went from a state of undernutrition to one of overnutrition in less than 100 years. At the beginning of the 20th century, deficiency diseases such as beriberi (thiamin deficiency), scurvy (vitamin C deficiency), and pellagra (niacin deficiency) were common. As time progressed the food supply improved, and, along with our continued economic development, the United States became a nation of plenty. It should be emphasized that undernutrition and overnutrition can coexist. As an example, those who are overweight may have iron deficiency if they consume too few iron-rich foods.

Today we face overnutrition as a result of uncontrolled supplementation with vitamins, minerals, and other compounds, or from consumption of too many Calories and not enough physical activity. Obesity is now the number one public health nutrition problem in the United States in adults and, alarmingly, in children and adolescents as well. Approximately two-thirds of American adults are either overweight or obese, with one-third being obese; approximately 17 percent of children and adolescents are obese (see Chapter 9). Along with nutrition concerns associated with obesity, health officials continue to express concern with Americans' general lack of physical activity, leading some health agencies to advocate inclusion of the importance of physical activity as a part of the study of nutrition. What makes this a problem is the strong link between obesity and heart disease, type 2 diabetes, stroke, and cancer. In addition, obesity is costing our nation financially. In 2008, it was estimated that approximately $147 billion was spent on health and medical care related to the effects of obesity.

malnutrition
Lack of proper nutrition resulting from deficient or excessive food or nutrient intake.

undernutrition
A type of malnutrition characterized by lack of specific nutrients.

overnutrition
A type of malnutrition characterized by too much of a specific nutrient; it is generally associated with excess energy intake and results in overweight or obesity.

NUTRITION AND DISEASE

How common is the connection between diet and disease?

Role of Nutrition in the Prevention of Disease

There is a strong connection between diet and illness. Although nutrient deficiencies are not as common in the United States as they were during the early part of the 20th century, they have not completely disappeared. For example, postmenopausal women have a higher risk of osteoporosis, and its occurrence has been attributed to inadequate amounts of calcium and vitamin D in the diet, among other factors. A problem found in countries where individuals consume a low-fiber diet is diverticulosis, a condition in which small pouches or sacs protrude from the wall of the colon. The diverticula may become infected and inflamed, resulting in pain and bleeding. While the direct link between a low-fiber diet and diverticulosis is not supported by all studies, it is believed that a high-fiber diet may prevent the inflammation of these pouches.

Do Americans eat as unhealthy as everyone says they do?

Many other common illnesses are also diet or weight related. Increasingly, modern science is discovering links between our dietary choices and/or weight status and the occurrence of heart disease, diabetes, and many types of cancer. Heart disease is the number one cause of death in the United States, and diet typically plays a role in its development. Along with heart disease, obesity is a risk factor for some cancers, type 2 diabetes, and musculoskeletal problems. However, even thin people can experience these diseases if they do not eat a healthy diet. Some people have genetic predispositions to these illnesses, but diet may modify their risk for certain diseases. Various compounds in the diet may decrease the risk of these diseases regardless of one's weight. For example, we believe the presence of *antioxidants* (substances that protect food from oxygen damage) in foods helps prevent heart disease and cancer. Along with proper nutrition, frequent exercise is an important factor in decreasing the risk and/or onset of disease, as heart disease and cancer, thus, the emphasis on healthy diet and lifestyle to promote health.

The link between diet and the increasing incidence of chronic diseases related to excess weight in Western societies, including the United States, has resulted in numerous studies being performed on the impact of foods and their nutritional content on health. Changes in industrial food production, changes in lifestyle, and increased availability and consumption of fast food are some aspects that are linked with diet and diseases prevalent in Western society.

While we are primarily afflicted with overnutrition and obesity, we still have inadequate intake of specific nutrients. Iron-deficiency anemia, for instance, remains one of the leading public health nutrition problems in the United States. Women of childbearing age, infants, and even some teenagers are at higher risk for this. Minority and economically disadvantaged populations often have inadequate nutrient intake compared to the rest of the population, resulting in them being disproportionately affected by iron-deficiency anemia compared to the rest of the population. There are multiple reasons for this inadequate intake, including lack of access to nutritious foods.

In summary, we have our work cut out for us. Our diet and lack of exercise are causing us to be afflicted with deadly diseases, as well as others that are simply debilitating, such as osteoporosis.

The Role of Nutrition in the Treatment of Disease

Monkey Business Images/Shutterstock.com

Nutrition is used in the modern medical setting to help the patient recover from illness or surgery.

Dietary modification is key in the prevention and treatment of chronic disease. For example, people with diabetes must follow a dietary regimen that spreads Calories and carbohydrates throughout the day to control the disease. People with cancer are often at risk for losing lean muscle mass, and they may drink special high-energy, high-protein beverages to prevent such loss. Many gastrointestinal disorders are treated by modifying dietary fiber and by spreading the patient's food intake among smaller, more frequent meals. Many people with kidney disease must limit their protein intake because their kidneys may not be able to excrete nitrogen, a by-product of protein utilization. Proper nutrition is critical to health care, both for preventing disease and for recovering from illness.

WHOM ARE WE TO BELIEVE ABOUT DIET ADVICE?

The Role of the Registered Dietitian (RD)/ Registered Dietitian Nutritionist (RDN)

The vast amount of nutrition information often overwhelms the consumer. You as a consumer must be prepared to decide whether the information is credible. This can be a difficult task since just about anyone can call himself or herself a nutritionist without having formal training in the field of nutrition. You should be skeptical about individuals who earn certificates and degrees in nutrition from mail-order or nonaccredited institutions. Surprisingly, many physicians have little training in nutrition, but this is improving as in-service training and medical school curriculums change. Conflicting information, sometimes generated from scientific studies, adds to the uncertainties and confusion surrounding what we should do about the poor state of our diets.

In this and the following chapters, we will offer summaries of what "experts" advocate. An expert in nutrition is someone with an advanced degree and credentials in the field. The **Registered Dietitian (RD)/Registered Dietitian Nutritionist (RDN)** is a health professional who has completed a degree in dietetics and nutrition from an accredited university; completes an accredited internship experience; and must pass a national examination to earn his or her credentials. Many states have also required that practitioners such as RDs/RDNs be licensed.

Registered Dietitian (RD)/ Registered Dietitian Nutritionist (RDN)

A professional who has the education and clinical training to make dietary recommendations and to counsel patients.

If you are unsure of something, ask the experts or consult a legitimate nutrition textbook.

With respect to certain illnesses, the RD/RDN is a key member of the health care team that must consider all angles of the recovery, including nutrition.

The Role of Government in Nutrition

You will find that the science of nutrition involves its share of politics from a legislative perspective as well as in public policy. Well into the 20th century, the federal government's role in nutrition was non-existent. In the 1940s, many men who were drafted to serve in World War II were rejected because of ailments related to deficiencies of specific nutrients. This led to the creation of the first **Recommended Dietary Allowances (RDAs)**) in 1941. After the war, the RDAs continued to be revised periodically by the Food and Nutrition Board under the National Research Council of the National Academy of Sciences. The initial RDAs were recommendations of known nutrients that were needed on a daily basis to maintain health and to prevent deficiencies. Later, the National Academy of Sciences expanded these recommendations to create the Dietary Reference Intakes (DRIs), which now includes limits of nutrient intake. You will learn more about the DRIs in chapter 2.

Recommended Dietary Allowances (RDAs)

The recommended nutrient intake required to meet the known nutrient needs of the healthy population.

With respect to certain illnesses, the RD/RDN is a key member of the health care team that must consider all angles of the recovery, including nutrition.

Several other government agencies are involved in nutrition recommendations. The U.S. Department of Agriculture (USDA) and the U.S. Department of Health and Human Services (HHS) also play a major role in food and nutrition policy. As the issue of overweight and obesity rose in the United States, the USDA and HHS published the first *Dietary Guidelines for Americans* (DGA) in 1980. The DGA is the recommendation for the American public on lifestyle and food choices in order to remain healthy. The agency updates them every 5 years, and we will discuss them throughout the text. The national school lunch and school breakfast programs are both funded by the USDA. The **Expanded Food and Nutrition Education Program (EFNEP)**, also USDA-funded, is a community-based program that helps people of limited financial means enhance their food and nutrient intake. Another government program is the **Special Supplemental Nutrition Program for Women, Infants, and Children (WIC)**, which is designed to improve the nutrition of pregnant and breastfeeding mothers, infants, and children up to age 5.

Expanded Food and Nutrition Education Program (EFNEP)

A government program to help people of limited financial means enhance their food and nutrient intake.

Special Supplemental Nutrition Program for Women, Infants, and Children (WIC)

A nutrition program run by the U.S. Department of Agriculture that is designed to improve the nutrition of pregnant and breastfeeding mothers, infants, and children up to age 5.

The involvement of government institutions in nutrition programs and policies means that knowledge of politics and political networking is important for RDs/RDNs. For example, even changing the RDA for a specific nutrient can be fraught with politics, as many government-sponsored feeding programs must meet the RDAs in terms of nutrient content. Lowering the RDA for one nutrient may mean less of a particular food required in a meal and less sales by the food producer of the foods rich in that particular nutrient.

BEFORE YOU GO ON...

1. Identify two major nutrition problems in the United States today and describe their primary causes.
2. When did the U.S. government first get involved with nutrition policy and why?
3. List two examples of government agencies involved in programs that help promote or maintain health.

THE SCIENCE OF NUTRITION

Compared to other disciplines, nutrition is a relatively young science. It initially formed in the early part of the 1900s from the combination of other sciences. At *land-grant universities,* which are federally funded to promote the agricultural sciences, professors in agricultural chemistry and animal science departments made many important discoveries. Each state has a land-grant institution. In Texas, it includes Texas A&M University; in California, it is the University of California at Davis; in New York, it is Cornell University; in Oklahoma, it includes Oklahoma State University; in Georgia, it is the

Nutrition is not immune from politics and legislation. Many food and nutrition programs have been developed by national and state governments in attempts to improve the health of our citizens.

© Andrea Izzotti/Shutterstock.com

University of Georgia. Do you know what your land-grant university is? See www.higher-ed.org/resources/land_grant_colleges.htm to determine which university is a land-grant institution in your state.

RDs/RDNs study many different aspects of nutrition, from genes to entire populations. Some focus on the impact of a nutrient at the gene or molecular level in a cell. For instance, recent work focuses on how nutrition influences our genes to make or not make certain proteins or compounds. This is known as *gene expression.* Some RDs/RDNs study the whole organism or individual, such as what people eat and why. Clinical researchers may look at certain diets related to particular diseases. Others examine cultural differences in eating behavior or specialize in the important relationship between nutrition and politics. These are just a few examples of the many topics that nutrition researchers explore.

More recently, as the obesity epidemic continues to grow, biobehavioral sciences have taken a more significant role in nutrition. Knowing what motivates people to make diet and physical activity choices, how to modify behavior to promote health, and how to prevent poor lifestyle choices are growing research areas within the field of nutrition. In addition, **nutrigenomics** is a newly emerging multidisciplinary field of medical science and clinical practice. It is an integrated science that attempts to understand a genetic and molecular connection for how dietary compounds alter the expression and/or structure of an individual's genetic makeup, thus affecting their health and risk of disease.

nutrigenomics

An integrated science that attempts to understand a genetic and molecular connection for how dietary compounds alter the expression and/or structure of an individual's genetic makeup, thus affecting their health and risk of disease.

How Can You Identify Reputable Sources of Nutrition Information?

No doubt you have had this problem before—you've read or heard conflicting information about what to eat. You are continually bombarded with claims made by weight-loss programs. Infomercials, radio and newspaper ads, magazines, websites with pop-up ads, diet centers and health-food stores, and even your local grocer all seem to have some type of advice regarding nutrition, and many say, "Studies show. . . ." With all this information, how do you wisely determine whom or what to trust? Are any of these sources believable? Some of the reputable nutrition journals include:

American Journal of Clinical Nutrition
Journal of Food Science
Journal of Nutrition
Journal of Nutrition Education and Behavior
Journal of Nutritional Biochemistry
Journal of the Academy of Nutrition and Dietetics
Nutrition and Cancer
Nutrition in the Elderly
Nutrition Research

Many other reputable nutrition journals and science journals also publish articles on nutrition.

Fortunately, the government is becoming more strict about nutrition claims that appear on food products. Any type of health claim appearing on a food product now must be backed by adherence to a stringent set of guidelines. The FDA has regulatory authority over these claims, and manufacturers of food products making these claims must now provide scientific evidence, including studies on humans, that the product provides the benefits promised. However, keep in mind that in a newspaper or magazine ad these regulations do not apply. Another factor that may surprise you is that dietary supplements are largely unregulated by any government agency; therefore, the same may not apply to claims included on supplement labels. We will discuss this in Chapter 8.

Some food producers attempt to take advantage of the consumer's lack of knowledge. For instance, have you noticed the claim on a bottle of vegetable oil that it is "cholesterol free"? If so, you may have concluded that the oil was a superior product, because cholesterol is bad for the heart. The part about the absence of cholesterol being good is true. However, all vegetables and vegetable oils are completely devoid of cholesterol; only foods of animal origin have cholesterol. So what is new about vegetable oil not having cholesterol? Absolutely nothing.

How Nutrition Recommendations Are Developed

New knowledge typically evolves from research conducted by scientists in a particular field. The process involves a scientist asking a question and then conducting research on cells, animals, or humans in an effort to answer that question. Therefore, when determining whether a source is reliable, make sure that research was conducted to generate the information and that the research was conducted under rigorous controls and methods. This approach is commonly referred to as the **scientific method**. For instance, if you want to know whether zinc supplements can lower blood cholesterol levels, you need to have one group of human subjects given zinc tablets and another group given a "fake" tablet called a **placebo**. The participants in a study who receive the treatment or substance being studied to determine whether it has an anticipated effect are called the **experimental group**. We need to have the second or **control group** (the one that receives the placebo) because sometimes people change their diets or other things in their life during the study period that could affect the results. Many times, participants and the investigator or researcher do not know who is receiving which treatment; this type of research is called a **double-blind study**. The number of subjects in each group is also important. Often a study will be repeated with other groups in order to verify the results of the first.

scientific method
A systematic method of research used in science in which an observation leads to a hypothesis; the hypothesis is tested via an experiment to attempt to prove or disprove.

placebo
In an experiment or research study, an inert substance or treatment given to subjects in the control group instead of the actual substance or treatment being studied.

experimental group
The participants in an experiment or research study who receive the treatment or substance being studied to determine whether it has an anticipated outcome.

control group
The participants in an experiment or research study who do not receive the treatment or substance being studied. A control group provides an "untreated" basis of comparison with the experimental group.

double-blind study
A study in which the participating subjects and the scientists conducting the experiment do not know who is receiving which treatment.

After the study is performed, the data are analyzed and written up as a manuscript and submitted to a science journal. The journal publisher gives the article to other experts in the field to review the study, judge its validity, and comment on whether the study was conducted appropriately and if the findings warrant publication. This is called the *peer review system.* If the manuscript is accepted and published, other scientists and professionals get to read it. The article must have enough information for other scientists to replicate the findings.

At this point, readers can access the article from many university libraries and/or government websites. However, much of what is published in these journals is too technical for the everyday layperson to grasp. Normally, science and health writers from the media then interpret the articles for the public. Eventually, this material may end up in nutrition textbooks and other media. As a by-product of this process, it may become more generalized and end up on the Internet. The best way to decide if something you are reading is reputable is to see whether it cites a journal where the original research was published, what is known as a *citation.* If no citation is included within the article, it may not be a reputable source.

© Evgeny Karandaev/Shutterstock.com

BEFORE YOU GO ON...

1. You've just read an article in a weekly magazine that describes how a particular vitamin may help prevent breast cancer. How would you determine whether the claim is valid?
2. Discuss the components of the scientific method and peer-review process.
3. What is a double-blind study?
4. Where would you look for accurate information about the effect of copper on the heart?

CHAPTER SUMMARY

- The major classes of nutrients are carbohydrate, fat, protein, water, vitamins, and minerals. The energy-yielding nutrients are carbohydrate, fat, and protein. Vitamins, minerals, and water do not provide energy, but support biochemical reactions and have structural functions in the body. Alcohol and phytochemicals are not nutrients but are important considerations when discussing nutrition and health. Phytochemicals are chemicals found in plant-based food that appear to have health benefit.
- Carbohydrate and protein supply 4 kcal per gram, and fat supplies 9 kcal per gram. The nonnutrient alcohol supplies 7 kcal per gram.
- Available food choices for any population are typically due to a wide variety of factors. For example, our living and working environment and lifestyle can determine what we eat, such as availability, variety, and convenience of fast-food establishments. Our likes and dislikes with respect to taste, family traditions, finances, media advertisement, and even our age are all contributing factors.
- The study of nutrition involves both undernutrition and overnutrition. In the United States, overnutrition has become a major public health problem as evidenced by the widespread increase in the percentage of the population who are either overweight or clinically obese.
- Chronic diseases have been linked to poor nutrition. Cancer, heart disease, fragile bones as we age (osteoporosis), and diabetes are primary examples.
- Several government programs, such as the Women, Infants, and Children (WIC) program and the Expanded Food and Nutrition Education Program (EFNEP), support better nutrition. Many of these are sponsored by the U.S. Department of Agriculture.
- Nutrition science grew out of many disciplines, including anthropology, food science and technology, psychology, physiology, economics, public health, sociology, organic chemistry, biochemistry, molecular biology, epidemiology, and law.
- Credible information on nutrition arises through use of the scientific method by nutrition experts and subsequent publication of their research in reputable journals. When you read a nutrition article in a lay publication, it is important to determine the source of the information reported and to see whether a specific scientific article is cited.

KEY TERMS

ALCOHOL A nonnutrient that has 7 kcal per gram.

CALORIE A scientific unit of energy; the Calories used to measure food energy are actually *kilocalories* (kcal). One kilocalorie, or food Calorie, equals 1,000 Calories.

CARBOHYDRATE A category of macronutrients that includes energy-yielding nutrients suchas starches and sugars, as well as non-energy-yielding nutrients such as fibers.

CONTROL GROUP The participants in an experiment or research study who do not receive the treatment or substance being studied. A control group provides an "untreated" basis of comparison with the *experimental group.*

DOUBLE-BLIND STUDY A study in which the participating subjects and the scientists conducting the experiment do not know who is receiving which treatment.

ELECTROLYTES Minerals such as sodium, potassium, and chlorine that assume a charge when dissolved in water.

EXPANDED FOOD AND NUTRITION EDUCATION PROGRAM (EFNEP) A government program to help people of limited financial means enhance their food and nutrient intake.

EXPERIMENTAL GROUP The participants in an experiment or research study who receive the treatment or substance being studied to determine whether it has an anticipated outcome.

FAT An energy-yielding nutrient that is insoluble in water; it provides more than twice as much energy as carbohydrate or protein.

FAT-SOLUBLE VITAMINS Vitamins that are insoluble in water, can be stored in the body for long periods of time, and do not need to be consumed daily.

FUNCTIONAL FOOD Foods that when added or present in a diet provide a health benefit beyond normal nutrition.

INORGANIC Compound or element not derived from living matter; also, does not contain carbon.

MACROMINERAL A mineral required by the body in excess of 100 mg per day; also called a major element.

MACRONUTRIENTS Nutrients needed in large amounts, such as carbohydrates, proteins, fats, and water.

MALNUTRITION Lack of proper nutrition resulting from deficient or excessive food or nutrient intake.

METABOLISM The biochemical activity that occurs in cells, releasing energy from nutrients or using energy to create other substances such as proteins.

MICROMINERAL A mineral required by the body in an amount less than 100 mg per day.

MICRONUTRIENTS Nutrients needed in small amounts, such as vitamins and numerals.

MINERALS Inorganic compounds required in small amounts for structure and regulating processes in the body.

NUTRIENT A substance that the body needs for energy, growth, and development.

NUTRIGENOMICS An integrated science that attempts to understand a genetic and molecular connection for how dietary compounds alter the expression and/or structure of an individual's genetic makeup, thus affecting their health and risk of disease.

ORGANIC Carbon-containing compound; derived from living matter.

OVERNUTRITION A type of malnutrition characterized by too much of a specific nutrient; it is generally associated with excess energy intake and results in overweight or obesity.

PHYTOCHEMICALS Chemical compounds in plants that have various effects on body functions; they are not nutrients in the classical sense.

PLACEBO In an experiment or research study, an inert substance or treatment given to subjects in the control group instead of the actual substance or treatment being studied.

PROTEIN An energy-yielding nutrient that contains nitrogen; its primary purpose is to support growth, maintenance, and repair of tissues.

RECOMMENDED DIETARY ALLOWANCES (RDAS) The recommended nutrient intake required to meet the known nutrient needs of the healthy population.

REGISTERED DIETITIAN NUTRITIONIST (RD/RDN) A professional who has the education and clinical training to make dietary recommendations and to counsel patients.

SCIENTIFIC METHOD A systematic method of research used in science in which an observation leads to a hypothesis; the hypothesis is tested via an experiment to attempt to prove or disprove the it.

SPECIAL SUPPLEMENTAL NUTRITION PROGRAM FOR WOMEN, INFANTS, AND CHILDREN (WIC) A nutrition program run by the U.S. Department of Agriculture that is designed to improve the nutrition of pregnant and breastfeeding mothers, infants, and children up to age 5.

UNDERNUTRITION A type of malnutrition characterized by lack of specific nutrients.

VITAMINS A group of nutrients that contain carbon and are required in small amounts to maintain normal body function.

WATER-SOLUBLE VITAMINS Vitamins that dissolve in water, are not stored in the body to any extent, and are excreted mostly through the urine.

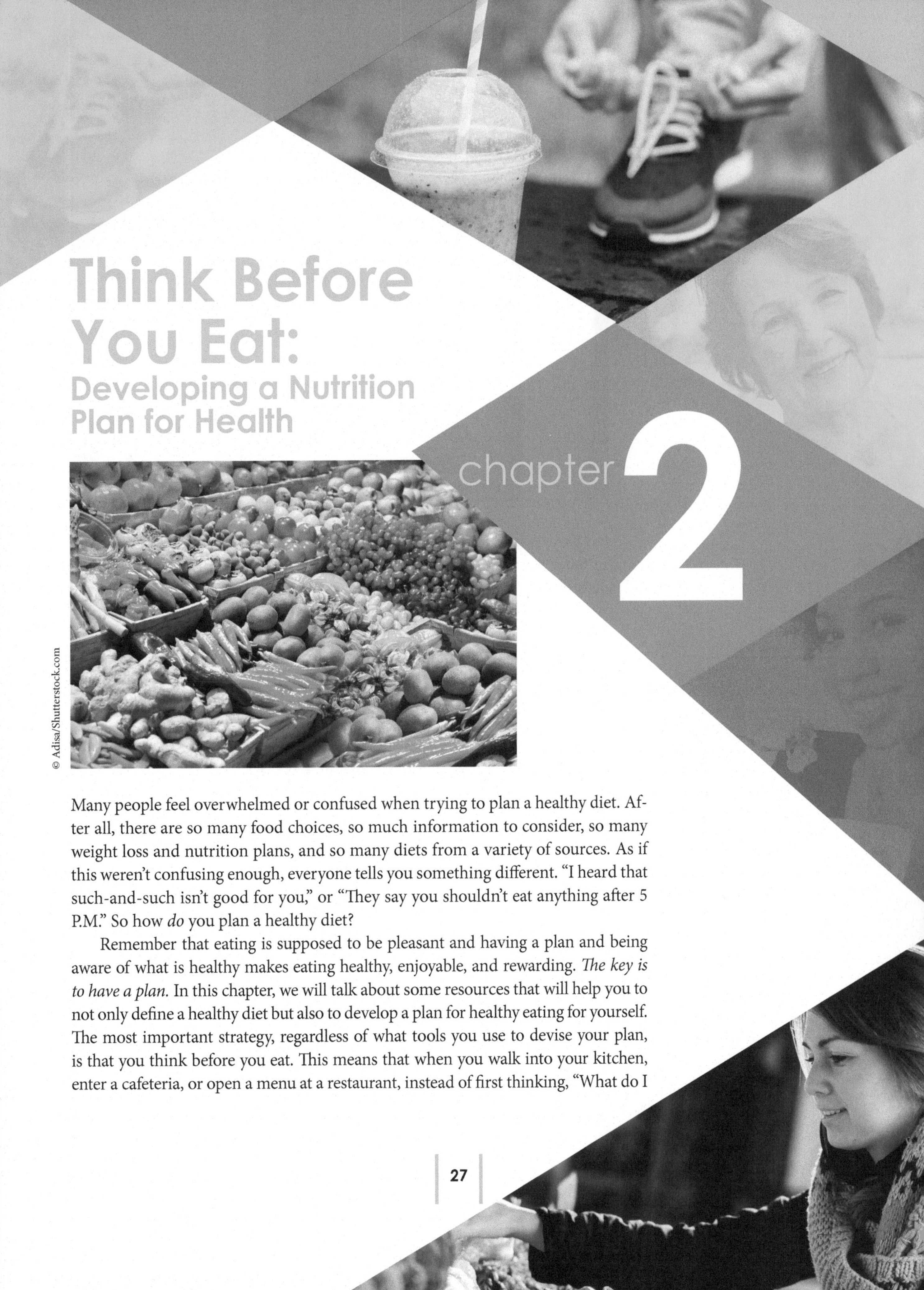

Think Before You Eat: Developing a Nutrition Plan for Health

chapter 2

© Adisa/Shutterstock.com

Many people feel overwhelmed or confused when trying to plan a healthy diet. After all, there are so many food choices, so much information to consider, so many weight loss and nutrition plans, and so many diets from a variety of sources. As if this weren't confusing enough, everyone tells you something different. "I heard that such-and-such isn't good for you," or "They say you shouldn't eat anything after 5 P.M." So how *do* you plan a healthy diet?

Remember that eating is supposed to be pleasant and having a plan and being aware of what is healthy makes eating healthy, enjoyable, and rewarding. *The key is to have a plan.* In this chapter, we will talk about some resources that will help you to not only define a healthy diet but also to develop a plan for healthy eating for yourself. The most important strategy, regardless of what tools you use to devise your plan, is that you think before you eat. This means that when you walk into your kitchen, enter a cafeteria, or open a menu at a restaurant, instead of first thinking, "What do I

Answer the question "What do I need to eat?" before making your choices.

© Christopher Boswell/Shutterstock.com

feel like eating?", you should begin by asking yourself, "What do I need to eat?" In other words, "Have I had enough vegetables today?" "Have I had enough dairy?" You should walk into these environments with a plan. Similarly, when you go grocery shopping, have a list and don't just look at foods in the aisle to see what looks good. After deciding what you need to eat, then you can ask, "What do I feel like eating?" After all, eating would probably be less enjoyable if all you did was eat strictly from the plan. Let's discuss some recommendations and tools available to help you answer these questions.

What does it mean to eat a healthy diet?

DEFINING A HEALTHY DIET

Scientists and health experts have spent decades trying to define a healthy diet. It is important to remember that nutritional needs change over the life span and can be different for athletes versus non-athletes or under special circumstances such as when a person is sick, pregnant, or taking certain medications. For everyone, one common theme remains constant: a healthy diet incorporates a variety of nutrient dense foods that include balance and moderation to help maintain a healthy body weight. Let's discuss what is meant by variety, balance, moderation, and nutrient density.

variety
Eating different types of foods within each food group.

balance
Incorporating foods from all food groups into your daily eating plan.

Variety means eating different types of foods within each food group. The reason for this: no one food does it all. For example, if you eat an adequate number of servings of vegetables every day, but eat only carrots, then you are not consuming a variety and therefore may be missing some important nutrients found in other vegetables. **Balance** means incorporating foods from *all* food groups into your daily plan so that you are eating fruits, vegetables, whole grains, dairy (or dairy substitutes), fats, and proteins. It means not relying on or favoring any one food group at the expense of another. It also can refer to balancing Calories you eat with Calories burned from physical activity. This helps you stay at a healthy weight. **Moderation** means not overconsuming any one food or food group. This term can also refer to *portion sizes.* We discuss the importance of portion sizes and portion control throughout this book, typically in reference to Calories, but it can be applied to any food or food group.

moderation
Avoiding overconsumption of any one food or food group.

empty calories
Calories with little or no nutrient content.

While it is important to incorporate the concepts of balance, variety, and moderation when planning a healthy diet, you must also consider the *nutrient density* of the foods you are eating. Nutrient density refers to the nutrient content of a food relative to its Calories. For example, suppose you are trying to decide what to have for a snack and you have the choice of eating candy or a banana. You determine that the portions you have both contain about 100 kcals, so what's the difference? Although both food choices provide the same number of Calories, the banana provides several essential nutrients, whereas the candy is essentially just sugar. The candy represents **empty Calories**, or Calories with little or no nutrient content. Therefore, the more nutrient-dense and healthier choice would be the banana.

© Africa Studio/Shutterstock.com

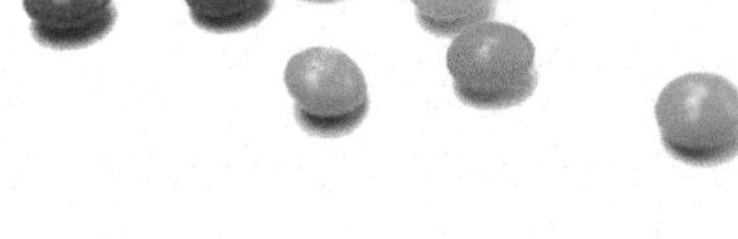

© FXQuadro/Shutterstock.com

Nutrient dense foods versus empty calories.

DIETARY GUIDELINES

Dietary Guidelines for Americans has been published jointly every 5 years since 1980 by the U.S. Department of Health and Human Services (HHS) and the U.S. Department of Agriculture (USDA). The latest guidelines, shown in Figure 2.1, were released December 2015. The *Dietary Guidelines for Americans* 2015 summarize the most current science-based recommendations to promote health through diet and physical activity to reduce risk for major *chronic diseases* for healthy people over age 2. *The Dietary Guidelines are used by health care professionals to assist Americans in planning a healthy, nutritionally adequate diet, to develop food and nutrition programs and program policies and to revise and develop public educational materials. The five *Dietary Guidelines for Americans 2015* are:

Dietary Guidelines for Americans
A summary of science-based advice to promote health through diet and physical activity and to reduce the risk for major chronic diseases in people over age 2.

1. Follow a healthy eating pattern across the lifespan.
2. Focus on variety, nutrient density, and amount.
3. Limit Calories from added sugars and saturated fats and reduce sodium intake.
4. Shift to healthier food and beverage choices.
5. Support healthy eating patterns for all.

FIGURE 2.1 The *2015 Dietary Guidelines for Americans* summarize scientific information in order to provide nutritional advice that promotes health and reduces the risk for cancer, diabetes, and major diseases associated with the heart.

Source: United States Department of Health and Human Services.

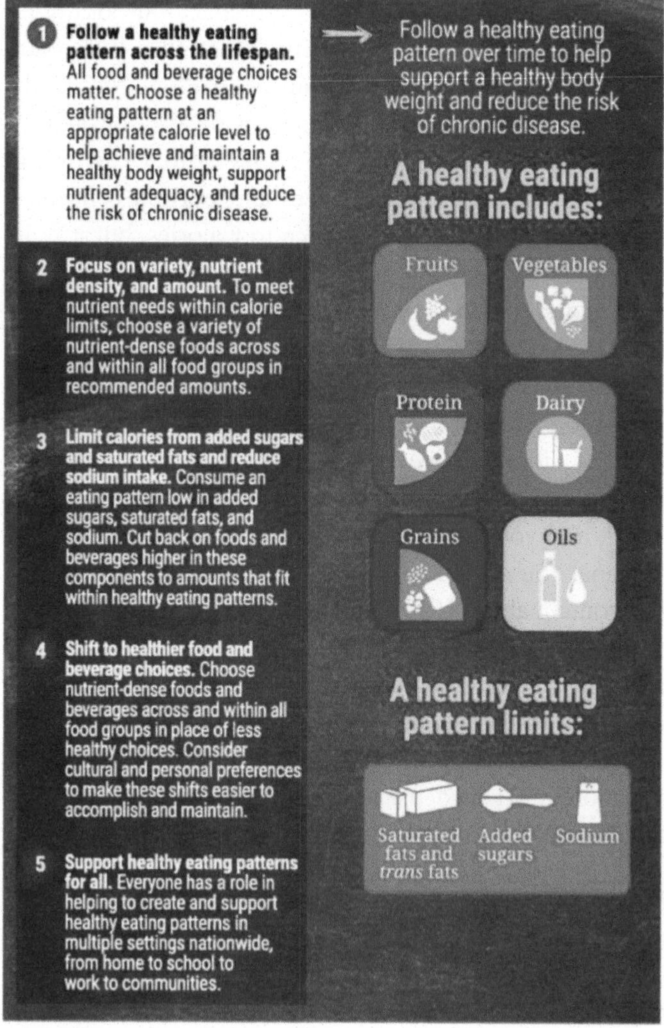

In order to help people follow the guidelines, Key Recommendations were developed. These include:

- Consume a healthy eating pattern that accounts for all foods and beverages within an appropriate Calorie level. A healthy eating pattern includes:
  - A variety of vegetables from all of the subgroups – dark green, red and orange, legumes (beans and peas), starchy, and other.
  - Fruits, especially whole fruits.
  - Grains, at least half of which are whole grains.
  - Fat-free or low-fat dairy, including milk, yogurt, cheese, and/or fortified soy beverages.
  - A variety of protein foods, including seafood, lean meats and poultry, eggs, legumes (beans and peas), and nuts, seeds, and soy products.
  - Oils
- A healthy eating pattern limits:
  - Saturated fats and trans fats, added sugars, and sodium

- In addition, several components of the diet should be limited:
  - Consume less than 10 percent of Calories per day from added sugars
  - Consume less than 10 percent of Calories per day from saturated fats
  - Consume less than 2,300 milligrams (mg) per day from sodium
  - If alcohol is consumed, it should be consumed in moderation – up to one drink per day for women and up to two drinks per day for men and only by adults of legal drinking age
- Americans of all ages – children, adolescents, adults, and older adults – should meet the Physical Activity Guidelines for Americans to help promote health and reduce the risk of chronic disease. *

Eating a healthy balance of nutritious foods is a central point in *Dietary Guidelines for Americans,* but the recommendations also recognize that balancing nutrients is not enough for health. Total Calories also count, especially as more Americans are gaining weight. Because almost two-thirds of Americans are now overweight or obese and more than half get too little physical activity, the 2015 *Dietary Guidelines for Americans* place a strong emphasis on Calorie control and physical activity. The guidelines serve as the foundation for federal food and nutrition education programs, such as MyPlate which will be discussed soon. The guidelines can also be adapted for special populations such as those with hypertension. For example, the **Dietary Approaches to Stop Hypertension (DASH)** diet plan is a tool to help individuals modify their diet to improve their blood pressure control and implement the *Dietary Guidelines.* The DASH diet is discussed in more detail in Chapter 7.

DASH (Dietary Approaches to Stop Hypertension)
A tool to help individuals lower sodium intake and implement the Dietary Guidelines.

Due to the critical role nutrition plays in the prevention of all major diseases, nutrition-related goals have been included in many health promotion initiatives. One such important effort is **Healthy People 2020**, which is a set of government objectives that include dietary and other goals that if attained could improve the overall health of the population, hopefully to be achieved by 2020. Although it is managed by the Office of Disease Prevention and Health Promotion, a division of the U.S. Department of Health and Human Services, Healthy People 2020 was created by a collaborative effort of scientists, federal and state agencies, and public feedback. The primary goals are to increase our quality of life through better health for all life stages, to eliminate health disparities and to create social and physical environments that promote good health. There are 42 topic areas with more than 1,200 ob-

Healthy
PEOPLE
2020

Healthy People 2020
A list of health objectives for the nation to achieve by 2020. It is designed to identify the most significant preventable threats to health and to establish national goals to reduce these threats.

jectives to strive for. It sets guidelines and prioritizes health promotion programs for states, communities, and organizations. The objectives are listed according to leading health indicators:

- Physical activity
- Overweight and obesity
- Tobacco use
- Substance abuse
- Responsible sexual behavior
- Mental health
- Injury and violence
- Environmental quality
- Immunization
- Access to health care

fortified foods
Foods with nutrients added to them that were not originally present. An example is orange juice fortified with calcium.

enriched foods
Foods that have had nutrients added back that were removed during processing. For example, enriched white rice has had some nutrients added back that were present before the outer brown husk was removed.

A basic premise of the *Dietary Guidelines* is that nutrient needs should be met primarily through consuming foods. However, the guidelines recognize that in certain cases **fortified foods** or foods with nutrients added to them (such as orange juice fortified with calcium) that were not originally present, may help meet nutrient needs, but they cannot replace a healthful diet. Of course, **enriched foods** also contribute to daily nutrient intakes. Enriched foods have had nutrients added back that were removed during processing. For example, enriched white rice has had some nutrients added back that were present before the outer brown husk was removed.

BEFORE YOU GO ON...

1. What are the components of a healthy diet?
2. Describe the difference between nutrient-dense Calories and empty Calories.
3. What does it mean to think before you eat?
4. Who issues Dietary Guidelines for Americans and what is their purpose?
5. Define Healthy People 2020.

RECOMMENDATIONS FOR SPECIFIC NUTRIENTS

v.s.anandhakrishna/Shutterstock.com

Thus far we have discussed the guidelines for developing a nutrition plan based solely on food and food groups. This plan is intended to be general and therefore does not provide information on the specific requirements of each nutrient. The requirements for each nutrient are listed in the dietary reference standards that have evolved since their creation in 1941. Dietary reference standards provide recommended intakes for specific nutrients. They can be used to plan diets for individuals and groups.

The Dietary Reference Intakes (DRIs)

In 1941, the Food and Nutrition Board published the first dietary reference standards, called the **Recommended Dietary Allowances (RDAs)**, for specific nutrients: Calories, protein, vitamin A, vitamin D, thiamin, riboflavin, niacin, vitamin C, calcium, and iron. The goal of the RDAs was to prevent diseases caused by nutrient deficiencies. Over the years, as more scientific evidence regarding what the body needs to stay healthy became available, a more complete set of standards was developed - the **Dietary Reference Intakes (DRIs)**. While the recommendations still have a focus on preventing nutrient deficiency, they have been expanded to include recommendations for disease prevention. These standards are used by healthcare workers, educators, and scientists to assess and improve the nutritional status of Americans. They are also used to interpret food consumption records of populations, to establish standards for food assistance programs, to plan menus for schools and the military, and to establish guidelines for nutrition labeling.

The DRIs are designed for healthy people and are categorized based on age group and life stage. They include four nutrient-based reference values: the RDAs, **Adequate Intake (AI)**, **Estimated Average Requirement (EAR)**, and **Tolerable Upper Intake Level (UL)**. See Table 2.1 for a complete description of each value and Figure 2.2 for a graphical representation of the differences. The current DRIs are listed in the back cover of your text. In addition—and as a response to common overconsumption of many nutrients, especially through supplements—the DRIs now include recommendations for maximum intake for any nutrient that has been shown to have toxic levels, the UL. Finally, components of food that have not traditionally been considered nutrients have been shown to have health benefits, such as phytochemicals (which we discussed in Chapter 1), are being reviewed. If sufficient evidence becomes available, reference intakes for them will also be established.

Recommended Dietary Allowances (RDAs)
The recommended intake required to meet the daily nutrient needs for 97–98 percent of all individuals in a given age or gender group.

Dietary Reference Intakes (DRIs)
Guidelines designed for healthy people, established to replace the original RDAs in the United States and the Recommended Nutrient Intakes (RNIs) in Canada.

Adequate Intake (AI)
The value assigned to a nutrient if some scientific evidence is available, but not quite enough to establish a recommendation with certainty.

Estimated Average Requirement (EAR)
The value assigned to a nutrient that would meet the needs of 50 percent of the people of a specific age or gender. It is used only by federal agencies for research and policy making.

Tolerable Upper Intake Level (UL)
The highest level of daily nutrient intake that poses little risk of adverse health effects to individuals in a specific age or gender group.

TABLE 2.1 Dietary Reference Intakes (DRIs)

Reference Value	What It Is	Why It Is Important
Estimated Average Requirement (EAR)	The value assigned to a nutrient that would meet the needs of 50 percent of the people of a specific age or life stage and gender. The EAR is established after careful review of the research published on the specific nutrient	The EAR by itself is used only by federal agencies for research and policy making. It may also be applied to epidemiological studies or community nutrition programs
Recommended Dietary Allowance (RDA)	The recommended intake required to meet the daily nutrient needs for 97–98 percent of all individuals in a given age or gender group. This level is based on the EAR of that nutrient	The RDA is used for diet planning for individuals and is the foundation of the DRI
Adequate Intake (AI)	The value assigned to a nutrient if some scientific evidence is available, but not quite enough to establish a recommendation with certainty	The AI is used to make recommendations for healthy individuals for nutrients with no RDA. AIs are also used in calculating the nutritional requirements of infants. For all nutrients except vitamin D, the AI for infants is based on intakes of healthy babies that are fed only breast milk
Tolerable Upper Intake Level (UL)	The highest level of daily nutrient intake that poses little risk of adverse health effects to healthy individuals in a specific age or gender group. As intake increases above the UL, the potential risk for adverse health effects goes up as well	The UL was established in response to potential toxic levels of nutrients being consumed, particularly by those taking dietary supplements or consuming foods with nutrients added to them. ULs are also used to set safe limits for nutrients added to our food and water, such as the fluoride added to tap water

Since the DRIs are established for healthy groups of people they may not be adequate for people with certain chronic or acute diseases. DRIs can also be used to ensure that menus for individuals and for institutions such as hospitals and school cafeterias provide adequate nutrition, but not too much of any one nutrient or too many Calories.

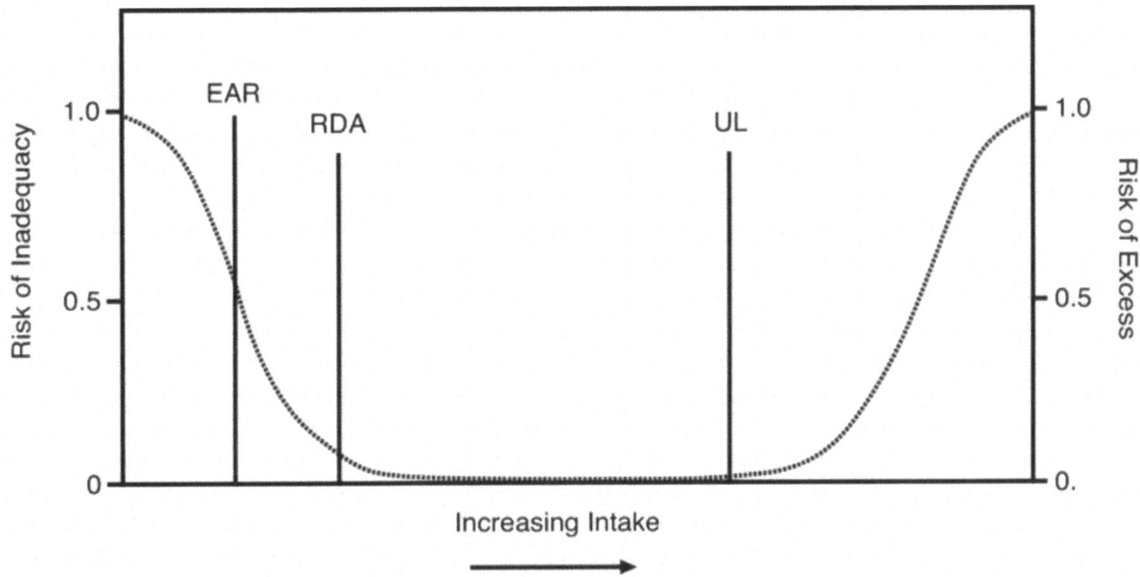

FIGURE 2.2 A graphic representation of the three reference values that are the DRI. The graph shows that the risk of adverse effects is greatest when intake is higher or lower than the recommended amounts.

Source: http://www.nap.edu/openbook.php?record_id=10872&page=84

The DRIs also influence the nutrition recommendations issued by the federal government; they are intended to work together. The nutrition recommendations and tools for healthy eating, such as MyPlate, translate the DRIs to meal planning. For instance, the DRIs suggest that adults consume 1,000 mg of calcium per day. This recommendation is reflected in the DASH diet and MyPlate, which suggest that adults consume three servings of dairy (a high source of calcium) per day. Similarly, the guidelines incorporate this information as part of the focus area "Key Recommendations" by stating, "Consume three cups per day of fat-free or low-fat milk or equivalent milk products."

ENERGY AND MACRONUTRIENT REQUIREMENTS

People often ask, "How many Calories should I eat?" To help answer that question there is a general recommendation called the Estimated Energy Requirement (EER). It is based on formulas designed to include individual characteristics such as age, gender, height, weight, and level of physical activity. These are all factors that influence the amount of energy expended on a daily basis. Because macronutrients contribute to Calories consumed, it is important to

Estimated Energy Requirement (EER)
A general recommendation for energy needs.

Acceptable Macronutrient Distribution Range (AMDR)
A recommended range of requirements for carbohydrates, fats, and proteins based on the total daily Calorie needs and balance of nutrients that are associated with a decreased risk of chronic disease.

provide guidelines for how much each macronutrient should contribute to overall Calorie intake. The recommendations for the amount of Calories from carbohydrates, fats, and proteins, the energy-yielding nutrients, are provided under the **Acceptable Macronutrient Distribution Range (AMDR)**. This is a recommended range of macronutrient requirements based on the total daily Calorie needs and balance of nutrients that are associated with a decreased risk of chronic disease:

Protein	10–35 percent of total daily Calories
Fat	20–35 percent of total daily Calories
Carbohydrates	45–65 percent of total daily Calories

APPLICATION TIP

According to the AMDR, a person on a 2,000-Calorie diet should consume 200–700 Calories from protein (50-175 grams), 400–700 Calories from fat (45-78 grams) and 900–1,300 Calories from carbohydrates (225-325 grams). The following is a sample daily menu.

Breakfast	Lunch	Dinner
¾ c. Cereal (not sweetened) 8 oz. Skim or 1% milk 1 Slice wheat bread 1 tbsp. peanut butter ½ Grapefruit Coffee or tea	1 c. lettuce ½ c. carrots (shredded) ¼ c. tomatoes (sliced) ¼ c. cucumbers (sliced) 2 oz. chicken (grilled) 2 tbsp. dressing (low-fat) 1 wheat pita 8 oz. milk (skim) 1 apple (small)	4 oz. salmon (baked with 1 tsp. olive oil) 1 c. rice (brown) ½ c. broccoli (steamed) ½ c. zucchini with 1 tsp. olive oil (sautéed) 1 ¼ c. strawberries Mineral water
Snack 1	**Snack 2**	
6 oz. yogurt (low-fat plain) 3 graham cracker squares	1 c. cantaloupe (in cubes) Half of a granola bar	

Source: Adapted from EBSCO Health Libraries.

BEFORE YOU GO ON...

1. What is the function of the DRIs, and how do they differ from the RDA standards?
2. What are the reference values established under the DRIs?
3. Define the Estimated Energy Requirement (EER) and explain its purpose.
4. What is the purpose of the Acceptable Macronutrient Distribution Range (AMDR)?

MYPLATE

Because we eat foods and not nutrients, it is important to translate the DRIs and the *Dietary Guidelines for* Americans into a daily plan for food intake. The USDA's MyPlate is designed to help implement the concepts of balance, moderation, nutrient density and variety. The most recent version, released in 2011, is pictured in Figure 2.3.

MyPlate
The nutrition guide designed by the U.S. Department of Agriculture that depicts the recommended food group distribution using a plate icon with the food groups divided among vegetables, fruit, grains, dairy, and protein.

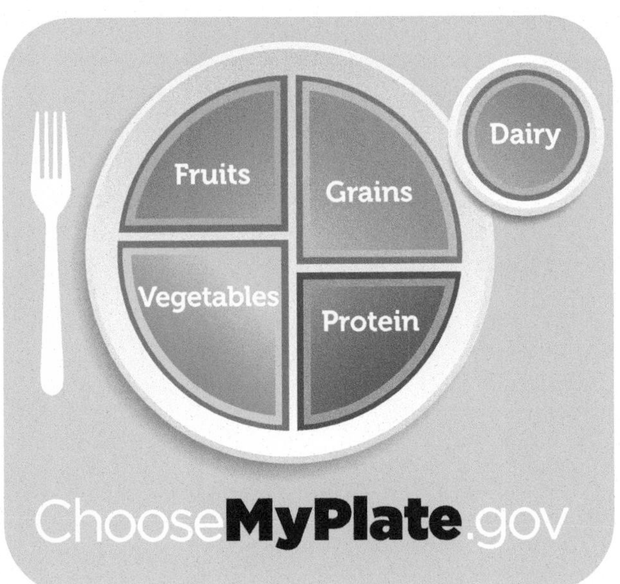

FIGURE 2.3 The USDA's MyPlate helps to translate the DRIs into an individualized guideline.
Source: http://www.choosemyplate.gov/images/MyPlateImages/PDF/myplate_green.pdf

The symbol resembling a plate is intentionally simple and is meant to be used with the interactive website and free handouts found at ChooseMyPlate.gov. The five food groups, colorful vegetables, fruits, grains, dairy and protein, are distributed on a plate icon and are portioned out to suggest the recommended serving amount of each of the food groups within a meal. Most of the meal should be based on the plant-based foods such as vegetables, fruits, and grains. Protein foods, such as meat, beans and peas, should only comprise a quarter of the plate. Dairy in the form of lowfat milk, cheese, yogurt, and calcium-fortified soymilk is encouraged daily. Oils are not displayed on the MyPlate icon as they were on MyPyramid, but the website emphasizes that the use of liquid oils rather than solid fats has not changed (Figures 2.4 and 2.5).

The MyPlate website at ChooseMyPlate.gov provides many tools to assist the consumer with meal planning, particularly the SuperTracker (Figure 2.6). At the SuperTracker website you can enter your personal information such as height, weight, age, gender, and activity level, and receive an individualized meal plan. In addition, you can track your diet over several days and compare it to what is recommended for you. Various meal plans are available at MyPlate, along with a list of foods within each food group. The meal plans include the recommended number of servings of each food group to emphasize the need for moderation and balance; the examples of foods within each food group assist in getting a variety of foods in each day to better meet the DRIs for vitamins and minerals. The importance of balance of Calories and energy expenditure is encouraged as well. Table 2.2 includes examples of various meal plans for those 18 years and older.

United States Department of Agriculture

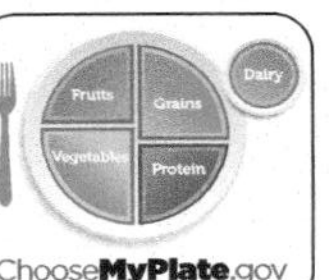

MyPlate Daily Checklist

Find your Healthy Eating Style

Everything you eat and drink matters. Find your healthy eating style that reflects your preferences, culture, traditions, and budget—and maintain it for a lifetime! The right mix can help you be healthier now and into the future. The key is choosing a variety of foods and beverages from each food group—*and making sure that each choice is limited in saturated fat, sodium, and added sugars.* Start with small changes—**"MyWins"**—to make healthier choices you can enjoy.

Food Group Amounts for 2,000 Calories a Day

Fruits	Vegetables	Grains	Protein	Dairy
2 cups	**2 1/2 cups**	**6 ounces**	**5 1/2 ounces**	**3 cups**
Focus on whole fruits	Vary your veggies	Make half your grains whole grains	Vary your protein routine	Move to low-fat or fat-free milk or yogurt
Focus on whole fruits that are fresh, frozen, canned, or dried.	Choose a variety of colorful fresh, frozen, and canned vegetables—make sure to include dark green, red, and orange choices.	Find whole-grain foods by reading the Nutrition Facts label and ingredients list.	Mix up your protein foods to include seafood, beans and peas, unsalted nuts and seeds, soy products, eggs, and lean meats and poultry.	Choose fat-free milk, yogurt, and soy beverages (soy milk) to cut back on your saturated fat.

Limit

Drink and eat less sodium, saturated fat, and added sugars. Limit:

- Sodium to **2,300 milligrams** a day.
- Saturated fat to **22 grams** a day.
- Added sugars to **50 grams** a day.

Be active your way: Children 6 to 17 years old should move **60 minutes** every day. Adults should be physically active at least **2 1/2 hours** per week.

Use SuperTracker to create a personal plan based on your age, sex, height, weight, and physical activity level.

SuperTracker.usda.gov

FIGURE 2.4 Specific recommendations for each group in MyPlate. Courtesy of www.choosemyplate.gov

FIGURE 2.5 SuperTracker is a dynamic tool provided by MyPlate to assist with meal planning. It allows the consumer to track their intake with their level of activity.
Source: https://www.supertracker.usda.gov/default.aspx

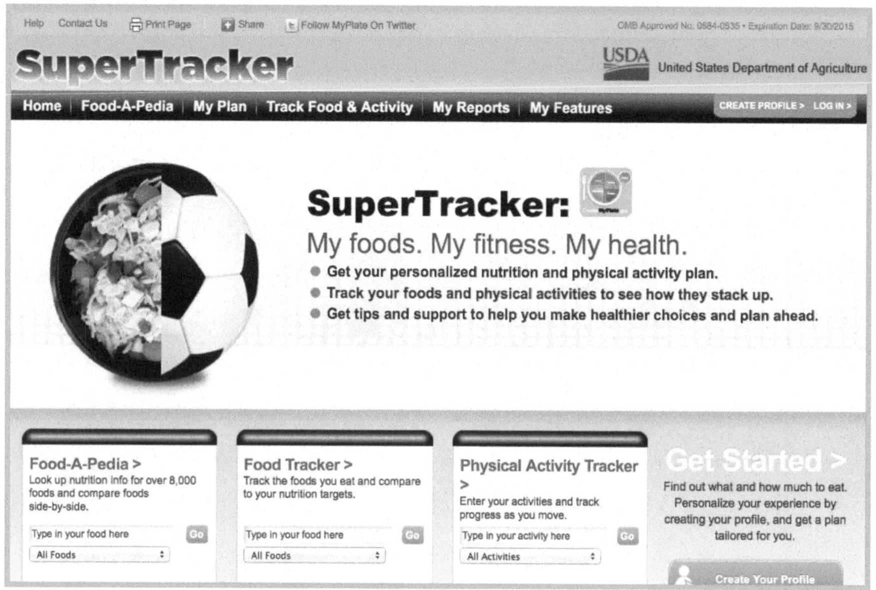

TABLE 2.2 MyPlate Recommendations for Specific Caloric Intake

Daily Amount of Food from Each Group					
Calorie Level	**1,600**	**1,800**	**2,000**	**2,200**	**2,400**
Fruits	1.5 c.	1.5 c.	2 c.	2 c.	2 c.
Vegetables	2 c.	2.5 c.	2.5 c.	3 c.	3 c.
Grains	5 oz. eq.	6 oz. eq.	6 oz. eq.	7 oz. eq.	8 oz. eq.
Protein	5 oz. eq.	5 oz. eq.	5.5 oz. eq.	6 oz. eq.	6.5 oz. eq.
Dairy	3 c.	3 c.	3 c.	3 c.	3 c.
Calorie Level	**2,600**	**2,800**	**3,000**	**3,200**	
Fruits	2 c.	2.5 c.	2.5 c.	2.5 c.	
Vegetables	3.5 c.	3.5 c.	4 c.	4 c.	
Grains	9 oz. eq.	10 oz. eq.	10 oz. eq.	10 oz. eq.	
Protein	6.5 oz. eq.	7 oz. eq.	7 oz. eq.	7 oz. eq.	
Milk	3 c.	3 c.	3 c.	3 c.	

Source: United States Department of Agriculture

SOLID FATS AND ADDED SUGARS

Is it OK
to eat sweets
and snacks
some-
times?

Is it okay to eat sweets and snacks sometimes? The answer is yes, but sweets, snack foods, and other empty Calorie foods tend to be high in added sugars and fat, particularly solid fats, which are linked to certain chronic diseases such as heart disease. These foods tend to be low in vitamins, minerals, fiber and phytochemicals, and are therefore considered empty Calories. Accordingly, they should contribute only a small amount of your total Calories for the day. Calories from solid fats and added sugars, also known as SoFAS, should be consumed in moderation and ideally consumed after you meet all your nutrient needs from foods that are more nutrient dense, without going over your total Calorie target for the day. Reducing your intake from these empty Calories allow for an increased intake of foods from any group, such as an extra glass of milk. In making this choice, be aware that most Americans already consume more than their recommended Calories. Of course, if your energy requirements are greater due to increased physical activity, the amount of additional Calories you can consume goes up, opening up the opportunity to consume additional foods from various food groups, as well as an energy dense food—in moderation. For example, if you require 2,000 Calories and typically meet your nutrient needs by consuming 1,800 Calories in your regular meals, then you have about 200 discretionary Calories, while a person who consumes 1,800 Calories but needs 2,100 Calories can add 300 Calories in snacks without gaining weight.

BEFORE YOU GO ON...

1. What is the purpose of MyPlate?
2. List the food groups included on the MyPlate food icon.
3. Why is it recommended to eat less foods with solid fats and added sugars?

THE NUTRITION FACTS LABEL

Nutrition Facts label

Part of the required information on a food label that provides the nutritional content of the product.

In 1990, the Nutrition Labeling and Education Act went into effect. Regulations for the contents of food labels are issued by two federal agencies: The United States Department of Agriculture (USDA) and the Food and Drug Administration (FDA). These agencies designed the label requirements so that consumers would have useful information about the food they eat. The USDA regulates and now requires the labeling of meat, poultry, and eggs. The FDA regulates food labeling, which is required for most packaged foods, such as breads, cereals, canned and frozen foods, snacks, desserts, and drinks. Nutrition labeling for fruits, vegetables, and fish is still voluntary but highly encouraged. Also, nutrition information is required for chain restaurants like McDonalds, Chipotle and Panera.

According to the Nutrition Labeling and Education Act, all food labels must contain the following information:

- A statement of identity: the common name of the product
- The net contents of the package: the accurate weight, volume, measure, or numerical count of the product in the package
- The name and address of the manufacturer
- A list of ingredients: ingredients must be listed by common name in descending order by weight; any food additives or preservatives are to be included here (see You Decide for more information)
- Identification of any of the major food allergens as one of the ingredients must be included on the label; major food allergens include milk, egg, fish, shellfish, tree nuts, wheat, peanuts, and soybeans
- Nutrition information; includes the Nutrition Facts label

Under the label's "Nutrition Facts" heading, manufacturers are required to provide information on certain nutrients, which were selected because they address today's health concerns. The order in which they must appear reflects the priority of current dietary recommendations. We will examine and discuss each part of the label, depicted in Figure 2.6.*

Some foods are exempt from nutrition labeling including the following:

- Food served for immediate consumption, such as that served in hospital cafeterias and airplanes, and that sold by food service vendors—for example, mall cookie counters, sidewalk vendors, and vending machines
- Medical foods, such as those used to meet the nutritional needs of patients with certain diseases or supplement drinks used in hospitals
- Coffee and tea, some spices, and other foods that contain no significant amounts of any nutrients

FOOD ADDITIVES—DO WE NEED THEM AND ARE THEY SAFE?

You DECIDE

Are some of the words in the ingredients list of many food labels unfamiliar to you or hard to pronounce? Per the FDA, food additives are "any substance the intended use of which results or may reasonably be expected to result, directly or indirectly, in its becoming a component or otherwise affecting the characteristics of any food." This definition includes any substance used to produce, process, treat, package, transport, or store food. Additives are used in foods to improve taste, texture, appearance, and quality. Food additives also improve the nutritional content as when food is fortified (for example, when iodine is added to salt). They can also be used to color food; they are used to make mint ice cream green, margarines yellow, and colas brown. While some of these additives have names that may be unfamiliar to you, some are nutrients you will learn about in the following chapters. For examples, antioxidants, such as vitamin C or vitamin E may be added to foods to preserve their freshness. They are listed as "ascorbic acid" and "tocopherol," respectively, in the list of ingredients, terms you may not associate with these vitamins (you will learn these terms and others in Chapter 8).

The FDA oversees substances added to food and is charged with the responsibility of monitoring their safe use. Under the federal Food, Drug, and Cosmetic Act (FDCA), the FDA must review the safety of food and color additives before manufacturers and distributors can market them. The agency also has a notification program for substances that are "Generally Recognized as Safe" (GRAS). Additives may be considered GRAS if they have been used in foods without harm for a significant period of time, such as prior to 1958. A food may also be categorized as GRAS if that food item has strong scientific backing that it is considered safe.

Food additives have been blamed for a variety of health conditions, from hyperactivity, including attention deficit hyperactivity disorder (ADHD), to cancer. Some of these concerns are based on the results of research done by professionals in either humans or animals, but there is often mixed results in the outcomes of these studies and/or the studies are not necessarily conducted in a manner that reduces bias. For example, researchers investigating the connection between food coloring and hyperactivity may ask parents if they believe their child's hyperactivity improved when reducing food coloring in their diet. The parent, wanting to find a solution to their child's hyperactivity, may believe there was improvement, when in reality, there was not. This is an example of potential bias in the study results. Some of the studies performed in animals, such as rats, may find that a particular additive caused cancer in the laboratory rats; however, these study animals are often exposed to high doses that we humans would not consume. Also, animals may respond differently to exposure to these additives compared to humans. These are all things to consider when seeing information in the news or Internet about how bad food additives are for humans.

Serving Size

The nutrition information on a Nutrition Facts label is based on the recommended serving size for a food. The serving sizes for common food items is standardized and must be expressed in both common household and metric measures to help make comparing different brands easier. The FDA allows the following as common household measures: the cup, tablespoon, teaspoon, piece, slice, and fraction (such as "¼ pizza"). Ounces may also be used, but only if a common household unit is not applicable and an appropriate visual unit is given—for example, 1 oz. (28 g/about ½ pickle).

Since it is not uncommon for people to consume more or less than the serving sizes listed, it is important to remember to adjust the nutrition information so it reflects the amount actually eaten. For example, a cola sold in a vending machine may list the serving size as 8-fl oz even though the soda is being sold in a 20-fl oz bottle. Consumers may drink the entire 20-fl oz bottle and not realize that they were consuming closer to 250 kcals rather than 100 kcals listed for the 8-fl oz serving.

CURRENT LABEL	
Nutrition Facts	
Serving Size 2/3 cup (55g)	
Servings Per Container About 8	
Amount Per Serving	
Calories 230	Calories from Fat 72
	% Daily Value*
Total Fat 8g	**12%**
Saturated Fat 1g	**5%**
Trans Fat 0g	
Cholesterol 0mg	**0%**
Sodium 160mg	**7%**
Total Carbohydrate 37g	**12%**
Dietary Fiber 4g	**16%**
Sugars 1g	
Protein 3g	
Vitamin A	10%
Vitamin C	8%
Calcium	20%
Iron	45%

* Percent Daily Values are based on a 2,000 calorie diet. Your daily value may be higher or lower depending on your calorie needs.

	Calories:	2,000	2,500
Total Fat	Less than	65g	80g
Sat Fat	Less than	20g	25g
Cholesterol	Less than	300mg	300mg
Sodium	Less than	2,400mg	2,400mg
Total Carbohydrate		300g	375g
Dietary Fiber		25g	30g

PROPOSED LABEL	
Nutrition Facts	
8 servings per container	
Serving size	2/3 cup (55g)
Amount per 2/3 cup	
Calories	**230**
% DV*	
12%	**Total Fat** 8g
5%	**Saturated Fat** 1g
	***Trans* Fat** 0g
0%	**Cholesterol** 0mg
7%	**Sodium** 160mg
12%	**Total Carbs** 37g
14%	**Dietary Fiber** 4g
	Sugars 1g
	Added Sugars 0g
	Protein 3g
10%	**Vitamin D** 2mcg
20%	**Calcium** 260mg
45%	**Iron** 8mg
5%	**Potassium** 235mg

* Footnote on Daily Values (DV) and calories reference to be inserted here.

FIGURE 2.6 The current Nutrition Facts label on the left was adopted in 1993. With the exception of adding trans fat to the label, it has not been modified since this time. The Nutrition Facts label on the right will be implemented in 2018, reflects more common serving sizes and emphasizes common nutrition concerns, including obesity and other chronic health conditions.

Source: http://www.fda.gov/Food/GuidanceRegulation/GuidanceDocumentsRegulatoryInformation/LabelingNutrition/ucm385663.htm }

APPLICATION TIP

One way to determine how many servings you are consuming is to compare the amount of food you are about to eat (your portion) to everyday objects. For example, 1 c. of cereal is about the size of your fist; ¼ c. of dried fruit is about the size of an egg; and ½ c. of pasta, rice, or potato is about half of a baseball. Therefore, if you eat a cup of rice (about the size of a baseball), you have consumed two servings of rice.

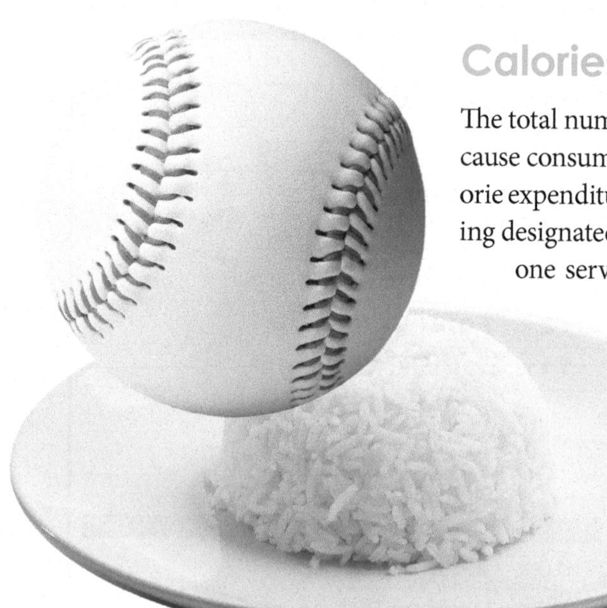

Calories

The total number of Calories in a labeled food is always listed first because consumers must be able to match daily Calorie intake with Calorie expenditure to avoid weight gain. Calories shown are for one serving designated by the serving size on the label, so if you eat more than one serving, remember that you are consuming more Calories than are listed on the label. The label also includes the Calories from fat, so the consumer can easily calculate the percent of Calories from fat the food provides.

Nutrients

The nutrients on the Nutrition Facts label are listed in order of nutrients that we should consume less of and those we should consume more of. The nutrients listed first are those that Americans tend to eat too much of and tied to developing chronic conditions when eaten in excess: total fat, saturated fat, trans fat, cholesterol, sodium, and sugars. As we have noted, consuming too much of these nutrients may increase your risk of heart disease and certain cancers. Protein is included next, a nutrient most Americans get enough of in their diet. Lastly, the American diet should strive to increase dietary fiber, calcium, vitamin A, vitamin C, and iron. Any nutrient fortified or enriched in the food product must also be included on the food label; other nutrients may be added voluntarily by the food manufacturer.

Daily Values
The nutrient standards used on food labels; they are based on a 2,000-Calorie diet.

Daily Value

Perhaps the key to using the Nutrition Facts label for diet planning is the percent Daily Value (%DV). The **Daily Values** are the nutrient standards used on food labels; they are based on a 2,000-Calorie diet. Why create yet another set of standards? Because many of the other standards vary for different age and gender groups. For labeling purposes, 2,000 Calories has been established as the reference for calculating percent DVs. This level was chosen, partly because many health experts say it approximates the maintenance Calorie requirements of the groups most often targeted for weight reduction, such as postmenopausal women. The DVs are set for the "average person" and are listed in Table 2.3. Because many people need more or less than 2,000 Calories, these values are best used to compare one product to another. If you compare products, make sure the serving sizes are similar, especially the weight (grams, milligrams, ounces). The percent DV helps you determine whether a serving of food is high or low in a nutrient. A 5% DV or less is *low* for all nutrients, those you want to limit (such as fat, saturated fat, cholesterol, and sodium), and even those that you want to consume in greater amounts (fiber, calcium, etc.). A 20% DV or more is *high* for all nutrients. Note that there is no percent DV for protein, sugar, or trans fats. A percent DV is required to be listed if a claim such as "high in protein" is made. Otherwise, unless the food is meant for use by infants and children under age 4, none is needed. No DV has been established for sugars because no recommendations currently exist for the total amount to eat in a day. Experts have also not provided a DV for trans fat; however, they recommend that you limit trans fats as much as possible.

TABLE 2.3 Daily Values

Food Component	Daily Value (DV)
Fat (based on 30% of total Calories)	65 g
Saturated fat (based on 10% of total Calories)	20 g
Cholesterol	300 mg
Total carbohydrate (based on 60% of total Calories)	300 g
Fiber (based on 11.5 g fiber per 1,000 Calories)	25 g*
Sodium	2,300 mg**
Vitamin A	5,000 IU
Calcium	1300 mg
Iron	18 mg
Vitamin C	60 mg

*The RDA for fiber is 14 g per 1000 kcal of energy needed. Your individual needs may be greater.

**Please note that the AI for sodium is 1,500 mg.

Note: DVs are given in grams (g), milligrams (mg), micrograms (μg), and international units (IU).

Claims on Labels

Every time you turn on the TV or go to the grocery store, you see a new product claiming that it helps prevent a disease or that it is high in a certain nutrient. These claims are often confusing and leave the consumer wondering what to believe. In an effort to regulate the use of such label claims, the FDA has established specific guidelines that manufacturers must follow to make certain claims on their food labels. There are three categories of label claims: health claims, nutrient content claims, and structure/function claims.

Health claims

Statements made about a product that link it or some of its ingredients to a reduced risk of disease, such as a claim that consuming fiber reduces your risk of heart disease.

Health claims are statements made about a product that link it or some of its ingredients to a reduced risk of disease, such as a claim that consuming fiber reduces your risk of heart disease. Such claims must be approved by the FDA prior to being placed on the label. There are three categories of health claims. One category of health claims are supported by extensive scientific evidence that has been reviewed by the FDA and a body of experts in the scientific community. These types of claims are known as Authorized Health Claims. Other types of claims are backed and requested by a body of scientific experts with the U.S. government or the National Academy of Sciences, but do not have the strong body of scientific evidence that Authorized Health Claims have. These types of claims are known as an Authoritative Health Claims. Lastly, some health claims have the support of a scientific body of experts and are based on emerging scientific evidence, but this evidence is relatively new compared to the other health claims. This "emerging evidence" may lead to a **Qualified Health Claim** and may be used on food or dietary supplement labels. The following are examples of some of these approved health claims.

Qualified Health Claim

A health claim based on new and emerging evidence among a food component, food or a dietary supplement, and the reduced risk of a disease.

Health Claims:

- Calcium—decreased risk of osteoporosis
- Fiber-containing grain products, fruits, and vegetables—decreased risk of cancer
- Folic acid—reduced risk of neural tube defects
- Fruits, vegetables, and grain products that contain fiber—lower risk of heart disease
- Fruits and vegetables—lower risk of cancer
- Soluble fiber from certain foods, such as whole oats and psyllium seed husk—decreased risk of heart disease
- Lower saturated fat and cholesterol—decreased risk of heart disease
- Higher potassium and lower in sodium—reduced risk of high blood pressure
- Whole grain foods with low saturated fat and cholesterol - reduced risk of some cancers

Qualified Health Claims:

- Tomatoes – reduced risk of prostate cancer
- Walnuts – reduced risk of coronary heart disease
- Omega-3 fatty acids – reduced risk for coronary heart disease

Another type of claim that may be placed on food or dietary supplement labels called a **structure/function claims**. These claims are commonly seen on dietary supplements and describe an association between a nutrient or food component and the structure or function in the body. For example, a claim on a fiber supplement may state that fiber helps "maintain bowel regularity" or for a calcium supplement, that calcium helps "build strong bones." Unlike the health claims, structure/functions claims do not need to be preapproved by the FDA; however, the manufacturer of the supplement must provide documentation to the FDA within 30 days following the marketing of the supplement with the claim. Documentation with proof that the claim is accurate must include this notification. In addition, the manufacturer must include on the label of the product that the FDA has not approved the structure/function claim (see Figure 2.7). The same disclaimer must also inform the consumer that the product is not intended to "diagnose, treat, cure, or prevent any disease" to distinguish the supplement from a medication.

Structure/function Claims
A claim on a dietary supplement or food product that describes the relationship between a nutrient or food component and the structure or function of the body.

The FDA also regulates food labeling that defines what terms may be used to describe the level of a nutrient in a food item. These types of claims are known as **nutrient content claims**. The nutrient content claims have been approved by the FDA and are useful in selecting food products that may be a healthier option because of the level of the nutrient described in the claim. See Figure 2.8 for a list of these types of claims.

Nutrient Content Claims
A claim on a food product that describes the level of a particular nutrient in that food product.

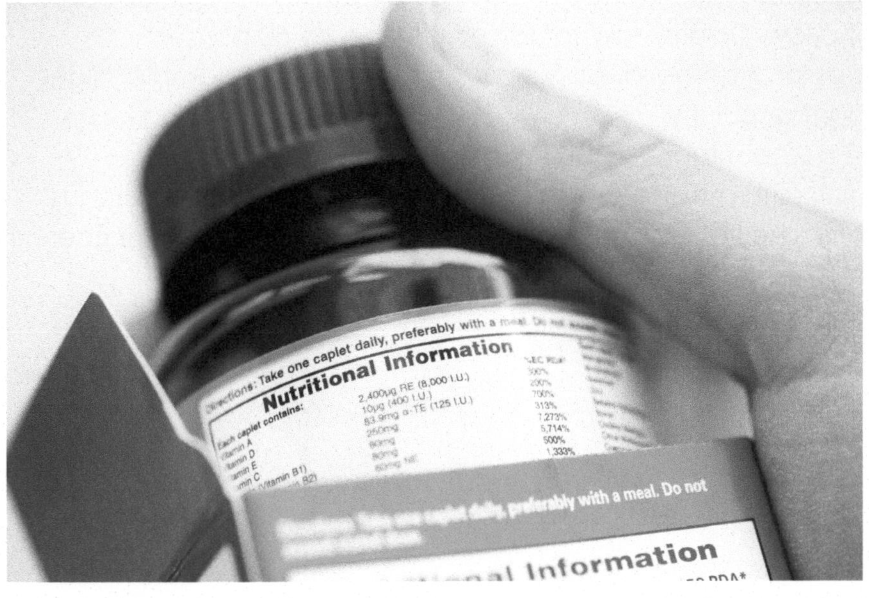

FIGURE 2.7 All structure/functions claims on dietary supplements and food products must include a disclaimer that informs the consumer that the claim has not been approved by the FDA and that the product is not to be treated as a medication that can treat or cure diseases.

FIGURE 2.8 Nutrient Content Claims

- *"Free":* No or trivial amounts of fat, saturated fat, cholesterol, sodium, sugars, or Calories. For example, "Calorie-free" means less than 5 Calories per serving, and "sugar-free" and "fat-free" both mean less than 0.5 g per serving.
- *"Low":*
  "low-fat": 3 g or less per serving
  "low-saturated-fat": 1 g or less per serving
  "low-sodium": 140 mg or less per serving
  "very-low-sodium": 35 mg or less per serving
  "low-cholesterol": 20 mg or less, and 2 g or less of saturated fat, per serving
  "low-Calorie": 40 Calories or less per serving
- *"Lean" and "extra lean":* These terms can be used to describe the fat content of meat, poultry, seafood, and game meats.
- *"Lean":* Less than 10 g fat, 4.5 g or less saturated fat, and less than 95 mg cholesterol per serving or per 100 g
- *"Extra lean":* Less than 5 g fat, less than 2 g saturated fat, and less than 95 mg cholesterol per serving or per 100 g
- *"High":* 20 percent or more of the DV for a particular nutrient in a serving
- *"Good source":* 10–19 percent of the DV for a particular nutrient.
- *"Reduced" or "Less":* At least 25 percent less of a nutrient or Calories than the regular product. A "reduced" claim can't be made on a product if its reference food already meets the requirement for a "low" claim. In other words, applesauce can't say "reduced in saturated fat" because it never had saturated fat in it to begin with.
- *"Light":* This term can mean one of three things:
  One-third fewer Calories or half the fat of the regular food
  Sodium content of a low-Calorie, low-fat food reduced by 50 percent
  Texture and color, as long as the label explains the intent—for example, "light brown sugar" or "light and fluffy"
- *"More":* At least 10 percent more of the DV than the original food.
- *"Healthy":* Low in fat, saturated fat, trans fat, cholesterol, and sodium. It must contain 10 percent of the DV of vitamin A or C, iron, calcium, protein, or fiber.

gopause/Shutterstock.com

Free-range eggs are produced by hens that are allowed to graze or roam outside for at least some portion of each day. Typically, egg-producing chickens are raised in cages.

Even claims that are regulated may often appear confusing or misleading at first glance. For example, some egg manufacturers sell "free-range" and "cage-free" eggs. These products typically display a picture of a farm or of chickens in a field. The consumer may get the visual of freely grazing, happy chickens. Is this really the case? It is important to understand the definitions and guidelines behind such claims and to understand that some "play on words" can be involved. See Sustainable Nutrition for more information.

BEFORE YOU GO ON...

1. Why are manufacturers required to provide information on selected nutrients on the food product's Nutrition Facts label?
2. How may the Nutrition Fact label help with following a healthy diet?
3. What are the differences between a health claim, qualified health claim, and structure/function claim?
4. What is the difference between the terms "fat-free" and "low-fat"?
5. What are the DVs used for?
6. What must occur before a manufacturer can make a structure/function claim about a product?

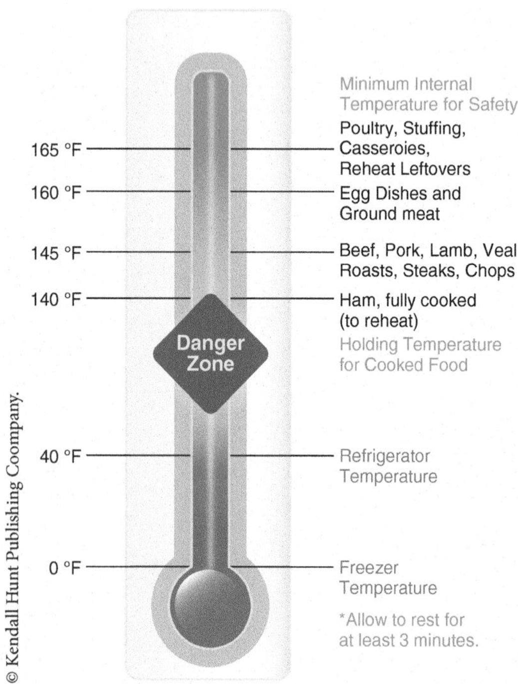

*OTHER THINGS TO THINK ABOUT WITH FOOD

FOOD SAFETY

Have you ever had a stomach flu but wondered if it was "something you ate"? We often confuse food poisoning (foodborne illness) with stomach flu. Americans enjoy one of the safest food supplies in the world, but still roughly 1 in 6 people (or approximately 48 million) will contract some form of food poisoning each year. Salmonella causes the most hospitalizations and deaths. Fortunately, there are several things that can be done to protect yourself and your family from foodborne illnesses.

According to *FightBac! Partnership for Food Safety Education*, keeping food safe includes four core practices: Clean, separate, cook and chill.

Clean focuses on reducing the amount of bacteria that can be spread in the work area by washing hands and surfaces often. *Separating* is also key since it helps prevent cross-contamination between raw meats, poultry, seafood and eggs with other fresh foods that will not be cooked. To prevent cross-contamination, food needs to be kept separate in the grocery cart, grocery bags and in the refrigerator. During preparation, one cutting board should be designated for fresh produce while another cutting board for raw meats. Never use the same plate for raw and cooked meats.

Proper *cooking* and *chilling* of foods is necessary to achieve and maintain appropriate temperatures that will reduce the growth of bacteria. Bacteria grow most rapidly in what is termed the Temperature Danger Zone (40°F to 140°F). The specific temperature a food needs to be cooked to is dictated by the type of food in question. For example, ground beef has a different temperature requirement than poultry. When chilling foods, refrigerate quickly to bring chilled food to a temperature of 40°F or below. Refrigeration only slows the growth of bacteria.

ORGANIC FOODS

© Shutterstock.com

As Americans are becoming more and more concerned about their food products and how they are produced, many people wonder if they should be buying organic food products. What exactly makes a food product organic? Organic refers to the way farmers grow and process their food products. For example, organic plant foods are free of synthetic fertilizers, chemical-based pesticides and any genetic engineering or modifications. Animals raised under organic guidelines are fed organic feed and are free of any antibiotics or growth hormones. In order to be certified organic, the U.S. Department of Agriculture (USDA) verifies farmers and ranchers are in compliance with organic standards, as defined by the USDA, to grow crops and raise livestock that:

- Preserve natural resources and biodiversity
- Support animal health and welfare
- Provide access to the outdoors so that animals can exercise their natural behaviors
- Only use approved materials
- Do not use genetically modified ingredients
- Receive annual onsite inspections
- Separate organic food from non-organic food

There are very specific guidelines and strict labeling requirements for organic food products. In order for a food to be labeled 100% organic, all ingredients must be certified by the USDA as organic. If a product is labeled "organic," at least 95% of the ingredients must be organically produced (except water and salt). Many food items are labeled that they are "made with" organic ingredients which means at least 70% of the product must be certified organic ingredients.

GENETICALLY MODIFIED ORGANISMS

Genetically modified organisms (GMOs) are foods that have been altered by manipulating the DNA (genes) to produce a targeted, and improved food product. Approximately 90% of corn, soybeans and cotton are genetically modified in the U.S.

There are many pros and cons to this farming practice. Genetically modified crops reduce the need for pesticides. Seeds are modified to resist certain insects. Better crop yields also result due to the ability to resist extreme weather and reduce crop failure. Genetically modified foods have the ability to increase the nutritional value of a food by modifying the vitamin or mineral content. Since our crops are often harvested and shipped distances, GMOs can increase shelf-life, reduce spoilage and extend flavor and nutritional value.

There are some negative results of GMOs. Proteins are often combined in the new organism that were not present previously. This can cause increased allergic reactions by humans. Also, there may be an altered resistance to antibiotics because GMOs may have antibiotic properties which lower the effectiveness of other antibiotics. Genes may migrate by passing from one species to another which could cause herbicide-resistant genes in weeds.

Currently, labeling of GMOs on food products is not required. A company can choose to state whether or not their product has been genetically modified. Certified organic foods are free of GMOs. There is a major movement in the U.S. to have labeling of genetically modified organisms in food products become mandatory.*

*SUSTAINABLE NUTRITION

Cage-free or free-range—what do they really mean?

While purchasing chicken or eggs at the grocery store, you may have noticed on the packaging that the chicken was raised either "cage-free" or "free range." This is in contrast to those chickens that are confined to a cage or pen of some kind, which is considered the conventional method. Both producers will claim benefits to either methods. Here is a description of some of the claims and what they may or may not mean.

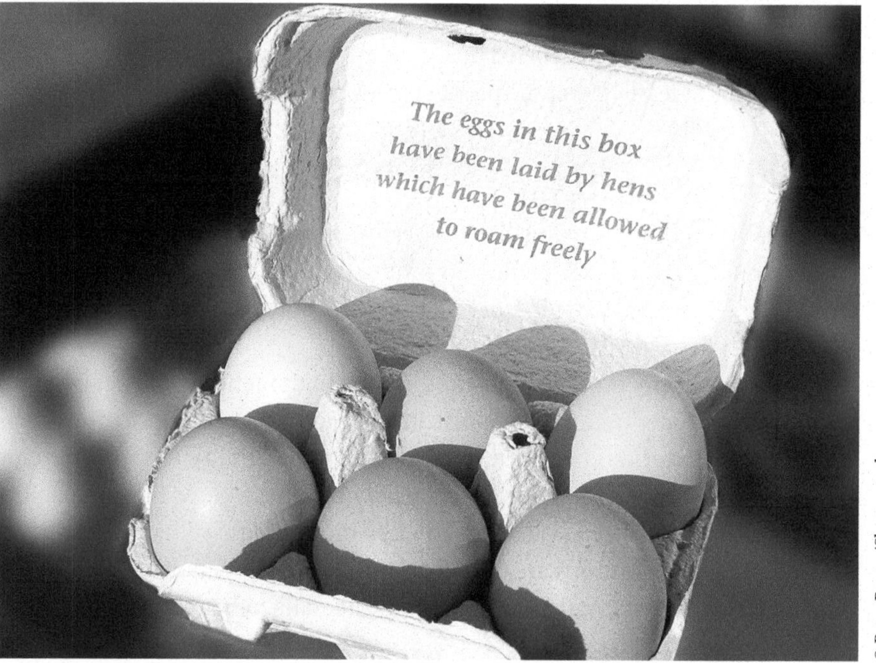

The eggs in this box
have been laid by hens
which have been allowed
to roam freely

© Peter Baxter/Shutterstock.com

Most eggs are obtained from caged hens. However, many consumers prefer to purchase eggs produced by hens that are not kept in cages.

Producers of the conventional method of raising chickens contend that caging hens has benefits for the birds, consumers, and their workers. The cages help separate the birds from their feces, which is said to help reduce the risk of disease and infections. Producers also contend that working conditions for their farmers and employees are better with caged hens than with other systems. Moreover, by using cages for egg-laying hens producers can employ automation, which decreases labor time, costs, and the prevalence of dust and ammonia. Eggs are laid on the sloping floor of the cage so that there is minimal contact between the egg and the hen, which producers say decreases the possibility of bacterial contamination of the egg.

Cage-free or free range, per the USDA definition, means the chickens are allowed exposure to the outside for some period of time during the day; however, the length of time the chickens are allowed outside is not specified or regulated. Reasons why people choose free-range or cage free chickens or eggs include desire to eat poultry and eggs raised in a more humane manner; reduced risk of exposure to salmonella, a bacterium commonly found on poultry; better nutritional quality of the chickens; and reduced exposure to antibiotics or hormones that are often used in poultry production. Research does not consistently support the notion that free-range or cage-free chickens and eggs are nutritionally superior to conventionally raised chickens and may depend on supplemental grain that chickens are exposed to. Lastly, levels of salmonella from free-range or cage-free chickens appeared to be no different than conventionally raised chickens.

So, which is better? Basically, it comes down to personal choice and financial status. One thing to consider is the greater production cost associated with raising free-range or cage-free hens is often reflected in the price of the meat or eggs of these hens. Being educated on what the claims on the nutrition packaging may help the consumer make a more informed choice.

PUTTING IT ALL TOGETHER

So far we have discussed the recommendations and the various tools available to help you plan a healthy diet. Now you have to incorporate this information into a menu of meals that fit your lifestyle, accommodate your schedule, and include foods you like. So the first step is to get out a sheet of paper and start listing the foods you normally eat. Second, make a list of the different categories represented by MyPlate. Third, place the foods you like into the various categories of MyPlate. Do you have foods from each category? Do you have a variety of foods in each group? If not, consider making a list of new foods to try. You can begin to construct a menu plan by incorporating the foods you like in the amounts recommended by MyPlate and other recommendations.*

CHAPTER SUMMARY

- A healthy diet includes balance, variety, and moderation. *Balance* means incorporating foods from all food groups into your plan daily. *Variety* means eating different types of foods within each food group. *Moderation* means not overconsuming any one food or food group.
- It is important to eat mostly nutrient-dense foods, or foods with a lot of nutrients for the number of Calories they contain, rather than empty Calories or foods that supply Calories but not many nutrients.
- Having a plan will help you think before you eat and accomplish your goal of eating a healthy diet.
- Guidelines exist that can help you develop a healthy eating plan, such as *Dietary Guidelines for Americans*, the DRIs, MyPlate, and the Nutrition Facts label.
- The *Dietary Guidelines* provide the general recommendations needed for planning a healthy diet.
- The DRIs, which include RDAs, AIs, EARs, and ULs, provide specific recommendations for nutrient intakes. The RDAs and the AIs are most often used.
- MyPlate translates the concepts of balance, variety, and moderation, along with the information from the *Dietary Guidelines* and the DRIs, into a usable diet plan. You can individualize it at the interactive MyPlate website.
- MyPlate includes discretionary Calories. These are the Calories you can consume after you meet all your nutrient needs without going over your total Calorie target for the day.
- MyPlate translates servings into understandable portions, such as 1 cup, to help consumers control portion sizes in an effort to control Calorie intake.
- The Nutrition Facts label found on many food products is intended to help you make choices regarding individual foods.
- Food labeling is required for most packaged foods such as breads, cereals, canned and frozen foods, snacks, desserts, and drinks. The USDA has only recently required labeling for meats, poultry, and eggs. Nutrition labeling for fruits, vegetables, and fish is voluntary but highly encouraged.
- Nutrition information is required for restaurant foods that make health or nutrient claims such as "low-fat" or "heart-healthy."
- The regulations for food labeling also define what terms may be used to describe the level of a nutrient in a food and how they can be used, such as "fat-free" or "low-sodium." These types of claims are known as Nutrient Content Claims.
- Health claims are statements made about a product that link it or some of its ingredients to a reduced risk of disease, such as a claim that consuming fiber reduces your risk of heart disease. Such claims must be approved by the FDA and supported by scientific evidence.
- Qualified Health Claims may also be found on the food label. The claims must be approved by the FDA and are based on emerging or new scientific research.
- Structure/function claims are frequently included on the labels of dietary supplements and do not need to be pre-approved by the FDA. The manufacturer of the supplement is required to include a disclaimer on the label that informs the consumer that the claim has not been approved by the FDA.
- All of the nutrient guidelines generated by federal agencies and the required Nutrition Facts label are designed to work together to help you plan a healthy diet.

KEY TERMS

ACCEPTABLE MACRONUTRIENT DISTRIBUTION RANGE (AMDR) A recommended range of requirements for carbohydrates, fats, and proteins based on the total daily Calorie needs and balance of nutrients that are associated with a decreased risk of chronic disease.

ADEQUATE INTAKE (AI) The value assigned to a nutrient if some scientific evidence is available, but not quite enough to establish a recommendation with certainty.

BALANCE Incorporating foods from all food groups into your daily eating plan.

DAILY VALUES The nutrient standards used on food labels; they are based on a 2,000-Calorie diet.

DASH (DIETARY APPROACHES TO STOP HYPERTENSION) A tool to help individuals lower sodium intake and implement the *Dietary Guidelines*.

DIETARY GUIDELINES FOR AMERICANS A summary of science-based advice to promote health through diet and physical activity and to reduce the risk for major chronic diseases in people over age 2.

DIETARY REFERENCE INTAKES (DRIS) Guidelines designed for healthy people, established to replace the original RDAs in the United States and the Recommended Nutrient Intakes (RNIs) in Canada.

EMPTY CALORIES Calories with little or no nutrient content.

ENRICHED FOODS Foods that have had nutrients added back that were removed during processing. For example, enriched white rice has had some nutrients added back that were present before the outer brown husk was removed.

ESTIMATED AVERAGE REQUIREMENT (EAR) The value assigned to a nutrient that would meet the needs of 50 percent of the people of a specific age or gender. It is used only by federal agencies for research and policy making.

ESTIMATED ENERGY REQUIREMENT (EER) A general recommendation for energy needs.

FOOD SAFETY Preventing foodborne illnesses by utilizing the practice of safely cleaning, separating, cooking and chilling foods

FOODBORNE ILLNESS An illness caused by ingesting food with a high level of bacteria or virus often caused by not following food safety guidelines

FORTIFIED FOODS Foods with nutrients added to them that were not originally present. An example is orange juice fortified with calcium.

GENETICALLY MODIFIED ORGANISMS An organism whose genetic material has been altered by manipulating the DNA (genes) to produce a targeted and improved food product.

HEALTH CLAIMS Statements made about a product that link it or some of its ingredients to a reduced risk of disease, such as a claim that consuming fiber reduces your risk of heart disease.

HEALTHY PEOPLE 2020 A list of health objectives for the nation to achieve by 2020. It is designed to identify the most significant preventable threats to health and to establish national goals to reduce these threats.

MODERATION Avoiding overconsumption of any one food or food group.

MYPLATE The nutrition guide designed by the U.S. Department of Agriculture that depicts the recommended food group distribution using a plate icon with the food groups divided among vegetables, fruit, grains, dairy, and protein.

NUTRIENT CONTENT CLAIMS A claim on a food product that describes the level of a particular nutrient in that food product.

NUTRITION FACTS LABEL Part of the required information on a food label that provides the nutritional content of the product.

ORGANIC FOODS Produce or other ingredients grown without the use of pesticides, synthetic fertilizers, or genetically modified organisms;

meat, poultry, eggs, and dairy products that do not take antibiotics or growth hormones.

QUALIFIED HEALTH CLAIM A health claim based on new and emerging evidence among a food component, food or a dietary supplement, and the reduced risk of a disease.

RECOMMENDED DIETARY ALLOWANCES (RDAS) The recommended intake required to meet the daily nutrient needs for 97–98 percent of all individuals in a given age or gender group. It is used for diet planning for individuals and is the foundation of the DRI.

STRUCTURE/FUNCTION CLAIMS A claim on a dietary supplement or food product that describes the relationship between a nutrient or food component and the structure or function of the body.

TOLERABLE UPPER INTAKE LEVEL (UL) The highest level of daily nutrient intake that poses little risk of adverse health effects to individuals in a specific age or gender group.

VARIETY Eating different types of foods within each food group.

REFERENCES

http://www.fda.gov/Food/GuidanceRegulation/GuidanceDocumentsRegulatoryInformation/LabelingNutrition/ucm2006828.htm#introduction

http://www.eatright.org/kids/article.aspx?id=6442478973&terms=food%20additive

http://www.fda.gov/food/ingredientspackaginglabeling/definitions/default.htm

http://www.fda.gov/Food/IngredientsPackagingLabeling/FoodAdditivesIngredients/ucm094211.htm#types

Centers for Disease Control and Prevention. (2014). Estimates of Foodborne Illness in the United States. Retrieved on April 13, 2016 from http://www.cdc.gov/foodborneburden/#

United States Department of Agriculture, Food Safety and Inspection Service. (October 2011). "Danger Zone" (40°F - 140°F).)

U.S. Department of Agriculture. (2015). Organic Agriculture. http://www.usda.gov/wps/portal/usda/usdahome?contentidonly=true&contentid=organic-agriculture.html

U.S. Department of Agriculture. (2012). Labeling Organic Products. https://www.ams.usda.gov/sites/default/files/media/Labeling%20Organic%20Products%20Fact%20Sheet.pdf)

Food and Drug Administration. (2015). Guidance for Industry: Voluntary Labeling Indicating Whether Foods Have or Have Not Been Derived from Genetically Engineered Plants http://www.fda.gov/food/guidanceregulation/guidancedocumentsregulatoryinformation/ucm059098.htm)

COOKING 101: QUICK, EASY, HEALTHY MEAL PLANNING AND PREPARATION

It's Easier Than You May Think!

Healthy eating is more than just consuming the right amounts of Calories, and fats, carbohydrates, and proteins and a balance of vitamins and minerals. It takes planning and execution, but for most people, especially students, the entire process needs to be quick and easy, too. Add that to adjusting to a new schedule, moving into a dorm or apartment, and juggling academics, family, job, and social life—and it can all be very stressful. Accordingly, it's little wonder that so many college students tend to put healthy eating and food preparation at the bottom of their priority list. But you shouldn't, and it doesn't have to be stressful. With a little bit of planning and very little cooking time, healthy meals can fit easily into your schedule. Preparing some of your own food can also save you money—so add that to its benefits.

Keeping It Simple: Some Tips to Get You Started

Tools of the Trade for the Beginner's Kitchen

If you are buying equipment for a kitchen in your first home or just trying to pick up the essentials for preparing quick meals in your apartment or dorm room, some basic tools can be very helpful (see Figure 2.9). The following checklist can help you get started.

- Something to cook on (many dorms have restrictions, so check before buying):
  - Microwave
  - Toaster and/or toaster oven
  - Hot plate (unless you have access to a stove)
  - Rice steamer
  - Slow cooker
- Silverware
- Cups, plates, bowls
- Spatula
- Dish soap and sponge
- Potholders or oven mitts
- Two knives (utility or chef's knife for cutting and chopping; paring knife for coring, seeding, etc.)
- Vegetable peeler
- Dry measuring cups and spoons
- Liquid measuring cup
- Two thermometers-one for your refrigerator and one for measuring the temperature/doneness of cooked poultry and meats)

- Cookware (avoid those with nonstick coatings):
  - Three pots with lids one small; (one medium; and one large or stockpot for cooking pasta)
  - Frying pan
  - Baking sheet
- Strainer
- Can opener
- Blender
- Basic spices/condiments:
  - Salt
  - Pepper
  - Cinnamon
  - Italian spices (you can usually find a blend of oregano, basil, etc.)
  - Vinegar
  - Vanilla
  - Garlic

FIGURE 2.9
You need only a few essential pieces of equipment for a functioning kitchen.

FIGURE 2.10
Measuring cups and spoons are important items to include in any kitchen.

Common Measurements

When reading recipes you may have noticed that the metric system and the U.S. system are both used, depending on what recipe you are following. Therefore, it is helpful to have measuring cups and spoons that use both systems, like those pictured here (Figure 2.10). If yours do not have both measurements see Table 2.4, which includes some common equivalents.

TABLE 2.4 Common Equivalents

dash	=	~1/8 tsp.
3 tsp.	=	1 tbsp.
2 tbsp.	=	1 fl. oz.
4 tbsp.	=	1/4 cup (2 fl. oz.)
5 $^{1}/_{2}$ tbsp.	=	1/3 cup (2 1/2 fl. oz.)
16 tbsp.	=	1 cup (8 fl. oz.)
2 cups	=	1 pint (16 fl. oz.)
2 pints	=	1 quart (32 fl. oz.)
4 quarts	=	1 gallon (128 fl. oz.)
1 g	=	0.035 oz. (1/30 oz.)
1 oz.	=	28.35 g (often rounded to 30 for convenience)
454 g	=	1 lb.
2.2 lb.	=	1 kg (1000 g)
1 tsp.	=	5 mL
1 tbsp.	=	15 mL
1 fluid oz.	=	28.35 mL (often rounded to 30 for convenience)
1 cup	=	0.24 L
1 gallon	=	3.80 L

In addition to conversions, it is helpful to be aware of common abbreviations used in recipes. Table 2.5 includes some of the more common ones.

TABLE 2.5 Common Abbreviations

teaspoon	=	tsp.
tablespoon	=	tbsp.
cup	=	c.
pint	=	pt.
quart	=	qt.
gram	=	g
milliliter	=	mL
liter	=	L
ounce	=	oz.
fluid ounce	=	fl. oz.
pound	=	lb.
kilogram	=	kg

Following is a list of common cooking terms.

Bake/Roast: To cook food uncovered in an oven or similar appliance.

Beat: To make a mixture smooth with rapid, regular motion using a wire whisk, spoon, hand beater, or mixer. When using a spoon, lift the mixture up and over with each stroke.

Blend: To mix two or more ingredients thoroughly.

Boil: To heat a liquid until bubbles break on the surface, or to cook in boiling water.

Braise: To slowly cook meat or poultry in a small amount of liquid in a covered pot.

Broil: To use direct heat above the food to cook.

Brown: To cook quickly until the surface of the food is brown.

Chop: To cut food into small pieces.

Coat: To cover the entire surface of a food with a mixture such as flour or breadcrumbs.

Core: To use a sharp knife to remove the core and seeds of fruit/vegetables.

Cream: To stir or blend one or more foods until they are soft (in a liquid state).

Crisp-tender: The "doneness" of vegetables when they are cooked only until tender and remain slightly crisp or crunchy in texture.

Crush: To use a garlic press or a blunt object to smash foods such as garlic until the fibers separate.

Cube: To cut food into 1/2-inch cubes (or size noted in recipe).

Dash: Less than 1/8 tsp.

Deep-fry: To cook in hot oil deep enough for food to float.

Dice: To cut into small, square pieces.

Drain: To put food and liquid into a strainer or colander, or pour liquid out of a pot by keeping the lid slightly away from the edge of the pan and pouring away from you.

Flute: To pinch the edges of dough, such as on piecrust.

Fold: To mix by gently turning over and over.

Fork-tender: The "doneness" of a food when a fork can easily penetrate it.

Fry: To pan-fry by cooking in a frying pan, usually over medium heat, using a small amount of oil.

Grate: To rub food on a grater, or chop it in a blender or food processor to produce fine, medium, or coarse particles.

Grease: To cover or lubricate with oil to keep food from sticking.

Knead: To work dough by folding and stretching with the heel of the hand.

Marinate: To allow food to soak in liquid before cooking in order to increase flavor and tenderness.

Mince: To cut or chop food into very small pieces.

Mix: To combine ingredients using a fork, spoon, or whisk.

Oil: To apply a thin layer of vegetable oil on a dish or pan; can substitute vegetable oil spray.

Peel: To remove the outer covering of foods by trimming away with a knife or vegetable peeler.

Poach: To cook food over low heat in a small amount of hot, simmering liquid.

Preheat: To heat the oven to the desired temperature before putting food in to bake.

Sauté: To cook in a small amount of oil or water.

Scald: To heat milk until bubbles appear. Bubbles should not be "breaking" on the surface.

Shred: To rub a food against a grater to divide it into small pieces.

Sift: To remove lumps or lighten the dry ingredients by putting them through a strainer or sifter.

Simmer: To cook at a temperature just below the boiling point. Bubbles form slowly but do not reach the surface.

Slice: To cut food into thin pieces.

Steam: To cook over boiling water.

Stew: To cook over low heat in a large amount of simmering liquid.

Stir-fry: To quickly fry food, usually at high heat, to a crisp-tender state while constantly stirring.

Stock: Water in which vegetables and/or meat and meat bones have been cooked; should be stored in the refrigerator.

Thaw: To slowly change from a frozen state to a liquid or unfrozen state.

Toss: To mix foods lightly with a lifting motion, using forks or spoons.

FIGURE 2.11
Mise en place means getting all the ingredients together before you start cooking.

BEFORE YOU GO START...

1. Make sure you read any recipe you are following carefully.
2. Check to see that you have all of the ingredients.
3. Gather and prep all ingredients; in other words, get them out and ready for cooking (the culinary term for this is mise en place, see Figure 2.11).
4. Use clear measuring cups for liquid ingredients and opaque (or clear) cups for dry.
5. Level all dry ingredients off and measure carefully.

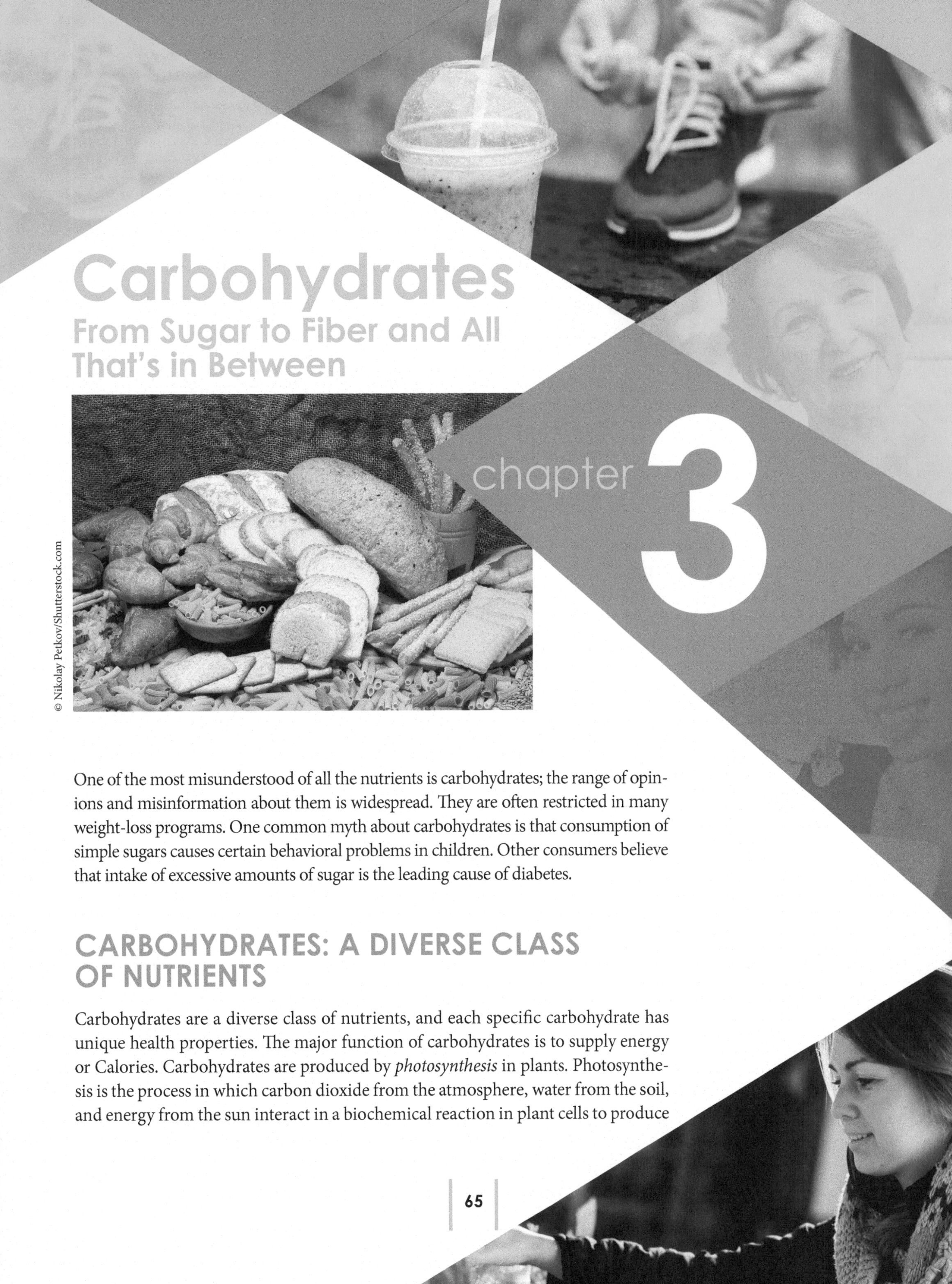

Carbohydrates

From Sugar to Fiber and All That's in Between

chapter 3

© Nikolay Petkov/Shutterstock.com

One of the most misunderstood of all the nutrients is carbohydrates; the range of opinions and misinformation about them is widespread. They are often restricted in many weight-loss programs. One common myth about carbohydrates is that consumption of simple sugars causes certain behavioral problems in children. Other consumers believe that intake of excessive amounts of sugar is the leading cause of diabetes.

CARBOHYDRATES: A DIVERSE CLASS OF NUTRIENTS

Carbohydrates are a diverse class of nutrients, and each specific carbohydrate has unique health properties. The major function of carbohydrates is to supply energy or Calories. Carbohydrates are produced by *photosynthesis* in plants. Photosynthesis is the process in which carbon dioxide from the atmosphere, water from the soil, and energy from the sun interact in a biochemical reaction in plant cells to produce the simplest of all carbohydrates, glucose (Figure 3.1). This process occurs with the assistance of the plant compound (pigment) chlorophyll. The energy from the sun is trapped chemically within the bonds of this sugar. Worldwide, dietary carbohydrates are the most important source of energy and are a cheap source of Calories. Many types of carbohydrates exist. Some carbohydrates, such as dietary fiber, provide little energy but have other health benefits. Because it is not digestible in the small intestine, dietary fiber promotes gastrointestinal health and may prevent some diseases that are prevalent in Western cultures, such as colon cancer. Other carbohydrates when consumed in excess, such as sugar, have been linked to disease and obesity.

Simple sugars are a significant source of carbohydrates in Westernized diets. A commonly consumed source of more complex carbohydrates in North America and Europe is wheat. However, this is not the case in other parts of the world where carbohydrate sources include rice in Asia, corn in South America, and cassava in Africa (Figure 3.2). Cassava is a shrub whose root is high in starch, and starch from this root is often used to make tapioca. Table 3.1 lists the percentages of carbohydrate content of selected foods.

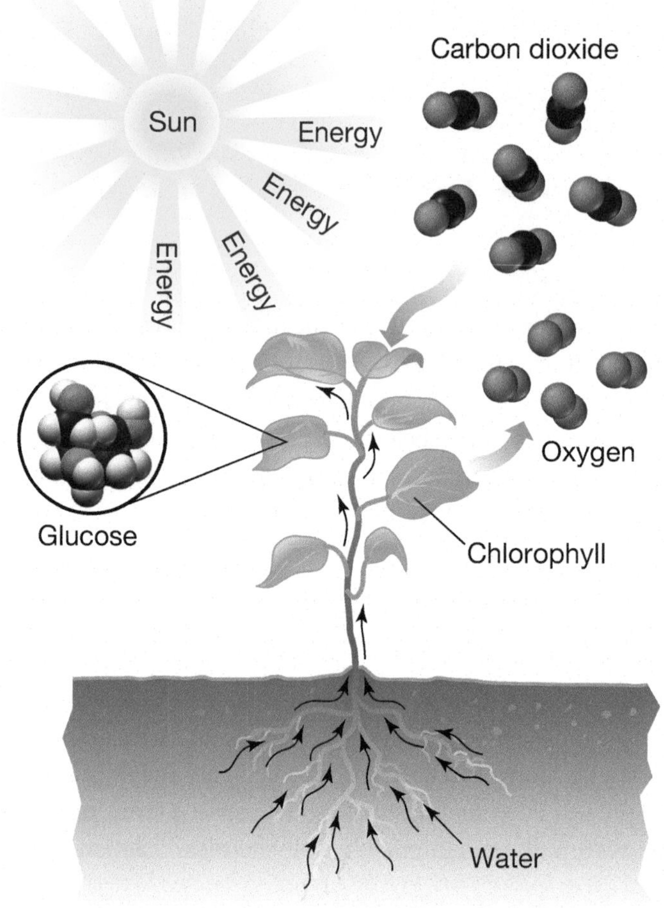

FIGURE 3.1 This illustration shows how glucose is produced in plants. It occurs through the biochemical reactions of water from the soil, carbon dioxide from the atmosphere, and energy from the sun. The reaction occurs in the chlorophyll-containing plant organelles called *chloroplasts*.

TABLE 3.1 Carbohydrate in Selected Foods by Weight

Food	Household Measure	Weight (g)	Amount of Carbohydrate (g)	Percentage of Carbohydrate in the Food (%)
Apple, with peel	1 apple	138	19	14
Banana	1 banana	118	27	23
Butter	1 tbsp.	15	<0.1	0
Cheddar cheese	1 oz.	28	1	0.04
Corn oil	1 tsp.	14	0	0
Ice cream	1/2 c.	66	16	24
Lima beans, cooked	1/2 c.	85	20	24
Milk, 2%	1 c.	244	11	4.5
Orange juice	1/2 c.	124	13	11
Peanuts, roasted	1/2 c.	37	8	22
Peanut butter, smooth	1 tbsp.	16	3	19
Rice, cooked	1/2 c.	79	22	28
Spaghetti noodles	1/2 c.	65	20	31
Tuna, water packed	2 oz.	57	0	0
Table sugar	1 tsp.	4	4	100
White bread	1 slice	25	13	52

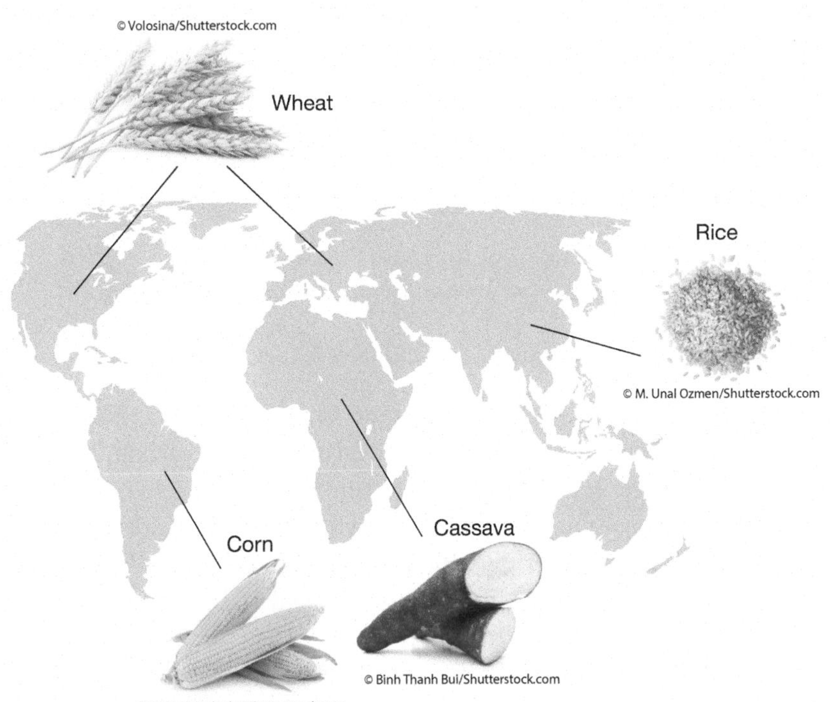

FIGURE 3.2 The primary sources of carbohydrates in different parts of the world are rice, corn, wheat, and cassava. The map indicates where many of the world's sources of each are grown.

Global
NUTRITION

SORGHUM—THE FORGOTTEN GRAIN

Ever hear of the grain sorghum? Thousands of acres of this grain are grown in the Midwest every year, but few Americans have ever heard of it. However, in many parts of the world, such as Africa and parts of Asia, sorghum is an important crop and is used in flours, snack foods and alcoholic beverages. It grows well in dry areas because it does not require much water and is therefore a very sustainable crop. There is increasing interest in sorghum in Western countries due to recent discoveries that it may have potential health benefits. Sorghum contains compounds similar to those present in blueberries, and these compounds have strong antioxidant activities. In fact, the antioxidant level in some varieties of sorghum is much higher than levels in most other grains, as well as many fruits and vegetables. Studies in animals reveal that it can lower blood cholesterol and can reduce colon carcinogenesis, and epidemiological studies suggest it is associated with reduced rates of esophageal cancer. Furthermore, when compared to other carbohydrates, it may result in less weight gain largely due to the inhibition of some digestive enzymes by the antioxidant compounds it contains. Another beneficial aspect of sorghum is that it is a gluten-free grain. The increasing number of individuals diagnosed as having celiac disease can use sorghum as an alternative flour source for cooking (see the section on celiac disease later in this chapter). As a result, sorghum is now found in some cereals and other grain-based products, and we are likely to hear more about sorghum as part of a healthy diet in the future.

HOW DO WE DEFINE A CARBOHYDRATE?

Scientists coined the term *carbohydrate* based on its chemical composition. Only three elements are contained in carbohydrates: carbon, hydrogen, and oxygen. For every atom of carbon, there is one molecule of water (H_2O). Literally, *carbohydrate* means "carbon with water." All carbohydrates supply approximately 4 kcal per gram of energy when digested. We must eat carbohydrates daily because our bodies store limited quantities of carbohydrate in the liver and muscle.

Types of Carbohydrates

Carbohydrates are chemically categorized as either simple or complex based on how many sugar units (monosaccharides) are linked together. For example, a carbohydrate with less than 10 monosaccharide units is classified as being a simple carbohydrate; a carbohydrate with more than 10 (all the way up to thousands) is classified as a complex carbohydrate.

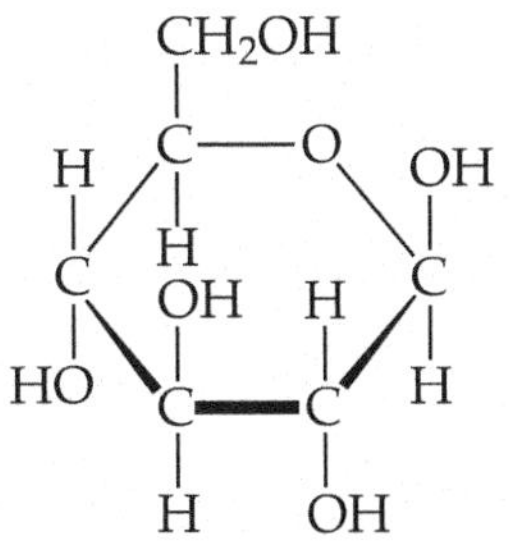

(a) Glucose

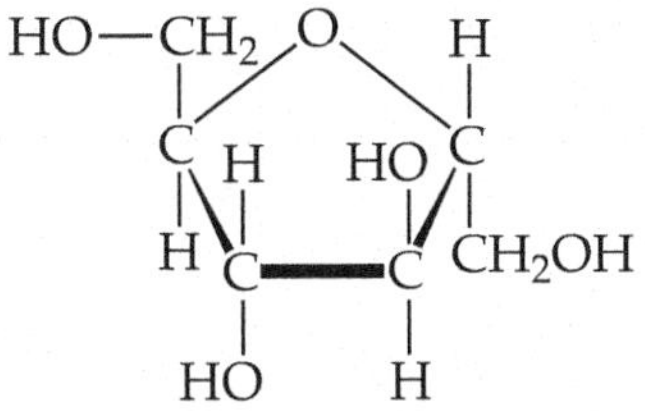

(b) Fructose

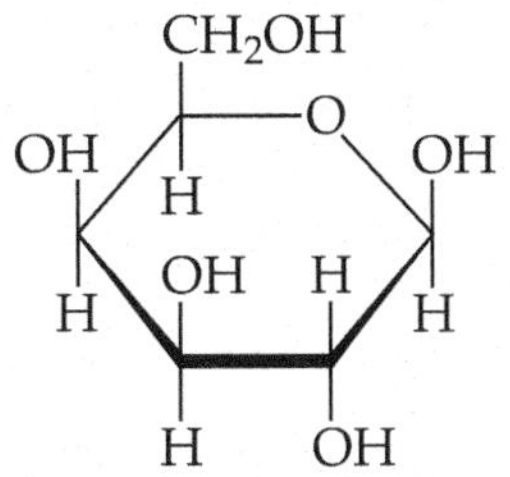

(c) Galactose

FIGURE 3.3 Chemical structures of the three basic monosaccharides: glucose, fructose, and galactose.

Simple Sugars

MONOSACCHARIDES. *Monosaccharides* are a group of single sugar molecules that are used to assemble all carbohydrates. They consist of one basic chemical ring . The three monosaccharides are glucose, fructose, and galactose (see Figure 3.3).

Biologically, the most important and common monosaccharide is **glucose**. Glucose circulates in the blood and is the main source of energy for the body. It is often referred to as *blood sugar*. Glucose units, when linked together, make up the more complex carbohydrates such as starches and fibers.

Fructose is a monosaccharide found abundantly in fruit, honey, and vegetables such as beets, sweet potatoes, parsnips, and onions, as well as grains such as corn.

Galactose is the third type of monosaccharide that is consumed as a part of the disaccharide lactose found in milk. Galactose rarely exists by itself. It may also be found as a type of fiber component of fruit (pectin). Fruits such as bananas, berries, and cherries are good sources. Vegetables such as broccoli, cabbage, cauliflower, cucumber, mushrooms, pumpkin, and spinach contain some galactose.

DISACCHARIDES. *Disaccharides* are composed of two monosaccharides linked together by a chemical bond. One disaccharide is **sucrose**, which is commonly known as table sugar and is composed of one glucose molecule and one fructose molecule (Figure 3.4). Sucrose comprises 25 percent of the total caloric intake of Western diets, or 500 Calories per day of a 2,000-Calorie diet!

Another disaccharide is **lactose**, or milk sugar (Figure 3.4), which is composed of glucose and galactose. Only mammals (including humans) produce milk and thus lactose, which is a major source of Calories for young animals

glucose
The monosaccharide that circulates in the blood, and is often referred to as blood sugar. It is the main source of energy for the body.

fructose
A monosaccharide that has a simple ring structure. It is the sugar found abundantly in fruit, honey, and also some vegetables such as beets, sweet potatoes, parsnips, and onions. It is the sweetest sugar.

galactose
A monosaccharide that is consumed as a part of the disaccharide lactose found in milk; it is a basic component of other, more complex carbohydrates.

sucrose
A disaccharide commonly known as table sugar; it is composed of one glucose molecule and one fructose molecule.

lactose
A disaccharide, commonly known as milk sugar that is composed of glucose and galactose.

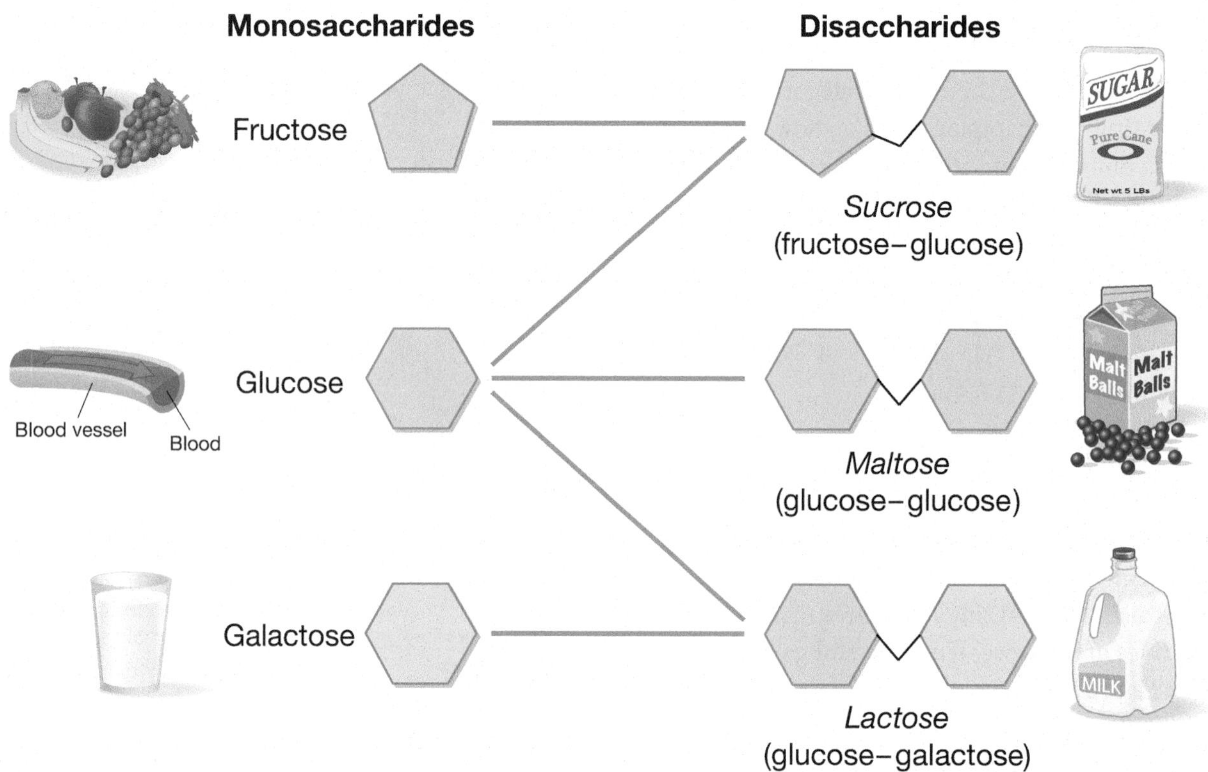

FIGURE 3.4 Disaccharides are composed of two monosaccharides as shown. Sucrose, or table sugar, is composed of glucose and fructose. Maltose is two glucose molecules linked together. Lactose, or milk sugar, is composed of glucose and galactose.

and infants. Lactose has other benefits, such as aiding in the absorption of the mineral calcium and favoring the growth of beneficial intestinal bacteria.

Maltose (Figure 3.4) is a disaccharide that is composed of two glucose units. Maltose is rather mysterious. In plants, it is found for only a brief time in germinating seeds. In animals, it is found when starches are broken down during digestion. The major source of this sugar in our diets may be malted candies or shakes; it can also be found in malt liquors and beer.

maltose
A disaccharide that is composed of two glucose units.

Complex Carbohydrates

Complex carbohydrates, also known as polysaccharides, include **starch, glycogen** and dietary fiber (Figure 3.5). Polysaccharides are composed of thousands of glucose molecules linked together by glycoside bonds. Dietary fiber is composed of repeating units of glucose and other monosaccharides that cannot be digested by human enzymes because they are not able to hydrolyze the beta 1-4 glycoside bonds it contains. Thus, glucose will not be released for absorption in the small intestine, and the dietary fiber passes through to the colon where the bacteria that reside there can metabolize some of it.

Starch is the storage form of carbohydrate found in plants. Generally, starches are either a long, straight chain or are a branched chain (Figure 3.5). Both types are composed of repeating glucose units that are bound together by alpha 1-4 glycoside bonds which we can easily digest. Potatoes and pasta contain significant levels of starch.

Glycogen, another polysaccharide, is the storage form of carbohydrate found in the liver and muscle of animals. On a carbohydrate-restricted diet or between meals, glycogen is broken down to provide glucose to support normal metabolism. In fact, the average human stores only approximately 2,000 Calories as glycogen. Therefore, glycogen can be depleted within less than a day by fasting, carbohydrate restriction, or extensive exercise.

polysaccharide
A carbohydrate composed of a chain with thousands of glucose molecules linked together.

dietary fiber
A carbohydrate composed of repeating units of glucose and other monosaccharides that cannot be digested by human enzymes and thus cannot be absorbed and used by the body. Dietary fiber is now part of the Institute of Medicine formal definition of fiber in the diet. Dietary fiber represents that fraction that is inherent in the intact food.

starch
The storage form of carbohydrate found in plants.

glycogen
The storage form of carbohydrate in animals, and is found in the liver and muscle.

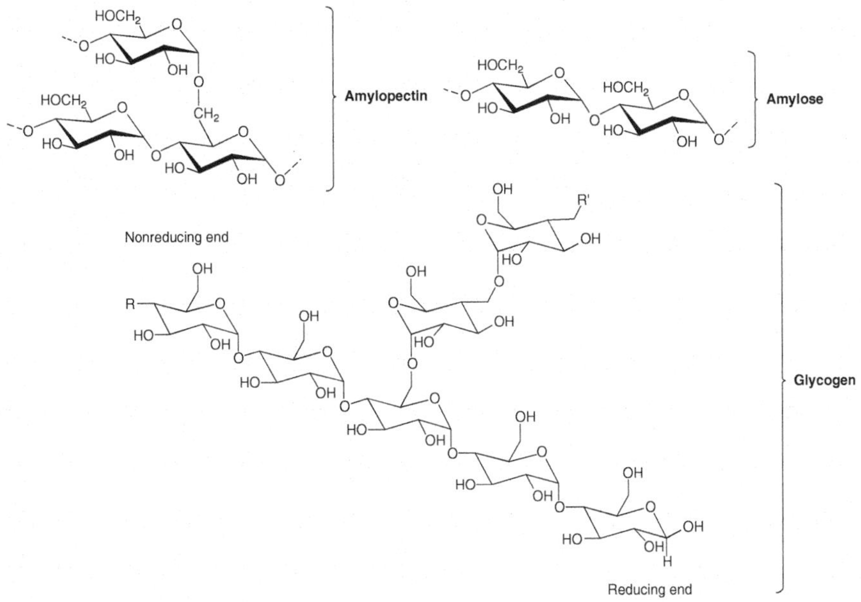

FIGURE 3.5
Illustrations of complex carbohydrates from plants (starch) and animals (glycogen). Notice that glycogen found in animals is much more highly branched than starch found in plants. The bonds between monosaccharides to form complex carbohydrates are glycoside bonds. The type of glycoside bond determines if we are able to digest the carbohydrate.

BEFORE YOU GO ON...

1. Explain the major difference between monosaccharides and disaccharides.
2. What sugars are found only in milk and its products?
3. Define starch and glycogen.

WHAT ARE THE PRIMARY SOURCES OF CARBOHYDRATES?

Where do we get carbohydrates in our diet and what foods contain simple sugars, starches, and fiber? Carbohydrates are naturally present in almost all plant foods (e.g., fruits, vegetables, grains, legumes) and in milk. Carbohydrates, many times in the form of simple sugars, are added to a wide variety of foods, some of which may surprise you: ketchup, low-fat salad dressing, and tomato sauce. What foods are high in sucrose? Obvious sources of sucrose are table sugar, cakes, cookies, pastries, certain breakfast cereals, and ice cream. In addition, simple carbohydrates such as high-fructose corn syrup and sucrose have been added to low-fat foods to enhance taste (see Figure 3.6). In many ways, doing so has substituted one problem (our high-fat diets) for another problem (overconsumption of simple sugars). However, some of the changes in our food preferences have contributed in an even more significant way to our consumption of excess Calories from carbohydrates. For example, the choice of drinking a 16 fl. oz. caramel macchiato means we are getting 34 grams of carbohydrate, of which 32 grams are sugars, whereas a 16 fl. oz. black coffee has no carbohydrates or sugars.

Regular Ranch Salad Dressing

Nutrition Facts	
Serving Size 2 tbsp (29.0 g)	
Amount Per Serving	
Calories 148 Calories from Fat 140	
	% Daily Value*
Total Fat 15.6g	**24%**
Saturated Fat 2.4g	**12%**
Cholesterol 8mg	**3%**
Sodium 287mg	**12%**
Total Carbohydrates 1.3g	**0%**
Dietary Fiber 0.1g	**0%**
Sugars 1.2g	
Protein 0.4g	
Vitamin A	**0%**
Vitamin C	**0%**
Calcium	**1%**
Iron	**0%**
Nutritional Units 4	
*Percent Daily Values are based on a 2,000 calorie diet. Your daily values may be higher or lower depending on your calorie needs.	

Fat-Free Ranch Dressing

Nutrition Facts	
Serving Size 2 tbsp (35.0 g)	
Amount Per Serving	
Calories 48 Calories from Fat 3	
	% Daily Value*
Total Fat 0.4g	**1%**
Saturated Fat 0.1g	**0%**
Cholesterol 0mg	**0%**
Sodium 354mg	**15%**
Total Carbohydrates 10.7g	**4%**
Dietary Fiber 0.2g	**1%**
Sugars 2.1g	
Protein 0.2g	
Vitamin A	**0%**
Vitamin C	**0%**
Calcium	**1%**
Iron	**0%**
Nutritional Units 1	
*Percent Daily Values are ` ased on a 2,000 calorie diet. Your daily values may be higher or lower depending on your calorie needs.	

FIGURE 3.6

Food labels. Fat-free products are provided for those who wish to limit fat intake, but the changes in taste and texture that occur with fat reduction is usually offset by adding carbohydrates. One product that uses this approach is salad dressing. Note that the total amount of carbohydrates in the fat-free salad dressing is 10.7 g whereas in the regular dressing it is 1.3 g. Have you ever tried the fat-free version? If so, did you notice a significant difference in the taste?

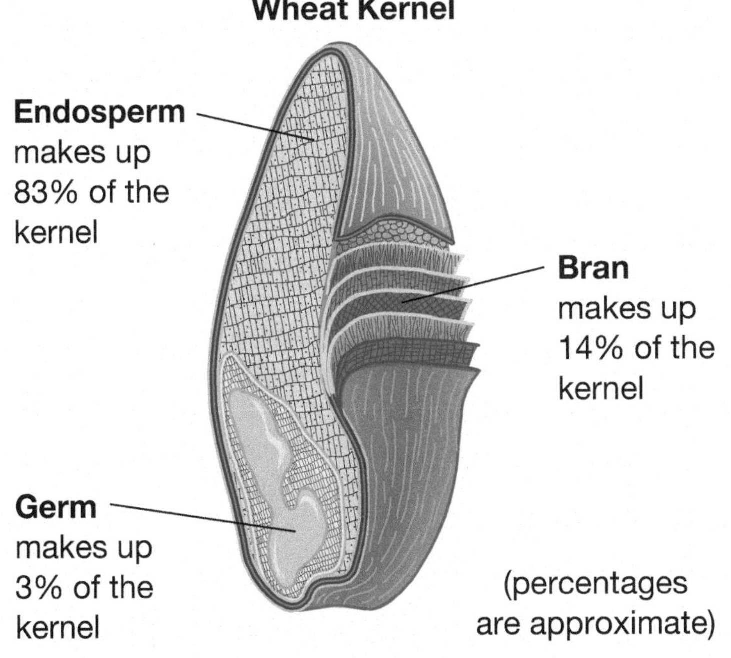
Wheat Kernel
Endosperm makes up 83% of the kernel
Bran makes up 14% of the kernel
Germ makes up 3% of the kernel
(percentages are approximate)

FIGURE 3.7

A kernel of grain showing its various components. There are three main parts of a kernel: germ, bran, and endosperm.

Make it a PRACTICE

CHOOSE WHOLE GRAINS

Eating whole grains, such as whole-wheat bread or cereal (those not refined by milling), is important for health because the parts of grain kernels normally lost in processing provide many nutrients. The germ of a grain kernel (the innermost part of the kernel) is rich in protein, oils, vitamins, and minerals (Figure 3.7). The *endosperm* is the middle portion of the kernel and it is very high in starch. The bran part of the grain is high in dietary fiber; the outer husk is not edible. When whole grains of wheat are milled to make white flour, the outer husk and bran layer, and even part of the germ layer, are removed, making the product much lower in dietary fiber and other nutrients. The end product is white flour, which is high in starch. White bread is typically made from white flour and is thus a good source of starch but nutritionally inferior to whole-wheat bread. Whole-wheat flour is preferable because the kernels have not undergone the same extensive milling process. Bread made with whole-wheat flour is high not only in starch, but also in dietary fiber. Whole-grain products are typically identified using an approved stamp on the package. However, consumers should carefully consider all nutritional characteristics of a food when making selections to be sure that the item chosen is beneficial for multiple reasons (Figure 3.8). As noted later in this chapter, fiber can help reduce heart disease and colon cancer, among other health benefits.

Examples of complex carbohydrates include whole-grain breads and pastas, as well as potatoes (try to avoid fried versions to limit fat intake), cassava, vegetables, and legumes.

If you wish to obtain more complex carbohydrates in your diet, including fiber, follow these simple rules:

- When possible, use bread made from whole grains instead of white flour. Be sure to look for "whole grain" on the food product label. In addition, look for products where whole grains are the first item in the ingredient list.
- Choose high-fiber cereals that have little or no sucrose or other Calorie containing sweeteners added (read the list of ingredients on the food product label).
- Use brown rice instead of white rice.
- In recipes, use more beans such as navy, kidney, black, or pinto beans. These beans can also be used as a meat substitute.

- Keep the edible peels on your fruits and vegetables because they are high in dietary fiber. Be sure to wash fresh fruits and vegetables before consuming them.
- Increase your intake of fresh vegetables and fruits.

To lower your intake of low-nutrient density foods containing rapidly digestible simple carbohydrates, follow these suggestions:

- Limit your intake of soda and other sugared drinks such as sports beverages, fruit punch, and other fruit drinks.
- Use canned fruits that are packed in natural juices; better yet, use fresh or frozen fruits for desserts and to sweeten baked goods such as pancakes and waffles, instead of syrup.
- Limit your intake of ice cream, high-sugar breakfast cereals, candy, and desserts.
- Decrease the use of added sugars, honey, and syrups.

Nutrition Facts
Serving Size 33g
Servings Per Container about 14

Amount Per Serving	
Calories 150 Calories from Fat 70	
	% Daily Value*
Total Fat 8g	12%
Saturated Fat 2.5g	13%
Trans Fat 0g	
Cholesterol 0mg	0%
Sodium 110mg	5%
Total Carbohydrate 22g	7%
Dietary Fiber 2g	8%
Sugars 10g	
Protein 2g	
Vitamin A	0%
Vitamin C	0%
Calcium	0%
Iron	4%

*Percent Daily Values are based on a 2,000 calorie diet. Your daily values may be higher or lower depending on your calorie needs:

	Calories:	2,000	2,500
Total Fat	Less than	65g	80g
Sat Fat	Less than	20g	25g
Cholest	Less than	300mg	300mg
Sodium	Less than	2,400mg	2,400mg
Total Carb		300g	375g
Fiber		25g	30g

(a)

Nutrition Facts
Serving Size 1 Bar (35g)
Servings Per Container about 14

Amount Per Serving	
Calories 140 Calories from Fat 45	
	% Daily Value*
Total Fat 5g	8%
Saturated Fat 0.5g	3%
Trans Fat 0g	
Cholesterol 0mg	0%
Sodium 105mg	4%
Potassium 100mg	3%
Total Carbohydrate 20g	7%
Dietary Fiber 4g	14%
Soluble Fiber 1g	
Insoluble Fiber 3g	
Sugars 5g	
Protein 6g	
Vitamin A	0%
Vitamin C	0%
Calcium	0%
Iron	6%

*Percent Daily Values are based on a 2,000 calorie diet. Your daily values may be higher or lower depending on your calorie needs.

(b)

FIGURE 3.8
Are all whole-grain products healthier for you? Notice that the product in (a) has whole grain, but also contains saturated fat and 10 g of sugar. The one in (b) is healthier because of the lower saturated fat and sugar content, and it contains twice the amount of fiber.

IS THERE A PROBLEM WITH WHEAT?

Some of the most widely consumed grains in the United States are wheat, rye, and barley. Grains provide fiber, calories, protein, and micronutrients. However, some people have a reaction to the protein gluten in these three grains. This disorder is called *celiac disease*. Celiac disease is an autoimmune disorder that causes a range of gastrointestinal problems including intestinal cramps and diarrhea. In more severe cases, damage to the intestine leads to a reduced ability to absorb nutrients. The only successful treatment is to eliminate all products made with wheat, rye, barley and most sources of oats (because of cross-contamination). Hidden sources of gluten include some medications. Eliminating all of these sources is difficult to achieve. Think of all the food made with wheat ingredients: some examples include bread, cereals, some artificial coffee creamers, crackers, pasta, cookies, and even soy sauce.

Until recently, celiac disease was considered relatively uncommon. Previous U.S. figures suggested that it affected one in 6,000 persons. However, more recent population studies suggest a much higher prevalence, particularly in persons of European ancestry. Approximately 1 in 100 to 200 people in the U.S. suffer from celiac disease. Why the increase in prevalence? One explanation is that physicians may be more familiar with this condition and tests to screen for it are more advanced. Thus, previously undiagnosed diarrhea and abdominal discomfort are now being diagnosed as celiac disease. It has also been suggested the increasing number of diagnosed cases could be related to the way grains are grown and processed or due to the fact that gluten is used more frequently as a filler in processed foods and medicines.

Still others suggest that the growing number of people who are saying they are "gluten sensitive" without an official diagnosis may make the growth in diagnosed cases appear larger than it is. Because the gluten-free diet dictates that you stay away from many fatty, fried, and pre-packaged foods, it has caught on in Hollywood and with the media as a fad diet. The increased popularity of a gluten-free diet has led to a greater variety of gluten-free products on the market, but many are just as processed as the foods they replace. According to a report from the market research group Packaged Facts, sales of gluten-free products in the United States grew by an average of 28 percent between 2008 and 2012. This is good news for true celiac patients who in the past had a difficult time finding gluten-free products and therefore had to make all of their food from scratch. Most people who stick to the gluten-free diet report that they "feel" better doing so, but this is strictly anecdotal and may be due to an increased consumption of fruits and vegetables. Whatever the cause, gluten-free eating has caught on in the mainstream and is no longer just for celiac patients.

BEFORE YOU GO ON...

1. What percentage of your Calories should come from carbohydrates, according to the DRIs?
2. List some practical ways to increase complex carbohydrates in your diet.
3. What is a whole-grain food, and why is whole grain important for our diets?
4. What is the most common type of carbohydrate we consume?

THE DIETARY ROLE OF CARBOHYDRATES

As we've discussed, carbohydrates are an important part of a healthy balanced diet. Based on the Dietary Reference Intakes and the AMDRs, between 45 to 65% of total Calories should come from carbohydrates. Of this amount, no more than 10% should come from added sugars. They provide the body with energy, vital nutrients and perform many other important functions. Most important is that our brain prefers to use glucose as an energy source and red blood cells are only able to use glucose for their energy source. In addition to supplying energy, carbohydrates spare protein, prevent ketosis, and regulate blood glucose levels. We will discuss each of these functions separately as follows.

Dietary Energy

Why
do we
need
carbohydrates?

We have already mentioned that half of the Calories we consume are in the form of carbohydrates. The processes of carbohydrate digestion and metabolism result in glucose. One gram of carbohydrate supplies 4 kcal of energy. The speed with which we obtain energy from carbohydrates depends on how quickly they are digested. Simple sugars are easily digested and absorbed, providing a quick source of energy. On the other hand, complex carbohydrates, which are more slowly digested and absorbed, are best when a more sustained level of energy is needed to get through the day and while we sleep.

Protein Sparing

A diet low in total calories and carbohydrates causes the body to obtain energy from other sources. If carbohydrates are restricted, the body begins to use protein (dietary and our own muscle protein) as a source of calories. This is not an ideal situation, since we need protein for growth and maintenance of muscle and organs and to maintain an adequate immune system (which will be discussed in Chapter 5). If sufficient carbohydrates are available, then the protein is spared from being used for energy and thus are available for growth and repair. However, if carbohydrate intake is insufficient, then protein will be broken down to maintain blood glucose levels. This process is called **gluconeogenesis**, which is the synthesis of new glucose from noncarbohydrate sources. Therefore, in order to prevent utilizing proteins stored in muscles to meet energy demands, it is important to consume sufficient dietary carbohydrates and total calories to meet your energy needs.

Preventing Ketosis

gluconeogenesis
Synthesis of new glucose from noncarbohydrate sources.

Another source of calories for energy is stored fat. Fat, carbohydrates, and protein can be broken down into a compound called *acetyl CoA*. From this point, acetyl CoA can be further broken down to obtain energy. However, to fully break down fats, we need a chemical derived from carbohydrates and certain amino acids called *oxaloacetate*. When oxaloacetate is not present the liver responds by making fats into ketone bodies. **Ketone bodies** are acidic fat derivatives that arise from the incomplete breakdown of fat. Although they can be a source of energy for some cells in the body, high levels can disrupt the acid–base balance of the blood, alter kidney function, and lead to dehydration - a condition called *ketosis*. Although the brain and nervous system prefer to use glucose as an energy source, those cells can adapt to using ketones if not enough glucose is available. However, people who do not have sufficient carbohydrates in their diets may show signs of compromised mental function, such as dizziness and even fainting, and their breath may smell fruity or foul because of the natural odor of ketone bodies.

ketone bodies
Acidic fat derivatives that arise from the incomplete breakdown of fat.

Regulating Blood Glucose Levels

The body has mechanisms to maintain a stable level of glucose in the blood. Once monosaccharides are absorbed in the bloodstream from the small intestine, they travel to the liver where galactose and fructose may be converted to glucose. Glucose will subsequently be re-released into the bloodstream, where other tissues can use it as a source of energy. If glucose concentrations exceed energy requirements, the body stores this excess energy as glycogen or as fat.

Insulin is a hormone released from the pancreas in response to increasing blood glucose after a meal. Insulin promotes cellular uptake of glucose, which results in a decrease of glucose in the blood. Insulin also has other functions, such as promoting protein synthesis and the conversion of extra glucose to glycogen and fat. When you have not eaten for a period of time and as blood glucose begins to fall, glucagon is released. **Glucagon** is a hormone that stimulates the breakdown of liver glycogen to glucose. As a result, blood sugar level rise to desirable levels. In essence, insulin and glucagon work together to keep blood glucose levels in the normal range (Figure 3.9).

insulin
A hormone released from the pancreas that allows glucose to enter cells to be used for energy.

glucagon
A hormone released from the pancreas that breaks down liver glycogen to glucose.

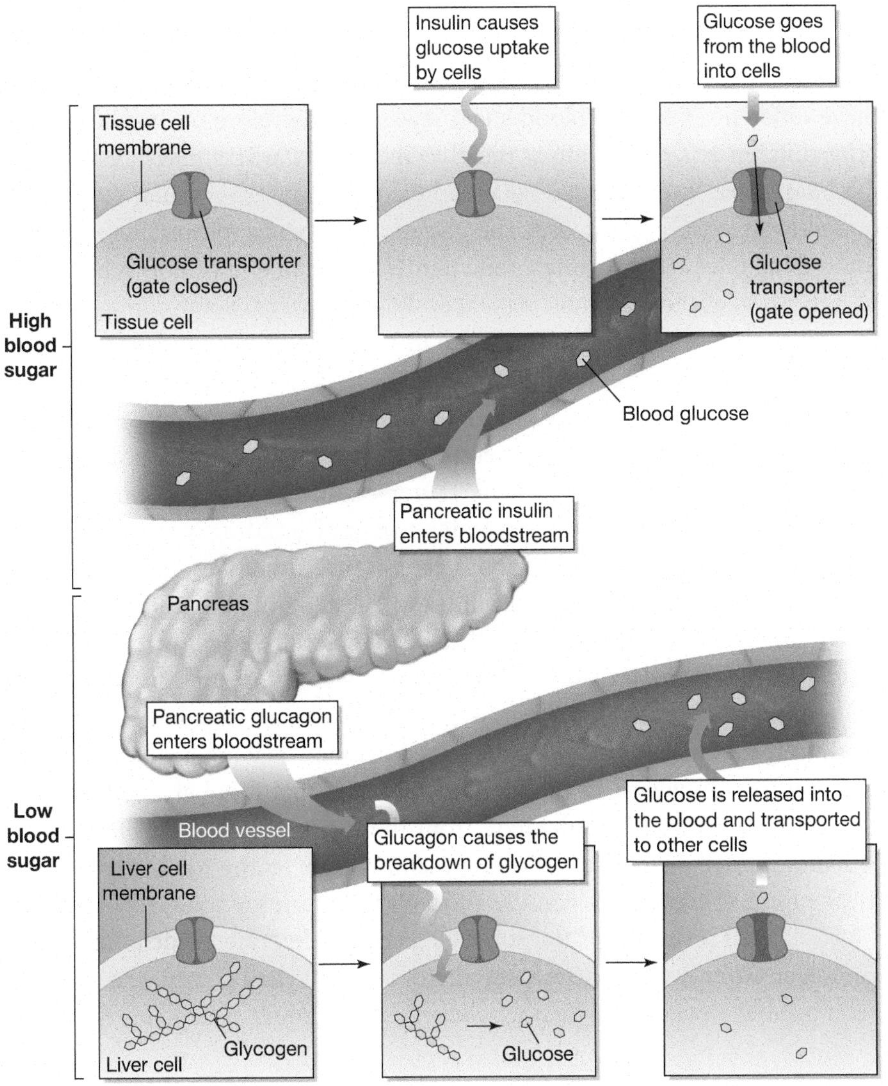

FIGURE 3.9
This illustration demonstrates how insulin and glucagon work to regulate blood glucose levels within normal limits. Insulin lowers blood glucose, and glucagon raises blood glucose. Both hormones are produced by the pancreas.

If you haven't eaten for a few hours and then you drink a soda or eat a candy bar, both of which are high in simple sugars, the quick digestion and absorption of glucose can cause a very large surge of blood sugar and insulin. This surge of insulin causes a rapid drop in blood glucose levels as the glucose is taken up in the cells. In fact, levels can drop very quickly and to such a low point that it can make you feel dizzy or even drowsy. It is known to happen to students who skip a meal and have a cookie or candy bar prior to class. If you consume a snack that includes a slowly digestible complex carbohydrate, or a mixed meal that also contains fat and protein, it will take longer to digest carbohydrates and glucose will be released into the blood much more slowly. This slower release of glucose prevents a surge in insulin levels and the resulting rapid drop in blood glucose levels. This does not happen in everyone, and apparently, some individuals are more sensitive to this reaction than others are.

Glycemic Response

glycemic index
A measure of how fast blood glucose increases when a person ingests a particular food, compared to ingestion of glucose.

No carbohydrates are really "bad" or "good" for you; carbohydrates simply have different effects on blood sugar levels and therefore on insulin release. This difference is referred to as the **glycemic index**, which measures how fast blood glucose levels increase when a person ingests a particular food, compared to ingestion of glucose. The glycemic index is appropriate only when describing the effect of a single food item itself on an empty stomach, making it difficult to use for a complete meal or dietary pattern. Some common foods and their glycemic index are presented in Table 3.2. A glycemic index of 70 or greater is considered high; 56–69 medium; and below 55 low.

The glycemic index has recently been of interest to both health professionals and consumers because of the belief that foods with a high glycemic index have a greater ability to cause weight gain. Therefore, many diet plans have suggested consuming foods with a low glycemic index and avoiding foods with a high glycemic index. As of yet, not enough long-term studies have been conducted to determine whether the glycemic index will be a useful weight-loss tool. However, many consumers appear to be keenly interested in learning about the glycemic index of particular foods. Since it was designed for single food items, the index is really being misused. When these items are consumed in the form of a meal or mixed with other foods, the glycemic index may not be that accurate.

Another drawback of the glycemic index is that it is based on the consumption of 50 g of carbohydrate from the food item. The *glycemic load* is a mathematical score that adjusts glycemic index to the total carbohydrate in the food consumed. If you use broccoli to determine the glycemic index, you will need several cups to get the 50 g of carbohydrate needed for the test. However, when we consume a serving of broccoli (half a cup), the glycemic load is much lower than when we consume the amount needed for the test.

BEFORE YOU GO ON...

1. What do we mean when we say that carbohydrate can "spare" protein, and when would this be relevant?
2. What is the cause of ketosis?
3. If you skip breakfast, go to class, and then snack on a candy bar and soda after class, you may feel dizzy and nervous. What causes this to happen in some people?

TABLE 3.2 Glycemic Index of Selected Food Items

Food	Glycemic Index
Maltose	105
Dates	103
Glucose	100
Boiled white potato	85
Cornflakes	83
Doughnut	76
Graham crackers	74
Soda	72
Corn chips	72
Watermelon	72
White bread	70
Grape-nuts	67
Wheat Thins crackers	67
Raisins	64
Table sugar	64
Oatmeal cookies	57
Banana	56
Potato chips	56
All-Bran cereal	51
Carrots	47
Orange juice	46
Grapes	46
Baked beans	44
Spaghetti	44
Orange	43
Apple	38
Skim milk	32
Whole milk	30
Grapefruit	25
Plain yogurt	14
Note: These are values for simple food items consumed on an empty stomach and not part of a mixed meal, which gives different results.	

> **APPLICATION TIP**
>
> Just because a food has a lower glycemic index does not mean that is healthier or that it has a higher nutrient content than a food that has a higher glycemic index.

DIETARY FIBER

Dietary fiber is made up of those carbohydrates that resist human digestive enzymes. Dietary fiber is important, as it prevents a number of chronic diseases. Fiber is mostly composed of polysaccharides, although one component of dietary fiber, *lignin,* is technically not a carbohydrate. A more accurate term to use instead of *dietary* fiber is *nonstarch polysaccharide.* Chemically, there are two types of dietary fiber: soluble and insoluble.

*Recommended Intakes

The DRI for fiber is 14 grams per 1000 Calories consumed. This translates into 38 grams/day for men and 25 grams/day for women up to age 50 years. Men and women over the age of 50 should reduce their daily fiber intake to 30 grams and 21 grams, respectively. The recommended intake is close to double the current fiber intake which ranges from 12 to 15 g/day for most Americans. In the United States, the fecal bulk (weight of feces excreted) per person is around 110 g/day. In underdeveloped nations where people have unrefined plant-based diets and dietary fiber is much greater, it is 500 g/day. The transit time (the time food takes to pass through the entire gastrointestinal system) in Western nations is around 70 hours. However, in some British populations, transit times of 2 weeks have been recorded! Generally, a shorter transit time is desirable. Fewer incidents of constipation and less contact of toxic compounds with the wall of the gastrointestinal tract are two benefits of a short transit time. In more underdeveloped societies, the average transit time is about 35 hours.*

soluble fiber

Fiber that can dissolve in water. It is composed of many repeating monosaccharides that are acid derivatives of galactose. It is a jellylike material that acts as a cement in plants.

insoluble fiber

A type of fiber that is mainly composed of plant cell walls. It cannot be dissolved in water and resists human digestive enzymes. It is composed of cellulose, hemicellulose, and lignin.

Soluble & Insoluble Fiber

Soluble fiber can dissolve in water. It is composed of many repeating monosaccharides that are acid derivatives of galactose. It is a jellylike material that acts as a cement in plants. **Insoluble fiber** is mainly present in plant cell walls and helps to provide structure to the plant, and it cannot be dissolved in water. It is composed of cellulose, hemicellulose, and lignin. Table 3.3 summarizes the types of dietary fiber, what they are composed of, and some food sourc-

© Africa Studio/Shutterstock.com

Green, leafy vegetables, and fresh and dried fruits—as well as whole-grain pastas, breads, and cereals—are all good sources of fiber.

es. Table 3.4 gives examples of the amounts of soluble and insoluble fibers in foods, showing that both fiber types are normally present.

Up until 2001, there were no formal definitions of dietary fiber. At that time the Institute of Medicine published a report that provided a proposed definition for use in the United States and Canada. This definition differentiated between fiber in the intact food (called *dietary fiber*) and fiber that had been extracted and/or synthesized and used in a prepared food (called **functional fiber**). These two classes of fibers, when added together, represented the total fiber content of a food. The committee created these categories of fiber based on our historical understanding of the health benefits associated with fiber present in foods. Because not all "added" fibers have been definitively demonstrated to improve our health, the committee did not want consumers to assume that the functional fibers contained in foods would always provide a health benefit.

functional fiber

The Institute of Medicine definition of fiber in our diet includes this form of fiber, which includes fiber that has been extracted and/or synthesized and is added to food.

APPLICATION TIP

If you want both soluble and insoluble fibers in one food item, try eating those peas your mother told you about when you were younger!

TABLE 3.3 Dietary Fiber Types, Composition, Food Sources, and Health Outcomes

Fiber Type	Soluble	Insoluble
Examples	Pectin, gums, mucilages	Cellulose, hemicellulose, lignin (not a carbohydrate)
What is it?	Soluble fiber is composed of many repeating monosaccharides that are acid derivatives of galactose; it is a jellylike material that acts as cement in plants; gums are normally found in plants at a site of injury and serve the same protective function as scar tissue in humans; mucilages are produced in plants at particular sites to prevent transpiration or evaporation of water	Insoluble fiber is mainly found in plant cell walls, and it cannot be dissolved in water; the chemical composition varies widely; cellulose, which is similar to starch, is composed of repeating glucose units; the chemical bonds in cellulose have a different shape than those found in starch, making it impossible for human digestive enzymes to break cellulose down; cellulose is found in the plant cell wall and gives structure to the plant; hemicellulose fiber has many subtypes and is found in plant cell walls; however, it is really not at all similar to cellulose; lignin is a compound that acts as a cement for cellulose in plants and plant cell walls
Food sources	Fruits, legumes, oats, oat bran, potatoes, and peas	Cereals, grains, legumes, kidney beans, green beans, wheat bran cereal, brown rice, carrots, and seeds
Health outcomes	Slows absorption of glucose and lipids, and lowers blood cholesterol levels Can help in reducing heart disease and controlling diabetes	Prevents some large intestine problems such as constipation and hemorrhoids; may also protect against cancer of the large intestine

TABLE 3.4 Soluble and Insoluble Fibers in Selected Foods

Food	Serving Size	Soluble Fiber (g)	Insoluble Fiber (g)
Apple	1 small	2.3	1.6
Brown rice	1/2 c. cooked	0.1	1.6
Corn	2/3 c.	0.2	1.4
Cornflakes	1 c.	0	0.5
Green beans	2/3 c.	0.6	3.3
Kidney beans	1/2 c. cooked	0.5	4.0
Oatmeal	1/3 c. uncooked	1.4	1.3
Orange	1 medium	1.3	1.9
Peas	1/2 c.	2.0	3.2
Popcorn	3 c.	0.8	2.0
Potatoes	1 small	2.2	1.6
Rye bread	1 slice	0.8	1.9
Whole-wheat bread	1 slice	0.3	1.2

Health Benefits of Fiber

Soluble fibers are known for their ability to lower blood cholesterol. Insoluble fibers tend to hold on to water in the gut and may soften stools and accelerate the passage of contents through the gastrointestinal tract, decreasing what is called *transit time*. Eating foods containing both forms of fiber is important in maintaining good health.

Although it is classified as a carbohydrate, dietary fiber does not yield energy as do the other carbohydrates. Despite this, we know that dietary fiber has many health benefits to the human body and is the focus of much research. Here are some of the currently understood health benefits of dietary fiber:

- Dietary fiber gives bulk to the contents of the digestive tract and improves the ability of the gastrointestinal tract to move food along its length. The time food takes to pass through the large intestine (transit time) is decreased.
- Dietary fiber dilutes toxic materials, which results in less contact between toxins and the intestinal wall.
- Dietary fiber allows for easier defecation. Fiber tends to hold on to water and makes the stools softer, resulting in easier bowel movements.
- Dietary fiber aids in weight control. The water-holding capacity of fiber may give a feeling of fullness or satiety. Fiber may also help in weight control as it displaces sugars and fats from the diet. High-dietary-fiber foods are generally also low in fat.
- Dietary fiber can bind with bile acids and enhance their excretion. Typically, bile acids (produced in the liver) secreted into the gastrointestinal

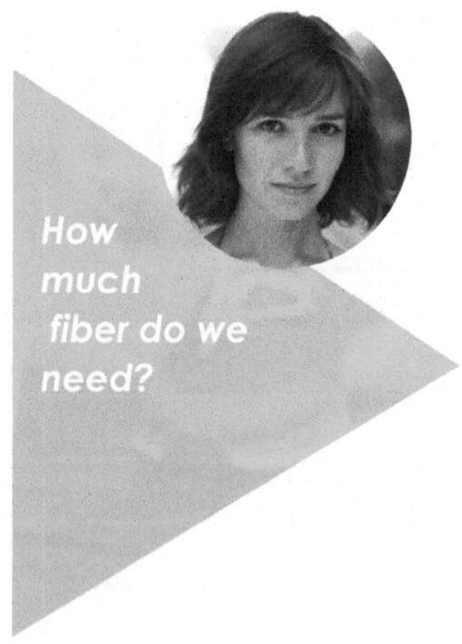
How
much
fiber do we
need?

tract can be reabsorbed to make cholesterol. Fiber reduces this reabsorption, which forces the liver to pull cholesterol from the blood to make the needed bile, which in turn lowers blood cholesterol levels.

The effects of dietary fiber typically decrease the following diseases or health problems:

- Diverticulosis, a condition in which pockets form in the colon wall due to increased intra-abdominal pressure exerted during defecation. These pockets can trap feces and become inflamed and infected.
- Constipation and diarrhea
- Colon cancer
- Ulcerative colitis or inflammation of the colon
- Appendicitis
- Hiatal hernia, or the pushing of part of the stomach up to the thoracic cavity
- Hemorrhoids and varicose veins
- Heart disease (particularly soluble fiber as it tends to lower blood cholesterol)
- Insulin requirements (fiber can help control blood glucose levels because it slows digestion and absorption of carbohydrates)

Resistant Starches

resistant starch
A starch that escapes digestion in the small intestine.

Another type of carbohydrate that is often grouped with dietary fiber is called **resistant starch**. This is an area of growing research as more health benefits of this type of starch are emerging. What is a resistant starch? Simply stated, it is a starch that escapes digestion within the small intestine. There are four classes of these starches: R1, R2, R3, and R4. R1 is the most non-digestible and may be found in seeds, unprocessed whole grains, and legumes. R2 is a more granular type of starch found in uncooked potatoes and green banana flours, for example. R3 is created by first cooking and then rapidly cooling a high-starch food. Breads, cornflakes, and cooked-then-cooled potatoes have this type of starch. R4 is chemically synthesized and not found in nature.

The resistant starches that have been researched the most have been R2 and R3 starches. R3 starches may enhance satiety (feeling of fullness), leading to decreased food intake. Other studies show that R2 and R3 can improve glucose tolerance. These two starch types can also improve large intestinal health by encouraging healthy bacteria to grow. Resistant starch does deliver calories, approximately 2 to 3 kcal/g as opposed to 4 kcal/g for typical starch. Because of their desirable taste and textures, resistant starch sources may be more palatable than other high fiber foods. About 3 to 7 g per day of resistant starch is consumed by Westerners, but more can be consumed without harmful effects. Navy beans are a good source of resistant starch, with half a cup cooked beans providing almost 10 g. Other good sources include unripe bananas, cold potatoes, cold pasta, lentils, oatmeal, and whole-grain bread.

Make it a PRACTICE

WHAT'S THE BEST WAY TO ADD FIBER TO YOUR DIET?

Increasing your intake of dietary fiber may not be as difficult as you think, but it does take some knowledge of food composition. A person who simply follows the recommendations of MyPlate by choosing fruits, vegetables, and whole grains will typically get about 25–30 g of fiber per day.

In general, the following foods are high in fiber:

- Legumes and lentils such as dried beans, peas, baked beans, kidney beans, split peas, garbanzo beans (chickpeas), lentils, pinto beans, black beans, green beans, snap beans, pole beans, lima beans, and broad beans
- Fruits such as blackberries, strawberries, cherries, plums, pears, apples, kiwifruit, guava, bananas, and dried fruits (dried figs, prunes, and raisins)
- Vegetables such as fresh or frozen green peas, broccoli, Brussels sprouts, sweet corn, beets, baked potato (with skin), and carrots; green leafy vegetables such as spinach, beet greens, kale, collards, Swiss chard, and turnip greens
- Nuts such as almonds, Brazil nuts, coconut, peanuts, and walnuts (high in fiber and calories)
- Whole wheat, barley, rye, oats, buckwheat, and cornmeal

If your current fiber intake is low, and you increase the fiber in your diet, the best advice is to increase the fiber content slowly, giving your gastrointestinal tract some time to adjust. In addition, be sure to consume plenty of water when making this change. Abruptly and substantially increasing fiber intake often results in diarrhea and other forms of gastrointestinal distress.

Can You Consume Too Much Fiber?

Overconsumption of fiber carries some health risks. Fiber can bind up minerals and interfere with their absorption. An intake of 50 g of fiber or more per day has been shown to significantly decrease the absorption of several minerals, including calcium, zinc, copper, and iron. Excess fiber intake causes an increased number of bowel movements, and some people may experience diarrhea, which can lead to dehydration. In people who increase fiber without increasing fluid, constipation may result.

To Supplement OR NOT

IS SUPPLEMENTAL FIBER IN PILL OR POWDER FORM THE SAME AS FIBER FOUND IN FOOD?

Many advertisements today urge us to purchase fiber pills to increase the dietary intake of this important nutrient. We have discussed the health benefits of dietary fiber, so why not get it from a pill? One reason to get your fiber from food is that foods high in fiber contain a variety of other nutrients along with important bioactive phytochemicals that have antioxidant activity. Sometimes when isolated fibers are put in pill form, they lose their antioxidant potential. Another issue is whether fiber pills can really dissolve in the stomach and intestines and have a significant impact. Purified sources of fiber may also bind up some minerals, whereas in food the level consumed may not cause such impairment. Some individuals (e.g., older adults) take fiber supplements to increase bowel movements and avoid constipation. Although these work, generally people become dependent on them. This is not necessarily bad, except that if you stop taking the supplements you may be more constipated than before you started taking them. In general, getting fiber from food sources is your best choice for health.

BEFORE YOU GO ON...

1. Can you distinguish between the health benefits of soluble fiber and insoluble fiber?
2. How does fiber affect the movement of food and waste components along the gastrointestinal tract?
3. How much fiber is recommended and how does this compare to what most Americans typically consume on a daily basis?
4. What pitfalls may occur if you consume too much fiber?
5. What is a resistant starch and what benefits do they have in a diet?

YOUR HEALTH AND CARBOHYDRATES

Empty Calories

We should clarify the difference between a food that is nutrient dense and one that contains empty calories. *Nutrient density* is the measure of the relative number of nutrients delivered per calorie in a given food. A candy bar and a banana may each provide 100 Calories. However, the banana has several other important nutrients while the candy bar does not, making the banana more nutrient dense. A goal should be to consume carbohydrate foods that are rich in nutrients, and to minimize consumption of foods with high calories but few nutrients. Unfortunately, this is not always the case in Western societies, and the issue is becoming much more worrisome. Health professionals are aware of the increased consumption of soft drinks that are high in sugar and have very little nutritive value. Cakes, cookies, pastries, and ice cream are other foods high in fat as well as sugar. Any positive effects from the presence of calcium in ice cream may be counterbalanced by its high caloric content.

© GWImages/Shutterstock.com

Soda vending machines in schools are controversial. Do you know if they are present in your local schools? Should public schools be obligated to provide or make available only foods that are considered nutritious and healthy? Why?

Nutrition & LIFESTAGES

WHAT'S SO BAD ABOUT SODA IN SCHOOLS?

Soda consumption in the United States increased from 22.2 gal. per person per year in 1970 to over 43 gal. a year in 2012, a jump of 197%. One 12-fl oz can of regular, sugar-sweetened soda contains approximately 140 calories. A study of 11- and 12-year-old adolescents monitored both their soda intake and body mass index (BMI). BMI is a measure that is used to determine overweight and obesity. This research revealed that BMI increased with increased sugared soda consumption. In other words, the more sugared soda a person drinks, the greater the risk of becoming overweight or obese. During the period from 1985 to 1997, consumption of soda in our schools increased by 1,200 percent, while the purchase of milk by students decreased by 30 percent. In a study using National Health and Nutrition Examination Survey data for 1999–2010, the heaviest consumers of carbonated beverages were adolescent and young-adult males. They consumed about 2.0 servings of regular carbonated soft drinks per day (1 serving = 12-fl oz). Females in the same age brackets were not far behind; they consumed about 1.2 servings per day. However, public concern over soda consumption may have made some impact. Per capita consumption of carbonated soft drinks has declined since its peak in 1998, according to the trade publication **Beverage Digest** and calculations by the Center for Science in the Public Interest (CSPI).

Since sodas are replacing healthier drink options, health officials are very concerned about the impact this will have on health. For example, the decrease in calcium intake in all ages due to decreased milk consumption, particularly during the adolescent years when peak bone mass is developing, may lead to osteoporosis in adulthood. Increased consumption of soda may also be linked to an upward spike in dental decay. Of course, the connection between obesity and excess caloric intake is a major problem that health officials must confront. In addition to a high level of sugar, the most routinely consumed soda beverages contain caffeine, and a concern over potential caffeine dependence, especially in children and adolescents, has also emerged. Those who consume soda may also be decreasing their intake of healthy foods and beverages. To make matters worse, many schools have multiple vending machines where students can select snacks that are also high in sugar and fat content. Because vending machines are profitable for schools, some school officials are reluctant to remove them. However, the availability of these food items is contrary to the goals of the federal school lunch program, which is designed to help schools provide nutritious meals and to educate students on proper nutrition.

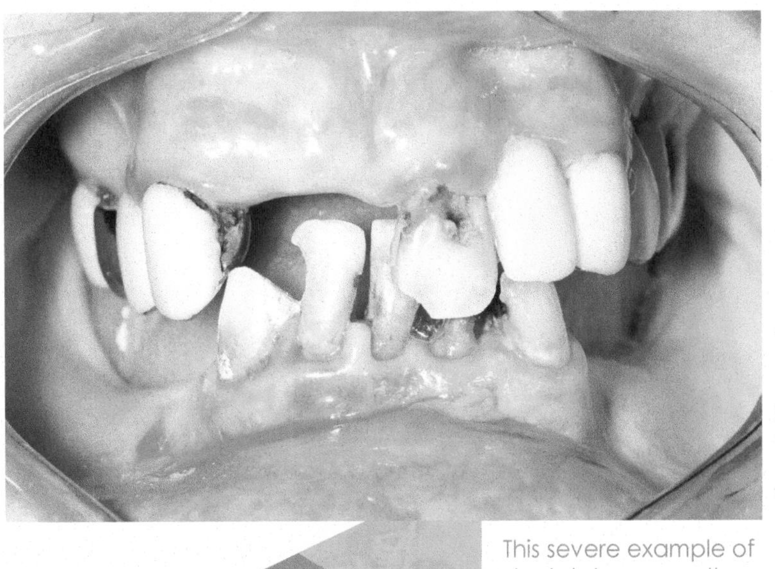

© botazsolti/Shutterstock.com

This severe example of dental decay resulted from poor food choices and poor eating habits. Much of this decay is due to the presence of a sticky carbohydrate on teeth. Bacteria adhere to and produce lactic acid, which dissolves the tooth enamel, leading to cavities.

Sugar Intake and Dental Decay

The association of sugar intake with dental decay or cavities has been documented for some time. The key factor is that a sticky carbohydrate can adhere to the enamel of the teeth and be metabolized by oral bacteria to produce lactic acid. Lactic acid degrades tooth enamel, allowing further infiltration of bacteria into the inner parts of the teeth. Fluoridation of water, practiced for more than 40 years in this country, has resulted in a dramatic decrease in the incidence of dental decay presumably due to the hardening effect of fluoride on tooth enamel. However, if our sugar consumption were decreased, perhaps we would observe an even further decline in dental disease.

APPLICATION TIP

Carbohydrates *alone* do not make you fat! Consuming more total calories than you need does.

Carbohydrate Intake and Obesity

Previously we discussed the issue of consuming empty calories through sugar intake. In addition to sugared soda, and based on the rapid increase in obesity in U.S. children and teens, nutrition experts are concerned about the availability of candy in our schools. How strong is this link? Obesity has a complex etiology. Therefore, the increasing obesity rate cannot be attributed entirely to increased sugar intake. Fat is also very high in calories (9 kcal/g) and thus a concentrated source of energy. The typical American diet is very high in animal protein, which can contain a lot of fat. While genetic predisposition also plays a significant role in a person's weight, physical inactivity and continued consumption of excessive amounts of calories set the stage for weight gain and ultimately obesity. Many consumers are also apparently unaware of how many calories are in the foods they eat. Frequently the caloric contents of foods are much higher than we think (see Chapter 9 for more information).

Low-Carbohydrate Diets and Weight Loss

Low-carbohydrate diets have been proposed as a great way to lose weight. The idea behind this approach is that severely reduced carbohydrate consumption forces the body into ketosis, in which products of fat are broken down and turned into ketone bodies. Protein and fat are less efficient sources of energy than carbohydrates. In addition, when consuming a low-carbohydrate diet, muscle glycogen is broken down to glucose. Glycogen holds on to water, but when it is broken down on a low-carbohydrate diet, the water is released. Water is lost as urine on these diets, which accounts for part of the weight loss that occurs.

The Atkins and South Beach diets are probably the two most popular examples of low-carbohydrate diets and have some similarities. Unfortunately, clinical trials on low-carbohydrate diets are not numerous. One study showed that after 6 months on an Atkins-like diet, compared to a traditional low-fat diet, the Atkins participants actually lost more weight. However, a lot of this reduced weight was attributable to water loss. Interestingly, as the study progressed further, the earlier difference in weight loss between the two diets was not observed after 12 months. In fact, both groups had a high dropout rate, suggesting the inability of subjects to sustain either type of diet.

One major concern about low-carbohydrate diets is the high intake of fat allowed on these diets, which research has shown can lead to increased risk for heart disease. However, data from the study just mentioned did not indicate that those on the low-carbohydrate, high-fat diet developed or experienced an increased risk for heart disease as compared to those on the conventional low-fat diet. No long-term controlled intake studies have as yet been reported on the correlation between low-carbohydrate diets and heart disease. In addition to being restrictive and difficult to maintain, low-carbohydrate diets may cause bad breath due to an increase of ketone bodies, constipation due to low intake of dietary fiber, and dehydration from induced water loss.

The controversy over carbohydrate restriction for weight loss is likely to continue for some time. Although many so-called fad diets do lead to weight loss, much of the reduction for many dieters is temporary. This problem of regaining lost weight is an important concern in our struggle against obesity. The key for anyone to lose weight and to keep the weight off is to identify a reasonable and healthy dietary pattern that works for them in the long term.

Myths & LEGENDS

DOES EATING SUGAR REALLY CAUSE OBESITY?

Simply stated, the more calories you consume (and sugar is often a prime source of excess calories) and the less energy you expend, the more weight you will gain. As noted earlier, research studies indicate that the more sugar one consumes, the greater the risk of becoming obese. But does that mean sugar causes the obesity, or simply that it provides extra calories? As low-fat products have become popular in recent years, the public may have been misled about their caloric content. Many of these low-fat products have extra sugar added, such as high-fructose corn syrup, in order to keep the flavor desirable. In an effort to reduce obesity and other negative impacts of added sugars, the Dietary Guidelines recommend no more than 10% of total Calories coming from added sugars. Even the research can contribute to uncertainty. One study suggested that women who consume soft drinks are more at risk of developing obesity. Remember that soda is the leading source of sugar in the American diet. However, another study failed to confirm a link between soda consumption and the incidence of obesity.

Flavoring and Sweetening Foods

Beyond our requirement for carbohydrate as a nutrient, the sweet taste of some carbohydrates adds flavor and enjoyment to our diets. Substances added to foods to enhance sweetness may be classified as either nutritive or nonnutritive sweeteners. **Nutritive sweeteners** can be digested and yield calories. **Nonnutritive sweeteners** are sometimes referred to as alternative sweeteners or sugar substitutes. They may be natural or synthetic and do not provide calories.

nutritive sweeteners
Sweeteners that can be digested and yield calories.

Nonnutritive sweeteners
Products that are sometimes referred to as alternative sweeteners or sugar substitutes. Most are synthetic and do not provide food energy.

Myths & LEGENDS

IS HONEY HEALTHIER FOR YOU THAN TABLE SUGAR?

Refined table sugar, or sucrose, is a disaccharide composed of glucose and fructose. Honey is composed of the same two monosaccharides, but they are not bonded together as in the case of sucrose. Fructose is sweeter than glucose and thus is often used to sweeten foods. However, fructose is not converted to energy as efficiently as glucose; this slower metabolic conversion means it is not as likely to raise blood glucose or insulin as readily. Because of this and the notion that honey is natural, many believe it is a healthier form of sweetener than table sugar. Honey, however, is not any healthier for you than table sugar. Honey may also accelerate tooth decay due to its sticky nature and adherence to the enamel of teeth. It has 21 kcal per teaspoon compared to 17 kcal for table sugar. One other aspect of honey that's important for parents and child caregivers to know is that it should never be given to infants less than 1 year old. Because it is made by bees, it can contain the spores of the bacterium *Clostridium botulinum*. Infants have much less acid in their stomachs, so these spores can germinate and lead to botulism, which is a deadly form of food-borne illness.

Substances such as fructose and sucrose are nutritive sweeteners. The intensity of the sweetness varies depending on the type of sugar (see Table 3.5 for the sweetness of sugars and sugar alternatives). For example, fructose is the sweetest simple sugar and lactose is the least sweet. Refined or processed sweeteners, such as molasses and high-fructose corn syrup are also used in foods. Molasses is a by-product of refined sugarcane or sugar beets that not only tastes sweet but also contains significantly higher levels of the minerals, iron and calcium, compared to other sweeteners. **High-fructose corn syrup** is a commonly used sweetener made from cornstarch that is one and a half times as sweet as sucrose. Cornstarch, which has a 50:50 ratio of fructose and glucose, is processed using enzymes to generate high-fructose corn syrup that typically contains 55% fructose and 45% glucose. You can find high-fructose corn syrup in sodas, desserts, low-fat yogurt, English muffins, ketchup, and other baked goods. It has become a concern for health professionals and consumer interest groups in that its prevalence in our diets is believed to contribute toward obesity by providing excess calories.

high-fructose corn syrup
A carbohydrate derived from cornstarch in which the level of fructose is increased using enzymes. In essence, cornstarch is made into a syrup that has slightly more fructose than glucose.

TABLE 3.5 Sweetness of Sugars and Sugar Alternatives

Type of Sweetener	Relative Sweetness to Sucrose	Typical Sources
Sugars		
Lactose	0.2	Dairy
Maltose	0.4	Sprouted seeds
Glucose	0.7	Corn syrup
Sucrose	1.0	Table sugar
Fructose	1.7	Fruit, honey, soft drinks
Sugar alcohols		
Sorbitol	0.6	Dietetic candies, sugarless gum, frozen desserts, baked goods
Mannitol	0.7	Dietetic candies, chocolate-flavored coating agents for ice cream and confections
Xylitol	0.9	Sugarless gums, hard candies, throat lozenges, toothpaste
Nonnutritive sweetener		
Stevia	30	Desserts, powdered sweeteners, liquids
Artificial sweeteners		
Aspartame (Nutrasweet or Equal)	200	Diet soft drinks and fruit drinks, powdered sweeteners
Acesulfame-K (Sunette)	150–200	Chewing gums, desserts, alcoholic beverages, syrups, candies, sauces, yogurt
Saccharin (Sweet' n Low)	500	Diet soft drinks
Sucralose (Splenda)	600	Soft drinks, baked goods

Sugar alcohols are either natural or derived from industrial processes. Sorbitol, mannitol, and xylitol are sweeteners that are not digested to the same extent as the other simple sugars, so they are less likely to cause dental caries. However, since some of these sugar alcohols pass through the intestines undigested, excess intake can lead to diarrhea and abdominal cramps. Although, they can be metabolized they yield fewer calories than glucose (4 kcal/g; sorbitol supplies 2.6 kcal/g, xylitol 2.4 kcal/g, and mannitol 1.6 kcal/g). You can find

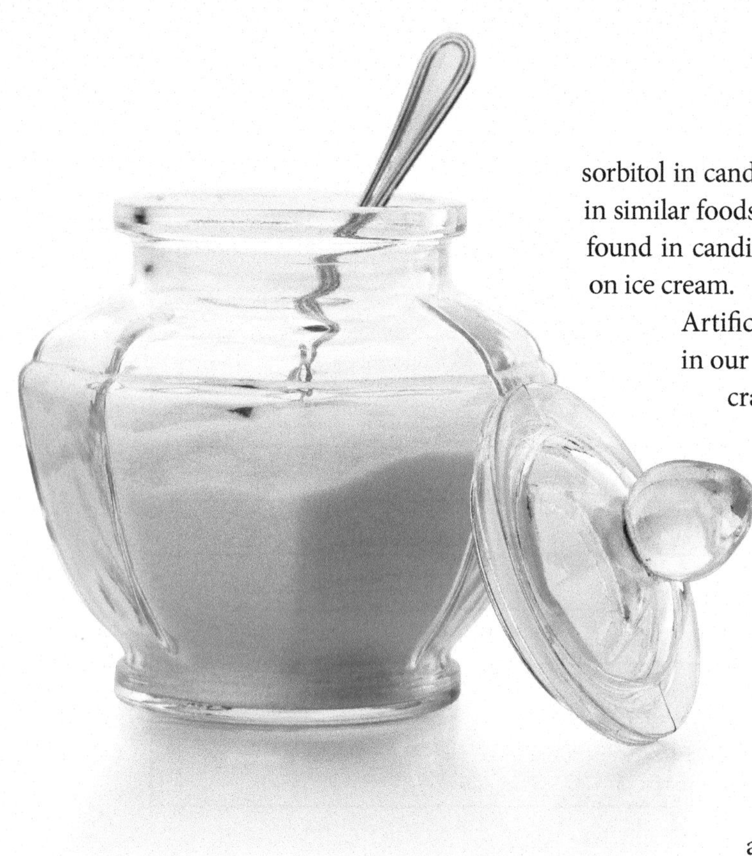

© fotogiunta/Shutterstock.com

sorbitol in candies, frozen desserts, and baked goods. Xylitol is found in similar foods, but also in mouthwashes and toothpaste. Mannitol is found in candies and the chocolate-flavored coating agent some like on ice cream.

Artificial or nonnutritive sweeteners are now quite prevalent in our food supply. Aspartame, acesulfame-K, saccharin, sucralose and stevia are examples. These compounds are much sweeter than natural sugars or sugar alcohols. Are artificial sweeteners safe? Based on the research to date, there is no evidence that artificial sweeteners cause cancer as long as they are consumed in amounts below the Acceptable Daily Intake (ADI). The ADI is the amount of an artificial that can be consumed on a daily basis based on the person's body weight. In the last few years, there has been some concern that artificial sweeteners may alter the type of bacteria in the gut and make some people more prone to insulin resistance or increased appetite. However, more research is needed to establish any definitive link.

APPLICATION TIP

Moderate caloric restriction and increased physical activity are still the best methods of losing weight and maintaining weight loss.

Lactose Intolerance

The inability of some people to digest milk sugar, or lactose, is commonly known as lactose intolerance. It is most often a genetic condition related to loss of function of the enzyme *lactase*. However, it can also result from aging, abdominal surgery in which part of the small intestine is removed, or use of certain medications. Lactase breaks down lactose into galactose and glucose, both of which can be absorbed. Virtually all infants have the ability to produce sufficient levels of lactase, but as they become older, the synthesis or function of this enzyme dramatically decreases, particularly in those of African and Asian descent, and even those of southern European ancestry.

Those who are lactose intolerant typically experience side effects such as diarrhea, bloating, and flatulence when they consume milk. These symptoms are caused by lactose entering the large intestine, where the bacteria ferment it, producing lactic acid and gas. The presence of lactose and lactic acid increases osmotic pressure (the pressure exerted by water moving into the gastrointestinal tract) and draws water into the large intestine, leading to diarrhea. The fermentation process leads to gas production, which causes bloating and flatulence. Many with this condition believe they must avoid milk entirely, which may limit their intake of specific nutrients, such as calcium and Vitamin D. Despite this condition, most RDs/RDNs believe that those who are lactose intolerant need not avoid milk and dairy products totally, because a large amount of milk or lactose must be consumed at one time to trigger the symptoms. For those who are more severely lactose intolerant, several options exist. Consuming three 8-fl oz glasses of milk spread throughout the day may not result in these symptoms in some people, whereas one 8-fl oz glass may produce symptoms in others. In lactose-hydrolyzed milk, lactase has been added to break down the lactose. Milk can be purchased in this form, or lactase drops or tablets can be added to regular milk to eliminate the lactose. Other products such as sweet acidophilus milk and buttermilk are low in lactose and may be safely consumed. Soy, rice, and almond milk are lower in calcium and Vitamin D, and may lack other nutrients unless they are fortified like some juices. Yogurt is yet another food that can be consumed to retain the nutritional benefits of dairy products. Another way to incorporate milk into a diet of a lactose-intolerant individual is to offer small amounts of milk (2–3-fl oz) with a mixed meal.

BEFORE YOU GO ON...

1. What is nutrient density?
2. How does sugar consumption contribute to dental decay?
3. Many people are lactose intolerant. Why does this occur?

There are many products on the market today that can be used by people with lactose intolerance to get the benefit of dairy products.

Checking blood sugar levels is important to properly manage diabetes and avoid complications of the disease.

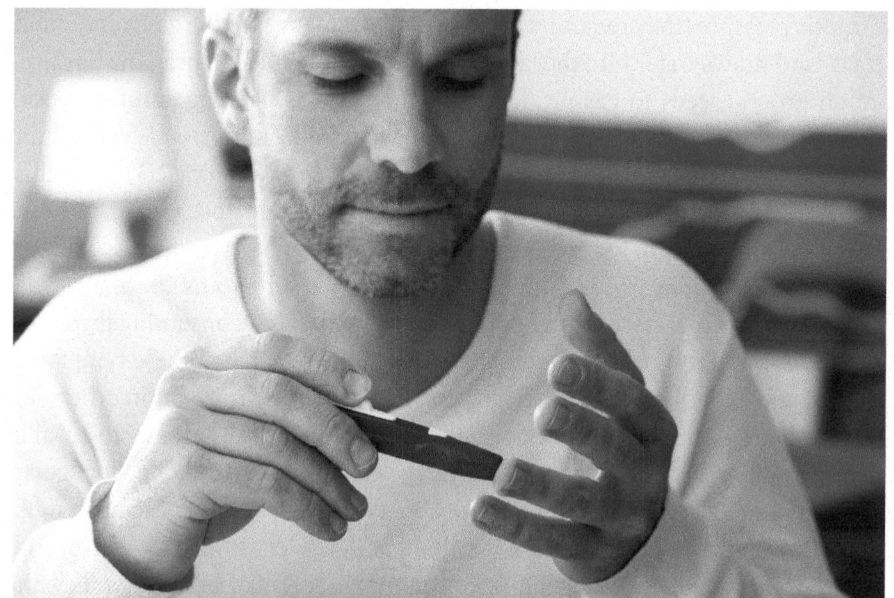

DIABETES MELLITUS

diabetes mellitus

The inability of the body to regulate blood glucose levels within normal limits (Fasting Blood Glucose >126 mg/dL).

prediabetes

A condition in which impaired glucose tolerance leads to elevated blood glucose levels (Fasting Blood Glucose between 100 mg/dL and 125 mg/dL), which if ignored, can result in development of diabetes mellitus.

hyperglycemia

An elevated blood glucose level (a Fasting Blood Glucose above the normal 99 mg/dL).

acidosis

A buildup of acids in body fluids such as blood.

Diabetes mellitus is the inability of the body to regulate blood glucose levels within normal limits and results in **hyperglycemia,** an elevated blood glucose level. Over 29 million Americans have diabetes and 86 million have prediabetes. As discussed, under normal conditions, after a meal the pancreas begins to release insulin as glucose levels in the blood become elevated. Insulin allows the body's cells to take up glucose and use it, which brings glucose in the blood down to normal levels. When this tightly regulated system is altered leading to an impaired glucose tolerance, blood glucose levels become elevated for prolonged periods. Depending upon the severity of this elevation dictates a diagnosis of either diabetes or prediabetes.

Hyperglycemia can lead to a variety of short-term or long-term problems. Short term, glucose spills over into the urine. When this occurs, water is removed from blood to produce urine to excrete the glucose. This water loss results in intense thirst and frequent urination. Often, persistent thirst and excessive urination are the first signs of diabetes. Because the body must obtain energy from somewhere other than glucose, the body starts to rely on fat. As noted earlier, fat cannot be fully metabolized without the presence of oxaloacetate derived from carbohydrates and some amino acids. The result is the production of ketones. Ketones have a sweet and fruity odor to them, so people with diabetes often have a fruity smell to their breath. Ketosis and acidosis are the result. Acidosis is the buildup of acids in body fluids such as blood. People who develop acidosis and ketosis become drowsy and lethargic, may feel nauseated, and have rapid breathing. In addition to fat, the body can break down proteins for energy. This increases the demands on the kidney through the increased excretion of nitrogen, which is a component of proteins. If protein breakdown continues, muscle wasting (atrophy) may occur.

Long term, hyperglycemia can increase the risk for coronary heart disease (due to elevated blood lipid levels), kidney failure, high blood pressure, and damage to the eyes and blood vessels. In addition, blood vessels that supply the arms, hands, legs, and feet become more narrow in people with diabetes, and this contributes to foot ulcers, which is the leading cause of non-accident-caused amputations of the limbs. People with more advanced stages of diabetes mellitus can also develop nerve damage due to the elevated levels of glucose in their bodies. The excess glucose leads to the glycation of proteins (a chemical reaction in which proteins are modified by being bound to glucose or fructose), which can induce inflammation and other physiological changes.

Despite some beliefs, at this time research does not support excess sugar intake as the primary cause of diabetes mellitus. Several types of diabetes mellitus exist, and their causes are complex. Some variations may be caused by genetic predisposition; others may be related to environmental and lifestyle factors.

FORMS OF DIABETES

Type 1 Diabetes

Type 1 diabetes, is most often diagnosed in children or adolescents. However, adults may develop this form as well. It constitutes about 10 percent of all cases of diabetes mellitus. Type 1 diabetes occurs when the pancreas is unable to produce insulin. It is thought to be an autoimmune disease. An autoimmune disease is one in which the body begins to see its own organs and proteins as foreign, and the immune system attacks its own organs and tissues. The condition generally develops suddenly and the person loses weight (protein and fat are lost). The patient experiences muscle wasting because muscle protein is being broken down to form glucose. Lifelong insulin injections or use of an insulin pump is the usual treatment, along with a carbohydrate-controlled diet to help regulate blood glucose levels and insulin requirements.

type 1 diabetes
A disease that occurs when the pancreas is unable to produce insulin. It was formerly known as juvenile-onset diabetes or insulin-dependent diabetes mellitus, because of its frequent diagnosis in children or adolescents.

Type 2 Diabetes

Type 2 diabetes accounts for more than 90 percent of all cases of diabetes mellitus. In type 2 diabetes, the individual may be able to produce insulin, even too much, but cells in the body do not respond to the insulin in our blood. Sometimes the term *insulin* resistance is applied to these individuals. People with type 2 diabetes are typically older than age 40 and overweight or obese when diagnosed. However, many overweight adolescents are now being diagnosed as well, and even children as young as 3 years old. The increase in type 2 diabetes has been linked with an increase in obesity for people of all ages. This type of diabetes also appears to have a genetic link, so obesity and overweight factors alone may not be completely responsible.

type 2 diabetes
A disease that occurs when the insulin produced by the pancreas does not function as effectively, leading to elevated blood glucose. It was formerly known as adult-onset diabetes or non-insulin-dependent diabetes mellitus.

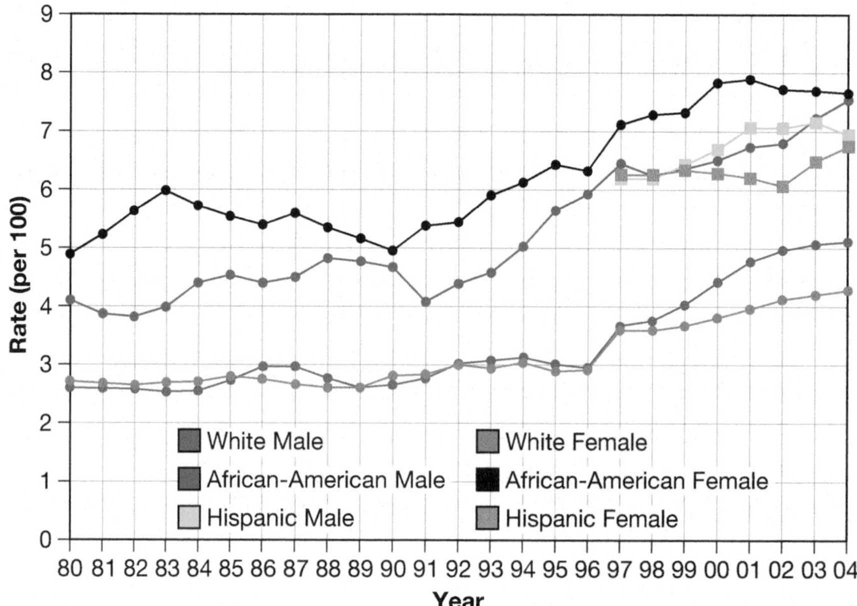

FIGURE 3.10
The rates of diabetes among various ethnic or racial groups. Note that African American females have the highest rate. According to the American Diabetes Association, treatment for people with diabetes cost $245 billion per year.
Source: http://professional.diabetes.org/admin/UserFiles/0%20-%20Sean/FastFacts%20March%202013.pdf

The percentage of a population that develops diabetes varies for different ethnic groups. African Americans, especially women, are almost twice as likely to develop type 2 diabetes as non-Hispanic whites. Hispanics also have a much higher risk for diabetes compared to whites (Figure 3.10). Nearly 19 percent of African Americans over the age of 20 have diabetes; this group also experiences a higher incidence of complications from diabetes. Researchers also believe that African American children may be at increased risk for type 2 diabetes due to genetic factors.

*Once diagnosed with diabetes, diet and lifestyle changes are a key component of treatment. In terms of diet, it is necessary to control the amount of carbohydrate consumed. This makes sense since carbohydrates are the nutrient that raises blood sugar. The American Diabetes Association recommends diabetics aim for 45-60 grams of carbohydrate per meal and adjust as needed based on blood sugar. See figure 3.11 for an example of how much carbohydrate is found in commonly eaten foods. In addition to dietary changes, exercise can help control blood sugar by improving insulin sensitivity. A good starting point is 30 minutes per day. Lastly, weight control or weight loss is needed. If overweight, aim for a weight loss of 5-10%. In addition to diet and lifestyle changes, type 2 diabetics often require oral medications to help control blood sugar.

Food	Amount
Bread	1 oz
Pasta or rice	1/3 cup
Flake cereal	1 cup
Hot cereal	½ cup
Tortilla	6 inch
Apple, peach, pear	1 small
Dried fruit	¼ cups
100% fruit juice	½ cup
Milk (whole, 2%, 1% or skim)	1 cup
Beans, potatoes, peas, corn	½ cup
Brownie or cake, no frosting	2 inch square
Ice cream	½ cup
Jam/jelly	1 tbsp

FIGURE 3.11
Amount of food that provides 15 grams of carbohydrate

note: meats, cheeses, fats and oils do not contain carbohydrate

Gestational Diabetes

Another type of diabetes is **gestational diabetes**, which is diabetes that occurs in some women during pregnancy. Hispanics and Native Americans have higher susceptibility for this. Physicians and dietitians alike must take extra care to ensure that the fetus is not harmed. This type of diabetes can cause fetal or infant illness or death. The risks of high infant birth weight or surgical birth are higher with gestational diabetes. After birth, the condition typically disappears. However, mothers with gestational diabetes are at higher risk for developing type 2 diabetes later in life, and their infants are more likely to develop diabetes as adults.

gestational diabetes
Diabetes that occurs in some women during pregnancy.

BEFORE YOU GO ON...

1. Define diabetes mellitus and describe why those who have it are at risk for coronary heart disease.
2. Differentiate between type 1 and type 2 diabetes.
3. Describe two risk factors that contribute to diabetes development.
4. What is gestational diabetes?

CHAPTER SUMMARY

- Carbohydrates are responsible for several major functions, the most important of which is serving as the major source of energy in our bodies. In addition, carbohydrates spare stored protein from being broken down so that muscle mass is maintained. Having ample carbohydrates and total calories in your diet prevents ketosis. Carbohydrates also provide flavoring or sweetness to foods we consume.
- The simple sugars are divided into two categories: monosaccharides and disaccharides. The monosaccharides are glucose, fructose, and galactose; the disaccharides are sucrose, lactose, and maltose. Glucose is sometimes referred to as blood sugar, and is the main source of energy for the body. Fructose is found primarily in fruits; galactose is a component of lactose or milk sugar. Simple table sugar is sucrose.
- Plant starches are composed of complex carbohydrates or polysaccharides. The animal version of stored complex carbohydrate, called *glycogen*, is found mainly in the liver and muscle.
- Dietary fiber is a complex carbohydrate that is not digested and has many health benefits and may lower the risk of many types of chronic diseases, such as cancer, heart disease, and diabetes. The DRI recommends 25–38 g/day of dietary fiber (14 g/1,000 kcal consumed). The average American consumes only about half the fiber recommended by several health agencies, or approximately 12–15 g/day.
- Food sources vary in levels of soluble and insoluble fiber. Fruits are excellent sources of soluble fiber, and whole-grain cereals and breads are good sources of insoluble fiber. Soluble fiber can lower blood cholesterol, whereas insoluble fiber is more likely to help prevent constipation and colon cancer.
- Resistant starch is another type of carbohydrate grouped with dietary fiber. There are four classes designated as R1, R2, R3, and R4, with R1 being the most non-digestible. R2 and R3 starches provide 2 to 3 kcal/g.
- Many diets contain excess sugars and insufficient levels of whole-grain carbohydrate sources. Excess intake of sugars may be one of the primary reasons why obesity has increased in the United States. Low intake of whole grains, fruits, and vegetables may contribute to heart disease, several types of cancer, and type 2 diabetes.
- Some people do not produce enough of the enzyme lactase to break down the milk sugar lactose. This can cause them to have gastrointestinal discomfort such as diarrhea, bloating, and flatulence. Despite these issues, lactose-intolerant people may still consume dairy products without ill effects if they ingest small amounts and/or spread their intake of dairy products throughout the day, or choose fermented dairy products that are lower in lactose, such as yogurt.

KEY TERMS

ACIDOSIS A buildup of acids in body fluids such as blood.

DIABETES MELLITUS The inability of the body to regulate blood glucose levels within normal limits.

DIETARY FIBER A carbohydrate composed of repeating units of glucose and other monosaccharides that cannot be digested by human enzymes and thus cannot be absorbed and used by the body. Dietary fiber is now part of the Institute of Medicine formal definition of fiber in the diet. Dietary fiber represents that fraction that is inherent in the intact food.

FRUCTOSE A monosaccharide that has a simple ring structure. It is the sugar found abundantly in fruit, honey, and also some vegetables such as beets, sweet potatoes, parsnips, and onions. It is the sweetest sugar.

FUNCTIONAL FIBER The Institute of Medicine definition of fiber in our diet includes this form of fiber, which includes fiber that has been extracted and/or synthesized and is added to food.

GALACTOSE A monosaccharide that is consumed as a part of the disaccharide lactose found in milk; it is a basic component of other, more complex carbohydrates.

GESTATIONAL DIABETES Diabetes that occurs in some women during pregnancy.

GLUCAGON A hormone released from the pancreas that breaksdown liver glycogen to glucose

GLUCONEOGENESIS Synthesis of new glucose from noncarbohydrate sources.

GLUCOSE The monosaccharide that circulates in the blood, and is often referred to as *blood sugar*. It is the main source of energy for the body.

GLYCEMIC INDEX A measure of how fast blood glucose increases when a person ingests a particular food, compared to ingestion of glucose.

GLYCOGEN The storage form of carbohydrate in animals, and is found in the liver and muscle.

HIGH-FRUCTOSE CORN SYRUP A carbohydrate derived from cornstarch in which the level of fructose is increased using enzymes. In essence, cornstarch is made into a syrup that has slightly more fructose than glucose.

HYPERGLYCEMIA An elevated blood glucose level.

INSOLUBLE FIBER A type of fiber that is mainly composed of plant cell walls. It cannot be dissolved in water and resists human digestive enzymes. It is composed of cellulose, hemicellulose, and lignin.

INSULIN A hormone released from the pancreas that allows glucose to enter cells to be used for energy.

KETONE BODIES Acidic fat derivatives that arise from the incomplete breakdown of fat.

LACTOSE A disaccharide, commonly known as milk sugar that is composed of glucose and galactose.

MALTOSE A disaccharide that is composed of two glucose units.

NONNUTRITIVE SWEETENERS Products that are sometimes referred to as alternative sweeteners or sugar substitutes. Most are synthetic and do not provide food energy.

NUTRITIVE SWEETENERS Sweeteners that can be digested and yield calories.

POLYSACCHARIDE A carbohydrate composed of a chain with thousands of glucose molecules linked together.

PREDIABETES A state in which impaired glucose tolerance leads to elevated blood glucose levels, which if ignored, can result in development of diabetes mellitus.

RESISTANT STARCH A starch that escapes digestion in the small intestine.

SOLUBLE FIBER Fiber that can dissolve in water. It is composed of many repeating monosaccharides that are acid derivatives of galactose. It is a jellylike material that acts as a cement in plants.

STARCH The storage form of carbohydrate found in plants.

SUCROSE A disaccharide commonly known as table sugar; it is composed of one glucose molecule and one fructose molecule.

TYPE 1 DIABETES A disease that occurs when the pancreas is unable to produce insulin. It was formerly known as juvenile-onset diabetes or insulin-dependent diabetes mellitus, because of its frequent diagnosis in children or adolescents.

TYPE 2 DIABETES A disease that occurs when the insulin produced by the pancreas does not function as effectively, leading to elevated blood glucose. It was formerly known as adult-onset diabetes or non-insulin-dependent diabetes mellitus.

REFERENCE

Turner ND, Lupton JR. (2011) Dietary fiber. *Adv Nutr* 2:151–152. http://www.usda.gov/factbook/chapter2.pdf

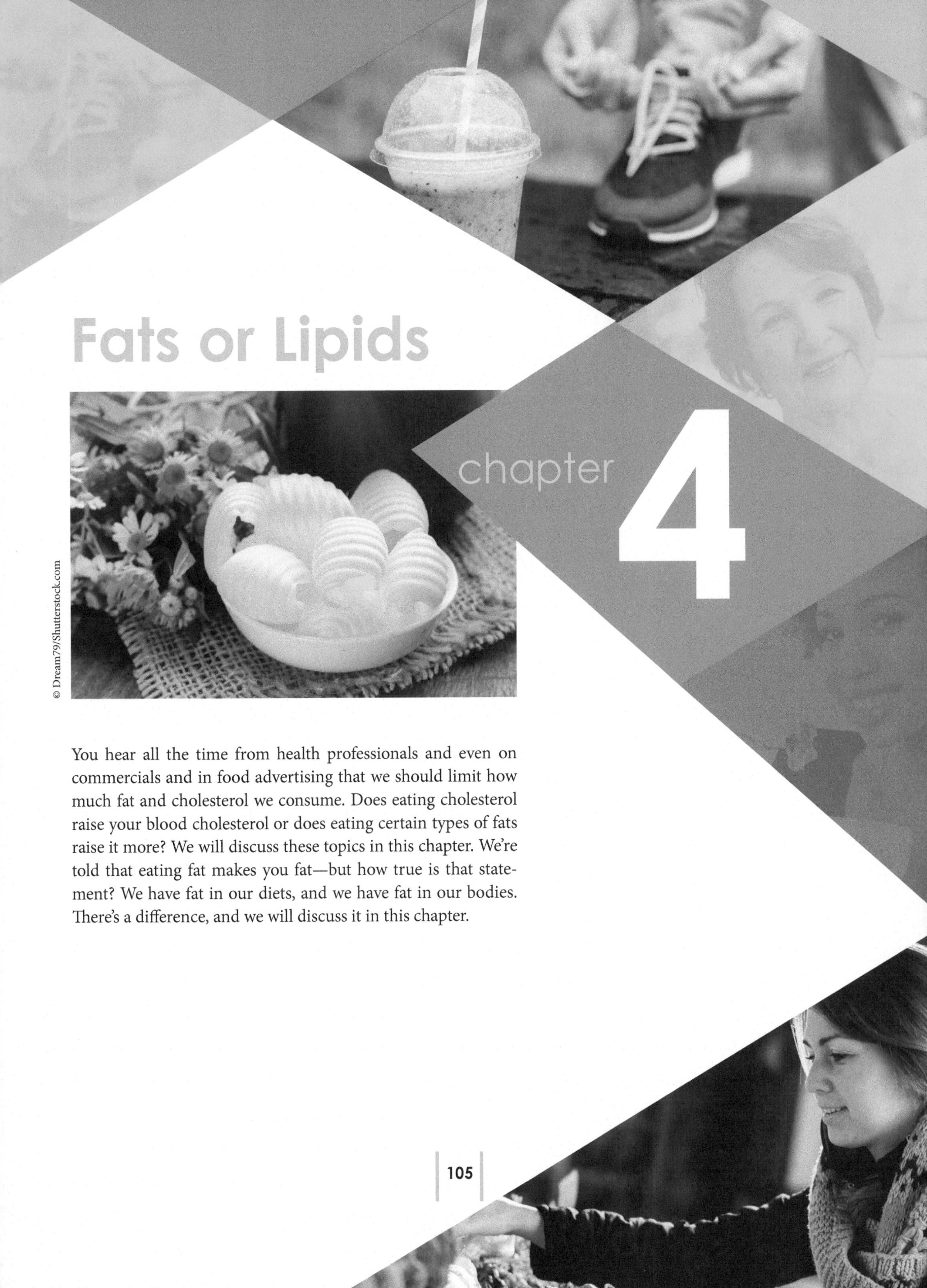

Fats or Lipids

chapter 4

© Dream79/Shutterstock.com

You hear all the time from health professionals and even on commercials and in food advertising that we should limit how much fat and cholesterol we consume. Does eating cholesterol raise your blood cholesterol or does eating certain types of fats raise it more? We will discuss these topics in this chapter. We're told that eating fat makes you fat—but how true is that statement? We have fat in our diets, and we have fat in our bodies. There's a difference, and we will discuss it in this chapter.

THE LIPIDS IN OUR FOOD AND OUR BODIES

What are fats? Fats, or the more scientific term *lipids,* are defined as substances that are insoluble in water but soluble in organic solvents such as ether, acetone, and chloroform. Just look at what happens when you add a drop of oil to water. It simply sits there on top of the water. A wide variety of lipids influence human health, such as the following:

- Fatty acids
- Triglycerides
- Phospholipids
- Sterols such as cholesterol

Triglycerides and phospholipids contain fatty acids. We will focus much of our attention on fatty acids, because these compounds affect triglyceride and phospholipid function and ultimately our health. Cholesterol is vital as it is converted to important hormones, but it also can lead to heart disease when present in the blood at too high a level.

Oil and water. Notice how the two do not mix.

Lipids are composed of the same elements that are contained in carbohydrates:

- Carbon (C)
- Hydrogen (H)
- Oxygen (O)

The major difference is that lipids, when compared to carbohydrates, contain almost twice as many hydrogen atoms. Why is this important? The number of hydrogen atoms is a good predictor of how much energy a substance has and is why lipids provide 9 kcal/gram compared to carbohydrates that provide 4 kcal/gram.

Fatty Acids

We will begin our discussion with fatty acids. Fatty acids are not only important lipid compounds by themselves but also as components of triglycerides and phospholipids.

Fatty acids play important roles in the body. What is a fatty acid? Fatty acids are simply a chain of carbons linked (or bonded) together. One end of the chain has a *carboxyl group* (see Figure 4.1), represented by COOH. This end allows fatty acids to mix a bit with water, and is thus called *hydrophilic.* The other end of the chain has a *methyl group* (Figure 4.1) represented by CH_3. This part of the chain does not like to be mixed with water, and is thus called *hydrophobic.* The long chain between the two ends tends to behave like the methyl end and is not soluble in water. This means that the shorter the chain, the more it likes water.

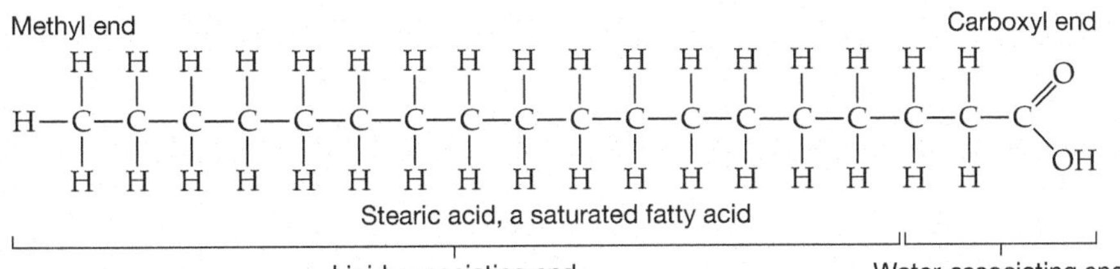

FIGURE 4.1 Structure of a fatty acid. The carboxyl end associates with water, and the methyl end and long carbon chain associate with lipid.

Fatty Acid Saturation

Fatty acid saturation refers to whether a fatty acid chain is occupied by all of the hydrogen atoms it can hold. If the chain is fully occupied by hydrogen atoms, then it is a **saturated fatty acid** (Figure 4.2). However, not all fatty acids contain carbons that are fully saturated with hydrogens. Some have areas where hydrogen atoms are missing; we refer to these fatty acids as *unsaturated.* These unsaturated fatty acids form a *double bond* between two carbon atoms when hydrogen atoms are not present. A fatty acid with one double bond

saturated fatty acid
Fatty acid that contains no double bonds.

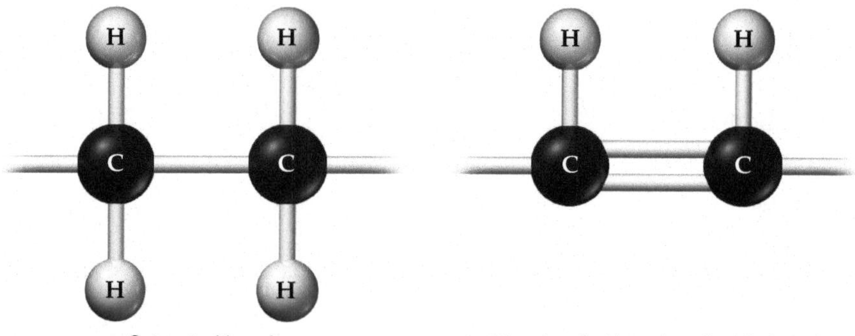

FIGURE 4.2 Saturated and unsaturated bonds connecting carbon atoms.

is called a **monounsaturated fatty acid;** one with two or more double bonds is called a **polyunsaturated fatty acid** (Figure 4.3). The level of saturation influences the fat's impact on health and its physical properties.

monounsaturated fatty acid
A fatty acid that contains only one double bond.

polyunsaturated fatty acid
A fatty acid that contains two or more double bonds.

Foods are composed of mixtures of all of these fatty acids, but some fatty acids are higher in some foods than others (Figure 4.4). Saturated fatty acids tend to be found in animal products and are usually solid at room temperature. Examples of foods with saturated fats are dairy products, meats, and some plants and tropical oils such as coconut, palm, and palm kernel oils.

FIGURE 4.3 Fatty acids that are saturated, mono-unsaturated, and polyunsaturated.

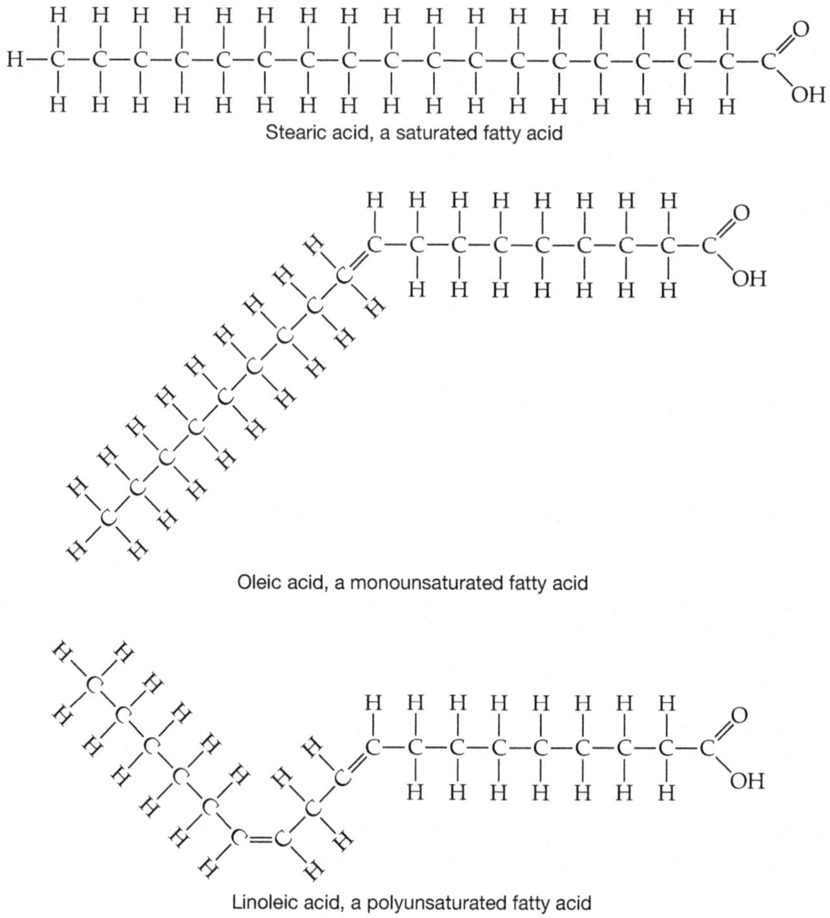

Stearic acid, a saturated fatty acid

Oleic acid, a monounsaturated fatty acid

Linoleic acid, a polyunsaturated fatty acid

Fats from these foods can increase blood cholesterol levels in some people. See the feature on page 135, What's Hot: Is Coconut Oil Bad for You or Not? Unsaturated fats tend to be found of plant origin and are liquid at room temperature. Some plant foods, such as canola and olive oils, are good sources of monounsaturated fatty acids. Polyunsaturated fatty acids can be found in vegetable oils, such as sunflower, flaxseed, corn, and safflower oils, and other foods, including vegetables, flax, and fish oils. Both monounsaturated and polyunsaturated fats can lower blood cholesterol levels in some people.

> **APPLICATION TIP**
>
> Read food labels to avoid tropical oils that are saturated; look for ingredients such as palm, palm kernel, or coconut oils. Even though they come from plants, they are saturated and less healthy for you than monounsaturated and polyunsaturated fats.

Essential and Nonessential Fatty Acids

essential fatty acid
Fatty acids that cannot be made by the body and can be provided only by the diet.

The concept of what is essential is rather simple. Nutrients that the body's tissues or cells cannot make, either at all or in an amount needed to maintain health, are said to be essential. Fatty acids that cannot be made by the body and must be provided by the diet are called **essential fatty acids**. The essential

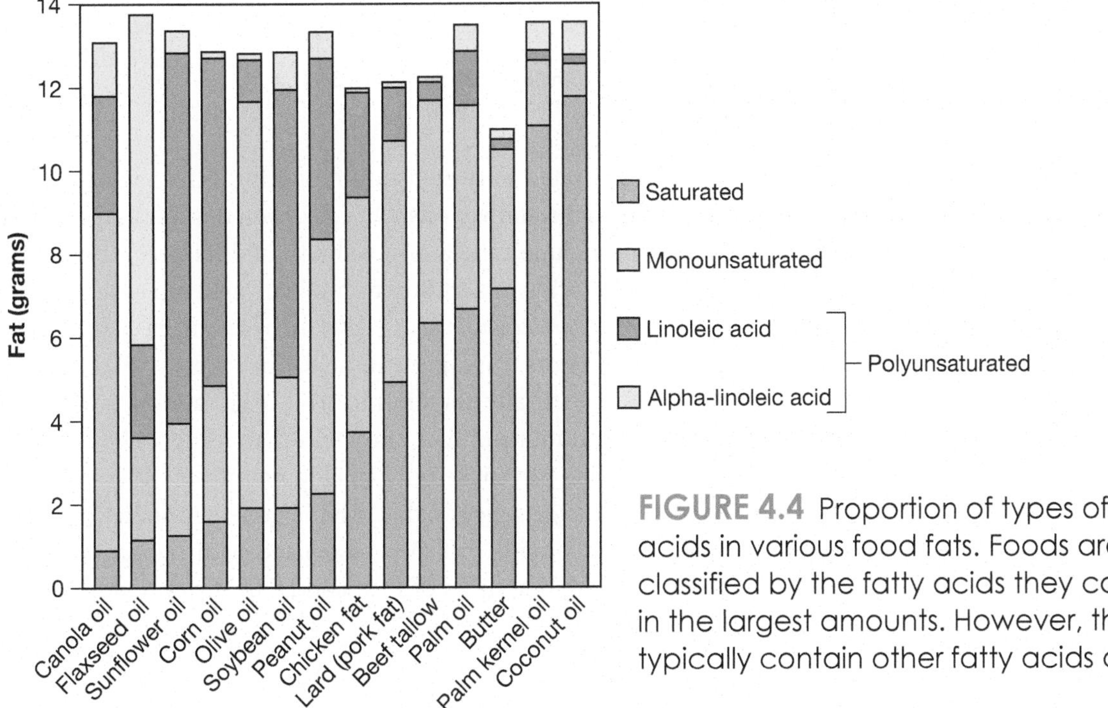

FIGURE 4.4 Proportion of types of fatty acids in various food fats. Foods are classified by the fatty acids they contain in the largest amounts. However, they typically contain other fatty acids as well.

fatty acids are *linoleic acid*, a member of the omega-6 fatty acid family and *linolenic acid*, a member of the omega-3 fatty acid family.

Omega-3 and Omega-6 Fatty Acids

You may have heard or read about these two fatty acid families through the media or advertisements. The numbers 3 and 6 refer to where the double bonds are located in the fatty acids (Figure 4.5). The location of the double bonds dramatically affects the function of the fatty acid.

*Both types of fatty acids play a crucial role in brain function and normal growth and development and are used as a starting point for **eicosanoids**, compounds that regulate a variety of body functions. For example, eicosanoids from omega-3 fats lower blood pressure, thin the blood and reduce inflammation. Eicosanoids from omega-6 fats do just the opposite – raise blood pressure, promote blood clotting and promote inflammation.

eicosanoids

Metabolically active chemicals synthesized from fatty acids. These chemicals have powerful physiological effects, including relaxing blood vessels and promoting blood clotting.*

Most Americans get plenty of omega-6 fatty acids but not enough omega-3s. The typical American diet tends to contain 14 to 25 times more omega-6 fatty acids than omega-3 fatty acids.

Carbon number from CH_3 end

1 2 3 4 5 6 7 8 9 10 11 12 13 14 15 16 17 18

$$CH_3{-}CH_2{-}CH_2{-}CH_2{-}CH_2{-}CH{=}CH{-}CH_2{-}CH{=}CH{-}CH_2{-}CH{-}CH{-}CH_2{-}CH_2{-}CH_2{-}CH_2{-}COOH$$

Omega end

Alpha end

First double bond is on sixth carbon from the omega end of the fatty acid

(a) An omega-6 fatty acid (linolenic acid)

Carbon number from CH_3 end

1 2 3 4 5 6 7 8 9 10 11 12 13 14 15 16 17 18

$$CH_3{-}CH_2{-}CH{=}CH{-}CH_2{-}CH{=}CH{-}CH_2{-}CH{=}CH{-}CH_2{-}CH_2{-}CH_2{-}CH_2{-}CH_2{-}CH_2{-}CH_2{-}COOH$$

Omega end

Alpha end

First double bond is on third carbon from the omega end of the fatty acid

(b) An omega-3 fatty acid (linolenic acid)

FIGURE 4.5
Differences between omega-6 and omega-3 fatty acids. Note where the double bonds occur.

Omega-6 polyunsaturated fatty acids are found in liquid vegetable oils, such as soybean, corn, and safflower oils. Omega-3 polyunsaturated fatty acids from plant sources include canola oils, walnuts, and flaxseed. Two other important omega-3 fatty acids in addition to linolenic acid are *eicosapentaenoic acid* (*EPA*) and *docosahexaenoic acid* (*DHA*). These omega-3 fatty acids can be made in small amounts from linolenic acid. They are also abundant in coldwater fish. Fish that naturally contain more oil (e.g., salmon, trout, herring) have higher concentrations of EPA and DHA than leaner fish (e.g., cod, haddock, catfish). Humans can make only small amounts of EPA and DHA from linolenic acid. Evidence suggests that for the general population, consumption of omega-3 fatty acids in fish is associated with reduced risks of cardiovascular disease. Other sources of EPA and DHA may provide similar benefits (see Table 4.1). Because very little linolenic acid is converted to EPA and DHA in humans, experts recommend that we consume more fish to get the health benefit of omega-3 fatty acids.

TABLE 4.1 Families of Fatty Acids and Food Sources

Fatty Acid Family	Food Sources
Omega-6 fatty acid	
Linoleic acid	Soybean, corn, and safflower oils; vegetables, seeds, whole grains.
Omega-3 fatty acids	
Linolenic acid	Flax seed and flax oil, pumpkin seed, walnut oil, chia seed, walnuts, canola oil.
EPA and DHA*	Fish such as lake trout, herring, sardines, Atlantic salmon, albacore tuna, bluefish, halibut, mackerel. *Caution:* Tuna may have high levels of mercury.
*Also found in breast milk.	

SOMETHING FISHY—OMEGA-3 FATTY ACIDS

Numerous research studies have validated the positive health benefits of omega-3 fatty acids, and RDs/RDNs continue to advocate an increased consumption of foods that contain them. Consuming omega-3 fatty acids is likely to decrease the risk of developing coronary heart disease. Physiologically, omega-3 fatty acids reduce inflammation, may lower blood pressure, reduce blood clotting, and lower blood triglyceride levels. However, one should be careful about taking excessive fish oil *supplements* because they can thin the blood and inhibit the normal blood clotting process. Those who take blood-thinning medications should ask their physician how much dietary omega-3 fatty acid is appropriate. Another important role for omega-3 fatty acids is improved cognition in infants fed formula containing omega-3 fatty acids. There is also some evidence to suggest it may delay the onset of dementia associated with aging.

How much omega-3 fatty acid should adults consume daily? It depends on whom you ask. For a typical 2,000-Calorie daily intake, about 3 g of omega-3 fatty acids are recommended, nearly twice the 1.6 g the average American consumes. Following are the American Heart Association recommendations to achieve healthy intake levels of omega-3 fatty acids:

Population	Recommendation
Patients without heart disease	Eat a variety of fatty fish at least twice per week. Include foods rich in linolenic acid (flaxseed, canola, and soybean oils, flaxseed and walnuts).
Patients with heart disease	Consume 1 g of EPA + DHA per day, preferably from fatty fish. Use supplements only after consultation with a physician.
Patients who need to lower blood triglycerides	Consume 2–4 g of EPA + DHA per day, provided in capsules under a physician's care.

These above recommendations are the best way to get omega-3 fatty acids.; However, food manufacturers are also adding these fatty acids to some products where they would not normally be found. For instance, some fruit juices, milk, cereals and even frozen pizzas can be found fortified with DHA and EPA at the supermarket.

Salmon, sardines, buffalo, walnuts, canola oil, and flax seed are examples of good sources of omega-3 fatty acids.

Trans Fatty Acids

What's
an example
of an
unhealthy
fat?

What are trans fatty acids? Most hydrogen atoms bonded to a carbon atom will be in a *cis* arrangement (see Figure 4.6). A **trans fatty acid** is an unhealthy fatty acid produced through addition of hydrogen atoms to the double bonds of fatty acids, which causes the molecule to assume an unnatural shape. Only a small amount of naturally occurring trans fatty acids are found in milk and meat – most are produced during food processing. Let's take margarine, for example. Margarines are typically made out of vegetable oils, which are liquid, yet most margarines are solids. So how do manufacturers take something that is liquid and make it into something solid? They do this through a process called *hydrogenation*. In hydrogenation, hydrogen atoms are added to the unsaturated fatty acid under intense heat so that there are fewer double bonds. This process serves two purposes: it makes the product into a solid and less susceptible to spoiling, which sounds great, but there is a downside. When you add the hydrogens back to the product, you change the configuration or arrangement of the bond and create trans fats.

trans fatty acid

An unhealthy fatty acid produced through the addition of hydrogen atoms to double bonds of fatty acids, which causes the molecule to assume an unnatural shape.

When hydrogenation is used for any product you will see the term *partially hydrogenated* on the food label in the ingredients list. The term *partial hydroge-*

cis and *trans* configuration
of unsaturated fatty acids:

cis *trans*

trans

cis

FIGURE 4.6
Differences between trans fatty acids and cis fatty acids.

nation is used because only some unsaturated fats are converted to saturated fats. Some unsaturated fatty acids remain in the *cis* form; others are converted to the trans form. The hydrogenated oils are often preferred for cooking because they don't break down under high cooking temperatures as quickly as other oils, and they are usually cheaper than butter. The higher cooking temperatures tolerated by these processed oils allow a crisp texture to be achieved, and most people enjoy the taste. As mentioned previously, partially hydrogenated fatty acids behave more like saturated fat and therefore have similar health consequences.

The primary concern with dietary trans fatty acids is that they raise the levels of "bad" or low-density lipoprotein (LDL) cholesterol in the body. This, in turn, is associated with an increased risk for heart disease. Trans fat consumption is also associated with a higher risk of diabetes. In 2006 the FDA implemented a requirement that food labels include the trans fatty acid content. More recently in 2013, a preliminary determination by the FDA stated that partially hydrogenated oils are no longer "generally recognized as safe." Other than the small amounts that occur naturally, this is a critical first step in having trans fatty acids eliminated from the food supply altogether. Between 2005 and 2013, manufacturers have voluntarily reduced the amount of trans fats in their products by nearly 75 percent. Thus far the decrease has mostly been driven by consumer awareness of the negative effects of trans fatty acids accompanied by the modification to food labels and not due to a government mandated reduction or ban. The Center for Disease Control estimates that further reducing trans fatty acids in the food supply can prevent 7,000 deaths from heart disease and 20,000 heart attacks each year. Due to the evidence that trans fatty acids have a negative impact on our well-being, health and nutrition professionals recommend that we limit our intake of trans fatty acids as much as possible. The American Heart Association recommends 2 g of trans fatty acids per day or less. This is less than 1 percent of Calories.

Spreadable products that are made with soy or omega-3 fatty acids and are lower in total fat and saturated fat are now available to consumers.

Myths & LEGENDS

HEALTHWISE, WHICH IS BETTER—BUTTER OR MARGARINE?

What's your answer? It may surprise you that non-hydrogenated spreads or those made from canola and/or olive oil is the answer. Here's why: the essential difference is that butter is an animal fat, while margarine is a fat produced from plants. In fact, margarine was developed as a substitute for butter. Both butter and margarine have the same number of Calories per serving. However, butter is high in cholesterol as well as saturated fat, which can raise your body's total blood cholesterol level. Because margarine is derived from a plant source, it does not contain cholesterol. The drawback to margarine is that even though it is a vegetable oil and high in unsaturated fat, it typically becomes liquid at room temperature and therefore is not easy to "spread" on breads and other foods. Thus manufacturers subject it to the hydrogenation process, which yields trans fatty acids. The more solid the margarine at room temperature, the more hydrogenated the product is.

Alternatives to partially hydrogenated margarines include a group of spreads that have emulsifiers (substances that facilitate mixture) added to enable unsaturated fats to be stable and spreadable in the product. They also have water added, which decreases the caloric content. These alternatives, unlike butter and traditional margarines, have fewer Calories, less saturated fat, and no cholesterol. With hydrogenated products containing trans fatty acids going out of vogue, these emulsified spreads are becoming more and more common. So the answer is that soft, tub margarine is best for you as long as it is not hydrogenated.

Triglycerides

Triglycerides are the primary form of lipid found in food and in the body. Simply stated, a **triglyceride** is a chemical structure composed of a three-carbon compound called *glycerol* in which fatty acids are bonded to each of the carbons (see Figure 4.7). The three fatty acids present are different from each other and the fatty acids in triglycerides found in the body often reflect dietary fatty acids consumed.

triglyceride

A form of fat found in food and in the body; chemically, it is composed of a three-carbon compound called glycerol in which fatty acids are bonded to each of the carbons.

FIGURE 4.7
General structure of a triglyceride fat.

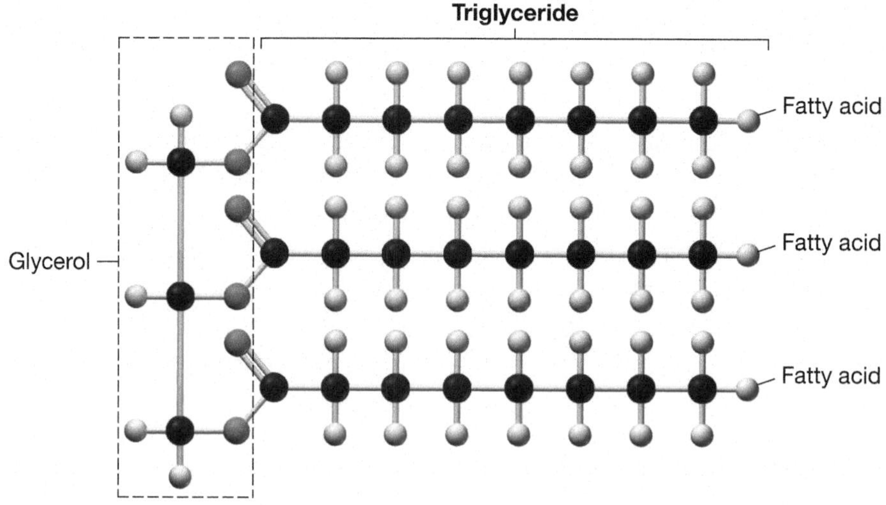

Phospholipids

As we mentioned in the beginning of the chapter, fat and water don't mix. Because your blood is mainly composed of water, your body has difficulty transporting fat through this watery substance. It accomplishes this task with assistance of a unique compound called a **phospholipid.** Chemically, phospholipids are very similar to triglycerides. Phospholipids have a three-carbon glycerol backbone; the first two carbons of the glycerol molecule have fatty acids bound to them, and the third carbon has a phosphate group bonded to it (see Figure 4.8). The presence of this phosphate group changes the physical properties of the structure so that the phosphate end mixes with water while the other end mixes with fat. This allows it to blend with fats in the watery

phospholipid
A lipid that has a three-carbon glycerol backbone; the first two carbons of the glycerol molecule have fatty acids bound to them, and the third carbon has a phosphate group bonded to it.

FIGURE 4.8
General structure of a phospholipid.

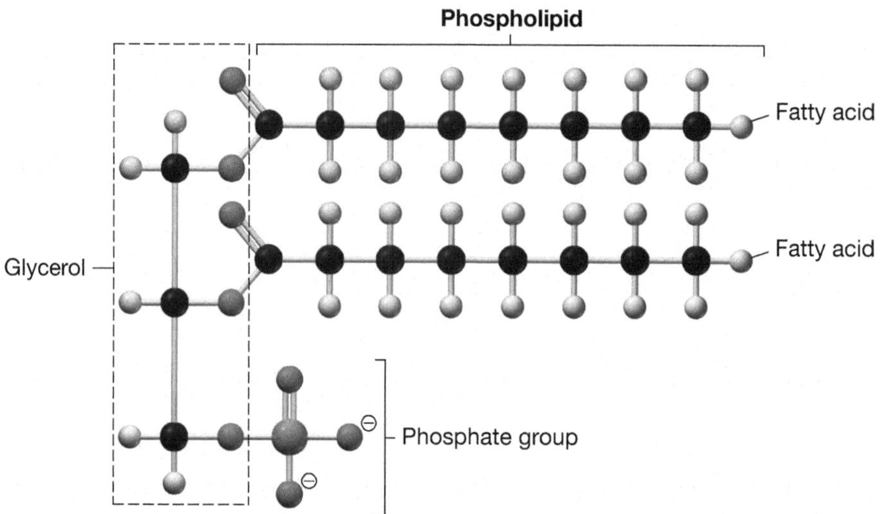

blood. We call the blending of fat and water *emulsification*. In food processing, many manufacturers add the emulsifier *lecithin* found in egg yolks to mix oil and water. An example of this is mayonnaise. Even though it is made from oil and water, it does not separate but stays mixed together because of the phospholipid lecithin.

We do not normally consume a lot of phospholipids in our diet. Only 2 percent of the fat consumed in the typical diet is from phospholipids and most of this comes from meat, poultry, and eggs. This is not a problem because the body can synthesize phospholipids from triglycerides present in cells. In the body phospholipids make up the majority of the molecules found in cell membranes and blood **lipoproteins**. Lipoproteins are molecules in the blood that help transport cholesterol and fatty acids to tissues.

lipoproteins
Molecules in the blood that help transport cholesterol and fatty acids to tissues.

Sterols/Cholesterol

Perhaps you have heard relatives or friends talk about their blood cholesterol levels and how they are trying to avoid too much cholesterol in the foods they eat. Most consumers have heard of cholesterol and its relation to heart disease. These groups of lipids are quite different chemically from the other lipids that we have discussed (see Figure 4.9). While cholesterol has received a lot of negative press, sterols are vital to health and basic metabolic functions. In fact, sex hormones such as *testosterone* and *estrogen* are sterols. Even vitamin D is a sterol. Some "stress hormones," such as *cortisol*, are also sterols. Cholesterol is a precursor to these compounds and is necessary for them to be produced in the body.

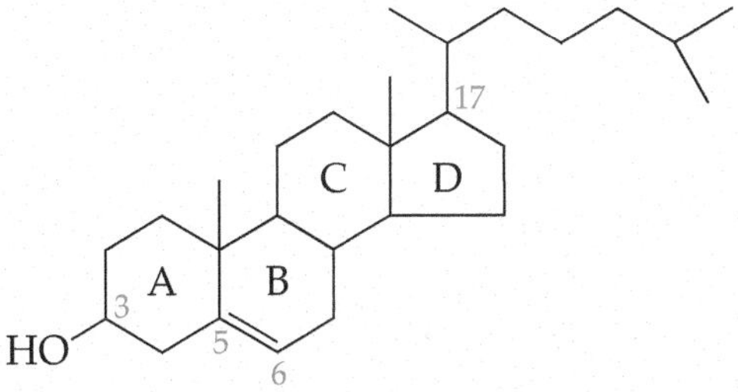

HO
3
A
5
B
6
C
D
17

FIGURE 4.9
Chemical structure of cholesterol.

The liver makes most of the cholesterol our bodies contain and, in fact, we do not need cholesterol in our diets. The types of fat in your diet, particularly saturated and trans fat, are more likely to raise your blood cholesterol than the amount of dietary cholesterol you consume. To help maintain your blood cholesterol levels within acceptable limits, many professionals recommend that you watch your intake of saturated fat and trans fat more carefully than your intake of cholesterol, as discussed later in this chapter.

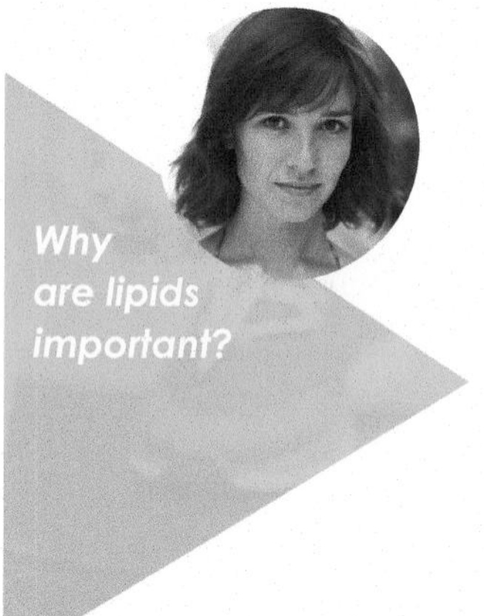

BEFORE YOU GO ON...

1. State the difference between saturated and unsaturated fatty acids.
2. Why are essential fatty acids so important?
3. What is a trans fatty acid and why is it no longer commonly found in foods?
4. List the benefits of consuming more omega-3 fatty acids in our diets.

LIPID FUNCTIONS

Lipids perform various functions in human nutrition, including storing energy, supplying essential fatty acids, absorbing and transporting fat-soluble vitamins, protecting and insulating vital organs, providing flavor in foods and promoting satiety, providing cell membrane structure, and serving as a precursor to steroid hormones (Figure 4.10).

Storage Form of Energy

Fats are the major form of stored energy in the body. The typical adult male of normal weight has 100,000 Calories stored as fat. Compare this to glycogen, the storage form of carbohydrates, which stores about 1,500 kcals. Fat is a concentrated energy source; it contains 9 Calories per gram, compared with 4 Calories per gram for carbohydrate and protein. A tablespoon of almost any type of vegetable oil has 120 Calories. With respect to the heart, lipids are significant because the heart uses fatty acids as its preferred source of energy.

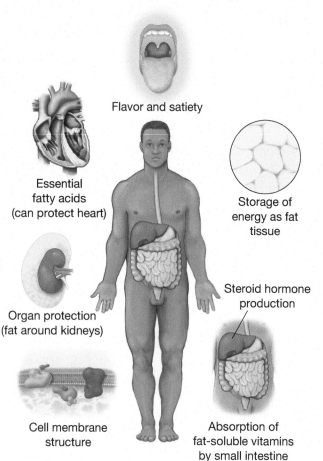

Flavor and satiety
Essential fatty acids (can protect heart)
Storage of energy as fat tissue
Organ protection (fat around kidneys)
Steroid hormone production
Cell membrane structure
Absorption of fat-soluble vitamins by small intestine

FIGURE 4.10
Fats carry out a number of functions in the human body.

© Viktor1/Shutterstock.com

Supply of Essential Fatty Acids

We have already mentioned that dietary fat supplies the body with essential fatty acids—linoleic and linolenic acids. The omega-3 fatty acid linolenic acid gives rise to the longer-chain fatty acids EPA and DHA. These fatty acids are converted to a group of metabolically active chemicals termed eicosanoids. Eicosanoids have powerful physiological effects, including relaxing blood vessels and promoting clotting.

Absorption and Transport of Fat-Soluble Vitamins

Fat is very important for the absorption of fat-soluble vitamins, which are vitamins A, D, E, and K. When conditions cause incomplete fat digestion or fat malabsorption, the amount of these vitamins absorbed decreases dramatically.

Organ Insulation and Protection

Fat has an important function in protecting and insulating the vital organs of the body, such as the fat deposits surrounding the kidney. The fat layer under the skin can also contribute to the insulating effects of fat. For reproductive reasons adult females have a greater percentage of body fat than males, and thus more insulating capacity as well.

Cell Membrane Structure

Phospholipids are the major component of cell membranes and membranes of organelles within cells. As you may recall, the phosphate group of these lipids allows the membranes to associate with a water environment, while the remainder of the molecule can associate with lipid phases of the cell. These phospholipids allow cells and organelles to have structure and act as barriers to selectively allow only certain compounds to enter and exit. Cholesterol is also involved with cell membranes in animals and helps maintain membrane integrity by keeping them from being too fluid or too dense.

Precursor to Steroid Hormones

Cholesterol is the precursor to many hormones. The two sex hormones estrogen and testosterone are made from cholesterol. Another hormone that controls salt balance in your body is aldosterone, also made from cholesterol. Later you will discover that vitamin D is also considered a steroid hormone and is made from cholesterol. We could not exist without cholesterol, because it gives rise to these very powerful hormones that affect our body's metabolism.

Why does food high in fat always taste so good?

Flavor and Satiety of Food

It would be difficult to overstate the contribution of fat to the taste of food. The most important aspect of fat in foods from a consumer perspective is sensory. Foods with fat have superior mouthfeel and texture. Have you noticed that regular ice cream has a smooth and creamy mouthfeel and the flavors linger longer than in the reduced-fat version? The flavor compounds in foods are generally interacting with the fat portion of food.

Fat in foods causes you to feel full longer. This means that you tend to be more satisfied and less hungry after consuming fat in a meal. This is called **satiety.** Satiety is the feeling of being satisfied after consuming food. One of the reasons for this effect is fat's tendency to slow the time it takes food to empty out of your stomach, so that the feeling of fullness is retained longer. Also, because they are fat soluble, the flavor compounds in food are dissolved in the fat, which contributes to satiety.

satiety
The feeling of fullness and satisfaction after a meal.

Low-fat diets can be problematic when weight control is an issue. Although it is important to reduce fat in a diet to effectively lose weight, some fat consumption is suggested because of fat's satiating effect. Moreover, fat slows **gastric emptying** (movement of food from the stomach to the small intestine), which blocks the return of the brain's hunger signals to us to consume more food. If you eat a salad without dressing, you are likely to feel hungry soon after finishing. However, if you add Italian dressing, nuts, or grated cheese that contain some fat, then you are less likely to become hungry as quickly. Remember that fat is an essential nutrient, so you cannot eliminate it from your diet.

BEFORE YOU GO ON...

1. What role does fat play in the absorption of certain vitamins?
2. Why do people feel more full and satisfied after consuming a meal with fat?
3. List at least five functions lipids perform in the body.

FAT CONTENT OF FOODS

What types of foods contain the most fat?

©Valentyn Volkov/Shutterstock.com

Fats are found in both animal *and* plant products. Meats, butter, and other dairy products contain significant levels of triglycerides with saturated fatty acids. Polyunsaturated fatty acids are present in larger amounts in fish and poultry than in red meat such as pork, lamb, and beef. Most vegetable oils are high in polyunsaturated fatty acids, but as noted earlier some tropical oils, such as coconut, are high in saturated fatty acids. Olive and canola oils are probably the best dietary sources of monounsaturated fatty acids. Table 4.2 lists the fat and cholesterol content of some commonly consumed foods.

Again, foods of animal origin are the *only* ones that contain cholesterol. Besides meats, foods such as cheese, butter, eggs, milk and shellfish all have cholesterol. Because cholesterol is made in the liver, eating cow, chicken, or any other animal's liver *will* give you a high intake of dietary cholesterol (see Table 4.2).

TABLE 4.2 Fat and Cholesterol Content of Selected Foods

	Serving Size	Fat (g)	Cholesterol (mg)
Foods with Cholesterol			
Cream, 31% fat*	1 c.	74	265
Shrimp, boiled	1 c.	3	283
Eggs, whole or yolk	1 large	5	212
Lobster, boiled	1 c.	1	104
Pork chops	3 oz.	14	78
Ground beef, cooked	3 oz.	15	76
Chicken breast, cooked	3 oz.	7	71
Ribeye steak	3 oz.	10	68
Butter, 81% fat	1 oz.	23	61
Ice cream, vanilla	1 c.	14	58
Bacon	3 oz.	38	58
Noodles, egg	1 c.	2	53
Beef hot dogs	2	27	48
Tuna, water-packed	1 c.	1	46
Cheese, cheddar	1 oz.	9	27
Milk, whole, 3.5% fat	1 c.	8	24
Milk, 2% fat	1 c.	5	20
Milk, 1% fat	1 c.	2	12
Mayonnaise, 78% fat	1 tbsp.	5	4
Foods High in Fat That Have No Cholesterol			
Coconut	1/4 c.	27	0
Avocado	1	26	0
Peanuts	1/4 c.	18	0
Almonds	1/4 c.	17	0
Soybeans	1/2 c.	8	0
Black olives	10	5	0
*A "serving size" of cream as an additive to coffee would typically be 1 tsp.			

Label Definitions

Consumers are often confused as to what certain terms regarding fat really indicate when they appear on a food label. We see labels such as "reduced fat" and "fat free" in the supermarket, but do we really know what they mean? As discussed in Chapter 2, the Food and Drug Administration (FDA) is responsible for the definitions of these terms and what food manufacturers are allowed to state on a label. Here are some claims and the requirements that must be met to use them on a food label:

- *Fat free*—less than 0.5 g of fat per serving, with no fat or oil added during processing
- *Low fat*—3 g or less of fat per serving
- *Less fat*—25 percent or less fat than the typical comparison food in its category of the same serving size
- *Light (fat)*—50 percent or less fat than in the comparison food (for example: 50 percent less fat than the producer's regular product)
- *Saturated fat free*—less than 0.5 g of saturated fat and 0.5 g of trans fatty acids per serving
- *Trans-fat free*—less than 0.5 g of trans fatty acids per serving
- *Cholesterol free*—less than 2 mg of cholesterol per serving, and 2 g or less of saturated fat per serving
- *Low cholesterol*—20 mg or less of cholesterol per serving and 2 g or less of saturated fat per serving
- *Lean*—Less than 10 g of fat, 4.5 g of saturated fat, and 95 mg of cholesterol per (100-g) serving of meat, poultry, or seafood
- *Extra lean*—Less than 5 g of fat, 2 g of saturated fat, and 95 mg of cholesterol per (100-g) serving of meat, poultry, or seafood

APPLICATION TIP

Learn to cook with and make salad dressings using extra virgin olive oil. It contains oleic acid, a monounsaturated fat that lowers total blood cholesterol, and antioxidants that protect against heart disease and certain types of cancers. However, it does contain the same amount of Calories as other oils.

Nutrition Facts	
Serving Size 1 cup (228g)	
Servings Per Container 2	
Amount Per Serving	
Calories 250 Calories from Fat 110	
	% Daily Value*
Total Fat 12g	**16%**
Saturated Fat 3g	**15%**
Trans Fat 1.5g	
Cholesterol 30mg	**10%**
Sodium 470mg	**20%**
Total Carbohydrate 0.1g	**10%**
Dietary Fiber 0g	**0%**
Sugars 5g	
Proteins 5g	
Vitamin A	4%
Vitamin C	2%
Calcium	20%
Iron	4%

*Percent Daily Values are based on a 2,000 calories diet. Your Daily Values may be higher or lower depending on your calorie needs.

	Calories	2,000	2,500
Total Fat	Less than	65g	80g
Sat Fat	Less than	20g	25g
Cholesterol	Less than	300mg	300mg
Sodium	Less than	2,400mg	2,400mg
Total Carbohydrates		300g	375g
Dietary Fiber		25g	30g

FIGURE 4.11
Nutrition facts label from macaroni and cheese. Note the amounts of fat, saturated fat, and trans fat listed on the label.

Identifying Fats on the Label

As you may recall from the discussions on food labeling in Chapter 2, the grams of total fat per serving size as well as saturated fat, trans fats, and cholesterol are present on food labels. The Calories from fat in a serving size plus the percentage of total fat, saturated fat, and cholesterol the food contributes towards the Daily Value (DV) are all listed on a food label (see Figure 4.11).

Trans-Fatty Acids

Food labels are now required to show the amount of trans fat per serving. Due to negative health effects associated with trans fatty acids, steps are being taken to slowly remove them from foods.

BEFORE YOU GO ON...

1. If you want to reduce intake of saturated fatty acids, which foods should you avoid?
2. Define *low-fat* food as used on food labels.

LIPIDS AND HEALTH

You have probably heard quite a bit about the link between too much fat in our diet and specific diseases. Government and health agencies have recommended how much and what type of fat we should consume to maintain health. Also, researchers have studied which diseases may be linked to too much fat intake. Here we consider these factors.

Recommendations for Dietary Intake of Fats

The USDA's 2015 *Dietary Guidelines for Americans* provides recommendations for all people over age 2. The AMDR recommends that total fat comprise 20 to 35 percent of total Calories. Going lower than 20 percent increases the risk of inadequate supply and absorption of important fat-soluble vitamins.

Saturated fat should constitute no more than 10 percent of your total caloric intake (Table 4.3). The balance should come from polyunsaturated and from monounsaturated fatty acids. For someone on a 2,000-Calorie diet, this means no more than 20 g of saturated fat per day and around 5 tsp of oil per day. Meat, cheese, and whole milk are the chief contributors to saturated fat in the American diet. Trans fat and products that are hydrogenated, including many crackers and snack foods, should be avoided. As an example, Figure 4.12 translates fat recommendations into a 2,000 Calorie single day meal plan.

TABLE 4.3 Fat Recommendations from the 2015 Dietary Guidelines for Americans

	Recommended Intake
Total fat	20–35% of daily Calories
Saturated fat	<10% of daily Calories
Trans fat	As low as possible

© Sea Wave/Shutterstock.com

© Teri Virbickis/Shutterstock.com

Visible and invisible sources of fat. Cookies have a great deal of fat, but it is not readily visible, unlike the fat in butter.

FIGURE 4.12 This menu provides approximately 2,000 Calories: ~35% Calories from fat, ~20% from protein, and ~45% carbohydrate. It is low in saturated fat (9%), high in fiber (25 g) and low in sodium (~1500 mg).

BREAKFAST
Breakfast taco with 1 oz. cheddar cheese, and 1 scrambled egg; 8 oz. orange juice

SNACK
Apple

LUNCH
Chicken salad made from 2 oz. fresh roasted chicken breast, chopped celery, pecans, sandwich spread, served on a bed of lettuce and tomato; low sodium Triscuits®; baby carrots and hummus; 8 oz. low fat yogurt; water to drink

DINNER
3 oz. baked salmon; ½ cup brown rice with sliced almonds; salad with mixed lettuce, tomato, chopped broccoli, chopped carrots and Italian dressing

SNACK
2 Graham crackers with 2 oz peanut butter

You may be consuming more fat than you realize since much of the fat we consume is invisible. Visible fat, such as what we can see on meat or poultry, allows us to easily visualize fat intake. Invisible fat is not readily apparent just by looking at the food item. Examples are the fat added to crackers and baked products. While many people concern themselves with reducing total fat intake, the average American is actually consuming very close to the correct percent of their daily Calories from fat. A more appropriate concern and emphasis should be improving on the *types* of fat consumed: limiting saturated and trans fatty acids and increasing mono and polyunsaturated fatty acids.

CHOOSING THE RIGHT FATS FOR YOUR DIET

In order to manage the amount and type of fat in your diet, follow these guidelines:

Make it a PRACTICE

Ways to reduce saturated and total fat intake

Think of meat as a side dish instead of the focus of your meal. When you eat poultry, remove the skin. It contains high levels of saturated fat.

- Choose 1% or skim milk.
- Carefully trim off fat from meats before cooking. Drain off fat after you brown meat. You can reduce the fat in hamburger by rinsing it under water after browning.
- Chill soups and stews after cooking so that you can skim off the hardened/congealed fat.

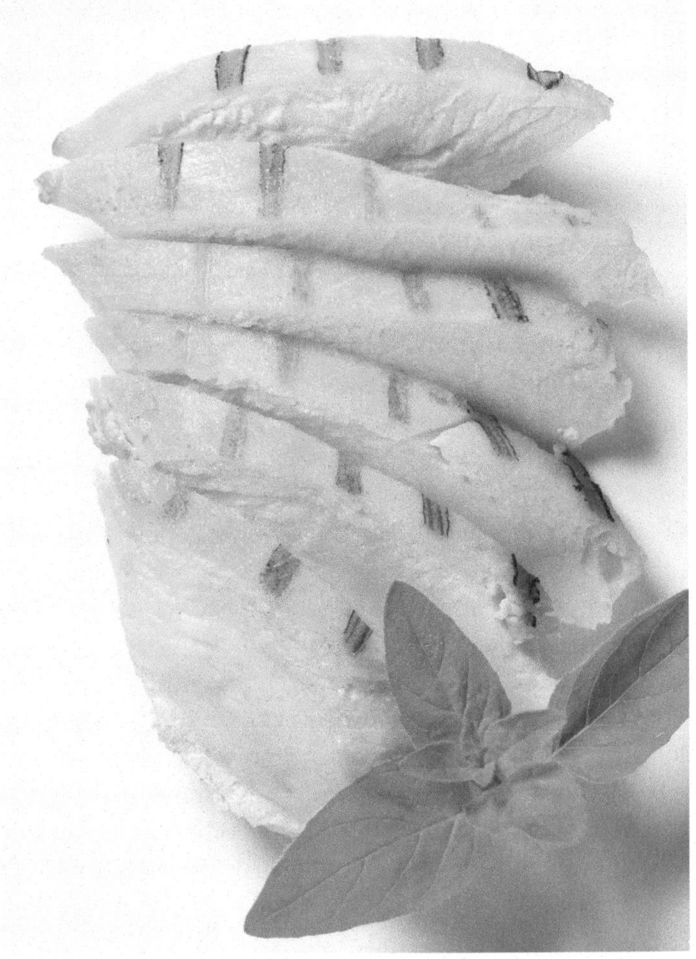

- When choosing beef or pork, select cuts with "loin" or "round" in the name. For example, pork tenderloin.
- Grill, broil or bake rather than fry meats and other food items.
- Eat foods without adding extra cheese.
- Cut down on consumption of bacon, sausage, hot dogs, and baked goods.
- Limit the intake of foods prepared with cream sauces or gravies.

Ways to increase intake of healthy fats

- Choose cold water fish options over beef, pork, and lamb.
- Use plant based oils, such as olive oil, canola oil and vegetable oil, when preparing food or choosing salad dressing.
- Snack on or add nuts and seeds (chia seeds, flax, sunflower seeds) to recipes and salads.
- Use soft tub spread or margarine instead of butter. Use trans-fat-free margarines or spreads with olive or canola oils, or Benecol, a soy-based spread, as an alternative.

Obesity

Is the obesity epidemic in the United States and other industrialized nations connected with an increased fat intake? Common sense would say yes—fats contain over twice the number of Calories by weight than carbohydrates and proteins. However in the United States, the *percentage* of Calories from fats in our diet has actually *decreased* over the last two decades.

Walter Willett of Harvard University has examined this relationship and found that a small reduction in body weight occurs in individuals who eat diets with a lower percentage of Calories from fat. After analyzing data from several short-term studies, he estimated that a decrease of 10 percent of Calories from fat would reduce weight by 16 g/day, which would result in a 9-kg (20-lb.) weight loss after 18 months. This was true only when the total amount of Calories consumed did not change. However, Willett points out that over longer periods of time, lower levels of fat consumed have not shown a decrease in body weight, suggesting that the body compensates in some way. Several studies indicate that when individuals consume a diet high in fruits, vegetables, and whole grains (low in fat and high in complex carbohydrates), they achieve an effective weight reduction. Lowering the amount of fat in one's diet may not be as difficult as many of us perceive it to be, as indicated in the tips listed previously. There are some concerns over restricting dietary fat too much. Some individuals with very low-fat diets may have an insufficient intake of vitamins A and E, iron, and zinc, because reduced-fat foods are often low in these nutrients. People may overcompensate on a low-fat diet by increasing their intake of carbohydrates with a false sense of security that they may not be getting as many Calories. Of course, replacing high-fat foods with pastries and chips made with low-fat substitutes may not constitute a low-Calorie diet. These foods often have more sugars and are high in Calories, leading to weight gain. In fact, one study revealed that increased intake of simple carbohydrates is associated with a decrease in the more healthy HDL cholesterol in the blood.

Low fat diets are not the only types of diets that promote weight loss. You may find it interesting that studies have shown that people who adhere to the Mediterranean diet are at a lower risk for being obese than people consuming the average American diet despite the total amount of daily Calories from fat being 35 percent. How can people consuming higher amounts of fat be less obese? It's because of the mix of foods being consumed. The majority of fat Calories in the Mediterranean diet come from monounsaturated fatty acids. In addition, the Mediterranean diet is higher in fish consumption as well as whole grains.

As will be discussed more in depth in Chapter 9, in the end, weight loss boils down to energy balance—Calories consumed versus Calories expended doing physical activities. Quantity and quality of fats and other dietary components as well as physical activity all influence the size of our waistlines.

Heart Disease

While the number of deaths from heart disease has steadily declined since the 1960s, it is still ranked as the leading cause of death. The main type of heart disease linked with fat intake is **atherosclerosis,** which is characterized by a buildup of fatty deposits and streaks in the arteries. This narrowing of the arteries can reduce and eventually cut off blood flow to the heart and create a condition referred to as **ischemia.** A related condition is called *angina pectoris*, or chest pains under the left arm that are normally caused by a partially blocked artery. If the artery becomes completely blocked, it is called a *myocardial infarct* or *heart attack*. If this occurs in the brain it is called a *stroke*. Collectively, these conditions are referred to as *cardiovascular diseases* (see table 4.4).

atherosclerosis
The process in which deposits of fatty substances, cholesterol, cellular waste products, calcium, and other substances (referred to as plaque) build up in the inner lining of an artery.

ischemia
A restriction in blood supply to the heart, generally due to factors in the blood vessels with resultant damage or dysfunction of tissue.

TABLE 4.4 Types of Cardiovascular Disease

Disease	Definition
Atherosclerosis	A form of heart disease in which deposits of fatty substances, cholesterol, cellular waste products, calcium, and other substances (referred to as plaque) build up in the inner lining of an artery.
Ischemia	A restriction in blood supply to the heart, generally due to factors in the blood vessels with resultant damage or dysfunction of tissue.
Angina pectoris	Pain in the chest, shoulder, or arm typically caused by insufficient blood flow to the heart.
Thrombosis	Formation of a blood clot in a blood vessel. The clot itself is called a thrombus.
Myocardial infarct	Destruction of heart tissue resulting from obstruction of the blood supply to the heart muscle (a heart attack).
Stroke	An event in which blood supply to the brain is suddenly interrupted by a blood clot, hemorrhage, or other cause.

Although no *single* factor leads to heart disease, certain attributes or *risk factors* increase one's likelihood of developing heart disease. Heredity or family history is one such strong risk factor for heart disease. *High blood pressure and diabetes increase the risk as well. Research confirms that diet plays a significant role. An increased intake of saturated and trans fats have been directly correlated to an increase in heart disease risk. Other dietary risk factors include inadequate fiber intake and excessive intake of added sugars which can lead to high blood cholesterol levels. Certain lifestyle behaviors impact risk. Smoking increases risk, whereas exercise decreases risk for all types of cardiovascular disease. *

Cholesterol is packaged into several different transport molecules in the body whose relative abundance have significant differential effects on health. We refer to these transport molecules as lipoproteins (see Figure 4.14) Lipoproteins are spherical structures that are a combination of lipids and proteins. A layer of phospholipids and proteins create a shell surrounding triglycerides and cholesterol in order to transport these lipids to various tissues. The blood contains four types of lipoproteins:

- Chylomicrons
- Very low-density lipoproteins (VLDLs)
- Low-density lipoproteins (LDLs)
- High-density lipoproteins (HDLs)

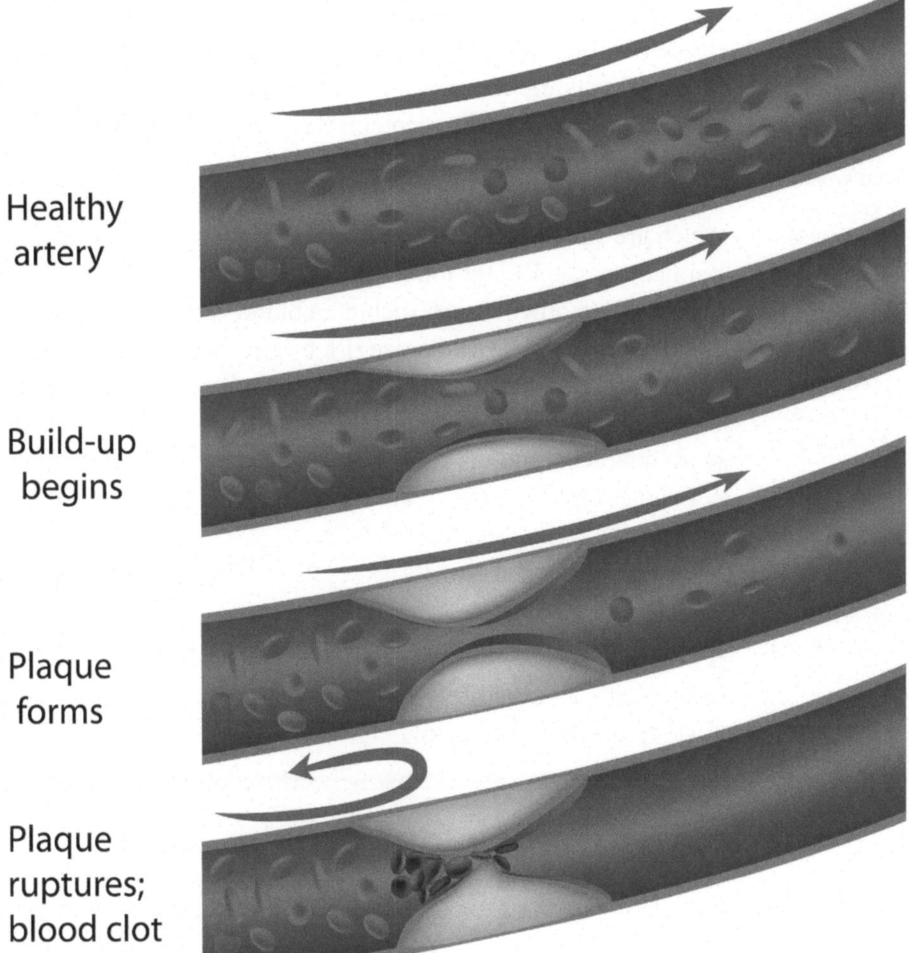

FIGURE 4.13
A normal artery (top image) and an artery showing early and advanced atherosclerosis. Note that the opening for blood flow is almost blocked.

chylomicrons

(kye-loh-MY-kronz) Lipoproteins formed in the cells lining the small intestine following absorption of fats. They are made in the small intestinal cells and transport dietary lipids to the liver.

very low-density lipoproteins (VLDLs)

Lipoproteins that are synthesized in the liver and contain both triglycerides and cholesterol. They function to deliver triglycerides to other tissues.

low-density lipoproteins (LDLs)

Remnants of the breakdown of VLDLs. They deliver cholesterol to other tissues, including blood vessels.

high-density lipoproteins (HDLs)

Lipoproteins that are made in the liver; they decrease heart disease risk by removing excess cholesterol from cells and blood vessels and returning it to the liver for breakdown and elimination.

Recall that lipids are not soluble in water. This is a problem for lipid transport in the blood, which is mostly water. To get around this problem, adding a protein to these lipids in a spherical structure allows them to be more soluble in blood so they can be transported throughout the body.

Chylomicrons are lipoproteins formed when one consumes a meal and the cells lining the small intestine absorb the fats. They are made in the small intestinal cells and transport dietary lipids to the liver. **Very low-density lipoproteins (VLDLs)** are lipoproteins that are synthesized in the liver and contain both triglycerides and cholesterol. They deliver triglycerides to other tissues. Once the VLDLs deposit triglycerides in other tissues, they become **LDLs**, which are smaller and denser, but now cholesterol rich. LDLs are, therefore, remnants of the VLDLs following the removal of triglycerides and will deliver cholesterol to other tissues, including blood vessels. **HDLs** are made in the liver. HDLs decrease heart disease risk by removing excess cholesterol from cells and blood vessels and returning it to the liver for breakdown and elimination.

It is important to keep in mind that while HDLs are commonly referred to as "good cholesterol" and LDLs as "bad cholesterol," these lipoproteins are not cholesterol themselves but rather the vehicle by which the cholesterol is transported throughout the body.

APPLICATION TIP

High HDL cholesterol is good and you can increase it through daily aerobic exercise.

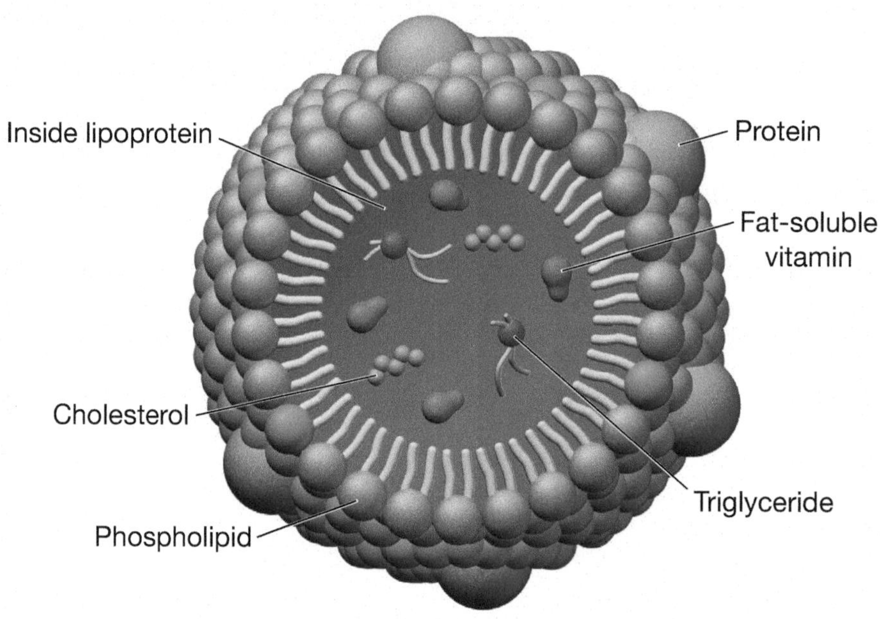

FIGURE 4.14
Diagram of a lipoprotein. Notice the spherical shape, with phospholipids and protein on the outer shell and triglycerides and cholesterol in the inner portion.

High HDL cholesterol levels decrease the risk of heart disease; high levels of LDL cholesterol have the opposite effect, which is why HDL cholesterol is referred to as the *good* or healthy cholesterol and LDL cholesterol as the *bad* cholesterol. HDL takes cholesterol from tissues, including blood vessels and dying cells, and brings it to the liver for breakdown. HDL cholesterol tries to keep the blood vessels from being clogged with fat, which helps prevent heart attacks. LDL does the opposite by bringing cholesterol from the liver and depositing it in other tissues, including the inner lining of blood vessels, leading to the appearance of fatty streaks or deposits in the vessels (see Figure 4.15). Over the years, lipids (fats) build up and the cells become rich in cholesterol. The smooth muscle cells lining the blood vessels then begin to divide, and

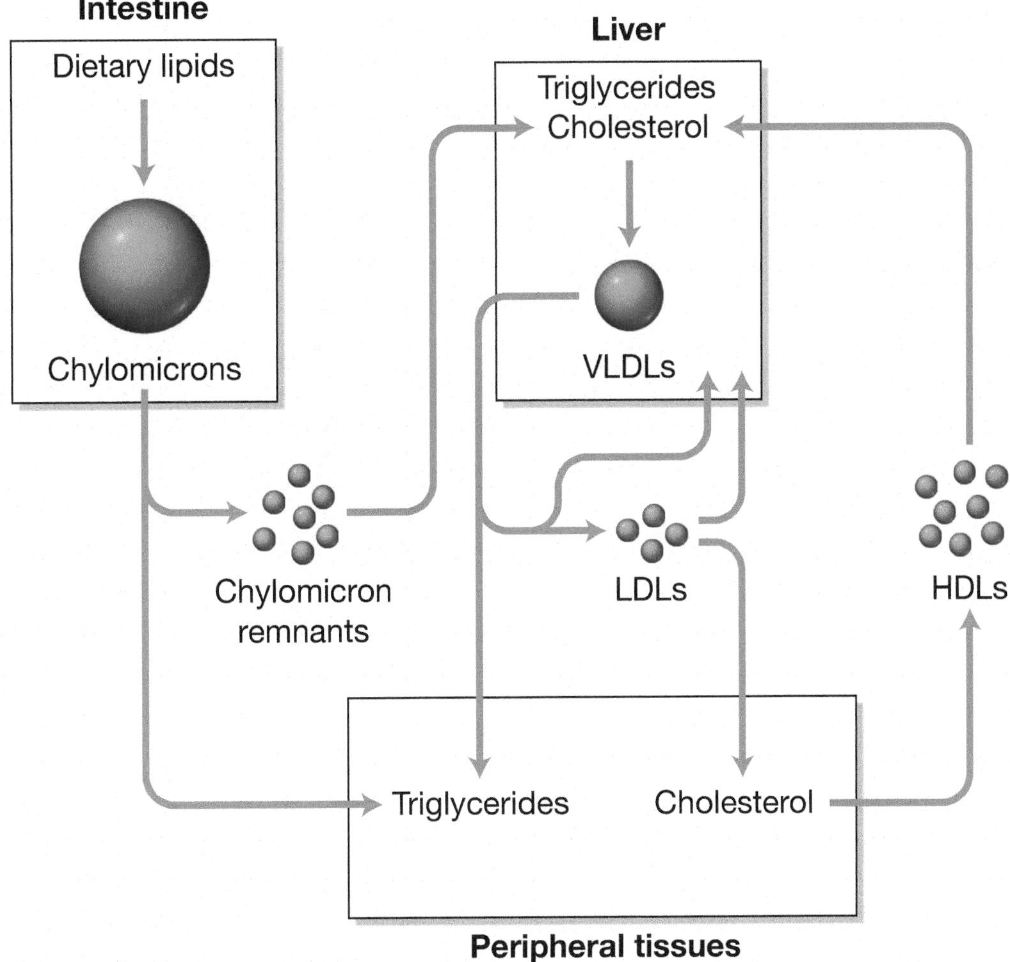

FIGURE 4.15
Overview of metabolism of the various lipoproteins present in our bodies with reference to diet, liver, and peripheral tissues.

the cholesterol-laden cells start to become calcified. As this *plaque* develops, the blood vessel becomes narrower and complete blockage can occur, cutting off the flow of blood to the heart muscle and resulting in a myocardial infarct (see Figure 4.13). Actually, the terms *bad* and *good* are not really appropriate, because we need both types and they are essential to good health. Table 4.5 provides a guide for the blood levels of total, LDL, and HDL cholesterol we should maintain for good health as recommended by the American Heart Association.

TABLE 4.5 American Heart Association Recommended Blood Cholesterol Levels

Total Cholesterol Level	**Category**
Less than 200mg/dL	Desirable
200-239 mg/dL	Borderline high
240mg/dL and above	High
LDL (Bad) Cholesterol Level	**LDL Cholesterol Category**
Less than 100mg/dL	Optimal
100-129mg/dL	Near optimal/above optimal
130-159 mg/dL	Borderline high
160-189 mg/dL	High
190 mg/dL and above	Very High
HDL (Good) Cholesterol Level	**LDL Cholesterol Category**
Less than 40 mg/dL	A major risk factor for heart disease
40—59 mg/dL	The higher, the better
60 mg/dL and higher	Considered protective against heart disease

Source: National Heart, Lung, and Blood Institute

Cancer

Research to date is inconclusive as to whether diets high in total Calories from fat promote cancer incidence. However, studies have found that specific types of fatty acids can influence the risk for developing cancer in different ways depending on the variety of fatty acid being consumed. For instance, high levels of saturated fat consumption has been linked to breast, ovarian, colon, and prostate cancers; however, the intake levels causing the observed increased risk were generally far higher than the 10 percent of daily Calories from saturated fat recommended in the Dietary Guidelines for Americans. As such, a diet that follows the guidelines should not put you at an increased risk for these cancers.

What's
HOT

IS COCONUT OIL BAD FOR YOU OR NOT?

Recently there have been a number of claims made about the health benefits of coconut oil. This may seem confusing since it is primarily a saturated fat, and in this chapter we say that a diet high in saturated fat may increase your risk for heart disease. Most of the saturated fats in coconut oil are medium chain fatty acids and are therefore absorbed differently than other saturated fats, most of which are long chain. In addition, virgin (unhyrogenated) coconut oil made from fresh coconut kernel contains antioxidants. It has been suggested that regular consumption of coconut milk can decrease your risk of heart disease, but well-controlled studies have failed to support this claim. If consumed in its unhydrogenated form it has been shown to increase HDL cholesterol levels. There are also claims that it boosts immune system function and helps the action of anti-HIV drugs, but these claims are not supported by research. There is clearly a need for further research before any recommendations for or against adding coconut oil to the diet can be made.

On the other hand, consumption of fatty fish high in omega-3 polyunsaturated fatty acids is linked to a lower incidence of colon, breast, lung, esophageal, skin, and pancreatic cancers. There are several proposed mechanisms by which fish oil reduces the risk of cancer. For instance, it may stimulate the immune system allowing the body to more readily eliminate cancerous cells. Other data suggest that fish oil may reduce the occurrence of metastasis in models of breast cancer, the spread of a tumor from the organ of origin to other locations in the body. In addition, it has been seen to improve the efficiency and reduce the side effects of some commonly used chemotherapeutic drugs.

Nutrition & DISEASE

WHO'S MORE SUSCEPTIBLE TO HEART DISEASE, MEN OR WOMEN?

Heart disease does not discriminate on the basis of gender. It is the number one cause of death for women, just as it is for men. Historically, many studies on heart disease were performed on white males and the treatment was designed for men. We now know that medical treatment for heart attacks is not the same for men and women.

Before menopause, women may have some natural protection against heart disease due to their body's production of estrogen. After menopause, when estrogen levels decline, their risk for heart disease is similar to that of men. Thirty-two percent of women ultimately die from heart disease, which translates into 500,000 women a year. More than 8 million adult women have heart disease, and 13 percent of women over age 45 have had at least one heart attack. Black women are at even greater risk than the general population; they experience a 72 percent higher rate of some form of the disease than do white women in the United States. Black women aged 55–64 are twice as likely as white women to have a heart attack and 35 percent more likely to suffer from coronary artery disease.

Notably, women do not do as well after a heart attack in comparison to men. The National Coalition for Women with Heart Disease lists the following as differences by gender:

- Thirty-eight percent of women and 25 percent of men will die within 1 year of a first recognized heart attack.
- Among heart attack survivors, 35 percent of women and 18 percent of men will have another heart attack within 6 years.
- Forty-six percent of women and 22 percent of men who initially survive heart attacks will be disabled with heart failure within 6 years.
- Women are almost twice as likely as men to die after heart bypass surgery.

While the exact cause behind the poorer outcomes for women with heart disease is still being investigated, it is thought to be at least partially because of delays in getting treatment due to non-recognition of warning signs and symptoms such as jaw pain, back pain and shortness of breath, that the disease is present.

Why Is The Mediterranean Diet So Widely Recommended?

Many health professionals recommend the Mediterranean diet. The term Mediterranean applies to nations from southern Europe, northern Africa, and the Middle East that border the Mediterranean Sea: Spain, Portugal, France (Provence region), Morocco, Italy, Malta, Greece, Turkey, Lebanon, Israel, Jordan, Egypt, the former Yugoslavia, Libya, and Algeria.

The Mediterranean diet is an example for how it is the types of fat, and not always the quantity that are important when it comes to health. Observational and intervention studies have found that the Mediterranean diet is protective against cardiovascular disease, even in cases where the total percent of Calories from fat is higher than the control diets. Other disease states that are also positively influenced by the Mediterranean diet include: some forms of cancer, strokes, and diabetes.

The countries that constitute the Mediterranean area are shown in Figure 4.16; the Food Guide Pyramid that has been developed for the Mediterranean diet is depicted in Figure 4.17.

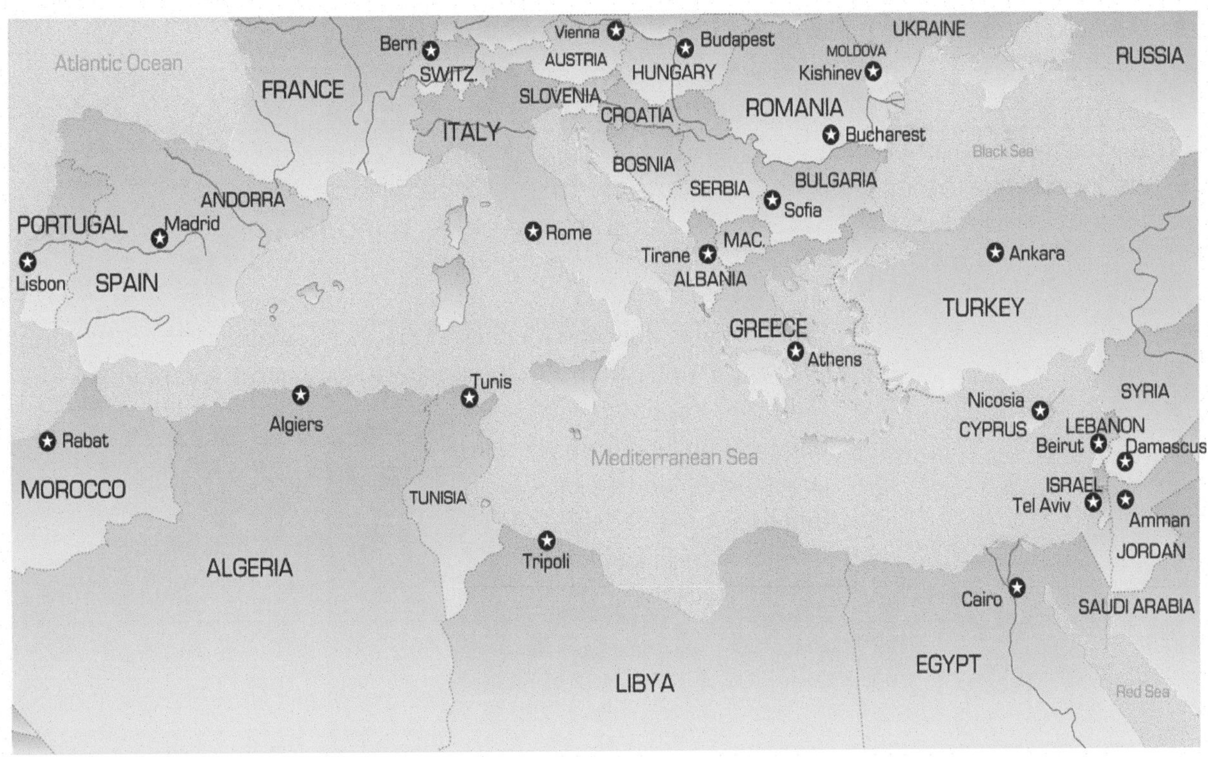

FIGURE 4.16 The Mediterranean countries.

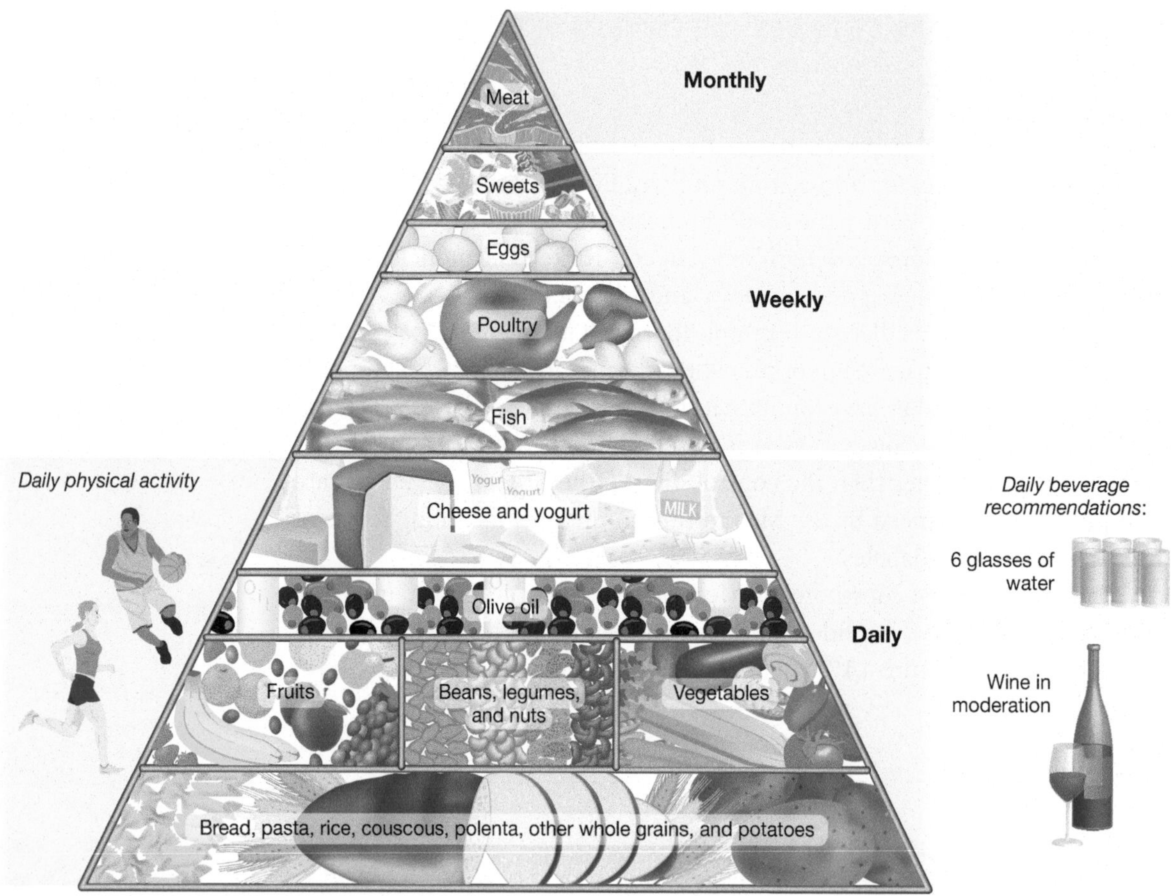

FIGURE 4.17

The Mediterranean Diet Food Guide Pyramid. Note the emphasis on whole grains, fruits, and vegetables at the base of the pyramid. Olive oil is an important component of this diet. Fish and poultry are consumed weekly, but beef is eaten only once a month.

What features does the Mediterranean diet contain? In practical terms, the following eating patterns in these countries are rather common:

- Daily physical activity
- Emphasis on food from plant sources, including fruits and vegetables, potatoes, breads and grains, beans, nuts, and seeds to be consumed daily
- Emphasis on a variety of minimally processed and, wherever possible, seasonally fresh and locally grown foods
- Olive oil (rich in monounsaturates) as the principal fat to be consumed daily; almost no butter, margarine, or other fats
- No trans fats or hydrogenated fats
- Total fat contributing 25–35 percent of Calories; saturated fat no more than 8 percent of Calories

- Daily consumption of low to moderate amounts of cheese and yogurt, frequently from goats and sheep—even camels
- Regular (weekly) consumption of small amounts of fish and poultry
- Fresh fruit as the typical daily dessert
- Very small amounts of red meat, eaten occasionally (monthly)
- With the exception of Muslims, moderate consumption of wine with meals—about one to two glasses per day for men and one glass per day for women

BEFORE YOU GO ON...

1. List the foods that contribute the most saturated fat to our diets.
2. Is too much fat in our diet a primary cause of obesity? Why or why not?
3. Describe atherosclerosis and its connection to cholesterol.
4. Give the recommended ranges for HDL, LDL, and total cholesterol.
5. What are some problems that could occur if your fat intake is too low?

CHAPTER SUMMARY

- Lipids are insoluble in water, but soluble in organic solvents such as ether, acetone, and chloroform. The major types of lipids in food and in our bodies are fatty acids, phospholipids, triglycerides, and cholesterol. Fatty acids are a source of energy; phospholipids are components of cell membranes. Triglycerides are the storage form of fat in our bodies and the major type of fat we consume in food. Cholesterol is found only in foods of animal origin, and it acts as a precursor to hormones.
- Fatty acids are classified based on the number of double bonds in the long carbon chain. If there are no double bonds, then the fatty acid is saturated. Meats and dairy products are sources of saturated fatty acids. Monounsaturated fatty acids have one double bond. Canola and olive oils are monounsaturated fatty acid sources. Polyunsaturated fatty acids have two or more double bonds and are found in most vegetables and vegetable oils such as corn oil.
- Dietary fats provide us with essential fatty acids such as linoleic acid and linolenic acid. These fatty acids are converted to powerful chemicals called *eicosanoids* that affect our health.
- Fat has several functions in the body including storing energy, supplying essential fatty acids, absorbing and transporting fat-soluble vitamins, protecting and insulating vital organs, providing flavor and satiety in food, providing cell membrane structure, and serving as a precursor to steroid hormones
- A major health concern has resulted from the manufacturing process of partial hydrogenation of polyunsaturated fatty acids. This process, used to create products such as margarine, leads to consumption of harmful trans fatty acids and more saturated fats in our diet.
- Health officials have published recommendations that adults consume not less than 20 percent and no more than 35 percent of their Calories in fat. The appropriate range for children and adolescents is between 30 and 35 percent, given their increased demands for energy and growth.
- There are four major cholesterol-containing lipoproteins: chylomicrons, VLDL, LDL, and HDL. Greater levels of HDL cholesterol in the blood are associated with reduced risk from heart disease, whereas the opposite is true of LDL cholesterol. High blood cholesterol levels and high LDL cholesterol levels can increase your risk for developing heart disease.

KEY TERMS

ATHEROSCLEROSIS (ath-er-oh-skler-O-sis) The process in which deposits of fatty substances, cholesterol, cellular waste products, calcium, and other substances (referred to as *plaque*) build up in the inner lining of an artery.

CHYLOMICRONS (kye-loh-MY-kronz) Lipoproteins formed in the cells lining the small intestine following absorption of fats. They are made in the small intestinal cells and transport dietary lipids to the liver.

EICOSANOIDS (eye-koh-sah-noydz) Metabolically active chemicals synthesized from fatty acids. These chemicals have powerful physiological effects, including relaxing blood vessels and promoting blood clotting.

ESSENTIAL FATTY ACIDS Fatty acids that cannot be made by the body and can be provided only by the diet.

HIGH-DENSITY LIPOPROTEINS (HDLS) Lipoproteins that are made mostly in the liver, but in the small intestine as well; they decrease heart disease risk by removing excess cholesterol from cells and blood vessels and returning it to the liver for breakdown and elimination.

ISCHEMIA (iss-KEE-mee-ah) A restriction in blood supply to the heart, generally due to factors in the blood vessels with resultant damage or dysfunction of tissue.

LIPOPROTEINS Molecules in the blood that help transport cholesterol and fatty acids to tissues.

LOW-DENSITY LIPOPROTEINS (LDLS) Remnants of the breakdown of VLDLs. They deliver cholesterol to other tissues, including blood vessels.

MONOUNSATURATED FATTY ACID A fatty acid that contains only one double bond.

PHOSPHOLIPID (fos-fo-LIP-id) A lipid that has a three-carbon glycerol backbone; the first two carbons of the glycerol molecule have fatty acids bound to them, and the third carbon has a phosphate group bonded to it.

POLYUNSATURATED FATTY ACID A fatty acid that contains two or more double bonds.

SATIETY (suh-TYE-eh-tee) The feeling of fullness and satisfaction after a meal.

SATURATED FATTY ACID Fatty acid that contains no double bonds.

TRANS FATTY ACID An unhealthy fatty acid produced through the addition of hydrogen atoms to double bonds of fatty acids, which causes the molecule to assume an unnatural shape.

TRIGLYCERIDE A form of fat found in food and in the body; chemically, it is composed of a three-carbon compound called *glycerol* in which fatty acids are bonded to each of the carbons.

VERY LOW-DENSITY LIPOPROTEINS (VLDLS) Lipoproteins that are synthesized in the liver and contain both triglycerides and cholesterol. They function to deliver triglycerides to other tissues.

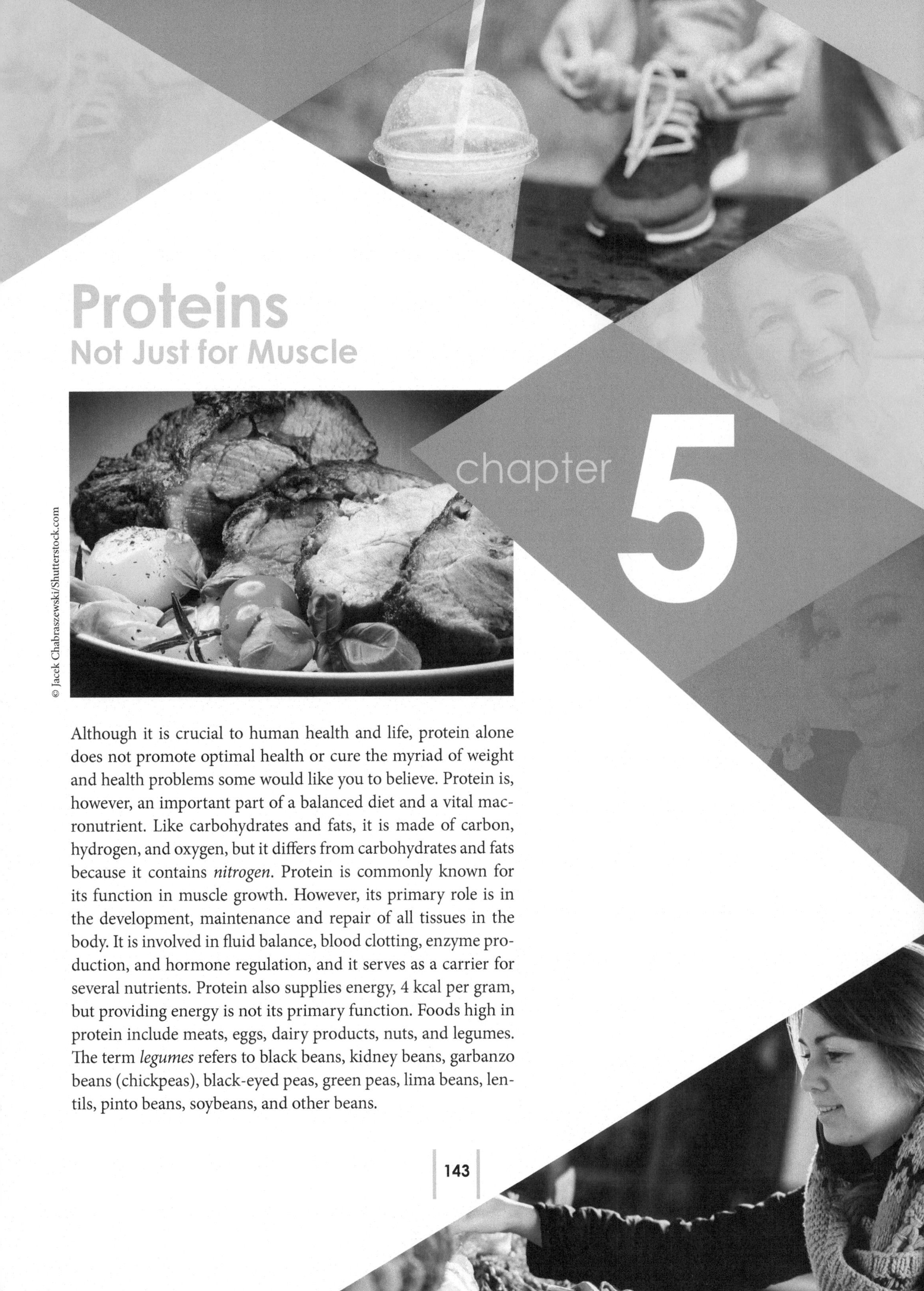

Proteins
Not Just for Muscle

chapter 5

© Jacek Chabraszewski/Shutterstock.com

Although it is crucial to human health and life, protein alone does not promote optimal health or cure the myriad of weight and health problems some would like you to believe. Protein is, however, an important part of a balanced diet and a vital macronutrient. Like carbohydrates and fats, it is made of carbon, hydrogen, and oxygen, but it differs from carbohydrates and fats because it contains *nitrogen*. Protein is commonly known for its function in muscle growth. However, its primary role is in the development, maintenance and repair of all tissues in the body. It is involved in fluid balance, blood clotting, enzyme production, and hormone regulation, and it serves as a carrier for several nutrients. Protein also supplies energy, 4 kcal per gram, but providing energy is not its primary function. Foods high in protein include meats, eggs, dairy products, nuts, and legumes. The term *legumes* refers to black beans, kidney beans, garbanzo beans (chickpeas), black-eyed peas, green peas, lima beans, lentils, pinto beans, soybeans, and other beans.

Amino acid structure

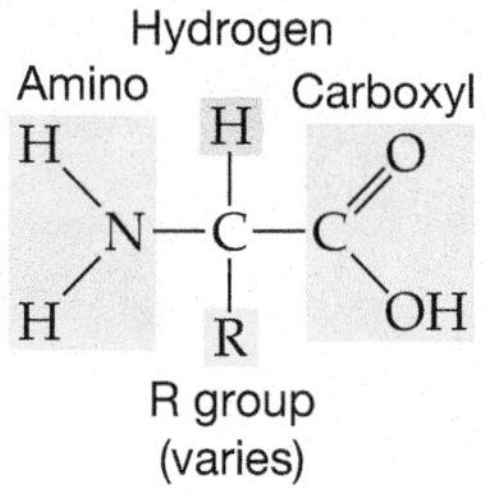

Hydrogen

Amino Carboxyl

R group (varies)

FIGURE 5.1
Chemical structure of an amino acid.

amino acids

The building blocks of protein. They contain nitrogen and link together to form proteins.

PROTEIN STRUCTURE AND FUNCTION

Amino Acids

How can protein, one nutrient, have so many functions in the body? In order to answer this question we must discuss some chemistry. Proteins are made of combinations of **amino acids** linked together. Basically, amino acids are the building blocks for protein. All amino acids are made of a central carbon connected to four different groups (see Figure 5.1). One group is called an *amine group* (this is where the nitrogen is located), one is an *acid group (carboxyl)*, one is *hydrogen*, and the fourth is a *side chain*, or *R group*.

The R groups are unique in each of the different amino acids (see Figure 5.2). This is how you can distinguish one amino acid from the other; the R group dictates the function of each amino acid. The R groups allow the different amino acids and the unique proteins made from them to vary in shape, size, and electrical charge. This variation allows proteins to serve so many important and different functions.

Some amino acids are positively charged, some are neutral, and some carry a negative charge. The charge plays an important role in the unique qualities of the amino acids and the proteins they make. There are 20 known amino acids that the body uses for various functions.

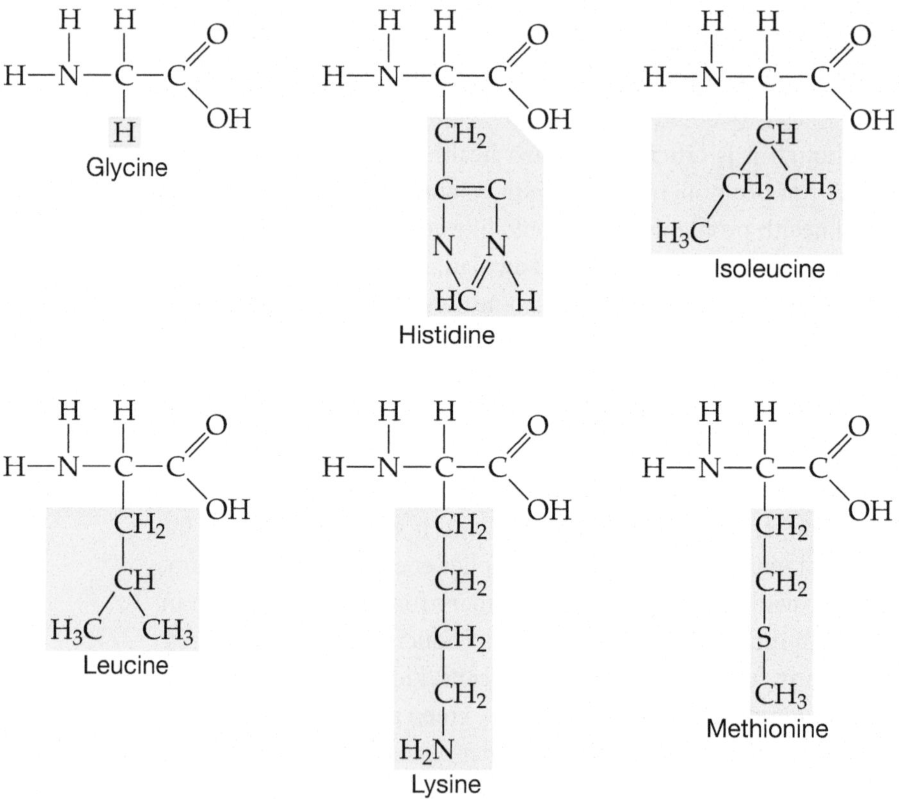

FIGURE 5.2
There are 20 different amino acids, each with a different R group (contained in the blue box) that makes the amino acid and the proteins it creates unique.

Glycine

Histidine

Isoleucine

Leucine

Lysine

Methionine

Nine of the amino acids are classified as **essential amino acids**. Essential amino acids are those that cannot be made in the body in the amounts sufficient to meet its physiological needs, so we must obtain them from the food we eat. If essential amino acids are not consumed in the diet, the body will not be able to make the proteins it needs for growth, maintenance, or any of the other functions mentioned previously without breaking down muscle tissue to acquire the needed essential amino acids. **Nonessential amino acids** are also needed in the body, but the body can produce them, so we do not have to obtain them from food. The body can make the nonessential amino acids by reusing the nitrogen groups of essential amino acids and other proteins that have been broken down. This process is called **transamination** because it involves transferring the amine group (the nitrogen-containing part) from one molecule to another to make an amino acid (see Table 5.1). However, it is not possible to use these transamination reactions to form essential amino acids using nonessential amino acids, which is why we have to get our essential amino acids from dietary sources.

essential amino acids
Amino acids that cannot be made in the body, so we must obtain them from the food we eat.

nonessential amino acids
Amino acids that can be made in the body by transferring the amine group, or nitrogen, from an essential amino acid to another compound containing a carbon, an acid group, a hydrogen, and an R group.

transamination
Transference of the amine group (the nitrogen-containing part) from one molecule to another to make an amino acid.

TABLE 5.1 Essential and Nonessential Amino Acids

Essential Amino Acids	Nonessential Amino Acids
Histidine	Alanine
Isoleucine	Arginine
Leucine	Asparagine
Lysine	Aspartic acid
Methionine	Cysteine
Phenylalanine	Glutamic acid
Threonine	Glutamine
Tryptophan	Glycine
Valine	Proline
	Serine
	Tyrosine
Note: Under certain circumstances, nonessential amino acids cannot be made by the body; then they are referred to as being *conditionally essential amino acids.*	

In rare circumstances, when nonessential amino acids cannot be made by the body in the quantities needed, those amino acids are considered to be **conditionally essential amino acids**. This can occur because of disease or when the essential amino acid needed to make the nonessential amino acid is limited in the diet. For example, in the inherited disease *phenylketonuria* (*PKU*), the

conditionally essential amino acids
Nonessential amino acids that under certain circumstances cannot be made in sufficient quantity by the body and therefore must be consumed in the diet.

enzyme that breaks down the amino acid *phenylalanine* is not produced or is deficient. This enzyme typically converts the essential amino acid phenylalanine to the nonessential amino acid *tyrosine.* Without this enzyme, phenylalanine accumulates in the blood and body tissues and can cause brain damage. Because people with PKU can't break down phenylalanine, they must avoid it in their diet. Tyrosine then becomes essential and therefore must be consumed in the diet. People with PKU must follow a strict diet with low protein and avoid aspartame (brand name NutraSweet) because it contains phenylalanine.

Protein Structure

peptide bonds

Bonds that link amino acids together to make proteins. The bond is formed between the acid group of one amino acid and the amine group of another.

Every protein in the body has a different chain of amino acids linked together in a specific order by peptide bonds. **Peptide bonds** are formed between the acid group of one amino acid and the amine group of another (see Figure 5.3). The sequence of amino acids in a protein determines the unique three dimensional shape of each protein in our diet and in our body (see Figure 5.4).

FIGURE 5.3 Amino acids are joined together by peptide bonds.

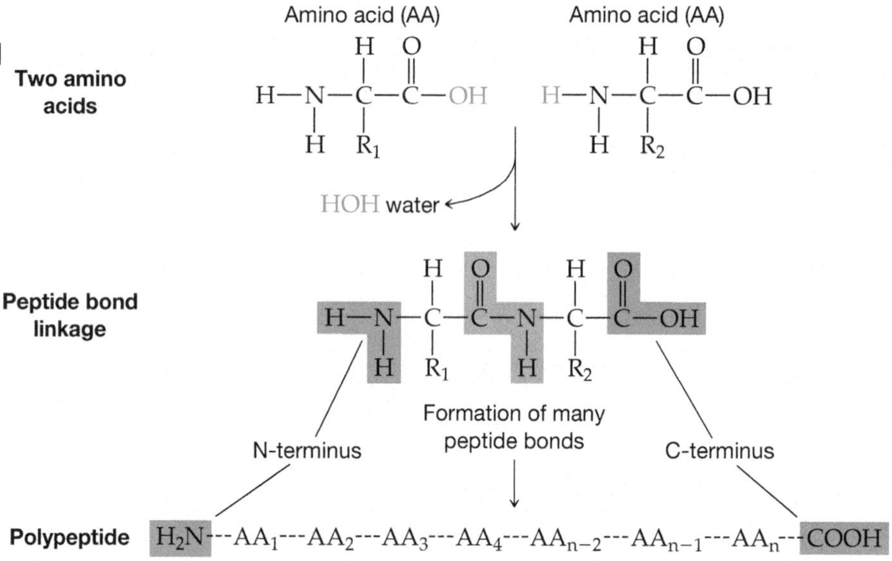

FIGURE 5.4 Amino acids linked to form a polypeptide.

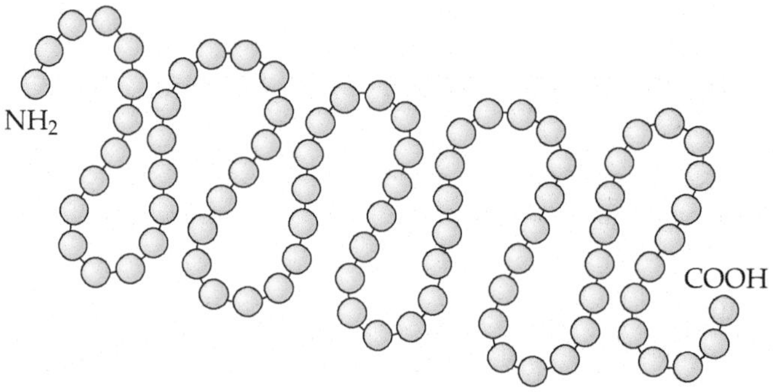

Shape Dictates Function

The specific order of the amino acids is part of what determines a protein's shape, which in turn dictates its function. Why does the order dictate the shape? Recall from our previous discussion that the R groups give the protein its unique and specific qualities. The charge of each amino acid influences how it interacts with the other amino acids in the protein and therefore its shape. For example, if an amino acid's R group is electrically charged, it will be positioned to the outside of the protein so that it can mix in the watery environment of the body. If an amino acid has a neutral charge, it won't mix with water and will move to the middle or core of the protein where it can mix with the other neutral amino acids, causing the chain to curl onto itself into a coil, a globule, or other shape.

What happens if the order of the amino acids in a protein gets messed up?

If the order of the amino acids is so important, how does the body know the order in which to place them? Our DNA determines the order or sequence in which the amino acids will be linked. Each of us has a genetic code that we inherit from our biological parents. This code determines the sequence of amino acids, that not only makes each protein unique, but also makes people unique from each other and other species. The nucleus of each cell in the body contains the DNA necessary to make every protein needed by the body. However, different cells make only the proteins needed for their specific functions. For instance, only the cells of the *pancreas* will link the amino acids in the order needed to make the protein that is the hormone insulin (see Figure 5.5). The cells make their needed proteins not just because the DNA is there, but in response to the ever-changing conditions of the body. The pancreas does not always make insulin just because the DNA for insulin is there. When blood sugar is low, the cells of the pancreas stop producing insulin so that your blood sugar will not keep falling.

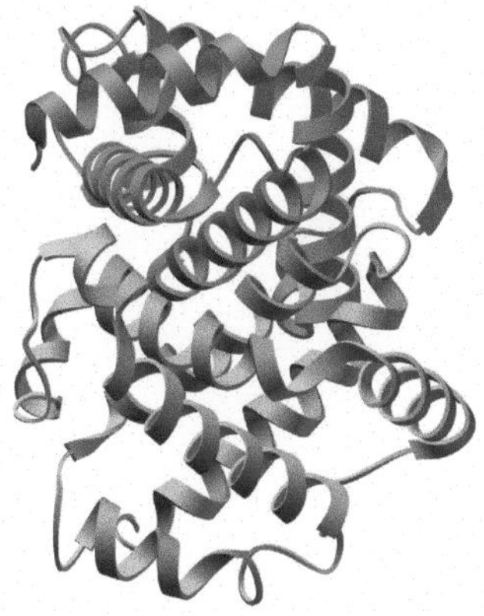

FIGURE 5.5
Three-dimensional structure of insulin.

If just one amino acid in the link is out of order, or an amino acid is skipped because of genetic error, the shape of the protein is changed and therefore the function is altered. For example, in the inherited disease **sickle-cell anemia**, an incorrect amino acid is incorporated into the protein chain. **Hemoglobin** is a protein in red blood cells that carries oxygen. Red blood cells are normally disc-like in shape. In the disease sickle-cell anemia, a single amino acid is altered and this causes hemoglobin to clump together forming strands. The clumps and strands of hemoglobin cause the red blood cell shape to change from a disc to a sickle shape. The sickle-shaped cells do not allow for complete bonding of hemoglobin and oxygen, and can easily stick to one another and block small blood vessels. This causes less blood to reach the part of the body that the blocked vessel supplies. Tissue that does not receive a normal blood flow eventually becomes damaged, which causes the complications of sickle-cell anemia.

sickle-cell anemia
A form of anemia that occurs when a person inherits two abnormal genes (one from each parent) that causes an incorrect amino acid to be incorporated in the sequence for the protein hemoglobin. The change in the amino acid causes the shape of the protein to change leading to the cell being more sickle shaped rather than disc shaped. The sickle-shaped cells do not allow for complete bonding of hemoglobin and oxygen and can easily stick together.

hemoglobin
A protein contained in the red blood cells that carries oxygen throughout the body.

The normal red blood cell is shaped correctly to maintain its function of carrying oxygen throughout the body. In the sickle cell, the shape of the red blood cell is changed and, therefore, it cannot function optimally.

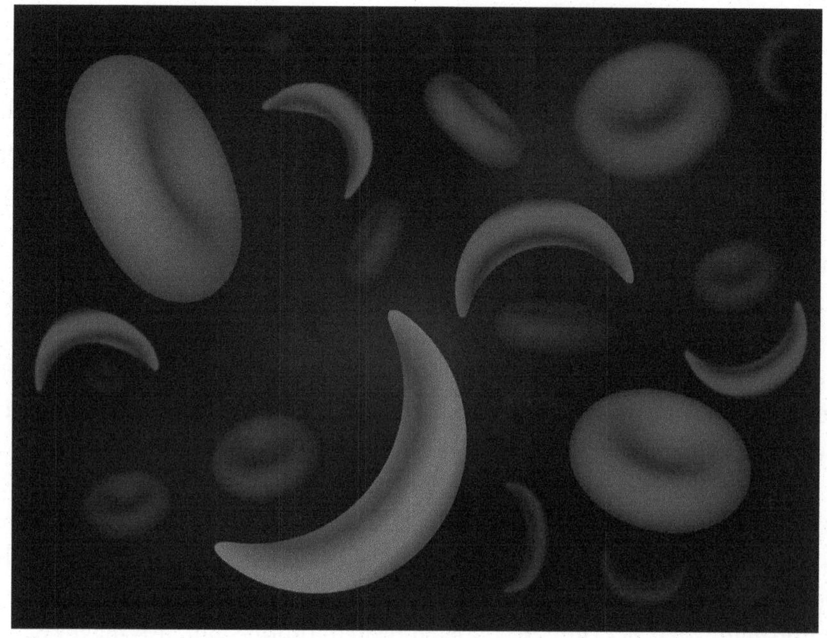

Denaturation

denaturation

A process in which a protein's structure and function are changed by heat, acid, enzymes, agitation, or alcohol.

Because a protein's shape determines its function, we can change a protein's ability to function by altering its shape. This occurs when we cook food, when we sterilize items such as bandages or a baby's bottle, or when we break down protein during digestion (see Chapter 6 for more information on digestion). A protein's structure and function can be changed by heat, acid, enzymes, agitation, or alcohol in a process called **denaturation.** Anyone who has ever cooked has a visual example of denaturation. For example, as you add heat while cooking a liquid egg, you change its shape by making it less liquid and its function by making it less soluble (think of mixing a raw egg in a recipe such as cookie dough as compared to mixing a cooked egg to make egg salad). Similarly, when we eat proteins we denature them with stomach acid. Stomach acid unravels the three-dimensional structure just as cooking does.

Denaturation allows more of the surface area of the protein to interact with digestive enzymes and thus helps with digestion. In addition to breaking down proteins in food, our stomach acid denatures the proteins of many of the bacteria found in foods. This in turn changes their function so that they can no longer harm us. This is an important concept to remember if you are taking medicines that block stomach acid production, such as antacids. In this case, you must exercise caution in consuming foods that are uncooked or have a high chance of containing bacteria, such as raw meat and fish. By taking medication to block stomach acid and by not cooking food, you have essentially eliminated two methods of denaturing the protein of potentially harmful bacteria: heat and stomach acid. This can increase your chances of getting a foodborne illness.

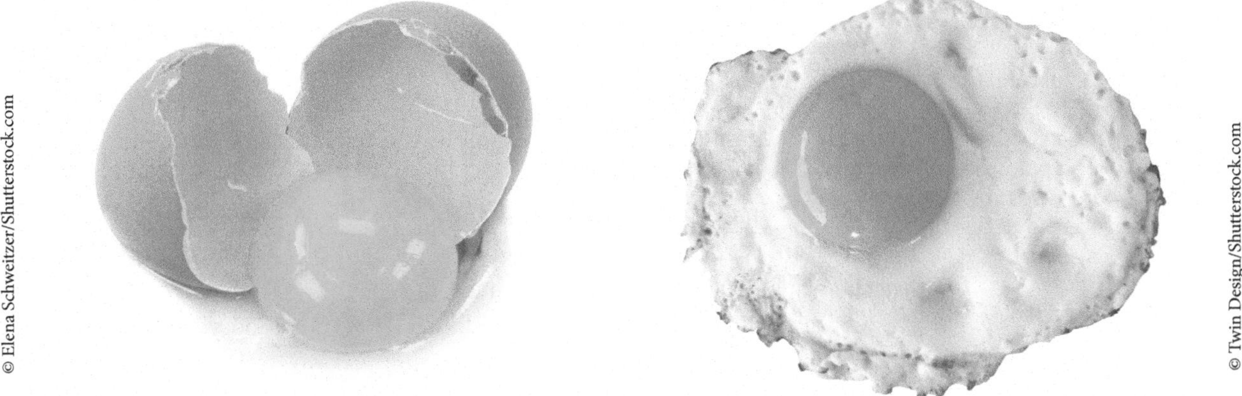

The structure and function of the raw egg is transformed—denatured by heat—in the fried egg.

Protein Function

Protein is needed for many functions in the body, and it is part of every physiological system. The following is a summary of some of the most important roles and tasks it performs (see also Figure 5.6).

Growth, Maintenance, and Repair

Protein is probably best known for its role in body growth, maintenance, and repair. Even adults who have reached their growth potential and who are not increasing muscle mass by weight resistant exercise must consistently consume adequate amounts of protein to supply the essential amino acids. The

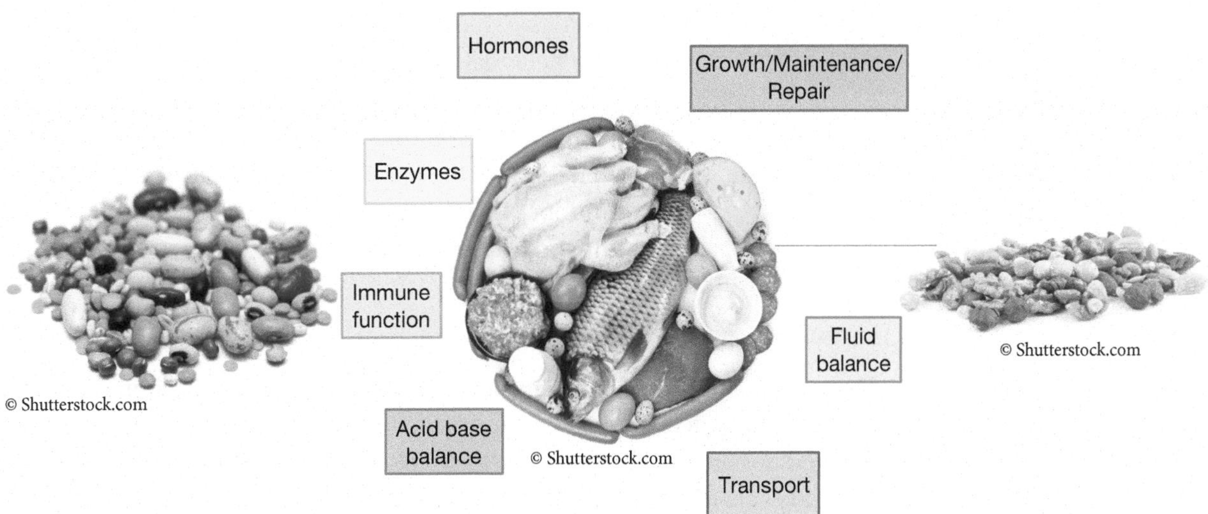

FIGURE 5.6 The many functions of protein

albumin

A protein that constitutes 60 percent of the body's plasma (the watery part of blood) proteins. Among albumin's many functions, it transports drugs and thyroid hormones and carries fatty acids from adipose tissue to the muscle cells for use as energy.

pH

A numerical scale that measures and reflects acid–base balance.

body is in a dynamic state where proteins are constantly being broken down and synthesized. Many amino acids are reused to make new proteins, but some must be replaced through the diet, particularly the essential ones. These amino acids are used to restore the proteins of the cells that are continually being broken down and renewed. For example, the cells that line your intestine are replaced about every 3 days, your red blood cells live only for about 4 months, and your skin cells are constantly sloughing off to be replaced by new skin.

Protein is also important in blood clotting and as part of connective tissue such as ligaments and tendons. Collagen is part of all the connective tissue in the body including tendons, bones, skin, teeth, and blood vessels; it is made of protein and constitutes the most abundant protein in the entire body. Hair and nails are made of protein and noticeably weaken when protein intake is insufficient.

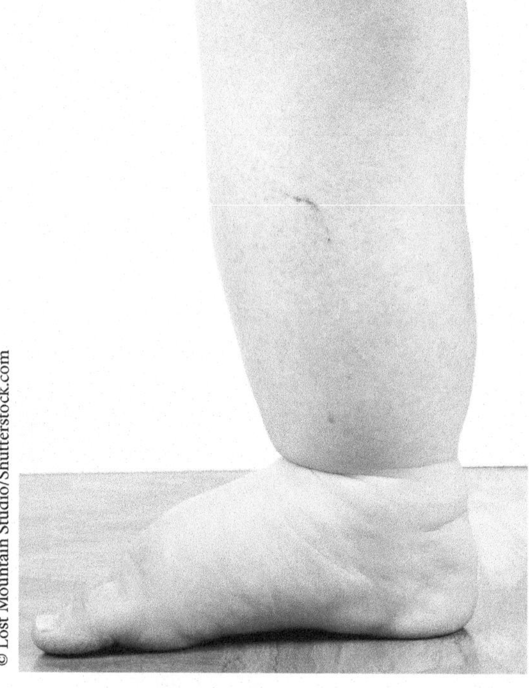

When protein levels are low, fluid balance is not maintained and swelling occurs.

Fluid Balance

Protein plays a crucial role in maintaining fluid balance. Proteins in the blood, such as albumin, help keep an optimal balance between the fluids inside and outside your cells and blood vessels. When blood is circulating, it delivers nutrients across the thin walls of the capillaries to the areas around and inside the cells. A balance of fluids between these spaces and the capillary vessels must be maintained at all times to prevent swelling (*edema*).

Acid–Base Balance

As a normal part of the body's chemical reactions, acids and bases are constantly being produced. The body strives to maintain its pH, or its acid–base balance, in a tight range. Proteins help maintain the very narrow range of pH in the body. In other words, they act as buffers, and help neutralize the pH when too many hydrogen ions are present and threaten to make the blood acidic. They also contribute hydrogen ions to make the blood more acidic when it is becoming too alkaline or basic.

acid–base balance

The mechanisms the body uses to keep its fluids close to neutral pH (i.e., neither basic nor acidic) so that the body can function normally.

Immune Function

Many of us tend to take our immune systems for granted. We shouldn't. Even when we don't feel sick, our immune systems are hard at work fighting off foreign substances called *antigens* that constantly threaten the body's health. *Antibodies* are the proteins that the body's immune system produces as a major defense against these antigens. However, many foreign substances never even make it into the body to cause a threat, thanks to one of the immune system's first defense mechanisms—the mucus present in the respiratory system and intestine. This mucus is made of amino acids and is constantly being secreted to trap bacteria and keep other foreign substances from invading the body. Without adequate protein, the immune system becomes weakened because it cannot produce enough mucus or enough antibodies to fight off antigens and keep you healthy.

Enzymes

Enzymes are proteins that speed up chemical reactions. They assist in very specific reactions in every cell of the body. Enzymes are made by stringing together hundreds to thousands of amino acids in a specific and unique order. Remember that the chain of amino acids then folds into a unique shape. It is this unique shape that allows each enzyme to carry out specific chemical reactions. Throughout the body, enzymes play vital roles that keep the body functioning optimally; when they are low, problems or symptoms develop.

Sometimes a particular enzyme is not created because of a problem in genetic coding. This is referred to as an inborn error of metabolism. Some genetic disorders produce relatively unimportant physical features or skeletal abnormalities. Others produce serious diseases and even death. For example, *hemophilia* is a disease that results in excessive bleeding and bruising from minor injuries. People with this disorder are missing the genetic code to make a protein (enzyme) needed for clotting to occur. Therefore, they must receive preventive injections of the clotting factor proteins or must inject them when they are cut to slow bleeding. Not all enzyme deficiencies are caused by genetic problems. Sometimes the enzyme is damaged or levels are reduced by medications, illness, or inadequate nutrition. For example, lactose intolerance often occurs after abdominal surgery or while taking certain medications (see Chapter 3 for more information on lactose intolerance).

Hormones

Hormones are like messengers that help regulate the various systems and functions of the body. Some hormones are made of lipids; some, like insulin, are made from proteins. Insulin has many functions but is perhaps best known for its role in maintaining blood sugar levels (see Chapter 3 for more information on blood glucose regulation).

Transport

Proteins help transport substances across cell walls by acting as pumps. Transport proteins in the cell membrane, called *sodium-potassium pumps*, help maintain the balance of sodium and potassium between the outside and inside of the cell. In addition, proteins serve as transporters of nutrients throughout the bloodstream. For example, the protein albumin constitutes 60 percent of the protein in the body's *plasma* (the watery part of blood). Among albumin's many functions, it transports drugs and thyroid hormones and it carries fatty acids from adipose tissue to muscle cells for use as energy. Proteins have water-repelling and water-attracting ends, which allow them to interact with the fat and the water. You may recall from Chapter 4 that proteins are part of the lipoproteins that carry fats from the liver to the body and are part of the chylomicrons that transport long-chain fatty acids after absorption. Without the presence of protein along with phospholipids, fat could not mix with the watery environment of the blood.

Energy

Perhaps the least efficient purpose for proteins is for energy production. In other words, because protein plays such an important role in so many other functions, it is not optimal use of this nutrient to use it for energy. However, if carbohydrate or Calorie intake is too low, protein will be used for energy or to make glucose to maintain blood glucose levels. This alternate use may compromise its contribution to the numerous other functions just discussed. This is why protein sparing is often listed among the functions of carbohydrates. Other than the very small amount of amino acids in the blood, protein has no storage form in the body like carbohydrates and fats. Therefore, when the body uses protein as an energy source for any prolonged period, the protein not supplied in the diet will be obtained from body tissue, especially muscle. In a short period of time a significant amount of muscle tissue can be lost. For that reason, it is crucial to consume adequate amounts of carbohydrates and fats to meet your Calorie needs to ensure that protein will be used only minimally for energy, thus conserving most protein for the various vital functions that depend on it.

BEFORE YOU GO ON...

1. Explain how protein differs chemically from carbohydrates and fats.
2. What determines the shape and function of amino acids?
3. What is the process of denaturation and why is it important?
4. List the functions of protein in the body.

FOOD SOURCES OF PROTEIN

Protein Quality

Although protein is found in both plant and animal foods, the source can vary in quality. A **high-quality protein,** also called a **complete protein,** is one that provides all of the essential amino acids in the amount that the body needs. Complete proteins are also easy to digest and absorb. Typically, animal proteins like those found in meats and dairy products and the vegetable protein in soy are considered highly digestible because the human body can absorb almost 90 percent. In contrast, some plant proteins are only 60 percent digestible.

high-quality protein/complete protein
A protein that provides all of the essential amino acids in the amount that the body needs and is easy to digest and absorb. Also called a complete protein.

Food sources of protein.

APPLICATION TIP

Sources of proteins that are low in fat	
Low-Fat Protein Choices	
Include regularly	*Include only occasionally*
Skim and low-fat dairy products (milk, yogurt, cheese)	Whole milk and dairy products (milk, yogurt, cheese)
Broiled, grilled, or baked skinless boneless chicken and turkey breast	Dark-meat chicken and fried chicken
Lean cuts of meat such as London broil	High-fat cuts of meat such as prime rib and other cuts with visible marbled fat, luncheon meats such as bologna and pastrami
White-meat pork tenderloin	Bacon, ham, sausage, hot dogs, and fried pork products
Broiled, grilled, baked, or sautéed shrimp	Fried shrimp
Broiled, grilled, baked, and sautéed fish, especially salmon and other coldwater fish	Fried fish
Egg whites or egg substitutes	Whole eggs
Soy and soy products	Deep-fried tofu
Beans, lentils, and legumes	Refried beans cooked with lard
Nuts and seeds (small portions)	

incomplete proteins
Foods that do not contain all of the essential amino acids in the amount needed by the body. They include fruits, legumes, grains, and vegetables.

complementary proteins
Two or more foods whose amino acid content, when combined, provides all of the essential amino acids.

Foods that do not contain all of the essential amino acids in the amount needed by the body are called **incomplete proteins**. Examples of incomplete proteins include legumes (except soy), grains (except quinoa), and vegetables. Because animal products are a traditional source of high-quality protein, many people think that in order to consume adequate protein you must eat meat, seafood, eggs, and dairy products. This is *not* true. You can obtain adequate protein by eating **complementary proteins. Complementary proteins** are foods that when eaten alone are not complete proteins, but when combined correctly provide all of the essential amino acids. Anyone who has eaten rice and beans together has consumed complementary proteins. When you eat beans, methionine is the limiting amino acid. Rice is rich in methionine and beans are low. Put them together and they complement each other and provide adequate methionine. For more examples of complementary proteins, see Figure 5.7.

ARE SOYBEANS A MIRACLE FOOD?

Nutrition & **DISEASE**

There are no magic bullets in our food supply capable of eliminating all health concerns. However, recent studies have suggested that the potential health benefits associated with consuming soy and soy products may include protection against some cancers, cardiovascular disease, and bone loss. See Table 5.2 for a list of soy products and suggestions for including them in your daily meals. How many of these are you familiar with, and how often do you consume them?

TABLE 5.2

Soy Foods	Meal Suggestions
Tofu	Chop extra-firm tofu into cubes, add to spaghetti sauce, and serve with whole-wheat pasta
Tempeh	Place on skewers with vegetables and season (or use barbecue sauce), grill, or broil
Soy nuts	Sprinkle over salads or cereal
Textured soy (substitute for ground meat)	Use in spaghetti, tacos, sloppy joes, chili, etc.
Soy dairy products	Soy milk, soy cheese, and soy yogurt can be substituted for cow's milk (i.e., as milk on your cereal)

Soy and soy products provide a complete source of protein with little saturated fat and no cholesterol. In fact, 1 c. of soy provides 57 percent of the DV for protein, less than 300 Calories, and only 2.2 g of saturated fat. In addition, it contains *isoflavones* which help protect cells against damage. Research has indicated that the *isoflavones* in soy may lower cholesterol, especially when soy products are used as a replacement for higher fat animal-based foods. Soy may also help prevent prostate and colon cancer. Some *isoflavones* in soy act as *phytoestrogens*, which may help prevent symptoms of menopause and osteoporosis in postmenopausal women. However, there is mixed information regarding soy's effect on the risk of breast cancer. The same phytoestrogens that can be beneficial to health may actually increase the risk of breast cancer in some women by raising estrogen levels. Therefore, overconsumption of soy supplements, which are concentrated sources of phytoestrogens, are not recommended. In order to balance the many health benefits associated with soy against the risks of overconsumption, it is recommended that intake of soy foods should be limited to 4 servings per day.

Soy is derived from soy beans and comes in many different forms, such as the popular Japanese dish edamame and the many products pictured here. Soybeans are high in protein and low in fat. They contain B vitamins, calcium, potassium, vitamin A, iron, isoflavones, and plant estrogens.

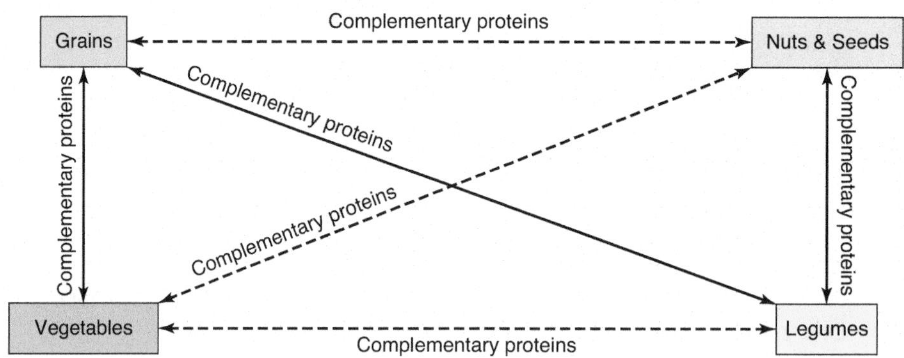

FIGURE 5.7 Complementary protein sources.

People who consume meats and/or dairy products generally don't have to worry about consciously consuming complementary proteins. However, vegetarians and those who infrequently consume meat and dairy products do need to pay close attention to complementary proteins to ensure that they are receiving adequate amounts of all of the essential amino acids. It is not necessary to eat the complementary proteins in the same meal, but it is best to consume them in the same day in order to have the amino acids necessary for protein synthesis.

Supplemental Protein

An additional source of protein for some people, especially vegetarians, highly active people, and those needing to gain weight, is supplemental protein. Most Americans, whether vegetarian or not, consume sufficient levels or even more dietary protein than they need, and yet protein and amino acid supplements have become very popular. Protein supplements are available as powders, shakes, drinks, bars, pills, puddings, and more. These sources can contribute to meeting daily protein requirements; however, they are not superior to food sources of protein and should be consumed with sufficient energy to support protein synthesis.

In other words, protein supplements do not magically stimulate muscle growth, optimize your immune system, or fulfill any of the other claims marketers may make. In fact, dietary protein is less expensive and provides a wider variety of vitamins and minerals when compared to supplements.

Some people consume protein from supplements rather than foods high in protein because they are concerned with the extra Calories from fat found in some protein-rich foods. However, many foods are low-fat sources of protein, such as chicken breast with no skin, low-fat or skim milk, and egg whites. See the Application Tip on page 154 for some additional suggestions.

As mentioned previously, consuming excess protein does not provide additional health benefits. The protein you eat beyond what your body needs for protein function will be used for energy or stored as fat. In addition, excess pro-

Protein supplements come in many different forms.

tein in the diet can create an imbalance, especially when you are eating protein in place of other healthy foods such as grains, vegetables, and fruits. Intake of too much protein means that the body has to rid itself of the nitrogen groups on the amino acids and excrete them as urea in the urine. This increases the body's water requirements as it attempts to essentially "flush out" the system.

Recommendations for Protein Intake

The DRI for protein for non-athletes is 0.8 g per kilogram of body weight of high-quality protein for men and women and is based on scientific nitrogen balance studies. Nitrogen balance studies assess the amount of nitrogen being consumed and compare it to the amount of nitrogen being excreted. This information can be used to determine protein needs. So, if you weigh 150 lb., divide your weight by 2.2 to get kilograms and then multiply by 0.8 for an RDA of 55 g of protein per day. This recommendation is meant for healthy adults. If you are recovering from an injury, are ill, stressed, or pregnant, or are a competitive athlete, then you may need to increase the DRI for protein.

You may notice that not all food labels list a % DV for protein. According to the FDA, a % DV is required to be listed only if a claim is made for protein, such as "high in protein." Otherwise, unless the food is meant for use by infants and children less than 4 years of age, an indication of the % DV is not needed. This is because most Americans over age 4 consume more than the recommended amount of protein, and therefore inadequate protein intake is not a public health concern.

Myths & LEGENDS

MORE PROTEIN = MORE MUSCLE— DO ATHLETES REALLY NEED MORE PROTEIN?

No specific DRI addresses protein needs for athletes, but sport nutritionists suggest that they need more protein than nonathletes for tissue and muscle repair and increased protein turnover. This requirement is especially true when you begin a new exercise program.

Whether an athlete needs more protein and how much additional protein is needed is influenced by how hard the athlete is training and the type of exercise. In 2009, a joint position statement by the American College of Sports Medicine, the Academy of Nutrition and Dietetics, and Dietitians of Canada stated that protein requirements for athletes are higher than for nonathletes. They recommended that endurance athletes consume 1.2–1.4 g per kilogram and resistance athletes should consume 1.2–1.7 g per kilogram.

Although these recommendations are higher than the DRI of 0.8 g per kilogram of body weight most athletes still do not need to make a special effort to get more protein in their diet. Because athletes tend to eat more food, they are naturally consuming more protein. However, some athletes such as those restricting Calories or those consuming vegetarian diets may need to assess their protein intake to make sure they are consuming adequate amounts. Sufficient protein is easy to obtain from a balanced diet that contains an adequate amount of Calories. Remember that in order to increase muscle mass you need several things: adequate Calorie intake, adequate protein intake, and exercise.

If Calorie intake is adequate, research suggests that muscle mass can be maintained within a wide range of protein intakes. Many attempt to achieve the extra edge by consuming excessive amounts of protein from supplements. However, there is no magic advantage to consuming protein supplements when compared to consuming protein-rich foods.

© Bojan656/Shutterstock.com

To promote muscle growth and recovery, strength and power athletes should consume 1.2–1.7 g of protein per kilogram of body weight daily.

BEFORE YOU GO ON...

1. What is the difference between a complete protein and an incomplete protein?
2. What health benefits are associated with consuming soy and soy products?
3. What is a complementary protein?
4. Do athletes need more protein than the DRI?
5. If you exercise, do you need to consume protein supplements?

APPLICATION TIP

Recent research suggests consuming a small amount of protein along with carbohydrates one hour before your workout in order to optimize protein synthesis. Try a glass of milk, a cup of yogurt, or a peanut butter sandwich

vegan

A person who eats only plant food and does not eat anything produced from animals. Also referred to as a strict vegetarian.

lacto-vegetarians

People who consume milk and dairy products, such as cheese and yogurt, but avoid eggs, seafood, and meat.

lacto-ovo vegetarians

People who consume eggs and dairy products, but no meat or seafood.

macrobiotic vegetarians

People who consume mostly whole grains, especially brown rice, in their diets along with vegetables, soy, legumes, fruits, and sometimes whitefish.

semivegetarians (or flexitarians)

People who occasionally eat meat and seafood, yet predominately practice a vegetarian diet.

VEGETARIANISM

Different Types of Vegetarian Diets

There are several types of vegetarians (see Table 5.3), and many people have different ideas about what being a vegetarian really means. One type of vegetarian is a **vegan.** According to the Academy of Nutrition and Dietetics, vegans eat only plant foods and do not consume meat, fish, poultry, milk or other dairy products, eggs, or use anything else produced from animals (e.g., leather). **Lacto-vegetarians** consume milk and dairy products, such as cheese and yogurt, but avoid eggs, seafood, and meat. **Lacto-ovo vegetarians** consume eggs and dairy products, but no meat or seafood. **Macrobiotic vegetarians** consume mostly whole grains, especially brown rice, in their diets along with vegetables, soy, legumes, fruits, and nuts and seeds to a lesser extent. They are not vegans because they eat limited amounts of fish. You may have noted that some people call themselves vegetarians although they eat fish, chicken, or even red meat. These people are sometimes identified as **semivegetarians (or flexitarians).** Loosely defined, a semivegetarian is someone who occasionally eats meat and seafood, yet predominately practices a vegetarian diet. The subtle differences in these diet practices are important because the more restrictive the vegetarian diet, the more knowledge and planning it takes to obtain all the essential nutrients to prevent deficiencies.

TABLE 5.3 Types of Vegetarians

Types of Vegetarians	Definition
Vegans	Omit all animal products from their diets, including dairy and eggs
Lacto-vegetarians	Include dairy products but no other animal foods
Lacto-ovo-vegetarians	Include eggs and dairy products but no meat
Macrobiotic vegetarians	Consume mostly whole grains, especially brown rice, in their diets along with vegetables, soy, legumes, fruits, and sometimes white-fish, but avoid meat, poultry, eggs, and dairy
Semivegetarians/ flexitarians	Occasionally eat meat and seafood, yet predominately practice a vegetarian diet

Why Do People Choose to Become Vegetarians?

People become vegetarians, or choose not to eat meat or fish, for a variety of reasons. In some areas of the world, not enough meat is available or meat is too expensive, and therefore people may have fewer choices. However, in countries that are more affluent, people usually choose to be vegetarians for more personal reasons, such as:

vegetarians
People who do not consume animal flesh but may eat eggs and dairy products.

- **Treatment of animals:** Some people do not believe we should consume animal tissues.
- **Hormones and antibiotics:** Some people want to limit their exposure to any residues of the hormones that are often given to promote growth or the antibiotics that are used to prevent illness in animals.
- **Health benefits:** Many people choose to be vegetarians because of the health benefits associated with diets rich in fruits, vegetables, and whole grains.
- **Environmental impact:** Many people choose to be vegetarian because there is a higher environmental impact to raise animal foods than plant foods.
- **Religion:** Many religions have dietary guidelines as part of their code of conduct. For example, Muslims are not permitted to consume alcohol or animals and birds that are carnivorous (meat-eating). Catholics were traditionally asked to abstain from eating meat on Fridays as a form of penance, and many still abstain during Lent. Vegetarianism is recommended in Hindu scriptures, although Hindus are free to choose their own diet. Of those who eat meat, most abstain from beef and pork.

Health Benefits of a Vegetarian Diet

Are vegetarians really healthier than people who eat meat are, and do they live longer?

Although there is still insufficient research to know whether vegetarians live longer than nonvegetarians do, they do appear to have a lower risk of heart disease. Some evidence suggests that a vegetarian diet may also help in the prevention of some cancers, but more studies need to be conducted before any definitive conclusions can be made. We do know that vegetarians typically have a lower body mass index (BMI) than nonvegetarians and are therefore much less likely to be obese. It is difficult to determine whether vegetarians are healthier than nonvegetarians due to their dietary intake. This is because most vegetarians also practice other healthy lifestyle behaviors such as abstaining from smoking and engaging in regular exercise.

Although only about 2–3% of Americans are vegetarians, and even fewer are vegan, the general population is more aware of the benefits of consuming a plant-based diet. This awareness is partly due to the change of focus in the research of vegetarian diets from one of assessing the nutritional quality of the diet to a recent focus on assessing its health benefits.

© DarZel/Shutterstock.com

A variety of delicious and healthy vegetarian meals is available from many different cultures. Do your local supermarkets offer a good selection of ethnic foods? Have you noticed an increase in the number of ethnic restaurants in your city or community?

Reflective of this change in research focus are the recommendations being made by many leading health organizations. Many agencies including the American Cancer Society, the American Heart Association, the National Institutes of Health, and the American Academy of Pediatrics recommend a diet based on a variety of plant foods, including grain products, vegetables, and fruits, to reduce the risk of chronic lifestyle diseases. A diet high in plant foods contains less saturated fat and cholesterol and potentially fewer Calories. It is also likely to be higher in phytochemicals, antioxidants, vitamins, minerals, and fiber. Therefore, consuming vegetarian meals may help reduce the risk of many serious diseases such as cancer, high blood pressure, heart disease, and obesity.

Challenges for Vegetarians

What do I need to do if I decide to become a vegetarian?

Although many health benefits result from consuming a balanced vegetarian diet, some potential health risks are associated with one that is poorly planned and too restrictive. The greatest risk is that of imbalance or nutritional deficiency. The more restrictive the diet, the greater the nutritional risk. Therefore, a vegan diet would likely have the greatest possible risks if not planned properly. When beginning a vegetarian diet, ask yourself why you are doing so. Adopting a vegetarian dietary pattern should be done after researching the subject to learn how to appropriately balance the diet to meet all nutrient requirements. If not planned adequately, vegetarian diets, especially vegan diets, can lead to anemia due to inadequate intake of iron or vitamin B_{12}. In addition, vegan diets can be low in zinc, calcium, protein, vitamin B_6, and devoid of vitamin B_{12} because these nutrients are most abundant in animal foods. Many resources are available to help you acquire some background information as well as helpful tips for easy menu planning. See Figure 5.8 for a food guide for North American vegetarians and meal-planning recommendations put forth by the Vegetarian Society. With even more careful planning a vegan diet can provide all of the required nutrients in sufficient amounts. See Chapter 2 for more tips on planning a healthy diet.

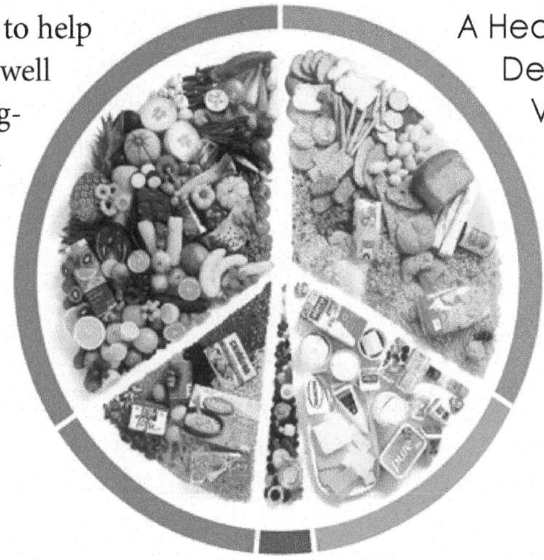

FIGURE 5.8 A Healthy Plate Description for Vegetarians

What's HOT

PROTEIN FOR WEIGHT LOSS

There is a lot of debate as to what diet is most effective for weight loss. High-protein diets have become highly discussed because several studies showed that high-protein diets resulted in more weight loss over 3–6 months than conventional high-carbohydrate low-fat diets. A smaller group of studies attempted to follow subjects for 12 months or more and found that there was no difference in body weight between those on a high protein diet and conventional diet and exercise weight loss plans. A Harvard study was conducted with 800 overweight and obese subjects who followed one of four diets for 2 years. Each diet resulted in a 750-Calorie deficit and varied in the amount of protein, carbohydrates, and fats consumed. The diets were equally successful in promoting weight loss and maintaining it over 2 years. Furthermore, they had similar effects on decreasing disease risk and improving cholesterol levels. The study emphasized behavioral counseling and support group activities provided equally across the groups. The authors suggest that behavioral factors, rather than the amount of carbohydrates or proteins one consumes, are the main influences on weight loss. In addition, they suggest that any type of diet, if presented with enthusiasm and persistence, can be effective. This is encouraging news as it makes sense that no one diet will work for everyone. Therefore, health practitioners can utilize a variety of diets to meet the cultural and individual food preferences of each patient they are working with. Perhaps as a society we can stop jumping from one fad to the next and be open to the possibilities to enhance weight loss efforts and help to reverse the obesity epidemic.

Daily food selections should include at least 5 portions of fruits and vegetables; 5 portions of grains and starchy vegetables; 2–3 portions of high protein foods; 2–3 portions of milk and dairy products; 0–3 portions of fatty or sugary foods. A "portion" is, for example, a slice of bread, an apple, a glass of milk, or two tablespoons of baked beans, but remember—it's the balance that matters, so if your daily caloric intake requirements are higher, increase the amount you eat in all categories, not just the fatty and sugary foods.

Source: Courtesy of The Vegetarian Society of the United Kingdom (www.vegsoc.org).

BEFORE YOU GO ON...

1. Name and differentiate between the different types of vegetarians.
2. What are the different reasons for choosing to become a vegetarian?
3. What are the health benefits and challenges of consuming a vegetarian diet?

PROTEIN IMBALANCE

Too Little Protein

After discussing the important roles of protein in the body, you can imagine how inadequate protein intake might affect overall health. Although it is possible, protein is rarely the only deficient nutrient in a malnourished person, so protein malnutrition is usually not an isolated problem. For example, we absorb much of the iron we need by consuming iron-rich proteins (see Chapter 7 for more details). **Protein energy malnutrition (PEM)** occurs when a person does not consume adequate amounts of protein and/or energy (Calories).

Although PEM is rare in the general population of most industrialized countries, it does exist in the United States in those with major illnesses such

protein energy malnutrition (PEM)
A disorder that occurs when a person does not consume adequate amounts of protein, Calories, or both.

PEM is the most common nutrient deficiency in hospital patients or nursing home residents in the United States.

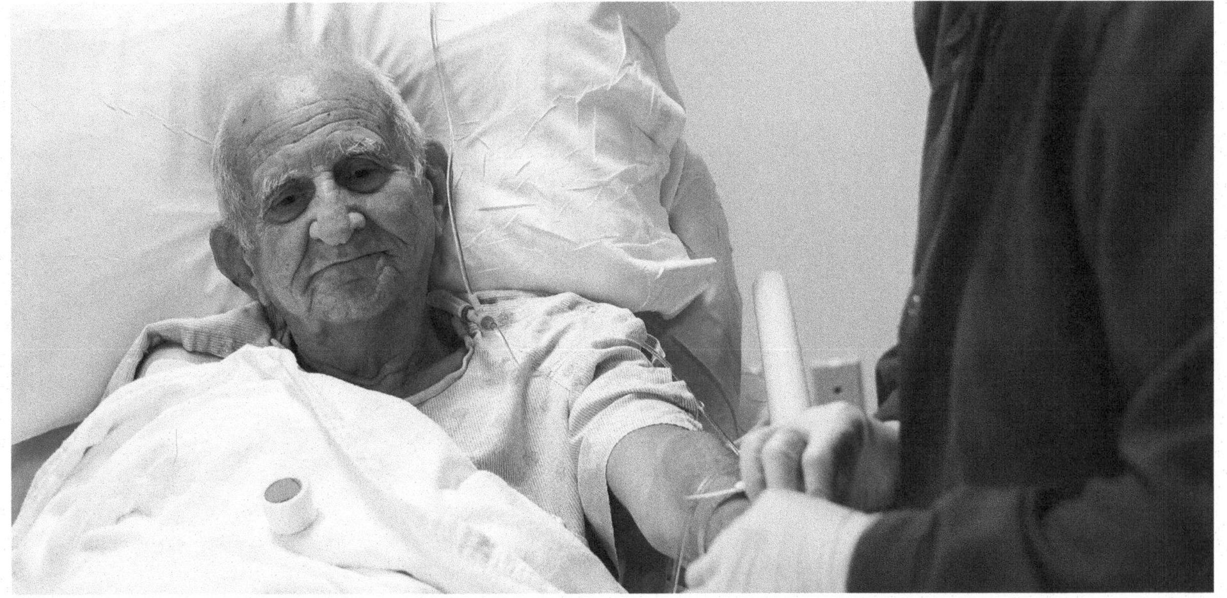

© Fotoluminate LLC/Shutterstock.com

as cancer, HIV, and anorexia nervosa and in children in low-income areas. In fact, PEM is the most common form of nutritional deficiency diagnosed in hospitalized patients in the United States. It is estimated that half of all patients admitted to the hospital have some degree of malnutrition in the form of PEM. In addition, several surveys conducted in low-income areas of the United States reported that 22–35 percent of children ages 2–6 had a slower than normal growth rate due to PEM. PEM is an even greater concern internationally. Although childhood malnutrition in developing countries has been declining since 1990, there are still roughly 16% of those children that are underweight and 33% that are stunted.

According to the World Health Organization (WHO), PEM is by far the most lethal form of malnutrition. Infants and young children are most susceptible to the devastating medical complications associated with PEM because of their high energy and protein needs and their vulnerability to infection. The two types of PEM are discussed in more detail next.

marasmus

A form of PEM characterized by emaciation, or a skeletal appearance due to inadequate intake of both protein and Calories.

kwashiorkor

A form of PEM characterized by a swollen appearance, especially in the abdomen. Historically, kwashiorkor was thought to be caused by a lack of protein, but in fact there may be other contributors to its development.

Marasmus and Kwashiorkor

People with **marasmus** are characterized by emaciation, or a skeletal appearance due to inadequate intake of protein and Calories. Essentially, it is a condition of starvation. Marasmus is most common in infants and children of impoverished regions, but can occur in adults as well. It can occur in industrialized nations, typically as a complication of cancer or HIV, in infants and children because of malabsorption because of gastrointestinal disease, or because of self-starvation associated with eating disorders such as anorexia nervosa.

The term **kwashiorkor** is taken from the language of Ghana and means "the sickness of the weaning." Kwashiorkor most frequently affects children who are being weaned from breast milk. Often these children are transitioned

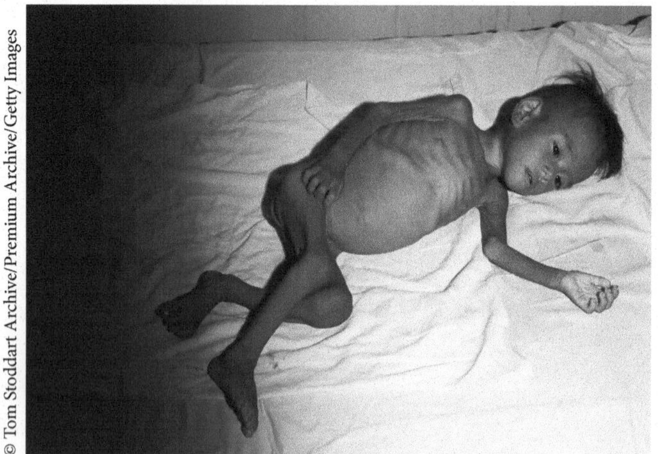

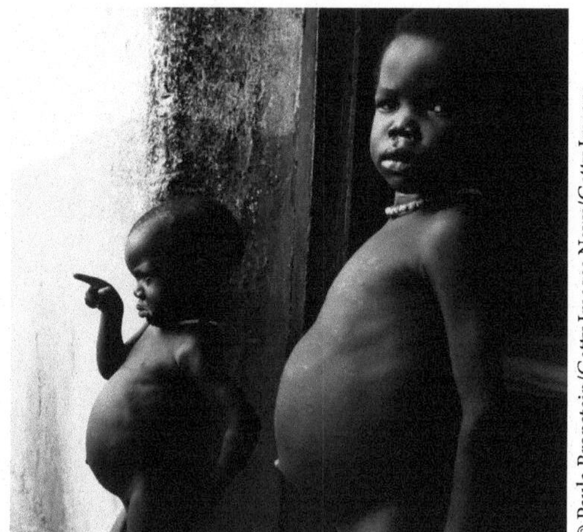

Marasmus (*left*) is a form of PEM common in children of impoverished nations. It is caused by inadequate protein and Calorie intake. The child at right, suffering from kwashiorkor, has a "potbelly" appearance due to inadequate protein intake.

from breast milk to a very starchy, low-protein cereal and kwashiorkor develops quickly. Although deficient levels of dietary protein may contribute to development of kwashiorkor, other factors may be involved including altered distributions of the bacteria that reside in the gut. Such children look as if they are developing a "potbelly" as fluid accumulates in the tissues creating edema, particularly in the abdomen. Those unfamiliar with malnutrition often mistake this for a child being overnourished. This is not the case. The children may be receiving enough Calories, but not enough protein, which is what causes the potbelly appearance. Cases have been observed among the poor in the United States, but are most common in underdeveloped regions worldwide. Some of the more consequential medical complications include impaired growth, edema, rash, and an impaired immune system.

Whether PEM occurs because of poverty, chronic disease, an eating disorder, or poor intake, the approach to rehabilitation is similar. The patient will need a medically supervised nutrition plan to correct the deficiency and to ensure proper fluid and electrolyte balance.

Too Much Protein

We seem to have a cultural obsession with dietary protein. Many labels and marketing slogans for food products use descriptions such as "high protein" or "good source of protein." Many fad diets and weight-loss programs also stress protein intake.

With all of this attention on protein, one might assume that Americans do not consume enough of it. As we have learned, the opposite is true—the typical American consumes more than the recommended amount. This fact raises the question—are we consuming too much protein? If we do eat too much, what are the consequences? Considerable disagreement exists among scientists and those claiming to be experts when they attempt to define how much protein is too much, and whether there is even such a thing as eating too much of it. Although several studies have suggested potential health risks associated with a high-protein diet, not enough evidence exists to conclude that consuming more than the recommended amount is harmful. In addition, there is no agreed upon definition of "high protein." It could mean above the DRI, which would cover a wide range of intakes, and therefore it would be difficult to make any conclusions on such a broad definition. It is difficult to determine whether protein itself causes many of the associated health problems, or other dietary components that may be limited in a high-protein diet. Therefore, it is important to discuss some of the suggested health concerns of consuming a high-protein diet.

One of the reasons a high protein diet may be problematic is related to the lack of balance. High-protein diets are often low in fruits, vegetables, whole grains, and fiber and may be high in saturated fat. This is not to say that all sources of protein are high in fat. There are many lean sources of protein and many high-quality plant sources of protein such as soy products. However, many high-protein diets are low in fiber, phytochemicals, and many vitamins and minerals. If by eating excess protein one is consuming excess Calories, then of course weight gain will occur. In addition, a high-protein diet that consists mainly of animal protein sources is likely to be high in saturated fat.

Research suggests that high protein diets can increase the risk of several chronic diseases. For example, several studies have suggested that a high-protein diet, especially one high in animal protein, may increase the risk for certain types of cancer. In particular, colon, prostate, breast, and pancreatic cancers have been linked to a high protein intake. However, researchers have had difficulty in determining whether this risk is associated with the excess protein or the dietary imbalances associated with eating less fiber, fewer fruits and vegetables, and more saturated fat. It has also been suggested that high protein diets may also cause bone loss, which can lead to osteoporosis, especially in those who consume inadequate amounts of calcium. The theory is that higher protein diets cause elevated urinary calcium excretion. However, there is little evidence to support that a high protein diet leads to bone loss and it may in fact benefit bone health by helping to offset muscle loss often experienced in the elderly. For some, an additional risk of increased calcium excretion associated with a high-protein diet is an elevated risk for the formation of kidney stones. Drinking plenty of fluids will help offset this potential problem by diluting the contents of the urine.

Some health professionals have suggested that high-protein diets may stress the kidneys and therefore lead to an increased risk of kidney disease. While this may be true for those who are susceptible to developing kidney stones and other kidney problems, such as diabetics, there does not appear to be a concern for the average healthy person. However, it can be a problem for infants and premature infants if there is insufficient water intake and for anyone taking multiple medications and supplements that may be putting stress on the kidneys.

Although experts disagree about the exact amount of protein required and the amount that determines excess, they generally agree that consuming 2 g of protein per kilogram of ideal body weight per day is safe for most healthy people. There is no information to suggest any benefits in eating amounts greater than this.

BEFORE YOU GO ON...

1. What is protein energy malnutrition (PEM)?
2. Describe the primary difference between the diseases kwashiorkor and marasmus.
3. Are there health concerns regarding consumption of too much protein, if so, describe them?

CHAPTER SUMMARY

- Chemically, proteins (amino acids) are made of carbon, hydrogen, oxygen, and nitrogen.
- Proteins are made up of combinations of amino acids that are linked together by peptide bonds. All amino acids are made of a central carbon connected to four different groups: an amine group (which contains nitrogen); an acid group; hydrogen; and the R group (or unique side chain).
- The R groups distinguish one amino acid from the other and dictate the functions of the different amino acids. They allow the different amino acids to vary in shape, size, and electrical charge, making each protein unique. So insulin and hemoglobin, although both proteins, have very specific functions.
- There are 20 known amino acids. Essential amino acids cannot be made in the body in sufficient quantities to meet physiological needs. We must obtain them from the foods we consume, such as dairy products, meat, eggs, soy, and vegetables. Nonessential amino acids can be made in the body. However, under certain circumstances, nonessential amino acids that cannot be made by the body in sufficient quantity are called *conditionally essential amino acids.*
- Our DNA determines the order or sequence in which the amino acids will be linked together in a specific protein. The specific order of amino acids in a protein is part of what determines the shape of the protein, which in turn dictates its function. Proteins form a three-dimensional shape that is unique for each protein.
- A protein's structure and function can be changed by heat, acid, enzymes, agitation, or alcohol in a process called *denaturation*. For example, stomach acid denatures the protein we eat during digestion.
- Proteins serve many important functions in the body, including growth, maintenance, repair, fluid balance, acid–base balance, immune function, enzymes, hormones, transport, and energy.
- All of the essential amino acids must be present in adequate amounts for protein synthesis to occur or cells will not be replaced as they die off.
- A high-quality protein, also called a complete protein, is a protein that provides all of the essential amino acids in the amount that the body needs and is easy to digest and absorb. Animal proteins, such as those found in meats and dairy products, and the vegetable protein in soy are examples of foods containing complete protein; they are considered highly digestible because the human body can absorb almost 90 percent of them.
- Foods that do not contain all of the essential amino acids are called *incomplete proteins*. Examples of incomplete proteins include legumes, grains, and vegetables. These foods, when combined with other incomplete proteins, can make a complete protein.
- Recent studies have suggested that a variety of health benefits are associated with consuming soy and soy products because of the phytoestrogens they contain.
- Most Americans consume more protein than they need and therefore supplements are not necessary. Many vegetarians in America consume sufficient protein levels, however, vegans may have marginal protein intakes. Therefore, vegetarian/vegan diets should be carefully balanced to include sufficient protein.
- Although supplements can contribute to meeting daily protein requirements, they are not superior to food sources of protein and generally not needed.
- The DRI for protein is 0.8 g per kilogram of body weight of high-quality protein for men and women. This accounts for about 10 percent of the total Calories for the day. Endurance athletes should consume 1.2–1.4 g per kilogram, and resistance athletes should consume 1.2–1.7 g per kilogram. However, most athletes already consume more protein than is recommended and therefore do not have to increase their intake.
- There are several types of vegetarians. Although health benefits result from consuming a balanced diet rich in plant foods, some potential health risks are associated with a vegetarian diet that is poorly planned and too restrictive. The greatest risk is that of imbalance or nutritional deficiency.

- PEM occurs when a person does not consume adequate amounts of protein and Calories. Infrequently, individuals may consume diets that are restrictive in protein, but provide adequate Calories. The two categories of PEM are kwashiorkor (due to inadequate protein intake), and marasmus (due to inadequate energy and protein intake).
- Although several studies have suggested potential health risks associated with a high-protein diet, not enough evidence exists to conclude that consuming more than the recommended amount is as harmful as was once thought. However, over consuming protein can lead to nutritional imbalances.

KEY TERMS

ACID-BASE BALANCE The mechanisms the body uses to keep its fluids close to neutral pH (i.e., neither basic nor acidic) so that the body can function normally.

ALBUMIN A protein that constitutes 60 percent of the body's *plasma* (the watery part of blood) proteins. Among albumin's many functions, it transports drugs and thyroid hormones and carries fatty acids from adipose tissue to the muscle cells for use as energy.

AMINO ACIDS The building blocks of protein. They contain nitrogen and link together to form proteins.

COMPLEMENTARY PROTEINS Two or more foods whose amino acid content, when combined, provides all of the essential amino acids.

COMPLETE PROTEIN A protein that provides all of the essential amino acids in the amount that the body needs and is easy to digest and absorb. Also called a *high-quality protein.*

CONDITIONALLY ESSENTIAL AMINO ACIDS Nonessential amino acids that under certain circumstances cannot be made in sufficient quantity by the body and therefore must be consumed in the diet.

DEAMINATION This process removes the amine group from amino acids.

DENATURATION A process in which a protein's structure and function are changed by heat, acid, enzymes, agitation, or alcohol.

ESSENTIAL AMINO ACIDS Amino acids that cannot be made in the body, so we must obtain them from the food we eat.

HEMOGLOBIN A protein contained in the red blood cells that carries oxygen throughout the body.

HIGH-QUALITY PROTEIN A protein that provides all of the essential amino acids in the amount that the body needs and is easy to digest and absorb. Also called a *complete protein.*

INCOMPLETE PROTEINS Foods that do not contain all of the essential amino acids in the amount needed by the body. They include fruits, legumes, grains, and vegetables.

KWASHIORKOR A form of PEM characterized by a swollen appearance, especially in the abdomen. Historically, kwashiorkor was thought to be caused by a lack of protein, but in fact there may be other contributors to its development.

LACTO-OVO VEGETARIANS People who consume eggs and dairy products, but no meat or seafood.

LACTO-VEGETARIANS People who consume milk and dairy products, such as cheese and yogurt, but avoid eggs, seafood, and meat.

LIMITING AMINO ACID An essential amino acid that is not present in sufficient amounts through dietary protein.

MACROBIOTIC VEGETARIANS People who consume mostly whole grains, especially brown rice, in their diets along with vegetables, soy, legumes, fruits, and sometimes whitefish.

MARASMUS A form of PEM characterized by emaciation, or a skeletal appearance due to inadequate intake of both protein and Calories.

NEGATIVE NITROGEN BALANCE A situation in which protein intake is less than what is needed or the body is breaking down more protein than it is producing, such as during a time of illness or injury.

NONESSENTIAL AMINO ACIDS Amino acids that can be made in the body by transferring the amine group, or nitrogen, from an essential amino acid to another compound containing a carbon, an acid group, a hydrogen, and an R group.

PEPTIDE BONDS Bonds that link amino acids together to make proteins. The bond is formed between the acid group of one amino acid and the amine group of another.

PH A numerical scale that measures and reflects acid–base balance.

POSITIVE NITROGEN BALANCE A situation in which protein intake exceeds what is excreted, such as during periods of growth, recovery from illness, and pregnancy.

PROTEIN BREAKDOWN A process in which proteins in the body are broken down into individual amino acids.

PROTEIN ENERGY MALNUTRITION (PEM) A disorder that occurs when a person does not consume adequate amounts of protein, Calories, or both.

PROTEIN SYNTHESIS A process in which amino acids are linked together using peptide bonds to make proteins.

SEMIVEGETARIANS (OR FLEXITARIANS) People who occasionally eat meat and seafood, yet predominately practice a vegetarian diet.

SICKLE-CELL ANEMIA A form of anemia that occurs when a person inherits two abnormal genes (one from each parent) that causes an incorrect amino acid to be incorporated in the sequence for the protein hemoglobin. The change in the amino acid causes the shape of the protein to change leading to the cell being more sickle shaped rather than disc shaped. The sickle-shaped cells do not allow for complete bonding of hemoglobin and oxygen and can easily stick together.

TRANSAMINATION Transference of the amine group (the nitrogen-containing part) from one molecule to another to make an amino acid.

VEGAN A person who eats only plant food and does not eat anything produced from animals. Also referred to as a *strict vegetarian*.

VEGETARIANS People who do not consume animal flesh but may eat eggs and dairy products.

REFERENCES

Craig WJ, Mangels AR. (2009) Position of the American Dietetic Association: vegetarian diets. *J Am Diet Assoc* 109:1266–1282.

Smith MI, Yatsunenko T, Manary MJ, Trehan I, Mkakosya R, Cheng J, et al. (2013) Gut microbiomes of Malawian twin pairs discordant for kwashiorkor. *Science* 339:548–554.

UNICEF-WHO-The World Bank Joint Child Malnutrition Estimates, 2012.

Watford M, Wu G. (2011) Protein. *Adv Nutr* 2:62–63.

Wu G. (2013) *Amino Acids: Biochemistry and Nutrition.* Boca Raton, FL: CRC Press.

Digestion and Absorption - The Link Between Food and Energy

Feature: Alcohol

Thus far we have discussed food in terms of what we put on our plates and, ultimately, in our mouths. We have not discussed what happens to the food once we can no longer see it. We must keep in mind that eating is only the initial step in generating energy for our body's use. Food that was on our plate needs to be digested into smaller components so that we can absorb its nutrients. After consumption, the next step in the process of converting food to energy is a complex series of chemical reactions and interactions combined with muscular movements that break down the food into smaller compounds. This process is called **digestion.** We must then move the smaller products of digestion across the lining of the intestinal tract and into our bodies, which is called **absorption.** Once absorbed into our bodies and transported into cells, these components have to be converted into **adenosine triphosphate (ATP),** a fuel source for the body. Multiple organs and several steps are involved in these

digestion

The first step in the process of converting food to energy; it is a complex series of chemical reactions and interactions combined with muscular movements that break the food down into smaller compounds.

absorption

The movement of the smaller products of digestion across the lining of the intestinal tract, into our bodies, and ultimately into our cells.

adenosine triphosphate (ATP)

A high-energy molecule that can be broken down to a usable form of energy.

complex processes. This chapter will give you an overview and understanding of these processes.

THE ORGANS AND THE FUNCTIONS OF DIGESTION

gastrointestinal (GI) tract
A series of organs with many complex outer layers of muscles and an inner mucosal layer of glands and absorptive cells.

Digestion occurs in the digestive or **gastrointestinal (GI) tract.** The GI tract consists of a series of organs with many complex outer layers of muscles (see Figure 6.1) and an inner mucosal layer of glands and absorptive cells. It starts with the mouth and ends with the anus. When food is in the digestive tract, it is still not "inside" the body. As noted earlier, before it can provide energy it must go through a series of steps that begin in the GI tract (Figure 6.2 and Table 6.1).

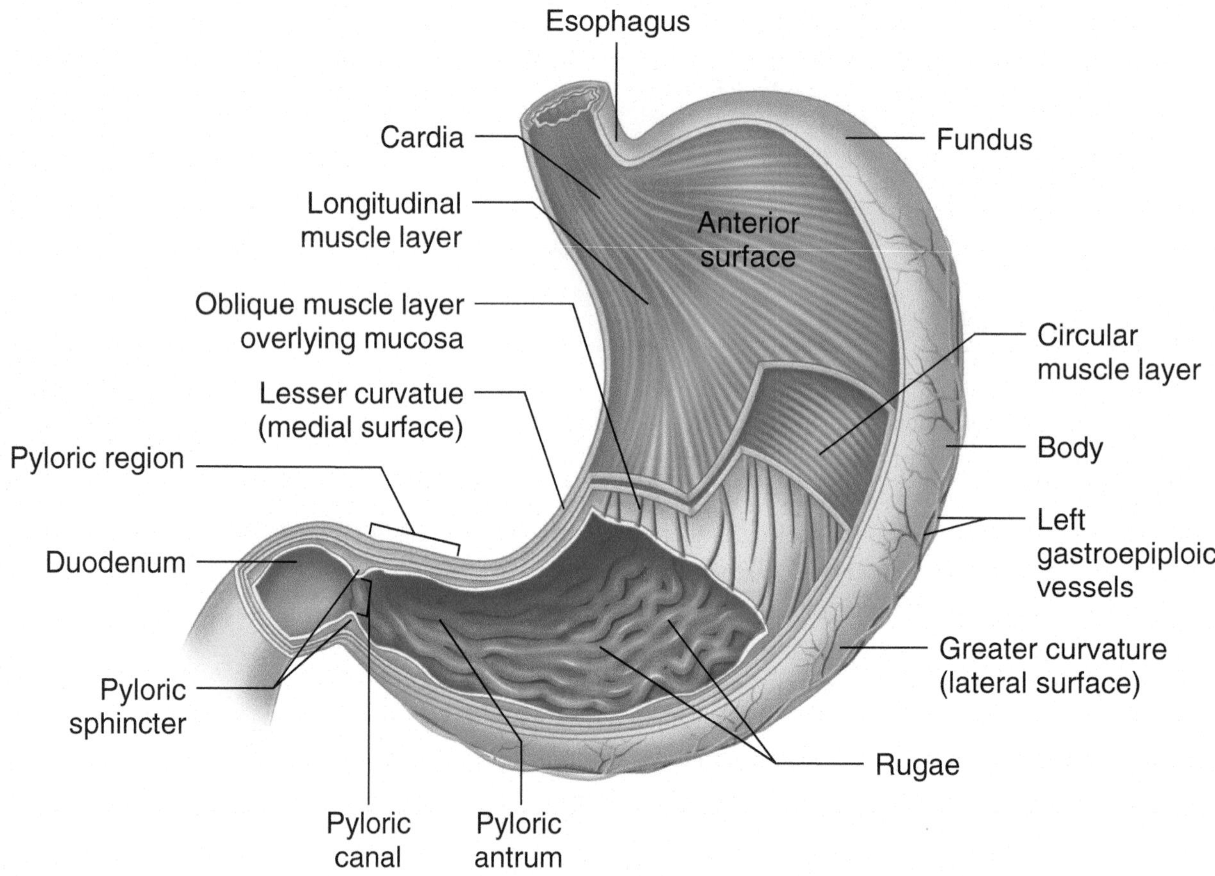

FIGURE 6.1
The GI tract has many complex outer layers of muscle and an inner mucosal

TABLE 6.1 Role of Each Organ in Digestion and Absorption

What It Is	What It Does
Mouth	Mechanically digests food by chewing and grinding; begins chemical digestion of carbohydrates with salivary amylase
Esophagus	Moves food from the mouth to the stomach
Stomach	Mechanically digests food by churning and mixing; releases hydrochloric acid (HCl) to denature proteins; begins chemical digestion of proteins with pepsin
Small intestine	Primary site of digestion; releases enzymes; completes chemical digestion of carbohydrates, fats, and proteins; is the primary site of absorption
Large intestine	Absorbs water; prepares indigestible wastes (feces) for defecation
Rectum	Temporarily stores feces
Anus	Eliminates feces from the body
Accessory Organs	
Tongue	Helps mix food with saliva; assists in swallowing; provides the sense of taste; helps with the initial swallowing process
Salivary glands	Produce saliva, which contains the enzyme salivary amylase that starts digestion of carbohydrates
Liver	Produces bile, which emulsifies fats; receives nutrients after absorption; major site for metabolism
Gallbladder	Stores bile, then releases it into the small intestine for emulsification of fats
Pancreas	Produces digestive enzymes that are released into the small intestine, where they help digest carbohydrates, fats, and protein

The main functions of the GI tract are to take in food, transport it, and secrete substances that help break it into smaller compounds so that they can be absorbed. The period of time it takes food to travel the length of the digestive tract is called **transit time**, and it depends on several factors. See the Myths and Legends feature for more information.

transit time
The period of time it takes food to travel the length of the digestive tract.

Myths & LEGENDS

IF YOU SWALLOW CHEWING GUM, WILL IT STAY IN YOUR STOMACH FOR 7 YEARS?

How long does food take to get "from one end to the other" of your digestive tract? The time varies widely from person to person and depends a lot on what you eat. Meals high in fat and/or protein take longer than those higher in carbohydrates, especially those high in fiber. The rate of passage through the GI tract is also influenced by the amount of fluid you drink. Of course, different health conditions influence transit time. If you have diarrhea, food moves through more quickly. On average, for a healthy adult, it takes anywhere from 12 to 40 hours from the time food is eaten until the undigested components and waste materials exit the body as feces. People who have a bowel movement immediately after a meal are not excreting what they just ate. Instead, the food they have just eaten has stimulated **peristalsis**, a muscular movement that propels food through the digestive tract. Therefore, if you swallow chewing gum, the powerful movements of peristalsis move it through the GI tract and it will be excreted normally with the remainder of the fecal waste.

peristalsis
A muscular movement that propels food through the digestive tract.

Digestion occurs through a combination of mechanical and chemical processes. The mechanical process involves chewing, mixing, and peristalsis. The chemical process involves mixing the food with the various secretions and enzymes of the GI tract that help break the larger compounds into smaller forms that can be absorbed. In addition, the digestive tract moves undigested or unabsorbed substances through its length and, ultimately, to elimination by defecation.

APPLICATION TIP

Many people think they are constipated if they do not have a bowel movement every day. However, constipation is defined as fewer than three bowel movements a week. It is not wise to correct the problem by taking laxatives or over-the-counter medicines. The best ways to prevent or correct constipation are to consume a high fiber diet, drink plenty of water, and participate in regular physical activity.

If the sphincters keep food from going in the wrong direction, then what happens when you throw up?

The digestive tract, as shown in Figure 6.2, is made up of several organs, including the mouth, esophagus, stomach, small intestine, large intestine, and the rectum. Other organs such as the salivary glands, liver, the pancreas, and the gallbladder assist these organs. The organs are connected by **sphincters**, which are circular muscles located throughout the digestive system that work like one-way doors to control the movement of its contents from one part to another. They relax to allow substances to enter and then close to keep them from moving backward. This is very important, as the contents of one organ of the digestive tract may be damaging to another area. For example, when substances from the stomach that are very acidic move back into the esophagus, a burning sensation in the chest called **heartburn** occurs. Over time this can damage the esophagus, which does not have the thick mucous lining that the stomach has to protect it from the hydrochloric acid it produces.

sphincters
Circular muscles located throughout the digestive system that work like one-way doors to control the movement of its contents from one part to another.

heartburn
A burning sensation that occurs in the chest when substances from the stomach reflux back into the esophagus

FIGURE 6.2
Chewing, digestion, and absorption involve many organs and glands.

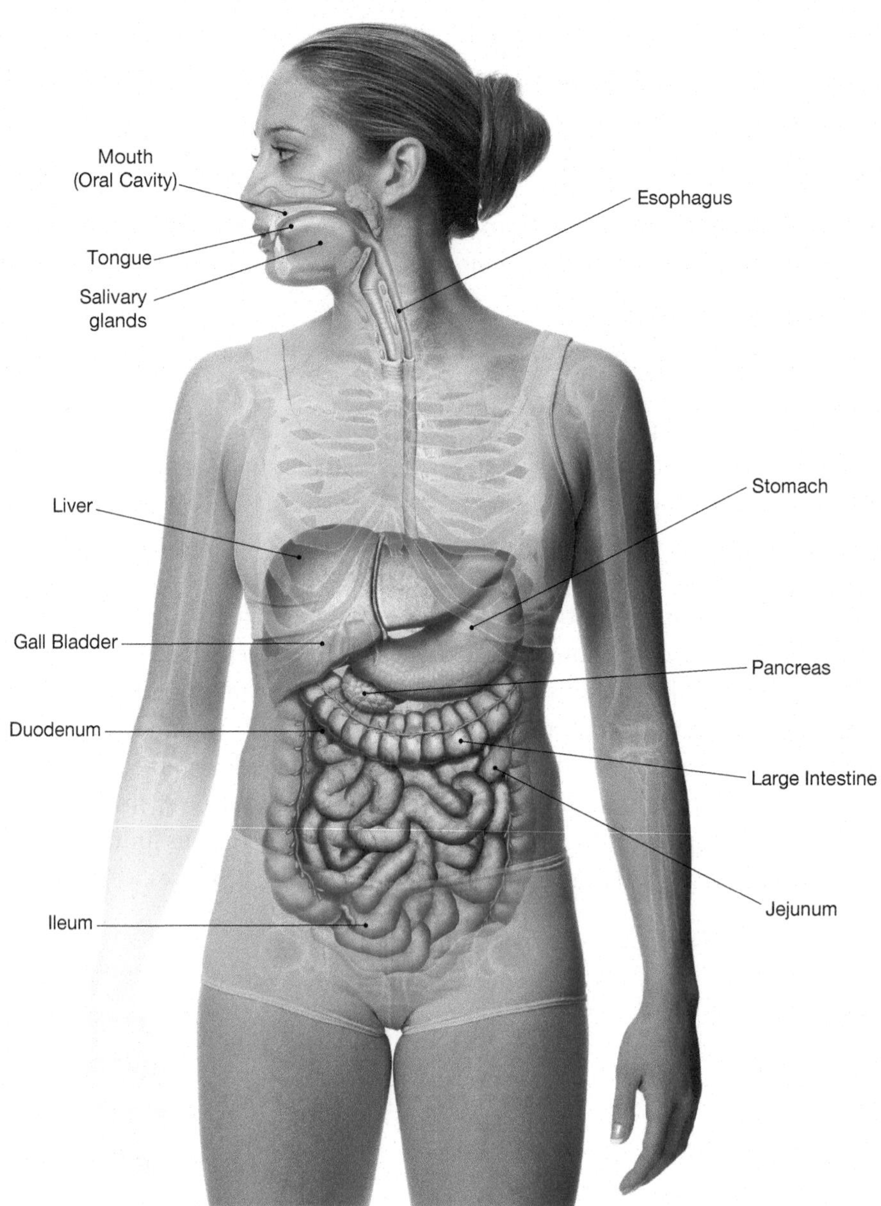

Absorption

Once the food on your plate has been broken into its smallest units, it is ready to be absorbed, or to cross the lining of the small intestine into the body, into the blood, and finally into the cells, where it can be used for energy or stored (see Figure 6.3). Water, vitamins, minerals, and small molecules such as glucose don't need to be digested or broken into smaller molecules before they are absorbed, but carbohydrates, fats, and proteins must be digested to smaller units before it is possible to absorb them.

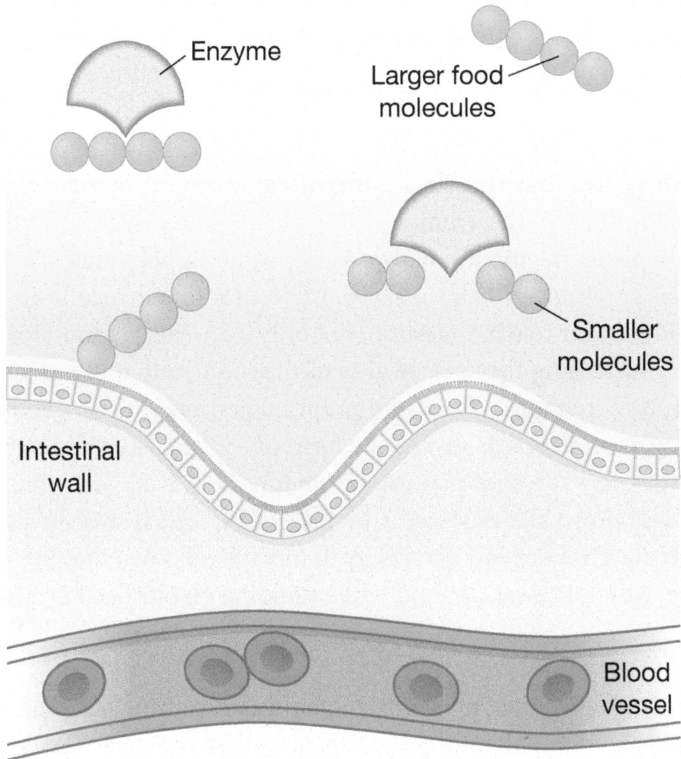

FIGURE 6.3
Large molecules must be broken into smaller ones before absorption can occur.

The Sum of the Parts

Now let's look at the different parts of the digestive tract and discuss the role they play in digestion and absorption. We will look at them in order, with the thought of the food on our plate as a mental guide to remember where we started.

The Nose

Some aspects of the digestive process begin before you even put food in your mouth. The sight, smell, and thought of food can trigger the digestive system to prepare for food. Close your eyes and imagine the smell of freshly baked chocolate chip cookies or of a pizza restaurant as you walk by. Can you almost taste the cookies and the pizza? There is a strong connection between our brain, digestive system, and sense of smell. In fact, digestive secretions and enzymes can be released in response to these smells as a way of preparing for the food that is about to be eaten. Our sense of taste and our ability to identify different flavors are strongly connected to our ability to smell these foods. In fact, taste is 80 percent smell. The rest of the sensation of taste is determined by the appearance, temperature, and texture of the food, and by the taste buds. Five primary tastes are now recognized: *salty, sweet, sour, bitter*, and *umami* (the taste associated with monosodium glutamate, or MSG).

The Mouth and Esophagus

The digestive process begins in the mouth, where food is chewed. Saliva is added during chewing to help lubricate the food, and enzymes are released to begin the digestive process. This process can start just before food enters the mouth as the release of saliva is increased by just the thought and smell of food. Again, think of the aromas of the cookies and pizza. Saliva does more than just moisten the mouth; it also digests some carbohydrates, helps inhibit bacterial growth, and helps dissolve molecules to enhance taste. Chewing plays an important role in digestion, not only by preparing food for swallowing but by increasing the surface area of the food so that digestive enzymes can reach it more rapidly to ensure proper digestion. The tongue helps with the mixing of food. Food, now in the form of a **bolus**, is swallowed in a process that involves the coordination of the tongue and 22 other muscles. The bolus travels down the esophagus by peristalsis, which was defined earlier. Peristalsis does not depend on gravity to move food down the digestive tract. Therefore, we could swallow food while standing on our head or in space.

bolus
A portion of food swallowed at one time.

The Stomach

After traveling down the esophagus, food must pass through the *lower esophageal sphincter* and into the stomach (Figure 6.4). The stomach is a J-shaped sac that mixes and liquefies food into a substance called **chyme.**

chyme
The substance that results after the stomach mixes and liquefies food.

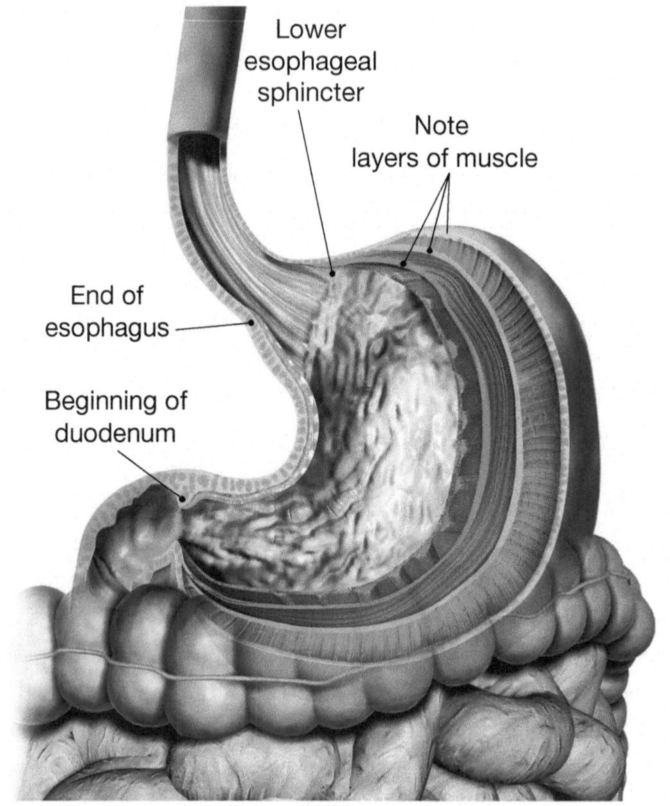

FIGURE 6.4
The stomach starts where the esophagus terminates at the lower esophageal sphincter and ends at the beginning of the duodenum. It consists of three parts, and it has several layers of muscles that help generate the churning and mixing motion.

The stomach's volume varies depending on the person but on average it holds about a liter after a normal meal. But because it has the capacity to expand, it can hold up to about 4 L when full. Once food enters the stomach, the cells of the stomach start producing gastric juice, which is composed of water, **hydrochloric acid (HCl)**, mucus, pepsinogen, gastric lipase, the hormone gastrin, and intrinsic factor. Hydrochloric acid is secreted to begin the breakdown of protein through a process called *denaturation.* As you recall from Chapter 5, denaturation is the unraveling of proteins from their three-dimensional shape, which changes their function. In addition to breaking down dietary protein, hydrochloric acid also denatures protein in potentially harmful bacteria that are often present in food.

hydrochloric acid (HCl)
A substance secreted in the stomach to denature protein.

The digestion that occurs in the stomach converts food into chyme. The stomach contains several layers of muscles running in different directions that allow it to churn and mix the chyme with the secretions while pushing it down toward the small intestine. These secretions, which include mucus, play a very important role in digestion. Mucus protects the stomach from the acid and the digestive enzymes it contains. Without mucus the stomach can be damaged, as when a person develops a stomach ulcer. The stomach secretions and their roles are listed in Table 6.2.

TABLE 6.2 The Secretions of the Stomach

What It Is	What It Does	Why It Is Important
Mucus	Protects the lining of the stomach from HCl	Without it, the stomach would be damaged by HCl and pepsin
Hydrochloric acid (HCl)	Denatures proteins; liquefies foods; activates the enzymes pepsin and lingual lipase; helps prepare iron for absorption	It helps neutralize bacteria and assists in digestion of proteins
Intrinsic factor	Is essential for the absorption of vitamin B_{12}	You need vitamin B12 to prevent a form of anemia called *pernicious anemia*
Pepsinogen	Is a proenzyme (inactive) that is converted to an active form called pepsin by stomach acid	It aids in protein digestion by breaking protein into shorter chains
Hormones (20 different chemical messengers)	Control movement of the stomach and secretion of HCl; communicate with the pancreas, liver, gallbladder, small intestine, and the rest of the body	Hormones regulate digestive processes and ensure that the right enzyme is released at the right time

Nutrition &
DISEASE

ulcer

Also called a peptic ulcer; an erosion that occurs in the lining of the stomach or the upper part of the small intestine.

Helicobacter pylori or *H. pylori*

A bacterium that can invade the stomach lining and cause peptic ulcers.

STOMACH ULCERS

An **ulcer**, also called a peptic ulcer, is an erosion that occurs in the lining of the stomach or the upper part of the small intestine. Stomach ulcers were once thought to be caused by stress and/or eating spicy food. However, we now know that 9 of 10 stomach ulcers are caused by a bacterium called ***Helicobacter pylori*** or ***H. pylori*** that is resistant to stomach acid. Half of the world's population has an *H. pylori* infection, and an estimated 30% of people in North America have it. *H. pylori* invades the protective mucus lining of the stomach and therefore allows the wall of the stomach to become damaged. Most people know they have an ulcer because of frequent and severe stomachaches. However, some individuals may have no symptoms.

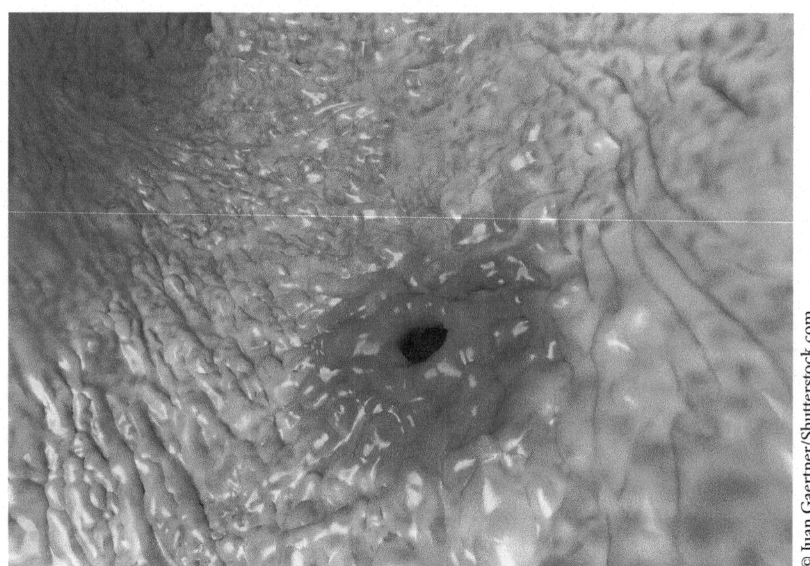

An ulcer is an erosion that occurs on the lining of the stomach or the upper part of the small intestine. Ninety percent of stomach ulcers are caused by a bacterium called *H. pylori*.

H. pylori is most likely spread from person to person through oral-oral or fecal-oral exposure. Infection may sometimes result from ingestion of food or water contaminated by fecal matter, such as the contaminated water supplies in some developing countries. Fortunately, *H. pylori* is easily treated with antibiotics. While *H. pylori* infection is the most common cause of ulcers, ulcers can also be caused by regular use of aspirin or ibuprofen, excessive consumption of alcohol, and smoking.

As the chyme reaches the end of the stomach, it must then pass through the *pyloric sphincter* into the small intestine. The stomach squirts a small amount, about 3 mL (~ 2/3 of a teaspoon), of chyme at a time into the small intestine to allow the highly acidic liquid to be neutralized. The contents typically empty completely within 4 hours of having finished a meal.

The time it takes for a meal to completely empty from the stomach varies based on the contents of the meal. For example, a high-fat meal of steak and French fries can take as long as 6 hours; and a lower-fat meal such as pasta and vegetables with no meat or sauce may only take 3 or 4 hours. Similarly, the consistency of the meal affects the rate of emptying, with liquids emptying more quickly than solid food. Therefore, if you drink a protein shake it may empty more quickly than a protein bar of similar nutrient content. Not much absorption takes place in the stomach. In fact, only aspirin, some fat-soluble drugs, the mineral copper, and a small amount of alcohol are absorbed in the stomach.

Why do I feel full for so long after I eat a steak, but feel hungry again soon after eating pasta?

The Small Intestine

Most digestion and absorption occurs in the small intestine (Figure 6.5). It is about 20' long when stretched and is divided into three sections: the **duodenum**, the **jejunum**, and the **ileum**. Of these three sections, the jejunum is where most digestion and absorption occurs. The small intestine is designed to maximize contact with nutrients so that the body can absorb as many of the

duodenum
The top part of the small intestine. It is about 25 cm long and starts at the pyloric sphincter.

jejunum
The middle part of the small intestine; the site where most absorption occurs.

ileum
The bottom part of the small intestine.

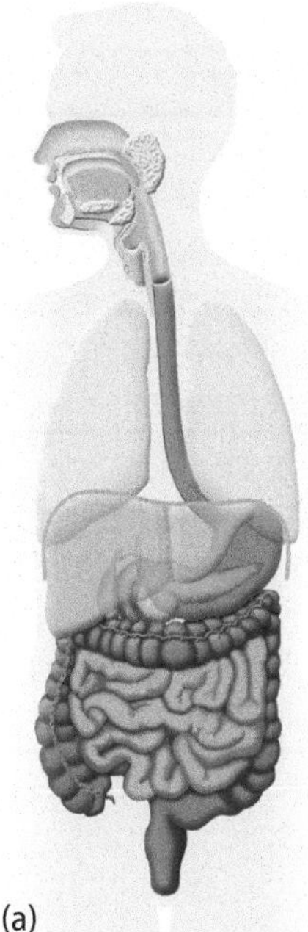

(a)

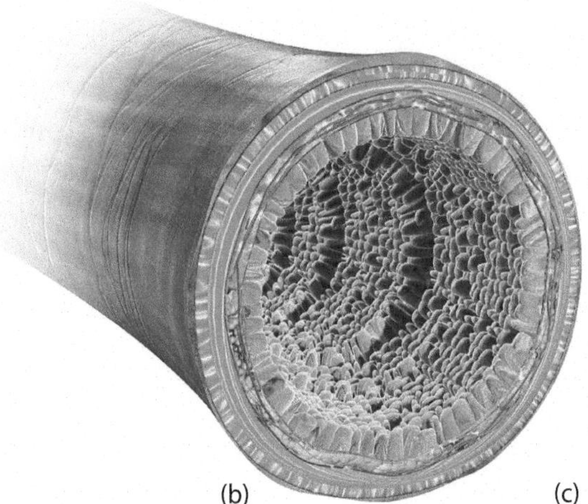

(b)

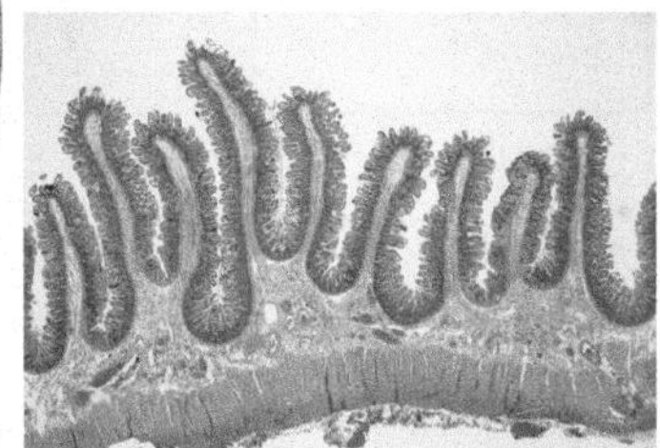

(c)

FIGURE 6.5
The small intestine is where most absorption occurs. It is divided into three sections: the duodenum, the jejunum, and the ileum. (b) The fingerlike projections of the small intestine, called the villi, enhance its surface area, which maximizes absorption into the capillaries that line it. (c) Close-up views of the villi, microvilli, and the veins, arteries, and capillaries.

villi

Fingerlike projections in the small intestine that increase the surface area to maximize absorption.

microvilli

Tiny hairlike projections extending from the villi into the inside of the small intestine to assist absorption and secrete digestive enzymes.

alkaline bicarbonate (bicarb)

A substance released from the pancreas into the small intestine to neutralize the acidic contents from the stomach.

gallbladder

An accessory organ for digestion that stores and releases bile.

bile

A substance made in the liver; it is stored in the gallbladder and released into the small intestine to help with fat digestion.

nutrients as possible; it folds back and forth several times. This results in huge surface area that is further increased by fingerlike projections called **villi.** Tiny hairlike projections, called **microvilli,** extend from the villi into the interior of the small intestine. The cells lining the villi and microvilli secrete digestive enzymes to facilitate digestion and are responsible for nutrient absorption.

Immediately upon entering the top of the small intestine, the acidic chyme from your stomach is neutralized by **alkaline bicarbonate (bicarb).** Bicarb is released from the pancreas to protect the lining of the small intestine. The pancreas also releases enzymes into the duodenum that help break down carbohydrates, fats, and proteins. The **gallbladder** releases **bile** into the duodenum. Bile is made in the liver and stored in the gallbladder; it assists in the digestion of fat. Bile contains water, cholesterol, fats, bile salts, proteins, and bilirubin. Bilirubin gives bile and feces a light brown/dark yellow color. If the bile contains too much cholesterol, bile salts, or bilirubin, it can sometimes harden into what are called gallstones (See Table 6.3).

The villi are absorptive cells that are lined with tiny blood vessels called *capillaries*. The capillaries "pick up" water-soluble nutrients once they are absorbed to carry them to the liver. The large vessels of the lymph system transport most fat-soluble molecules into the blood via two ducts in vessels in the neck. Fat-soluble molecules, therefore, bypass the liver and are available to the cells of the body without first being metabolized by the liver.

TABLE 6.3 Diseases and Syndromes of the Digestive Tract

What It Is	What It Does	What Causes It	How To Treat It
Constipation	Makes having a bowel movement difficult (fewer than three times per week)	Low fiber; not enough exercise; medication; dehydration; ignoring the urge to defecate; disease	Try to eat 25 g of fiber per day; limit high fat foods; drink plenty of fluids; exercise; can use stool softeners to ease elimination; however, consult with a physician first
Diarrhea	Produces loose, watery stools occurring more than three times per day	Bacterial or viral infections from contaminated food or water; food intolerances; medication; disease	Prevent dehydration; avoid dairy, high-fat, and high-sugar foods; take medication if symptoms are prolonged or severe; and if more than 2–3 days consult a physician
Heartburn/ gastroesophageal reflux disease (GERD)	Produces pain in the chest when stomach acid refluxes back into the esophagus	Being overweight; pregnancy; hiatal hernia (part of the stomach pushing on the esophagus); diet	Limit foods that increase symptoms (spicy foods, high-fat foods, alcohol); lose weight; consult physician who may prescribe antacids, or acid-pump inhibitors

What It Is	What It Does	What Causes It	How To Treat It
Lactose intolerance	Inability to break down lactose (the sugar found in dairy products) because of a lack of the enzyme lactase	Genetic ethnicity (African Americans and Asians are more likely than Caucasians to have this condition); surgery; medication	Limit intake of dairy products not treated to remove lactose; use lactase pills
Irritable bowel syndrome	Affects the large intestine and leads to cramping, diarrhea, and constipation	Overly sensitive muscles and nerves of the large intestine that may react more to stress or certain foods	Increase fiber in the diet; eat small, frequent meals; consume probiotics; avoid foods that aggravate the condition; medications can be prescribed based on the most troublesome symptom
Ulcerative colitis	Chronically inflames the large intestine (in the manner of an ulceration)	Heredity and an autoimmune disorder	Eat plenty of omega-3 fatty acid containing foods such as salmon; during flare-ups, decrease consumption of foods that aggravate the condition, such as grain products, spicy foods, alcohol, and dairy products; medical therapies include corticosteroids, immunomodulators, antibiotics and biologic therapies
Crohn's disease	Inflames the small and/or large intestine	Heredity and an autoimmune disorder	Eat plenty of omega-3 fatty acid containing foods such as salmon; during flare-ups, decrease consumption of foods that aggravate the condition such as grain products, spicy foods, alcohol, and dairy products; medical therapies include corticosteroids, immunomodulators, antibiotics and biologic therapies
Gallstones	Stones form from bile in the gallbladder that can cause pain, jaundice, and pancreatitis	High cholesterol; obesity; fasting; more frequent in women than men	Surgically remove gallbladder
Celiac disease	Causes malabsorption	Autoimmune response to gluten	100% avoidance of gluten

Almost all of the nutrients consumed are absorbed in the small intestine. Most minerals, except for the electrolytes (see Chapter 7 for more information on electrolytes) are absorbed in the duodenum and upper part of the jejunum. The jejunum is where the majority of carbohydrates, amino acids, and water-soluble vitamins are absorbed. Lipids and fat-soluble vitamins are absorbed throughout the ileum, with vitamin B_{12} being absorbed in the terminal segment of the ileum. By the time digestive contents reach the end of the ileum and beginning of the colon, it includes some water, some indigestible items, plant fibers such as cellulose and pectin, and bacteria.

Some individuals have part of the lower small intestine removed because of disease or trauma, which causes short bowel syndrome. Because fat-soluble vitamins and vitamin B_{12} are absorbed in the ileum, if this segment of the small intestine is removed, then it will be difficult to meet the requirements for fat-soluble vitamins and B_{12}. As a result, individuals with short bowel syndrome must take a fat-soluble vitamin supplement formulated to increase water solubility. They also must take intramuscular shots of vitamin B_{12} because they are unable to absorb this vitamin at all. Individuals with Crohn's disease and other inflammatory bowel diseases suffer from frequent bouts of diarrhea. Remember that with diarrhea, food moves quickly through the intestine; therefore, they also can have impaired ability to absorb many nutrients, including protein, fat, carbohydrates, water, vitamins, and minerals.

The Large Intestine

Once digestive contents reach the large intestine very little break down occurs, but the contents may take as long as 12–24 hours to travel through it. The large intestine is about 5' long, and its main roles in the digestive process are propulsion of contents, absorption of sodium and water, and preparation of waste for defecation. In addition, the large intestine contains a very large number of bacteria (~ 100 trillion).

The bacterial flora in your intestine is actually a good thing, and you don't need or want to get rid of them. Therefore, colon cleansing is not a good idea. (We'll discuss this further in the What's Hot feature that follows.) The bacteria metabolize any nutrients that remain in the large intestine. For example, they break down plant fibers such as cellulose and pectin to *short-chain fatty acids* and gases. So, yes, the downside is that they produce gas or *flatus*. However, short-chain fatty acids are important for the health of the lining of your large intestine.

In addition to breaking down certain plant fibers, the intestinal bacteria also produce vitamin K and some B vitamins. Vitamin K is necessary for our blood to clot properly. Without the bacteria to produce it, we would most likely not get enough vitamin K from the foods we eat. Much like stomach health is compromised by an infection of *H. pylori*, the colon can be inhabited by pathogenic bacteria that cause diarrhea and other diseases.

What's HOT

COLON CLEANSING: BEWARE

As we've periodically described, misinformation on health and nutrition abounds. Perhaps none is greater than that associated with the process of "colon cleansing." Many products and many ways to supposedly cleanse the colon are available. Some natural-health practitioners claim that "death begins in the colon" and that "90 percent of all diseases are caused by improperly working bowels." The practices they recommend include fasting, periodic cleansing of the intestines, and colonic irrigation.

The websites, companies, and "natural health" groups that encourage this cleansing have several things in common (besides a high price for their services). They all suggest that as a modern society we are living with dangerous compounds in our colons as a result of a diet high in processed foods. Our food choices have resulted in hard, crusty, clogging black matter lining the walls of our colons. So all you have to do is buy their product and any health ailment imaginable is cured. Sounds too good to be true? Well, it is, and more.

Colon cleansing may be extremely harmful to your health, leading to the very problems it supposedly treats. The Mayo Clinic, the National Institutes of Health, and most reputable health professionals strongly recommend against colon cleansing of any type. Doing so, particularly on a regular basis, can lead to fluid and electrolyte loss, a decrease in the ability of the colon to contract and regulate bowel movements, disruption of the bacteria in your colon, heart problems, and, in the case of those already weakened (such as the elderly and those with HIV), death. In addition, many of the more invasive colon cleansing techniques can result in bowel perforation, bacterial infection, and severe illness. If you think you have an intestinal problem, see a doctor. The physician may prescribe medications or refer you to a Registered Dietitian to alter your diet to encourage the "friendly colon bacteria" that are necessary for optimal health and bowel function. An example of one of the dietary changes you can make is to include food sources of probiotics into your daily food intake. See the feature, To Supplement or Not for more information.

Gross! I have bacteria in my intestine? Is that what you are getting rid of when you do colon cleansing?

APPLICATION TIP

The average person passes gas 6 to 20 times per day. If you are passing more gas than that, examine your diet. Although foods that cause gas in some people may not cause it in others, foods that are typically high in carbohydrates and fiber are more likely to cause gas than those high in protein or fat. Common gas-producing foods include beans, vegetables, fruits, wheat, and corn. You can decrease gas production by reducing your intake of uncooked beans, as cooking helps reduce the indigestible carbohydrates in the beans. If you still have problems it is possible to use enzyme tablets (e.g., containing lactase, alpha-galactosidase) that help digest the fermentable carbohydrates that contribute to gas production.

To Supplement OR NOT

PROBIOTICS AND PREBIOTICS

Probiotics are food products and supplements that contain live bacteria (microbiota) that may improve the health and microbial balance of the intestines. These substances have gained attention as functional foods (foods that provide health benefits beyond their original nutritional function) because of the now recognized link between the microbiota in the gut and our health. It is because of this health link that probiotic products have been widely used in other parts of the world for years. Although probiotic products contain several different kinds of bacteria, most contain *Lactobacillus* and *Bifidobacterium*. The most common sources of probiotic bacteria are yogurt and other fermented milk products such as kefir. However, they can be found in a variety of products.

Prebiotics are typically carbohydrate sources that evade digestion in the small intestine and reach the colon where they can be used to feed the bacteria. By doing so, prebiotics are able to support the growth and activity of desirable bacterial populations, which may improve intestinal and systemic health.

Synbiotics are combinations of probiotics and prebiotics that are designed so that the prebiotics specifically support the growth of the probiotic cultures they contain.

© Christopher Gardiner/Shutterstock.com

probiotics
Live microbial food products and supplements that improve the health and microbial balance of the intestine; most contain Lactobacillus and Bifidobacterium.

prebiotics
Indigestible carbohydrate sources that reach the colon and support the growth and activity of desirable bacteria.

synbiotics
Combinations of prebiotics and probiotics designed to support health.

Foods containing probiotics such as the yogurt pictured here may have health benefits, particularly for symptoms associated with gastrointestinal problems.

Limited evidence suggests that probiotics may have many beneficial effects on our health, including the following:

- Decreased symptoms associated with many gastrointestinal diseases:
    - Irritable bowel syndrome
    - Inflammatory bowel disease
    - Ulcerative colitis
    - Crohn's disease
- Decreased diarrhea, especially in children
- Decreased diarrhea as a result of taking antibiotics
- Decreased growth of the bacterium *H. pylori*, which is responsible for many stomach ulcers and other problems
- Decreased constipation
- Increased intestinal motility
- Enhanced immune response
- Increased absorption of nutrients such as folate, niacin, vitamin B_{12}, and riboflavin
- Increased ability of people who are lactose intolerant to consume some dairy products

In addition, preliminary evidence from animal studies and human studies suggests the following benefits:

- Decreased incidence of colon cancer
- Decreased allergies, especially in children
- Decreased incidence of bacterial vaginosis in women
- Decreased total cholesterol and triglycerides
- Improved HDL/LDL ratio
- Decreased blood pressure

Scientists have yet to determine exactly how probiotics produce these benefits, and they are not yet certain exactly how much we need to consume. The benefits achieved may be due to a synergistic effect of the probiotics with other compounds in the food. Look for the words *live cultures* or *active cultures* on packages of yogurt and other products, as not all of them contain active bacterial cultures. *Lactobacillus bulgaricus, Streptococcus thermophilus,* and *Lactobacillus acidophilus* are the most common cultures added to yogurt. A lot of research still needs to be done before an exact recommendation can be made for consumption of probiotics. In the meantime, including yogurt and other sources of probiotics in a balanced diet is your best bet for experiencing the potential health benefits.

BEFORE YOU GO ON...

1. Describe how food that is in the digestive tract ultimately gets into the body.
2. Once digested food is absorbed, it travels through the blood to the cells, where it is converted to a usable form of energy. What is this energy source called?
3. List the main functions of the GI tract.
4. Where does most food absorption take place?

DIGESTION AND ABSORPTION: FROM TONGUE TO BLOOD

Now that we have had a brief discussion of the major organs and processes involved in digestion and absorption, let's get back to considering the food on our plate. Let's suppose that in an effort to maintain a healthy diet and to meet current dietary recommendations, we have eaten a balanced meal. What happens to that meal once we have chewed and swallowed it?

Carbohydrates

The enzymatic breakdown of carbohydrates begins as soon as you put food in your mouth. The enzyme called *salivary amylase* in the saliva breaks carbohydrates into smaller glucose links. To experience amylase at work, slowly chew a piece of bread; you'll notice that it gets sweeter the longer it stays in your mouth. This is because the smaller links of glucose are sweeter than the larger links that make up the bread. Amylase continues to work until it reaches the stomach where hydrochloric acid inactivates it. Once food is in the stomach, no further carbohydrate break down occurs. Therefore, when carbohydrates are consumed alone, particularly those low in fiber, they empty quickly from the stomach. (See Chapter 3 for a review of carbohydrates.)

Once they enter the small intestine, carbohydrates are broken down by an enzyme released from the pancreas called *pancreatic amylase* into smaller chains of glucose. Next, several enzymes from the lining of the small intestine continue the breakdown. An example of one of these enzymes is *lactase,* the enzyme that breaks down the disaccharide lactose found in milk. People who lack this enzyme have *lactose intolerance* and may experience gas, cramps, and diarrhea if they consume too much lactose. An enzyme called *sucrase* breaks down the disaccharide sucrose, and the enzyme *maltase* breaks down the disaccharide maltose. See Table 6.3 for more information on lactose intolerance and other problems associated with the digestive tract.

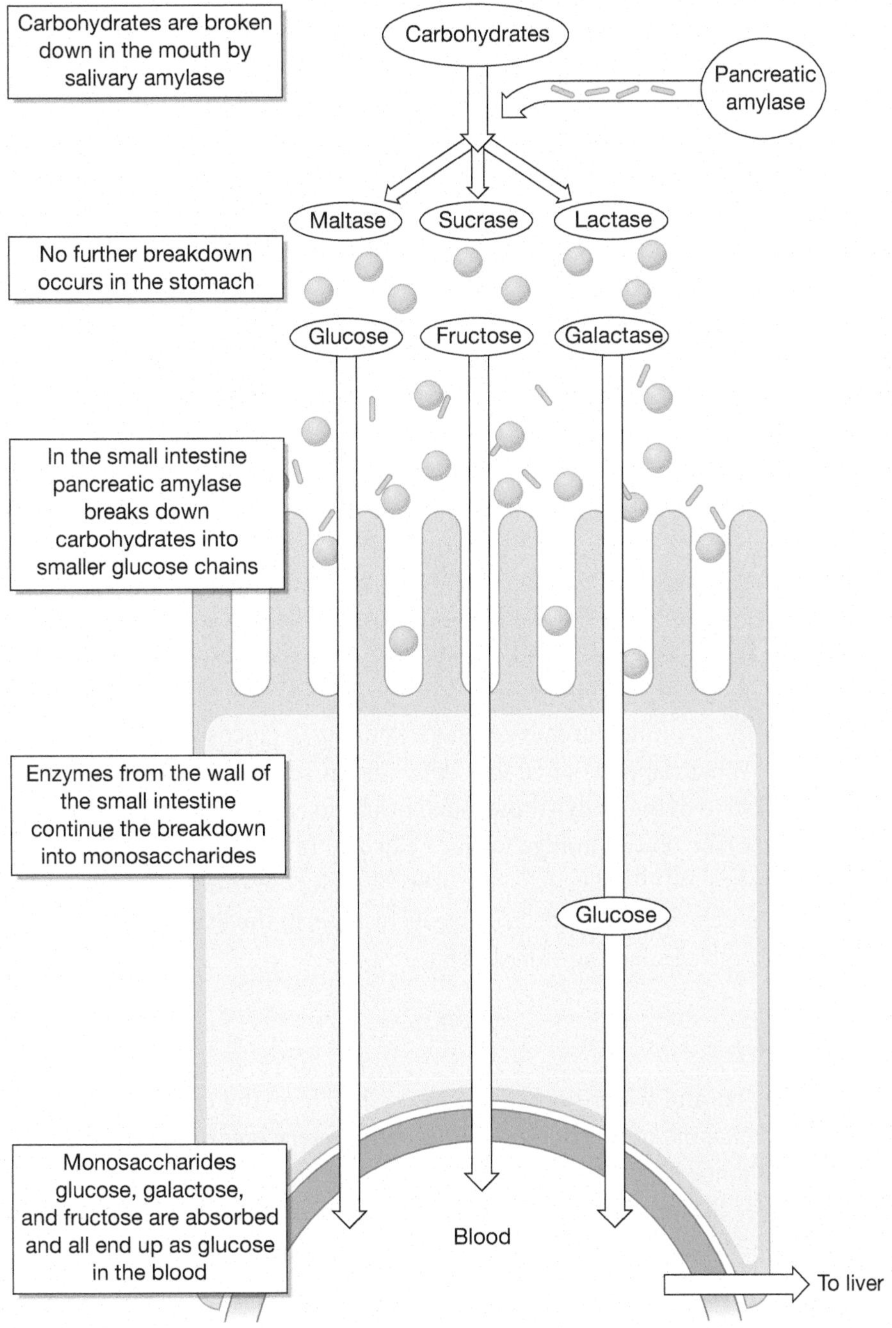

Carbohydrates are broken down in the mouth by salivary amylase
Carbohydrates
Pancreatic amylase
Maltase
Sucrase
Lactase
No further breakdown occurs in the stomach
Glucose
Fructose
Galactase
In the small intestine pancreatic amylase breaks down carbohydrates into smaller glucose chains
Enzymes from the wall of the small intestine continue the breakdown into monosaccharides
Glucose
Monosaccharides glucose, galactose, and fructose are absorbed and all end up as glucose in the blood
Blood
To liver

FIGURE 6.6
Carbohydrates are broken down into monosaccharides before they are absorbed.

© gosphotodesign/Shutterstock.com

The end products of carbohydrate digestion are single sugars *(monosaccharides)* ready for absorption (see Figure 6.6). The single sugars glucose and galactose are transported across the wall of the small intestine. Fructose is absorbed by a different process but is ultimately made into glucose in the liver. So, eventually, all of the starches and sugars end up as glucose when they reach the blood. What happens after that depends on several factors, mainly the nutritional state of the body—how much has been eaten and whether the glycogen stores (the body's storage form of glucose) in the muscles and liver are full. Depending on these factors, the absorbed glucose can be used to maintain blood glucose, used to replace glycogen stores in the liver and muscle, or made into triglycerides and stored as fat.

Fats

Put simply, fat and water don't easily mix. Therefore, the digestion, absorption, and transport of fats in a predominantly watery environment present a unique challenge for the body. Although chewing and combining with watery secretions of the stomach are important to increase the surface area of fats, most enzymatic digestion and absorption occur in the small intestine.

When chyme enters the duodenum, bile released from the gallbladder acts on large fat molecules in a process called *emulsification* and mixes them in the watery environment of the small intestine. This mixing allows the enzyme *pancreatic lipase* to break down the fat molecules into smaller molecules—fatty acids and glycerol (Figure 6.7). Some free fatty acids enter the capillaries, but the larger triglycerides must enter the larger vessels of the lymphatic system. Remember that fat and water don't mix. Therefore, before the larger triglycerides can be transported through the body they are formed into special carriers, called *chylomicrons,* that enable the fat to travel in the watery environment of the blood. The triglycerides can then pass into the cells of the body to be broken down and used for energy or stored as fat. After the fat is absorbed, the bile continues through the intestine and most is reabsorbed in the ileum or bound by fiber and excreted. (See Chapter 4 for a review of fats.)

© bonchan/Shutterstock.com

Protein

Enzymatic digestion of protein begins in the stomach when *pepsinogen* is released from the wall of the stomach and converted to its active form, *pepsin,* when exposed to stomach acid. The enzyme pepsin then breaks the peptide bonds in proteins into smaller units. Stomach acid also assists in the digestive process by denaturing the proteins, or unraveling their three-dimensional shape. The smaller units then empty into the small intestine, where enzymes secreted by the pancreas break them into still smaller units. Then, enzymes from the wall of the small intestine act on the peptides to break off one amino acid at a time, and the individual amino acids are absorbed (Figure 6.9). The amino acids then travel through the blood to the liver. Once in the liver, their fate depends on several circumstances, such as how much carbohydrate you have consumed. The absorbed amino acids can be used to make proteins, or, if you have not consumed enough carbohydrates, the amino acids can be used to make glucose. Any amino acids in excess of the body's needs can be made into fat and stored. (See Chapter 5 for a review of proteins.)

Alcohol

Some alcohol is absorbed right away in the stomach, especially when it is consumed without food, but most is absorbed in the small intestine. It travels to the liver, where it is detoxified. Alcohol will be discussed later in this chapter.

FIGURE 6.7
Fats are broken down into fatty acids and glycerol before they are absorbed.

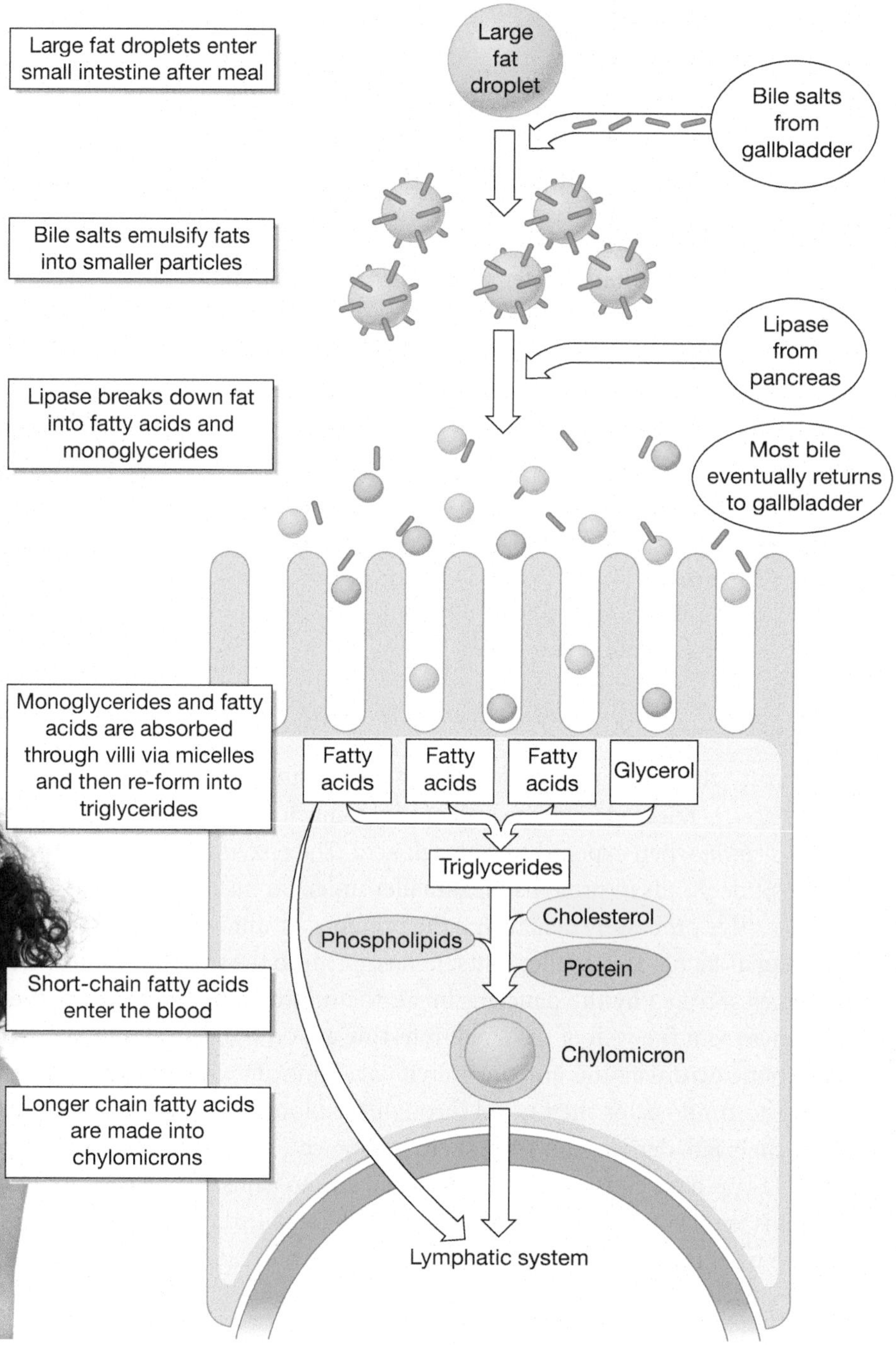

Vitamins and Minerals

Vitamins are absorbed unchanged from the form in which they are found in the food we eat. Absorption of fat-soluble vitamins (vitamins A, D, E, and K) is facilitated by the presence of lipid in our diets. Just like larger lipid molecules, fat-soluble vitamins must be transported by chylomicrons in lymph before entering the bloodstream. Therefore, if you do not consume fat with them, they

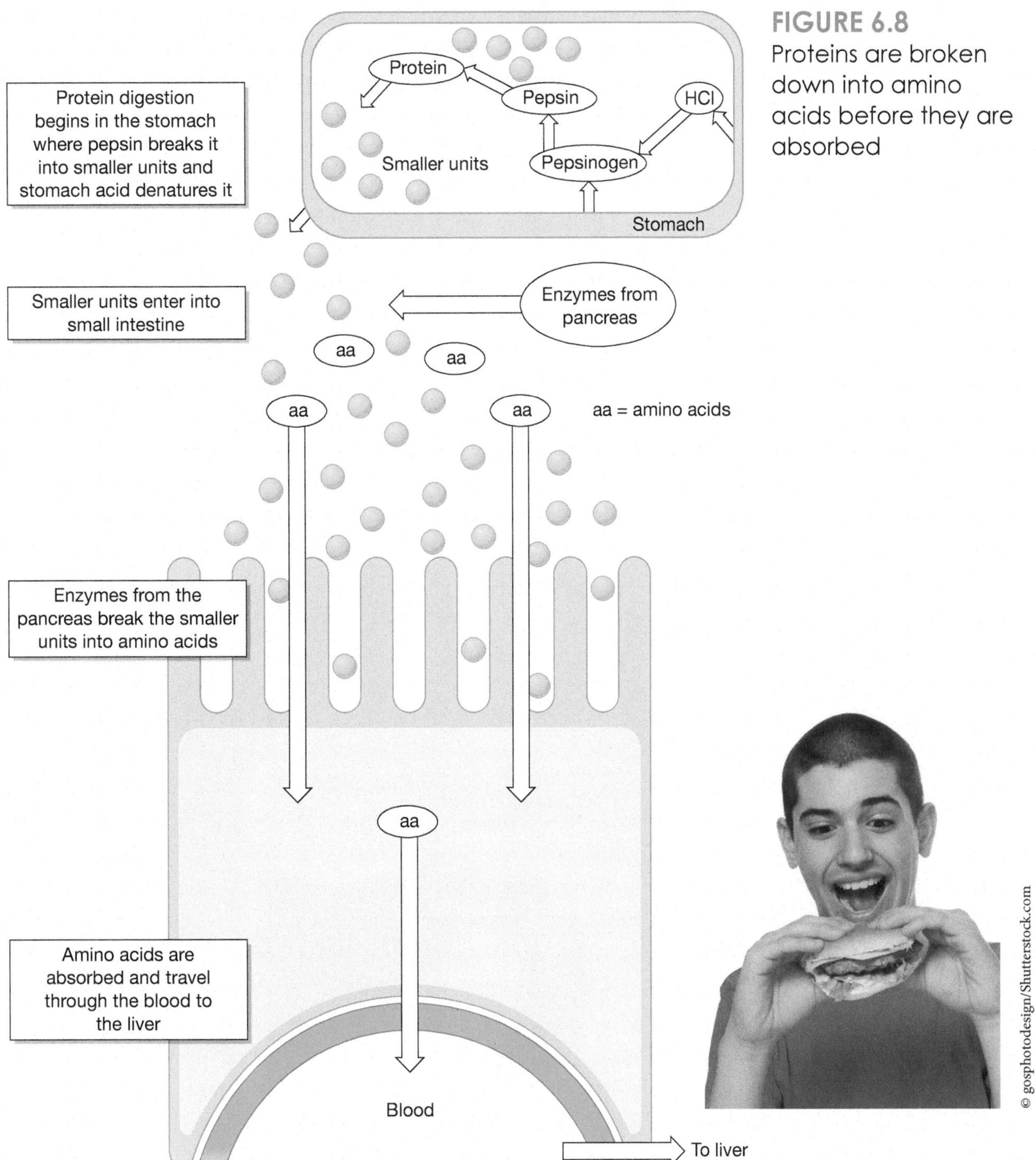
Protein digestion begins in the stomach where pepsin breaks it into smaller units and stomach acid denatures it
Protein
Pepsin
HCl
Smaller units
Pepsinogen
Stomach
Smaller units enter into small intestine
Enzymes from pancreas
aa
aa
aa
aa
aa = amino acids
Enzymes from the pancreas break the smaller units into amino acids
aa
Amino acids are absorbed and travel through the blood to the liver
Blood
To liver

FIGURE 6.8
Proteins are broken down into amino acids before they are absorbed

are not absorbed but are excreted in the feces. The water-soluble vitamins can be absorbed without food and are freely transported in the blood. Absorption of vitamin B_{12} requires *intrinsic factor,* which is released in the stomach. Once it binds with this, it is absorbed in the ileum.

Minerals are absorbed all along the small intestine. Sodium is best absorbed with glucose and amino acids, which is why you will often find these nutrients together in sports drinks. Some nutrients such as iron and calcium are absorbed based on need, so that when your body's stores are low you absorb more from the food you eat. (See Chapters 7 and 8 for a thorough discussion of vitamins and minerals.)

Water

You may think that the water we are referring to is the water you drink. However, the digestive system contains water from the food we eat, the fluids we drink, our saliva, and all the secretions of digestion. Most is absorbed in the small intestine; a small amount is absorbed in the large intestine, and the rest is excreted in the feces. Water is absorbed by following sodium and other nutrients such as glucose across the wall of the intestine.

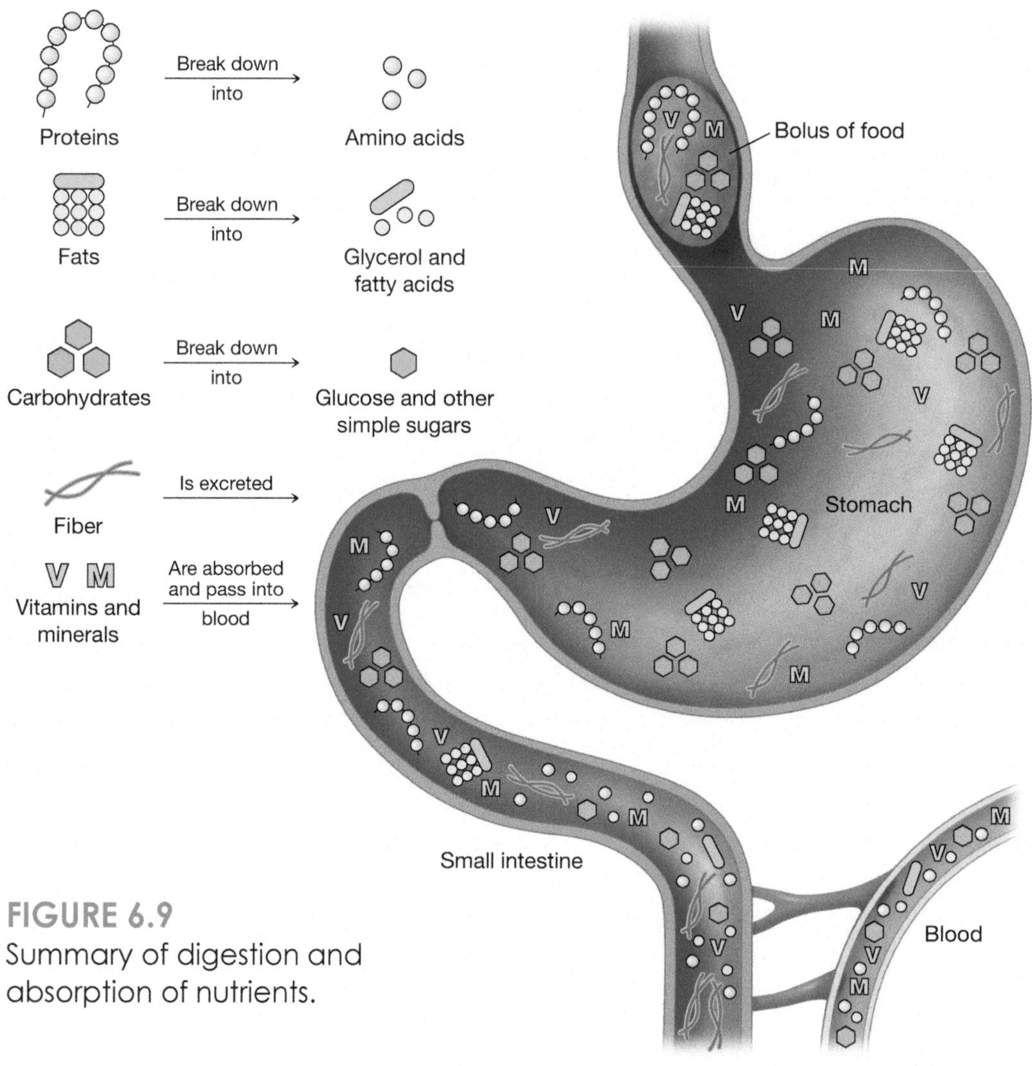

FIGURE 6.9
Summary of digestion and absorption of nutrients.

The information within this section of the chapter demonstrates the various processes that must be used in order to digest and absorb the nutrients we require to live. An overview of digestion and absorption of all nutrients is provided in Figure 6.9. It demonstrates where each class of nutrient is digested, absorbed, and the form in which it is transported in the blood.

BEFORE YOU GO ON...

1. Carbohydrates, fats, proteins, vitamins, and minerals must be broken down into what form before they can be absorbed?
2. Identify at least three diseases of the GI tract and describe their causes.
3. What process helps the body mix fat in its watery environment?
4. What nutrients help enhance water absorption?

ALCOHOL - EASILY ABSORBED BUT NOT A NUTRIENT

Do you think alcohol is a nutrient? As you may remember, nutrients promote growth and maintenance of your body and organs. Alcohol does not promote growth or maintenance, nor does it have any critical function in the body, therefore, it is not a nutrient. However, because alcohol does provide Calories, we discuss alcohol in this text. Alcohol provides approximately 7 kcal per gram—less than the 9 kcal per gram for fat, but greater than the 4 kcal per gram for carbohydrate or protein.

Consuming alcohol as an energy source is *not* recommended. Overconsumption often leads to many health problems, as well as social and mental debilitation. Chronic drinkers have many nutritional problems, as alcohol intake can depress appetite, interfere with nutrient absorption, and increase excretion of several vitamins and minerals. Once the body absorbs alcohol, it can also interfere with the ability of tissues and cells to fully utilize nutrients.

Some consumers measure the quality of a beverage by the proof.

Alcohol Consumption and Its Influence on Blood Alcohol Concentration (BAC)

Blood alcohol concentration (BAC), sometimes referred to as *blood alcohol level (BAL)*, is simply the percentage of alcohol present in your blood. A blood alcohol concentration of 0.1 percent means that there is one part alcohol for 1,000 parts blood in the body (one divided by 1,000 = 0.001 or 0.1 percent). The higher the level, the more negative physiological effects on the body. How much a single drink will raise your blood alcohol level depends on several factors, such as whether you are male or female, how much you weigh, whether you have eaten or have consumed the alcohol on an empty stomach, and your physical condition. The U.S. Department of Health and Human Services defines "one drink" as 1.5 oz. of 80-proof liquor, 12 oz. of regular beer, or 5 oz. of table wine. Based on these definitions, each drink contains roughly the same amount of alcohol (about 0.5 oz.). That is why there is such a difference in serving sizes for these various drinks (Figure 6.10). Table 6.4 provides a description of the changes in behavior and physical skills that occur with different levels of BAC.

blood alcohol concentration (BAC)

The percentage of alcohol present in the blood. It is used to measure the amount of intake and to predict correlations with physiological effects.

FIGURE 6.10

Each of these servings of alcoholic beverages is equivalent to one drink and contains approximately the same amount of alcohol.

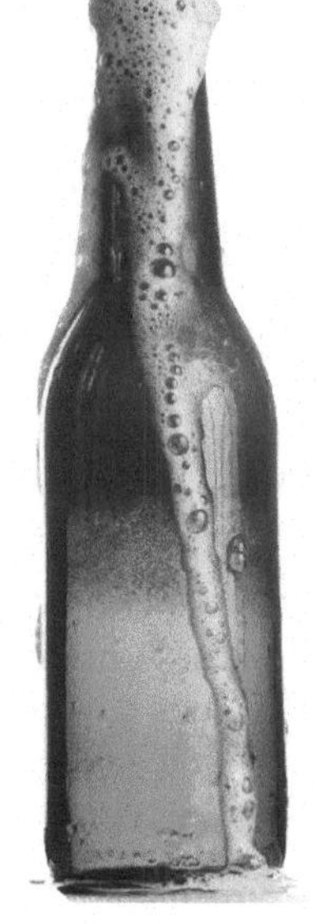

APPLICATION TIP

Never consume alcohol on an empty stomach. A full stomach significantly slows absorption of alcohol into the blood.

All states have cracked down on both under age drinking, and drinking and driving under the influence of alcohol. Sobriety tests such as this one are common.

© Lisa F. Young/Shutterstock.com

TABLE 6.4 Blood Alcohol Level and Behavioral Effects

BAC%	Behavioral Effect(s)
0.02–0.03	Alcohol starts to relax the drinker.
0.04	Often drinkers at this stage are relaxed, happier, and chatty.
0.05	Judgment, attention, control, and physical skills begin to diminish. Decision-making ability (such as whether to drive) is impaired, as are sensory-motor skills.
0.08	All states recognize this as the legal point of intoxication. Driving skills and coordination are impaired.
0.10–0.125	Several effects are likely at this point, such as balance, vision, speech, and control problems. Reaction time increases.
0.12–0.15	Peripheral vision is diminished, so less detail is visible. Balance and coordination are problematic. A sense of tiredness, displays of unstable emotions, diminished perception, memory, and comprehension are seen at this level. A person may vomit if not accustomed to drinking or if this BAC level has been reached too quickly.
0.18–0.25	Often, the drinker is in a state of apathy and lethargy and is less likely to feel pain. Vision is certainly diminished in the areas of color, form, motion, and dimensions. Drinkers are intense with emotions, confused, dizzy, and disoriented. Walking is often difficult or impossible as muscle coordination is diminished and speech is slurred.
0.25–0.30	Drinkers may lose consciousness during this stage. They have almost completely lost motor functions, have little response to stimuli, can't stand or walk, and experience vomiting and incontinence.
0.30–0.50	Once the BAC reaches 0.45 percent, alcohol poisoning is almost always fatal, and death may occur at a level as low as 0.37 percent. Unconsciousness, diminished or absent reflexes, lower than normal body temperature, circulatory and respiratory problems, and incontinence commonly occur.

Alcohol Poisoning—The Ultimate Danger

Numerous deaths have resulted from excessive alcohol intake among college students. A well-known case involved a 19-year-old Colorado State University student, Samantha Spady, who died of alcohol poisoning, with a BAC of 0.436 percent. Investigation by the coroner's office suggested that she had consumed alcohol over an 11-hour period and ended the day at a fraternity house, where she consumed significant additional amounts of alcohol while playing drinking games. She had consumed an amount of alcohol equivalent to 30–40 12-oz. beers.

Do you think a cup of black coffee will sober you up? Think again!

Myths & LEGENDS

WILL DRINKING COFFEE MAKE YOU SOBER?

Many people think that you can "sober up" someone who is under the influence of alcohol by having him or her consume coffee, particularly black coffee. Many drinking establishments and other places where alcohol is served keep coffee on hand for this purpose. The active ingredient in coffee, caffeine, does stimulate the central nervous system. But does giving black coffee to an intoxicated person really help? Actually, neither coffee nor caffeine is helpful in sobering an individual who is under the influence of alcohol. Consuming coffee when inebriated may actually increase alcohol's adverse effects and make it harder for the person to recognize that they are drunk. Only time will help, as most alcohol is broken down gradually in the liver or expelled from the body through respiration (breathing) or urine. The bottom line on consuming coffee when intoxicated is that you will be a wide-awake drunk!

Levels of Consumption

Aren't there different definitions of what's moderate?

In establishing relative alcohol consumption, the Centers for Disease Control (CDC) uses the following definitions for moderate, heavy, and binge drinking:

- Moderate use is up to one drink per day for women and up to two drinks per day for men.
- Heavy use is 15 drinks or more a week for men and 8 drinks or more a week for women.
- Binge drinking usually corresponds to more than five drinks on a single occasion for men or more than four drinks on a single occasion for women, generally within about 2 hours.

Edyta Pawlowska/Shutterstock.com

A national epidemic? Concerns over an increase in the number of college students who consume alcohol several times a week have recently received considerable attention in the media and from college administrators. Does this scene look familiar to you? What would you suggest is the best way to address the problems of excessive alcohol consumption and binge drinking?

Based on these definitions, of those who do drink, 7 percent are heavy drinkers, 22 percent are moderate drinkers, and 71 percent are light drinkers.

BEFORE YOU GO ON...

1. In the United States, what is the typical range of alcohol content in beer, expressed as a percentage?
2. What does BAC stand for, and what do the numbers mean?
3. Give the CDC's definitions of moderate, heavy, and binge drinking.

DIGESTION AND METABOLISM

Alcohol, Absorption, and the Liver

Alcohol is absorbed by the gastrointestinal tract, primarily in the small intestine, and then enters the bloodstream. In fact, the body absorbs alcohol more rapidly than nutrients. Moreover, when consumed on an empty stomach, alcohol enters the bloodstream faster than when the stomach is full.

The only organ in the body capable of metabolizing alcohol is the liver, but only 90 percent of blood alcohol is metabolized by the liver (Figure 6.11). The remaining 10 percent is eliminated through the lungs and urine.

FIGURE 6.11
Alcohol is absorbed in the stomach. From the stomach, the alcohol enters the bloodstream and then travels to the liver, where liver cells break it down. When alcohol is broken down by the liver, it is either used as a source of energy or, more likely, converted into fat.

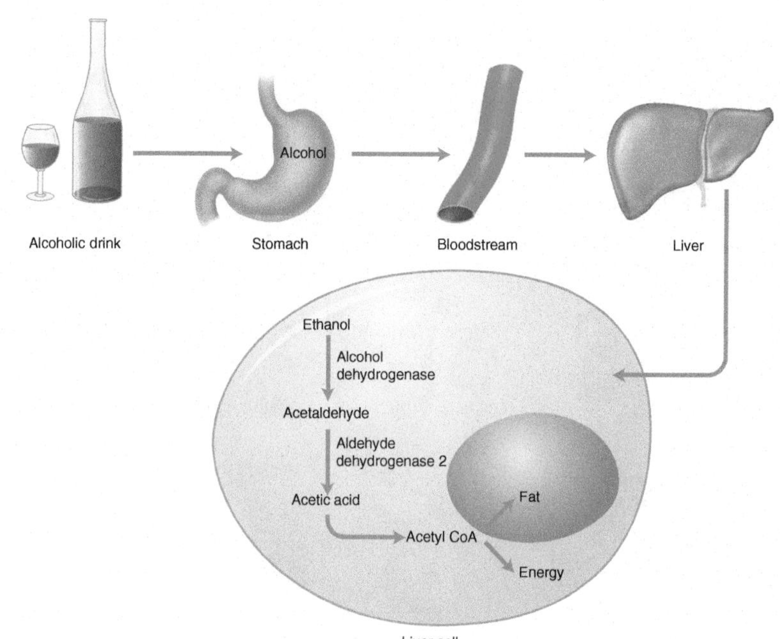

Nutrition & CULTURE

ALCOHOL AND LIVER DISEASE

Alcohol can affect many organs. As we have already observed, the central nervous system is impaired by alcohol intake. However, of the many potential health consequences of alcoholism, the most well known is its impact on the liver. Remember that alcohol goes to the liver, where it is processed, and its metabolites are toxic to cells. Three types of liver conditions/diseases may result from alcohol abuse:

1. Fatty liver
2. **Alcoholic Hepatitis**
3. **Cirrhosis**

alcoholic hepatitis
Inflammation of the liver resulting from excessive alcohol consumption over an extended period of time.

cirrhosis
A disease resulting in the hardening and scarring of the liver.

Fatty liver is simply the accumulation of fat within liver cells. For reasons other than alcohol consumption, obese people or individuals who consume too much added sugar can experience the same condition. The good thing here is that if the person stops drinking, it is reversible. This condition can lead to inflammation of the liver in the short term, but if alcohol intake continues, fatty liver disease can contribute to permanent liver damage.

Alcoholic hepatitis is an inflammation of the liver that is caused by excessive intake of alcohol over an extended period of time. Individuals with this condition can experience fluid accumulation in the abdomen, jaundice (yellowing of

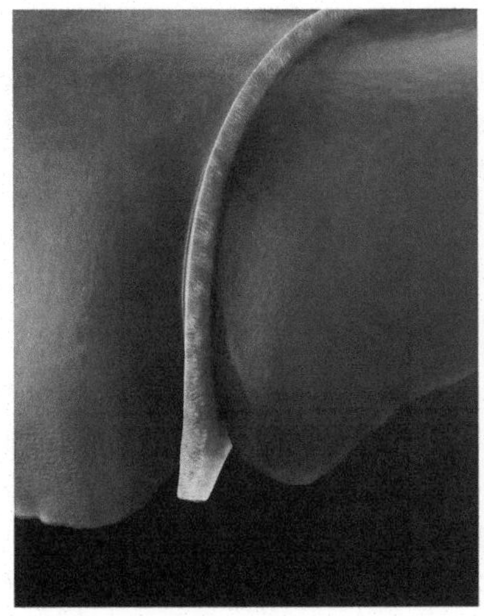

healthy

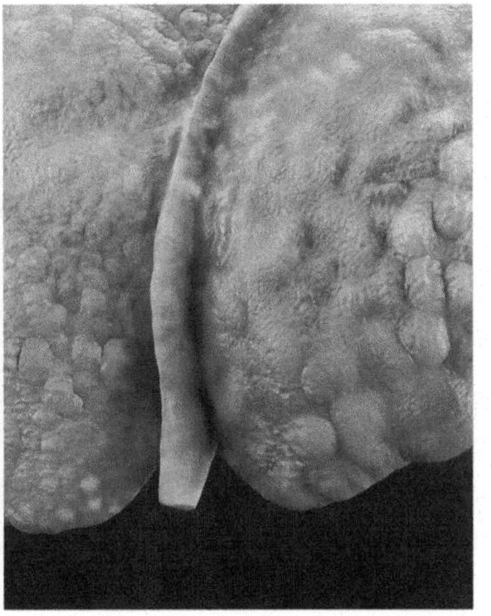

cirrhosis

© eranicle/Shutterstock.com

The effects of long-term alcohol consumption on the liver. Cirrhosis of the liver (right) may be irreversible if the damage is severe. A healthy liver is shown on the left.

the skin), and neurological problems when the condition advances and results in liver failure. Because the liver has the ability to create new cells, hepatitis is reversible if the person abstains from alcohol and consumes an adequate diet.

In cirrhosis, the liver becomes hardened and scarred. Cirrhosis is a serious, often fatal liver condition. The early stage of liver cirrhosis is reversible, but not the late stage. Ten to 15 percent of alcoholics develop liver cirrhosis by the time they die. In fact, liver cirrhosis resulting from alcohol abuse is one of the 10 leading causes of death in the United States. Women who consume the same amount of alcohol as men are even more likely to develop liver disease perhaps related to differences in how alcohol is processed between the genders.

Alcohol and the Brain

Alcohol has a profound impact on the brain's ability to function that results in behavior changes. The frontal lobe, the area of the brain that handles reasoning and judgment, is compromised. One of the prime effects of alcohol is that the brain's normal processes to inhibit risky behaviors are decreased. People often appear more relaxed and say things they normally would not without alcohol. As more alcohol is consumed, other parts of the brain that control speech, vision, and muscle movement are impaired. Intoxicated people may be unable to walk and thus stagger; they slur their speech; and their eyes may not be able to focus. With higher alcohol levels in the blood and consequently in the brain, the parts of the brain that control respiration and heart contractions are impaired, and the person becomes unconscious. If too much alcohol has been consumed before becoming unconscious, death can occur. In essence, alcohol is toxic, and it causes brain cells to die. Unlike liver cells that can be replaced, brain cells are seldom regenerated, which leads to permanently impaired neurological functioning.

What's HOT

BINGE DRINKING ON COLLEGE CAMPUSES

Binge drinking has steadily increased among adolescents and young adults. As noted earlier, binge drinking usually corresponds to more than five drinks on a single occasion for men or more than four drinks on a single occasion for women, generally within about 2 hours. Today, research indicates that binge drinking may begin as early as age 12. It is higher in males than females but that is not to say that females do not do their share of binge drinking. The 18–34 age group has the highest percentage of binge drinkers, about 56 percent overall. Among college students, one study reported that half admitted having four to five drinks in one sitting within a 2-week period. Those living in fraternity or sorority houses had the largest incidence, with 86 and 80 percent, respectively, admitting to having engaged in an episode of binge drinking. The behavior is highest among whites and lowest among African Americans.

Many college students who binge drink do not realize that they are in fact binge drinking. Many actually consider themselves light to moderate drinkers. Studies also show that college students who binge drink have more difficulties in their studies and experience depression and anxiety more frequently. Binge drinkers may become abusive to others, and many sexual assaults on college campuses have been linked to this behavior. According to the National Institute of Alcohol Abuse and Alcoholism, about 1,825 deaths per year among college students can be attributed to binge drinking and the resulting behavior.

Although the effects of a hangover are not totally understood, some possibilities exist. A hangover could be partly due to the dehydration effects of alcohol. As alcohol is consumed, the brain blocks a hormone that promotes water retention by the kidneys (see Chapter 7). The hangover effect of a dry mouth and a headache is due to this dehydrating effect. Excess fluid loss via frequent urination results in a loss of potassium, magnesium, and other electrolytes The electrolyte imbalance can lead to further fluid imbalance and muscle soreness, which are common with hangovers. Rehydration will help in recovering from some of the hangover effects. One glass of water for each alcoholic beverage serving consumed is a good rule of thumb. Impurities in alcoholic beverages that are really toxins may also contribute to hangovers. Beer and red wines contain some of these toxins, which can lead to a headache. These toxins are termed congeners, which are by-products of the fermentation process.

APPLICATION TIP

Among college students, research shows that nondrinkers get better grades than drinkers, especially those who binge drink.

BEFORE YOU GO ON...

1. Name and distinguish between three diseases of the liver that can result from alcohol abuse.
2. What is the liver disease that can be caused by chronic alcohol intake and may be irreversible?
3. What are some possible causes of a hangover?

HEALTH AND ALCOHOL CONSUMPTION

A curse and a cure? We've already discussed some of the serious consequences of excess alcohol intake. Conversely, are there health benefits to *moderate* alcohol consumption? Is it the *type* of alcoholic beverage consumed that determines whether it is a curse or a cure, or the alcohol itself? As we further explore potential health risks and benefits of alcohol consumption, keep in mind that these questions are all difficult to answer with absolute certainty.

Health Risks

The negative health outcomes of excess alcohol intake definitely outweigh the benefits simply because many Americans are not moderate but heavy drinkers. For heavy drinkers, the quality of life, which we will discuss later, is compromised. Alcohol intake also has physiological consequences.

Disease Risk

Excess alcohol intake can lead to high blood pressure and weakening of the heart muscle *(cardiomyopathy)*. A number of cancers have also been linked to alcohol abuse, particularly cancers of the esophagus, mouth, throat, colon, liver, and breast. For example, women who consume more than two drinks per day have a 25 percent increased risk of developing cancer. Digestive issues as well as learning and memory problems can occur as well. As discussed earlier, the biggest health issue is to the liver, where alcohol abuse can cause inflammation (hepatitis), degeneration, and hardening or scarring (cirrhosis). An even more serious issue is the combination of alcohol consumption and cigarette smoking. This combination can increase the risk of cancer even more.

Interactions with Medications

Another negative and dangerous aspect of alcohol intake is its potential interaction with medications. Medications prescribed for depression or anxiety, painkillers, or sedatives can have an enhanced and even deadly interaction with the effects of alcohol. Alcohol and many medications may make you sleepy, and the combination of both only intensifies this effect. Combinations of drugs and alcohol are a prescription for accidents involving motor vehicles and machinery. People are more likely to fall or lose the ability to concentrate even on simple tasks. Alcohol can influence the potency of some medications and render others ineffective. Also, some drugs become toxic when alcohol is metabolized first, allowing the drugs to accumulate in the blood and tissues to dangerous levels. The National Institute on Alcohol Abuse and Alcoholism has information on common medications that can negatively interact with alcohol. This information may be found at http://pubs.niaaa.nih.gov/publications/Medicine/medicine.htm.

ALCOHOL AND PREGNANCY

Nutrition & LIFESTAGES

All alcohol intake should be avoided during pregnancy and several months before you plan to become pregnant. Alcohol intake during pregnancy can lead to a range of physical, mental and behavioral abnormalities (deviations from the norm) in the infant, which are referred to as fetal alcohol spectrum disorder (FASD). Infants who are born to mothers who consumed alcohol regularly during pregnancy may exhibit slow growth; smaller heads; irregular facial features, defective hearts and organs; mental impairment; and malformed arms, legs, and genital organs. Later in life these children tend to be hyperactive, have limited attention spans, have difficulty in reasoning, and are unable to view cause-and-effect relationships. When severe physical, mental and neurobehavioral symptoms are present, the child is diagnosed as having **fetal alcohol syndrome** or FAS (see Figure 6.12). These conditions are not reversible, as the alcohol affects the developing fetus directly. The danger from alcohol is most problematic during the first 3 months of pregnancy, and mothers are often unaware that they are pregnant when consuming alcohol during this critical time. In addition, it may not be the amount of alcohol, but the presence of any alcohol at the wrong time that matters. This means that only one drink consumed at a certain time during pregnancy can result in FASD. For some organs, the period of critical development may be only a few hours long, and alcohol intake during these few hours could cause lifelong defects in the body. Thus, FASD is the primary reason the medical community now recommends complete abstinence from alcohol during pregnancy.

fetal alcohol syndrome (FAS)
A set of birth abnormalities in babies born to mothers who consume alcohol during pregnancy, characterized by abnormal facial features, abnormal arms and legs, and lower-than-normal intelligence.

FIGURE 6.12
Fetal alcohol syndrome (FASD) has long been known to occur in pregnant mothers who consume alcohol. The effects of FASD on the facial features are not reversible, and often the child has cognitive deficits. This child has FASD and is pictured with his adoptive parents.

Nutritional Implications

People who consume alcohol in excess may develop nutritional problems. First, because alcohol contains a significant amount of Calories, the energy intake without proper caloric expenditure leads to weight gain. On the other hand, many drinkers satisfy their caloric needs at the expense of a well balanced diet. This can lead to displacement of Calories from these foods by alcohol. Alcohol has few other nutrients, and not consuming other foods with vitamins and minerals may lead to inadequate intake. Alcoholics frequently experience vitamin and mineral deficiencies because of decreased consumption of nutrient-dense foods, reduced absorption of nutrients (e.g., thiamin), and the inability to properly metabolize nutrients as a result of liver malfunction.

As discussed, alcohol is a diuretic. Water-soluble vitamins may be excreted at a greater rate through the urine. Since these vitamins are not stored in the body to any significant extent, the B vitamins (thiamin and folate in particular) and vitamin C status may be compromised in those with heavy alcohol intakes. The group of symptoms that result from the loss of these water-soluble vitamins, particularly thiamin, is called **Wernicke–Korsakoff syndrome**; these symptoms include eye muscle paralysis, loss of memory, and damaged nerves. Another vitamin that is lost with alcohol, especially in the liver, is folate. Because one of the enzymes (alcohol dehydrogenase) used to metabolize alcohol contains zinc, decreased zinc stores are common among heavy alcohol users. Potassium, magnesium, and phosphates are other nutrients lost through alcohol abuse.

Wernicke–Korsakoff syndrome

The symptoms that result from the loss of water-soluble vitamins, particularly thiamine, from excess alcohol consumption over time.

Health Benefits

Researchers have discovered some possible health benefits associated with moderate alcohol consumption (one drink per day for women and two drinks per day for men). The most consistently identified benefit of alcohol intake on human health has been associated with the heart and circulatory system. More than 100 studies have indicated that *moderate* consumption of alcohol can reduce the risk of heart attack, stroke, and peripheral vascular disease. Depending on the study, a 25–40 percent reduction in risk can be achieved, which is quite significant. This reduction applies to both men and women. Alcohol may contribute to this improvement by reducing factors that lead to blood clotting, and by increasing the protective type of cholesterol, we mentioned in Chapter 4, HDL cholesterol. We do not see this relationship or benefit in heavy drinkers; therefore, more alcohol intake is not a plus. In fact, excess alcohol intake can lead to increased blood pressure and a greater risk of cardiovascular disease.

DO YOU HAVE A PROBLEM WITH ALCOHOL?

Self-
ASSESSMENT

Various screening tools can be used to determine whether you have a problem with drinking, are an alcoholic, or are in the stages of developing the disorder. Figure 6.13 is the Alcohol Use Disorder Identification Test, one of many screening tests used by professionals in counseling.

FIGURE 6.13
Alcohol Use Disorder Identification Test (AUDIT)

1. How often do you have a drink containing alcohol?
   - ❑ Never
   - ❑ Monthly
   - ❑ 2 to 4 times a month
   - ❑ 2 to 3 times a week
   - ❑ 4 or more times a week

2. How many drinks containing alcohol do you have on a typical day when you are drinking?
   - ❑ 1 or 2
   - ❑ 3 or 4
   - ❑ 5 or 6
   - ❑ 7 to 9
   - ❑ 10 or more

3. How often do you have 6 or more drinks on one occasion?
   - ❑ Never
   - ❑ Less than monthly
   - ❑ Monthly
   - ❑ Weekly
   - ❑ Daily or almost daily

4. How often during the past year have you found that you were not able to stop drinking once you started?
   - ❑ Never
   - ❑ Less than monthly
   - ❑ Monthly
   - ❑ Weekly
   - ❑ Daily or almost daily

5. How often during the past year have you failed to do what was normally expected from you because of drinking?
   - ❑ Never
   - ❑ Less than monthly
   - ❑ Monthly
   - ❑ Weekly
   - ❑ Daily or almost daily

6. How often during the past year have you needed an alcoholic drink in the morning to get yourself going after a heavy drinking session?
   - ❑ Never
   - ❑ Less than monthly
   - ❑ Monthly
   - ❑ Weekly
   - ❑ Daily or almost daily

7. How often during the past year have you had a feeling of guilt or remorse after drinking?
   ❑ Never ❑ Weekly
   ❑ Less than monthly ❑ Daily or almost daily
   ❑ Monthly

8. How often during the past year have you been unable to remember what happened the night before because you had been drinking?
   ❑ Never ❑ Weekly
   ❑ Less than monthly ❑ Daily or almost daily
   ❑ Monthly

9. Have you or someone else been injured as a result of your drinking?
   ❑ No ❑ Yes, during the past year
   ❑ Yes, but not in the past year

10. Has a relative, friend, a doctor or other health worker been concerned about your drinking or suggested you cut down?
    ❑ No ❑ Yes, during the past year
    ❑ Yes, but not in the past year

Procedure for scoring:
Questions 1–8 are scored 0, 1, 2, 3, or 4. Questions 9 and 10 are scored 0, 2, or 4. The maximum possible score is 40. A score of 8 or more is suggestive of problem drinking.

Source: Reprinted courtesy of the World Health Organization, http://whqlibdoc.who.int/hq/2001/who_msd_msb_01.6a.pdf

Are there any health benefits from alcohol consumption?

Red Wine and Phytochemicals

Since the 1970s, there has been an increased interest in the potential health-promoting benefits of wine. Research has focused on the compounds in grapes and wine that may produce these benefits. These compounds are termed *phytochemicals* (*phyto* means "plant"), as discussed in Chapter 1. It appears that red wines have more of these phytochemicals than white wines, and research suggests that, accordingly, dark-colored wines may provide somewhat greater health benefits than their white counterparts. The primary reason for this is that red wines are made with longer contact between the juice and grape skins during fermentation. The healthy compounds are found in the grape skins and seeds, and so with extended contact with the grape juice, more of them are extracted in red wine.

Some of the phytochemicals involved in health promotion are called *polyphenols.* This class of plant chemicals protects cells against free radical damage. Two polyphenols in our food supply are **catechin** and **resveratrol**. Catechin and resveratrol are found in grapes from which wine is made, but they are present in many other foods. Therefore, it is not necessary to consume wine to derive health benefits provided by these molecules.

© Africa Studio/Shutterstock.com

Wine *may* offer some beneficial health effects—both from the alcohol and the various antioxidant chemicals found in red wines.

catechin
A polyphenol found in grapes and other plants that protects against free radical damage.

resveratrol
A polyphenol found in grapes and other plants that protects against free radical damage.

BEFORE YOU GO ON . . .

1. Which vitamins will be deficient because of excess alcohol intake, and why?
2. Explain why researchers think moderate wine consumption may provide cardiovascular health benefits.

CHAPTER SUMMARY

- When food is in the digestive tract, it is still not "inside" the body. It must be digested and absorbed from the GI tract, which runs from the mouth to the anus.
- Once digested food is absorbed, it travels through the blood to the cells, where it is converted to a usable form of energy called ATP.
- The main functions of the GI tract are to take in food, transport it, and secrete substances that help break it into smaller compounds so that they can be absorbed.
- On average, for a healthy adult, it takes anywhere from 12 to 40 hours from the time food is eaten until the undigested components and waste materials exit the body as feces.
- Digestion begins in the mouth with chewing and the mixing of food with saliva. Saliva lubricates food and contains enzymes.
- Peristalsis is a muscular movement that propels food through the digestive tract and explains why we can swallow and digest without using gravity.
- The stomach churns and mixes food with its secretions, including HCl and enzymes.
- Mucus is one of the stomach's secretions; it protects the stomach from being damaged by the acid and digestive enzymes it contains.
- The time it takes for a meal to completely empty from the stomach varies based on the contents and consistency of the meal.
- Most absorption occurs in the small intestine. The small intestine is designed to maximize contact with nutrients so that the body can absorb as many of the nutrients as possible. It folds back and forth several times and contains fingerlike projections called *villi* and *microvilli* to increase the absorptive surface area.
- The pancreas releases several enzymes for digestion and bicarbonate to help neutralize the acid contents coming from the stomach.
- Bile is synthesized in the liver and stored in the gallbladder; the gallbladder releases bile to assist with fat digestion.
- The large intestine has important bacteria that produce vitamins. It also absorbs water, sodium, and short-chain fatty acids.
- Carbohydrates, fats, and proteins must be digested into smaller units in order to be absorbed.
- Alcohol is not considered a nutrient because it does not promote growth or maintenance or have any critical function in the body. However, it does contain substantial Calories, contributing 7 kcal per gram.
- Excess alcohol intake can cause serious liver diseases such as fatty liver, hepatitis, and cirrhosis.
- Alcohol consumption during pregnancy is not recommended. A common result of alcohol intake during pregnancy is a condition called FAS, in which the baby has facial, leg, and arm abnormalities and lower-than-normal intelligence.
- Researchers increasingly think that moderate consumption of alcohol, especially in red wine, has some potential health benefits.

KEY TERMS

ABSORPTION The movement of the smaller products of digestion across the lining of the intestinal tract, into our bodies, and ultimately into our cells.

ADENOSINE TRIPHOSPHATE (ATP) A high-energy molecule that can be broken down to a usable form of energy.

ALKALINE BICARBONATE (BICARB) A substance released from the pancreas into the small intestine to neutralize the acidic contents from the stomach.

ALCOHOL DEHYDROGENASE A liver enzyme that converts ethanol into the toxic acetaldehyde.

ALCOHOLIC HEPATITIS Inflammation of the liver resulting from excessive alcohol consumption over an extended period of time.

BILE A substance made in the liver; it is stored in the gallbladder and released into the small intestine to help with fat digestion.

BLOOD ALCOHOL CONCENTRATION (BAC) The percentage of alcohol present in the blood. It is used to measure the amount of intake and to predict correlations with physiological effects.

BOLUS A portion of food swallowed at one time.

CATECHIN A polyphenol found in grapes and other plants that protects against free radical damage.

CHEMICAL ENERGY Energy contained in a molecule that has not yet been released; it is also called potential energy.

CHYME The substance that results after the stomach mixes and liquefies food.

CIRRHOSIS A disease resulting in the hardening and scarring of the liver.

DIGESTION The first step in the process of converting food to energy; it is a complex series of chemical reactions and interactions combined with muscular movements that break the food down into smaller compounds.

DIURETIC A compound that, when consumed, causes you to urinate more and can lead to dehydration.

DUODENUM The top part of the small intestine. It is about 25 cm long and starts at the pyloric sphincter.

FETAL ALCOHOL SYNDROME (FAS) A set of birth abnormalities in babies born to mothers who consume alcohol during pregnancy, characterized by abnormal facial features, abnormal arms and legs, and lower-than-normal intelligence.

GALLBLADDER An accessory organ for digestion that stores and releases bile.

GASTROINTESTINAL (GI) TRACT A series of organs with many complex outer layers of muscles and an inner mucosal layer of glands and absorptive cells.

GLYCOGEN The storage form of glucose; it is stored in the liver and the muscles.

HEARTBURN A burning sensation that occurs in the chest when substances from the stomach reflux back into the esophagus.

HELICOBACTER PYLORI OR H. PYLORI A bacterium that can invade the stomach lining and cause peptic ulcers.

HYDROCHLORIC ACID (HCL) A substance secreted in the stomach to denature protein.

ILEUM The bottom part of the small intestine.

JEJUNUM The middle part of the small intestine; the site where most absorption occurs.

MICROVILLI Tiny hairlike projections extending from the villi into the inside of the small intestine to assist absorption and secrete digestive enzymes.

PERISTALSIS A muscular movement that propels food through the digestive tract.

PREBIOTICS Indigestible carbohydrate sources that reach the colon and support the growth and activity of desirable bacteria.

PROBIOTICS Live microbial food products and supplements that improve the health and microbial balance of the intestine; most contain *Lactobacillus* and *Bifidobacterium*.

RESVERATROL A polyphenol found in grapes and other plants that protects against free radical damage.

SPHINCTERS Circular muscles located throughout the digestive system that work like one-way doors to control the movement of its contents from one part to another.

SYNBIOTICS Combinations of prebiotics and probiotics designed to support health.

TRANSIT TIME The period of time it takes food to travel the length of the digestive tract.

ULCER Also called a peptic ulcer; an erosion that occurs in the lining of the stomach or the upper part of the small intestine.

VILLI Fingerlike projections in the small intestine that increase the surface area to maximize absorption.

WERNICKE-KORSAKOFF SYNDROME The symptoms that result from the loss of water-soluble vitamins, particularly thiamine, from excess alcohol consumption over time.

REFERENCES

CDC. Binge drinking. http://www.cdc.gov/alcohol/fact-sheets/binge-drinking.htm.

Chartier, K., and R. Caetano. Ethnicity and health disparities in alcohol research. NIH, National Institute on Alcohol Abuse and Alcoholism. http://pubs.niaaa.nih.gov/publications/arh40/152-160.htm. Accessed 9/11/14.

Crohn's and Colitis Foundation of America. Crohn's treatment options. http://www.ccfa.org/what-are-crohns-and-colitis/what-is-crohns-disease/crohns-treatment-options.html.

MedicineNet.Com. Alcohol impairment chart. http://www.medicinenet.com/script/main/art.asp?articlekey=52905

Turner ND, Ritchie LE, Bresalier RS, Chapkin RS. (2013) The microbiome and colorectal neoplasia: environmental modifiers of dysbiosis. *Curr Gasteroenerol Rep* 15:346–355.

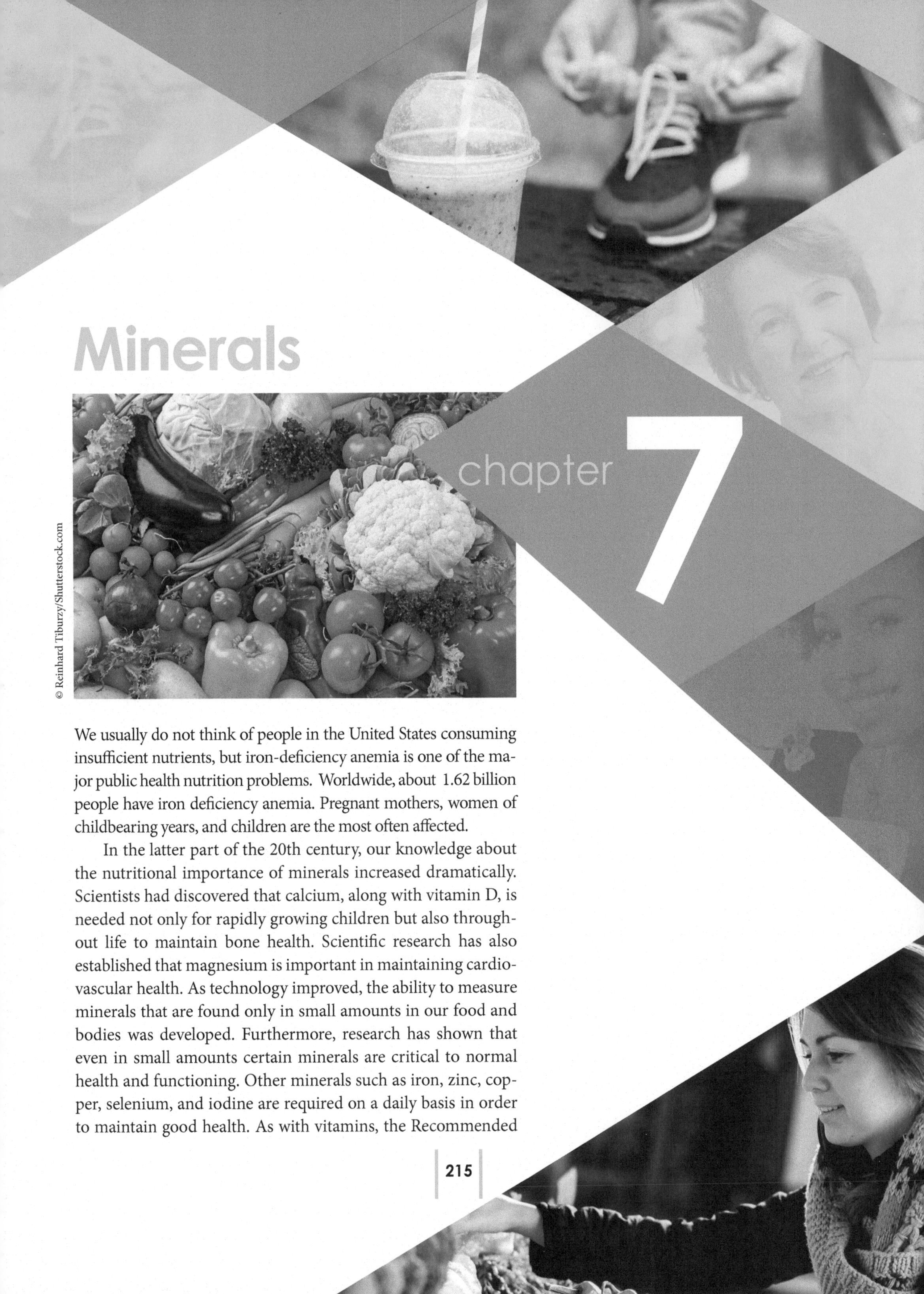

Minerals

chapter 7

© Reinhard Tiburzy/Shutterstock.com

We usually do not think of people in the United States consuming insufficient nutrients, but iron-deficiency anemia is one of the major public health nutrition problems. Worldwide, about 1.62 billion people have iron deficiency anemia. Pregnant mothers, women of childbearing years, and children are the most often affected.

In the latter part of the 20th century, our knowledge about the nutritional importance of minerals increased dramatically. Scientists had discovered that calcium, along with vitamin D, is needed not only for rapidly growing children but also throughout life to maintain bone health. Scientific research has also established that magnesium is important in maintaining cardiovascular health. As technology improved, the ability to measure minerals that are found only in small amounts in our food and bodies was developed. Furthermore, research has shown that even in small amounts certain minerals are critical to normal health and functioning. Other minerals such as iron, zinc, copper, selenium, and iodine are required on a daily basis in order to maintain good health. As with vitamins, the Recommended

Dietary Allowances (RDAs) for many minerals have now been determined, and as research and knowledge continues to evolve, some DRIs are likely to continue to change. In some instances, sufficient information on which to base a specific RDA recommendation is lacking, and therefore, only a range or Adequate Intake (AI) is given. This chapter will explore the function of many of these minerals, what occurs when consumption is too high or too low, and the primary food sources of each.

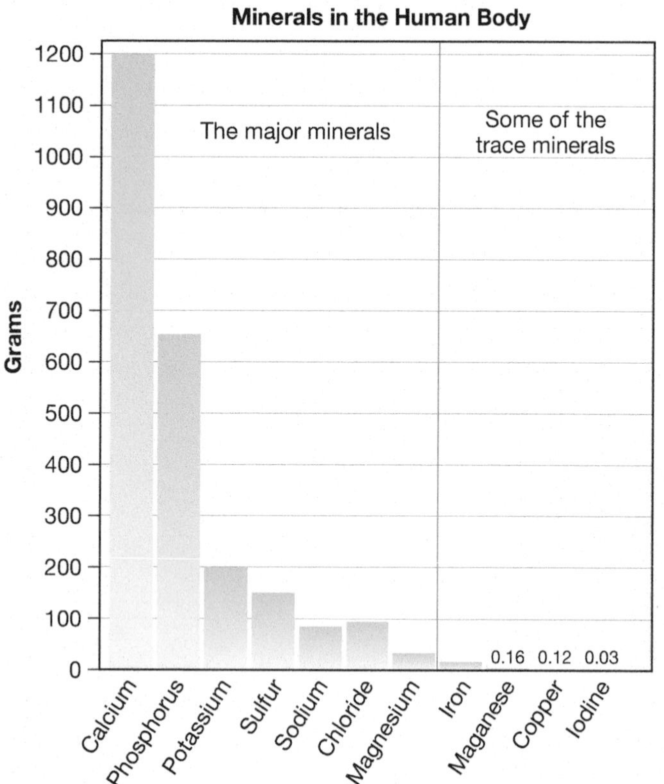

FIGURE 7.1 The amount of minerals in the average human body. The differences in levels do not mean that one is more important than another.

Minerals are inorganic nutrients that are essential components in the diet. Minerals are classified based on their content in the body and recommended level of dietary intake (Table 7.1). The major minerals are found in greater amounts in the body, and each contributes a total mass of about 5 g (approximately a teaspoon). Their dietary recommendation is at least 100 mg per day. Each trace mineral contributes less than 5 g to your body weight and the recommended intake for each is less than 100 mg per day. Figure 7.1 displays the contributions made by the individual minerals to our body. See Table 7.4 at the end of this chapter for a summary of all minerals and their food sources and functions.

TABLE 7.1 Essential Minerals Needed to Sustain Optimal Health

Major Minerals	Trace Minerals
Calcium	Iron
Phosphorus	Zinc
Sodium	Copper
Potassium	Selenium
Chloride	Iodine
Magnesium	Fluoride
Sulfur	Chromium
	Manganese
	Molybdenum

The list of minerals has grown over the years and includes nutrients that are recognizable, such as calcium, iron, and potassium, as well as more obscure nutrients such as copper, selenium, and chromium. Researchers continue to study how and why minerals are essential to the body.

THE MAJOR MINERALS

Calcium

Calcium is the most abundant mineral in the body. It represents 40 percent of all the minerals in the body which contributes 1.5 percent of total body weight. More than 99 percent of the calcium is found in the bones and teeth. Calcium may be released from the bone to be used for other purposes, such as muscle contraction and nerve transmission. Calcium is constantly being placed in the bone and released to the blood from the bone. Therefore, bone may be sacrificed when blood calcium levels are low.

Calcium in Bone

A critical role for calcium is the building and maintenance of bone. While calcium is an important component of bone, other nutrients are vital for appropriate bone formation. Bone is composed of a combination of two types of building materials: minerals—primarily calcium and phosphorus—and the connective tissue collagen. Protein collagen provides the major structural framework for bone and can be thought of as the frame of a house. Once the frame of a house is in place, drywall can be attached. In a similar manner, once the collagen framework is established, mineral complexes can be added to bone. Calcium makes up a crystal in bone called **hydroxyapatite.** This bone crystal is large and complex and gives bone its strength. When calcium is absent, bone becomes weak because of lack of these crystals. Magnesium, sodium, phosphorus, and fluoride are also part of this crystal. Fluoride plays a role in making teeth and bones harder; its hardening effect on tooth enamel is one of the reasons its use is recommended in preventing decay. Nutrients and information are delivered to bone via blood vessels and nerves in a complex network of canals (Figure 7.2).

hydroxyapatite
The large and complex crystal in bone that contains calcium and gives bone its strength.

FIGURE 7.2
Bone anatomy is complex. Bones are composed of a series of networks and cells. Most bone is made up of collagen. The key role calcium plays in bone is the formation of calcium crystals, called *hydroxyapatite*, which gives bone its strength.

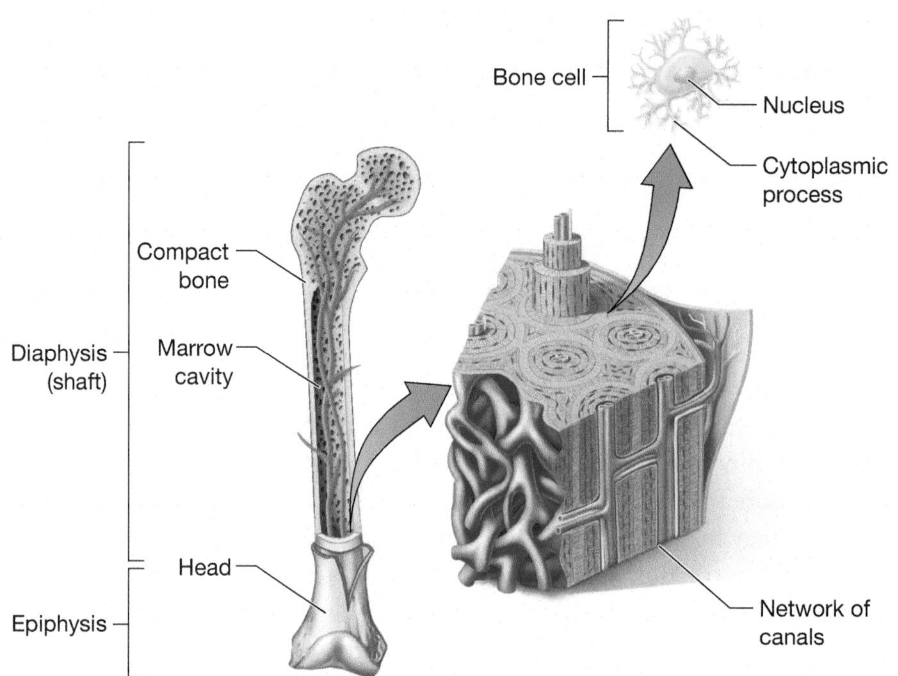

Calcium in Muscle and Nerve Cells

While less than 1 percent of calcium is found in muscle and nerve cells, its role there cannot be underestimated. Calcium plays a fundamental role in muscle contraction. When we want a muscle to contract, calcium enters the cells to initiate the contraction. In nerve cells, calcium is critical in allowing the release of neurotransmitters for conduction of nerve impulses. Calcium also regulates the levels of sodium and potassium ions across the nerve membrane, both of which are necessary for nerve conduction.

Nutrition & DISEASE

CALCIUM AND VITAMIN D IN BONE HEALTH

Bone exists in a constant state of remodeling or turnover, meaning that bone is always being simultaneously broken down and rebuilt. This process allows bone to adapt to physical stress, injury, growth, and nutritional changes. Bone turnover can be thought of as a simple mathematical equation, with the result being bone loss, gain, or maintenance (Figure 7.3). When bone loss begins to exceed bone gain or maintenance, the bone may begin to lose its structure and "density" (Figure 7.4). This can result in bone that is fragile and easily fractured, a condition known as osteoporosis.

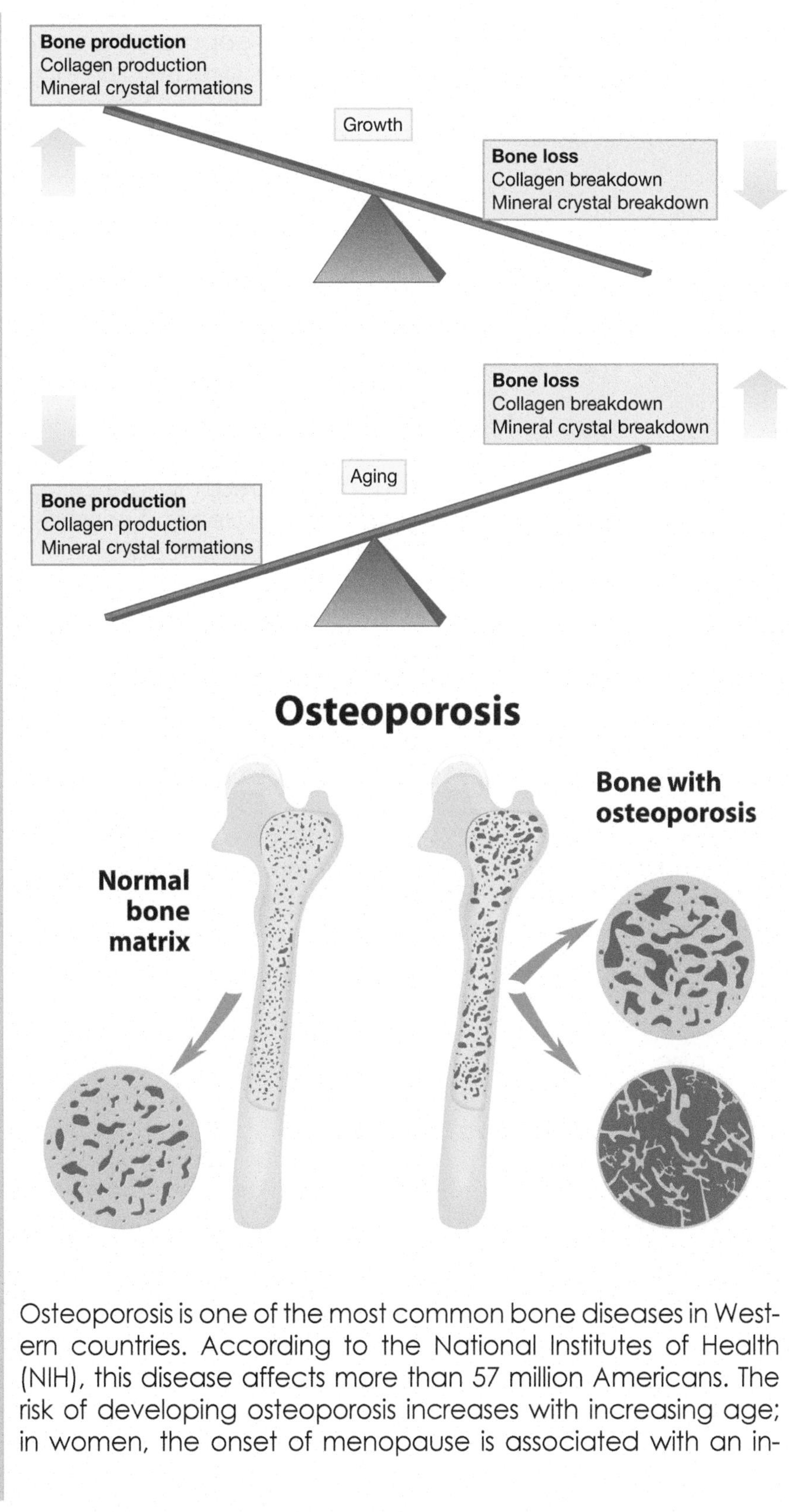

FIGURE 7.3
Bone "remodeling" illustrated. There are times when, under normal conditions, bone is being broken down and built up at the same time. During growth, more bone is built than lost; as we age, more bone is lost than built.

FIGURE 7.4
Osteoporosis illustrated. The diagrams demonstrate what appears to be loss of total bone. However, in the microscopic structure, osteoporotic bone develops (right) a honeycomb appearance, with reduced bone density compared to normal bone (left).

Osteoporosis is one of the most common bone diseases in Western countries. According to the National Institutes of Health (NIH), this disease affects more than 57 million Americans. The risk of developing osteoporosis increases with increasing age; in women, the onset of menopause is associated with an increased rate of bone loss as estrogen levels decline. Although it is more prevalent in people over age 50, osteoporosis can occur at any age, even as early as the 20s. This disease develops gradually over a lifetime, and there are no obvious symptoms until the bone becomes so weak that frequent fractures occur. Although there have been significant advances in medications to help slow the rate of bone loss in individuals who've been diagnosed with osteoporosis, there is no cure.

To prevent osteoporosis, both men and women should acquire as much bone mass as possible during youth and adolescence. The young teen years are the most important, because at around age 18 for women and age 20 for men, you will have achieved 90 percent of your peak bone mass. You will continue to add a small amount in your 20s, reaching your peak at about age 30. After age 30 you gradually begin to lose bone mass. Whether you develop osteoporosis will depend primarily on how much bone mass you accumulated as a teen.

When you are a teenager, calcium intake and sufficient vitamin D are critical in making sure you gain as much bone mass as possible. Women are at greater risk for this bone disease than men. Compared to men, women have lower bone mass to begin with. Many women, especially young women, are likely to diet and in an effort to cut Calories, often avoid foods rich in calcium and vitamin D, such as milk. Females may also lose calcium during frequent pregnancies. Also, men have greater muscle mass and tend to do more weight-bearing exercise, which helps build bones and slows the rate of breakdown. Other risk factors for osteoporosis include tobacco use, excess alcohol intake, being Caucasian, and having a small body frame size.

As you age, it is important that you take as many actions as possible to slow your rate of bone loss. What does this mean? You should consume sufficient quantities of calcium and vitamin D and exercise regularly, engaging specifically in weight-bearing exercise. Estrogen also has a positive effect on bone; postmenopausal women should discuss with their doctor to see if hormone replacement therapy is appropriate for them.

Osteoporosis is a much more serious disease than many people think. The elderly are more likely to fall and break a bone. Those who fracture a hip often die within a year because of the complications resulting from the injury. In the case of bone health, lifelong prevention is the key.

APPLICATION TIP

To prevent osteoporosis:

- Consume two to three servings per day from the milk and dairy group from MyPlate.gov.
- For those who do not consume dairy, include other high-calcium foods in the diet each day. (Table 7.2)
- Participate in weight-bearing exercise such as strength training, walking, and running.
- Maintain a healthy weight.
- Avoid excess alcohol or caffeine intake and stop smoking if you smoke.

TABLE 7.2 Calcium-Rich Foods

Food	Serving Size	Calcium (mg)	Fat (g)	Calories
Milk				
Skim*	8 oz.	301	0.4	86
2%*	8 oz.	298	4.7	121
Whole*	8 oz.	290	8.2	149
Yogurt				
Plain, fat-free*	8 oz.	488	0.4	137
Plain, low-fat*	8 oz.	448	3.8	154
w/ Fruit, low-fat*	8 oz.	338	2.8	243
Cheese				
American	1 oz.	163	6.9	93
Cheddar*	1 oz.	204	9.4	114
Cottage, 2%	1 c.	156	4.4	203
Mozzarella, part skim	1 oz.	183	4.5	72
Ricotta, part skim*	1/2 c.	337	9.8	171
Ricotta, whole milk*	1/2 c.	257	16.1	216

Fish and Shellfish				
Sardines, canned in oil, drained, including bones*	3.75 oz.	351	10.5	191
Salmon, pink, canned, including bones	3 oz.	181	5.1	118
Vegetables				
Bok choy, raw (Chinese cabbage)	1 c.	74	0	9
Broccoli, cooked, drained, from raw	1 c.	74	0.6	44
Soybeans, mature, boiled	1 c.	175	15	298
Collards, cooked, drained, from raw*	1 c.	226	0.7	49
Turnip greens, cooked, drained, from raw, leaves and stems	1 c.	197	0.3	29
Others				
Tofu, raw, regular, prepared with calcium*	1/2 c.	434	5.9	94
Almonds (dry-roasted)	1 oz.	75	15	169
Dried figs, uncooked*	1 c.	287	2.3	507
Source: USDA Nutrient Data Laboratory, 2002.				

Note: You also can increase the calcium in foods by following these suggestions:

1. Add nonfat powdered milk to all soups, casseroles, and drinks.
2. Add reduced-fat cheese to soups, salads, or vegetables.
3. Buy juices, cereals, breads, and rice that are fortified with calcium.
4. Replace sour cream with yogurt in recipes.
5. Add almonds, tofu or salmon to salads.
6. Some bottled waters contain calcium; check the labels for more information.

*Indicates a high calcium source

APPLICATION TIP

Drinking one 8-oz. glass of milk provides 300 mg of calcium, which is about one-third the DRI for younger children and about one-fourth the DRI for teens. In addition, milk supplies other minerals and vitamins needed by the body. To reduce the amount of fat, replace whole milk and cream with reduced fat, low-fat, or skim milk in recipes.

Calcium's Role in Blood Clotting

In Chapter 8, we will discuss the importance of vitamin K in blood clotting. Calcium also is central to blood clotting. Like vitamin K, calcium is needed to convert the protein prothrombin into thrombin. Thrombin is an enzyme that converts fibrinogen into fibrin. Both vitamin K and calcium play roles in the blood-clotting process by making fibrin (see Figure 8.5).

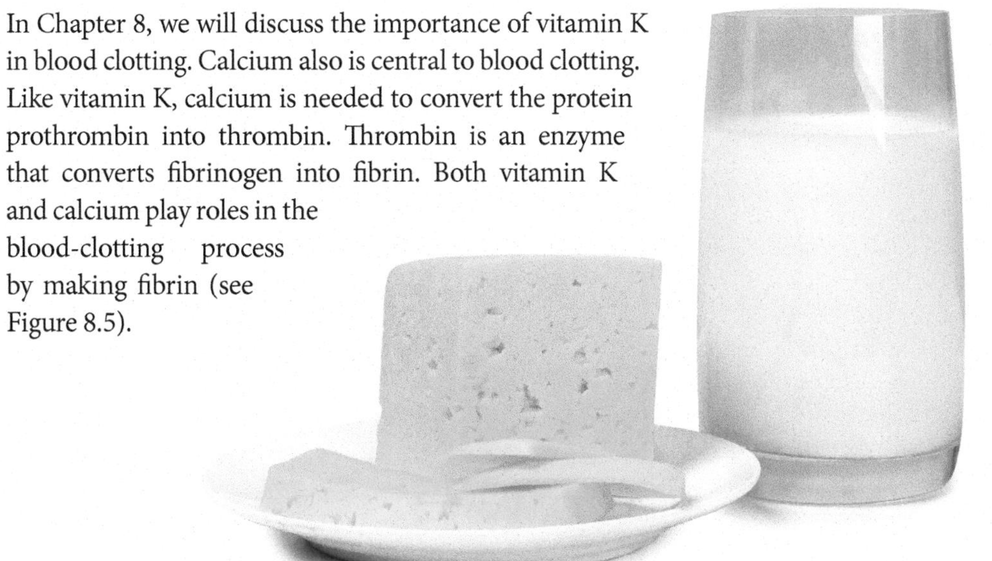

© grynoid/Shutterstock.com

> **APPLICATION TIP**
>
> To get the most out of calcium-rich foods and increase your overall absorption, spread your consumption of them throughout the day. For example, rather than having a glass of milk and a yogurt for breakfast, have the milk for breakfast and the yogurt for lunch.

Calcium and Blood Pressure

Calcium can have a protective effect against hypertension. Years ago, it was discovered that some women suffered from a serious condition during pregnancy called toxemia of pregnancy or **pre-eclampsia** (see Chapter 10 for more information). It is characterized by headache, fatigue, protein in the urine, and high blood pressure. Women who are overweight and teenagers who are pregnant are especially prone to this condition. Scientists reported that mothers who had a lower chance of pre-eclampsia had higher dietary calcium intake, primarily from dairy products. Further studies were conducted to determine whether calcium could be used to lower blood pressure in other groups of people with hypertension. The results were promising. Hypertensive subjects who consumed greater levels (more than 800 mg per day) of calcium had significantly lower blood pressure. These benefits may be related to other nutrients in the diet as well, such as potassium and magnesium.

pre-eclampsia
A serious blood disorder in pregnancy characterized by headache, fatigue, protein in the urine, and high blood pressure.

© Hank Shiffman/Shutterstock.com

Calcium Absorption and Blood Levels

Dietary factors can decrease the absorption of calcium. Some plant-based foods contain a compound called phytate. This substance looks like a sugar molecule and is found in soy products and the husk of whole grains and cereals. Phytate binds certain minerals—calcium and zinc in particular—making them unavailable to cells. Oxalate is another compound with negative charges that binds calcium and other minerals that have positive charges, limiting their absorption. Spinach contains a good amount of calcium, but it is also high in oxalates, making this food's role as a calcium source questionable.

Other factors increase calcium absorption. For example, adequate vitamin D is necessary for calcium absorption. Spreading your calcium intake more evenly throughout the day results in more calcium being absorbed. Also the presence of the milk sugar lactose in the gut at the same time as calcium results in greater absorption. The increased physiological need for calcium, such as during growth, pregnancy, and lactation enhances absorption as well.

phytate

A substance that looks like a sugar molecule and is found inside the husk of whole grains and cereals; it binds certain minerals—calcium and zinc in particular—making them unavailable to cells.

oxalate

A compound with negative charges that binds calcium and other minerals that have positive charges.

Requirements and Food Sources

In setting recommendations for calcium, the level needed to achieve peak bone mass during the late teen to early adult years is a primary factor. The recommended dietary allowance (RDA) for calcium is 1,000 mg per day for adults between the ages of 19 and 50 and 1,200 mg per day for women over the age of 50 and men over the age of 70. For adolescents, the recommendation is 1,300 mg per day; this is the age group that most often does not meet the recommended levels.

Ca^{+2} Mg^{+2} Fe^{+2} Zn^{+} Cu^{+2}

Phytate **Oxalate**

FIGURE 7.5

Phytate and oxalate can decrease the absorption of several minerals. This illustration shows how the negative charge of phytate and oxalate can attract and bind up the positive-charged minerals.

Dairy products are the best calcium sources, but other sources are available for those who do not tolerate dairy. These foods include canned sardines and salmon if the bones are eaten, turnip greens, broccoli and other green leafy vegetables (Table 7.2). Absorption of calcium from dietary sources or supplements depends on several factors. For example, the lactose in milk may enhance absorptionso that approximately 50% of the calcium is absorbed. However, plant sources of calcium may not be as absorbable, as discussed previously. A number of calcium supplements are on the market. The two most common types of calcium supplements are calcium citrate and calcium carbonate. To improve the calcium absorption from calcium carbonate, it is best to take the supplement with food. Whether from dietary sources or supplements, the vitamin D status of the person is also important for optimal calcium absorption.

functional foods
Foods and beverages that have been developed or altered in some way in order to optimize health.*

Many food manufacturers have begun to address a lack of calcium in our diet by adding calcium to beverages. The most well-known practice is the addition of calcium to orange juice. The practice of adding a nutrient to a food or beverage has led to the development of a new area of nutrition known as **functional foods**. Simply defined, functional foods are foods and beverages that have been developed or altered in some way in order to optimize health. Calcium is added to food products such as soy milk, almond milk, tofu, frozen waffles and breakfast cereals.

$$O^{-}-\overset{\overset{\displaystyle O}{\|}}{P}-O^{-}$$
$$\quad\;|\;\; O^{-}$$

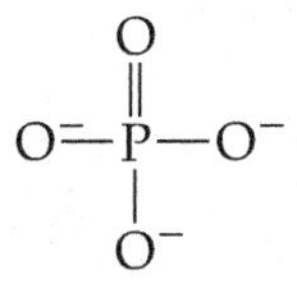

FIGURE 7.6
The chemical structure of phosphate, showing negative charges associated with the oxygen. The negative charge allows the phosphate groups to bond to other positively charged atoms to form larger compounds.

Phosphorus

Phosphorus ranks second after calcium in terms of abundance in our bodies. Approximately 85 percent of the phosphorus is in our bones, with the remainder in soft tissues such as muscle. Phosphorus is not normally found by itself but as a compound with four oxygen atoms. The resulting structure is referred to as phosphate (see Figure 7.6).

Roles of Phosphorus

Phosphorus plays many roles in our bodies. It is part of bone and teeth. It is also a part of the molecule adenosine triphosphate (ATP), the "usable" form of energy (Figure 7.7). Without phosphorus, our bodies would be unable to deliver energy or store it.

As an element of phospholipids, it is a part of cell membranes and lipoproteins. In Chapter 4, we discussed the role of phosphorus, as a part of the phospholipid, to help cell membranes mix with water in the body. Phosphorus is a critical part of lipoproteins, whose role it is to transport lipids in our blood to tissues.

Requirements and Food Sources

The RDA for phosphorus for adults is 700 mg per day. Getting sufficient phosphorus from our diet is no problem because it is so abundant in our food sup-

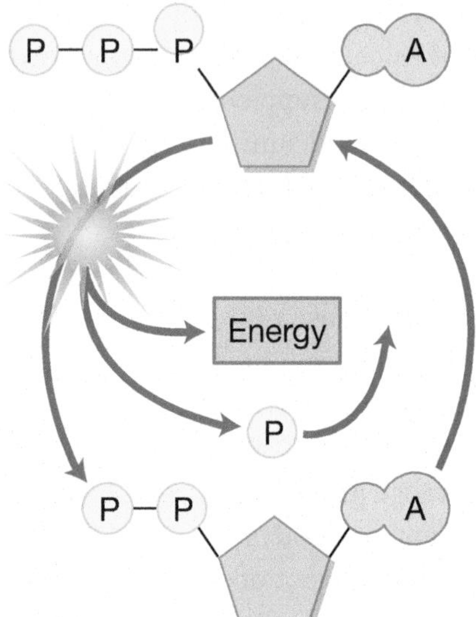

FIGURE 7.7
Role of phosphorus in a cell's energy metabolism. Most of the energy produced in a cell ends up in the form of ATP. When a phosphate group is liberated from ATP to produce ADP, a great deal of energy is released to drive energy-requiring biochemical processes.

ply. Phosphorus deficiency in healthy people is rarely reported. Good sources include meat, fish, poultry, eggs, milk and milk products, cereals, legumes, and grains. Other sources include tea, coffee, chocolate, and soft drinks. Many soft drinks contain considerable amounts of phosphorus in the form of phosphoric acid, particularly dark soft drinks or colas. There have been reports that cola intake can increase the loss of calcium and contribute to osteoporosis, an affect often attributed to the high level of phosphorus and low level of calcium in the soft drink. However, this is controversial. Some scientists do not agree that the phosphorus content in colas, or the amount consumed, will increase calcium loss. The issue may not be the actual amount of cola consumed but that those who drink colas are not consuming enough calcium-rich dairy products.

Magnesium

Of all the major minerals, magnesium is the one found in the smallest amount in the body. The average adult human has approximately 35 g of magnesium in his or her body. About half of the magnesium is located in bone. The remainder is in soft tissues, such as skeletal muscle, heart, liver, and body fluids.

Roles of Magnesium

Magnesium is part of the bone crystals that give our skeleton strength and serve as storage for magnesium when other areas, such as the blood, need it. Magnesium is important in maintaining the integrity of DNA and RNA by working with phosphorus in maintaining the genetic material. It is also very important in stabilizing ATP.

Magnesium plays the opposite role to calcium in muscle contraction. Whereas calcium is involved in contraction, magnesium is involved in relaxation. Some health experts advocate consuming more dietary magnesium because this effect on relaxing muscles may result in dilation of the blood vessels, thus lowering blood pressure. This, in turn, may reduce the risk of heart disease and stroke.

Magnesium deficiency, although rare, can occur in cases of severe diarrhea, vomiting, or heavy sweating, all of which result in excess fluid loss. In some instances, people on medications to help eliminate fluid from the body, a class of medications known as *diuretics*, may lose magnesium and can become deficient. They should have their blood levels of magnesium checked periodically by their health care provider. Some alcoholics may also become magnesium deficient because alcohol is a diuretic and causes nutrient loss through the kidneys.

Requirements and Food Sources

The DRI for magnesium is 400 mg per day for men and 320 mg per day for women. Unfortunately, 75 percent of Americans consume below these lev-

els. There are a variety of dietary sources of magnesium, one of the best being green leafy vegetables (spinach, collards, and turnip greens). Magnesium is part of the plant pigment chlorophyll, making green plants high in magnesium. Other sources of magnesium are unpolished grains, nuts, and legumes. Wholegrain cereals and breads are good sources of magnesium, but the refined products are not; therefore, one reason for the suboptimal intake of magnesium in the U.S. population is the increased consumption of refined foods. About half of the magnesium we eat can be absorbed by the small intestine.

BEFORE YOU GO ON...

1. How does calcium give strength and structure to bone?
2. What are 2 major roles that phosphorus plays in our body?
3. Which foods would you choose to get enough magnesium?
4. Which minerals have been shown to lower blood pressure in hypertensive people?

THE TRACE MINERALS

As mentioned previously, breakthroughs in analytical techniques have allowed scientists to detect smaller quantities of minerals and are the primary reason for the expansion of new knowledge about the trace minerals which play many roles in body functions and health. Even though we need less than 100 mg of each of these minerals per day, a lack of these nutrients can be just as problematic as with any of the other nutrients discussed so far. A number of diseases and conditions have been linked to a deficiency of these trace minerals in our diets. Conversely, excess intake of many of these minerals is known to cause harm. The trace minerals are listed in Table 7.1. Some of these trace minerals are highlighted in this chapter.

Iron

We have only a total of 2–4 g of iron in our body, but it is one of the most important trace minerals and also one that is the most lacking in the United

States and worldwide. Its role in delivering oxygen to cells in our body is well known. However, iron has roles beyond simply preventing anemia.

Roles of Iron

One of the most important roles of iron is to help deliver oxygen to the tissues and cells of our bodies. Oxygen is bound to hemoglobin and is circulated in the blood as part of a red blood cell (RBC). Every second, your body's bone marrow produces 2.5 million RBCs, which matches the number of RBCs destroyed in your liver, spleen, and lymph nodes. A typical RBC might circulate for only 120 days before being replaced to maintain a balance of approximately 25 trillion circulating RBCs.

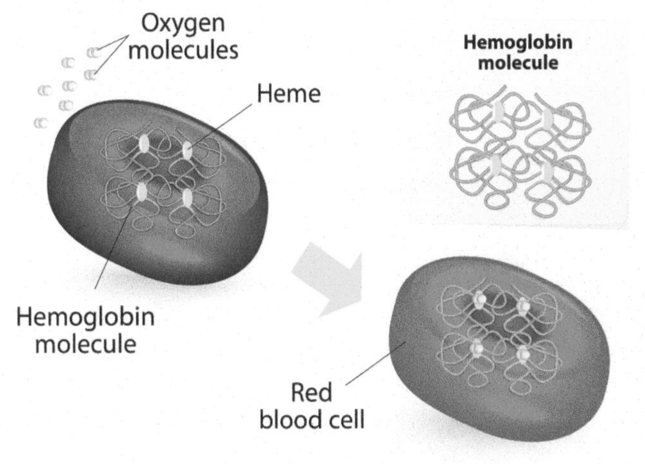

FIGURE 7.8 Hemoglobin

RBCs have been described as "bags of hemoglobin." Each RBC contains approximately 250 million hemoglobin units and contributes as much as a third of cell weight. Hemoglobin is the iron-containing protein that carries oxygen to the tissues and cells throughout your body, and picks carbon dioxide, a waste product, to be eliminated from the body. It contains four heme units. At the core of each heme unit is iron, which binds oxygen to be delivered to tissues and cells.

Iron is stored primarily in the liver bound to the protein **ferritin**; it is also stored in the spleen and bone marrow. In order for iron to be used to make heme and hemoglobin, it must be transported to the bone marrow aboard a protein called **transferrin**.

Hemoglobin is vital to effective oxygen circulation and delivery to all parts of the body. **Anemia** refers to a clinical condition in which the level of hemoglobin is too low. It can be caused by poor hemoglobin production, decreased RBC formation, or increased blood loss (as in hemorrhage). Iron-deficiency anemia is a form of anemia that is caused by low levels of hemoglobin due to reduced iron stores or inability to utilize iron to make hemoglobin. This is why your physician may measure your hemoglobin level as part of a routine checkup to screen for anemia. **Hematocrit** is another test your physician may wish to measure; it is the percentage of blood that is composed of red blood cells. A low value of hemoglobin and hematocrit may be a sign that anemia may be setting in, but other factors can affect both other than anemia. By the time low blood levels of hemoglobin or hematocrit are detected in a person who has iron-deficiency anemia, the body's stores of iron have already become depleted. Other tests may detect dropping iron levels earlier. Because ferritin levels in blood directly correlate to

ferritin
A protein that binds iron for storage and is a good indicator of iron status.

transferrin
A blood protein that carries iron to organs.

anemia
A condition characterized by below-normal levels of red blood cells, hemoglobin, or both.

hematocrit
The percentage of blood that is composed of red blood cells.

iron stores (in most cases), measuring ferritin levels may detect low iron stores before hemoglobin and hematocrit levels drop. Another test for iron levels may be the amount of iron transferrin is transporting, what is known as **transferrin saturation**.

transferrin saturation
The percent of iron that is bound to available transferrin. With other laboratory data, often used to assist in diagnosing iron-deficiency anemia.

Decreased immune response, fatigue, inability to regulate body temperature, decreased thyroid gland metabolism, and decreased ability to synthesize neurotransmitters are all conditions associated with iron deficiency. Iron deficiency anemia during pregnancy can lead to premature delivery. Intake of iron at this time is important so that the newborn baby will have at least 6 months of iron stores in the liver. Iron deficiency during childhood is also an issue and can affect cognitive function and the ability to learn.

APPLICATION TIP

Vitamin C can help with iron absorption. To enhance absorption of nonheme iron such as that found in iron-fortified breakfast cereal or an iron supplement, drink a glass of orange juice with them.

Iron Absorption

Compared to other minerals, the amount of iron absorbed in a typical diet is very low. To complicate matters, the form of the iron is important in determining the amount of iron absorbed by the small intestine. There are two major forms of iron in our diets. One is **heme iron,** an organic form of iron that is still part of the complex ring structure that makes up hemoglobin. Twenty-five to 35 percent of this form of iron is absorbed. The second form is **nonheme iron,** or the elemental form of iron that is not a part of hemoglobin. The amount of nonheme iron absorbed ranges from 2 to 20 percent.

heme iron
An organic form of iron that is still part of the complex ring structure that makes up hemoglobin.

nonheme iron
The elemental form of iron that is not a part of hemoglobin.

The heme form of iron is found only in meats, fish, and poultry. Of the iron found in these foods, 60 percent is in the heme form and the rest in the elemental or nonheme form. The heme form can cross the cells of the small intestine much more easily than the nonheme form. Nonheme iron is found in both plant and animal foods. Two factors that enhance the absorption of nonheme iron are the presence of vitamin C and the presence of meat, fish, and poultry in the diet. Vitamin C increases the solubility of nonheme iron and allows it to be better absorbed. In practical terms, this means that having orange juice along with your cereal in the morning will result in more iron absorbed. When meat, fish, and poultry are consumed, the absorption of nonheme iron is enhanced. This phenomenon has been referred to as the **meat, fish, and poultry factor (MFP)**.

meat, fish, and poultry factor (MFP)
A factor in these foods that enhances the absorption of elemental iron.

The presence of meat, fish, or poultry in a meal or a food high in vitamin C (e.g., one cup of orange juice) can increase the amount of nonheme iron absorbed from about 2 percent to nearly 8 percent. To some extent, the small intestine can regulate the amount of iron absorbed based on need. If you go to a high altitude where there is less oxygen, your body responds by making more red blood cells, which means more iron is required. The small intestine absorbs more iron as a result. A diet too high in fiber (more than 30 g per day) and phytate can impair iron absorption. Also, too much dietary calcium decreases iron absorption.

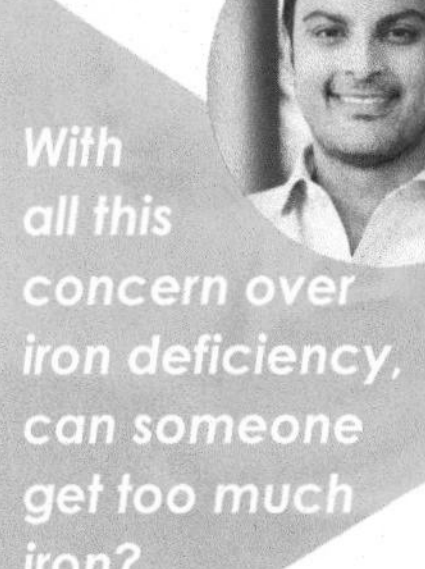

With all this concern over iron deficiency, can someone get too much iron?

Requirements and Food Sources

How much iron should we consume? The recommended amounts have changed over the years. Generally speaking, the recommended amounts are higher for women than men. Monthly blood loss through the menstrual cycle accounts for some of the higher requirements. In addition to the monthly blood loss, women of childbearing age tend to have lower iron intakes, which compound the problem of iron-deficiency anemia. Men and women over 50 years of age have an RDA of 8 mg per day. Women of childbearing age (ages 19–50) have an RDA of 18 mg per day. During pregnancy, the DRI goes up to 27 mg per day. It is often difficult to attain this level in typical diet patterns. There is much debate as to whether women should supplement with iron because of the difficulty of getting the RDA amounts from the diet alone. For pregnant women, physicians often prescribe prenatal vitamins, which contain the RDA for iron. Some health professionals advocate for an iron supplement for women of childbearing age. Of course, whenever possible everyone should try to obtain iron from food. Men consuming a 2,500-Calorie diet should not have any problems reaching the RDA for iron.

Women who are vegetarians need to be extra diligent about their diet because they do not consume foods that contain heme iron. It has been suggested that they multiply their RDA for iron by a factor of 1.8 to compensate for the lack of heme iron in their diets. For a woman of childbearing age, this would mean 18 mg per day × 1.8 = 32 mg per day, which would require a supplement. Vegetarian men would need 14 mg per day, which they should be able to get from their diets. It is recommended to discuss the use of any supplement with your physician before taking them.

APPLICATION TIP

To best absorb the iron in your food, avoid drinking coffee, tea, or milk with your meal.

Good iron sources include not only meat, fish, and poultry but also shellfish (especially oysters), beans, enriched cereal, green leafy vegetables, eggs, and even dried fruit, such as apricots. Coffee and tea should be avoided or limited when consuming these foods because they contain substances that bind up iron and make them unavailable for absorption.

Toxicity

Iron can be toxic if too much enters the body. The Tolerable Upper Intake Level (UL) for iron is 45 mg per day. In some individuals, the levels of iron absorbed cannot be regulated, and iron builds up to dangerous levels. Iron toxicity often occurs as a result of a genetic disorder called *hemochromatosis*. An individual who has two copies of a certain defective gene is at risk for hemochromatosis. Many people may have this genetic disorder. Up to 10 percent of those of northern European descent may have one copy of the gene, meaning that they are carriers, and 1 out of 250 have both copies, which is rather high for a genetic disorder. Symptoms of iron overload include abdominal pain, fatigue, and mental depression in the early stages, and advance to liver damage in the later stages due to iron accumulation. Infections, joint pain, skin pigmentation due to iron deposits, diabetes, blood in the stools, and shock are symptoms of iron toxicity. High iron in tissues or even in the diet may be a risk factor for heart disease. Those with hereditary hemochromatosis need to be careful about iron intake, especially when many foods are either enriched or fortified with iron. These individuals should not take iron supplements. They should avoid vitamin C supplements and limit their intake of foods high in vitamin C. Many health professionals advocate better screening of this disorder. The tests used to screen for hemochromatosis are the transferrin saturation and ferritin, as well as blood tests for liver damage. If these indicators suggest high iron stores, you can be tested to determine whether you carry the gene for hereditary hemochromatosis.

I am a vegetarian. Can I get enough iron from my diet alone?

Zinc

Zinc has been the subject of a great amount of research in the last 30 years. Deficiencies of zinc have been known to occur worldwide. Zinc is important for the function of nearly 200 different enzymes. It was also one of the first nutrients known to exert its effects at the genetic level.

Roles of Zinc

Trace minerals function as cofactors for many enzymes, and zinc exerts much of its physiological effects through enzyme activities. It is involved in enzymes that break down alcohol in the liver, is a cofactor for an antioxidant enzyme that fights against free radicals, helps enzymes involved with protein digestion, works with enzymes that replicate DNA, and is a cofactor for enzymes involved with blood pressure regulation. Many of the enzymes in which zinc plays a role are involved with protein synthesis, and when there is a lack of dietary zinc, protein synthesis and growth are markedly reduced. Zinc plays a critical role in wound healing; therefore, zinc supplements are often given to patients recovering from burns and bed sores. Although, benefits of zinc supplementation in these patients may be limited to those who are zinc deficient. Zinc is a component of proteins that turn genes on and off. When we make hemoglobin, there is an enzyme that is zinc dependent. Insulin depends on zinc for storage and function. It is also a very important nutrient in supporting the immune system. Sexual development and the growth of bones are zinc dependent.

Zinc Deficiency Signs

Zinc deficiency was originally seen among adolescent males in the Middle East in places such as Egypt and Iran. It has also been found among the Hispanic population of Denver, Colorado—again, primarily among adolescent males. The most notable deficiency signs were dwarfism and delayed sexual development (see the *Nutrition and Lifestages* feature that follows). Some people have a genetic defect that limits the ability to absorb zinc, and alcoholics may also have a mild zinc deficiency.

Worldwide, zinc deficiency remains a large concern, especially among children. Children with zinc deficiency have mental disabilities and a reduced ability to recover from infection. Infection itself increases the requirement for zinc, creating a cycle that makes recovery difficult. Many international aid programs have focused on supplementing foods with micronutrients such as zinc to prevent some of these problems from occurring.

Signs of zinc deficiency include the following:

- Dwarfism in young teens, particularly males
- Poor sexual development (underdeveloped testes in males)
- Deformed bones
- Poor healing of wounds
- Abnormal hair and nails; loss of hair
- Hypogeusia, or the reduced ability to taste food
- Gastrointestinal disturbances, impaired lipid absorption
- Central nervous system defects
- Impaired folate and vitamin A absorption

Nutrition & LIFESTAGES

ZINC IN TEENAGE MALES

Trace minerals exist in your diet in small amounts. What could possibly happen if you didn't have enough of the metal zinc in your diet? Well, plenty can happen if you are a young adolescent boy. Years ago, nutritionists discovered that some boys around age 11–12 years living in certain areas of the world were short compared to others in the same country. They could not blame this entirely on the culture because some boys were normal height and others were dwarfed. Areas that were affected included Middle Eastern countries such as Iran and Egypt. However, a young group of Hispanic males living in Denver, Colorado, showed similar signs. Besides being short for their age, they appeared to be sexually underdeveloped.

It was later learned that the boys had a zinc deficiency. This puzzled some, because it looked as if they had enough zinc in their diets. However, in the Middle East and in some Hispanic cultures, it is common to consume unleavened, or flatbreads. These breads contain phytate. The phytate in the flat bread or tortillas in the young boys' diets was binding up the zinc and making it unavailable for absorption by the intestine. Fortunately, this was not permanent. When the nutritionists gave these boys zinc supplements, they grew about 6–8" in 6 months! It was clear that zinc is needed to support growth and sexual development. However, you should be aware that taking a zinc supplement will not make you grow taller or improve sexual performance if you are not deficient, and too much could be toxic.

Zinc Absorption

About 40 percent of dietary zinc can be absorbed in the small intestine. When there is a sufficient store of zinc, the small intestine makes a protein to bind up the zinc and prevent it from being absorbed. The cells that line the gastrointestinal tract are sloughed off every 3–5 days. The zinc is lost this way when it binds to the proteins in the cells. When you need more zinc, the protein is not made and zinc is absorbed into the bloodstream. As with iron, the presence of meat, fish, and poultry in the diet improves the amount of zinc absorbed.

Requirements and Food Sources

Remember that zinc is needed for protein synthesis. Men have a higher RDA for zinc than women due to the greater muscle mass of men and thus their greater dependence on increased protein synthesis to maintain that muscle mass. The RDA for zinc is 11 mg per day for men and 8 mg per day for women. Requirements increase during pregnancy and lactation. The UL for zinc is 40 mg per day; consuming more than this amount can lead to decreased copper absorption. A decrease in HDL cholesterol has been reported in men receiving 50 mg of zinc per day over a 3-month period. Excess zinc supplementation has been implicated in increased rates of infection in those people. Vomiting, diarrhea, and cramps can occur at dosages greater than 100 mg per day.

Meats, poultry (turkey in particular), oysters, herring, eggs, legumes, and whole-grain cereals are good sources of zinc. Fruits are very poor zinc sources. The refinement of grains can result in significant zinc loss that is not enriched back to the grain. Some breakfast cereals and soymilks are fortified with zinc; therefore, reading food labels is important to help prevent a zinc deficiency.

Copper

Roles of Copper

Copper, like zinc, exerts its physiological effects as a cofactor for enzymes. Copper has several well-known functions. First, it is needed for absorption, storage, and metabolism of iron. Here again, we can see how one nutrient depends on the function of another. In copper deficiency, animals and humans can become anemic, and it appears to be iron-deficiency anemia. Without copper, iron cannot be incorporated into hemoglobin and red blood cells.

Another important role for copper is that of strengthening connective tissue. Collagen depends on a copper-containing enzyme to enhance its strength by promoting cross-linking among the various collagen proteins. In copper deficiency, connective tissue is weakened. Another important function of copper is that it is needed for enzymes involved in the production of neurotransmitters, for an enzyme involved in the production of ATP, and as an enzyme that fights against free radicals in the body.

Copper Absorption

Approximately half of the dietary copper is absorbed. A small amount of copper may be absorbed by the stomach, but most is absorbed by the small intestine. The same protein that regulates zinc uptake regulates how much copper is absorbed. As a consequence, too much zinc can interfere with copper absorption.

Requirements and Food Sources

The RDA for copper is 900 μg per day for adult men and women. Few cases of copper deficiency have been reported.

The UL for copper is 10 mg per day. Vomiting and liver damage can occur at this or higher levels.

Good food sources of copper include organ meats, shellfish, mushrooms, chocolate, nuts, legumes, and the germ and bran portions of cereals. Drinking water, especially where water runs through copper pipes, is a good source of dietary copper.

Selenium

Selenium has received a lot of attention in the past 30 years, as we have learned more about it. Selenium was thought to be a toxic metal only. Today, we know that selenium is essential for good health and can prevent several diseases.

Roles of Selenium

The most important role that selenium plays is in the antioxidant defense system against free radical damage to cells and tissues. Selenium is part of an antioxidant enzyme called *glutathione peroxidase*. The activity of this enzyme depends on how much selenium is present. Glutathione peroxidase works with vitamin E in protecting against free radical damage. In fact, many selenium deficiency symptoms resemble those of vitamin E deficiency.

Selenium also plays an important role in the production of active thyroid hormone. Selenium deficiency can mimic thyroid dysfunction to some extent.

Requirements and Food Sources

The RDA for selenium is 55 µg per day for adults. Requirements increase during pregnancy and lactation. The UL is 400 µg per day. Seafood is an excellent source of selenium. Fish (especially tuna), meats, organ meat, and eggs are also good selenium food sources. Wheat-based cereals and sunflower seeds are good sources, but only if these plants are grown in areas where there is adequate selenium in the soil.

Iodine

The most important role of iodine involves thyroid gland and the production of a hormone with powerful effects, **thyroid hormone or thyroxine**. Thyroxine is a hormone that controls the basal metabolic rate and heat production in our bodies. Although we need only very small quantities of iodine, the amount is critical for the activity of this powerful chemical. Thyroxine is made from an amino acid, tyrosine, and iodine in the thyroid gland found in our neck.

When iodine is lacking in our diets, the cells of the thyroid gland become enlarged in an attempt to absorb more iodine from the blood. Over time, this results in an enlarged thyroid gland, called **goiter** (Figure 7.9). People with goiter tire easily and may gain weight because of decreased basal metabolism. People are more likely to develop goiter in areas where the soil has low levels of iodine.

thyroid hormone or thyroxine
A hormone that controls the basal metabolic rate and heat production in our bodies.

goiter
An enlarged thyroid gland due to an iodine deficiency.

FIGURE 7.9
Iodine deficiency leads to enlarged thyroid glands. Here we see the results of iodine deficiency, called *goiter*.

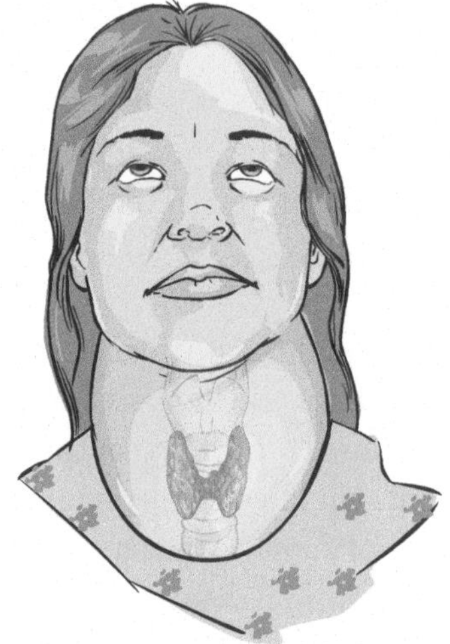
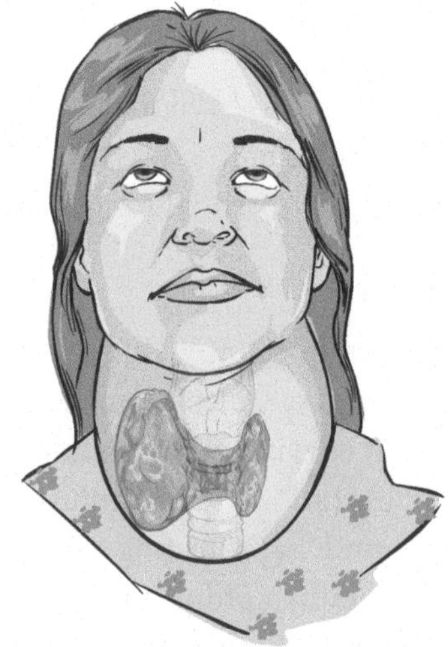

cretinism
The mental and physical retardation of children whose mothers were iodine deficient during pregnancy.

Mothers who are iodine deficient during pregnancy have offspring who are mentally and physically impaired. This is called **cretinism,** and it is not normally reversible.

Currently, iodine deficiency in the United States is not common. Most table salt has iodine added to it in order to combat iodine deficiency; however, it is still a major problem in some parts of the world. Health relief organizations are trying to fortify foods with iodine to help relieve iodine deficiency. Many in the United States consume iodine from iodized table salt. Iodized salt is not generally used in processed foods. Therefore, reducing your intake of processed foods will not negatively affect your iodine status.

Requirements and Food Sources

The RDA for iodine is 150 μg per day. The UL is 1,100 μg per day. Iodine can be toxic in large amounts. Excess intake of iodine can lead to enlargement of the thyroid gland just as iodine deficiency does. Food sources are seafood and iodized salt. Plants grown in areas with sufficient iodine in the soil are also good sources of iodine.

Fluoride

Fluoride is a mineral that is associated with healthy teeth. Recall that bone and teeth are composed of crystals. These crystals are composed primarily of calcium and phosphorus. However, fluoride can be incorporated into the crystal at certain places, which makes the crystal harder and more stable. Thus, the overall effect of fluoride incorporation into teeth is a hardening of the enamel, which makes the teeth more resistant to tooth decay. Tooth decay is caused when bacteria and a sticky sugar substance adhere to teeth and acid is produced. Normally the acid causes the enamel to erode, but fluoride makes tooth enamel more resistant to acid. People living in areas with greater fluoride levels in the water have a much lower incidence of tooth decay.

Too much fluoride can result in **fluorosis**, which causes discoloration and mottling (blotchy appearance) of the teeth. It occurs only when teeth are being developed and cannot be reversed. While this may be cosmetically unappealing, it does not result in physical harm. Fluoridated water is the best diet source of fluoride. However, most toothpastes and mouthwashes also contain small amounts. More foods may contain fluoride if they have been processed or canned with fluoridated water. The AI for fluoride is 4 mg per day for men and 3 mg per day for women. The UL for those older than age 8 is 10 mg per day.

fluorosis
Fluoride toxicity that causes discoloration and mottling of the teeth.

In the United States, water is routinely fluoridated. The evidence suggests that this is both effective and inexpensive in preventing tooth decay. However, the practice of water fluoridation was and still remains controversial.

Chromium

The major function of chromium is facilitating glucose uptake by improving the function of the hormone insulin, which assists with the transport of glucose across cell membranes. Studies have reported that insulin function is impaired when chromium is lacking, and it is thought to be helpful to some people with diabetes.

The AI for chromium is 35 μg per day for men ages 19–50 and 25 μg per day for women between 19 and 50 years. No UL has been established for chromium because toxicity has not been reported. Chromium is found widely distributed in the food supply, but most foods provide a small amount. Foods that are good sources of chromium include meat and whole-grain products, as well as some fruits and vegetables, brewer's yeast, liver, nuts, and cheese.

Myths & LEGENDS

CAN CHROMIUM PICOLINATE SUPPLEMENTS INCREASE LEAN TISSUE IN YOUR BODY?

Chromium picolinate has been advocated as a supplement to increase lean body mass while decreasing fat mass. Does it really work? Human studies have been performed to answer this question. One small study on older men (ages 56–69) had them take chromium picolinate while going through resistance training. Over a 12-week period, while undergoing a twice-per-week intensive resistance training program, one group of nine men took the supplement and another group of nine men were given a placebo. The researchers concluded that chromium picolinate did not improve muscle size, strength, power, or lean tissue. Another study with football players did show that those taking a chromium picolinate supplement developed more lean body mass and experienced a decrease in body fat. However, a similar study on another group of football players produced different results. Players did not see a change in body composition as a result of supplementation. Overall, there are more studies showing no effect on body composition than those with positive results.

BEFORE YOU GO ON...

1. Which trace mineral is most likely to be lacking in our diets?
2. What are some good food sources of copper?
3. How do zinc and copper exert their physiological effects?
4. What minerals are likely to be involved with protection against free radicals as antioxidants?
5. Which trace mineral is important for the utilization of iron?
6. What is the relationship between iodine and energy expenditure?

WATER AND WATER BALANCE

Water is essential for life. A good, clean, and convenient water supply is taken for granted in many parts of the world. However, in some regions of the world, obtaining water to live is a major part of daily activities. For many people, carrying jugs of water for drinking and cooking each day is a way of life.

Although balance among all nutrients is important, water is essential to life and is required in the greatest amount. It is so crucial that signs of *dehydration* (excessive water loss in the body) can begin after just one day without water, and a person generally cannot survive for more than 6 days without consuming some water.

The adult human body is composed of 56–64 percent water (by weight), most of which is found in muscle tissues. Because men have more muscle tissue than women do, the male body has a greater percentage of water by weight. In fact, if you compared a man and a woman who both weigh 150 lbs. the man's body would contain 10 percent more water. Whether male or female, an adult requires 9–13 cups of water every day to maintain water balance. Water is important for controlling body temperature, maintaining the body's acid–base balance, and regulating blood pressure. Although dehydration is the water-related condition you tend to hear about most, overhydration can occur as well. In diseases in which the kidneys and heart are affected, water retention can be a serious problem.

Water, like minerals, is an **inorganic** substance meaning that it does not contain carbon. In contrast, fats, proteins, carbohydrates, and vitamins are **organic** substances that contain carbon. Water consists of two hydrogen atoms and one oxygen atom bonded together. This bond between the hydrogen and oxygen atoms is different from those found in many other compounds. In water, the bonding causes a shift in charge among the individual atoms. The hydrogen side of the molecules has a slight positive charge, and the oxygen side has a slight negative charge. This distribution of electrical charge allows water to attract other water molecules. Because water is charged, other substances that are also charged can dissolve in it. A good example is sodium chloride (table salt), which also has positive and negative charges (Figure 7.10).

inorganic

Describes a substance that does not contain carbon.

organic

Describes a substance that contains carbon.

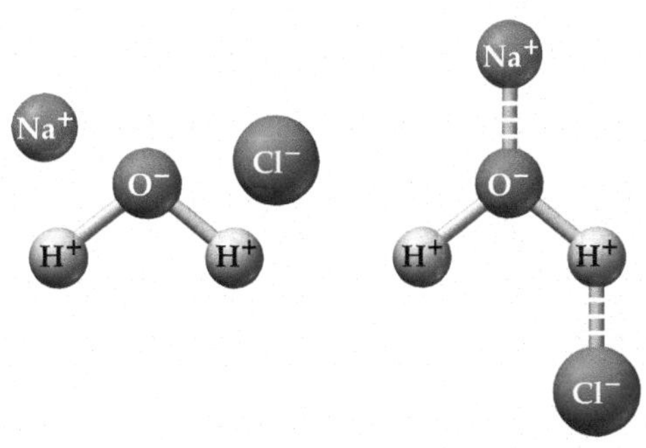

FIGURE 7.10

Ever wonder why substances can dissolve in water so easily? Because of the bonding properties of hydrogen with oxygen, oxygen has a slight negative charge, whereas hydrogen's charge is positive. The charge distribution of water allows other charged elements to dissolve in water. For example, the positive charge of sodium is attracted to the negative charge of water, as illustrated here.

intracellular

Inside a cell.

extracellular

Outside a cell.

metabolic water

Water that is produced during the breakdown of carbohydrate, fats, and proteins.

Within the body, water is found in two major compartments: inside cells as **intracellular** water and outside cells as **extracellular** water. As shown in Table 7.3, 60 percent of the body's total water is intracellular and 40 percent is extracellular. Extracellular water includes the water between tissue cells (*interstitial fluid*) and in the *lymph system*, connective tissues, and joints, as well as plasma, cerebrospinal fluid, mucous secretions, and the fluid within the eye (Figure 7.11). Water that is produced during the breakdown of carbohydrate, fats, and proteins is called **metabolic water.** We acquire about 1 ½ cups of water per day from metabolic water.

TABLE 7.3 Distribution of Body Water

Compartment	Percentage of Total Body Water
Intracellular (such as muscle cells)	60%
Extracellular	
Interstitial fluid and lymph	20
Connective tissues and joints	8
Plasma	7
Eyes, mucous secretions, and other	3
Cerebrospinal fluid	1
Intestinal secretions	1

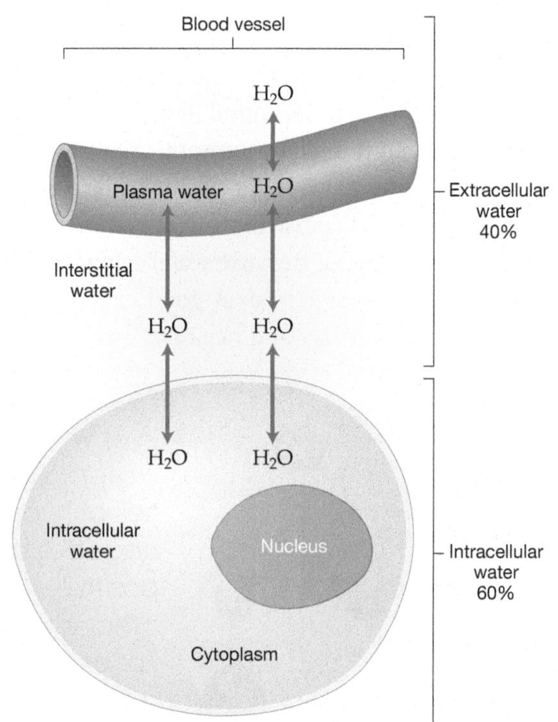

FIGURE 7.11
How is water distributed in the body's compartments? Extracellular water can be found in blood and interstitial spaces, the spaces between cells of tissues. Most of the water in our body is intracellular.

IS BOTTLED WATER SAFER AND BETTER FOR YOU?

Myths & LEGENDS

Much of the popularity of bottled water is based on the assumption that it is cleaner and healthier than tap water. Is this assumption valid? Bottled water, which is sold in a sanitary container, is considered a food and must meet federal and other local regulations. The Food and Drug Administration (FDA) regulates bottled water if it crosses state lines. Although bottled water contains no Calories, added chemicals, sweeteners, or sugar, the FDA has identified different standards of identity for bottled water, such as "spring," "sparkling," and "mineral" water. Water products that contain added ingredients are classified as soft drinks or dietary supplements.

In general, spring water comes from an underground source. Bottled spring water must retain the composition found at its source. Spring water contains less than 250 parts per million (ppm) solids. Mineral water is the same as spring water but contains more than 250 ppm solids. No minerals may be added to mineral water, however, it must be bottled as it exists from its original source. The solids in spring water and mineral water are mostly from minerals such as calcium, magnesium, and trace elements. Sparkling water is similar to spring water, with the additional regulation that it must have the same amount of dissolved carbon dioxide present as at its source.

Bottled water manufacturers are not permitted to make any health claims. No therapeutic benefits from bottled water have been documented. Nevertheless, consumers apparently believe that bottled water tastes better and is healthier for them than tap water. Ironically, about 25 percent of the bottled water sold today originates from tap water sources.

To answer the question, bottled water is likely to be safe because of the packaging requirements imposed by the FDA, but no more than tap water. Public water supplies also are tightly regulated in order to provide safe and clean water for consumption. Routine sampling and analysis of tap water assures safe supplies. In addition, tap water contains fluoride, which is important in dental health.

Look familiar? Bottled water is a very popular beverage in the food industry today.

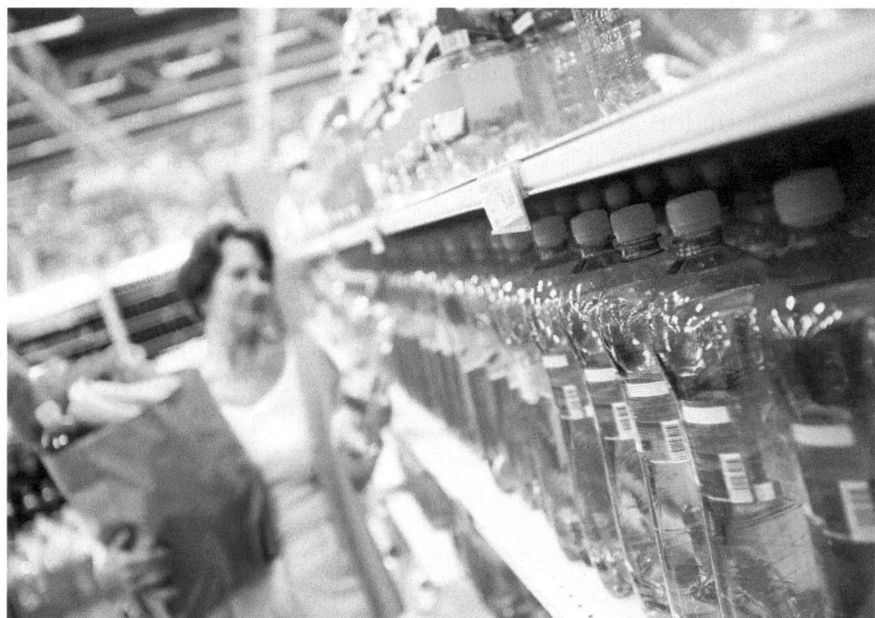

Water Balance

No other nutrient fluctuates within the body as much as water. Water loss depends on many factors. For instance, the temperature of your environment, your age, your activity level, and other factors all influence how much water your body loses daily. Some days people tend to retain more water, but they may eliminate more water a few days later. Athletes typically have a much greater water loss than nonathletes, but this varies with environmental conditions and the type of activity the athlete performs. In addition, athletes tend to be able to adapt and are more efficient at using the body's water. However, they still have higher water requirements than those who do not exercise. Infants tend to lose proportionately more body water than adults and are thus more likely to experience dehydration than adults. To avoid dehydration, you must balance water losses with water ingestion. Unlike some essential nutrients, water has no storage mechanism. When extracellular water is lost, you cannot replenish it from some a storage site within your body. In fact, a decreased concentration of extracellular fluid pulls water out of your cells, eventually dehydrating them. Consequently, even a slight inadequacy in your water supply can change the way your body functions. Thus, you must consume fluids on a regular basis.

The most critical role water plays in the body's functioning is temperature regulation. Water is used to cool the body through sweating. The many biochemical reactions that occur within the body generate a lot of heat. Water within the body absorbs this heat and carries it to the skin where it can be transferred to ambient air, in order to maintain the body's temperature at 98.6 °F (37 °C). Excess heat is then released through sweating. Sweating itself doesn't cool you; rather the body is cooled when the sweat evaporates from your skin.

Sources of Water Loss in the Body

insensible water loss
Water lost through daily sweating, exhalation of air, and other mechanisms that are not easily sensed.

Your body loses water every day in a variety of ways. In addition to sweating, you excrete it in urine and feces, and release it through the lungs each time you exhale. Generally, about 900–1,200 mL (3.8–5 cups) of water are lost daily as urine. The amount of urine produced is proportional to the amount of water you drink. Water loss through the lungs is typically 300 mL per day, or less than 1 cup, but it is influenced by environmental conditions. Water loss via feces can be significant when one is experiencing diarrhea.

Water balance from input to output is summarized in Table 7.4. Because mild daily sweating and the exhalation of air humidified by the lungs generally go unnoticed, these processes and other minor water loss mechanisms, such as secretions of the eyes, are often referred to as insensible water loss. In addition, mild sweating is often separated from activity-induced sweat, which has a higher mineral content and is visually obvious. Sweat can be a significant route of water loss for athletes and for people who live in warm climates. Interestingly, if you change your activity level or environment, your sweat glands adapt to ensure that you stay in balance.

© somchaij/Shutterstock.com

TABLE 7.4 Daily Water Balance from Intake and Output

	Water Intake*			Water Loss	
Source	**mL**	**cups**	**Source**	**mL**	**cups**
Drinking water (from beverages)	1,000	4.2	Urine	900–1,200	3.8–5
Water in food	600–800	2.5–3.4	Insensible:		
Metabolic water (from digestion)	200–300	0.9–1.3	Mild sweating	400	1.7
Total	1,800–2,100	7.6–8.9	Lungs	300	1.3
			Feces	200	0.9
			Total	1,800–2,100	7.7–8.9

*These are estimates for adults and can vary widely.

Hydration: Water Intake and Retention

A region of the brain called the *hypothalamus* controls the body's perceived need for water, commonly called *thirst*. The brain monitors the body's fluid salt concentration and responds with a signal to take in fluid when water levels are low or salt concentration is high. Thirst is not always the best indicator of water needs though as our perception of thirst lags behind the time when water is needed. In addition to thirst, the body produces two hormones to help maintain hydration. **Antidiuretic hormone** is released by the pituitary gland in the brain to signal the kidneys to retain water. **Aldosterone** is produced by the adrenal glands above the kidneys; it induces the kidneys to retain more sodium and water.

antidiuretic hormone
A hormone released by the pituitary gland in the brain to signal the kidneys to retain water.

aldosterone
Hormone produced by the adrenal glands located above the kidneys. It induces the kidneys to retain more sodium and, consequently, more water.

Although the body has mechanisms to retain and conserve water in some situations and excrete it in others, fluid intake is necessary every day. How much water should we consume? General recommendations for water consumption for adults are 1–1.5 mL/kcal of energy expenditure under average environmental conditions (8–12 cups of water per day total, including beverages and the water contained in food). This guideline has some exceptions. Pregnant women have an increased requirement of about 30 mL per day (an ounce per day more) to accommodate the expanded extracellular fluid, the fluid needs of the fetus, and the amniotic fluid. Breastfeeding mothers need approximately 600–700 mL more water per day (2½–3 cups). They need this water to produce breast milk.

If you are on a low-Calorie, low-carbohydrate or high-protein diet, drinking extra water is advisable. It will help your body remove potentially harmful excess nitrogen and the ketone bodies that these diets produce. In addition to fluids or drinks, several foods are excellent sources of water. For instance, many fruits and vegetables are 85–95 percent water by mass.

APPLICATION TIP

In order to stay hydrated during exercise, you should consume about 1 cup of fluids for every 15–20 minutes of activity.

The Dangers of Dehydration

Even mild or early dehydration can result in significant changes in how your body works. For example, a decrease of 1–2 percent body weight from water loss signals thirst and can cause lack of mental concentration and mild fatigue. A loss of water approximating 2 percent of body weight can significantly reduce athletic ability. If dehydration reaches approximately 5 percent of body weight, cramping and heat exhaustion can result. At the 7–10 percent level, hallucinations and heatstroke are common (see Table 7.5 for signs of dehydration). Dehydration can occur from excessive loss through sweating without adequate fluid replacement. In athletes who exercise in hot environments, dehydration progresses due to continued sweating. Dehydration also occurs in temperate environments but stabilizes more easily because it is easier to transfer heat to cooler air temperatures. Dehydration can also occur because of vomiting and diarrhea. Initially, dehydration is characterized by a shift in fluid from intracellular and interstitial areas to the blood. As dehydration becomes more severe, blood volume is reduced. This means that less blood is returned from the body to the heart and the heart pumps less blood, which decreases blood pressure. In addition, dehydration reduces your ability to remove excessive heat through sweat, leaving you vulnerable to **hyperthermia** (increased body temperature) and heatstroke because your body does not have enough water to cool itself.

hyperthermia
Increased body temperature.

TABLE 7.5 Signs of Dehydration

Mild Dehydration	Moderate to Severe Dehydration
Dry and sticky mouth	Extreme thirst
Feeling of tiredness and sleepiness	Lack of sweating
Thirst	Very dry mouth and skin
Decreased urine	Little or no urine; dark-colored urine
Lack of tears when crying	Sunken eyes
Muscle weakness	Shriveled skin and lack of elasticity
Headache	Low blood pressure
Dizziness	Rapid heartbeat
Cramping in arms and legs	Rapid deep breathing
	Fever
	Unconsciousness and convulsions

The Role of the Kidneys and Urine in Water Balance

Urine is the major source of water loss and is the primary path for excretion of metabolic waste and the regulation of extracellular fluid composition. The kidneys control the composition of urine and blood through microscopic structures called **nephrons.** Each kidney is composed of about 1 million nephrons (Figure 7.12), which collectively generate approximately 1–2 L (4–8 cups) of urine daily. Urine has several components, the most significant being water, electrolytes, urea, and creatinine. Urea and creatinine are by-products of protein and muscle metabolism, respectively, and are the major nitrogen waste products.

nephrons
Microscopic structures in the kidneys that control the composition of urine and blood.

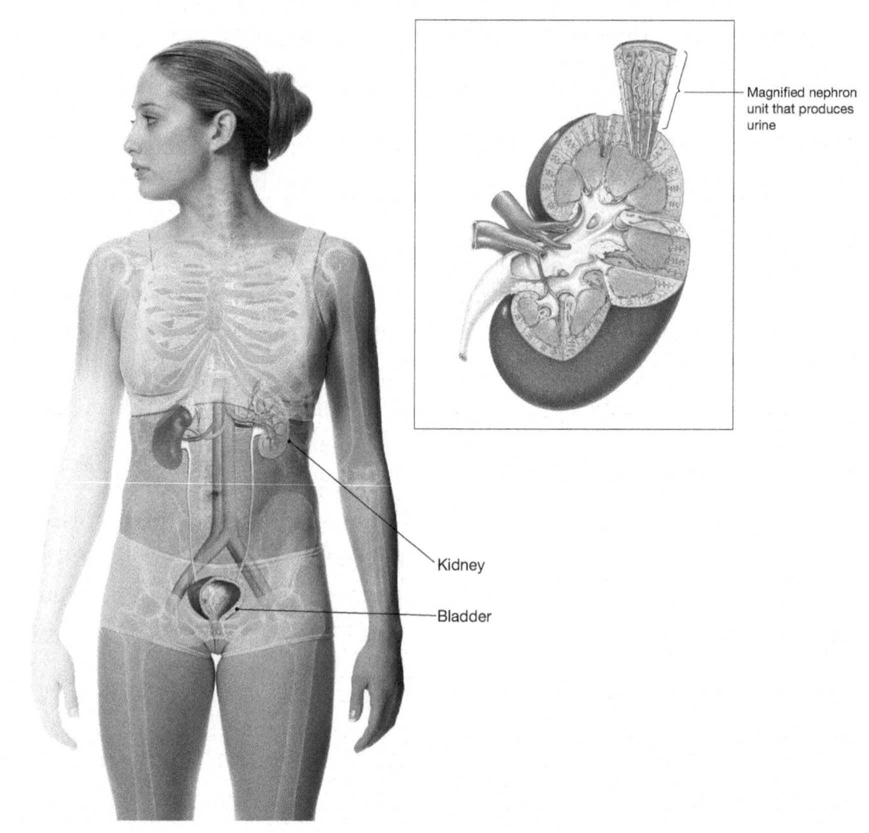

FIGURE 7.12 The kidney and the microscopic nephron structures are the components that regulate water and salt in our bodies. Blood is filtered through the glomerulus of the nephron and the materials we want to keep are reabsorbed from the nephron back into the blood supply.

BEFORE YOU GO ON...

1. Why is water considered an inorganic nutrient?
2. What is the most critical role of water in the body?
3. What part of the brain controls thirst?
4. Describe some of the effects of dehydration on the body.

ELECTROLYTES: SODIUM, POTASSIUM, AND CHLORIDE

Electrolytes are minerals that, when placed in water, become charged particles.

Sodium, potassium, and chloride are some of the most recognized electrolytes important to humans. They are often discussed together and are commonly called *electrolytes* because their metabolic and biochemical functions are interrelated. Sodium (Na+) is primarily found in the extracellular fluid and potassium (K+) is found predominately in the intracellular fluid (Figure 7.13). Chloride (Cl^-), is usually associated with sodium and therefore is more concentrated in the extracellular fluid. These elements, particularly sodium and potassium, are heavily involved in the proper maintenance of water balance.

The DRI for sodium for adolescents and adults up to age 50 is 1,500 mg per day. The DRI for those over age 70 is 1200 mg. The average American takes in much more than the estimated daily requirement for sodium because salt (40 percent sodium) intake averages 8.5 g per day (which equals 3400 mg of sodium). Therefore, someone who does not exercise does not need to worry about sodium intake because we get more than enough in our diets. However, this is not the case for potassium. The adequate intake level for potassium is 4,700 mg for teenagers and adults. Many Americans, especially those not consuming five servings of fresh fruits and vegetables per day, do not meet the *adequate* daily intake requirement of potassium. For reference purposes, one banana contains 450 mg of potassium.

Should someone who does not exercise be concerned about electrolytes?

FIGURE 7.13
Cells are high in potassium. The extracellular, or outside, area surrounding the cell is high in sodium and chloride. The cell pumps sodium out and potassium in to maintain this distribution. What would happen to this distribution if the cell died?

Chloride has a DRI of 2,300 mg per day for teenagers and adults up to age 50; it declines to 1800 mg per day for those over 70 years of age. Table salt, or sodium chloride, is a major contributor of chloride to our diets. Therefore, we typically get enough chloride from our diets.

Dietary Sodium

Most people who are trying to reduce sodium intake cut back on the salt they add to their food. However, most of the sodium we consume comes from processed foods rather than table salt. As much as 50–75 percent of sodium in the American diet is added to foods by manufacturers for taste or as a preservative. Individuals add another 15 percent during cooking and by salting food at the table. The sodium occurring naturally in foods such as eggs, milk, meats, and vegetables may supply only about 10–15 percent of your total sodium intake. Drinking water may also contribute to our sodium consumption, as do certain medicines, mouthwash, and toothpaste. Foods with the highest sodium content include luncheon meats (ham, turkey, salami, and pepperoni), snack chips, French fries, hot dogs, cheeses, soups, and gravies. Table 7.6 and Figure 7.14 illustrate some common foods and their sodium content.

Although Table 7.6 gives you the level of sodium in select serving sizes for particular foods, following the tips listed in Figure 7.14 may be more practical if you are trying to reduce your sodium intake.

FIGURE 7.14
High-Sodium Foods to Limit or Avoid.

1. Cured, processed, or smoked meats and fish such as ham, bacon, corned beef, cold cuts, hot dogs, chipped beef, pickled herring, sardines, tuna, and anchovies
2. Meat sauces, bouillon cubes, and meat extracts
3. Salted snacks such as potato chips, corn chips, pretzels, salted popcorn, nuts, and crackers
4. Salad dressings, relishes, Worcestershire sauce, barbecue sauce, soy sauce, salsa, and ketchup
5. Packaged frozen foods; packaged sauce mixes, gravies, and casseroles; and packaged noodle, rice, and potato dishes
6. Canned soup
7. Cheese, including processed cheese and cheese spreads

TABLE 7.6 Sodium Content of Selected Foods

Food	Sodium (mg)	Food	Sodium (mg)
Meat and Alternatives		**Other**	
Corned beef (3 oz.)	827	Salt (1 tsp.)	2132
Ham (3 oz.)	800	Pickle, dill, large	1181
Tuna, canned in oil (3 oz.)	337	Broth, chicken (1 cup)	924
Sausage, pork (3 links)	362	Ravioli, canned (1 cup)	741
Hot dog	527	Broth, beef (1 cup)	893
Bologna (1 slice)	304	Gravy (1/3 cup)	374
Milk and Milk Products		Italian dressing (2 tbsp.)	292
Cream soup (1 cup)	871	Pretzels, thin (1 oz.)	326
Cottage cheese (½ cup)	382	Olives, green (5)	210
Cheese, American (1 oz.)	445	Pizza, cheese (1 slice)	362
Cheese, Parmesan (1 oz.)	433	Soy sauce (1 tsp.)	409
Milk, skim (1 cup)	103	Bacon (3 slices)	581
Milk, whole (1 cup)	105	French dressing (2 tbsp.)	268
Grains		Potato chips (1 oz.)	128
Bran flakes (1 cup)	180	Ketchup (1 tbsp.)	154
Corn flakes (1 cup)	204	**Fast Foods**	
Bagel, medium	561	McDonald's cheeseburger	745
English muffin	264	Big Mac	1007
Bread, white (1 slice)	137	Pizza Hut Supreme pizza (1 slice)	875
Bread, whole-wheat (1 slice)	146	Taco Bell taco	274
Crackers, saltine (4)	112		

Dietary Chloride

As with sodium, the natural chloride content of most foods is low. However, sodium chloride, or table salt, is approximately 60 percent chloride. As discussed, it is frequently added to foods in substantial amounts as a flavor enhancer or preservative. A food containing 1 g of sodium chloride includes approximately 600 mg of chloride. Because we typically consume 8.5 g of salt per day, it's easy to see how we are exceeding the DRI of 2,300 mg for chloride.

Dietary Potassium

Unlike sodium and chloride, potassium is not routinely added to foods. Rich sources of potassium are typically fresh, unprocessed foods. Fresh fruits and vegetables are ranked among the best potassium sources. Tomatoes, carrots, potatoes, beans, peaches, pears, squash, oranges, and bananas are all notable for their high potassium content (Table 7.7). Milk, meats, whole grains, coffee, and tea are also among the most significant contributors to our daily consumption of potassium.

Make it a
PRACTICE

MINIMIZING SALT IN YOUR DIET

Health professionals universally advise moderating our salt intake. Many of us have acquired a taste for salt, which makes adhering to a low-salt diet challenging. Next time you go out to eat with family or friends, observe how many people salt their food before they even taste it. Here are some simple steps for reducing salt in your diet:

- Avoid consuming too many processed foods. Canned foods such as vegetables and soups typically contain much more salt than fresh or frozen foods. Check the labels.
- Cut down on the use of salt when cooking. Even when cooking pasta or rice, there is no need to add salt to the water.
- Try to avoid adding salt to your food at the table. At least taste your food first. The only benefit of this salt source is it provides iodine (a required nutrient) if iodized salt is used.
- Learn to use other flavor enhancers such as lemon juice and salt-free herb mixtures.
- When cooking, use sodium-free herbs, spices, and flavorings such as allspice, garlic, garlic powder, mustard powder, onion powder, paprika, parsley, pepper, rosemary, sage, thyme, and vinegar. Try using other flavor enhancers. However, be cautious when using dried celery or parsley, as they may have added sodium. The best option is to use fresh herbs whenever possible.

Following a low-salt diet will likely be difficult at first. However, our taste perception of salt does change, so slowly alter salt levels and you will find you think lower salt foods taste normal to you. Give yourself at least two months for your taste buds to adapt.

TABLE 7.7 Potassium Content of Selected Foods

Food	Potassium (mg)
Vegetables	
Potato, medium, baked	941
Squash, summer, raw (2 cups)	592
Tomato, medium whole	292
Celery (1 medium stalk)	104
Carrot, small whole	160
Broccoli (2 cups raw)	575
Fruit	
Avocado (1)	975
Orange juice (1 cup)	496
Banana, medium	422
Raisins (1 oz.)	212
Prunes (3)	209
Watermelon (1 cup)	170
Milk and Milk Products	
Yogurt, whole milk (1 cup)	380
Milk, skim (1 cup)	410
Meats	
Tuna, canned in oil (3 oz.)	283
Ground beef patty 85% lean, broiled (3 oz.)	270
Lamb, loin, roasted (3 oz.)	209
Pork, loin, roasted (3 oz.)	268
Chicken, breast, roasted (3 oz.)	133
Grains	
Bran buds (1 cup)	731
Bran flakes (1 cup)	221
Raisin bran (1 cup)	352
Wheat flakes (1 cup)	200

© paulista/Shutterstock.com

© Julie Clopper/Shutterstock.com

© Perry Correll/Shutterstock.com

© Nattika/Shutterstock.com

Sodium is hidden in many food items. To reduce your sodium intake, try to avoid adding salt to your food and limit consumption of salty snacks and processed foods. Do you consume many of the foods shown here?

Hypertension and Sodium

hypertension
High blood pressure.

Medical research suggests that for certain individuals, a diet high in sodium may increase the risk of developing high blood pressure or **hypertension.** Therefore, the U.S. government requires food manufacturers to list the per-serving sodium content on food labels. Manufacturer claims regarding sodium content must follow the labeling criteria given in Table 7.8. Terms such as *sodium-free, low sodium,* and *unsalted* must adhere to a strict definition.

TABLE 7.8 Sodium Labeling

Label Claim	Sodium Content
Sodium free	Must contain <5 mg sodium/serving
Very low sodium	Must contain ≤35 mg sodium/serving
Low sodium	Must contain ≤140 mg sodium/serving
Reduced sodium	At least 25% less sodium than the original product
Light in sodium or lightly salted	At least 50% less sodium than the original product
Unsalted or no added salt	No salt added to recipe—does not mean sodium free

essential hypertension
High blood pressure that is due to an unknown cause.

secondary hypertension
High blood pressure that is due to other diseases such as kidney disease.

Roughly one in three American adults have high blood pressure, a confirmed risk factor for coronary heart disease and stroke. Millions of Americans have these diseases. The exact cause behind the majority of hypertension cases is unknown; high blood pressure that is due to an unknown cause is called **essential hypertension.** *Many factors are thought to play a role in essential hypertension. Diet, inactivity, obesity, stress, genetics, increasing age, and male gender are just some of the factors that increase the risk.*

The remaining cases, known as **secondary hypertension**, have known causes such as kidney disease. Fortunately, most hypertension is treatable with lifestyle modifications (diet and exercise) and/or medication. Everyone should have his or her blood pressure checked annually.

Much debate among health professionals has centered on what constitutes high blood pressure. Because blood pressure increases with age, what may be normal for an adult may be considered high for a child or teenager. Blood pressure readings consist of two components. When the heart contracts and forces blood to move because of an increase in pressure from the pumping action, the peak pressure generated is called the **systolic blood pressure.** When the heart relaxes and blood pressure falls, the lowest blood pressure reading during cardiac relaxation is called **diastolic blood pressure.** Normally, a person with a systolic reading of 140 mm Hg or greater, or a diastolic reading of 90 mm Hg or greater, or both, is considered hypertensive. Table 7.9 outlines normal and high blood pressure readings for adults age 18 or older. People in Stages 1 and 2 are at increased risk for a heart attack or kidney disease. Normalizing blood pressure, through lifestyle change, medication, or a combination, is an important step in reducing the risk of these diseases.

systolic blood pressure
The peak pressure generated when the heart contracts and forces blood to move because of an increase in pressure from the pumping action.

diastolic blood pressure
When the heart relaxes and blood pressure falls; this is the lowest blood pressure reading during cardiac relaxation.

TABLE 7.9 Normal and High Blood Pressure Measurements for Adults Age 18 or Older

	Blood Pressure, mm Hg		
Category	**Systolic**		**Diastolic**
Normal	<120	and	<80
Prehypertension	120–139	or	80–89
High			
Stage 1	140–159		90–99
Stage 2	160 or higher	or	100 or higher
Hypertensive crisis	Higher than 180	or	Higher than 110

Source: Reprinted with permission from the American Heart Association.

Regardless of the classification, the role of diet in the control of hypertension has been studied and debated for years. Hypertension is often associated with obesity, and losing weight can result in a significant drop in blood pressure. Sodium has long been linked with an increased incidence of hypertension. For many years, health professionals advocated reducing salt intake to decrease the incidence of hypertension. But continued research has shown that not all individuals with a high sodium intake develop hypertension. Some studies have shown that individuals who have a difficult time excreting the sodium they consume experience higher blood pressure. Other studies suggest that the greater the reduction of sodium in the diet, the greater the reduction in blood pressure. People whose blood pressure responds well (declines) to a low-sodium diet are called *salt sensitive.* However, many factors are involved with high blood pressure, besides the food choices we make, such as our level of physical activity.

Potassium appears to exert an antihypertensive effect by relaxing blood vessels. Maintaining the proper balance of sodium and potassium is therefore very important. However, the typical American diet is high in sodium and low in potassium. Nutrition experts often identify the sodium–potassium consumption ratio as a critical determinant of hypertension.

Do you have your blood pressure checked on a regular basis? This is done quickly and easily and is a painless process.

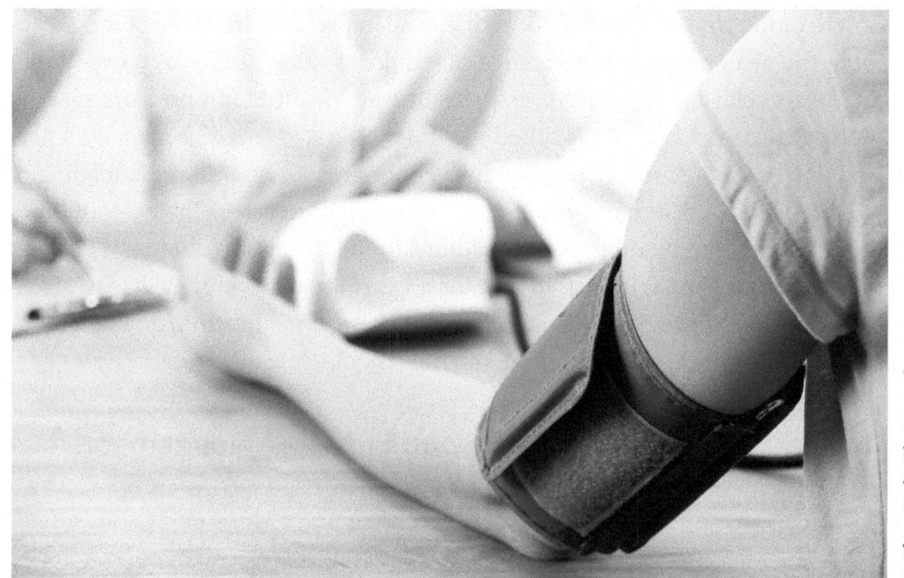

© Africa Studio/Shutterstock.com

Other minerals may also play a role in determining a person's blood pressure. Studies suggest that a high intake of dietary calcium and magnesium may be as important in controlling hypertension as limiting sodium. A diet high in calcium from dairy products has been shown to lower blood pressure significantly in people with hypertension.

One of the most effective campaigns against hypertension is called the **Dietary Approaches to Stop Hypertension (DASH) eating plan**, which is rich in fruits, vegetables, and low-fat dairy products, and is low in fat and saturated fat.

Dietary Approaches to Stop Hypertension (DASH)
A diet pattern promoted for the prevention and control of hypertension.

Nutrition & DISEASE

One of the most effective diet and lifestyle changes to manage hypertension is called the **Dietary Approaches to Stop Hypertension (DASH)** eating plan, which is rich in fruits, vegetables, whole grains, legumes, nuts, seeds, and low-fat dairy products and is low in fat and saturated fat. When used in combination with moderate salt intake, the DASH plan (Table 7.10) lowers blood pressure significantly, as well as improves blood cholesterol levels (i.e., lowers LDL cholesterol). Following the DASH plan results in a higher intake of calcium, magnesium, potassium and fiber and a lower intake of sodium. Given these findings and those outlined earlier, a diet that conforms to DASH would seem to go a long way in reducing high blood pressure.

Table 7.10 The DASH Eating Plan

Food Group	Daily Servings	Serving Sizes	Examples and Notes	Significance of Each Food Group to the DASH Eating Pattern
Grains	6–8	1 slice bread 1 oz. dry cereal 1/2 cup cooked rice, pasta, or cereal	Whole wheat bread and rolls, English muffin, pita bread and bagel, whole wheat pasta, bran cereals, grits, oatmeal, brown rice, unsalted pretzels, and popcorn	Major sources of energy and fiber
Vegetables	4–5	1 cup raw leafy vegetable ½ cup cut-up raw or cooked vegetable ½ cup vegetable juice	Broccoli, carrots, collards, green beans, green peas, kale, lima beans, potatoes, spinach, squash, sweet potatoes, and tomatoes	Rich sources of potassium, magnesium, and fiber
Fruits	4–5	1 medium fruit ¼ cup dried fruit ½ cup fresh, frozen, or canned fruit ½ cup fruit juice	Apples, apricots, bananas, dates, grapes, oranges, grapefruit, grapefruit juice, mangoes, melons, peaches, pineapples, raisins, strawberries, and tangerines	Important sources of potassium, magnesium, and fiber
Fat-free or low-fat milk and milk products	2–3	1 cup milk or yogurt 1 ½ oz. cheese	Fat-free (skim) or low-fat (1%) milk or buttermilk, fat-free, low-fat, or reduced-fat cheese, fat-free, or low-fat regular yogurt	Major sources of calcium and protein
Lean meats, poultry, and fish	6 or less	1 oz. cooked meats, poultry, or fish 1 egg	Select only lean; trim away visible fats; broil, roast, or poach; and remove skin from poultry	Rich sources of protein and magnesium

Nuts, seeds, and legumes	4–5 per week	1/3 cup or 1-½ oz. nuts 2 tbsp. peanut butter 2 tbsp. or ½ oz. seeds ½ cup cooked legumes (dry beans and peas)	Almonds, hazelnuts, mixed nuts, peanuts, walnuts, sunflower seeds, peanut butter, kidney beans, lentils, and split peas	Rich sources of energy, potassium, magnesium, protein, and fiber
Fats and oils	2–3	1 tsp. soft margarine 1 tsp. vegetable oil 1 tbsp. mayonnaise 2 tbsp. salad dressing	Soft margarine, vegetable oil (such as canola, corn, olive, or safflower), low-fat mayonnaise, and light salad dressing	The DASH study had 27 percent of Calories as fat, including fat in or added to foods
Sweets and added sugars	5 or less per week	1 tbsp. sugar 1 tbsp. jelly or jam 1/2 cup sorbet, gelatin 1 cup lemonade	Fruit-flavored gelatin, fruit punch, hard candy, jelly, maple syrup, sorbet and ices, and sugar	Sweets should be low in fat

Source: National Heart, Lung, and Blood Institute, www.nhlbi.nih.gov/health/public/heart/hbp/dash/how_make_dash.html.

BEFORE YOU GO ON...

1. How much sodium per day is recommended for an adult, and how much sodium do we typically consume per day in the United States?
2. What is the difference between a reduced-sodium and a low-sodium product?
3. Where does most of the sodium in our diets come from and why?

FUNCTIONS OF ELECTROLYTES

Absorption of electrolytes in the body is high, and their function affects our water balance. In addition to their role in water balance, electrolytes perform other important physiological functions.

Physiological Functions

The movement of water and electrolytes across the cells of your body is extremely important for basic bodily functions. Water and electrolytes are moved across cells through two processes, diffusion and osmosis. **Diffusion** is the movement of electrolytes from an area of greater concentration to an area of lesser concentration. **Osmosis** is the movement of water across a membrane from an area where there are fewer particles to an area where there are more particles in order to equalize the concentration (Figure 7.15). Physiologically, this means that if sodium builds up outside the cells of a tissue, water moves from the inside to the outside of the cells to equalize the concentration of sodium. In practical terms, this means that excess salt intake can lead to edema, which is swelling in the extracellular tissues due to excess fluid retention.

diffusion

The movement of electrolytes from an area of greater concentration to an area of lesser concentration.

osmosis

The movement of water across a membrane from an area where there are fewer particles to an area where there are more particles in order to equalize the concentration of those particles.

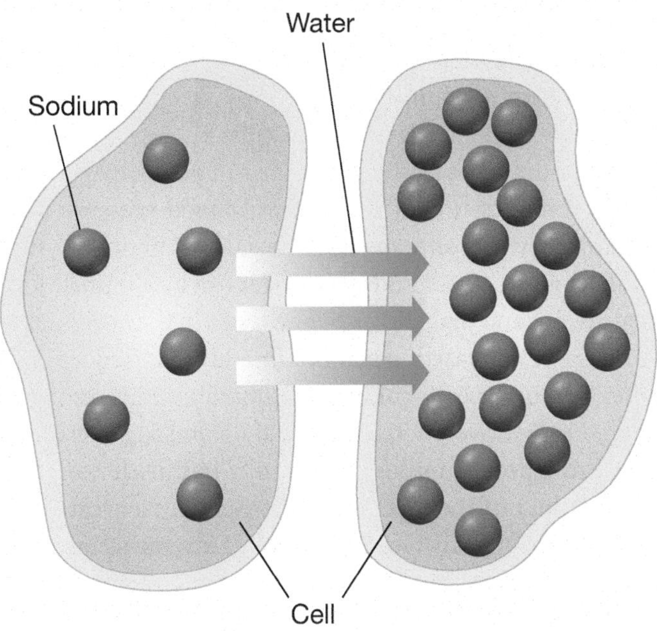

FIGURE 7.15
Osmosis is a fundamental principle of biology whereby water is distributed among organs, tissues, cells, and the blood. Water moves into an area of greater salt concentration to equalize the concentration in both cells. The cell membrane is permeable to water but not to the sodium in this example.

Because sodium and potassium have charges when they dissolve in water, they can carry electrical currents which allows the body to contract muscles and transmit nerve impulses.

Chloride, as a component of hydrochloric acid (HCl), establishes and maintains the acidic nature of the stomach. Cells within the stomach wall secrete HCl. This is especially important to help with the digestion of protein.

Deficiencies

A sodium deficiency rarely occurs, but it can happen. Loss of sodium is often accompanied by loss of body water or dehydration. Loss of sodium through sweat, followed by replacement of water *without* adequate sodium, can lead to water intoxication. This occurs because the sodium concentration in the extracellular fluids is diluted. This condition is called **hyponatremia** or low blood sodium. Another way of stating this is that the blood becomes too dilute. Drinking several gallons of water in a few hours can lead to this. Common symptoms include loss of appetite, weakness, mental apathy, uncontrolled muscle twitching, and brain swelling. Death can result if the condition is severe. **Water intoxication**, or *overhydration* has been reported in marathon runners and other endurance athletes. They often consume plenty of water without electrolytes, and the water consumption dilutes the electrolyte content in their body fluids.

hyponatremia
Low blood sodium.

water intoxication
A condition caused by excess water consumption that results in dilution of blood electrolytes, particularly sodium.

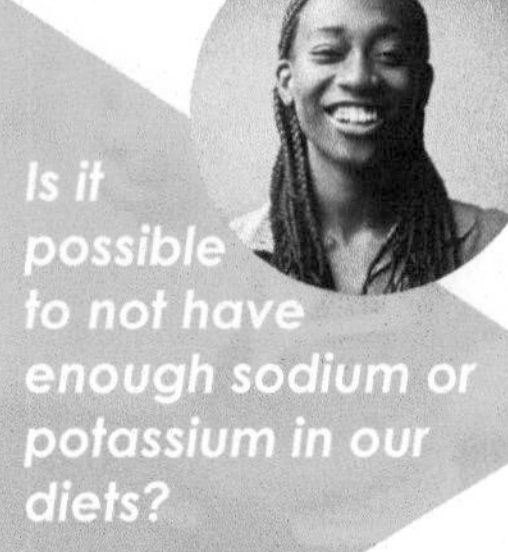

Is it possible to not have enough sodium or potassium in our diets?

Although your potassium intake may be adequate, some situations can result in a potassium deficiency. For example, persistent use of laxatives can decrease the amount of potassium absorbed in your digestive tract. Chronic use of certain diuretics intended to control blood pressure may also result in increased urinary loss of potassium. Because diuretics are substances that increase urine volume, water and electrolytes can be eliminated through their use. Kidney disease and diabetes also may result in the excess excretion of potassium because of increased urination. In addition, frequent vomiting after eating, either involuntarily or voluntarily, ultimately reduces the absorption of potassium in the digestive tract. Diarrhea and vomiting over a period of a few days can lead to a potassium loss that results in muscle weakness, complete paralysis and failure of the digestive tract muscle, tachycardia (rapid heartbeat), and hypotension (low blood pressure). Extreme weight loss can lead to loss of muscle and potassium, which can contribute to a potassium deficiency. In most cases, when you see your physician for an annual checkup, he or she will order blood tests that will include an assessment of your blood levels of sodium, potassium, and chloride.

SHOULD YOU USE SPORTS DRINKS WHEN YOU EXERCISE?

What's HOT

The issue of consuming sports drinks to improve performance when exercising or competing has been and continues to be a subject of much debate. Proper hydration is always critical for athletic performance because temperature regulation is highly dependent on hydration and the capacity to sweat. The amount of water lost during many events is tremendous, and it may take several days to replace what is lost. For instance, in endurance activities such as running, 2 quarts of fluid can be lost per hour. If you are involved in an event that lasts less than an hour in a mild climate, plain water will do fine. However, if you are participating in a longer event or one in which the intensity of exercise or performance is high or excess sweating is likely, then a sports drink may help. Not only do these beverages have electrolytes to replace those lost during sweating, some contain compounds (such as glucose) that help with water absorption in the small intestine. Even the presence of sodium in the beverage increases the body's absorption of water. However, a word of caution is in order. When these beverages are consumed during an event, gastrointestinal cramping may occur if their glucose content is too high. Weighing before and after a strenuous physical activity can help determine how much fluid replacement is needed. In general, 2 ½ cups of fluid are needed to replace 1 lb. of weight lost due to water depletion.

When you choose a sports drink, the carbohydrate concentration should be about 6 percent (from a combination of sucrose, fructose, and glucose) for optimal water absorption and to minimize gastrointestinal issues. Fructose-only drinks should be avoided because they can decrease water absorption and cause abdominal cramping. The drink should contain sodium (which will give it a somewhat salty taste) in order to increase the desire to take in fluids.

BEFORE YOU GO ON...

1. What is the difference between diffusion and osmosis?
2. What is the relationship between dietary sodium, potassium, and calcium intake and blood pressure?
3. When can you be at risk for potassium deficiency?
4. Describe a potential benefit and potential problem of consuming a sports drink in connection with exercise.

CHAPTER SUMMARY

- Our knowledge of minerals, especially trace minerals, continues to evolve, with most of the information obtained in the latter part of the 20th century. New analytical methods for detecting small quantities of minerals were a primary force behind these new findings.
- Minerals can act as structural parts of the body or as cofactors for enzymes. Some minerals exert their influence at the gene level. The amount of many minerals absorbed depends on the body's storage level. More minerals are absorbed when stores are decreased.
- Calcium is the most abundant mineral in the body. It is well known for its role in bone development. It also plays important roles in the physiology of cells, muscle contraction, and nerve impulse transmission.
- A lack of calcium over a period of time, particularly during adolescence, can lead to osteoporosis later in life. New research suggests that calcium, especially from dairy products, may lower body weight in obese individuals.
- Phosphorus is present in the body and in foods as phosphate. In this form, phosphorus stabilizes DNA, RNA, and ATP. It is a component of cell membranes and lipoproteins. It plays a central role in blood pH balance.
- Most Americans do not consume the RDA for magnesium. However, severe magnesium deficiency is observed only in cases of extended vomiting, diarrhea, excessive sweating or prolonged use of diuretics. Magnesium is a cofactor for about 300 different enzymes. It plays a role in muscle contraction that leads to relaxation of the muscle, and it is part of a pump that moves sodium out of a cell and potassium into the cell.
- One of the most effective diet and lifestyle changes to control hypertension is the Dietary Approaches to Stop Hypertension. This diet places an emphasis on eating more fruits, vegetables, whole grains and low-fat dairy, while eating less saturated fat and sugar. Following this meal plan leads to consuming more potassium, magnesium, calcium and fiber, and assists with lowering blood pressure as well as blood cholesterol levels.
- Iron-deficiency anemia is a too common public health nutrition problem in the United States and the number one problem worldwide. Women of childbearing years, infants, and children are especially vulnerable to iron-deficiency anemia.
- Iron toxicity is more common than previously thought. Consuming high quantities of iron can cause liver and red blood cell damage called *hemochromatosis*. However, a significant cause is genetic and involves the inability to regulate the amount of iron absorbed by the small intestine.
- Zinc was one of the first nutrients known to function at the genetic level. Zinc exerts its function as a cofactor for about 200 enzymes. Zinc deficiency has been documented in young boys showing symptoms of poor growth, poor sexual development, lack of taste, impaired wound healing, and compromised immunity.
- Copper is essential as a cofactor for fewer than 20 enzymes. It is involved in enzymes that improve the utilization of iron, increase the strength of connective tissue, and increase the synthesis of neurotransmitters. Copper is part of an enzyme that protects against free radical damage and is involved with ATP production.
- Selenium is a critical part of the body's antioxidant system. Deficiencies of selenium have been reported to lead to weakening of the heart muscle. Selenium is thought to decrease the risk of certain cancers, such as prostate cancer.

- Iodine's main function is to produce thyroid hormone, which regulates basal metabolism. Iodine deficiency results in goiter or enlarged thyroid. Infants born to mothers with low iodine develop cretinism, in which irreversible mental and physical retardations occur.
- The drop in tooth decay in this country has largely been a result of water fluoridation. Too much fluoride during tooth development can harm teeth and leave them discolored.
- Chromium is an essential mineral that is believed to help insulin transport glucose across cell membranes and consequently is thought to be helpful to some people with diabetes. Reported signs of deficiency are elevated blood cholesterol and triglyceride levels.
- Fifty-six to 64 percent (by weight) of the adult human body is composed of water. Women have less water than men because of their higher body fat percentage.
- Water consists of two hydrogen atoms and one oxygen atom. Hydrogen has a slight positive charge, whereas oxygen has a slight negative charge. This difference in charges makes water an ideal medium for dissolving elements that have charges.
- Water is the largest component of both intracellular fluids (inside cells) and extracellular fluids (outside cells). It serves as a medium in which other nutrients are carried and in which biochemical reactions occur. These biochemical reactions generate body heat, which water absorbs to maintain the body's temperature at 98.6 °F or (37 °C).
- Water loss occurs in several ways: urine, mild to severe sweating, feces, and lungs (breathing). Losses should be balanced with intake of water in food, and beverages, which not only contain water but also produce metabolic water when they are metabolized.
- The hypothalamus within the brain controls our sensation of thirst and monitors the body's fluid salt concentration. If the salt concentration is high, antidiuretic hormone is released by the pituitary gland to signal the kidneys to retain water. Aldosterone is produced by the adrenal glands; it induces the kidneys to retain more sodium and water.
- Dehydration is dangerous. During exercise, dehydration can occur rapidly along with electrolyte loss. Dehydration may also occur through vomiting and diarrhea. It can lead to cramping, heat exhaustion, stroke, and death. Drinking fluids with electrolytes is the best way to compensate for dehydration.
- Urine is the chief excretory route for body water and metabolic waste. The kidneys control the composition of urine and blood through microscopic structures called *nephrons.*
- Electrolytes are minerals that when placed in water become charged particles. Some minerals are positively charged (cations); others are negatively charged (anions).
- Sodium is the primary cation found outside cells, whereas potassium is the primary cation found inside cells. Chloride, an anion, is usually associated with sodium and therefore is more concentrated outside cells. These elements are heavily involved in the proper maintenance of water balance. If sodium builds up outside cells, water moves from inside the cells and blood compartment to outside the cells via osmosis
- The adult (not elderly) dietary requirement for sodium is 1,500 mg per day. Americans tend to consume about 8.5 g per day of salt or 3400 mg of sodium—well above the estimated requirement. The sodium occurring naturally in foods such as eggs, milk, meats, and vegetables may supply only about 10–15 percent of sodium intake. The remainder comes from salt added to food in processing, in cooking, and at the table.
- Populations that consume a high level of salt normally experience a greater incidence of hypertension. For many years, health professionals have advocated reducing salt intake to decrease the incidence of hypertension. The DASH diet is frequently recommended to people who need to lower their sodium intake.

KEY TERMS

ALDOSTERONE Hormone produced by the adrenal glands located above the kidneys. It induces the kidneys to retain more sodium and, consequently, more water.

ANEMIA A condition characterized by below-normal levels of red blood cells, hemoglobin, or both.

ANTIDIURETIC HORMONE A hormone released by the pituitary gland in the brain to signal the kidneys to retain water.

CRETINISM The mental and physical retardation of children whose mothers were iodine deficient during pregnancy.

DIASTOLIC BLOOD PRESSURE When the heart relaxes and blood pressure falls; this is the lowest blood pressure reading during cardiac relaxation.

DIETARY APPROACHES TO STOP HYPERTENSION (DASH) A diet pattern promoted for the prevention and control of hypertension.

DIFFUSION The movement of electrolytes from an area of greater concentration to an area of lesser concentration.

ESSENTIAL HYPERTENSION High blood pressure that is due to an unknown cause.

EXTRACELLULAR Outside a cell.

FERRITIN A protein that binds iron for storage and is a good indicator of iron status.

FLUOROSIS Fluoride toxicity that causes discoloration and mottling of the teeth.

FUNCTIONAL FOODS Foods and beverages that have been developed or altered in some way in order to optimize health.

GOITER An enlarged thyroid gland due to an iodine deficiency.

HEMATOCRIT The percentage of blood that is composed of red blood cells.

HEME IRON An organic form of iron that is still part of the complex ring structure that makes up hemoglobin.

HYDROXYAPATITE The large and complex crystal in bone that contains calcium and gives bone its strength.

HYPERTENSION High blood pressure.

HYPERTHERMIA Increased body temperature.

HYPONATREMIA Low blood sodium.

INORGANIC Describes a substance that does not contain carbon.

INSENSIBLE WATER LOSS Water lost through daily sweating, exhalation of air, and other mechanisms that are not easily sensed.

INTRACELLULAR Inside a cell.

MEAT, FISH, AND POULTRY FACTOR (MFP) A factor in these foods that enhances the absorption of elemental iron.

METABOLIC WATER Water that is produced during the breakdown of carbohydrate, fats, and proteins.

NEPHRONS Microscopic structures in the kidneys that control the composition of urine and blood.

NONHEME IRON The elemental form of iron that is not a part of hemoglobin.

ORGANIC Describes a substance that contains carbon.

OSMOSIS The movement of water across a membrane from an area where there are fewer particles to an area where there are more particles in order to equalize the concentration of those particles.

OXALATE A compound with negative charges that binds calcium and other minerals that have positive charges.

PARATHYROID HORMONE A hormone produced by the parathyroid glands located next to the thyroid glands in the neck; it is released if blood calcium levels decrease.

PHYTATE A substance that looks like a sugar molecule and is found inside the husk of whole grains and cereals; it binds certain minerals—calcium and zinc in particular—making them unavailable to cells.

PRE-ECLAMPSIA A serious blood disorder in pregnancy characterized by headache, fatigue, protein in the urine, and high blood pressure.

SECONDARY HYPERTENSION High blood pressure that is due to other diseases such as kidney disease.

SYSTOLIC BLOOD PRESSURE The peak pressure generated when the heart contracts and forces blood to move because of an increase in pressure from the pumping action.

THYROID HORMONE OR THYROXINE A hormone that controls the basal metabolic rate and heat production in our bodies.

TRANSFERRIN A blood protein that carries iron to organs.

TRANSFERRIN SATURATION the percent of iron that is bound to available transferrin. With other laboratory data, often used to assist in diagnosing iron-deficiency anemia.

WATER INTOXICATION A condition caused by excess water consumption that results in dilution of blood electrolytes, particularly sodium.

REFERENCES

http://www.cdc.gov/nutrition/everyone/basics/vitamins/calcium.html

http://ods.od.nih.gov/factsheets/Calcium-HealthProfessional/

FDA. Sodium in Your Diet: Using the Nutrition Facts Label to Reduce Your Intake. http://www.fda.gov/Food/ResourcesForYou/Consumers/ucm315393.htm.

USDA. National Nutrient Database for Standard Reference. http://ndb.nal.usda.gov/

TABLE 7.11 Summary Table for Minerals

Mineral	What It Does and Why It Is Important	Deficiency: What Happens If You Get Too Little	Toxicity: What Happens If You Get Too Much	Food Sources[1]		
Calcium	Component of mineral crystals in bone and teeth; involved in muscle contraction, initiation of heartbeat, blood clotting, and release and function of several hormones and neurotransmitters	Rickets in children; bone softening and osteoporosis in adults	Constipation, kidney stones, calcium deposits in body tissues; hinders absorption of iron and other minerals	**Food Item**	**Serving Size**	**Amount**
				Yogurt, plain	1 c.	488 mg
				Milk, 2%	1 c.	271 mg
				Cheddar cheese	1 oz.	192 mg
				Sardines, canned	2	108 mg
				Turnip greens, boiled	½ c.	99 mg
				Spinach, raw	1 c.	30 mg
				Broccoli, raw	½ c.	21 mg
Phosphorus	As phosphate, a component of mineral crystals in bone and teeth; part of high-energy molecules (ATP and CP) in cells; and part of cell membrane molecules	Weakness, bone pain, and anorexia (rare)	Hinders absorption of calcium (rare)	**Food Item**	**Serving Size**	**Amount**
				Lentils, cooked	½ c.	356 mg
				Milk, skim	1 c.	247 mg
				Chicken breast	3 oz.	155 mg
				Almonds	1 oz.	139 mg
				Mozzarella cheese	1 oz.	131 mg
				Egg, boiled	1 large	104 mg
Magnesium	Involved in energy metabolism; component of enzymes involved in numerous bodily operations	Nausea, irritability, muscle weakness, twitching, cramps, and cardiac arrhythmia	Nausea, vomiting, low blood pressure, and nervous system disorders (Warning: Overdose can be fatal to people with kidney disease.)	**Food Item**	**Serving Size**	**Amount**
				Cashews	1/4 c.	89 mg
				Whole-wheat bread	1 slice	37 mg
				Tofu	3 oz.	33 mg
				Spinach, raw	1 c.	24 mg
				Rib steak	3 oz.	22 mg
				Collard greens, boiled	½ c.	19 mg
				Turnip greens, boiled	½ c.	16 mg
				Cereal (special K)	1 c.	16 mg

Mineral	What It Does and Why It Is Important	Deficiency: What Happens If You Get Too Little	Toxicity: What Happens If You Get Too Much	Food Sources[1]		
Sulfur	Element in amino acids methionine and cysteine; assists with protein structure; found in thiamin and biotin; and antioxidant activity as part of glutathione.	Unknown	No known in humans	Primarily protein	n/a	
Iron	Component of heme structures found in hemoglobin, myoglobin, and cytochromes, which transport oxygen in the blood or store and handle oxygen in cells; found in molecules that are involved in collagen production, antioxidation, and energy metabolism	Skin pallor, weakness; fatigue, headaches, shortness of breath (all signs of iron-deficiency anemia), occurs during lead poisoning	Toxic buildup in liver and (in rare instances) heart	**Food Item**	**Serving Size**	**Amount**
				Cereal (special K)	1 c.	8.70 mg
				Beef liver	3 oz.	5.24 mg[1]
				Chuck roast	3 oz.	3.12 mg
				Rib steak	3 oz.	2.18 mg
				Great northern beans	1/2 c.	1.89 mg
				Red kidney beans, boiled	1/2 c.	1.61 mg
				Whole-wheat bread	1 slice	1.43 mg
				Raisins	1/4 c.	1.07 mg
				Chicken, white meat, roasted	3 oz.	0.92 mg
Zinc	Component of numerous enzymes	Slow healing of wounds, loss of taste, and retarded growth and delayed sexual development in children	Nausea, vomiting, diarrhea, abdominal pain, and gastric bleeding	**Food Item**	**Serving Size**	**Amount**
				Total whole Bran cereal	1 c.	19.95 mg
				Oysters, raw	3 oz.	14.14 mg
				Rib steak	3 oz.	5.94 mg
				Beef liver	3 oz.	4.45 mg
				Turkey, dark meat	3 oz.	3.79 mg
				Blue crab, canned	2 oz.	2.28 mg
				Shrimp, cooked	3 oz.	1.33 mg
				Peanuts, roasted	¼ c.	1.20 mg
				Cereal (special K)	1 c	0.90 mg
				Great northern beans	½ c.	0.78 mg
				Whole-wheat bread	1 slice	0.64 mg

Mineral	What It Does and Why It Is Important	Deficiency: What Happens If You Get Too Little	Toxicity: What Happens If You Get Too Much	Food Sources[1]		
Copper	Component of several enzymes involved in energy metabolism, antioxidant activity, collagen production, and hormone and neurotransmitter production	Rare in adults; in infants, rare type of anemia marked by abnormal development of bones, nerve tissue, and lungs	Liver disease, vomiting, and diarrhea	**Food Item**	**Serving Size**	**Amount**
				Beef liver	3 oz.	12.4 mg
				Oyster	1 medium	0.67 mg
				Clams, cooked	3 oz.	0.59 mg
				Sunflower seeds	¼ c.	0.57 mg
				Great northern beans, boiled	1 c.	0.43 mg
				Pecans	1 oz.	0.34 mg
				Shrimp, canned	3 oz.	0.23 mg
				Mushrooms, raw	1 c.	0.22 mg
				Peanuts, roasted	1 oz.	0.19 mg
				Cereal (special K)	1 c.	0.06 mg
Selenium	Component of antioxidant enzyme; involved in thyroid hormone function	Weakened heart	Fingernail changes, hair loss	**Food Item**	**Serving Size**	**Amount**
				Tuna, canned, packed in water	2 oz.	46 μg
				Rice, brown (medium grain)	½ c.	38 μg
				Beef liver	3 oz.	28 μg
				Sunflower seeds	¼ c.	21 μg
				Whole-wheat bread	1 slice	18 μg
				Crab, boiled	3 oz.	17 μg
				Cereal (special K)	1 c.	7 μg
				Rice, white (long grain)	½ c.	6 μg
Iodine	Component of thyroid hormone	Goiter (enlargement of thyroid gland)	Results from overdose of medications or supplements; burning in mouth, throat and stomach and/or abdominal pain, nausea, vomiting, diarrhea, weak pulse, and coma	**Food Item**	**Serving Size**	**Amount**
				Codfish	3 oz.	99 μg
				Iodized salt	1 g	77 μg
				Shrimp	3 oz.	35 μg
				Potato, baked, with skin	1	62 μg
				Egg, hard-boiled	1 large	29 μg
				Tuna, canned, packed in water	3 oz.	17 μg

Mineral	What It Does and Why It Is Important	Deficiency: What Happens If You Get Too Little	Toxicity: What Happens If You Get Too Much	Food Sources[1]		
Fluoride	Involved in strengthening teeth and bones	Dental caries	Mottling of teeth	**Food Item**	**Serving Size**	**Amount**
				Shrimp, canned	3 oz.	169 µg
				Fluoridated water	1 c.	159 µg[1]
				Carrots, cooked	½ c.	53 µg
				Spinach, cooked	½ c.	43 µg
				Potatoes, boiled	3 oz.	42 µg
				Cheese	1 oz.	9.8 µg
				Milk, 2% fat	1 c.	6.8 µg
				Tomatoes, canned	½ c.	6.7 µg
				Broccoli, boiled	½ c.	4.5 µg
				Egg, hard-boiled	1 large	2.5 µg
				Cabbage, boiled	½ c.	1.1 µg
				Toothpaste		5001500 µg/g
Chromium	Involved in glucose metabolism	Elevated blood glucose, cholesterol, and triglycerides	Unknown	**Food Item**	**Serving Size**	**Amount**
				Broccoli	½ c.	11 µg
				Grape juice	1 c.	7.5 µg
				Potatoes, mashed	1 c.	2.7 µg
				Rib steak	3 oz.	2.0 µg
				Green beans	½ c.	1.1 µg
				Banana	1 medium	1.0 µg

[1]*Source:* USDA National Nutrient Database for Standard Reference, Release 19.

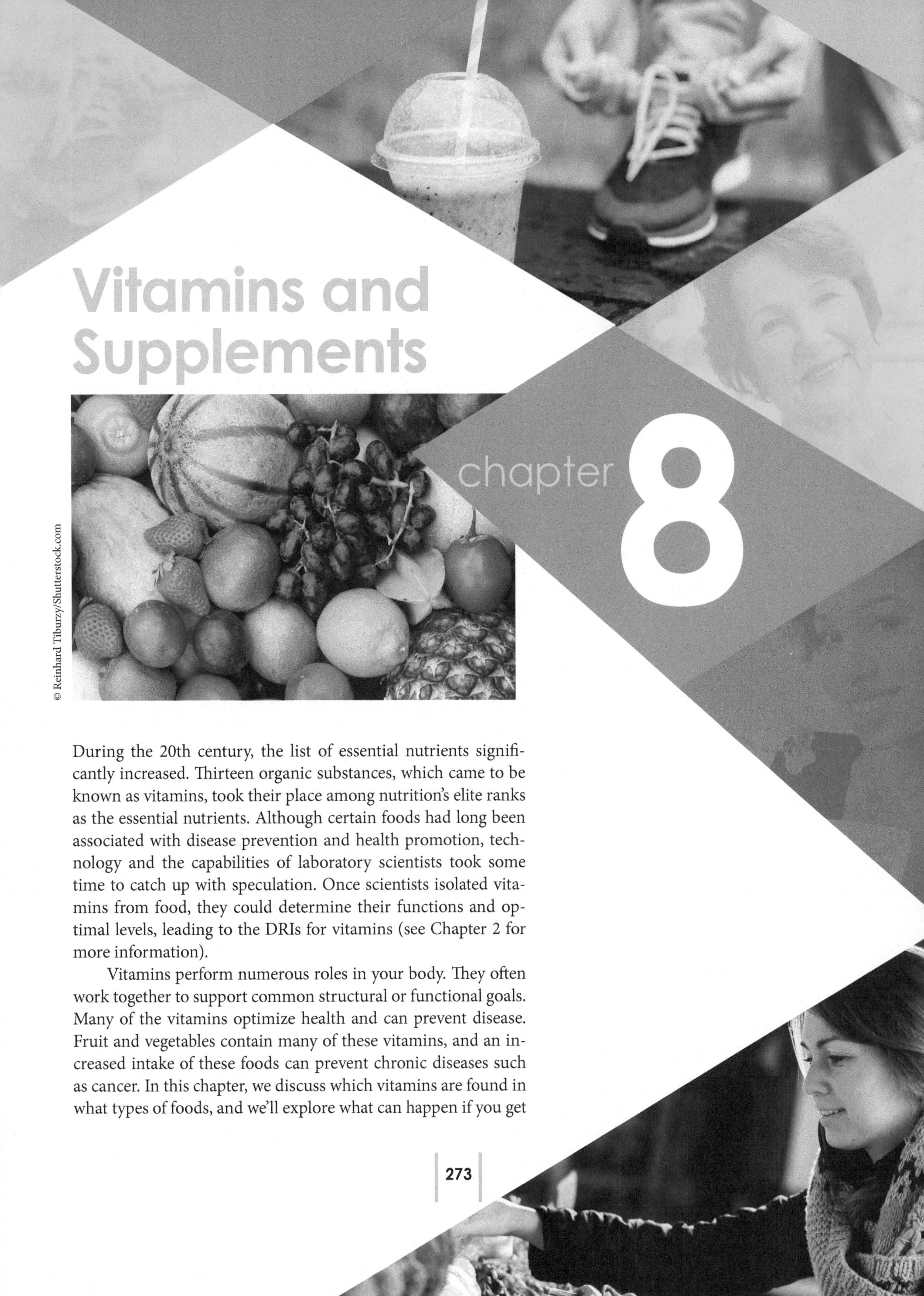

Vitamins and Supplements

chapter 8

© Reinhard Tiburzy/Shutterstock.com

During the 20th century, the list of essential nutrients significantly increased. Thirteen organic substances, which came to be known as vitamins, took their place among nutrition's elite ranks as the essential nutrients. Although certain foods had long been associated with disease prevention and health promotion, technology and the capabilities of laboratory scientists took some time to catch up with speculation. Once scientists isolated vitamins from food, they could determine their functions and optimal levels, leading to the DRIs for vitamins (see Chapter 2 for more information).

Vitamins perform numerous roles in your body. They often work together to support common structural or functional goals. Many of the vitamins optimize health and can prevent disease. Fruit and vegetables contain many of these vitamins, and an increased intake of these foods can prevent chronic diseases such as cancer. In this chapter, we discuss which vitamins are found in what types of foods, and we'll explore what can happen if you get too much or too little of these nutrients. Supplements will also be addressed. Today, vitamins and minerals are among the most popular dietary supplements, accounting for approximately $23 billion in sales in 2012. Although our current knowledge and understanding of vitamins may seem complete to the general public, we still have a lot to learn. As a result, DRI levels for vitamins continue to evolve.

Vitamins: A Little Goes a Long Way

As we discussed in Chapter 1, the macronutrients (carbohydrates, proteins, and fats) are required in your diet in *gram* amounts. In contrast, micronutrients such as vitamins are found in your body in much lower levels and are required in your diet only in milligram and microgram amounts. One reason for this difference is that carbohydrates, proteins, and fats serve major structural roles in the body and provide the fuel that powers your cells. Vitamins, however, are involved with biochemical reactions or metabolism and therefore are needed in much smaller amounts. This does not mean that they are less important than macronutrients; in fact, macronutrients need vitamins to function properly. For example, the B vitamins are needed in the pathways used to break down macronutrients into a usable form of energy—ATP.

Although several vitamins are involved in regulating energy metabolism, they are not a fuel source and do not provide energy. Carbohydrates, fats, and proteins are stored in the body and serve as readily available fuel resources. An adult male can store about a pound of carbohydrate as glycogen and, depending on diet and activity, can store 10, 50, or 100 or more pounds of fat. In contrast, although vitamin B_1, which is known as thiamin, is critical for proper energy metabolism, your body contains less than a teaspoon of this nutrient.

Origins of the Term "Vitamin"

Originally, the term *vitamine* was developed in reference to essential or vital (*vita*) and the presence of nitrogen (*amine*). As more "vitamines" were identified, scientists learned that not all of them contain nitrogen. Thus, the term *vitamine* was shortened to the more familiar term *vitamin.*

As they were discovered, vitamins were assigned a letter (A, B, C, D, E, and K). This system became complicated, however, when researchers realized that vitamin B wasn't a single vitamin, but rather several different ones involved in similar functions in the body. Each vitamin was therefore assigned a subscript. Thus, thiamin is also known as vitamin B_1, riboflavin as B_2, niacin as B_3, pyridoxine as B_6, and cobalamin as B_{12}. Pantothenic acid (B_5), biotin (B_7), and folate (B_9) are also B vitamins.

In addition to being assigned a letter and a subscript, vitamins are also categorized into two groups based on solubility (see Table 8.1). Thiamin, riboflavin, niacin, folate, biotin, pantothenic acid, pyridoxine, cobalamin and vitamin C are classified as water soluble. Vitamins A, D, E, and K do not dissolve well in water and are classified as fat soluble. There are also some molecules called **provitamins** or precursors; these substances need to be converted in order to be vitamins. Examples include **beta-carotene**, which can be converted into vitamin A, and *tryptophan* (an essential amino acid), which can be converted into niacin.

provitamins
Substances that need to be converted in order to have vitamin-like activity in the body.

beta-carotene
A precursor of vitamin A found in plants.

TABLE 8.1 Water-Soluble and Fat-Soluble Vitamins

Vitamins	
Water Soluble	**Fat Soluble**
Vitamin C (ascorbic acid)	Vitamin A
Thiamin (vitamin B_1)	Vitamin D
Riboflavin (vitamin B_2)	Vitamin E
Niacin (vitamin B_3)	Vitamin K
Pantothenic acid (vitamin B_5)	
Pyridoxine (vitamin B_6)	
Biotin (vitamin B_7)	
Folate (vitamin B_9)	
Cobalamin (vitamin B_{12})	

BEFORE YOU GO ON...

1. List the water-soluble vitamins.
2. Why are vitamins A, D, E, and K called fat-soluble vitamins?
3. What is the origin of the term vitamin?
4. What is a provitamin?

FAT-SOLUBLE VITAMINS

As mentioned previously, the four fat-soluble vitamins are A, D, E, and K. Fat-soluble vitamins are more likely to be toxic than water-soluble vitamins because they are stored for longer periods of time and in larger amounts. Because of this you do not need to consume fat-soluble vitamins daily. Fat-soluble vitamins are stored in the liver and the body's fat cells, which are not renewed as quickly as the body's water. Although these vitamins are stored longer and in larger amounts than the water-soluble vitamins, people can develop deficiency signs for them if they do not consume adequate amounts. It usually takes longer for the deficiency to occur, months compared to days.

Vitamin A

My grand-mother always told me that eating carrots was good for my eyesight. Is that true?

Vitamin A occurs in nature in three different chemical forms: retinol, retinal, and retinoic acid. These three forms are found in animal tissues. Retinol is the most active form of vitamin A and is stored in the liver. It can go to other tissues, and specific cells convert it into one of the other two forms. Beta-carotene is an antioxidant found in plants. This plant pigment can be converted into vitamin A in the small intestine if needed, and thus it is referred to as a precursor to vitamin A. The units in which beta-carotene are measured are called **retinol activity equivalents** or **RAE**. About 12 μg (micrograms) of beta-carotene will produce 1 μg of retinol; thus, you need 12 times as much beta-carotene to get the same benefit as retinol.

retinol activity equivalents or RAE
The units in which beta-carotene is measured.

Vitamin A has many functions. It is involved in vision, gene regulation, immune function, bone growth, reproduction, cell membrane stability, integrity of epithelial cells (cells that make up the skin and lining of the digestive tract), synthesis of the hormone cortisol by the adrenal glands, maintenance of the lining that insulates nerves, production of red blood cells, and production of thyroid hormone. Let's consider some of these functions of vitamin A in more detail.

Vitamin A and Eyesight

Vitamin A is so crucial to normal vision that a deficiency results in blindness. In fact, vitamin A deficiency is the leading cause of non-accidental blindness throughout the world. An early sign of a vitamin A deficiency is poor vision in dim lighting. This is often coupled with poor flash recovery, such as when the lights are turned on in a dark room and you must adjust your eyes to seeing in the bright light. A person with a marginal vitamin A deficiency takes longer to recover from the flash and to reestablish vision. In fact, the eyes are so sensitive to vitamin A status that an injection of vitamin A can alleviate night blindness within minutes.

Vitamin A is also involved in the maintenance of healthy *cornea* tissue (the outer layer of the eye). During short term vitamin A deficiency, the cornea becomes dry and hardened. Normal cells, which secrete mucus to help keep the cornea moist, become keratin-forming cells that dry out the eye covering. *Keratin* is a protein that is hard and tough and is what your fingernails are made of. This leads to a condition called night blindness, which is reversible with vitamin A supplementation.

One of the most common age-related eye disorders is **macular degenerative disease**. It is actually a group of disorders characterized by the breakdown of the *macula*, the center portion of the retina that makes basic visual acuity possible. Several micronutrients are thought to be helpful in slowing this progressive disorder, including vitamin A.

macular degenerative disease
A group of eye disorders characterized by the breakdown of the macula, the center portion of the retina that makes basic visual acuity possible.

Vitamin A and Disease Resistance

Vitamin A plays an important role in disease resistance, particularly for children. A vitamin A-deficient child has a weakened immune system and is more likely to become ill from a bacterial infection than a child who has ample stores of vitamin A. Vitamin A is important in the production of white blood cells, which destroy harmful bacteria and viruses. In addition, epithelial cells found in the skin, lungs, and lining the gastrointestinal tract require vitamin A for proper function. In vitamin A deficiency, epithelial tissue is often compromised. **Cell differentiation** is the process by which specialized cells develop that are capable of performing specific functions. These cells become specialized as they mature. This process depends on vitamin A.

cell differentiation
The process by which specialized cells develop that are capable of performing specific functions.

Bone Development and Growth

The role of vitamin A in the development of bone cannot be underestimated. Bone undergoes a process known as remodeling. This means that for bone to grow, it must be constantly broken down and rebuilt. Your body does not simply add more bone material on top of existing bone; the inner part of the bone is broken down and new bone is laid on the top and ends of the bone to make them wider and longer. Vitamin A stimulates the bone cells that break down the inner part of bone. Therefore, children who are deficient in vitamin A will most likely fail to grow.

Vitamin A Toxicity

Vitamin A has toxic effects because it is stored in the fat tissue and liver and therefore can be stored in the body for a long time and potentially accumulate to high levels. Eskimos are a primary example of people who have experienced the results of such accumulated levels. Historically, they consumed a lot of polar bear liver, which contains high levels of vitamin A. As a result, they experienced *hypervitaminosis* or vitamin A toxicity. The tissues and cells affected by excess vitamin A are often the same ones affected by vitamin A deficiency. Symptoms of vitamin A toxicity include headache, abdominal pain, skin rashes, liver damage, diarrhea, nausea, hair loss, joint pain, and bone and muscle soreness. Itching skin, blurred vision, growth failure in children, and increased bone fractures are also common.

Pregnant women should be particularly concerned about consuming excessive amounts of vitamin A because toxicity can cause fetal malformations of the heart, head, brain, and spinal cord. Consuming three to four times, the DRI for vitamin A can lead to these birth defects in newborns. For this reason, pregnant women are advised to consume beta-carotene to get their vitamin A. Vitamin A toxicity can come from sources other than food. For example, Accutane, a drug used to treat acne, is a vitamin A derivative. Women who are pregnant or planning to become pregnant should *not* take this medication because of the high risks of vitamin A toxicity.

Recommended Intakes for Vitamin A

The DRI for vitamin A is 900 μg per day for men and 700 μg per day for women. Children have lower requirements. Women who are breast-feeding will need more vitamin A, ranging from 1,200 to 1,300 μg per day depending on age. These amounts can easily be met through a balanced diet. Most healthy people do not require a vitamin A supplement. As mentioned previously, care should be taken not to exceed the Tolerable Upper Intake Level of 3,000 μg per day, as there is a risk of toxicity.

Food Sources of Vitamin A

Vitamin A, as retinol, can be found in animal foods and products such as fortified milk, cheese, cream, butter, eggs, liver, and margarine with vitamin A added. Plant sources of beta-carotene include spinach, dark green leafy vegetables, and broccoli. Beta-carotene is also abundant in orange and red foods such as apricots, cantaloupe, and certain vegetables such as winter squash, carrots, sweet potatoes, and pumpkins.

SHOULD I TAKE BETA-CAROTENE AS A SUPPLEMENT?

You DECIDE

Although vitamin A is toxic if taken in large doses, beta-carotene is not. When you have enough vitamin A stores, your body is not as efficient at converting beta-carotene to vitamin A, and thus a toxicity problem is not likely. This is not to say that overconsuming beta-carotene has no side effects. Taking large doses of beta-carotene can turn your skin orange, especially the palms of your hands and soles of your feet. In fact, health food stores once sold "sun-tanning" pills that turned out to contain high levels of beta-carotene.

Because vitamin A is needed for health, yet can be toxic, it seems logical that beta-carotene supplementation may be safer than consuming large amounts of vitamin A. Furthermore, research has suggested that beta-carotene may help prevent heart disease and cancer. According to one significant study, a higher intake of certain green and yellow vegetables, which are rich sources of beta-carotene, may decrease the risk of lung cancer. Many bright red and orange fruits and vegetables are also good sources of beta-carotene.

It appears, however, that taking beta-carotene supplements does not prevent disease and may lead to some adverse effects. For example, one study that evaluated both vitamin E and beta-carotene supplementation in 30,000 men who smoked cigarettes reported that those who took just the beta-carotene supplement had an 18 percent increase in the incidence of lung cancer over a 5- to 8-year trial period compared to those who took no supplement, a vitamin E supplement, or a combination of beta-carotene and vitamin E supplement.

Because of scientific studies, health professionals do not recommend beta-carotene supplementation for the general public. Bottom Line: Get your nutrients from food!

Vitamin D

A Vitamin with Many Roles

Another name for vitamin D is *cholecalciferol*. In addition to being a vitamin, vitamin D is also classified as a hormone and a steroid. Its precursor is cholesterol, as mentioned in Chapter 4.

In recent years, scientists have discovered many new functions of vitamin D. Traditionally, it was known for its important role in bone development and maintenance. The main effect of vitamin D on bone is its ability to control metabolism of both calcium and phosphorus, two minerals involved in bone integrity (see Chapter 7).

Vitamin D plays a crucial role in the regulation of calcium metabolism. It stimulates the cells of the small intestine to produce a calcium-binding protein which increases calcium absorption from food. In addition, when blood levels of calcium begin to drop, vitamin D stimulates the kidneys to conserve calcium by decreasing urinary excretion. Vitamin D also causes the bones to release calcium to help maintain blood calcium levels.

Vitamin D has many important functions besides bone health. Vitamin D also plays a role in cell differentiation by activating or repressing certain genes.

Vitamin D Deficiency and Bone Effects

rickets

A softening and deformity of long bones that results from vitamin D deficiency in children.

Vitamin D deficiency in children results in a disease called **rickets** (see Figure 8.1). Rickets is a softening and deformity of long bones, such as the femur and tibia in your legs, due to the inability to deposit calcium in newly formed bone. This results in a "bowlegged" appearance from the pressure placed on these softer bones. The bone is unable to support the body weight and it "bows" outward.

Recent studies have observed that the number of children developing rickets has increased in both the United States and Great Britain dramatically over the past several years. In fact, between 1997 and 2011, England had nearly a fivefold increase in rickets cases. Scientists propose that this disturbing trend could be related to several factors including increased amount of time children spend indoors watching TV or playing video games and the use of sunscreen. Both of these would limit exposure to UV radiation from the sun, which is required for your body to convert cholesterol into vitamin D.

osteomalacia

A softening of the bones in adults that results from vitamin D deficiency.

In adults, a lack of vitamin D leads to softening of bone called **osteomalacia** caused by decalcification. Because adult bones are already developed, the bowlegged appearance is not present. Older adults, particularly older women, are often at high risk when they do not get enough vitamin D in their diets or adequate exposure to sunlight.

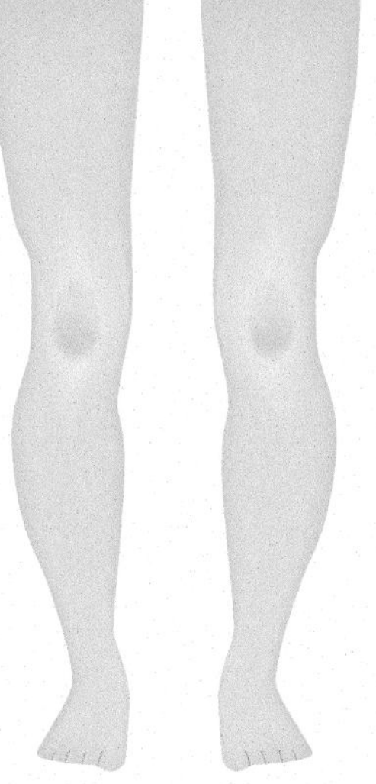

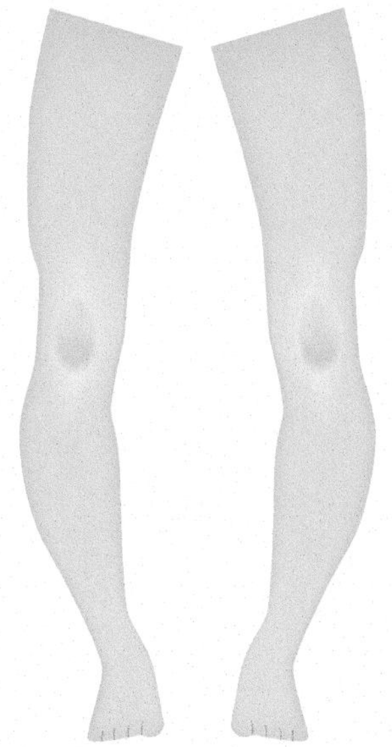

FIGURE 8.1 Normal legs vs. legs with rickets. Note the classical bowlegged appearance.

Making Your Own Vitamin D

Although vitamin D is a nutrient, some contend that it is not essential. The human body can make vitamin D as long as it has adequate exposure to sunlight. Cholesterol produced in the liver and found in the skin combines with ultraviolet rays (from sunlight) and is converted into a precursor of vitamin D. Through a series of steps, it is ultimately converted into the active form of vitamin D (see Figure 8.2). Despite the ability to obtain vitamin D from sunlight, you should also consume vitamin D–rich foods because many people do not get enough sunlight.

Those who live in areas of the world with limited daylight during winter months may be at risk for vitamin D deficiency. The farther you live from the equator, the longer the exposure time needed to get enough vitamin D. Therefore, without adequate dietary intake, those who live in northern areas with long winters may be at risk for vitamin D deficiency. Cloud cover, smog, clothing, and sunscreen all interfere with or block UV rays. A sunscreen with

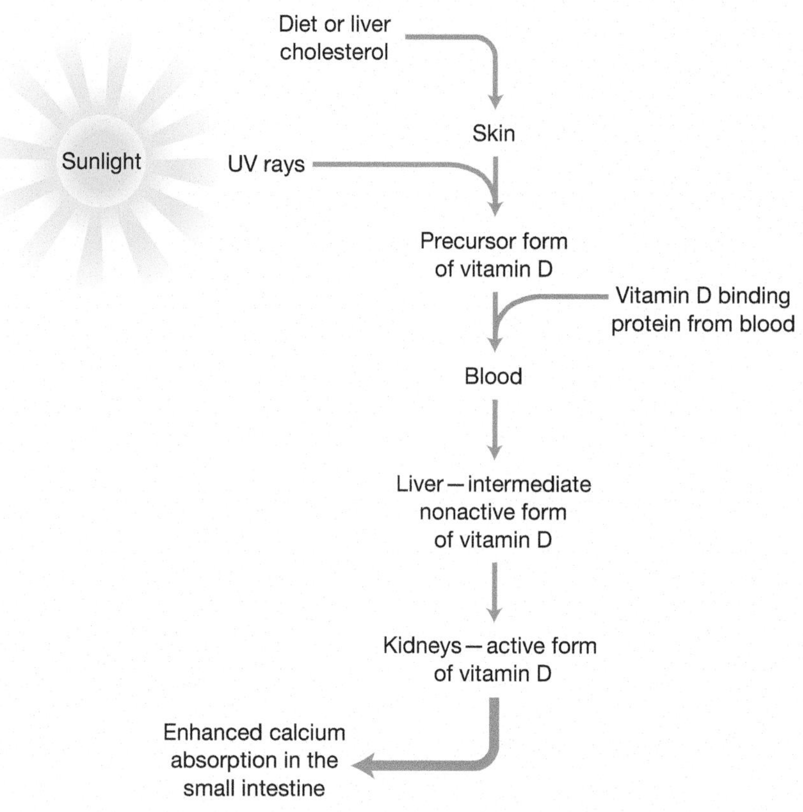

FIGURE 8.2 Production of vitamin D in the body, starting with exposure to sunlight.

SPF 8 can block the body's ability to produce vitamin D by 95 percent. In addition, those with darker complexions require longer periods under UV rays to convert cholesterol into the vitamin D precursor. People with light skin may require only 10–15 minutes of sunlight per day to get several days' worth of vitamin D, whereas people with darker skin may need several hours of sun exposure to get the same amount. In order to receive the benefits of exposure to sunlight, 20 percent of the skin should be exposed. Therefore, people who wear clothing that covers much of their body may need to receive more vitamin D from their diet. Tanning beds have UV light and contribute to the formation of vitamin D. However, the use of tanning beds to get UV exposure is not recommended because of its link to skin cancer.

Vitamin D Toxicity

Although uncommon, high consumption levels of vitamin D can be toxic because it is stored in fat and is not readily excreted from the body. The tolerable upper intake level (UL) for vitamin D is set at 100 μg daily. Symptoms of vitamin D toxicity include nausea, vomiting, and diarrhea. It may also lead to the calcification of soft tissues. For instance, the heart, blood vessels, brain, and kidneys may be targeted for calcium deposition with excess vitamin D intake. The ability to fortify foods with vitamin D is strictly regulated because of the potential risk of toxicity. In addition, one must be careful not to over supplement with vitamin D.

Recommended Intakes for Vitamin D

The DRI for vitamin D is set at 15 μg per day for children, adolescents, and adults up to 70 years of age. Infants need 10 μg per day and for adults older than 70, the DRI increases to 20 μg per day because of their decreased ability to convert vitamin D into its active form and decreased likelihood of adequate exposure to sunlight. The Tolerable Upper Intake Level for vitamin D has been increased to 100 μg per day.

APPLICATION TIP

Exposure of a person in a bathing suit to a minimal dose of sunlight, no more than 15–20 minutes at noon time, is the equivalent to taking 500 mcg of vitamin D orally.

Food Sources of Vitamin D

Other than oily fish, vitamin D is difficult to find in many foods. Therefore, it is often fortified in milk, margarine, cereal and juices. For teens, 3 cups of milk per day will provide 50 percent of the DRI for vitamin D. Remember that a combination of sunlight and food sources will *best* meet the daily requirement for vitamin D.

Vitamin E

A Vitamin That Fights Against Free Radicals

Vitamin E is not just one compound, but a group of compounds called **tocopherols**. There are four different types of tocopherols The Greek letters *alpha, beta, gamma,* and *delta* are used to identify them. They all have different degrees of vitamin E activity, with alpha-tocopherol having the greatest vitamin E activity.

Vitamin E fights against **free radicals** and is thus an **antioxidant** nutrient. Free radicals are unstable compounds with an unpaired electron that attack other molecules and break them down, damaging cell membranes, proteins, enzymes, molecules, and DNA. Free radicals can increase the risk of several different chronic diseases such as cancer and heart disease. They have also been associated with accelerated aging. Vitamin E acts as a "free radical buffer" by donating one of its unpaired electrons to the free radical to neutralize it. If left unpaired, free radicals cause a chain reaction in which one free radical sets off other compounds to becoming free radicals, leading to deterioration of the compounds and cells (see Figure 8.3).

Because vitamin E is fat soluble, it affords greater protection to lipid membranes or other fat-soluble compounds in a cell as opposed to free radicals found in the watery parts of cells and tissues. In addition to its potent role as

tocopherols
A group of compounds with vitamin E activity.

antioxidant
A compound that has the ability to help prevent or repair damage from oxidation by free radicals

free radicals
Unstable compounds with an unpaired electron that attack other molecules and break them down.

FIGURE 8.3
Free radicals can damage cells in the body. Notice the various sources that can cause free radical damage.

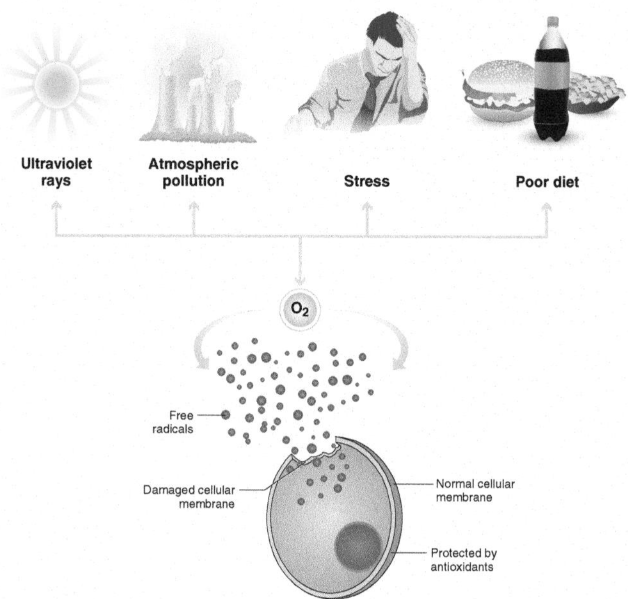

an antioxidant, vitamin E also enhances the immune system and is needed for nerve cell development.

Vitamin E Deficiency

Vitamin E deficiency has been reported in laboratory animals but rarely occurs in humans. This is because vitamin E is abundant in the food supply, the human body has large stores of it, and the body recycles what it does have. In adults, deficiency is most likely to appear in those who have malabsorption of the fat-soluble vitamins due to medications or disease. In addition, those on an extremely low-fat diet for prolonged periods can experience deficiency. Signs of vitamin E deficiency include loss of muscle coordination and reflexes, muscle weakness, and impaired vision. All of these are reversible with vitamin E supplementation.

Vitamin E Toxicity

Vitamin E can be toxic. Years ago popular literature advocated the benefits of vitamin E for its ability to enhance sexual pleasure and as an anti-aging nutrient. At that time, many people taking vitamin E supplements began to show signs of toxicity. These included headache and nausea, blurred vision, reduced sexual function in men, accelerated signs of aging, inflammation of the mouth, chapped lips, fatigue, gastrointestinal disturbances, muscle weakness, and increased bleeding. Research shows that extra vitamin E does not enhance sexual performance or slow the aging process. Supplements may also increase the risk of premature death from all causes.

Recommended Intakes for Vitamin E

The DRI for vitamin E is 15 mg per day for adults. Since vitamin E protects fats, the requirement increases among those who have a diet high in polyunsaturated fatty acids. The Tolerable Upper Intake Level for vitamin E is 1,000 mg per day. It may be lower for some people, such as those who smoke, because some research suggests an increased incidence of brain hemorrhage among smokers who take vitamin E supplements.

© Oksana Shufrych/Shutterstock.com

Food Sources of Vitamin E

Foods that are good sources of vitamin E include vegetable oils and products made with them, such as margarine and salad dressings. Wheat germ, nuts, seeds, and green leafy vegetables are also good sources of vitamin E.

Vitamin K

Roles in Blood Clotting and Bone Development

Vitamin K is best known for its role in blood clotting (see Figure 8.4). Vitamin K is indirectly involved with the production of the protein **fibrin**, which forms blood clots. Those without sufficient vitamin K stores may have trouble clotting when they bleed.

Of more recent interest has been the role of vitamin K in bone development because it is needed for the synthesis of some key bone proteins. Without the presence of these proteins, minerals such as calcium cannot bind to the bone. Thus, bone becomes soft, as in vitamin D deficiency.

fibrin
A protein that forms blood clots.

Vitamin K Deficiency, Toxicity, and Intake Recommendations

Vitamin K deficiency is rare in adults. The DRI for vitamin K is 120 μg per day for men and 90 μg per day for women. There is no Tolerable Upper Intake Level. However, this does not mean that excess consumption has no negative effects because large amounts have been shown to cause red blood cells to break apart.

Food and Other Sources of Vitamin K

Good sources of vitamin K include green leafy vegetables such as spinach and collard greens and vegetables from the cabbage family such as broccoli and Brussel sprouts. Soybeans and vegetable oils also contain vitamin K.

© Binh Thanh Bui/Shutterstock.com

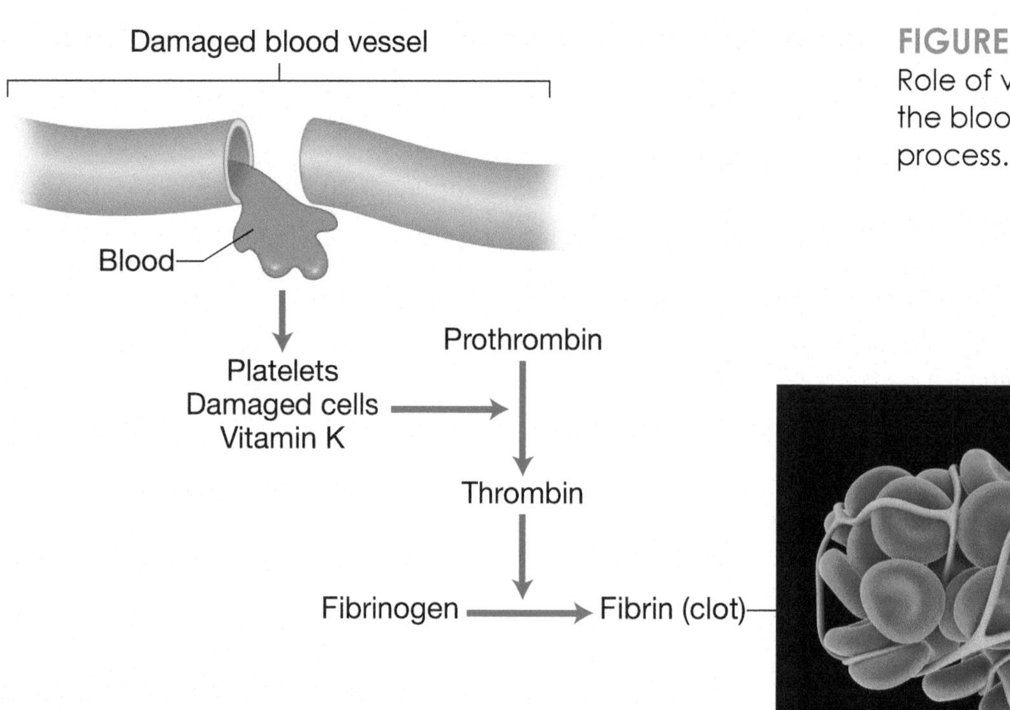

FIGURE 8.4
Role of vitamin K in the blood clotting process.

BEFORE YOU GO ON...

1. List the food sources of vitamin A.
2. How does vitamin A deficiency influence the eye and vision?
3. What is rickets and why might it be becoming more common?
4. What are some health concerns that may be associated with vitamin D insufficiency?
5. What is the major role of vitamin E?
6. What is the primary role of vitamin K, and why is deficiency rare?

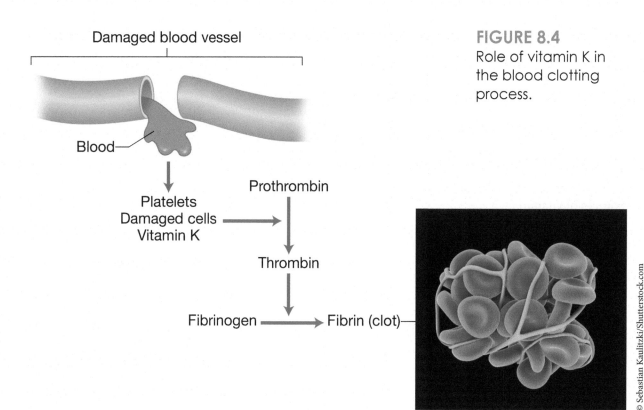

WATER-SOLUBLE VITAMINS

As indicated previously, water-soluble vitamins are not as toxic as fat-soluble vitamins because they are rapidly excreted with the urine. Therefore, it is difficult to get toxic levels of these vitamins from food sources. However, some water-soluble vitamins can be toxic if taken in large enough quantities, such as those that may occur with extreme supplement use. People often take large doses of vitamins to prevent or treat various conditions. For example, vitamin C is often taken in large doses to prevent or treat the common cold.

Vitamin C

Another name for vitamin C is **ascorbic acid**. Its use goes back several centuries to when sailors on long voyages came down with **scurvy**, a disease noted for bleeding gums that eventually leads to death that is caused by a vitamin C deficiency. Consumption of limes was found to prevent and treat it, and British sailors started consuming the fruits on long voyages, which is how they got the nickname "limeys." Other foods such as lemons, which are actually higher in vitamin C than limes, and cabbage were also recognized at the time for preventing scurvy even though vitamin C itself had not been identified.

ascorbic acid
Another name for vitamin C.

scurvy
A disease caused by vitamin C deficiency.

Role of Vitamin C

Vitamin C plays several roles. Like vitamin E, vitamin C is an antioxidant. However, because it is water soluble, it protects cell constituents in the watery part of the cell. For example, immune system cells have a lot of vitamin C in order to protect themselves against free radicals. This is important because a lot of free radical production occurs when the white blood cells of the immune system attack and kill bacteria and other foreign substances that cause illness.

Another important function of vitamin C is the production of the protein **collagen**. Collagen forms connective tissues such as tendons, bone, teeth, and skin and is necessary for proper wound healing and maintaining blood vessel structure. Vitamin C helps with the enzyme functions that are involved with the synthesis of collagen. Without vitamin C, the collagen that is made is abnormal.

collagen
A protein that forms connective tissues such as tendons, bone, teeth, and skin.

Vitamin C Deficiency

Scurvy is the result of severe vitamin C deficiency. Most of its symptoms are due to the improper formation of collagen. Bleeding gums, a classic sign, is caused by a lack of collagen in the structure of the blood vessels of the gums. Other signs of deficiency include loss of appetite, impaired growth, weakness, swollen wrists and ankles, and tiny hemorrhages on the skin surface that look like red spots. Anemia can also occur because vitamin C helps enhance iron absorption from nonmeat sources in the small intestine, and without it iron may not be adequately absorbed.

Vitamin C Toxicity

Although the Tolerable Upper Intake Level is 2,000 mg per day, there is controversy as to whether vitamin C is actually toxic. Many individuals supplement far in excess of the DRI and show no signs of vitamin C toxicity. For some individuals, however, supplementing at greater than 1,000 mg per day may lead to diarrhea and bloating.

Vitamin C contributes to a healthy immune system, but does consuming an amount beyond the DRI provide any benefit? Studies examining this issue have found that people who supplement their intake of vitamin C are just as likely to get a cold as those who do not. In addition, in very large doses, it can cause adverse symptoms such as diarrhea and other gastrointestinal issues. In addition, there is concern that excess vitamin C may lead to kidney stones; those with compromised kidney function should refrain from supplementing and should consume less than 200 mg per day. Vitamin C excess can also affect certain diagnostic tests. For instance, people who consume excess vitamin C may not have any evidence of blood in their stools but may have internal bleeding. Physicians usually ask patients to refrain from high levels of vitamin C during such tests.

Is it true that taking vitamin C will keep you from getting a cold?

Recommended Intakes for Vitamin C

The DRI for vitamin C is 90 mg per day for men and 75 mg per day for women. This is much higher than the 10–15 mg needed to prevent scurvy.

One population is at risk for low vitamin C stores: people who smoke and people who are around secondhand smoke. Studies have demonstrated that smokers consistently have lower blood levels of vitamin C because their bodies use vitamin C to help protect against the damaging compounds introduced by the tobacco smoke. Therefore, male smokers should consume 125 mg of vitamin C per day and female smokers 110 mg per day.

Food Sources of Vitamin C

The best sources of vitamin C are fruits and vegetables. Orange juice is perhaps the best-known source. Foods such as peppers, Brussels sprouts, broccoli, citrus fruits, strawberries, and sweet potatoes are also excellent sources of vitamin C. However, cooking can affect the level of vitamin C in these foods because heat and exposure to air can destroy or diminish it. The health benefits associated with the various methods for preparing and cooking vegetables are discussed in the following Make It a Practice feature.

Is there anything that I can eat or drink, other than orange juice, to get more vitamin C?

Make it a **PRACTICE**

HOW TO COOK YOUR VEGETABLES

There's more than one way to cook a vegetable, and all methods do not yield the same nutritional results. For example, boiling vegetables can result in loss of vitamins (especially water-soluble vitamins) and minerals into the cooking water. Microwaving, stir-frying, and steaming are more nutritious alternatives. Some experts maintain that steaming is superior to microwaving because it helps retain health-promoting flavonoids. On the other hand, microwaving's reduced cooking time can mean greater retention of vitamins that are sensitive to heat, such as vitamin C. When cooking vegetables, it is best to keep them as whole as possible; this results in less surface area being exposed, and thus fewer nutrients are lost. Regardless of cooking style, eating some vegetables every day is better than having no vegetables at all!

B Vitamins

The B vitamins play multiple roles in energy metabolism. For example, thiamin, riboflavin, niacin, pantothenic acid, and biotin participate in the release of energy from carbohydrate, protein, and fat (Figure 8.5). Vitamins B_6 and B_{12} are key nutrients in the metabolism and release of energy from amino acids. Vitamin B_{12} is also involved in the breakdown of glycogen stores to provide fuel during fasting and exercise.

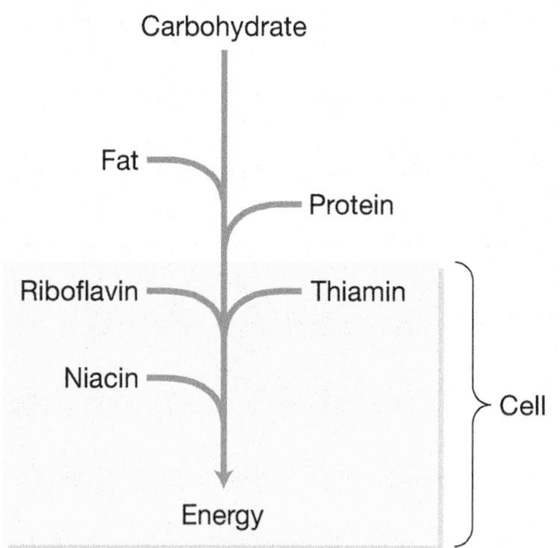

FIGURE 8.5
The B-vitamins, such as thiamin, riboflavin, and niacin, help cells derive energy from the energy-yielding macronutrients (carbohydrates, fats, and proteins), but vitamins do not supply energy themselves.

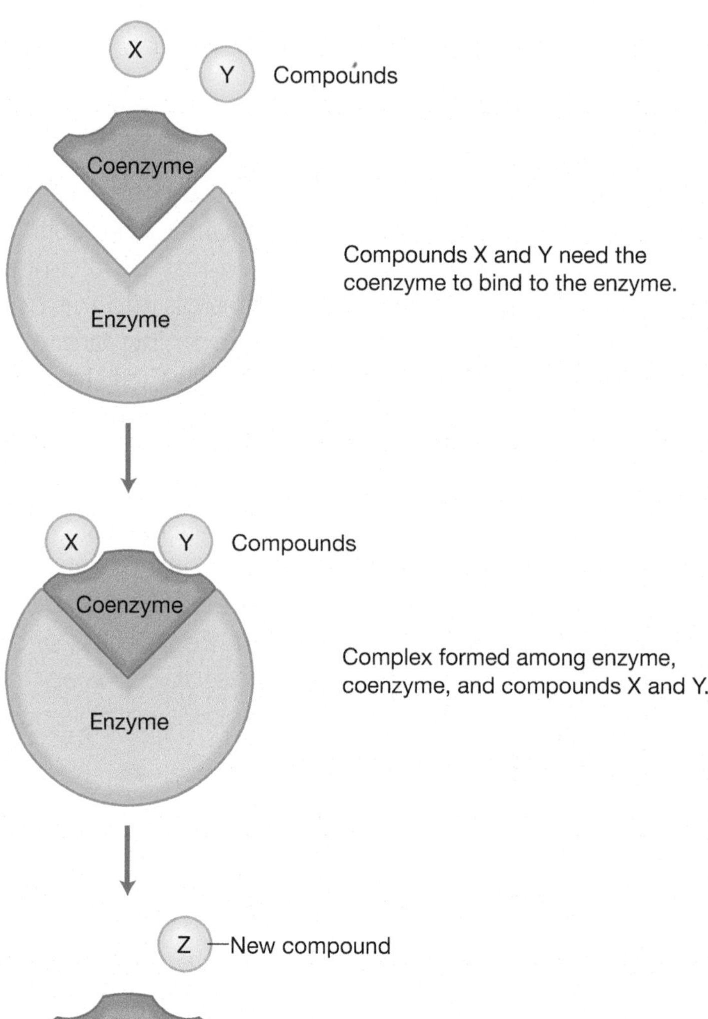

FIGURE 8.6
Some vitamins take part in biochemical reactions by acting as coenzymes. This scheme illustrates how a coenzyme helps an enzyme bind to a compound to create a biochemical reaction, which usually means that less energy is needed for the reaction to occur.

The B vitamins function in energy metabolism as **coenzymes** (see Figure 8.6). Coenzymes combine with an enzyme to increase its activity. As coenzymes, the B vitamins help release energy from foods although they don't provide energy directly.

coenzymes
Molecules that combine with an enzyme to increase its activity.

Because of their role in releasing energy, B vitamins are often added to energy drinks and other supplements marketed as energy boosters. Little scientific evidence suggests that B vitamins in excess of the DRI provide any extra "energy." Furthermore, without adequate Calories, macronutrients, and other nutrients, B vitamins alone will not increase energy.

Thiamin (B_1)

Thiamin, riboflavin, and niacin, as they are more commonly known, are also referred to as vitamins B_1, B_2, and B_3, respectively. They are all involved in the processes used to obtain usable energy, or ATP, from carbohydrates, fats, and proteins. Despite their similar functions, deficiencies in each can produce different physical signs in humans.

Function

Thiamin, or B1, was the first of the B vitamins to be identified as a unique compound from the other B vitamins. Thiamin plays a role in releasing energy stored in carbohydrates and some amino acids. In addition to its function in energy production, thiamin can also be found in the cell membranes of nerve and muscle cells and is required for proper function of these tissues.

Thiamin Deficiency

Beriberi, the result of thiamin deficiency, is a condition in which the heart becomes enlarged, fluid under the skin can accumulate, and the muscles become weak and may atrophy.

beriberi
The result of thiamin deficiency.

Another disease, **Wernicke-Korsakoff syndrome,** is due to severe thiamin deficiency in alcoholics. In addition to reducing thiamin absorption and increasing its excretion, high levels of alcohol consumption can also replace nutritious foods in the diet that contain the nutrient. Symptoms of Wernicke-Korsakoff syndrome include disorientation, loss of short-term memory, a staggering gait, and jerky eye movement.

Wenicke–Korsakoff syndrome
A neurological disorder associated with chronic alcoholism and thiamin deficiency.

Recommended Intakes and Food Sources

The DRI for thiamin is 1.2 mg per day for men and 1.1 mg per day for women. There is no Tolerable Upper Intake Level as no adverse effects have been observed with excess thiamin consumption. Some good food sources include pork, whole grains, breakfast cereals, enriched grains and pasta, green beans, milk, orange juice, organ meats, peanuts, dried beans, and seeds.

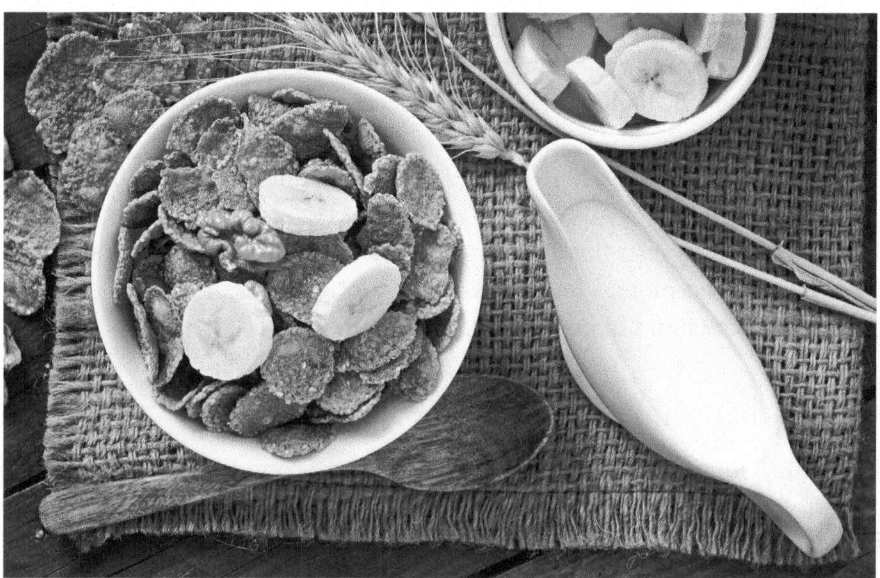
© Timolina/Shutterstock.com

Riboflavin (B_2)

Riboflavin, also called B_2, is another coenzyme involved in the release of energy from foods.

Riboflavin Deficiency

Deficiency of riboflavin often occurs in conjunction with deficiencies of other water-soluble vitamins. It results in a sore throat, cracks in the corner of the mouth, a swollen, glossy tongue, skin rashes, and hypersensitivity to light.

Recommended Intakes and Food Sources

The recommended daily intake of riboflavin for men is 1.3 mg and for women is 1.1 mg. Good food sources for riboflavin are milk, enriched breads, cereals, and pasta. Ultraviolet light can destroy riboflavin and this is one of the reasons milk comes in cardboard or opaque containers. In contrast, it is stable at high temperatures so cooking foods will not affect their riboflavin content unlike with some other nutrients. No Tolerable Upper Intake Level is set for riboflavin. However, while not detrimental to health, consumption of high levels of riboflavin supplements can turn urine bright yellow.

Niacin (B_3)

Function

Niacin can be found in two chemical forms: nicotinamide and nicotinic acid. Like thiamin and riboflavin, niacin is used to release energy from macronutrients. It is also involved in the synthesis of fatty acids.

Niacin Deficiency

Niacin deficiency leads to a condition called **pellagra**. The symptoms of pellagra are often referred to as "the four Ds": diarrhea, dermatitis, dementia, and death Pellagra was a major problem in the southeastern part of the United States in the early 1900s through the 1930s. Many impoverished Southerners at that time had three basic items in their diets: fatback (the layer of fat along the back of a pig), grits (white corn), and molasses. All three of these food items are devoid of niacin.

pellagra
A disease caused by a niacin deficiency.

Niacin Toxicity

Niacin is one of the few water-soluble vitamins to have toxicity symptoms. Overconsumption of supplements or fortified foods can result in "niacin flush." This temporary condition occurs when three to four times the RDA has been consumed and results in redness of the face, arms, and chest due to dilation of capillaries. The redness is accompanied by a tingling sensation that may be painful.

Nicotinic acid is often prescribed in conjunction with cholesterol-lowering medications called statins to help lower blood cholesterol and prevent heart disease in at-risk patients. The doses of niacin prescribed to these people often results in niacin flush.

In addition to niacin flush, overconsumption of niacin has been linked to an increased risk for liver injury, stomach ulcers, and vision loss.

Recommended Intakes and Food Sources

The recommendation for niacin consumption is 16 mg per day for men and 14 mg per day for women. The Tolerable Upper Intake Level is 35 mg per day. Sources include milk, eggs, meat, poultry, fish, whole-grain and enriched breads and cereals, and nuts. Niacin can also be synthesized in the body from an essential amino acid known as tryptophan. People who consume sufficient levels of protein, as do most people in the United States, are not likely to develop pellagra because the level of tryptophan in protein-rich foods is sufficient to make the needed amount of niacin.

Vitamin B_6

Function

Vitamin B_6 has seven forms. The most common and most active of these is called *pyridoxine*. Vitamin B_6 participates in many biochemical reactions. One of the most important functions is the conversion of one type of amino acid into another. This involves the nonessential amino acids discussed in Chapter 5. Vitamin B_6 also helps convert tryptophan into niacin and is involved in the synthesis of glucose and some types of lipids. It is important in the production of a neurotransmitter called *serotonin* that is derived from the amino acid tryptophan, as well as in hemoglobin synthesis. Therefore, a vitamin B_6 deficiency can lead to anemia. Other important roles for this vitamin include aiding immune function by helping in the synthesis of white blood cells, assisting in the release of glucose from glycogen, and development of the fetal brain.

Vitamin B_6 Deficiency

Similar to riboflavin, vitamin B_6 deficiency often occurs along with deficiency of other B vitamins. Because this vitamin is used in so many reactions, deficiency signs are diverse and include depression, vomiting, dermatitis, convulsions, anemia, and decreased immune response.

Vitamin B_6 Toxicity

Numb feet, loss of sensation in the hands, depression, fatigue, headache, nerve damage that progresses to the inability to walk, and convulsions have been reported in women taking 2 g per day or more of vitamin B_6. Many of these symptoms are not reversible.

Recommended Intakes and Food Sources

The DRI for vitamin B_6 is 1.3 mg per day for adults. The Tolerable Upper Intake Level is 100 mg per day. Sources of vitamin B_6 include beef liver, meats and poultry, baked potatoes, bananas, broccoli, spinach, watermelons, salmon, and navy beans.

Folate (B_9)

Folate

Folate is crucial to the maintenance of numerous tissues in the body, in particular hair, skin, and linings of the digestive and urinary tracts. Folate is import-

ant in cell division because DNA needs folate to make copies of itself during this process.

Folate Deficiency

In folate deficiency, macrocytic anemia occurs which is when the red blood cells cannot mature or form properly because of the inability to synthesize DNA. These immature cells grow in size rather than number. Other signs of folate deficiency are heartburn, diarrhea, frequent infection, inflammation of the tongue, depression, fatigue, irritability, and headache.

macrocytic anemia
Anemia characterized by enlarged, immature red blood cells that are fewer in number than normal cells.

Folate is so important to the developing central nervous system that deficiencies during pregnancy can result in severe abnormalities of the brain and spinal cord called neural tube defects. Spina bifida, the most frequently occurring and disabling birth defect, affects approximately one out of every 1,000 newborns in this country. Spina bifida results from the failure of the spine to close properly during the first month of pregnancy. As shown in Figure 8.7, the spinal cord can protrude through the back. Surgery is needed within 24 hours after birth to minimize the risk of infection and to preserve existing function in the spinal cord.

spina bifida
A birth defect that results from the failure of the spine to close properly during the first month of pregnancy.

Anencephaly, another form of neural tube defect, is a fatal congenital malformation and results in the incomplete or lack of development of the brain and skull.

Recommended Intakes and Food Sources

A distinction is made between dietary folate and the synthetic form of folate called folic acid used in supplements and enriched foods. Folic acid is more potent than folate because more of it is absorbed in the small intestine. Therefore, there is a greater chance of toxicity caused by consuming large amounts

folic acid
The synthetic form of folate that is used in dietary supplements and enriched foods.

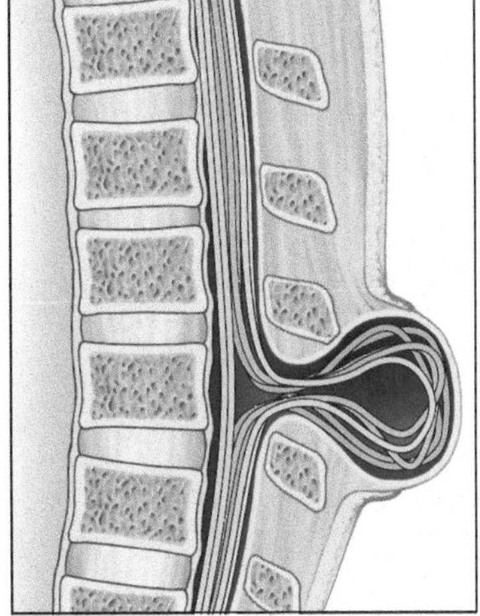

FIGURE 8.7
Neural tube defects can be caused by a lack of folate in pregnant mothers. The diagram shows how spina bifida results when the canal that houses the spinal cord fails to close, exposing the spinal cord to the external environment.

dietary folate equivalent

A unit of measure used to represent the conversion of folic acid into folate.

of the synthetic form compared to the naturally occurring form found in food. For this reason, the DRI is based on folic acid and not folate. A **dietary folate equivalent or DFE** is a unit of measure used to represent the conversion of folic acid to folate.

The DRI for folate (as DFE) is 400 μg per day for adults. Women who are pregnant or are planning to become pregnant should have 600 μg of folate per day. Some health professionals recommend that *all* women of childbearing age consume 600 μg of folate per day because adequate folate is most critical in the very beginning of pregnancy, before most women realize they are pregnant.

The Tolerable Upper Intake Level of folate is 1,000 μg (1 mg) from the synthetic source, folic acid. One reason for this limit is that higher doses may mask a vitamin B_{12} deficiency. Too much folic acid can cause convulsions in people with epilepsy.

Orange juice and green leafy vegetables are excellent sources of folate. Other good sources are organ meats, sprouts, beans, and vegetables. Breakfast cereals and bread are also good sources. A drawback is that folate is unstable and can be easily destroyed by heat, so much of it is destroyed through food processing. Preparation methods for vegetables that minimize the destruction of folate include microwaving, steaming, and stir-frying. Boiling vegetables in water too long destroys most of the folate in them.

APPLICATION TIP

Are frozen or canned vegetables an acceptable substitute for fresh ones? Frozen vegetables are considered a good alternative if you cannot purchase fresh vegetables. Most products are flash frozen close to the time of harvest so nutrient loss is minimal. Canned vegetables can be used, but since they are heat treated, the nutrient levels are not comparable to fresh or frozen. In addition, be aware that canned vegetables contain sodium. Check the label and look for low-sodium options.

Vitamin B_{12}

Function

Vitamin B_{12} is unique in several ways. First, it contains the mineral cobalt as part of its structure. Second, it is synthesized by bacteria and other microorganisms. Third, it is found only in foods of animal origin and not in plant foods.

One of the most important roles of vitamin B_{12} is to convert folate coenzymes into active forms. In other words, vitamin B_{12} is essential in converting folate into forms that the cell can use. Thus, a vitamin B_{12} deficiency can result in a folate deficiency. However, vitamin B_{12} has a separate function; it maintains the insulating lining that covers nerve fibers known as the **myelin sheath.** People with a vitamin B_{12} deficiency have a breakdown in the myelin sheath that disrupts nerve conduction, which can lead to paralysis and even death. Vitamin B_{12} is also involved with amino acid metabolism, bone metabolism, and the synthesis of DNA.

myelin sheath
An insulating sheath for nerve fibers that enhances conduction.

Vitamin B_{12} Deficiency

Vitamin B_{12} deficiency can occur because of factors other than insufficient diet levels. To utilize vitamin B_{12}, the stomach secretes a protein called **intrinsic factor** that binds to vitamin B_{12} and protects it from degradation until it can be absorbed. Some individuals have a genetic condition that causes an inability to produce intrinsic factor. As a result, vitamin B_{12} is destroyed by digestive enzymes without protection from its intrinsic factor, and very little is absorbed. This genetic defect becomes apparent in early adulthood. Many people lose the ability to produce intrinsic factor because of aging.

intrinsic factor
A protein produced by stomach cells that binds to vitamin B12 and protects it from degradation until it can be absorbed.

People who are affected by vitamin B_{12} deficiency because of the lack of intrinsic factor develop an anemia known as **pernicious anemia.** The red blood cells look the same as those found in folate deficiency. The cells, termed **megaloblasts**, are immature, larger in size, but fewer in number. Other symptoms of pernicious anemia include weakness, sore tongue, back pain, apathy, and tingling and numbness in the hands and feet. To overcome this problem, injections of vitamin B_{12} are given to patients lacking intrinsic factor. However, in many cases, nerve damage has already occurred and is irreversible. Pernicious anemia results in death if not treated.

pernicious anemia
Anemia that results from a vitamin B12 deficiency because of a lack of intrinsic factor.

megaloblasts
Immature, enlarged red blood cells.

Recommended Intakes and Food Sources

The DRI for vitamin B_{12} is 2.4 µg per day. Toxicity for vitamin B_{12} has not been reported. As mentioned earlier, naturally occurring vitamin B_{12} is only found in foods of animal origin. Milk, cheese, meat, poultry, and seafood are all excellent sources. Cereals and soy products are often fortified with vitamin B_{12} so can be a good source as well. Vegans and particularly those who are pregnant or lactating must make an extra effort to consume sufficient vitamin

© alexpro 9500/Shutterstock.com

B_{12}, as a fetus without enough of it from the mother can suffer irreversible nerve damage. People older than 50 are encouraged to take a vitamin B_{12} supplement because of decreased intrinsic factor synthesis.

APPLICATION TIP

To ensure that you consume sufficient folate in your diet, drink orange juice, add sunflower seeds to your salad, include beans in a meal, or eat strawberries for dessert.

Biotin (B_7)

Function

Biotin is involved with fatty acid synthesis and the breakdown of amino acids and some fatty acids. It is also important for the production of glucose and may also be involved with gene expression.

Biotin Deficiency

Deficiency of biotin occurs rarely. Consumption of raw eggs is known to induce biotin deficiency due to the fact that one of the proteins in eggs, avidin, binds to biotin causing it to not be absorbed. In an adult human, it would take the consumption of over two dozen raw eggs daily for several months to cause an effect. Cooking eggs denatures this protein. Symptoms of biotin deficiency include neurological impairment, hair loss, and skin rashes.

Recommended Intakes and Food Sources

Adults are recommended to consume 30 μg per day. It is widespread in foods; however, liver, soybeans, fish, and whole grains are considered to be particularly good sources. There is no Tolerable Upper Intake Level set.

Pantothenic Acid (B_5)

Function

Pantothenic acid is a part of a much larger molecule that is critical for harnessing energy. It is involved in the synthesis of lipids, steroid hormones, neurotransmitters, and hemoglobin.

Pantothenic Acid Deficiency

Deficiency of pantothenic acid is very rare. Its symptoms are nonspecific and include fatigue, neurological disturbances, and gastrointestinal distress.

Recommended Intakes and Food Sources

The RDA for pantothenic acid is 5 mg a day for both men and women. It is widespread in many foods and in fact, the word *pantothenic* is derived from the Greek word *pantothen* which means "from everywhere."

Pantothenic acid is known to be easily destroyed by food processing methods.

APPLICATION TIP

> If you have a hard time getting enough fruits and vegetables into your diet because you just don't like them, try adding them in with other foods or "hiding them." Frozen fruits can be used to make nutrient-dense smoothies and shakes by blending them with milk and/or yogurt. It is easy to create different flavors and textures. Vegetables can be chopped into small pieces and easily added to spaghetti sauces, soups, and stews or baked into casseroles, lasagnas, omelets, and pizzas.

See Table 8.4 at the end of this chapter for a summary of the functions, deficiency and toxicity symptoms, and food sources of the vitamins discussed in this chapter.

BEFORE YOU GO ON...

1. What are pellagra and beriberi?
2. In general, what foods are good sources of vitamin B_{12} and why?
3. What is spina bifida and what nutrient deficiency causes it?
4. List two functions of vitamin B_6.
5. Which vitamin plays a significant role in cell division be cause of its impact on DNA?

ENRICHMENT, FORTIFICATION, AND SUPPLEMENTATION

We have discussed the various vitamins and the foods that contain them. It is important to remember that supplemental forms of vitamins also contribute to our daily intake.

Enrichment

Food manufacturers enhance the vitamin and mineral content of many of their products by enrichment and fortification. **Enrichment** is the restoration of micronutrients that were originally present in the food but were lost during processing. Enrichment is mandatory when a manufacturer uses grain-based ingredients that have been milled, refined, or polished. These processes strip away the bran and germ, leaving only the starchy center region of the grain, which is referred to as the endosperm (see Figure 8.8). Flour made with the endosperm only is fluffier than whole-grain flour and easier to use in food manufacturing and home baking.

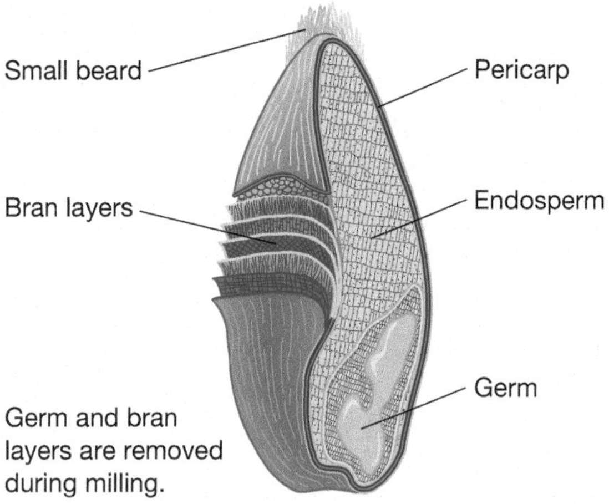

FIGURE 8.8 Nutrients are lost during the grain milling process. Germ and bran layers, rich in nutrients, are also lost during the milling process. The lost nutrients are often added back (enrichment).

enrichment
The restoration of micronutrients that were originally present in the food but were lost during processing.

From a nutritional perspective, however, the endosperm contains few vitamins. Most of the vitamins are found in the germ and the bran. For example, white rice is more refined than brown rice, which has more natural nutrients. In white rice, enrichment is needed to replace what has been lost through the refinement process. Not all of the nutrients that were lost are actually replaced, which means that brown rice is more nutrient dense than white rice. During the 19th and early 20th centuries, the widespread use of milled grains lead to serious nutritional deficiencies such as pellagra and beriberi, discussed earlier.

The Enrichment Act of 1942 states that U.S. food manufacturers must add thiamin, riboflavin, niacin, and iron to refined grain products. Although enrichment has eradicated many B vitamin deficiencies in countries such as the United States, they are still found in several underdeveloped countries.

Fortification

fortification
The addition of vitamins and minerals to foods that are not naturally present in those foods.

Some food manufacturers add vitamins and minerals to foods that are not naturally present in those foods. This process is called **fortification**. Breakfast cereals are an excellent example. The calcium added to orange juice is another example. Law mandates some fortification, such as vitamins A and D in milk and folic acid in enriched cereal and grain products. Fortification makes a significant contribution to the daily intake of vitamins. In addition to enrichment and fortification, many people supplement their diet with pills that contain individual vitamins or combinations of vitamins.

TO SUPPLEMENT OR NOT

Want to gain muscle? Improve athletic performance? Improve sexual performance? Lose weight? Grow stronger fingernails and hair? Obtain more energy? Increase concentration? Relieve depression? If you believe the advertising, whatever you desire to change about your health or appearance, you can seemingly achieve it by taking a supplement. We have all seen promotions for supplements on television, on the Internet, and in newspapers and magazines. With so many claims and promises, is it any wonder that millions of us fall prey to their marketing hype? In fact, marketing data shows a dramatic increase in the sales of supplements in the United States since 1997. Sales from supplements hit $32 billion in 2012 and is predicted to reach $60 billion by 2021 (Figure 8.9). As another indication of how successful these companies are, a recent study of 1,280 teenagers ages 14–19 reported that 46 percent admitted to having taken a dietary supplement.

Dietary supplements are a multi-billion dollar industry.

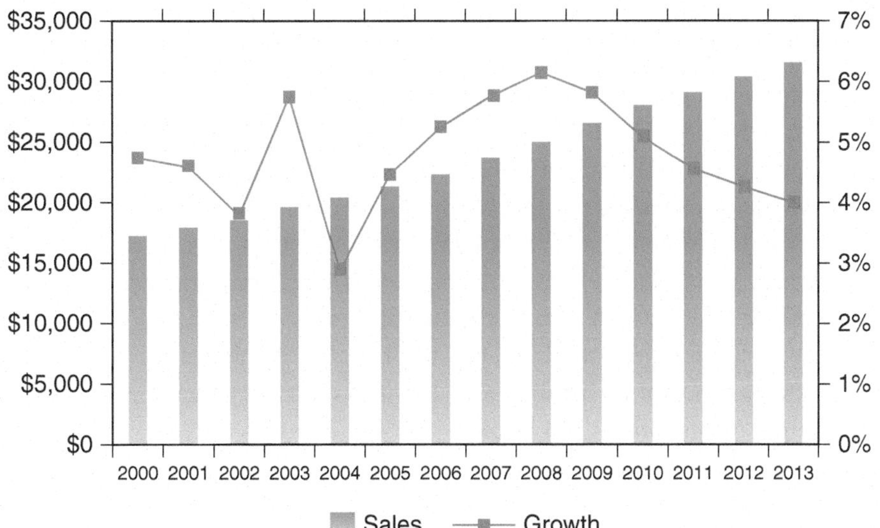

Source: Nutrition Business Journal estimates ($mill., consumer sale)

FIGURE 8.9 Growth in dietary supplement sales since passage of DSHEA Act of 1994.

Not all supplements provide false claims; several supplement manufacturers have honestly represented their product. The difficult part is telling the beneficial ones from those that are potentially harmful and those that simply fail to do what they claim. In this chapter, we review some tips on deciding whether to take a supplement and some guidelines that can be followed when trying to select a supplement. As this industry continues to grow, the scientific research into the validity of its claims grows as well. Therefore, you need to keep up-to-date on the latest information.

HISTORY OF DIETARY SUPPLEMENTS

Dietary supplements and herbs (or botanicals) are not new. In fact, the personal effects of the mummified prehistoric "Ice Man" found in the Italian Alps in 1991 included medicinal herbs. By the Middle Ages, thousands of botanical products had been used for their medicinal effects, many of which form the basis of modern drugs. In China, herbs and other unconventional treatments have been used for thousands of years as a form of treatment and is a still considered part of the Chinese culture and healing. Before the Nutrition Labeling and Education Act of 1990, supplements consisted only of vitamins, minerals, and other essential nutrients. In 1990, "herbs or similar nutritional substances" were added to the official definition of a "dietary supplement." The expanded meaning then included such substances as ginseng, garlic, fish oils, psyllium, enzymes, glandulars, and mixtures of these. At that time, dietary supplements were still regulated by the Food and Drug Administration (FDA) and subject to reviews similar to those for medicines. In the early 1990s, Congress debated various bills to revise the laws governing dietary supplements. The supplement industry took action and lobbied to ensure that the FDA did not acquire any more regulatory control. The supplement industry's efforts resulted in the **Dietary Supplement Health and Education Act of 1994 (DSHEA)**. In addition to drastically changing the role the FDA plays in supplement regulation, the DSHEA further expanded the formal definition of *dietary supplement*. According to the DSHEA, a supplement is as follows:

- A product (other than tobacco) that contains one or more of the following dietary ingredients: a vitamin, a mineral, an herb or botanical, an amino acid, or a constituent of any of these substances.
- Intended for ingestion in pill, capsule, tablet, or liquid form.
- Used to supplement the diet, rather than for use as a conventional food or as the sole item of a meal or diet.
- Labeled as a dietary supplement.

Dietary Supplement Health and Education Act of 1994 (DSHEA)
A federal law that significantly changed the role the FDA plays in supplement regulation and further expanded the formal definition of "dietary supplement."

Dietary supplements are often taken as a pill, capsule, or liquid; however, some foods are marketed that have the dietary ingredient of the supplement added to food. Obvious examples of this include bottled drinks that have vitamins added to them. They are often promoted to help boost your energy levels, a claim that is not supported by scientific research. Some botanicals are sold as tea, such as chamomile tea. You may find health food stores and smoothie bars that prepare drinks that contain ginseng or acai. It is apparent that the packaging of dietary supplements and botanicals has evolved over the years to include more than a bottle of pills as the demand for these produced increased.

Supplement Regulation

Since the passing of the DSHEA in 1994, the FDA regulates dietary supplements under a different set of regulations from those covering "conventional" foods and drugs (prescription and over-the-counter). Under the DSHEA, the supplement manufacturer must ensure that a dietary supplement is safe before it is marketed and, with the exception of a "new dietary ingredient," the manufacturer does not need approval from the FDA before selling their supplement to consumers. This is in contrast to drugs, which have to submit safety data to the FDA and receive approval before the release of a new drug. Any adverse side effect caused by the supplement may be reported to the manufacturer or the FDA The manufacturer is then required to forward these reports to the FDA. The FDA can then track and monitor adverse effects and take action to prohibit the sale of the supplement, but this is only after the supplement has been marketed and sold to the public, and after harm has occurred.

So who is responsible for making sure the supplements that we buy are actually safe?

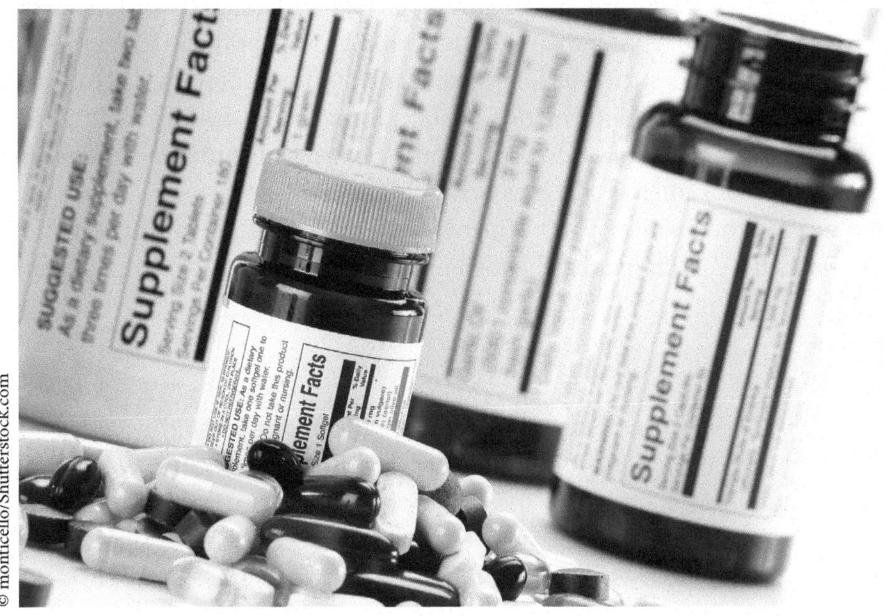

The FDA does not get involved in determining the safety of dietary supplements until after they are marketed. Nor does the FDA restrict any substance unless it poses a "significant and unreasonable risk."

BUYER BEWARE

Examples of Supplements That Have Carried FDA Cautions About Safety

- Colloidal silver
- Aristolochic acid
- Certain products marketed for sexual enhancement that claimed to be "natural" versions of the drug Viagra and were found to contain an unlabeled drug (sildenafil or tadalafil)
- Comfrey
- Ephedra
- Kava
- St. John's wort
- Some "dieter's teas"
- Red yeast rice

The important thing to remember is that the FDA does not get involved until *after* the product has been on the market. In other words, the FDA does *postmarketing surveillance* of supplements but does not ensure their safety or effectiveness. The agency may restrict a substance only if it poses a "significant and unreasonable risk" after it is being sold and used. The FDA handles consumer complaints of unsafe products, improper or illegal labeling claims, and package inserts.

Federal Trade Commission
The federal agency that has the responsibility for monitoring the accuracy of the advertising and labeling of supplements.

The **Federal Trade Commission** is responsible for monitoring the accuracy of the advertising and labeling of supplements. Although manufacturers are not required to register their products with the FDA or the FTC or get FDA approval before producing or selling supplements, they are supposed to make sure that product label information is truthful and not misleading. This would seem to be an adequate way to prevent false claims. Unfortunately, it does not protect the consumer as much as many think. The federal government does not oversee the *quality* of supplements from manufacturer to manufacturer or even between different batches of a product from the same manufacturer.

APPLICATION TIP

Don't be fooled by "fake science"! Manufacturers often say, "Studies show that . . .," but they never provide a reference. Or it was only one study underwritten by the company, conducted by company employees in their facility. Therefore, before purchasing and taking these products, always go to an outside source and search independent scientific journals for information about such claims.

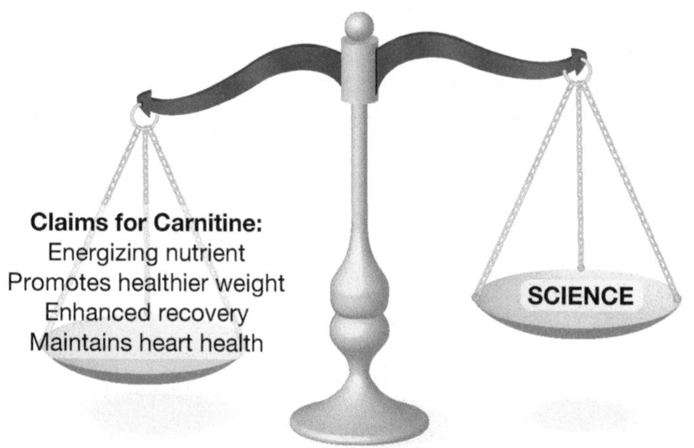

FIGURE 8.10 Claims made about supplements are often "sort of true"—as in the case of carnitine. It is always important to research and evaluate the scientific evidence regarding the claim's validity.

Partially True Claims

carnitine
The substance that transports long-chain fatty acids into the mitochondria for metabolism. Carnitine supplementation is said to enhance fat burning, but it appears to be ineffective.

Although it is important to be aware that the contents of the bottle may not match the label, it is also important to understand that manufacturers' health-related claims for many supplements are only partially true. Frequently, the claims are "sort of true" - a manufacturer takes a scientific fact but applies it incorrectly. For example, products containing the B-complex vitamins are often advertised as energy boosters. It is a scientific fact that B-vitamins are needed to extract energy from the macronutrients. Without adequate B-vitamins, a person will feel fatigued. However, unless a person is deficient in these nutrients, there is no scientific data supporting the claim that taking B-complex vitamins will give you extra energy. Another example is the claim made that **carnitine** will increase fat burning. In truth, carnitine does carry long-chain fatty acids from one part of the cell to another part where it can be used in energy metabolism. However, carnitine is needed in very small amounts, which are easily obtained in food and made in the body. There is no evidence that supplemental use of carnitine enhances fat metabolism in any way. Therefore, the claim on the bottle is not accurate.

DHEA is a supplement that has gained popularity in our youth-obsessed society.

dehydroepiandrosterone (DHEA)
A steroid hormone that is synthesized and secreted by the adrenal glands.

Another example of a claim that is based on the function of the components but lacks evidence that the supplement is effective is **dehydroepiandrosterone (DHEA)**, discussed in the Nutrition and Lifestages feature.

Nutrition & LIFESTAGES

THE FOUNTAIN OF YOUTH IN A BOTTLE?

We are a nation obsessed with youth and its maintenance, almost without regard to the cost of doing so. Everywhere you look there are advertisements for wrinkle creams and other products to make you look younger. Plastic surgery is more popular than ever. The supplements market has definitely made note of and cashed in on our youth-obsessed society. An ever-increasing number of products promise to help you retain or recapture your youthful appearance. One of the best known of these is DHEA. DHEA is a steroid hormone that is synthesized and secreted by the adrenal glands. DHEA is ultimately converted into estrogen (the female sex hormone) and androgen (the male sex hormone). It has been marketed as a virtual fountain of youth, with miraculous claims that it can slow aging, melt away fat, enhance memory, prevent osteoporosis, and increase libido. The level of circulating DHEA usually peaks during the 20s and 30s and then declines steadily thereafter.

Interest in DHEA as a supplement was boosted after several investigators reported that increased DHEA levels were associated with a decreased incidence of heart disease, various cancers, and several other age-related diseases. Alternatively, the further scientific evidence regarding its effectiveness is inconclusive at this time. Furthermore, this hormone can have potentially dangerous and undesirable side effects, including male sex characteristics (such as facial hair in women) and breast, ovarian, or prostate cancer. Therefore, you should not take DHEA until you have consulted with your physician. More clinical investigations are warranted before general dose recommendations can be made.

BEFORE YOU GO ON...

1. To what extent are supplements regulated and by whom?
2. What is the formal definition of a dietary supplement, and what federal legislation established it?
3. List the potential hazards of relying on the accuracy of supplement labels.
4. Since the DSHEA was passed, what role does the FDA play in ensuring that supplements are safe?

WHO TAKES SUPPLEMENTS AND WHY

Who's Buying Them?

According to the National Health and Nutrition Examination Survey (NHANES), over half of the United States population take at least one dietary supplement. The most commonly consumed supplements appear to be multivitamins or minerals. Use of supplements may be even more prevalent in certain populations. It is highest in women, people age 60 or older, whites, those who have more than a high school education, and those who exercise. In addition, it appears that the higher an individual's BMI, the less likely he or she is to use supplements. This is interesting because many supplements are marketed for weight loss.

Athletes are often looking for an extra edge in competition and training and are therefore a vulnerable target of supplement marketers. In fact, in one study of 513 athletes, 88.4 percent of those surveyed reported using at least one type of supplement. Sports drinks, multivitamin/multimineral supplements, and energy bars were the most common dietary supplements reported.

Supplement use is so prevalent among athletes that the National College Athletic Association (NCAA), the International Olympic Committee, and other governing bodies for many sports have had to establish rules and guidelines about their use. In addition to identifying banned drugs, they have issued regulations regarding what supplements may be provided to athletes by coaches and trainers. Categories of banned substances include stimulants, such as caffeine; anabolic agents, such as DHEA and androstenedione; alcohol and beta-blockers (typically, drugs); and peptide hormones and analogs, such as growth hormone and erythropoietin. NCAA provides a list of examples of drugs and supplements that are banned substances, but warn that the list is not definitive. NCAA discourages the use of dietary supplements and warns students and coaches that some dietary supplements not found on this list may result in a positive test for a banned substance. Also, supplements may be contaminated with a banned substance, which may not be listed on the label.

© Peter Weber/Shutterstock.com

Use of banned substances is prevalent among athletes at all levels, prompting the governing bodies of most sports to conduct strict testing for all banned substances. Floyd Landis of the United States won the 2006 Tour de France, the world's most prestigious cycling race. However, shortly after he was awarded the trophy, he was accused of a violation due to the presence of elevated levels of testosterone found in his urinalysis. He lost an appeal in 2007 of the French lab's analysis and was stripped of the title. He has since implicated other cyclists as using similar substances.

Supplement Use by College Students

Few studies have been done to determine the prevalence of supplement use by college students. This limited research suggests that use may be similar or higher in college students compared to their same-age peers who are not attending college and the older adult population. One study surveyed 272 students, of which 48.5 percent reported that they took a nonvitamin and mineral supplement during the past 12 months. The most frequently used products were echinacea, ginseng, and St. John's wort. Ten percent of the students took supplements to promote weight loss. Interestingly, most of those taking weight-loss supplements had BMIs in the recommended range and therefore did not need to lose weight. Eleven of the 19 participants who reported an adverse reaction to a supplement continued to take the products despite negative effects. Users and nonusers of supplements did not differ significantly by ethnicity, gender, or exercise habits or in how balanced they thought their diets were. More research needs to be conducted on college students, as they are often the target of supplement marketing claims such as those made for the many popular "energy drinks" discussed in the What's Hot feature.

ENERGY DRINKS—DO THEY GIVE YOU WINGS OR LEAVE YOU HANGIN'?

What's HOT

Energy drinks such as Red Bull, Venom, Monster, Adrenaline Rush, and WhoopAss are intentionally marketed to people under age 30, especially to teens and college students. They seem to have replaced coffee as the study companion for the average college student's all-nighter. Indeed, they are very popular, and as a verification of this, consider that worldwide revenues for Red Bull exceeded $6.5 billion in 2012, up from just over $1 billion in 2006.

Most energy drinks contain large doses of caffeine and other stimulants such as ephedrine, guarana, and ginseng. Some may provide more than the 80 mg of caffeine in a typical cup of coffee. Compared to the 37 mg of caffeine in a Mountain Dew or the 23 mg in a Coca-Cola Classic, that's one wide-eyed jolt. Caffeine may seem benign, but it is a drug—albeit a legal one—and can be associated with negative responses. These responses can include a rapid heart rate, increased blood pressure, dizziness, inability to concentrate, and insomnia. The response will not be the same for everyone and will be stronger for those who do not regularly consume caffeine and for children. The risk of having a negative response to these drinks may be increased if one drinks them too fast. Consider this: coffee is normally sipped slowly, delaying the caffeine ingestion, yet a Monster energy drink may be downed quickly and rapidly deliver caffeine into the body.

In addition to the stimulants, most drinks contain sugar and quite a few empty Calories. Depending on the brand, many also contain taurine (an amino acid said to act as an "energy booster"), guarana (a caffeine derivative), and B vitamins (said to boost energy). Despite their resemblance to sodas, the name and the marketing campaigns make energy drinks seem somehow healthier than sodas and coffee. When one considers the caffeine and Calorie content, as listed in Table 8.2, the energy drinks are definitely not healthier.

Many energy drinks are even sold as sports drinks. In fact, it is not unusual to see a Red Bull van or tent handing out free product to participants at local sporting events. This is of particular concern because the high caffeine content along with the high sugar concentration could lead to cramping and impairment in fluid absorption. Energy drinks have also become popular on the club and party scene. They are promoted as a healthier mix for vodka than sodas or juices. It is never a good idea to mix the two because alcohol is a depressant and the drinks are stimulants. Therefore, they tend to mask the intoxicating effects of alcohol, and people are more likely to overdrink and think that they are sober when in fact they are not.

The bottom line is: beware of popular energy drinks that "give you wings." Although the associated evidence is inconclusive, some of these products have been blamed for several deaths in Europe and are now banned in France, Denmark, Canada, and Iceland.

These are just a few of the energy drinks on the market! What do the number of choices shown here say about the popularity of these beverages?

© Chones/Shutterstock.com

Why Are They Buying Them?

Whether young, old, athletes, or college students, people take supplements for many reasons. Most do so in order to be healthier or to make up for nutrients they believe that they are lacking. Interestingly, results from large-scale nutrition surveys indicate that those most inclined to take supplements also have a healthier lifestyle, including diet. This means that they have an increased likelihood of ob-

TABLE 8.2 Caffeine and Calorie Content of Selected Drinks

Soda (12 oz.)	Caffeine (mg)	Calories	Sugar (g)
Dr Pepper	39	150	39
Coca-Cola Classic	34	144	30
Diet Coke	45	0	0
Pepsi	38	150	37
Diet Pepsi	36	0	0
Mountain Dew	55	165	46
Diet Mountain Dew	55	0	0
Energy Drink (12 oz.)	**Caffeine (mg)**	**Calories**	**Sugar (g)**
Amp	112	171	42
Monster Assault	120	150	39
Red Bull	115.5	165	40
Rockstar	120	180	45
SoBe Adrenaline Rush	114.2	180	47
Hype	115	171	38
Jolt Energy	150	100	40
Full Throttle	100	0	0
Coffee		**Caffeine (mg)**	
Percolated (7 oz.)		140	
Drip (7 oz.)		115–175	
Espresso (1.5–2 oz.)		100	
Brewed (7 oz.)		80–135	
Instant (7 oz.)		65–100	
Decaf, brewed (6 oz.)		5	
Decaf, instant (6 oz.)		3	
Tea		**Caffeine (mg)**	
Iced (12 oz.)		70	
Black (6 oz.)		70	
Green (6 oz.)		35	
Instant (7 oz.)		30	

taining more vitamins and minerals in their diet than those who don't. Perhaps people who take supplements are just more concerned with their health in general. A study published in the *Journal of the American Medical Association* surveyed more than 2,500 Americans regarding their use of supplements (given the two categories of vitamins/minerals and herbal products/natural supplements) and for what reasons. Their responses are summarized in Table 8.3. As the table indicates, most took vitamin and herbal supplements because they believed that such supplements were healthy or good for them. However, many people take supplements hoping for a quick fix or magical cure. Many marketing campaigns pick up on these reasons and the emotions that can be tied to them, with slogans such as "Lose weight in one week" and "Find the new you." They play on the hopelessness and desperation many dieters feel after repeated attempts to lose weight. Perhaps even more disturbing are the many supplements marketed to those who have potentially life-threatening diseases such as cancer and HIV. These people often fall victim to expensive supplements that promise to alleviate symptoms, prolong life, or even cure the disease.

Not all supplements have negative side effects, and some can be helpful if taken correctly. For example, the following groups of individuals may benefit from a vitamin supplement.

- Women who are pregnant or hoping to become pregnant need extra folic acid
- Older adults, people with dark skin, and people who get insufficient exposure to sunlight should consume extra vitamin D from vitamin D-fortified foods and/or supplements.
- Someone diagnosed with iron deficiency anemia or another nutritional deficiency
- An individual who has undergone a weight loss surgery
- Individuals with celiac disease, Crohn's disease or other issues that impact the absorption of nutrients.
- Elderly may need vitamin B12
- Vegans

Before you take a supplement, consider the following tips:

- *Think about your total diet.* The concept of "too much of a good thing" certainly applies when it comes to supplements. Before you decide to take a vitamin, mineral, or other supplement, consider *everything* in your diet. This is important because it all adds up. For example, if you eat foods that are fortified, such as cereal, you are getting added vitamins and minerals. Then, in addition to that fortified cereal, suppose you have a smoothie made with a supplement that contains added vitamins. You might take a daily multivitamin and then, of course, you eat food with nutrients in it. As you can see, you can easily consume an excessive amount of vitamins and minerals without even realizing it.

- *Check with your health care practitioner.* Many supplements that are safe under normal conditions may not be advisable for children; teenagers; or those who are ill, pregnant, having surgery, or taking certain medications. Therefore, always check with your health care practitioner before taking a new supplement. Furthermore, be sure to tell your practitioner what you are taking before any medications are prescribed, as some supplements interfere with the action of some medications. Also be careful about who you are defining as a "health care practitioner." Many who call themselves health care experts have a vested interest in whether you take a supplement because they are selling them and, therefore, receive a financial gain from your purchase. So, before you even consult a practitioner, find out what his or her credentials are and whether he or she sells supplements. A reputable practitioner does not profit from your taking a medicine or supplement.

APPLICATION TIP

The best course of action before taking any supplement is to make sure you are making that decision based on facts, following a consultation with your physician, and without your emotions.

TABLE 8.3 Reasons People Take Supplements

Vitamins/Minerals	% of Responses	Herbals/Supplements	% of Responses
Health/good for you	35	Health/good for you	16
Dietary supplement	11	Arthritis	7
Vitamin/mineral supplement	8	Memory improvement	6
Prevent osteoporosis	6	Energy	5
Physician recommended	6	Immune booster	5
Prevent colds/influenza	3	Joint	4
Don't know/no reason specified	3	Supplement diet	4
Immune system booster	2	Sleep aid	3
Recommended by friend/family/ media	2	Prostate	3
Energy	2	Don't know/no reason specified	2
All others	22	All others	45

Source: Adapted from Kaufman DW, Kelly JP, Rosenberg L, Anderson TE, Mitchell AA (2002). Recent patterns of medication use in the ambulatory adult population of the United States: the Slone survey. 287(3):337–344.

Make it a
PRACTICE

LEARN TO RECOGNIZE FRADULENT LABEL CLAIMS

The FDA and FTC provide the following guidelines to help consumers recognize fraudulent claims by supplements manufacturers and retailers.

1. Statements that the product is a quick and effective "cure-all" or diagnostic tool for a wide variety of ailments—for example, "Extremely beneficial in the treatment of rheumatism, arthritis, infections, prostate problems, ulcers, cancer, heart trouble, hardening of the arteries, and more." What exactly does "extremely beneficial" mean anyway? If it meant that symptoms were alleviated or a disease was cured, wouldn't they say that instead of using such a vague statement? Furthermore, drugs that are effective are rarely effective for such a wide variety of conditions; they are usually very specific. So, the fact that a supplement says it is effective for so many different conditions should be a warning sign.
2. Statements that suggest the product can treat or cure diseases—for example, "Shrinks tumors" or "Cures impotence."
3. Promotions that use words such as "scientific breakthrough," "miraculous cure," "exclusive product," "secret ingredient," or "ancient remedy"—for example, "A revolutionary innovation formulated by using proven principles of natural health-based medical science."
4. Advertising that uses impressive-sounding terms, such as these for a weight-loss product: "hunger stimulation point" and "-thermogenesis."
5. Undocumented case histories or personal testimonials by consumers or doctors claiming amazing results—for example, "My husband has Alzheimer's disease. He began taking a teaspoonful of this product each day. And now, in just 22 days, he is mowing the grass, cleaning out the garage, weeding the flower beds, and taking his morning walk again."
6. Limited availability and advance-payment requirements—for example, "Hurry. This offer will not last. Send us a check now to reserve your supply."
7. Promises of no-risk "money-back guarantees"—for example, "If after 30 days you have not lost at least 4 lb. each week, your uncashed check will be returned to you."
8. Don't assume the term "natural" means the product is safe.

- *Be skeptical.* Research any health claims about the benefits of a product; don't just take the word of a friend, co-worker, or personal trainer at the gym. Ask yourself, what is his training? Is she just telling me this because she thinks it worked for her? Then do some research of your own. Search for scientific studies done on the product and reported in reputable peer-reviewed scientific journals. You can do this by consulting a trained and licensed health professional or by searching PubMed, the Office of Dietary Supplements and the National Center for Complementary and Alternative Medicine. Also, choose supplements that have been purity and potency tested by an independent testing group like Consumer Labs or United States Pharmacopeia.

BEFORE YOU GO ON...

1. What is the NCAA's guideline for coaches and trainers in supplying supplements to their athletes?
2. Why should consumers be cautious about consuming so-called energy drinks such as Red Bull?
3. Who is taking supplements?
4. What are three signs of a fraudulent claim by a supplement manufacturer?

Always check with your healthcare practitioner before taking a supplement.

APPLICATION TIP

If you think you have experienced any adverse health effects from taking any supplement, you, your health care provider, or anyone else can and should report the adverse event or illness directly to the FDA by calling 1-800-FDA-1088, by faxing 1-800-FDA-0178, or online.

CHAPTER SUMMARY

- Vitamins are found in our bodies in much lower levels than the macronutrients and are required in our diets in only milligrams and micrograms. DRIs have been determined for all of the vitamins, although information continues to evolve as new discoveries are made.
- Vitamins interact so that several of them may affect a similar bodily function. Many are directly involved in metabolic pathways; others are cofactors or coenzymes for biochemical reactions.
- Vitamins can be toxic if consumed in large enough amounts. Fat-soluble vitamins and minerals can be more toxic when taken in large amounts because they can be stored in the body. Water-soluble vitamins are not as toxic because they are easier to excrete.
- Vitamins do not provide your body with energy but may facilitate the body's breakdown and release of energy from carbohydrates, fats, and proteins. The B vitamins are all involved in chemical pathways that aid in energy metabolism.
- Vitamins A and D are tightly connected to protein synthesis and can turn genes on and off. Bone strength and development depend to a large extent on vitamins A, C, D, and K.
- Vitamins can play a role as antioxidants. Vitamins C and E and beta-carotene are all antioxidants that protect us from harmful free radicals.
- Reproduction, growth, development, and even repair are heavily dependent on vitamins A, D, and C. Folate is involved because it promotes cell division.
- Deficiencies of thiamin, riboflavin, and niacin were once much more widespread in the United States than they are today.
- Thiamin deficiency leads to a disease called beriberi, and niacin deficiency leads to a disease called pellagra.
- The signs of folate and vitamin B_{12} deficiencies are similar. Folate deficiency during pregnancy can lead to spina bifida in infants. A lack of intrinsic factor can prevent absorption of vitamin B_{12} and lead to pernicious anemia in some people.
- Food processing, prolonged storage, or prolonged cooking can result in a loss of vitamins.
- Enrichment is the restoration of micro-nutrients that were originally present in a food but were lost during processing. Fortification is the addition of a nutrient to a food that did not originally contain it.
- Supplements are regulated under the Dietary Supplement Health and Education Act of 1994 (DSHEA).
- The FDA does not approve supplements before they are marketed. It gets involved only in postmarketing surveillance and, therefore, handles claims of adverse effects only after a supplement is made available to consumers.
- Manufacturers of supplements have to make sure that product label information is truthful and not misleading.
- Because no strict regulations protect consumers from potentially harmful supplements, it is up to you, the consumer, to beware.
- When researching information about supplements on the Internet, be sure the sites you check are reputable.
- Vitamin and mineral supplements are the most popular type of supplement. Limited evidence suggests that people who are healthy will achieve additional protection against disease by supplementing above the DRI.
- Beware of popular "energy drinks," as they are marketed to look like health or sports drinks but often contain amounts of caffeine higher than most sodas. In addition, they contain other stimulants that may lead to negative side effects such as rapid heart rate, elevated blood pressure, and dehydration. They should be consumed cautiously and not mixed with alcohol.
- Herbs and botanicals are becoming more and more popular. They are supplements that contain extracts or active ingredients from the roots, berries, seeds, stems, leaves, buds, or flowers of plants.
- Consult your health care practitioner before taking any supplement, vitamin, herb, and so on, just as you would before taking any medication.

KEY TERMS

ANEMIA A condition characterized by below-normal levels of red blood cells, hemoglobin, or both.

ASCORBIC ACID Another name for vitamin C.

BERIBERI The result of thiamin deficiency.

BETA-CAROTENE A precursor of vitamin A found in plants.

CARNITINE (CAR-nih-teen) The substance that transports long-chain fatty acids into the mitochondria for metabolism. Carnitine supplementation is said to enhance fat burning, but it appears to be ineffective.

CELL DIFFERENTIATION The process by which specialized cells develop that are capable of performing specific functions.

COENZYMES Molecules that combine with an enzyme to increase its activity.

COLLAGEN A protein that forms connective tissues such as tendons, bone, teeth, and skin.

DEHYDROEPIANDROSTERONE (DHEA) (dee-hy-droh-ep-ee-ann-DRAHS-ter-own) A steroid hormone that is synthesized and secreted by the adrenal glands.

DIETARY FOLATE EQUIVALENT A unit of measure used to represent the conversion of folic acid into folate.

DIETARY SUPPLEMENT HEALTH AND EDUCATION ACT OF 1994 (DSHEA) A federal law that significantly changed the role the FDA plays in supplement regulation and further expanded the formal definition of "dietary supplement."

ENRICHMENT The restoration of micronutrients that were originally present in the food but were lost during processing.

FEDERAL TRADE COMMISSION The federal agency that has the responsibility for monitoring the accuracy of the advertising and labeling of supplements.

FIBRIN A protein that forms blood clots.

FOLIC ACID The synthetic form of folate that is used in dietary supplements and enriched foods.

FORTIFICATION The addition of vitamins and minerals to foods that are not naturally present in those foods.

FREE RADICALS Unstable compounds with an unpaired electron that attack other molecules and break them down.

INTRINSIC FACTOR A protein produced by stomach cells that binds to vitamin B_{12} and protects it from degradation until it can be absorbed.

MACROCYTIC ANEMIA Anemia characterized by enlarged, immature red blood cells that are fewer in number than normal cells.

MACULAR DEGENERATIVE DISEASE A group of eye disorders characterized by the breakdown of the macula, the center portion of the retina that makes basic visual acuity possible.

MEGALOBLASTS Immature, enlarged red blood cells.

MYELIN SHEATH An insulating sheath for nerve fibers that enhances conduction.

OSTEOMALACIA A softening of the bones in adults that results from vitamin D deficiency.

PELLAGRA A disease caused by a niacin deficiency.

PERNICIOUS ANEMIA Anemia that results from a vitamin B_{12} deficiency because of a lack of intrinsic factor.

PROVITAMINS Substances that need to be converted in order to have vitamin-like activity in the body.

RETINOL ACTIVITY EQUIVALENTS OR RAE The units in which carotenoids are measured.

RICKETS A softening and deformity of long bones that results from vitamin D deficiency in children.

SCURVY A disease caused by vitamin C deficiency.

SPINA BIFIDA A birth defect that results from the failure of the spine to close properly during the first month of pregnancy.

TOCOPHEROLS A group of compounds with vitamin E activity.

WENICKE-KORSAKOFF SYNDROME A neurological disorder associated with chronic alcoholism and thiamin deficiency.

TABLE 8.4 Summary Table of Vitamins

Vitamin	What It Does and Why It Is Important	Deficiency: What Happens If You Get Too Little	Toxicity: What Happens If You Get Too Much	Food Sources[1]		
Vitamin A	Essential for proper development and maintenance of eyes and vision; needed to maintain the integrity of skin, digestive tract, and other tissues; needed for proper function of the immune system; and cell differentiation	Night blindness, reduced hair growth in children, loss of appetite, dry/rough skin, lowered resistance to infection, dry eyes, and xerophthalmia	Headaches, blurred vision, fatigue, diarrhea, irregular periods, joint and bone pain, dry/cracked skin, rashes, loss of hair, vomiting, and liver damage	**Food Item** Beef liver Vitamin A fortified milk Margarine Butter Egg, hard-boiled Cheddar cheese	**Serving Size** 3 oz. 1 c. 1 tbsp. 1 tbsp. 1 1 oz.	**Amount** 6852 µg 137 µg 115 µg 103 µg 85 µg 74 µg
Beta-carotene (provitamin A)	Antioxidant; like other provitamin A carotenoids (alpha-carotene and beta-cryptoxanthin), can be converted into vitamin A in the body	No direct effects; may cause symptoms associated with vitamin A deficiency	No known toxic effects; may cause yellowish discoloration of skin; may increase lung cancer in smokers	**Food Item** 1 REA equals (1 µg retinal) Sweet potatoes Pumpkin, canned Squash, butternut Kale Collards Carrots, raw Cantaloupe Apricots Broccoli	**Serving Size** 1 baked ½ c. ½ c. ½ c. ½ c. ½ c. ½ c. 4 ½ c.	**Amount** 961 RAE 953 RAE 572 RAE 478 RAE 386 RAE 367 RAE 136 RAE 134 RAE 52 RAE

Vitamin	What It Does and Why It Is Important	Deficiency: What Happens If You Get Too Little	Toxicity: What Happens If You Get Too Much	Food Sources[1]		
				Food Item	**Serving Size**	**Amount**
Vitamin D	Helps maintain adequate calcium in the blood by increasing calcium absorption from digestive tract; decreases calcium loss in urine	Rickets in children; bone softening and osteomalacia in adults	Calcium deposits in organs, fragile bones, renal, and cardiovascular damage	Cod liver oil Pacific oysters Salmon Sardines Vitamin D fortified milk, 2% Shrimp Egg, cooked Beef Yogurt Cheddar cheese Margarine Liver	1 tbsp. 3.5 oz. 3 oz. 1–¾ oz. 1 c. 3 oz. 1 3.5 oz. 1 c. 1 oz. 1 oz. 3.5 oz.	34 µg 16 µg 8.0 µg 6.25 µg 2.45 µg 2.25 µg 0.65 µg 0.18 µg 0.10 µg 0.09 µg 1.68 µg 0.38 µg
				Food Item	**Serving Size**	**Amount**
Vitamin E	Antioxidant; helps protect red blood cells, muscles, and other tissues from free radical damage	Rare; seen primarily in premature or low-birth weight babies or children who do not absorb fat properly; causes nerve abnormalities	Unknown	Corn oil Salad dressing, French Wheat germ Margarine Peanuts, roasted Spinach Pistachio nuts Collards Pumpkin seeds	1 tbsp. 2 tbsp. 2 tbsp. 1 tbsp. ¼ c. ½ c. ¼ c. ½ c. ¼ c.	2.87 mg 2.63 mg 2.04 mg 1.80 mg 2.27 mg 1.42 mg 1.36 mg 0.84 mg 0.57 mg

Vitamin	What It Does and Why It Is Important	Deficiency: What Happens If You Get Too Little	Toxicity: What Happens If You Get Too Much	Food Sources[1]		
Vitamin K	Needed for normal blood clotting; bone strength	Defective blood coagulation	Jaundice in infants	**Food Item** Collards Spinach Brussels sprouts Broccoli Cabbage Asparagus	**Serving Size** ½ c. ½ c. ½ c. ½ c. ½ c. ½ c.	**Amount** 530 µg 514 µg 150 µg 110 µg 82 µg 72 µg
Vitamin C (ascorbic acid)	Antioxidant; involved in collagen formation; aids in iron absorption	Muscle weakness, bleeding gums, easy bruising, and scurvy (in extreme cases)	Largely unknown; some concerns over kidney stones	**Food Item** Orange juice Green peppers Broccoli, cooked Strawberries Brussels sprouts Grapefruit Sweet potato, baked	**Serving Size** ½ c. ½ c. ½ c. ½ c. ½ c. ½ c. 1	**Amount** 62 mg 60 mg 51 mg 50 mg 48 mg 36 mg 20 mg
Thiamin (vitamin B_1)	Coenzyme for several reactions in energy metabolism; necessary for muscle coordination and proper development and maintenance of the central nervous system	Anxiety, hysteria, depression, muscle cramps, loss of appetite, beriberi, and Wernicke–Korsakoff syndrome (mostly in alcoholics)	Unknown (Note: Excess of one B vitamin may cause deficiency of others.)	**Food Item** Cereal (special K) Pork chop Beef liver Peanuts, roasted Great northern beans, boiled Spaghetti Orange juice White bread Brown rice (long grain) Milk, 2% Lima beans, cooked Pumpkin seeds	**Serving Size** 1 c. 3 oz. 3 oz. ¼ c. ½ c. ½ c. ½ c. 1 slice ½ c. 1 c. ½ c. 1 tbsp.	**Amount** 1.13 mg 0.53 mg 0.15 mg 0.15 mg 0.14 mg 0.12 mg 0.11 mg 0.11 mg 0.09 mg 0.09 mg 0.06 mg 0.05 mg

Vitamin	What It Does and Why It Is Important	Deficiency: What Happens If You Get Too Little	Toxicity: What Happens If You Get Too Much	Food Sources[1]		
Riboflavin (vitamin B_2)	Coenzyme for several reactions in energy metabolism	Cracks/sores around mouth and nose, visual problems	Unknown	**Food Item** Cereals (special K) Milk, 2% Spaghetti White bread	**Serving Size** 1 c. 1 c. ½ c. 1 slice	**Amount** 1.28 mg 0.45 mg 0.12 mg 0.08 mg
Niacin (vitamin B_3)	Coenzyme for several reactions in energy metabolism; in very large doses, lowers cholesterol (*Note: Large doses should be taken under the care of a physician.*)	In extreme cases, pellagra (a disease characterized by dermatitis, diarrhea, and mouth sores)	Hot flashes, ulcers, liver disorders, high blood sugar and uric acid, and cardiac arrhythmia	**Food Item** Peanuts, roasted Rib steak Whole-wheat flour Cereal (special K) Brown rice (long grain) Codfish, baked White bread Egg, hard-boiled Milk, 2%	**Serving Size** ¼ c. 3 oz. ½ c. 1 c. ½ c. 3 oz. 1 slice 1 1 c.	**Amount** 4.94 mg 4.08 mg 3.82 mg 1.50 mg 1.49 mg 1.11 mg 1.10 mg 0.26 mg 0.22 mg
Vitamin B_6 (pyridoxine)	Coenzyme for reactions involving the processing of amino acids; involved in the breakdown of carbohydrate stores (glycogen) in muscles and liver	Anemia, irritability, patches of itchy/scaling skin, and convulsions	Nerve damage	**Food Item** Beef liver Spinach, cooked Potato, baked Chicken, white meat, roasted Banana Rib steak Salmon, broiled Broccoli Navy beans Watermelon	**Serving Size** 3 oz. ½ c. 1 3 oz. 1 3 oz. 3 oz. ½ c. ½ c. ½ c.	**Amount** 0.87 mg 0.86 mg 0.70 mg 0.46 mg 0.43 mg 0.34 mg 0.19 mg 0.16 mg 0.15 mg 0.03 mg

Vitamin	What It Does and Why It Is Important	Deficiency: What Happens If You Get Too Little	Toxicity: What Happens If You Get Too Much	Food Sources[1]		
Folic acid (folacin)	Essential for manufacture of genetic material; helps form red blood cells; and cell division	Impaired cell division, anemia, diarrhea, and gastrointestinal upsets	Convulsions in people with epilepsy; may mask pernicious anemia	**Food Item** Cereal (special K) Beef liver Navy beans, cooked Collards, cooked Brussels sprouts Orange juice Spinach, raw Lettuce, iceberg White bread Kale, cooked	**Serving Size** 1 c. 3 oz. ½ c. ½ c. ½ c. ½ c. 1 c. 1 c. 1 slice ½ c.	**Amount** 300 μg 221 μg 127 μg 88 μg 78 μg 62 μg 58 μg 31 μg 28 μg 9 μg
Vitamin B_{12} (cobalamin)	Essential for building blocks of DNA; helps form red blood cells; and maintains myelin sheath or insulation of nerves	Pernicious anemia, nerve damage *(Note: Deficiency is rare except in strict vegetarians, the elderly, or people with malabsorption disorders.)*	Skin problems	**Food Item** Clams Beef liver Oysters Cereal (special K) Rib steak Tuna, canned Milk, 2% Cheddar cheese Chicken, white meat, roasted	**Serving Size** 3 oz. 3 oz. 3 oz. 1 c. 3 oz. 2 oz. 1 c. 1 oz. 3 oz.	**Amount** 84 μg 71 μg 15 μg 6 μg 3 μg 2 μg 1 μg <1 μg <1 μg
Pantothenic acid	Coenzyme for several reactions in energy metabolism	Fatigue, vomiting and abdominal cramps	Sensitivity of teeth	Abundant in many foods		
Biotin	Involved in energy metabolism	Seborrhea (greasy scales) in infants; anorexia, nausea, vomiting, dry/scaly skin in adults *(Note: Can be induced in adults by consuming large amounts of egg whites.)*	Unknown	Abundant in many foods		

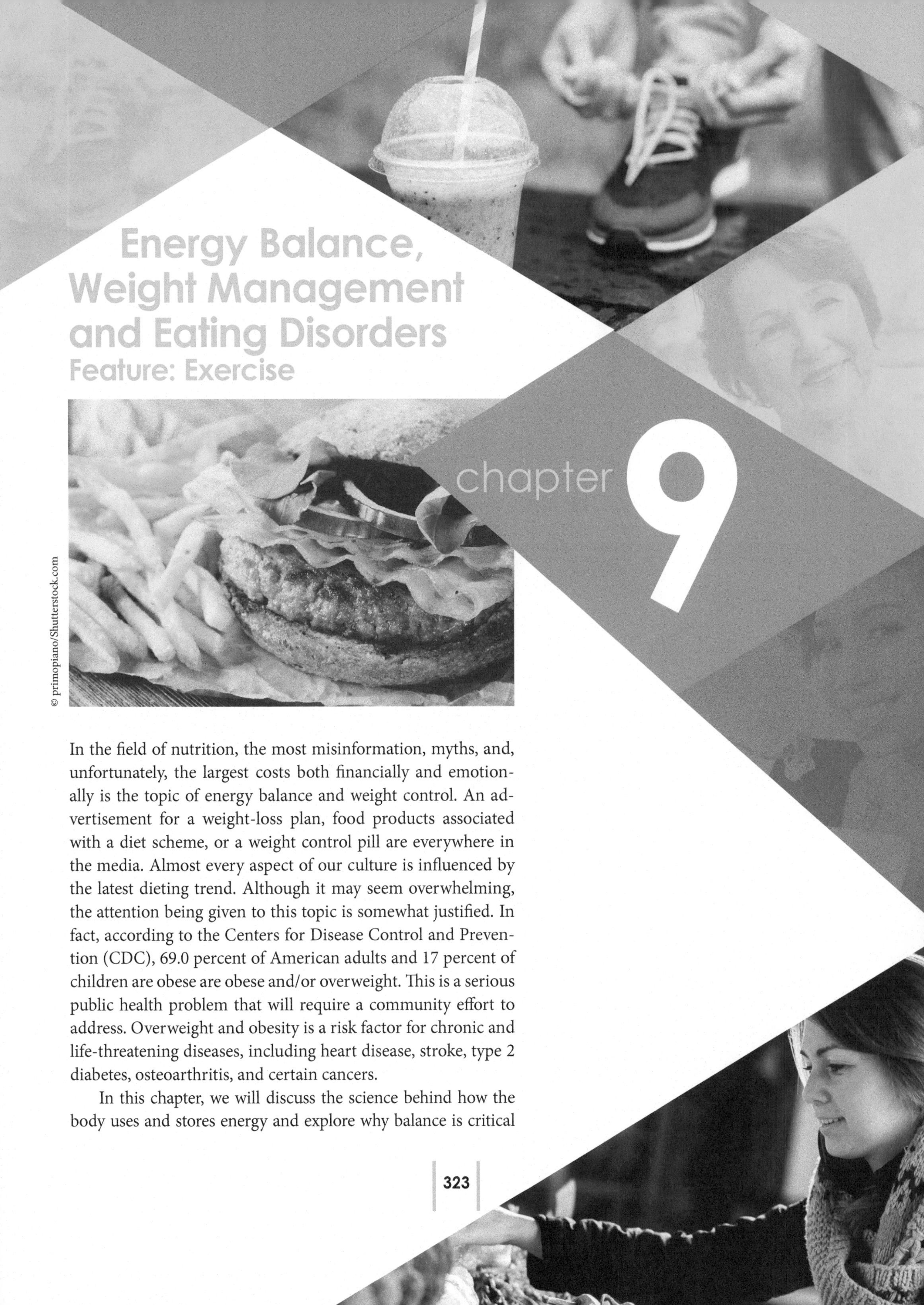

Energy Balance, Weight Management and Eating Disorders

Feature: Exercise

chapter 9

In the field of nutrition, the most misinformation, myths, and, unfortunately, the largest costs both financially and emotionally is the topic of energy balance and weight control. An advertisement for a weight-loss plan, food products associated with a diet scheme, or a weight control pill are everywhere in the media. Almost every aspect of our culture is influenced by the latest dieting trend. Although it may seem overwhelming, the attention being given to this topic is somewhat justified. In fact, according to the Centers for Disease Control and Prevention (CDC), 69.0 percent of American adults and 17 percent of children are obese are obese and/or overweight. This is a serious public health problem that will require a community effort to address. Overweight and obesity is a risk factor for chronic and life-threatening diseases, including heart disease, stroke, type 2 diabetes, osteoarthritis, and certain cancers.

In this chapter, we will discuss the science behind how the body uses and stores energy and explore why balance is critical

to maintaining a healthy weight. Popular treatments for weight loss and weight maintenance will be examined to see how and why they do or do not work. In addition, the pros and cons of many weight-loss programs will be discussed.

> **APPLICATION TIP**
>
> Many portions of commercially sold French fries, hamburgers, and sodas are two to five times larger than when they were first produced.

CALORIES IN VERSUS CALORIES OUT

In order to lose weight you must burn more Calories than you consume. To maintain weight you must burn as many Calories as you consume. To gain weight you must consume more than you burn. So, Calories in versus Calories out is an oversimplified explanation of a complex issue. However, this simple statement is fundamentally true and summarizes the fact that maintaining weight is an issue of balance.

Calories In: The Food We Eat

The "Calories in" side of the equation comes from the food we eat. We have easy access to a wide variety of food choices, both healthy and unhealthy. The downside of this easily accessible food supply is that many fast and convenient foods are high in fat, sugar, and Calories. Choosing these foods on a regular basis can easily contribute to an excessive Calorie intake. Foods that are marketed as low-fat or fat-free can be deceiving, because they often contain more Calories than the products they are designed to replace. It is important to read food labels for nutritional information and to eat Calorie dense foods in moderation.

In addition to availability, portion size has increased over time. In the food marketplace, the concept of getting more for your money seems to have eliminated the concept of eating a reasonable portion size.

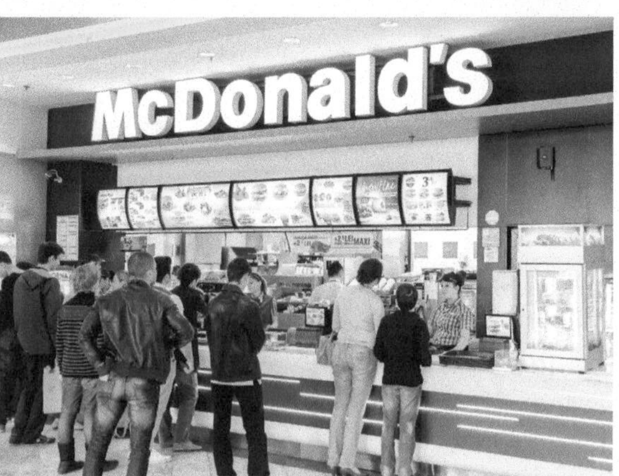

The concept of getting more for your money has contributed to the increasing portion sizes provided by many restaurants.

This trend has contributed to the obesity epidemic because larger portion sizes contribute to consuming more Calories as well.

Eating a larger meal away from home on occasion may not be a big problem, but Americans are dining out now more than ever. According to the United States Department of Agriculture (USDA) in 2012, food consumed outside the home accounted for about 43 percent of the family food budget, whereas in 1970 it accounted for only 26 percent. This may be attributed to the increased affordability and availability of fast food, advertising, and the faster paced lifestyle of today that makes it difficult to find the time to cook at home. In addition, the increased portion sizes in restaurant meals and beverages contribute to our excessive caloric intake.

There is a high density of fast food establishments in low income neighborhoods. It has been suggested that this is a partial explanation for higher obesity rates in lower income populations. Increasing the portion size of a product is an effective marketing tool. If people think they are getting more for their money, they are more likely to buy the product or patronize the restaurant.

Portion sizes and our idea of what is a reasonable portion size have been distorted. One way to combat this distortion is to educate ourselves as to what constitutes a reasonable portion size. See the Make It a Practice feature on portion sizes for guidelines on judging them.

Make it a PRACTICE

ACHIEVING A HEALTHY WEIGHT STARTS HERE: PORTION SIZES

ChooseMyPlate.gov gives recommendations for how much of each food group should be consumed for each age and gender group. Table 9.1 is taken from that website and describes the recommended daily equivalents of meat for each group.

TABLE 9.1 Recommended Daily Equivalents for Protein from ChooseMyPlate.gov

	Age Range	Daily Recommendation
Children	2–3 years old	2 oz. equivalents
	4–8 years old	3–4 oz. equivalents
Girls	9–13 years old	5 oz. equivalents
	14–18 years old	5 oz. equivalents
Boys	9–13 years old	5 oz. equivalents
	14–18 years old	6 oz. equivalents
Women	19–30 years old	5 1/2 oz. equivalents
	31–50 years old	5 oz. equivalents
	51+ years old	5 oz. equivalents
Men	19–30 years old	6 1/2 oz. equivalents
	31–50 years old	6 oz. equivalents
	51+ years old	5 oz. equivalents

Estimating an ounce equivalent when you are eating in a restaurant or cafeteria or even just making a quick dinner at home can be confusing. ChooseMyPlate.gov provides some examples of how much of each food group should be consumed. The website says, "In general, 1 oz. of meat, poultry or fish, 1/4 cup cooked beans, 1 egg, 1 tbsp. of peanut butter, or 1/2 oz. of nuts or seeds can be considered as 1 oz. equivalent from the Protein Foods Group." Let's say you are a 19-year-old male. You see on the chart that you should eat the equivalent of about 6.5 oz. of protein. What does that look like in terms of actual food?

If you have a chicken sandwich with a small chicken breast, like the one pictured in Figure 9.1a, for lunch. This is 6 oz. equivalents. For a snack you have an ounce of cashews (13 nuts) which is 2 oz. equivalents (Figure 9.1b). And for dinner, you have black beans with rice. Assuming you had 1/2 c. of black beans, as pictured in Figure 9.1c, this is 2 oz. equivalents. You have consumed 10 oz. equivalents and therefore have exceeded the recommended 6.5 oz. equivalents for the day. It is easy to see why so many people eat too much from some of the food groups and, therefore, too many Calories. If you are not sure how big the serving size on your plate is, you can compare it to real-world objects in several ways to get a better idea (see Table 9.2).

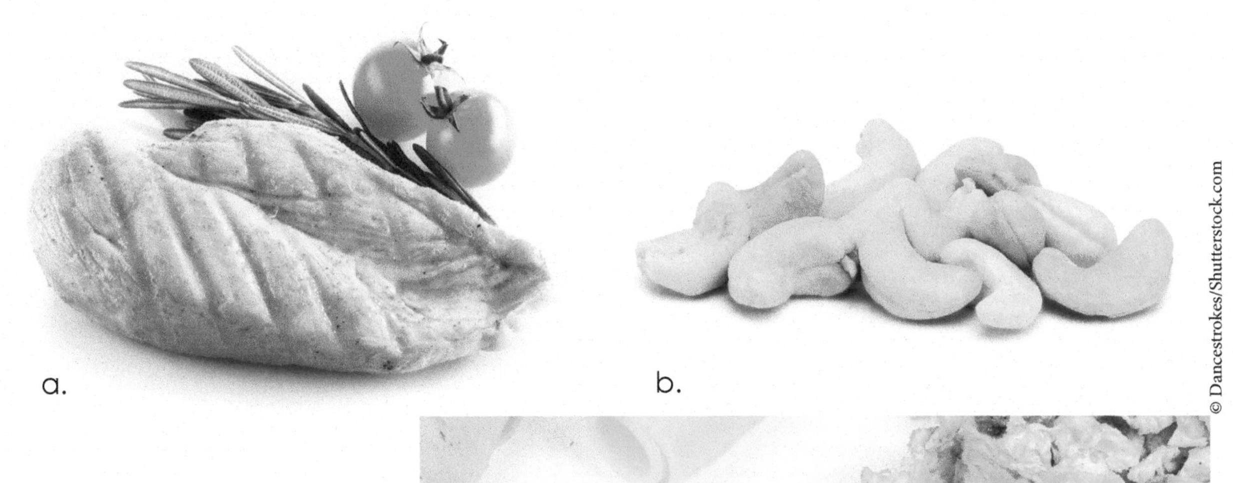

a. b.

c.

FIGURE 9.1
(a) A 6-oz chicken breast represents 6 oz. equivalents; (b) 1 oz. of cashews represents 2 oz. equivalents; (c) 1/2 cup of black beans represents 2 oz. equivalents.

TABLE 9.2 Some Real-World Objects to Help Judge Portion Sizes

One Serving of . . .	Real-World Object	MyPlate Equivalent
Apple	Baseball	1 c. (1 serving)
Bagel	Hockey puck (mini bagel)	1 oz. equivalent
Butter	Thumb (joint to tip)	2 oz.
Cheese	Pair of dice	1 1/2 oz. (1 serving)
Fish, grilled	iPhone	4 oz. equivalent
Fruit, chopped	Tennis ball	1 c. (1 serving)
Pancake	(4 1/2-in. diameter)	1 oz. equivalent
Potato	Computer mouse	1 c. (1 serving)
Meat:	Matchbox	1 oz.
	Bar of soap	3 oz.
	Thin paperback book	8 oz.
Rice, steamed	Small cupcake	1/2 c. (1 oz.) equivalent
Vegetables, cooked	Tennis ball	1 c. (1 serving)

APPLICATION TIP

Go to ChooseMyPlate.gov for more examples of what counts as an ounce equivalent, and then see if you can devise your own real-world-object examples to help you judge adequate portion sizes without taking time to weigh and measure foods.

Calories Out: Energy Expenditure

One of the first aspects to examine when discussing body weight is the "Calories out" or energy expenditure side of our *balance* equation. Individuals vary widely in the number of Calories burned each day. However, everybody expends energy or Calories in three ways: basal metabolic rate (BMR), physical activity, and the thermic effect of food (TEF). The relative significance of these variables varies somewhat depending on your individual circumstances.

© bikeriderlondon/Shutterstock.com

Basal Metabolic Rate

Did you know that we burn Calories even while we are just sitting or sleeping? These Calories make up most of the Calories we burn in a day and are part of what we call **basal metabolic rate (BMR)**. The Calories that contribute to BMR are used for your heartbeat, breathing, nerve impulse transmission, kidney function, growth and repair, and other basic functions and are defined as the amount of energy needed to maintain the body when it is at rest. Although BMR varies from one person to another, it generally makes up approximately two-thirds of the total Calories expended in a day by the average person. Someone who has a relatively slow or efficient metabolism requires fewer Calories to conduct the body functions listed above that contribute to BMR than does someone with a faster metabolism and the same lifestyle. The person with a slower metabolism will have a more difficult time keeping excess weight off.

basal metabolic rate (BMR)
Amount of energy that a person needs to keep the body functioning at rest.

Organs such as the brain, liver, and muscle burn most of the Calories that make up your daily BMR. In comparison, fat tissue does not require very many Calories for maintenance. Therefore, how much of your body is muscle and how much is fat influences how many Calories you burn in a day. The more muscle you have, the more Calories you burn, even when you are just sitting still. In individuals of similar age, sex, height, and weight, differences in muscle mass account for approximately 80 percent of the variance in BMR. Differences in muscle mass also account for most of the difference in BMR between men and women, and between younger and older adults of similar heights and weights. Several factors can influence your BMR. For example, food restriction, particularly chronic dieting, lowers BMR, especially when muscle mass is lost. Building muscle mass, exercising, and eating regular meals are the best ways to increase BMR (see Table 9.3).

TABLE 9.3 Factors Affecting Basal Metabolic Rate (BMR)

Factors That Increase BMR	Factors That Decrease BMR
Increased muscle mass Being taller Exposure to hot or cold temperatures	Loss of muscle mass Being female (lower muscle mass) Aging (especially if accompanied with loss of muscle mass)
Regular or frequent meals (by increasing TEF)	Skipping meals, dieting, meal restriction
Exercise (if increasing muscle mass)	Starvation, fasting intensity, duration, and type
	Sleep (BMR at its lowest while sleeping)
Fever	
Caffeine	
Stress	
Pregnancy and breastfeeding	
Hormones	
Nicotine	

Physical Activity

Physical activity refers to energy expenditure through all *voluntary* physical effort—in other words, daily activities, exercise, or physical labor. Physical activity is the component of daily caloric expenditure that varies the most from day to day in the same person and from person to person. The more muscles you contract and the more frequently you contract them, the more Calories you burn. Body weight, muscle mass, number of muscles used, duration, intensity, the exerciser's fitness, and the type of activity determine how much energy is used. Figure 9.2 lists the amount of time it takes to burn 150 Calories while participating in various activities. Note that this varies based on the size of the person. For example, running a mile burns more Calories in a 200 lb. person than a 150 lb. person simply because the heavier person has more weight to carry.

All activities expend energy but the amount will vary based on their intensity. Table 9.4 lists an estimate of energy expenditure for various activities. Although it may seem discouraging that many moderate activities don't appear to burn a lot of Calories, there are more reasons to exercise than just to burn Calories. Participation in regular physical activity increases muscle mass, which increases your caloric expenditure by increasing your BMR. Ex-

www.cdc.gov/nccdphp/dnpa/physical/

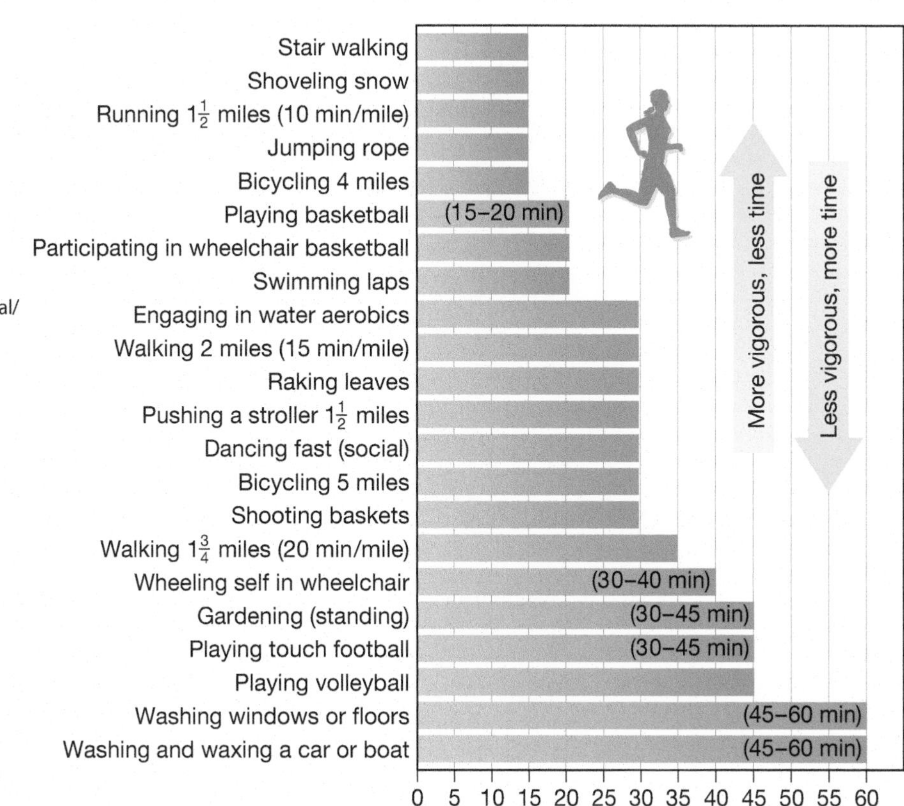

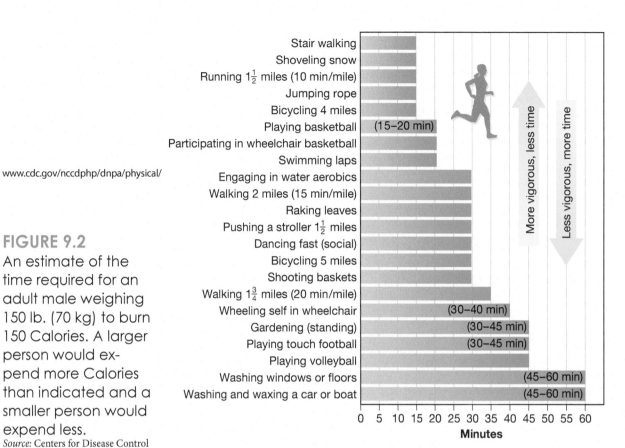

FIGURE 9.2
An estimate of the time required for an adult male weighing 150 lb. (70 kg) to burn 150 Calories. A larger person would expend more Calories than indicated and a smaller person would expend less.
Source: Centers for Disease Control

ercise has also been shown to decrease the risk of high blood pressure, heart disease, cancer, diabetes, osteoporosis, and obesity. The 2015 Dietary Guidelines for Americans recommend that adults perform 2.5 hours of moderate intensity or 75 minutes of vigorous intensity aerobic exercise or an equivalent combination of moderate and vigorous exercise spread throughout the week. Despite the known health benefits, only 49 percent of adult Americans report that they participate in regular physical activity. Regardless of whether you need to lose weight, gain weight, or just maintain weight, it is important to your health and well-being to participate in regular physical activity.

Thermic Effect of Food – Calories for Digestion

Did you know that you actually burn Calories when you eat? Research shows that your body burns about 10 percent of Calories consumed, depending on the type and quantity of food eaten (a little higher for protein, a little lower for fat). The process of burning Calories as you digest, absorb, transport, store, and metabolize food is called the **thermic effect of food (TEF)**. Dieting makes many claims about TEF. For example, some diets claim that there are "weight-loss foods," that is, foods that burn more Calories than they provide. But no evidence supports the idea that any food makes the body burn more Calories than the food provides. Other diets claim that eating a high-protein diet will make

thermic effect of food (TEF)
The energy expended by the body in digesting, absorbing, transporting, storing, metabolizing and otherwise processing food; it amounts to about 10 percent of Calories consumed.

TABLE 9.4 Energy Costs of Various Physical Activities

Activity	Intensity	Kilocalories Used per Pound per Hour
Sitting, quietly watching television	Light	0.48
Sitting, reading	Light	0.62
Sitting, studying including reading or writing	Light	0.86
Cooking or food preparation (standing or sitting)	Light	0.95
Walking, shopping	Light	1.09
Walking, 2 mph (slow pace)	Light	1.20
Cleaning (dusting, straightening up, vacuuming, changing linen, or carrying out trash)	Moderate	1.20
Stretching—Hatha Yoga	Moderate	1.20
Weight lifting (free weights, Nautilus, or Universal type)	Light or moderate	1.42
Bicycling <10 mph	Leisure (work or pleasure)	1.90
Walking, 4 mph (brisk pace)	Moderate	2.40
Aerobics	Low impact	2.40
Weight lifting (free weights, Nautilus, or Universal type)	Vigorous	2.86
Bicycling 12 to 13.9 mph	Moderate	3.82
Running, 5 mph (12 min per mile)	Moderate	3.82
Running, 6 mph (10 min per mile)	Moderate	4.77
Running, 8.6 mph (7 min per mile)	Vigorous	6.68

Source: Ainsworth BE, Haskell WL, Whitt MC, Irwin ML, Swartz AM, Strath SJ, O'Brien WL, Bassett DR Jr., Schmitz KH, Emplaincourt PO, Jacobs DR Jr., Leon AS. (2000) Compendium of physical activities: an update of activity codes and MET intensities. *Med Sci Sports Exerc* 32:S498–S516.

one lose weight because of the greater TEF of protein compared to fat or carbohydrates. Recent studies have indicated that if you consume the same amount of Calories on a diet that contains 25 percent of total Calories from protein as you do on a diet that contains 12 percent of total Calories from protein, you will not lose more weight or body fat. However, people who eat a higher protein diet may eat less because the protein makes them feel fuller longer.

Total Energy Expenditure

total energy expenditure (TEE) The sum of BMR, physical activity, and TEF.

Total energy expenditure (TEE) is the sum of BMR, physical activity, and TEF. Figure 9.3 shows how the differences in energy expenditure among people of the same size and sex can be explained by physical activity.

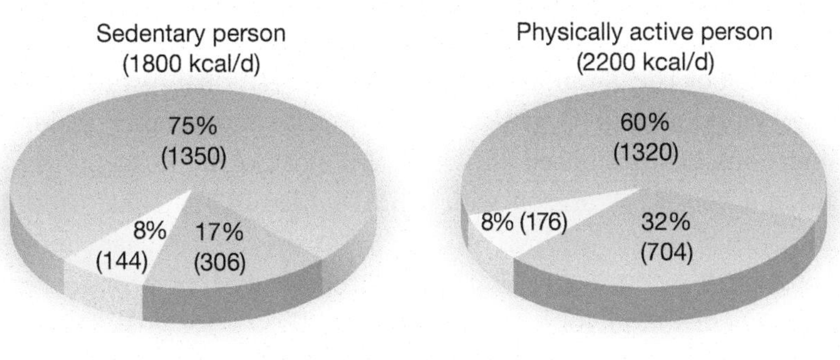

FIGURE 9.3 Comparison of the components of daily energy expenditure between an active person and a sedentary person of the same weight.

To measure BMR directly requires expensive specialized equipment that is usually found in research facilities. Estimating the Calories you burn in physical activity is a bit more difficult because it varies depending on intensity, duration, your fitness level, the environmental temperature, your body size, and the amount of muscle mass you have. One way to account for activity is to make an estimate based on activity factors. This approach is not precise, but it is a quick and useful calculation.

BEFORE YOU GO ON...

1. What is the bottom line to achieve weight loss?
2. List the factors that contribute to daily energy expenditure.
3. Which factor contributing to energy expenditure varies the most?
4. What factor may help explain why more Americans are overweight now than in the past?

OUT OF BALANCE: OVERWEIGHT, OBESITY, AND UNDERWEIGHT

body mass index (BMI)

A height–weight relationship used to assess obesity; it equals (weight in kilograms) / divided by (height in meters squared), or (weight in pounds × 703) / divided by (height in inches squared).

overweight

The condition of having a BMI of 25-29.9.

obesity

The condition of having a BMI of 30 or greater.

We can measure and define overweight and obesity in a number of ways. The body mass index (BMI) is the simplest calculation. It can be done anywhere with a tape measure and a scale; however, it has the limitation of not taking into account body composition. To be more accurate than BMI alone, we can estimate the actual amount of fat on the body, and, finally, we can examine how that fat is distributed.

Body Mass Index (BMI)

The **body mass index (BMI)** is a height–weight relationship. It equals (weight in kilograms) divided by (height in meters squared), or (weight in pounds × 703) divided by (height in inches squared). The National Institutes of Health and the World Health Organization, as well as many other major health organizations, have proposed the use of BMI as a tool in the diagnosis of overweight and obesity. A person with a BMI under 18.5 is considered underweight, normal weight is a BMI of 18.5-24.9, **overweight** is characterized by a BMI of 25-29.9 , while **obesity** is characterized by a BMI of 30 or greater. Table 9.5 is a convenient tool for looking up your BMI.

TABLE 9.5 Body Mass Index (BMI) Chart

	19	20	21	22	23	24	25	26	27	28	29	30	31	32	33	34	35
Height (in.)	**Body Weight (lbs)**																
58	91	96	100	105	110	115	119	124	129	134	138	143	148	153	158	162	167
59	94	99	104	109	114	110	124	128	133	138	143	148	153	158	163	168	173
60	97	102	107	112	118	123	128	133	138	143	148	153	158	163	168	174	179
61	100	106	111	116	122	127	132	137	143	148	153	158	164	169	174	180	185
62	104	109	115	120	126	131	136	142	147	153	158	164	169	175	180	186	191
63	107	113	118	124	130	135	141	146	152	158	163	169	175	180	186	191	197
64	110	116	122	128	134	140	145	151	157	163	169	174	180	186	192	197	204
65	114	120	126	132	138	144	150	156	162	168	174	180	186	192	198	204	210
66	118	124	130	136	142	148	155	161	167	173	179	186	192	198	204	210	216
67	121	127	134	140	146	153	159	166	172	178	185	191	198	204	211	217	223
68	125	131	138	144	151	158	164	171	177	184	190	197	203	210	216	223	230
69	128	135	142	149	155	162	169	176	182	189	196	203	209	216	223	230	236
70	132	139	146	153	160	167	174	181	188	195	202	209	216	222	229	236	243
71	136	143	150	157	165	172	179	186	193	200	208	215	222	229	236	243	250
72	140	147	154	162	169	177	184	191	199	206	213	221	228	235	242	250	258
73	144	151	159	166	174	182	189	197	204	212	210	227	235	242	250	257	265
74	148	155	163	171	179	186	194	202	210	218	225	233	241	249	256	264	272
75	152	160	168	176	184	192	200	208	216	224	232	240	248	256	264	272	279
76	156	164	172	180	189	197	205	213	221	230	238	246	254	263	271	279	287

APPLICATION TIP

Did you know that according to the latest national statistics published by the CDC, the average adult American woman is 63.8" tall and weighs 166 lbs. The average man is 69.3 in. tall and weighs 196 lbs. These figures correlate with an average BMI of 29, which puts the average American at an increased risk for many health problems, according to Table 9.6.

BMI and Disease Risk

Scientists studying the relationship between BMI and health have associated being overweight or obese with certain disease risks (Table 9.7). Being overweight or obese raises the risk for diseases such as cardiovascular disease; hypertension; type 2 diabetes; chronic inflammation; stroke; gallbladder disease; osteoarthritis; sleep apnea; respiratory problems; and endometrial, breast, prostate, and colon cancers. Obesity is also associated with complications during pregnancy, menstrual irregularities leading to infertility, and psychological disorders such as depression. The classification system used in Table 9.6 is based on research that shows that the risk of disease usually begins to increase at a BMI of 25–29.9, and increases further at a BMI of 30. The death rate increases with BMIs greater than 25; the increase is greatest with a BMI of 30 and greater. For people with a BMI of 30, death rates from all causes, and especially from cardiovascular disease, are increased by 50 to 100 percent above that of people with BMIs of 20–25 (see Figure 9.4).

TABLE 9.6 Body Mass Index (BMI) and Disease Risk

Body Mass Index	Disease Risks
25–29.9 (overweight)	• High blood pressure (hypertension)
	• High blood cholesterol (dyslipidemia)
	• Type 2 (non-insulin-dependent) diabetes
	• Insulin resistance, glucose intolerance
	• High blood insulin (hyperinsulinemia)
	• Coronary heart disease
	• Congestive heart failure
	• Sleep apnea and other breathing problems
	• Stroke
	• Gallbladder disease and gallstones
	• Gout
	• Osteoarthritis (degeneration of cartilage and bone in joints)

	• Certain types of cancer (such as endometrial, uterine, breast, prostate, colon, kidney, gallbladder, and esophageal)
	• Kidney stones
30 and greater (obese)	• All of the risks noted above
	• Kidney disease
	• Liver disease
	• Back problems
	• Restricted mobility
	• Complications of pregnancy
	• Poor female reproductive health (such as menstrual irregularities, infertility, irregular ovulation)
	• Hirsutism (presence of excess body and facial hair)
	• Bladder control problems (such as stress incontinence)
	• Psychological disorders (such as depression, eating disorders, distorted body image, and low self-esteem)
	• Increased risk of complications during surgery
	• **50–150% greater risk of premature death from any cause**

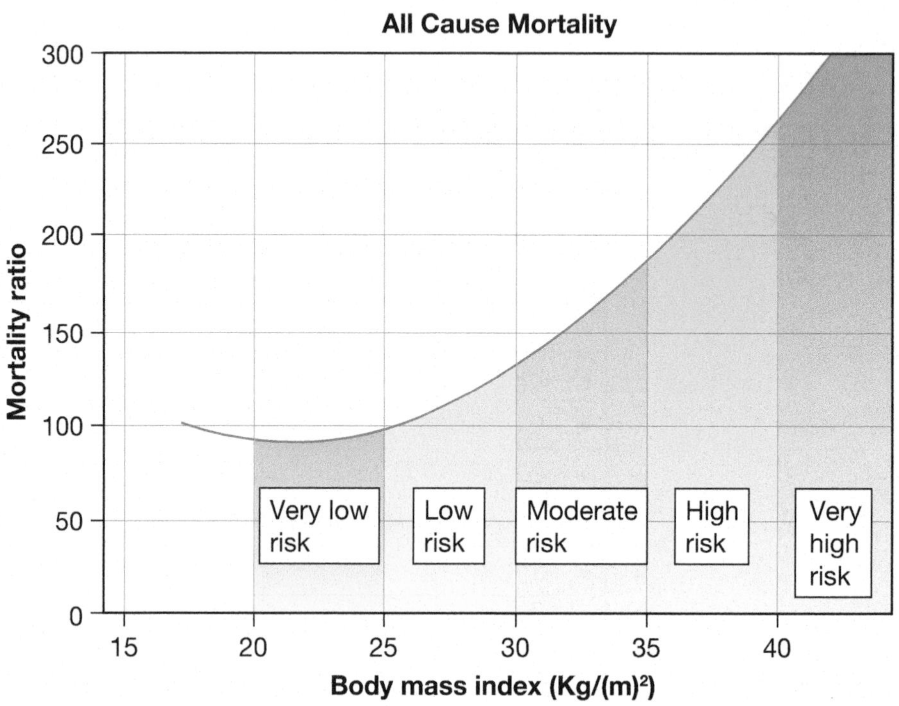

FIGURE 9.4
Relationship between BMI and mortality.

Underweight

Overweight and obesity are not the only potential problems associated with weight. It is also possible to weigh too little. If you have a BMI of <18.5, you are considered **underweight**. As you can see in Figure 9.4, the relationship between BMI and prevalence of disease and death is U-shaped. This means that just as risk goes up with an increasing BMI, it increases with a BMI below the recommended level as well. Being underweight is typically associated with inadequate nutritional intake, which can result in decreased overall energy, a weakened immune system, respiratory complications, heart irregularities, infertility, and delayed wound healing.

underweight
A BMI of <18.5

Some people are simply born with fewer fat cells and are genetically predisposed to being extremely thin. Other factors that can cause underweight include stress, depression, bereavement, smoking, and eating disorders. Some diseases cause sudden and dramatic weight loss, such as hyperthyroidism, HIV/AIDS, some cancers, and some conditions of the digestive system.

Limitations of BMI

Although BMI is a simple and convenient tool, it has some limitations in its utility as a method to diagnose overweight and obesity and therefore to determine disease risk. BMI fails to distinguish between fat and muscle mass. For example, the BMI of the athlete in Figure 9.5 indicates that he is obese; however, he is a lean and muscular individual. Athletes aside, most of the time people with high BMIs are obese. To be certain, measuring body composition is a better indicator for determining disease risk. In addition, the relationship between BMI and body fat differs according to sex and ethnic group. Women have a higher percentage of body fat than men at the same BMI.

FIGURE 9.5
A BMI of 32 suggests that this man is obese. However, on further assessment we discover that his body fat is estimated to be very low. BMI is not always an accurate indicator of obesity, especially for very lean and muscular individuals.

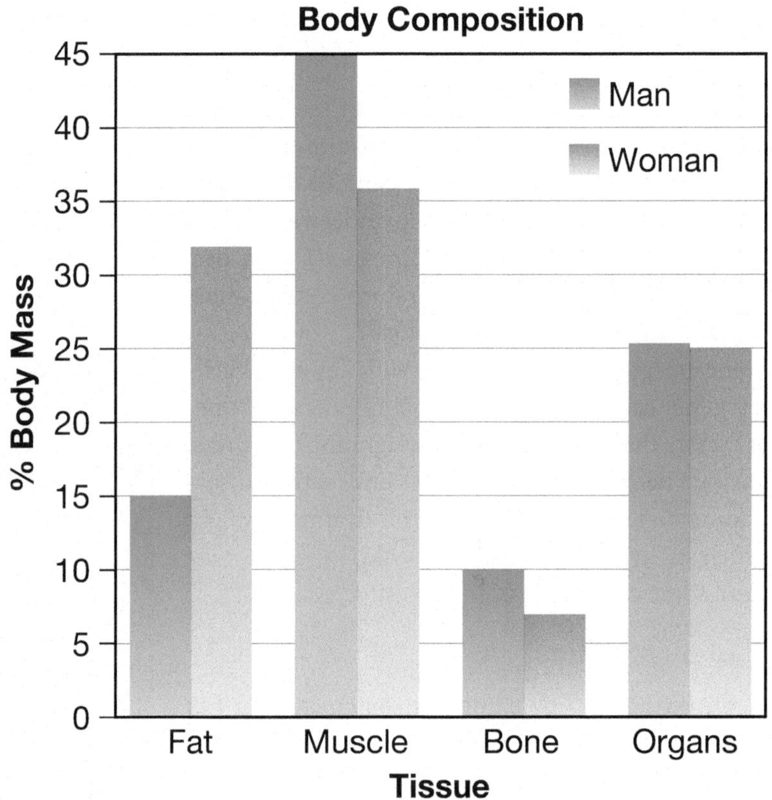

FIGURE 9.6

A comparison of the components of body composition between men and women. Note that men have a higher percentage of muscle mass and women have a higher percentage of body fat. Women require more body fat for reproduction.

Source: Republished from *Advanced Human Nutrition* by Wildman and Medeiros. © 2000 by CRC Press.

Body Composition

Total body mass is the sum of lean tissue mass and fat mass. The problems associated with obesity stem from extra body fat. Thus, it is helpful to know what percentage of your body weight is composed of fat. Although athletes have a lower percentage of body fat, the acceptable ranges of body fat percentage for the general population are roughly 18-24 percent for men and 25-31 percent for women. Maintaining body fat in these ranges is associated with a reduced risk of chronic disease.

Body fat is a combination of *essential fat* and *storage fat.* Essential fat is the amount of fat required for normal physiological functioning. It consists of the fat needed for the body's organs, central nervous system, muscles, and bone marrow.

In women it also includes sex-specific essential fat, or the amount of fat needed for optimal reproductive function. Storage fat consists mostly of fat from adipose tissue, tissue under the skin, and the fat that "pads" essential organs. Women have more essential body fat than men because of the added sex-specific fat, but they have similar amounts of storage fat. Men with more than 25 percent body fat and women with more than 32 percent body fat are considered obese.

Techniques to Estimate Body Composition

Although body composition is a much more informative statistic than BMI, it is much more difficult to determine. Several techniques are used to estimate body fat. None are 100 percent accurate and all are based on equations that make certain assumptions, which may not be true for every person. **Underwater weighing** is often referred to as the gold standard for estimating body composition. This technique measures the density of the body by comparing weight on land to underwater weight and the volume of water displaced by the body. The person is lowered into a tank of water after exhaling all air from the lungs. He or she is then weighed in the water. Because fat floats and lean tissue sinks, density predicts fatness. Although this test is accurate, it is not convenient and is usually available only in university and research laboratories.

Although they are not as accurate as underwater weighing, **skinfold calipers** are a more convenient alternative. The calipers are used to measure the thickness of the fat layer under the skin in several locations, such as the triceps, shoulder blade, and abdomen. Plugging these values into an equation yields the percentage of body fat. Although using calipers is much easier and less expensive than underwater weighing, the caliper method requires a trained and skilled operator. It is most accurate with people close to the normal range of body fat and less accurate for the extremely lean and the extremely obese.

One of the most recently developed techniques to estimate body composition is the **Bod Pod**. It uses similar techniques to underwater weighing, except that it uses air displacement instead of water displacement. The subject is able to breathe freely increasing the accuracy of the results. Of all the alternative techniques to underwater weighing, it is considered the most accurate.

underwater weighing
A technique for estimating body composition by comparing weight on land to underwater weight and the volume of water displaced by the body.

skinfold calipers
A technique for estimating body composition by measuring thickness of fat layer under the skin in several locations.

Bod Pod
A technique for estimating body composition by sitting within the Bod Pod and measuring displacement of air.

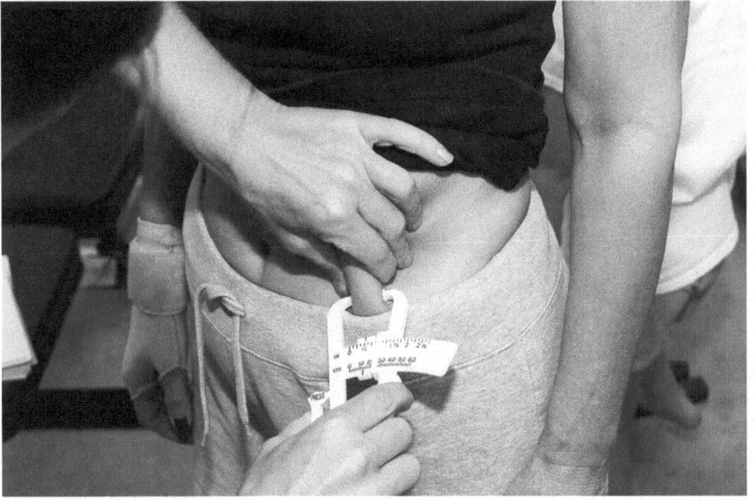

The underwater weighing technique is considered the gold standard for estimating body composition. Although not as accurate as the underwater weighing technique, skinfold calipers are a more convenient technique for estimating body composition.

Bathroom scales often use BIA to estimate body fat. It is not a very accurate technique because it is influenced by body water, which can fluctuate significantly.

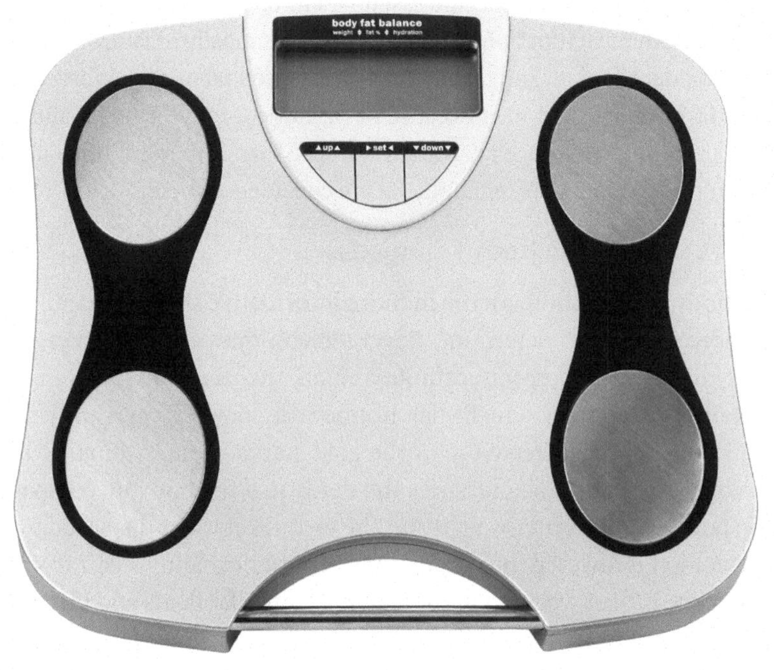

© cretolamna/Shutterstock.com

My bathroom scale tells me what I weigh and what my body fat is. Is it accurate?

Bioelectrical impedance analysis (BIA), another way to measure body composition, is based on the fact that lean tissue, with high water content, conducts electricity relatively well, while fat tissue, with low water content, conducts electricity poorly. It is often used in scales and hand-held devices. This method is even less accurate than skinfolds as it is greatly affected by changes in body water. Using this method, small electrodes are attached to a hand and a foot and a mild electric current is passed through the body. (Subjects do not feel anything.) By measuring the body's impedance, or resistance to current, a technician can determine the amount of lean tissue and the amount of fat.

bioelectrical impedance analysis (BIA)
A method of measuring body composition based on the fact that lean tissue, with high water content, conducts electricity relatively well while fat tissue, with low water content, conducts electricity poorly.

Body Fat Distribution

Where you store fat on your body has a significant influence on health and disease risk. Each person carries fat in their own pattern, which is largely genetically determined. In general, there are two kinds of distributions. In the **android** pattern, the "apple shape," most body fat is carried in the abdomen. In the **gynoid** pattern, the "pear shape," most body fat is carried on the hips and thighs. Either pattern can occur but the android pattern is more common in men and the gynoid pattern more common in women.

android
A pattern of body fat distribution in which most body fat is carried in the abdomen; the "apple" shape.

gynoid
A pattern of body fat distribution in which most body fat is carried on the hips and thighs; the "pear" shape.

In terms of disease risk, android obesity carries a much higher risk for hypertension, type 2 diabetes, and heart disease than gynoid obesity. Thus, given two people with exactly the same degree of obesity, the one with android obesity probably will have greater health problems. In android obesity, body fat can be stored under

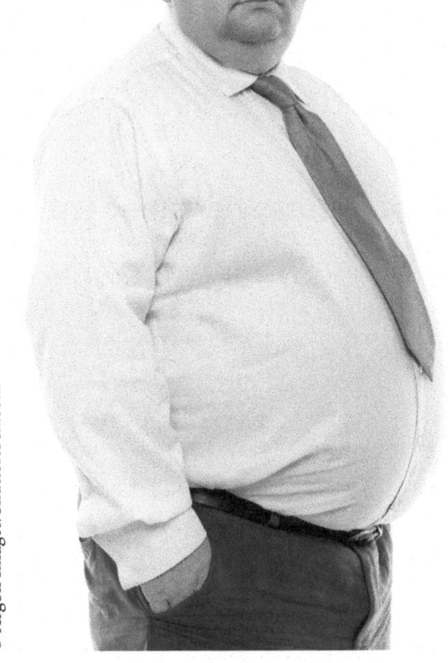
© Argon Images/Shutterstock.com

© Peter Elvidge/Shutterstock.com

The android pattern of obesity, most common in men, describes those who tend to carry fat in the abdomen. The gynoid pattern of obesity, more common in women, describes those who tend to carry body fat in the hips and thighs. Android obesity is associated with greater health risks than is gynoid obesity.

the abdominal muscle around the internal organs (**visceral fat**) or over the muscle and under the skin (**subcutaneous fat**). Visceral fat is associated with greater health risks than subcutaneous fat. Among those with android obesity, those with more abdominal visceral fat are at greater risk than those with subcutaneous abdominal fat. The **waist-to-hip ratio** measures this risk. In general, men with a waist-to-hip ratio of greater than 1.0 and women with a ratio greater than 0.8 are considered to have an excess accumulation of fat in their abdomen.

Although waist-to-hip ratio is a useful tool, health professionals often use waist circumference by itself as an accurate predictor of disease risk. Risk increases with a waist measurement greater than 40" for men and 35" for women. This is of particular concernbecause the most recent CDC data indicate that the average adult waist circumference is 39.7" for men and 37.5" for women.

visceral fat
Body fat stored under the abdominal muscle.

subcutaneous fat
(sub-kyoo-TAY-nee-us fat) Body fat stored over the muscle and under the skin.

waist-to-hip ratio
A measure of the health risks associated with android obesity.

APPLICATION TIP

You can determine whether your body fat distribution is putting you at risk by measuring your waist just above the hip bone, with the tape measure snug but not compressed. Women with a waist of 35" or greater and men with a waist of 40" or greater are at a greater health risk than those with smaller waist measurements.

BEFORE YOU GO ON...

1. How is BMI used to define obesity?
2. Why were the recommendations for BMI set where they are?
3. What are the recommendations for body fat percentage for men and women, and why are they different?
4. How does body fat distribution affect risk of disease?

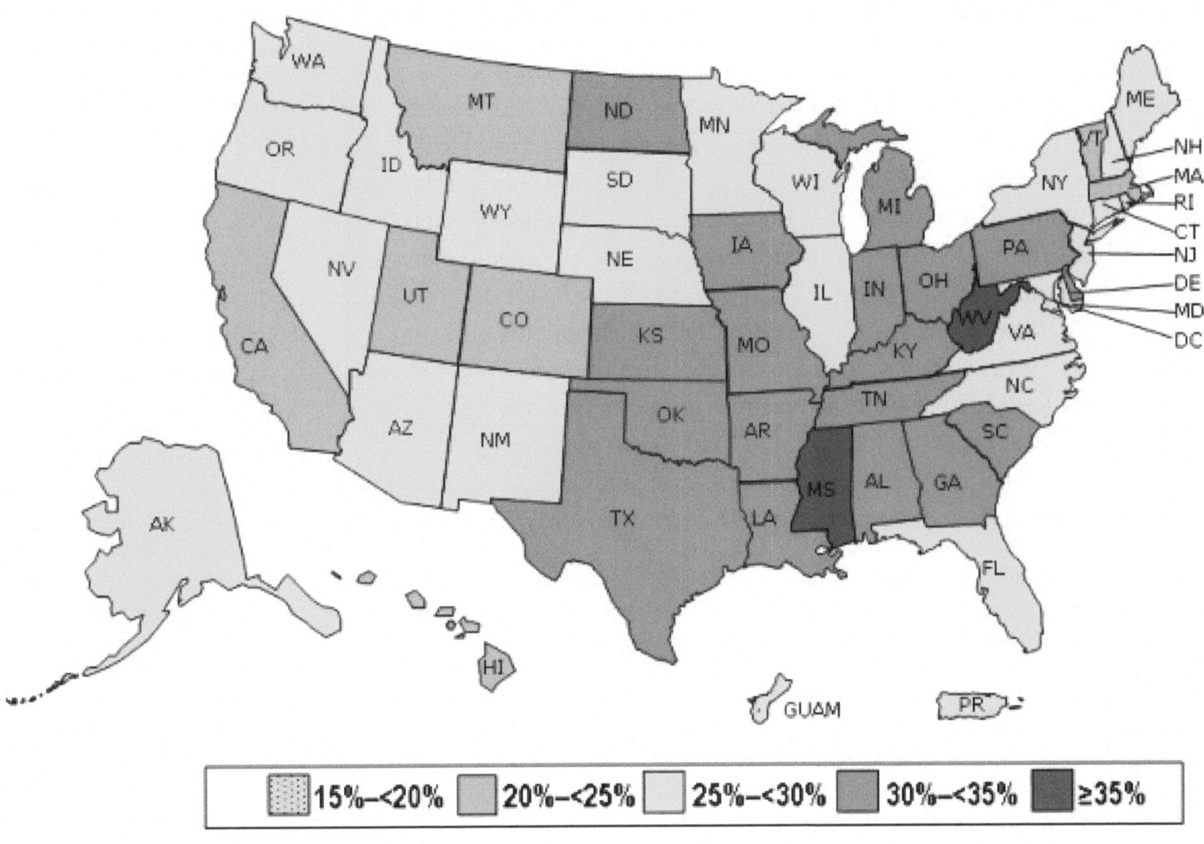

FIGURE 9.7
Increasing prevalence of obesity (BMI ≥ 30) in adults in the United States

OBESITY: AN ALARMING TREND

Years from now when health historians look back on this time in history, they will see a society that grew increasingly obese. In 1995, obesity prevalence, or the number of cases in a given population, in each of the 50 states was less than 20 percent. In 2000, only 28 states had obesity prevalence rates of less than 20 percent, and by 2005 there were only four! In 2012, 42 states had obesity prevalence rates equal to or greater than 25 percent, with 13 of those greater than 30 percent. That's over double the number of states that had obesity rates above 30 percent in 2008 (See Figure 9.7.)

"THE FRESHMAN FIFTEEN"—FACT OR FICTION?

Nutrition & LIFESTAGES

Students entering their first year of college are faced with many stresses and changes, including changes in eating and exercise behavior. A common fear among college students is the reported high risk of gaining 15 lbs. during their freshman year—the dreaded "Freshman Fifteen." Despite the common belief that this is as much a reality of college life as all-night studying and questionable cafeteria food, little documented evidence indicates that a 15 lb. weight gain is common. But don't breathe a sigh of relief yet. Although research has not found that freshmen gain an average of 15 lbs., it does support the perspective that many freshmen add weight. In fact, studies report average weight gains of anywhere from 2 to 9 lbs. Why the weight gain? The stress of handling social life and studies that are new and more challenging; being away from parents for the first time; an environment with unlimited access to food; and a less regular eating, sleeping, and exercising schedule can quickly lead to weight gain. In addition, if you use food to soothe emotional needs that may result from dealing with all of these changes, putting on 15 lbs. is quite possible.

You can do some things to prevent weight gain during college or any other time. You are already using one of the most important prevention techniques—educating yourself about nutrition and health. Here are a few more tips you can use:

- Stay active.
- Be aware of what you are eating.

- Stock your fridge with healthy snacks such as yogurt, vegetables, and fruit.
- Don't skip meals.
- Limit your intake of alcohol.
- Limit your intake of high-Calorie beverages such as sodas, and energy or coffee drinks.
- Have a plan for days when you may be too busy to eat regular meals, such as stocking your backpack with healthy snacks for between classes.
- Watch portion sizes.
- Get enough sleep; it helps to go to sleep at the same time every night, regardless of your class and/or work schedule.

Nutritional studies from 2012 indicate that 35 percent of adults in the United States were obese and 69 percent are either overweight or obese with almost 6 percent being extremely obese. The data also suggest that significant differences in obesity among ethnic groups remain. The prevalence of overweight was highest in Mexican American children compared to African American and Caucasian children. Among adults, similar differences existed. Approximately 33 percent of white adults were obese, compared to 48 percent of non-Hispanic black adults and 43 percent of Hispanic American adults. As a major health concern is obesity limited to the United States? The following Global Nutrition feature provides the answer.

© wavebreakmedia/Shutterstock.com

Some colleges are addressing the dreaded weight gain that many college students experience by providing state-of-the-art fitness facilities, by making physical education classes a requirement for graduation, and by offering healthy menu selections in the cafeterias.

© Kietr/Shutterstock.com

Obesity and its associated health risks have dramatically increased health care costs in the United States. In 2012, more than 190 billion dollars were spent in the United States for medical costs related to obesity. To these costs can be added time lost from work and spending on weight loss methods. This is no longer predominantly an adult concern. The trend toward obesity in younger people is alarming as more and more children and teens are diagnosed with health problems, such as heart disease and type 2 diabetes, which used to occur much later in life. For more information on children and obesity, see Chapter 10.

BEFORE YOU GO ON...

1. Which diseases are associated with obesity?
2. List the health risks associated with being underweight.
3. What can be interpreted from the U-shaped curve that represents the relationship between obesity and disease? (See Figure 9.5.)

OBESITY: CHOICE OR DESTINY?

Causes of Obesity

While the increasing numbers of obese and overweight adults and children have raised public awareness of the issue, the causes of obesity are still not completely understood. It is a subject of ongoing scientific research and debate with widely varying views and opinions. Modern research reports offer conflicting information about the issue. The popular media further add to the confusion in their effort to make quick and strongly worded headlines from the already confusing literature. Regardless, one thing is for sure: Obesity is a complex, multifaceted problem with no easy cause or solution.

Social & Environmental Causes of Obesity

Excess Food Intake

As a simple explanation, obesity is caused by a positive energy balance, which results from eating more Calories than you burn. We discussed the various sides of the "energy equation" in the beginning of the chapter. It makes sense that an unbalanced energy equation is connected to weight gain, especially when you consider that statistics suggest the average adult gains approximately 20 lbs. from age 25 to 55. If you assume that all the weight gain comes from fat tissue with an energy density of 3,500 kcal/lb that would equal 70,000 kcal of stored fat over the 30-year period. This is accumulated from an excess of just 97 kcal per day. If you can increase energy expenditure by just 100 kcal per day, perhaps you can offset this excess and prevent the weight gain statistically seen over time.

Environment

While the cause of obesity is complex and multidimensional, one thing is for sure. As a society, we eat more and do less physical activity. This has directly paralleled the increase in obesity prevalence over time. Studies have shown that rising car ownership and increasing television viewing, which are an indirect way to measure level of physical activity, have also closely paralleled trends in obesity. A study by Dietz et al. showed that prevalence of obesity increased by 2 percent for each additional hour of television viewed. There is also evidence that demonstrates the availability and price of food, particularly healthy foods such as fruits and vegetables, significantly impact food selection. In addition to being more readily available, the higher fat, higher Calorie fast food tends to be less expensive than healthier alternatives. Lack of safe walking and biking routes, the poor quality of local parks and decreased physical activity in schools have also been suggested as contributing factors to the obesity epidemic particularly among those of lower socioeconomic status.

Social Connections & Weight

Interestingly, at least one study suggests that an individual's social connections may have a stronger impact on obesity than geographical location or genetics. The study found that a person's chances of becoming obese increased 57 percent if a friend was obese, 40 percent if a sibling was, and 37 percent if a spouse was. In the closest friendships, the risk almost tripled. The study concluded that, when a person is part of a social network of people who are obese, that individual's idea of what is an acceptable weight increases. This is not to say that if you have overweight friends you should find new ones, but it does suggest that social relationships do have a strong impact on our eating behavior.

Genetics

We know that obesity is the product of genetics and environment. Studies that compare identical twins separated at birth and raised in different homes reveal that they are likely to have similar body weights despite their different environments. Obesity often runs in families, but many influences other than genes also run in families, including lifestyle practices and attitudes toward food and health. What is certain is that human genetics has not changed very much in the last 50 years, yet obesity prevalence has greatly increased during that time. It has been said that one's environment allows the genetics for obesity to "express" itself. In other words, while we cannot do much about our genetics, we have a tremendous degree of freedom in choosing our lifestyle and environment.

When a person gains weight in the form of fat, both the number and the size of fat storing cells, called adipocytes, increases. When a person is burning Calories and losing fat, however, only the size of these cells decreases. Not the number. This may partly explain why it is so difficult for some people to maintain weight loss. Even though they may have reduced the fat stored in adipocytes, the higher number of these cells available makes it easier for the body to store excess Calories the next time the person overeats.

One of the genetic theories of obesity is the **set point theory** which says that the body is programmed to gravitate toward a particular weight. The metabolism may adjust upward or downward to ensure that weight is neither lost nor gained. So if a person attempts to drastically reduce caloric intake, his or her metabolism slows down in an attempt to maintain the "set point weight" on fewer Calories. Conversely, if a person overeats, metabolism increases perhaps by increasing the TEF to use the extra Calories to prevent weight gain. This may help explain why some people cannot lose weight even when reducing caloric intake. Set point theory appears to have some merit but cannot be entirely true, as some people do change their set point in either direction by consistently eating less (or more) than they burn.

set point theory
A theory that states that the body is programmed to gravitate toward a particular weight; the metabolism may adjust upward or downward to ensure that weight is neither lost nor gained.

Certain hormones can also impact weight status. For example, fat tissue produces the hormone **leptin**, which is released into the blood to signal the brain that the body has had enough to eat. When body fat increases, it triggers an increase in leptin and the brain is signaled to decrease appetite to bring body fat back to a desired level. In turn, when body fat is low and leptin is low, the brain is signaled to increase appetite. Obese individuals generally produce enough leptin, but it is thought that the brain does not respond to the leptin that is in the blood. Although leptin is important, it explains only the alterations in hunger and appetite that may contribute to obesity and not all of the other factors.

***leptin**
Hormone produced by fat cells and released into the blood to signal the brain to decrease appetite; when body fat is low, production of leptin decreases and appetite increases.

FOOD ADDICTION

Obesity may be caused by things other than larger portion sizes and decreasing physical activity. There is some evidence to indicate that, in certain people, obesity may be a direct result of a food addiction. New studies have focused on a chemical in the brain called dopamine that is released in association with pleasure and reward. If there is a disturbance in its function, obesity may result. This would explain the behavior of some obese people who are so driven by food and the pleasure that they associate with eating that food comes before pursuit of other rewarding behaviors, similar to the experiences of people with drug and alcohol addictions. Food addiction and its role in the development of obesity remains a topic of controversy due to the fact that hunger, appetite, and body weight are controlled by many systems and chemicals in the body, not just dopamine. Furthermore, many experts contend there is no such thing as food addiction and that the term is simply an overuse of the word addiction. Nevertheless, it is now one of many theories regarding causes of obesity.

BEFORE YOU GO ON...

1. What does it mean to say that environment allows the genetics of obesity to express themselves?
2. Explain set point theory.
3. Explain the role of leptin in regulating body fat.

APPLICATION TIP

Tips for weight loss

- Create a deficit of about 500 Calories per day by: increasing exercise, decreasing portion sizes, avoiding beverages that are high in Calories.
- Set a realistic weight loss of 1–2 lbs per week.
- Eat a balanced diet.
- Eat small regular meals (about every 3 to 4 hours).
- Eat breakfast.
- Emphasize the health benefits of weight loss, not the pounds on the scale.
- Remember: this is a lifestyle change, not a short-term fix.

WEIGHT MANAGEMENT: A BALANCING ACT

Hunger, Appetite, and Satiety

Eating behavior is a combination of physiological and psychological factors. When your body needs fuel (food), your stomach and intestines send signals to the brain. The terms *hunger* and *appetite* are often used interchangeably, but they really mean two different things. Put simply, hunger is the need to eat and appetite is the desire to eat.

Hunger refers to the physiological mechanisms that determine how much and when we eat. This is a complex and not yet entirely understood combination of systems in the body. Low blood sugar levels and low glycogen (carbohydrate stores) levels are believed to increase hunger. However, the interaction of hormones, stomach distension, and nervous system stimuli also make our stomachs rumble. What complicates the clear understanding of the definition of hunger is our "desire" to eat. How many times did you feel "hungry," as in your stomach growling, when you ate dessert after a meal?

hunger
The physiological mechanisms that determine how much and when we eat.

Appetite refers to the psychological mechanisms that determine how much we eat and is therefore not the same as hunger. You can have a desire (appetite) for a certain food without having any physiological hunger. The sight or smell of food can stimulate your appetite. Talking about food or reading about it can have an effect on appetite, too. A connection between food and an event or memory can increase appetite (such as the desire for pumpkin pie around Thanksgiving or popcorn at the movies).

appetite
The psychological mechanisms that determine how much we eat.

satiation
The feeling of fullness at the end of a meal that tells you to stop eating.

satiety
How long you feel satisfied and full between meals.

Satiation and **satiety** signals take a while to reach the brain, so if you eat too quickly, you may overeat—at least in terms of what your body needs to satisfy its hunger. Satiation is the feeling of fullness at the end of a meal that tells you that you are full and to stop eating. Foods that are high in protein

How much do abundance, availability, and choice contribute to the rapid rise of obesity in the United States? What health consequences do you think will result if this trend continues?

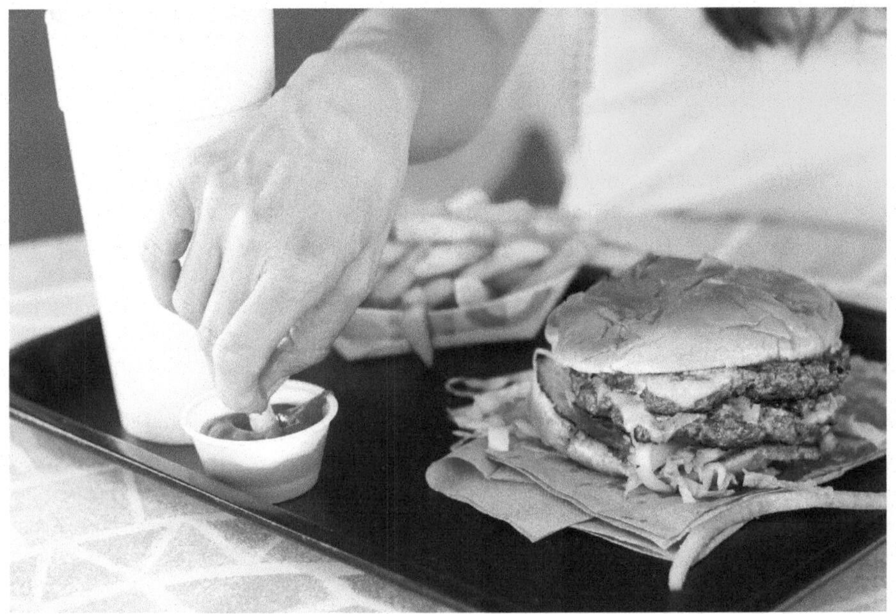

© Matthew Ennis/Shutterstock.com

are the most satiating. Satiety refers to how long you stay satisfied and full between meals. Many factors influence satiety. For example, the length of time food stays in your stomach affects how quickly you will be hungry again. This is why foods high in fat keep you full longer. Foods that are high in fiber also have a high satiety value. Typically, people who eat a lot of vegetables, fruit, and whole grains—all foods rich in fiber—do not get hungry as soon after eating as people who eat highly processed foods.

Weight Loss: What Doesn't Work

To date, treatments for obesity have not been very successful. In fact, most people who lose weight gain it back within a short time period. According to a report by the Institute of Medicine, typically two-thirds or more of weight lost by an individual will be regained within 1 year, and almost all will be regained within 5 years. Many people lose and regain weight many times in their efforts to battle obesity. As discussed earlier, dieting can lead to a lower BMR, which will make it hard to lose weight in the future. Regardless of any negative physical health consequences related to losing and regaining weight, the psychological consequences and negative impact on self-esteem are unquestionable.

Why Don't Diets Work?

The advice given in most diet books and plans contrasts sharply with recommendations discussed so far—with good reason. The recommendations in this book are based on scientific information. In order to lose weight and keep it off, there needs to be permanent changes in eating and exercise habits. In addition, most diets do not allow for real-life situations such as holidays, celebrations, and dining out. Many categorize foods as "good" or "bad" and encourage dieters to eliminate certain foods. This, of course, is not realistic for a lifetime. Table 9.7 provides information about some of the problems associated with fad diets.

Most of the diet books and plans don't recommend the same thing as MyPlate and the other recommendations we've been talking about in class. It's really confusing! How can we know what to believe?

TABLE 9.7 Problems with Common Fad Dieting Techniques

Technique	Effect
Skipping meals	Lowers BMR
Fasting	Lowers BMR
Restricting Calories with no exercise involved	Loss of lean body mass, which lowers BMR
Eliminating entire food groups	Likelihood of nutritional inadequacy; poor long-term compliance
Restricting variety of foods	Likelihood of nutritional inadequacy; poor long-term compliance
Relying on a single food	Certain nutritional inadequacy; poor long-term compliance
Liquid diet	Low satiety; nutritional inadequacy; not sustainable over the long term
Foods with so-called magical properties (e.g., "fat burners")	Not proven to be effective
Very low-Calorie diet	Lowers BMR; poor long-term compliance
Unusual food choices or eating patterns	Nutritional inadequacy; poor long-term compliance

Many diets instruct dieters to follow extremely low-Calorie meal plans, which may lower their metabolism. When this happens, the dieter ends up needing fewer Calories for BMR. Because they need fewer Calories for basic functions, it becomes more difficult to burn more Calories than they take in, which is the bottom line for losing weight. Lowering the metabolism also means that any short-term weight loss will likely be regained. In part, this is why increasing physical activity while dieting is so important, because doing so helps maintain total energy expenditure.

Loss of body water compounds the situation. Diets that result in an initial rapid weight loss do so from a loss of body water and lean muscle mass. The only way to lose fat is to expend Calories and that takes time. Although many dieters are encouraged by such a rapid weight loss on the scale, water loss is not permanent or desirable.

In addition, losing muscle is not desirable, if only because muscle is metabolically active tissue that uses Calories. Losing muscle lowers metabolism. And to make matters worse, if you lose a large amount of weight from muscle, typically you gain back fat weight before muscle. So even though your weight may go back to being the same as before you started dieting, in terms of body composition you are actually fatter and have a potentially lower metabolism because of lost muscle.

Simply put, most diets fail because they are not lifetime approaches to healthful eating.

APPLICATION TIP

Beware of these "red flags" for weight loss plans . . .

- Promise dramatic weight loss ("Lose 30 lbs in 30 days")
- Promise one easy permanent solution
- Promise permanent weight loss with no effort
- Say "Studies show that . . ." but provide no references from reputable scientific journals
- Tell you to eliminate or drastically reduce intake of any one food or food group
- Promise weight loss with no exercise
- Encourage consuming less than 1,200 Calories per day
- Encourage liquid meals
- Include pills, creams, or patches
- Say you can lose weight and eat all you want
- Suggest you take pills or drinks to "block absorption" of certain foods
- Encourage you to buy their food or supplements
- Use the word miracle
- Use testimonials to sell their plan
- Use dramatic before-and-after photos as selling techniques
- Provide no maintenance or follow-up plan
- Do not encourage permanent lifestyle changes

What Does Work

The best weight loss regimens promote making small, moderate lifestyle changes that can be maintained throughout life even after the desired weight is achieved. Studies from the National Weight Control Registry suggest that those who are successful in maintaining weight loss share some commonalities in the way they lost the weight. They ate a low-fat diet (less than 30 percent of Calories from fat), they regularly monitored their weight and food intake, they ate breakfast, and they participated in physical activity.

Eat Less, Burn More

The secret to successful weight loss is simple in principle, but more difficult to actually do. You must burn more than you eat, and you must be patient—weight loss takes a while. If the key equation of energy balance is that energy intake equals energy expenditure, then it stands to reason that the way to lose weight is to go into *negative* energy balance. This can be achieved most effectively by working both sides of the equation—increasing expenditure and reducing intake just enough, without going to the extreme and starving yourself. Creating a deficit of about 500 Calories per day is realistic and appropriate as long as the decrease in Calories does not go below the minimum of about 1,200 Calories for women and 1,500 for men. Of course, if exercising, these numbers are too low. One of the easiest, most effective ways to decrease intake is to decrease portion sizes.

A balanced diet integrating all food groups is viewed as necessary to promote long-term adherence to a weight management program. First, review current dietary intake and assess what are the areas of overconsumption. As far as the best distribution of fats, carbohydrates and proteins to achieve optimal weight loss, it appears that consistently reduced Calorie diets will result in weight loss regardless of which macronutrient is emphasized. The bottom line is that it is best to stick to a macronutrient distribution that can be adhered to. If you can't "live without" pasta or steak, and so on, don't try to; just limit the portions you consume.

Many people do not realize how many Calories they drink in a day. It is often the first place to look at cutting back. The awareness that the Calories we drink contribute significantly to weight gain has caused some consumer groups to call for government legislation such as banning vending machines

Calories in the beverages you consume can add up quickly.

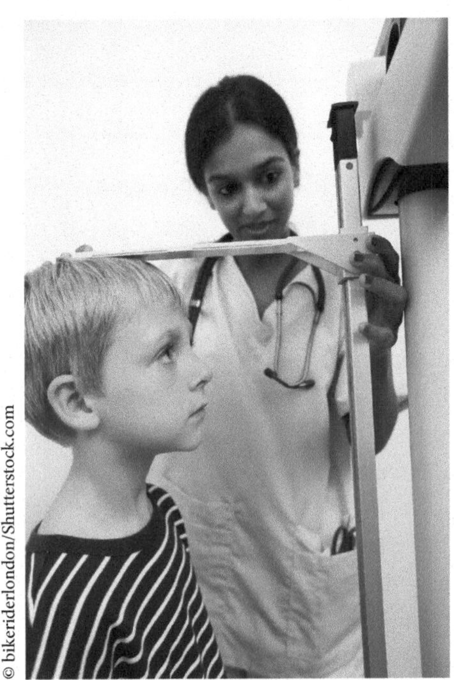

Because of the increase in the number of children who are overweight, many states are now requiring that students be screened for BMI to warn parents when their children are becoming overweight.

in public schools, BMI scanning in schools, or taxing the sale of sodas.

ChooseMyPlate.gov is a great place to start when planning your diet (see Chapter 2). Of course, when trying to lose weight, there will be less room for sweets and desserts, but these foods can be enjoyed in moderation as long as Calorie needs are not exceeded.

Physical Activity

To increase energy expenditure incorporate more activity into your daily routine and set time aside for exercise. The Center for Disease Control (CDC) recommends that, for weight maintenance, all adults engage in a minimum of 150 minutes of moderately intense physical activity each week. If you need to lose weight, up to 250 minutes per week may be needed. Parking the car farther away and walking, taking the stairs instead of the elevator, and walking instead of driving are simple ways to increase daily activity. It pays to make these simple lifestyle changes even in addition to a full-fledged exercise program.

About 30 minutes of activity, no matter how you divide it, burns the same number of Calories. A 30-minute walk is the same as three 10-minute walks in terms of energy expenditure. However, for optimum cardiovascular benefits, you must exercise vigorously enough to increase your heart rate for at least 20 minutes at a time. Although weight lifting often does not burn as many Calories as aerobic exercise (running, walking, cycling), it does have a positive long-term effect on body weight and body composition. Muscle is often lost when dieting. Therefore, including weight training of all muscle groups at least 2 days a week will reduce the loss of muscle while losing weight.

APPLICATION TIP

Beverages are often a source of "hidden" Calories. What do you drink? Add up everything you drink in a day and determine how many Calories you are drinking. Cutting back on these Calories can be a great way to create the caloric deficit necessary for weight loss. These can include empty Calories and therefore provide few nutrients.

Behavior Modification

When trying to lose weight it is just as important to examine *why* you eat as *what* you eat. Food intake is governed not only by internal cues of hunger and satiety, but also by social or emotional forces, not to mention just the pleasure of tasting something delicious. Based on appetite, people often eat food

FIGURE 9.8 Weight loss and management strategies.

Remember that weight loss must be individualized. Try these ideas and see what works for you.

Have regular meals. In addition to keeping your metabolism high, eating small regular meals helps keep your intake low. Research shows that restrained eaters—those who suppress hunger to skip meals and starve themselves—frequently end up bingeing or overeating. This response is a physiological reaction to both hunger and deprivation. Eat three to six meals a day, spaced at fairly regular intervals, about 3 to 4 hours apart.

Eat in a calm, conscious, and relaxed manner. As the Japanese dietary guidelines suggest, "Make all activities pertaining to food and eating pleasurable." Chew your food, so you get to taste it. Avoid stress-driven eating by paying more attention to what you are doing—eating—than to what is going on around you. By doing so, you will be more receptive to the internal cues that let you know when you have eaten enough. Make mealtime an oasis of peace and quiet. If time is short, calmly eat what you can.

Make your life easier with limits. At the grocery store, make your food purchases wisely. Bring home only foods that will contribute to a healthy diet. Most people tend to overeat certain foods, usually sweets and salty snacks. You can control how much you eat of these foods by limiting serving size or frequency of consumption. You can limit a food to certain situations, such as having a beer only when out with friends.

Learn to cook. Satisfying food offers a variety of tastes and textures. When its natural flavor has not been killed by overcooking or overprocessing, it does not require as much added fat or sugar to taste good. This food is hard to find in the commercial world. Your best bet is to cook it yourself. The Internet is an excellent resource for quick, easy, and healthy meals. Experiment and be ready for a few failures. The best cooks will tell you that making mistakes here and there is the best way to learn. See Chapter 2 for simple meal preparation tips.

Make cooking easy. Try to cook when you have time, rather than when you are starved and rushed. Learn a repertoire of quick and easy meals. Prepare foods ahead of time as much as possible, and keep a good supply of basic ingredients in the pantry.

Don't clean your plate. There are two ways to waste extra food: throw it out or eat it. If you feel guilty about throwing food out, save it for tomorrow's lunch or compost it. Either alternative is better than consuming unwanted and unneeded Calories. The best alternative is to reduce serving sizes on your plate to begin with, which eliminates the guilt associated with throwing food away.

When you cook, go for it. Cook as if you are cooking for several people and then portion the food out before you eat. Put all but the one portion you are eating into freezer-safe containers and refrigerate or freeze. You have just eliminated the excuse that you have no time to cook a healthy meal, as you will have several available throughout the week.

Don't wait until you are famished to eat. You will tend to overeat if you wait until you are so hungry; also, you will eat anything.

Plan. If you know that you tend to get really hungry at 3 P.M. and end up heading for the candy to satisfy your hunger, eat a small healthy snack at 2:30 to prevent that hunger. If you know you are going to come home from work or class at 6 P.M. and be so hungry you will eat anything, keep a snack with you and eat it as you head home.

Mix your meals. Carbohydrates, fats, and proteins together will help keep you fuller longer and will provide a balance of nutrients.

Don't eat out of a pot or serving dish; fix your plate. People are more likely to overeat and not even be aware that they are doing so if they don't fix a set portion size on their plate.

Don't read or watch TV while eating. You will tend to be distracted and may overeat as a result.
Eat slowly. It takes time for the brain to get the signal that you are full. If you eat too fast, by the time you feel full you will end up being stuffed!
Set realistic goals. Don't attempt to lose a lot of weight in a short period of time just to fit into an outfit or to wear a swim suit for spring break. This sets you up for unhealthy weight loss techniques and for weight gain after the event.
Pick a plan you can stick with. This could be a sensible commercial weight loss program or one you design to fit your own lifestyle.
Eat smaller portions. See Chapter 2.
Decrease Calories.
Beware of the Calories you drink.
Exercise. Include regular cardiovascular and strength-training exercise.
Don't eliminate any one food group.

the body does not need. This non-physiological eating may occur in social situations in which food is the medium of social exchange. Figure 9.8 offers behavior modification tips for weight loss.

Other Interventions for Obesity

Medications to Treat Obesity

Drug therapy may be used as a component of weight-loss treatment, along with diet, physical activity, and behavior modification. However, few medications are currently available. These drugs have potentially serious side effects. A physician should supervise anyone taking weight loss medications. None of them are a permanent solution or can be used without changing behaviors.

Two weight loss medications that may be prescribed by a physician are Orlistat (Xenical®) and Lorcaserin HCl (Belviq®). Orlistat is also sold over-the counter as Alli®. Orlistat works by inhibiting an enzyme produced by the pancreas that breaks down triglycerides and disrupts absorption of fat in the small intestines. Studies have shown that if one follows a reduced-Calorie diet and takes this drug, a weight loss of almost seven more pounds over one year can be achieved when compared to following the same reduced-Calorie diet without taking the drug. However, it is not without its side-effects. There is a warning on the package of the medication not to wear light clothing when taking this drug as anal seepage of stool is possible. This is due to the fact that stool contains a lot of undigested fat that make bowel movements loose. The fact that fat is not being digested creates another problem. The fat soluble vitamins A, D, E, and K may not be absorbed as well since they tend to dissolve in the fat that is being passed into the large intestine.

*Belviq works on the hunger receptors in the brain and helps people feel more satisfied with a smaller amount of food. Research has found that Belviq,

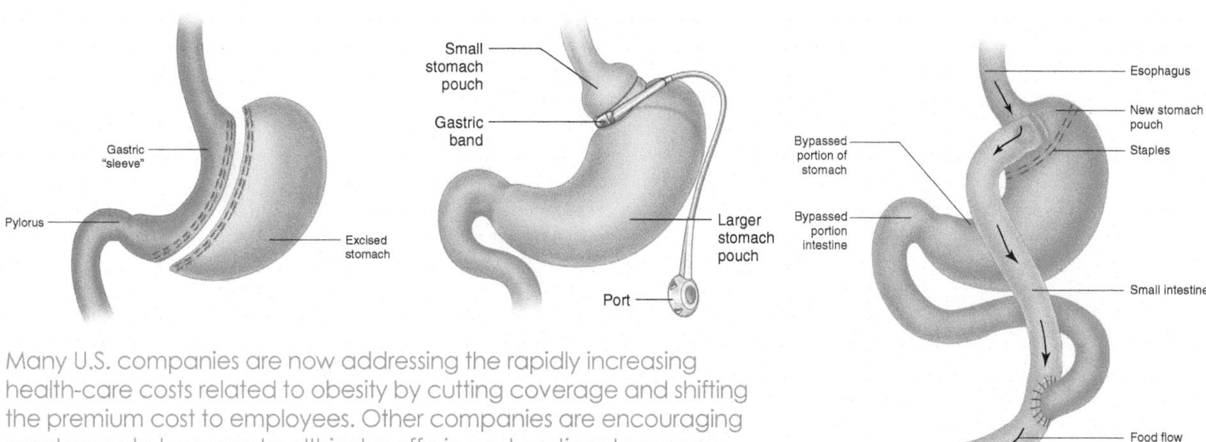

Many U.S. companies are now addressing the rapidly increasing health-care costs related to obesity by cutting coverage and shifting the premium cost to employees. Other companies are encouraging employees to become healthier by offering educational programs, by providing healthier foods in cafeterias and vending machines, and even by offering incentives for those who successfully make changes.

in combination with diet and exercise, can help people lose 5% or more of their body weight after 1 year of treatment when compared to diet and exercise alone.

For either weight loss medication, individuals must have a BMI of 27 or higher with medical issues related to body weight or a BMI above 30.*

Surgery

Surgery is sometimes prescribed for the severely obese—those with a BMI of 40 or greater or a BMI of 35 or greater with other serious health conditions. Surgery as a treatment for obesity is growing in popularity, even with those who are not extremely obese. Surgery should be considered as a last resort for those who have been unable to lose weight through long-term dietary changes and physical activity. There are several types:

- **Vertical Sleeve Gastrectomy** is performed laproscopically. Most of the stomach is removed and a vertical sleeve or tube is fashioned from the remaining stomach. Because the stomach is so much smaller, patients are forced to eat less. In addition, production of a hormone that promotes appetite is reduced so the individual feels less hungry.
- **Adjustable Gastric Band Procedure** is a type of bariatric surgery that uses an adjustable band that fits around the upper part of the stomach. The band divides the upper portion of the stomach into a pouch and separates it from the lower. This limits food intake. The band can be adjusted to allow more or less food to pass through to individualize weight loss.
- **Roux-en-Y Gastric Bypass** is the most commonly performed bariatric surgery in the United States. In this procedure, stapling creates a small stomach pouch. The remainder of the stomach is not removed, but is completely stapled shut and divided from the stomach pouch. The outlet from this newly formed pouch empties directly into the lower portion of the jejunum (part of the small intestine), thus creating some malabsorption as well as limiting intake.

vertical sleeve gastrectomy
Performed laproscopically. Most of the stomach is removed and a vertical sleeve or tube is fashioned from the remaining stomach. Because the stomach is so much smaller, patients are forced to eat less.

adjustable gastric band procedure
Type of bariatric surgery that uses an adjustable band that fits around the upper part of the stomach. The band divides the upper portion of the stomach into a pouch and separates it from the lower. This limits food intake. The band can be adjusted to allow more or less food to pass through to individualize weight loss.

Roux-en-Y gastric bypass
In this procedure, stapling creates a small stomach pouch. The remainder of the stomach is not removed, but is completely stapled shut and divided from the stomach pouch. The outlet from this newly formed pouch empties directly into the lower portion of the jejunum (part of the small intestine), thus creating some malabsorption as well as limiting intake.

© Candy Box Images/Shutterstock.com

Patients do lose weight as a result of the surgery. About one-third to one-half of those who have surgery lose about 50–60 percent of their initial weight and keep it off. Many do not keep the weight off in the long term because they are unable to eat less or the stomach expands over time. The surgery is associated with tremendous risks, including potential short- and long-term complications. Hair loss, nutrient deficiencies, vomiting, nausea and diarrhea are not uncommon. Surgery patients require lifelong medical monitoring.

BEFORE YOU GO ON...

1. Why don't diets typically work for long-term weight loss?
2. What are hunger, appetite, and satiety?
3. What does work in terms of weight loss?
4. List some characteristics of a healthy weight-loss plan.

anorexia nervosa
An eating disorder characterized by refusal to maintain a healthy body weight, an intense fear of weight gain, distorted body image, and loss of menstrual periods.

bulimia nervosa
An eating disorder characterized by recurrent episodes of abnormal food intake, loss of sense of control over that intake, persistent and prolonged weight compensation behaviors, and body image disturbance.

disordered eating
The general term covering a range of eating disorders or behaviors that are not severe enough to be medically diagnosed as an eating disorder (such as anorexia nervosa).

EATING DISORDERS

Popular misconceptions state that eating disorders always involve starving oneself or throwing up after meals. Although these practices are certainly symptomatic of a disorder, they represent a mere fraction of the various behaviors and attitudes that health professionals regard as disordered eating. In fact, disordered eating behaviors and attitudes range on a continuum from being unhappy with one's shape or weight to clinical diagnoses of **anorexia nervosa** and **bulimia nervosa** (depicted in Figure 9.9). The continuum encompasses a variety of unhealthy eating or compensatory habits and may include frequent dieting; binge eating; the use of unhealthy weight-loss methods such as vomiting, restricting food, and even exercising excessively. This continuum also includes extremes of these unhealthy patterns with some being very evident, while others hidden from those around the person affected by it. The entire continuum falls under the umbrella term **disordered eating.**

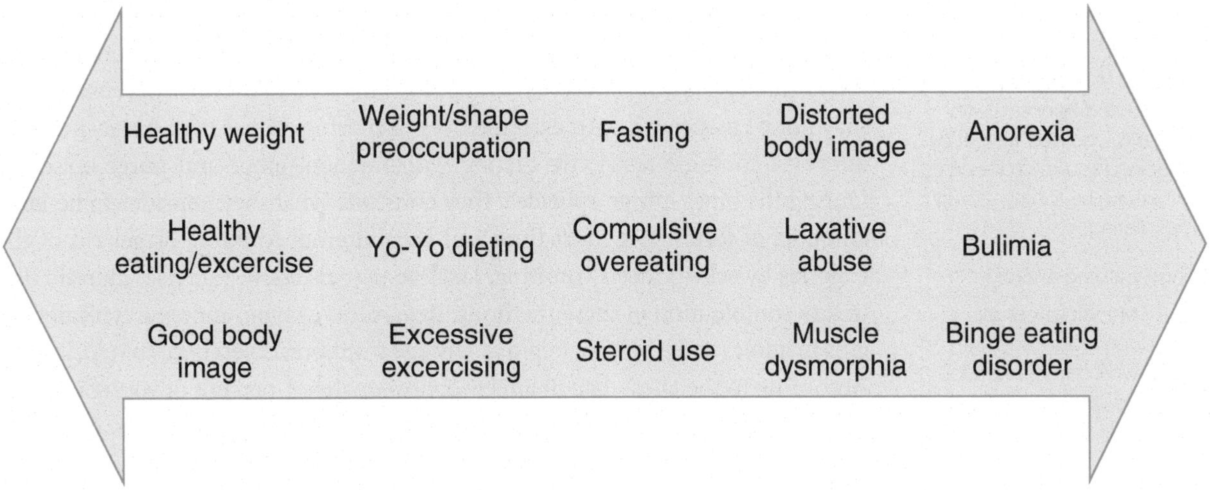

Healthy weight | Weight/shape preoccupation | Fasting | Distorted body image | Anorexia

Healthy eating/excercise | Yo-Yo dieting | Compulsive overeating | Laxative abuse | Bulimia

Good body image | Excessive excercising | Steroid use | Muscle dysmorphia | Binge eating disorder

FIGURE 9.9

Disordered eating behaviors occur on a continuum, with diagnosable eating disorders on one end and healthy eating on the other.

HOW DO WE DEFINE EATING DISORDERS?

In order to be diagnosed with an eating disorder, a patient must be assessed by a physician or psychologist to determine whether he or she meets the strict criteria set forth in the *Diagnostic and Statistical Manual, Fifth Edition (DSM-V)*. The *DSM* is a comprehensive manual that lists the symptoms and criteria of the various psychological disorders. Before making a diagnosis, physicians and psychologists use the *DSM* to determine whether a patient meets the criteria for a specific disorder.

Anorexia Nervosa

Anorexia includes an unwillingness to maintain normal body weight, intense fear of weight gain, and distorted body image. Symptoms of anorexia include fear of eating in public and reduced social interactions, particularly if planned at the last minute. Because of the low body fat, **amenorrhea** (missing three consecutive menstrual periods) may occur. Amenorrhea is a complex problem without an easy solution. The disorder is typically associated with an intense fear of weight gain that allows the sufferer to overpower his or her physical hunger and his or her body's desire to survive.

amenorrhea

Loss of menstrual flow for at least three consecutive cycles.

restricting anorexia
The DSM-V designation for individuals diagnosed with anorexia who lose weight by reducing food and overall caloric intake by fasting or very strict dieting.

binge-purging anorexia
The DSM-V diagnosis for individuals diagnosed with anorexia who combine periodic restrictive dieting with frequent binge-and-purge episodes.

Anorexia nervosa has two subtypes: restricting and binge-purging. Individuals with **restricting anorexia** lose weight by reducing food and overall caloric intake through fasting or very strict dieting. This type of anorexia nervosa may or may not be associated with extreme over exercising. Those with **binge-purging anorexia** combine restrictive dieting with frequent binge-and-purge episodes. During the binge-purge episodes, they consume what they consider to be large amounts of foods in a short time and then attempt to purge or get rid of the Calories by self-induced vomiting, laxative use, excessive exercise, diuretic use, or any combination of these methods. Regardless of type, anorexia typically begins in adolescence but can begin at any age from preadolescence to middle-age. According to the latest data, it affects approximately 1 percent of young women. While anorexia nervosa primarily affects women, men are also susceptible to developing it. Five to ten percent of those with anorexia nervosa are male.

Anorexia nervosa has a multitude of medical complications ranging from mild to severe. In fact, anorexia nervosa has the highest mortality rate of any psychological disorder due to the complications associated with self-starvation, such as heart, kidney, or multiple organ failure, or illnesses such as pneumonia, which may be due to an inability to fight infection. Other complications are as follows:

- Heart problems
- Gastrointestinal issues
- Cease in menstruation in females; decreased testicular function in males
- Anemia
- Profound tiredness
- Tendency to bruise
- Dental problems
- Decreased immune system functioning
- Dizzy spells and fainting
- Dry skin, hair and nails; yellow skin
- Water retention
- Insomnia
- Kidney and liver damage
- Growth of fine hair on the body; but hair loss on head
- Hyperactivity
- Hypoglycemia
- Pancreatitits
- Muscle cramps and weakness
- Light and sound sensitivity

Bulimia Nervosa

Bulimia is defined by recurrent binge eating episodes characterized by large amounts of food being eaten in a relatively short period of time and a feeling of loss of control over this behavior. This is followed by inappropriate weight compensatory behaviors such as purging, laxative use, dieting, or excessive exercise. Those with bulimia nervosa have a distorted body image, but appear to have a normal weight. Subtypes include **purging bulimia** (by means of laxatives, diuretics, or vomiting) and **nonpurging bulimia** (excessive exercise or dieting).

purging bulimia

The DSM-V diagnosis for individuals diagnosed with bulimia who have regularly engaged in a purging method such as self-induced vomiting or the abuse of laxatives, diuretics, or enemas.

nonpurging bulimia

The DSM-V diagnosis for individuals with bulimia who have used compensatory behaviors such as fasting or excessive exercise, but have not regularly engaged in self-induced vomiting or the misuse of laxatives, diuretics, or enemas.

Although the most recognizable symptoms of bulimia nervosa are related to food behaviors, bulimia can be thought of as a coping mechanism—a way to deal with distress and emotional pain. For some, bingeing provides a temporary escape from feelings of unhappiness and is an attempt to self-medicate. Purging provides a feeling of control and safety and often seems as a release from the stress and guilt experienced after the binge. Many bulimics report feeling a tremendous sense of relief and relaxation immediately following a purge. The purging can be thought of as symbolic—a way to expel that which the sufferer considers bad or negative.

Medical complications that may result from bulimia include, but are not limited to, the following:

- Stomach rupture
- Heart failure due to loss of vital minerals, such as potassium, caused by purging
- Irregular menstrual periods
- Diminished libido (sex drive)
- Addictions and/or compulsive behavior
- Clinical depression, anxiety, obsessive-compulsive disorder, and other psychiatric illnesses
- Increased risk for suicidal behavior
- Less deadly but serious problems caused by vomiting, including the following:
    - Loss of tooth enamel from exposure to stomach acid
    - Scarring on fingers from being pushed down the throat to induce vomiting
    - The esophagus becomes inflamed
    - Glands near the cheeks become swollen

Binge Eating Disorder

Binge eating disorder is now classified as an eating disorder in the new *DSM-V*. Binge eating disorder is characterized by recurrent episodes of binge eating that occur without regular purging or other compensatory behaviors intended to prevent weight gain. The prevalence of binge eating disorder among the general population is approximately 3 percent. However, the rate of binge eating disorder is difficult to estimate because it often goes unreported and may be higher among obese individuals, thus potentially making binge eating disorder one of the most common eating disorders.

binge eating disorder

An eating disorder characterized by recurrent episodes of binge eating that occur without regular compensatory or purging behaviors intended to prevent weight gain.

Medical complications that may result from binge eating disorder are generally associated with obesity and include, but are not limited to, the following:

- High blood pressure
- High cholesterol
- Cardiovascular disease
- Type 2 diabetes
- Gallbladder disease
- Joint problems
- Depression

RISK FACTORS

It is important to recognize the complexity of eating disorders. They are not caused by any one thing, and they are different in each individual. However, a number of common traits and behaviors have been identified in people with eating disorders. These characteristics and behaviors are called *risk factors.* **Risk factors** are characteristics or behaviors that increase the likelihood that you will develop a disease, though they do not necessarily cause the disease. The identification of risk factors, or triggers, for the development of eating disorders is important for prevention, early diagnosis, and intervention. Identifying certain groups at risk may also help increase awareness and identify target groups for intervention. The following risk factors have been identified as increasing one's risk of developing an eating disorder.

risk factors
Characteristics, situations, or triggers that identify individuals or groups as being at risk for developing eating disorders.

Studies show that dieting is a common weight management strategy for female college students. Interestingly, weight has little, if any, bearing on whether they engage in dieting. In one large study, there was no difference in the prevalence of dieting among overweight, obese, and normal weight females. Eighty percent of female students whose weight was classified as normal reported dieting.

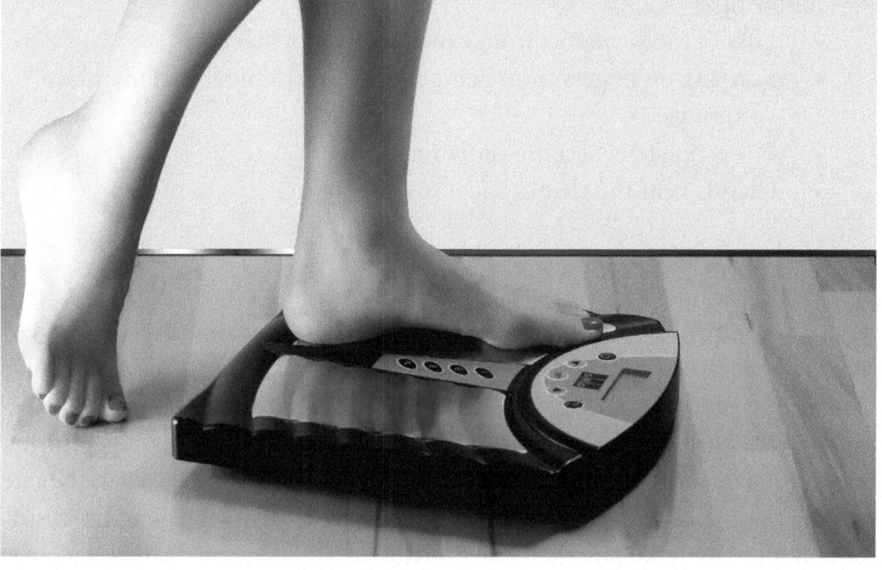

Dieting

Although dieting may seem harmless, if it goes too far, it may potentially have harmful consequences such as fatigue, anxiety, depression, low self-esteem, disturbed body image, amenorrhea, mental sluggishness, impaired performance in school and impaired growth. In addition, dieting for weight loss is strongly associated with later development of clinical eating disorders.

When it comes to dieting, perceiving oneself as overweight appears to be more important than actually being overweight. A study to define characteristics of dieters discovered that what distinguishes them from non-dieters is a personal experience of perceiving themselves to be overweight at any stage of life. The best predictor of the development of an eating disorder in adolescent girls is the presence of weight concerns, which encompasses fear of weight gain, worry over body weight and/or shape, and perceived fatness.

Cultural Pressure

Historically, women have tried to change their bodies to conform to a given era's image of beauty. The portrayal of female body ideals through the decades—in movies, magazines, and books—says it all. For example, in the past, female plumpness was associated with fertility. The current trend seems to be the fit, toned body that appears healthy, but may still be thin. There has always been a female ideal and pressure to attain it. What makes today's culture different is that the media have become much more powerful and information is easily disseminated.

The media tend to equate thinness with beauty, which is in turn equated with success. This focus on beauty and thinness in women as their most important assets for success can influence children at a very young age. How to reverse or successfully resist this cultural pressure to achieve a healthier, less pathogenic ideal is a complex problem. If it were simply this unrealistic and unattainable ideal that leads people down such a destructive path, everyone exposed to it would be victims—but not all are. Science has not yet determined exactly what separates those who fall victim to it from those who don't.

People who have a poor body image or body dissatisfaction may see themselves as fat even when they are very thin.

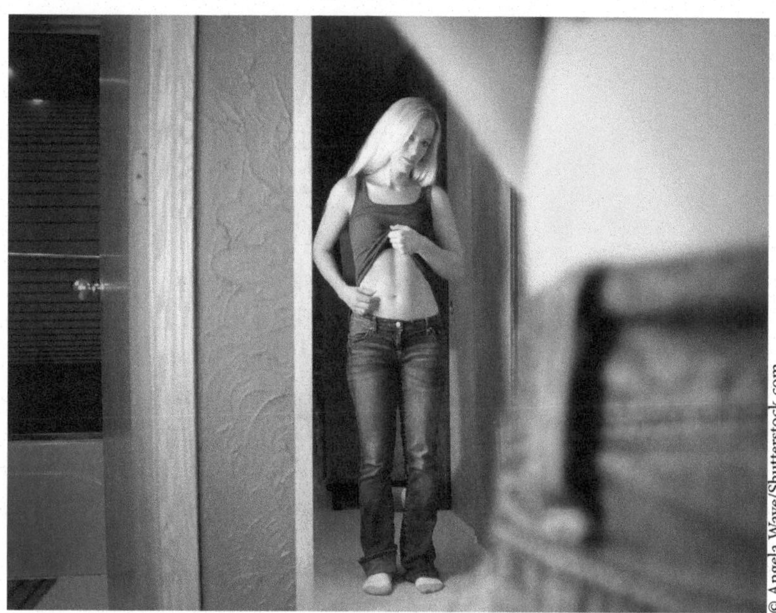

Body Dissatisfaction

Body dissatisfaction, or a poor body image, is a strong risk factor for developing disordered eating behavior. **Body image** is basically how we picture ourselves or how we "feel" about how we look. It can change from day to day and from situation to situation. It is what many people are expressing when they say they "feel fat." Our body image is influenced by many factors, including our level of self-esteem, societal pressure, media, culture, family, and peers. It tends to develop and evolve over time.

This altered impression of one's body can lead to a psychological condition known as **body dysmorphic disorder (BDD)**. People with BDD are preoccupied with the thought that some aspect of their appearance is unattractive, deformed, or "not right" in some way. In extreme cases, this can result in those affected to miss work, avoid social situations, and may even attempt suicide.

body dissatisfaction
A poor body image; being unhappy with one's body.

body image
A multifaceted psychological concept that refers to a person's perceptions, attitudes, and experiences about the appearance of his or her body.

body dysmorphic disorder (BDD)
(bah-dee dis-MOR-fic dis-OR-der) A psychological disorder in which an individual is preoccupied with the thought that some aspect of his or her appearance is unattractive, deformed, or "not right" in some way.

Self-Esteem

People with anorexia and bulimia typically have lower self-esteem than their non-eating-disordered peers. In addition, their self-esteem appears to be unduly connected to body size. Most are highly self-critical and perceive themselves as inadequate in most areas of social and personal functioning. In addition to being self-critical, people with anorexia tend to be highly reliant on external feedback either from others or from numbers on the scale. This external reliance makes them extremely vulnerable to media messages. Lack of self-esteem typically occurs despite above-average performance in academics and/or athletics. Nothing, including their weight, ever seems good enough.

Family

No evidence indicates that family problems are the primary or only cause of an eating disorder. However, families of people with anorexia appear to interact more dysfunctionally than the families of non-eating-disordered individuals. Some common characteristics in families of people with anorexia nervosa have been identified: not accepting individuality, overprotectiveness, inflexibility in rules, lack of ability to solve conflicts, inadequate boundaries, rejection of communication or expression of feelings, and over involvement of the anorexic child in parental conflicts. Women who are part of such families may turn to eating disorders or substances such as alcohol and drugs to cope with the family problems. The family connection to eating disorder risk may also be genetic. Many of the first-degree relatives of eating-disordered women are either eating-disordered or have associated disorders.

Athletes

Does being an athlete increase one's risk of developing an eating disorder? The answer is that being an athlete in general may not increase one's risk, but participation in certain sports may. Athletes of any sport, from recreational exercisers to elite athletes, can have this condition. However, endurance athletes and athletes in appearance-based sports (such as gymnastics, ballet, figure skating, and diving) are particularly prone to disordered eating and its associated health risks. Recognition of the increased risk in female athletes of developing disorders led to the coining of the term **female athlete triad** (Figure 9.10). This term has been used to describe the compilation of three interrelated serious health problems associated with prolonged caloric restriction: disordered eating, amenorrhea, and osteoporosis.

This phenomenon and the potential deficiencies and long-term health problems that may result have a serious impact on the athlete's performance and overall health. Many who have this condition engage in disordered eating behavior, which may include severe dietary restriction. This creates the potential for deficiency in any nutrient, depending on the severity of restriction and the types of foods restricted or omitted from the diet. The extreme demands of training and competing may increase the nutrient needs of many athletes and thus put them at an even greater risk of deficiency and long-term health problems than a restricting non-athlete.

female athlete triad
A serious health problem among female athletes that encompasses three interrelated health issues: disordered eating, amenorrhea, and osteoporosis.

estrogen
The predominate female sex hormone, which is also important for the development and formation of bone.

The development of one component of the female athlete triad, osteoporosis, is due to multiple factors. As previously mentioned, nutrient intake may be low in these girls due to overall energy restriction. Of particular concern is the fact that many female athletes restrict their intake of the most nutrient-dense source of calcium—dairy products. In addition, these athletes are more likely to have the other confounding risk factor of amenorrhea. Amenorrhea is not a normal consequence of training and should be recognized as a serious health problem. It is symptomatic of low estrogen levels. **Estrogen**, the predominant female sex hormone, is important in the development and formation of bone; however, in females with low body fat, blood estrogen levels may be low, increasing the risk for osteoporosis. The longer the amenorrhea lasts or the more frequently it occurs, the greater the risk for osteoporosis. In many athletes, low levels of estrogen result from a delayed onset of menses.

Although the preceding discussion focused on the onset of the triad of health conditions in athletes, the associated conditions can also occur in non-athletes with disordered eating.

FIGURE 9.10 The female athlete triad.

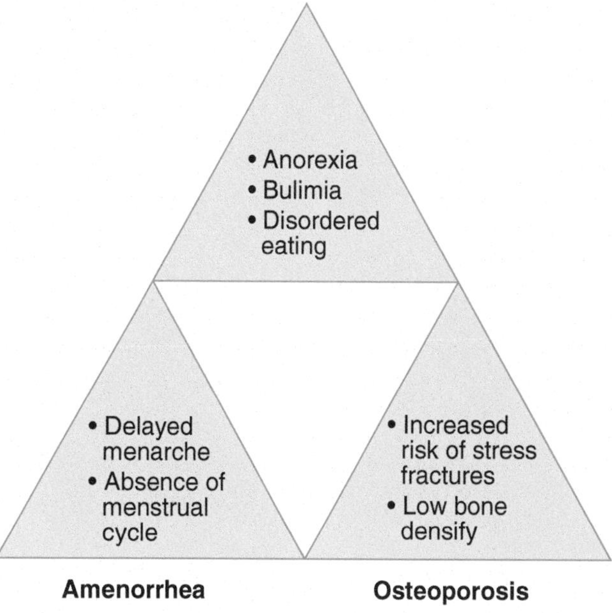

© Sergey Nivens/Shutterstock.com

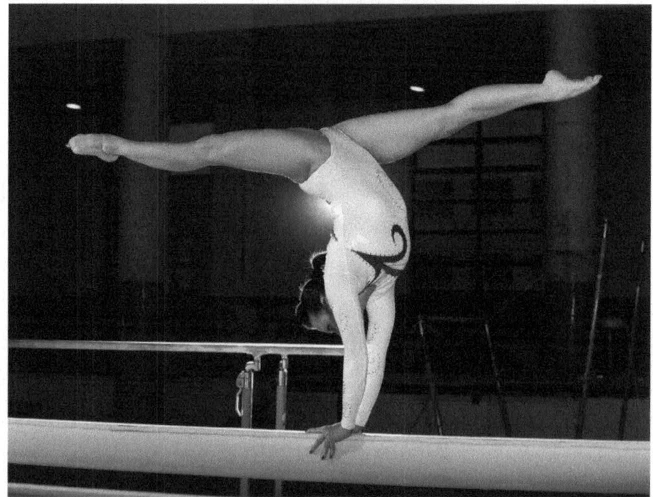

© ITALO/Shutterstock.com

Female athletes involved in all sports are at risk for developing disordered eating; however, athletes in appearance-based sports such as gymnastics may be at even greater risk.

Treatment

Considering the serious medical complications and life-threatening nature of eating disorders, rapid and successful treatment seems crucial. Unfortunately, success rates in the treatment of anorexia nervosa and bulimia are among the worst in the practice of psychological medicine.

It has been recognized for some time that children and adolescents with eating disorders require management by an interdisciplinary team consisting of physicians, nurses, dietitians, and mental health professionals.

Treatment goals for anorexia and other eating disorders are established on an individual basis. Goals are gradual and focus on stopping harmful behaviors, understanding the thoughts and feelings associated with those behaviors, and learning new ways to deal with the related emotions. For patients with anorexia nervosa, the first goal is to make sure that the patient is medically stable. This may be done in a physician's office or in the hospital; the evaluation typically includes close monitoring of electrolytes, fluid balance, and weight status. After medical stabilization, patients typically progress to either an inpatient or outpatient treatment center. Several centers across the United States have varying philosophies and approaches to treatment. Most embrace the **multidisciplinary treatment** approach and therefore use a variety of behavioral/psychological treatments, including individual counseling, group counseling, family therapy, behavior modification, and cognitive/behavioral therapy. Some also use complementary therapeutic approaches such as art, movement, music, nutrition, yoga, meditation, and exercise. In addition, medications have played a role in treatment and have benefited many patients, especially those who also have depression and anxiety. Others seek outpatient care through a mental health professional who specializes in working with people with eating disorders. These professionals will still most likely use a multidisciplinary approach whenever possible.

multidisciplinary treatment

Approach that incorporates health professionals from many different areas and therefore uses a variety of behavioral, psychological, and physical treatment philosophies; such teams can include physicians, psychiatrists, psychologists, registered dietitians, nurses, physical therapists, movement therapists, art therapists, and exercise physiologists.

Many organizations such as the National Eating Disorders Association have launched large-scale annual campaigns to raise awareness and promote the prevention of eating disorders. Each year they provide a strong message of self-acceptance and prevention.

FIGURE 9.11 Selected Web Resources Regarding Eating Disorders

The Renfrew Center
A nationally recognized treatment center with a good website that contains resources, information, and links to treatment centers, professionals, and support groups.
http://renfrewcenter.com/

Gürze Books
Offers a selection of books and resources on eating disorders and related topics.
http://www.gurzebooks.com

Alliance for Eating Disorders Awareness
Provides educational information for parents and caregivers about the warning signs, dangers, and consequences of anorexia, bulimia, and other related disorders.
http://www.allianceforeatingdisorders.com

National Association for Anorexia Nervosa and Associated Eating Disorders
The National Association for Anorexia Nervosa and Associated Disorders, Inc. is a nonprofit corporation that seeks to alleviate the problems of eating disorders, especially anorexia nervosa and bulimia nervosa.
http://www.anad.org/

BodyImageHealth.org
Includes tools for preventing body image, eating, fitness, and weight problems before they start. Based on a program called the Model for Healthy Body Image by Kathy Kater.
BodyImageHealth.org

Eating Disorders Anonymous
A fellowship of individuals who share their experiences, strengths, and hopes that they may solve their common problems and help others recover from their eating disorders. Includes articles, discussion, and tools for recovery.
http://www.eatingdisordersanonymous.org/

Largely Positive
Promotes health and self-esteem for people of all sizes.
http://www.largelypositive.com/

National Eating Disorders Association
Information on eating disorders and helpful links to treatment centers and professionals.
http://www.nationaleatingdisorders.org/

BEFORE YOU GO ON...

1. Why is treatment of eating disorders so difficult to measure?
2. Define the multidisciplinary approach to treating eating disorders.

EXERCISE

The Benefits of Exercise

RDs/RDNs and other health professionals have a number of reasons for promoting exercise. Exercise is an important factor in chronic disease prevention. It raises HDL cholesterol (the "good" cholesterol), lowers resting heart rate and blood pressure, and essentially makes the heart much more efficient so that it works less. Exercise helps prevent other chronic diseases as well, including type 2 diabetes and a number of cancers, particularly of the breast and colon. Weight-bearing exercise, such as working with weights or running, strengthens bone thus delaying the onset of *osteoporosis*, a disease in which bones become fragile and more likely to break. In addition, exercise has several psychological benefits. It can reduce stress and may help alleviate symptoms of mild depression and anxiety. For some, it may even improve their self-esteem. An improved sense of well-being generated by exercise frequently motivates individuals to improve their diet, thus increasing the likelihood that they are meeting, but not exceeding, their nutrient requirements.

It is important to find a form of exercise that you enjoy. Sometimes exercising with a friend or enjoying a peaceful environment help to make it a positive experience.

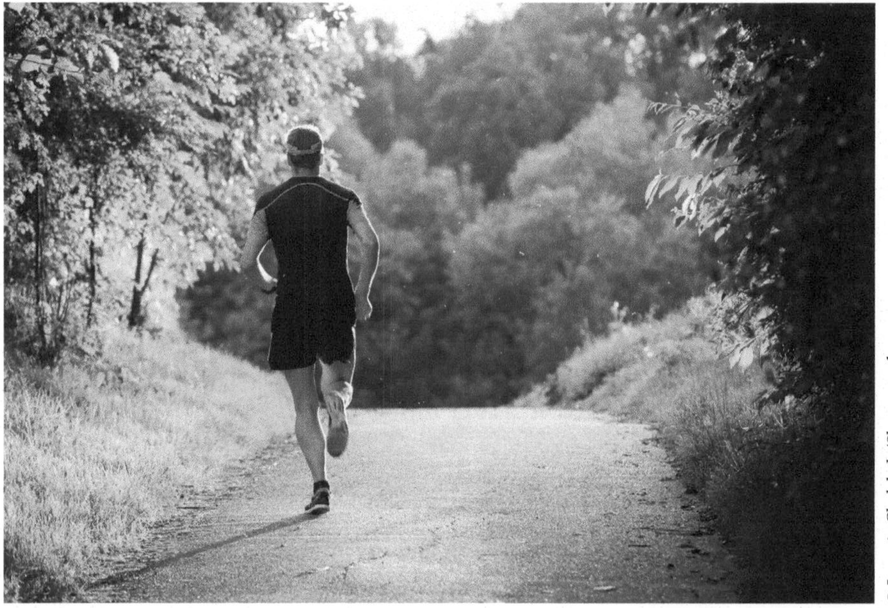

© Jaromir Chalabala/Shutterstock.com

HOW DO YOU CHOOSE THE RIGHT EXERCISE?

Self-
ASSESSMENT

An ideal exercise program includes some aerobic exercise such as walking, jogging, cycling, or swimming as well as stretching and strength training. The most important factor in choosing an exercise is finding one that suits you. Think about the changes exercise can offer and think about what appeals to you. The next thing to keep in mind is to be realistic. If you have only 1 hour to exercise, don't join a gym that is 30 minutes away. Avoid signing up for an activity you know or think you will hate because doing so will make failure more likely. We all have some time—so plan and then do something you enjoy.

There is also the nature of the activity itself to consider. Some people prefer the mental and physical state they experience by performing a technically challenging activity such as skiing or rollerblading. Some prefer games of strategy and teamwork, such as soccer, basketball, or bike racing. Other people choose activities that are more of a solo endeavor, such as running or walking. Many like a broad range of activities and would rather do something different each day.

Finding a match between exercise and your everyday life is a matter of meeting your needs in a way that creates balance. If the exercise helps establish that balance, you are likely to keep at it. It's also a matter of having an adventurous spirit, trying new experiences at every opportunity.

Self-Assessment Questions

- Have I found an exercise I really enjoy, that meets my needs on physical, social, and even emotional levels? If not, what other activities could I try to achieve these goals?
- Do I get at least 20–30 minutes of aerobic exercise at least three to five times per week?
- Do I make certain not to go into exercise sessions when hungry?
- Do I take in adequate carbohydrates, water, and electrolytes to recover from exercise?
    - Do I eat a balanced diet?

The Role of Exercise in Weight Management and Strength Training

Weight Management

Many people exercise because they want to lose weight or keep from gaining weight. Exercise may also help control weight by regulating appetite. Some evidence shows that formerly sedentary people who begin exercising often decrease their energy intake. Although exercise is essential in weight control, it should not be the only reason for participating in physical activity. Exercise provides many health benefits, as listed earlier, and it helps maintain weight by increasing the number of Calories burned each day, that is, your *metabolic rate*. This increase in daily metabolism results not just from the activity itself, which sometimes can actually burn a minimal number of Calories, but from building or maintaining muscle mass. Maintaining muscle mass requires more Calories than fat, even while you are just sitting in class, and therefore it keeps your metabolism increased. Maintaining muscle mass becomes very important as you age because it keeps your metabolism from decreasing too much, thus preventing the weight gain often thought to be a normal part of aging.

Which is better for you, high-intensity or low-intensity exercise?

Recommendations: How Much Exercise Is Enough?

fitness

The ability to perform moderate-to-vigorous levels of physical activity without undue fatigue, and the capability of maintaining this capacity throughout life.

Before we discuss recommendations for how much exercise is enough, it is important to define **fitness**. Fitness is more than being able to do push-ups or run a certain distance without being out of breath. The American College of Sports Medicine (ACSM), one of the leading professional organizations in

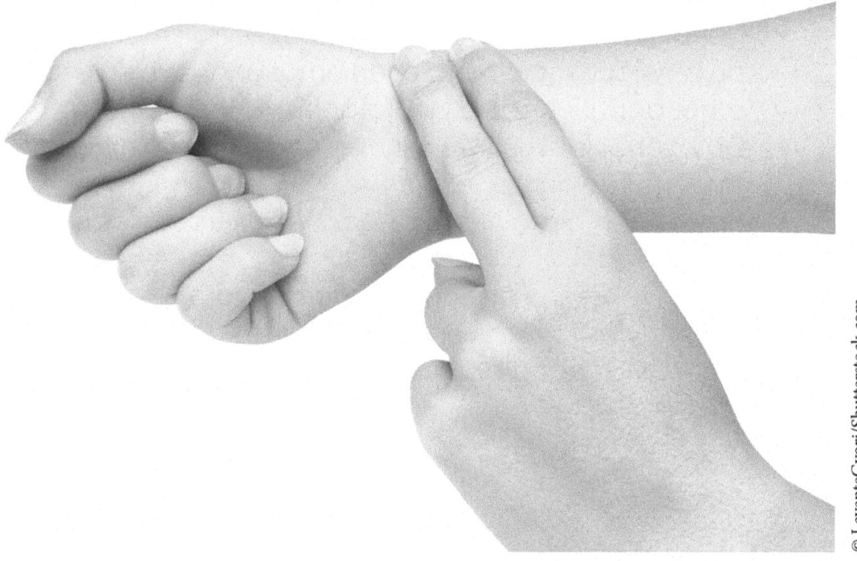

To determine whether you are exercising within the heart rate target zone, take your pulse at your neck, wrist, or chest; the Centers for Disease Control and Prevention (CDC) recommends the wrist. You can feel the radial pulse on the artery of the wrist in line with the thumb, as shown in the photo. Place the tips of your index and middle fingers over your artery and press lightly; do not use your thumb. Take a full 60-second count of your heartbeats, or count your heartbeats for 30 seconds and multiply by 2. Start the count on a beat, which is counted as zero.

the health and fitness field, defines fitness as "the ability to perform moderate-to-vigorous levels of physical activity without undue fatigue and the capability of maintaining this capacity throughout life."

Many people think of fitness as being able to exercise for a certain period of time. However, there are actually several components to fitness:

- Cardiorespiratory endurance
- Muscular strength
- Muscular endurance
- Flexibility

How long you exercise and the level of intensity achieved should depend on your goals and whether you are training for a specific sport or event or just trying to achieve or maintain the basic health benefits of exercise. The ACSM recommends that in order to achieve a cardiovascular benefit you should exercise for 150 minutes each week at a **moderate intensity**, which is about 55–70 percent of your **age-predicted maximum heart rate**. (See the application tip on how to determine your age-predicted maximum heart rate.) This means that when exercising you need to keep your heart rate up within the specified range (see the application tip to determine your personal values) for 20–60 minutes during continuous or intermittent (minimum of two to six 10-minute sessions throughout the day) aerobic activity.

As you probably know or suspect, there are many myths and recommendations about exercise. Although it's very difficult to keep up with all of them, we address three of the more common ones in the Myths and Legends feature that follows.

moderate intensity
A level of activity that increases your heart rate to 55–70 percent of your age-predicted maximum heart rate.

age-predicted maximum heart rate
The maximum heart rate you can achieve while exercising; it is calculated by subtracting your age from 220.

APPLICATION TIP

To estimate your age-predicted maximum heart rate, subtract your age from 220. In order to exercise at a moderate intensity, take 55–70 percent of that number:
Max heart rate x .55 = lower end of training range
Max heart rate x .70 = upper end of training range
This will give you the heart rate range you should maintain while exercising in order to achieve an optimal cardiovascular benefit.

Myths & LEGENDS

WHAT NOT TO BELIEVE!

"To burn more fat, exercise at a lower intensity." This is also not true. This myth is related to the previous one, anddespite solid scientific evidence to prove otherwise, it is advice still given in gyms and some fitness magazines. Fat is the predominant fuel used in low-intensity exercise, while high-intensity exercise burns carbohydrates. Because this is true, it is often suggested that in order to lose weight, you should work out at a lower intensity. An associated myth is that high-intensity exercise burns only carbohydrates and therefore does not contribute to weight loss.

Physiological facts explain why this is not so. The first involves energy balance. What matters is energy expenditure versus energy intake. If your intake is less than your expenditure, you will lose weight. It doesn't matter which form of Calories you burn. Higher intensity exercise burns more Calories per hour. Walking, you might expend 300 Calories per hour, while you might burn 600 Calories or more running for the same amount of time. An hour of high-intensity exercise contributes more to weight loss than the same time spent doing low-intensity exercise. If time is limited, increase your intensity. In addition, high-intensity exercise burns more Calories after exercise, as it keeps your metabolism elevated.

The best athletes are the ones with the lowest body fat. Not true. Every person has an ideal percentage of body fat (which allows them to perform at their best), and many athletes have compromised their performance by trying to lower their body fat to achieve unrealistic ideals. Assuming an athlete is not obese, no evidence suggests a direct link between percentage of body fat and performance.

Strength Training

If you have ever done strength training, you're probably aware that there is no shortage of sources for advice. Predictably, many supposed experts and manufacturers claim that their way of training and/or use of their equipment is the best way to gain optimal strength. The truth is that there are many different and effective ways of strength training. According to the ACSM, to achieve the maximum benefits from strength training, you should perform 8–12 repetitions each of 8–10 different exercises (conditioning all major muscle groups) on a minimum of two non-consecutive days per week.

Benefits of strength training include the following:

- Build muscle mass
- Increase metabolism (due to increased muscle mass)
- Control weight (due to increased metabolism)
- Build and maintain bone mass
- Prevent injury
- Improve daily functioning, especially in the elderly
- Enhance sport performance
- Prevent chronic diseases:
  Type 2 diabetes
  Heart disease
  Cancer
  High blood pressure

In order to maintain range of motion and to prevent injury and soreness, the ACSM recommends that you incorporate stretching into all workouts. Before stretching, warm up with 5–10 minutes of light cycling, walking, rowing, and so on. Each stretch should be held for 15–30 seconds and repeated two to four times, alternating sides. Figure 9.12 represents the basic recommendations to achieve fitness.

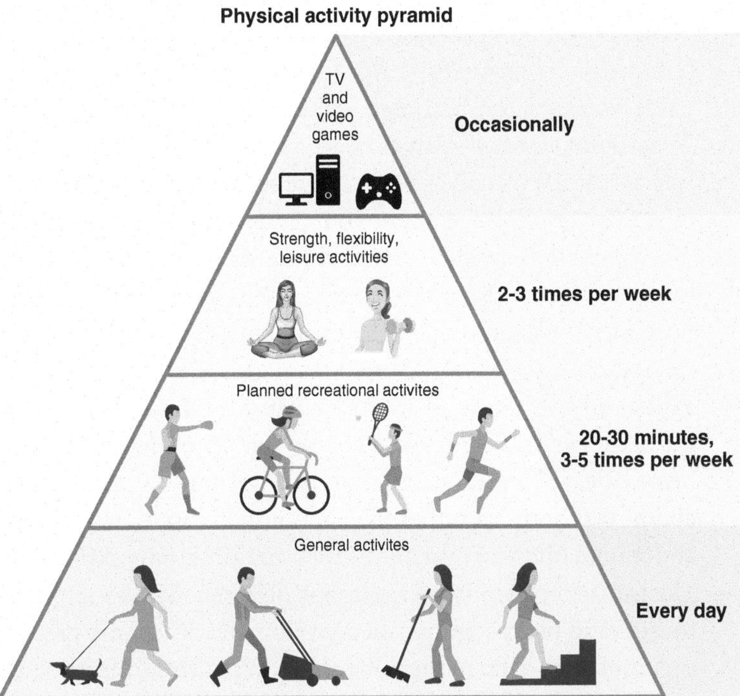

FIGURE 9.12 Physical activity pyramid.

BEFORE YOU GO ON . . .

1. List at least eight health benefits of exercise.
2. What is the ACSM and what are its recommendations for exercise?
3. Define fitness.
4. Explain why the statement "To burn more fat, exercise at lower intensity" is false.

CHAPTER SUMMARY

- Maintaining weight is an issue of energy balance. "Calories in" versus "Calories out" means that if you want to lose weight you have to burn more Calories than you eat. This can be done by increasing physical activity or decreasing food intake.
- In the food marketplace, the concept of getting more for your money seems to have eliminated the concept of eating a reasonable portion size; this trend has contributed to the obesity epidemic.
- Everybody expends energy or Calories in three ways: BMR, physical activity, and the TEF.
- Exercise can help you increase your BMR by increasing muscle mass. The more muscle you have, the more Calories you burn—even when you are just sitting still.
- We can measure and define overweight and obesity in a number of ways. The body mass index (BMI) is the simplest calculation; it is a height–weight relationship but has the drawback of not taking into account body composition.
- Overweight is characterized by a BMI of 25 or greater; obesity is characterized by a BMI of 30 or greater. Underweight is characterized as a BMI less than 18.5.
- The risk for diseases such as heart disease, cancers, high blood pressure, and diabetes usually begins to increase at a BMI of 25–29.9, and increases further at a BMI of 30.
- Being underweight increases your risk of disease also.
- The desirable ranges of body fat percentage are roughly 10–20 percent for men and 18–25 percent for women. Women should have more essential body fat than men to maintain optimal reproductive function. Men with more than 25 percent body fat and women with more than 30 percent body fat are considered obese.
- Where on your body you store fat has a significant influence on health and disease risk. Storing fat in the abdomen, called *android obesity*, carries a much higher risk for hypertension, type 2 diabetes, and heart disease than storing fat on the hips and thighs, which is called *gynoid obesity*. Those who store abdominal body fat under the abdominal muscle (visceral fat) are at greater risk than those who store abdominal body fat over the muscle and under the skin (subcutaneous fat).
- The waist-to-hip ratio measures the disease risk associated with abdominal body fat. Men with a waist-to-hip ratio of greater than 1.0 and women with a ratio greater than 0.8 are considered to have an excess accumulation of fat in their abdomen. Waist circumference alone is an accurate predictor of disease risk and is often used instead of the waist-to-hip ratio. Risk increases with a waist measurement of greater than 40" in men and 35" in women.
- Two-thirds of American adults are either overweight or obese. The increase in obesity prevalence is similar in adults and children. There are significant differences in obesity among ethnic groups.
- Weight is a complex phenomenon influenced by genetics, physiological factors, psychological factors, lifestyle behaviors, and social and economic factors.
- Many theories attempt to explain weight gain.
- Losing weight is usually not the biggest problem; keeping it off is the real challenge.
- Diets do not work because they are not lifetime approaches to healthful eating. Fad diets are unhealthy, disruptive to social and family life, and boring. Rapid weight loss usually results from a loss of body water and muscle mass, and the weight is quickly regained. Dieting can lead to a lower BMR, which makes it hard to lose weight in the future. Dieting can lead to psychological consequences such as depression, eating disorders, and negative self-esteem.

- In order to lose weight and keep it off you have to make permanent changes in your eating and exercise habits. Exercise is the key to maintaining weight loss.
- When you are trying to lose weight, it is just as important to examine *why* you eat as *what* you eat. You can do several things to modify your behaviors and environment to help manage your weight.
- The best treatment for obesity may be prevention.
- Anorexia nervosa is characterized by abnormally low body weight and intense fear of weight gain. There are two subtypes of anorexia nervosa.
  - Restricting-type anorexia describes an individual who restricts intake of food without purging.
  - Binge-eating/purging-type anorexia describes an individual who cycles between restricting and binge eating with purging.
- Bulimia nervosa is characterized by the consumption of an abnormally large amount of food in a short period of time, feelings of lack of control over this behavior and followed by compensatory behaviors to purge the Calories. There are two subtypes of bulimia.
  - In purging-type bulimia, an individual engages in self-induced vomiting and uses laxatives, enemas, or diuretics following a binge.
  - In nonpurging bulimia, a person engages in behaviors such as fasting or excessive exercise after bingeing, but does not regularly engage in self-induced vomiting or use of laxatives, enemas, or diuretics.
- The cause of an eating disorder is always complex.
- Risk factors can help identify individuals who may be prone to developing an eating disorder. Risk factors include dieting, cultural pressure, body dissatisfaction, and dysfunctional family dynamics. Each one of these risk factors is complex; together, they make the prevention and treatment of eating disorders a daunting task.
- Anorexia, bulimia, binge eating, and other disordered eating patterns are associated with many medical complications ranging from mild to severe. These disorders are among the most difficult psychological conditions to treat. Successful treatment requires the attention of an interdisciplinary team of healthcare experts. A registered dietitian is an important member of this team. He or she will teach the patient how to reconnect with food in a healthy way.
- Exercise plays a big role in chronic disease prevention.
- The American College of Sports Medicine (ACSM) recommends that you participate in physical activity at 60–90 percent of your age-predicted maximum heart rate for 20–60 minutes 3–5 days per week.
- According to the ACSM, to achieve maximum benefit from strength training, you should perform 8–12 repetitions each of 8–10 different exercises (conditioning all major muscle groups) on a minimum of two non-consecutive days per week.

KEY TERMS

ADJUSTABLE GASTRIC BAND PROCEDURE Performed laproscopically. Most of the stomach is removed and a vertical sleeve or tube is fashioned from the remaining stomach. Because the stomach is so much smaller, patients are forced to eat less.

AGE-PREDICTED MAXIMUM HEART RATE The maximum heart rate you can achieve while exercising; it is calculated by subtracting your age from 220.

AMENORRHEA Loss of menstrual flow for at least three consecutive cycles.

ANDROID A pattern of body fat distribution in which most body fat is carried in the abdomen; the "apple" shape.

ANOREXIA NERVOSA An eating disorder characterized by refusal to maintain a healthy body weight, an intense fear of weight gain, distorted body image, and loss of menstrual periods.

APPETITE The psychological mechanisms that determine how much we eat.

BASAL METABOLIC RATE (BMR) The rate at which basal metabolism occurs; it is more precisely defined as the REE measured after waking in the morning, at least 12 hours after the last meal.

BASAL METABOLISM Body processes involving involuntary activities only, such as heartbeat, breathing, and chemical reactions.

BINGE EATING DISORDER An eating disorder characterized by recurrent episodes of binge eating that occur without regular compensatory or purging behaviors intended to prevent weight gain.

BINGE-PURGING ANOREXIA The *DSM-V* diagnosis for individuals diagnosed with anorexia who combine periodic restrictive dieting with frequent binge-and-purge episodes.

BIOELECTRICAL IMPEDANCE ANALYSIS (BIA) A method of measuring body composition based on the fact that lean tissue, with high water content, conducts electricity relatively well while fat tissue, with low water content, conducts electricity poorly. When a mild electric current is passed through the body, the body's impedance, or resistance to current, indirectly indicates the amount of lean tissue and the amount of fat.

BOD POD A technique for estimating body composition by sitting within the Bod Pod and measuring displacement of air.

BODY DISSATISFACTION A poor body image; being unhappy with one's body.

BODY DYSMORPHIC DISORDER (BDD) (bah-dee dis-MOR-fic dis-OR-der) A psychological disorder in which an individual is preoccupied with the thought that some aspect of his or her appearance is unattractive, deformed, or "not right" in some way.

BODY IMAGE A multifaceted psychological concept that refers to a person's perceptions, attitudes, and experiences about the appearance of his or her body.

BODY MASS INDEX (BMI) A height–weight relationship used to assess obesity; it equals (weight in kilograms)/(height in meters squared), or (weight in pounds × 704.5)/(height in inches squared).

BULIMIA NERVOSA An eating disorder characterized by recurrent episodes of abnormal food intake, loss of sense of control over that intake, persistent and prolonged weight compensation behaviors, and body image disturbance.

DISORDERED EATING The general term covering a range of eating disorders or behaviors that are not severe enough to be medically diagnosed as an eating disorder (such as anorexia nervosa).

ESTROGEN The predominate female sex hormone, which is also important for the development and formation of bone.

FEMALE ATHLETE TRIAD A serious health problem among female athletes that encompasses three interrelated health issues: disordered eating, amenorrhea, and osteoporosis.

FITNESS The ability to perform moderate-to-vigorous levels of physical activity without undue fatigue, and the capability of maintaining this capacity throughout life.

GYNOID A pattern of body fat distribution in which most body fat is carried on the hips and thighs; the "pear" shape.

HUNGER The physiological mechanisms that determine how much and when we eat.

LEPTIN A hormone produced by fat cells that plays a role in body weight regulation.

LOW INTENSITY A level of activity in which you stay below 55 percent of your age-predicted maximum heart rate.

MULTIDISCIPLINARY TREATMENT Approach that incorporates health professionals from many different areas and therefore uses a variety of behavioral, psychological, and physical treatment philosophies; such teams can include physicians, psychiatrists, psychologists, registered dietitians, nurses, physical therapists, movement therapists, art therapists, and exercise physiologists.

MUSCLE DYSMORPHIA A form of body dysmorphic disorder characterized by a preoccupation with the idea that one is thin when he is actually very muscular.

NONPURGING BULIMIA The *DSM-V* diagnosis for individuals with bulimia who have used compensatory behaviors such as fasting or excessive exercise, but have not regularly engaged in self-induced vomiting or the misuse of laxatives, diuretics, or enemas.

OBESITY The condition of having a BMI of 30 or greater.

OSTEOPOROSIS A condition that affects older women in particular and is characterized by a decrease in bone mass and density and an enlargement of bone spaces, producing porosity and brittleness.

OVERWEIGHT The condition of having a BMI of 25 or greater.

PURGING BULIMIA The *DSM-V* diagnosis for individuals diagnosed with bulimia who have regularly engaged in a purging method such as self-induced vomiting or the abuse of laxatives, diuretics, or enemas.

RESTRICTING ANOREXIA The *DSM-V* designation for individuals diagnosed with anorexia who lose weight by reducing food and overall caloric intake by fasting or very strict dieting.

RISK FACTORS Characteristics, situations, or triggers that identify individuals or groups as being at risk for developing eating disorders.

ROUX-EN-Y GASTRIC BYPASS In this procedure, stapling creates a small stomach pouch. The remainder of the stomach is not removed, but is completely stapled shut and divided from the stomach pouch. The outlet from this newly formed pouch empties directly into the lower portion of the jejunum (part of the small intestine), thus creating some malabsorption as well as limiting intake.

SATIATION The feeling of fullness at the end of a meal that tells you to stop eating.

SATIETY How long you feel satisfied and full between meals.

SET POINT THEORY A theory that states that the body is programmed to gravitate toward a particular weight; the metabolism may adjust upward or downward to ensure that weight is neither lost nor gained.

SKINFOLD CALIPERS A technique for estimating body composition by measuring thickness of fat layer under the skin in several locations.

SUBCUTANEOUS FAT (sub-kyoo-TAY-nee-us fat) Body fat stored over the muscle and under the skin.

THERMIC EFFECT OF FOOD (TEF) The energy expended by the body in digesting, absorbing, transporting, storing, metabolizing and otherwise processing food; it amounts to about 10 percent of Calories consumed.

TOTAL ENERGY EXPENDITURE (TEE) The sum of REE, physical activity, and TEF.

UNDERWATER WEIGHING A technique for estimating body composition by comparing weight on land to underwater weight and the volume of water displaced by the body.

UNDERWEIGHT The condition of being 10 percent below what is considered a healthy weight for your height and build, associated with inadequate nutritional intake.

VERTICAL SLEEVE GASTRECTOMY Type of bariatric surgery that uses an adjustable band that fits around the upper part of the stomach. The band divides the upper portion of the stomach into a pouch and separates it from the lower. This limits food intake. The band can be adjusted to allow more or less food to pass through to individualize weight loss.

VISCERAL FAT Body fat stored under the abdominal muscle.

WAIST-TO-HIP RATIO A measure of the health risks associated with android obesity.

REFERENCES

APA DSM V: ooks.google.com/books?hl=en&lr=&id=_VzzAgAAQBAJ&oi=fnd&pg=PT2&dq=dsm+v+eating+disorder&ots=oTXnqcP42u&sig=zYfvRaE1isBJsVjKwpSnPiiCkQE#v=onepage&q=nonpurging&f=false

National Eating Disorder Association: https://www.nationaleatingdisorders.org/anorexia-nervosa

http://www.washingtonpost.com/wp-dyn/content/article/2007/03/09/AR2007030901870.html

National Eating Disorder Association. https://www.nationaleatingdisorders.org/silent-epidemic

Youth Risk Surveillance Survey – United States 2013. Accessed from http://stacks.cdc.gov/view/cdc/23483

ACSM http://www.acsm.org/search-results?q=anabolic%20steroid%20use

Nutrition from Pregnancy to Older Adults

chapter 10

© Gayvoronskaya_Yana/Shutterstock.com

You may be surprised to hear that a healthy pregnancy starts before a woman even becomes pregnant. In fact, being either overweight or underweight can severely reduce a woman's chance of conceiving a child. At no point during life will a human grow as rapidly as they do between conception through the end of infancy. Of the many things that can impact development and growth, nutrition is one that you can influence. Ensuring a healthy outcome for the developing child involves both the mother and the father and can include the entire family. Even if you are a cousin, aunt, uncle, or friend, you can help by being a positive role model to the child by living a healthy life and pursuing a balanced, adequate and varied diet.

Of the millions of pregnancies that occur each year in the United States, most result in a happy and healthy outcome for both the parents and the baby. According to the Centers for Disease Control and Prevention (CDC), the infant mortality rate in the United States was 6.17 deaths per 1,000 births in 2014. That is twice the rate in Finland, Iceland, or Norway. The rate is even higher for minority and impoverished women, reaching 13.6 per 1,000 for non-Hispanic black women. Experts believe the United States trails behind other developed countries most likely because of a lack of access to quality prenatal care for minorities and those without health insurance. Although the United States observed a 99 percent reduction in maternal deaths during the 20th century, 29 developed nations still had lower maternal mortality rates than the United States.

Although maternal death is the most extreme adverse pregnancy outcome, a much greater number of women are affected by pregnancy-related complications, such as bleeding, pregnancy-induced high blood pressure, infection, and depression after delivery. As many as half of all deaths and complications from pregnancy could be prevented if women had better access to health care before, during, and after pregnancy, received better quality of care, and made changes in their nutrition and lifestyle habits.

NUTRITION DURING PRECONCEPTION

Nutrition and overall health are important for all stages of pregnancy, including the time when a couple is trying to conceive a child. Both women's and men's fertility relies on several different factors ranging from genetics to the environment to lifestyle, including nutritional choices.

Women

Several nutritional related factors can negatively impact a woman's fertility. Undernutrition can result in the loss of the menstrual cycle due to changes in hormone levels. Similarly, extreme levels of exercise and eating disorders such as bulimia nervosa and anorexia nervosa can also disrupt the menstrual cycle. In each of these cases, it is believed to be the result of caloric deficit.

On the other end of the spectrum, obesity and overweight also negatively impact a woman's chance of conceiving. Obese women have higher hormone levels that result in irregular menstrual cycles.

Men

As with women, both obesity and undernutrition negatively impact male fertility. Undernutrition reduces sperm count and motility and can also affect sperm maturation. Obesity causes shifts in hormone levels; testosterone is lower while estrogen is increased, which reduces sperm production.

STAGES OF PREGNANCY

Once a couple has successfully conceived a child, full-term pregnancy lasts for 38–42 weeks, which is divided into three stages of approximately 13 weeks each called trimesters. These stages mark different phases of development for the fetus (see Figure 10.2) and therefore may be associated with different health implications and different physical sensations for the woman.

First Trimester (Weeks 1–13)

The first trimester is when the sperm fertilizes the egg and rapid cell division occurs, leading to the development of an embryo. After about 8 weeks of growth, organs are formed and the embryo becomes a fetus. In the initial stages of development, the embryo obtains nutrients from the lining of the uterus. Thereafter, the **placenta** forms as a connection between the mother's and fetus's blood vessels. This is how the developing fetus receives nutrients from the mother and rids itself of waste products. The placenta delivers these nutrients to the fetus through the **umbilical cord** which is connected to the fetus through the navel (or belly button). Considering this, it makes sense that any substances that appear in the mother's body will also influence the very

placenta
The organ formed in the uterus and that provides for nourishment of the fetus and elimination of waste products.

umbilical cord
A cord full of arteries and veins that connects the baby to the mother through the placenta.

About one and a half days later, the fertilized egg splits into two cells.
About three to four days later, the fertilized egg is now 64 separate cells.
Five to six days later, the embryo floats in the womb.
About two days later, the cells divide again.
Womb
Fallopian tube
Ovary
The embryo starts to embed itself in the womb wall. This is about 8 to 10 days after ovulation and pregnancy begins.
START HERE
Ovulation occurs; an egg is released from the ovary into the fallopian tube. It lives for 12 to 24 hours.
Twelve to 24 hours after ovulation, if unprotected sex has taken place, sperm surrounds the egg. One sperm breaks through to fertilize the egg.
Cervix
Vagina

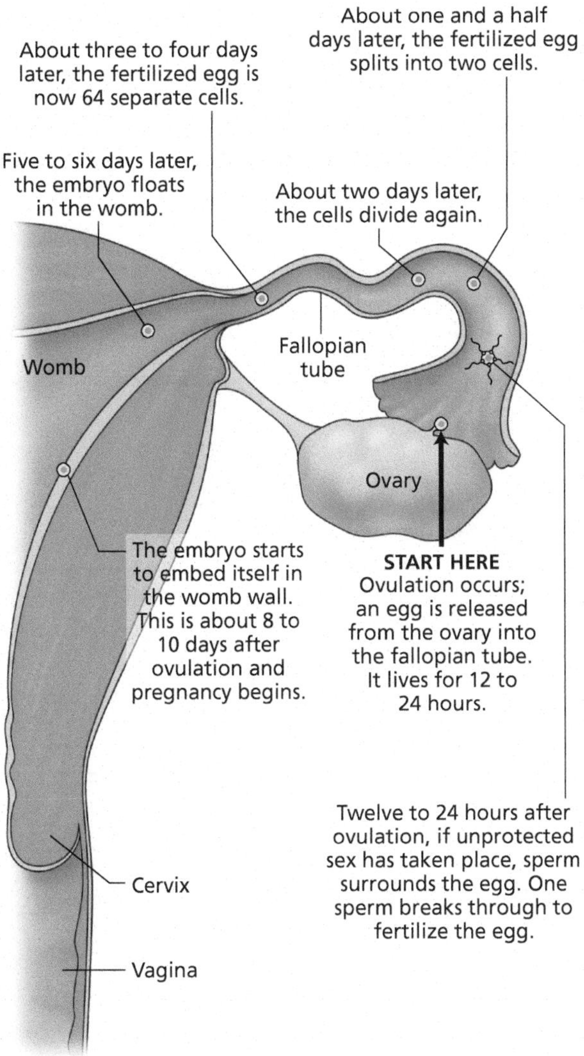

FIGURE 10.1
The first trimester is when the sperm fertilizes the egg and rapid development occurs, leading to the development of an embryo.

sensitive, rapidly developing fetus before a woman even knows she is pregnant. This is the time when the fetus is perhaps most vulnerable to inadequate nutrition and harmful substances such as drugs and alcohol in the mother. That is why it is critical to ensure adequate nutrient intake and to consider any medications or supplements if there is even a chance you could get pregnant.

Second Trimester (Weeks 14–27)

During the entire second trimester, a fetus gains roughly 2 lbs (only about 1 kg). The mother usually begins gaining about a pound (0.5 kg) per week at this point and by the end of the second trimester, she weighs roughly 16 lbs (7 kg) more than her prepregnancy weight. Much of this weight gain is due to the 30 percent increase in blood volume that occurs with pregnancy. The fetus can begin to hear sounds and to respond to light during this time.

Third Trimester (Week 28 to Birth)

The third trimester fully equips the fetus for survival outside the womb. Growth and development is dramatic for the fetus during this period. Toward the end of pregnancy, the fetus gains about half a pound (250 kg) per week, so that the baby is typically born weighing 7-9 lbs (3-4 kg). The skin, lungs, and suck-and-swallow reflex mature, and the fetus accumulates vital fat and nutrient stores.

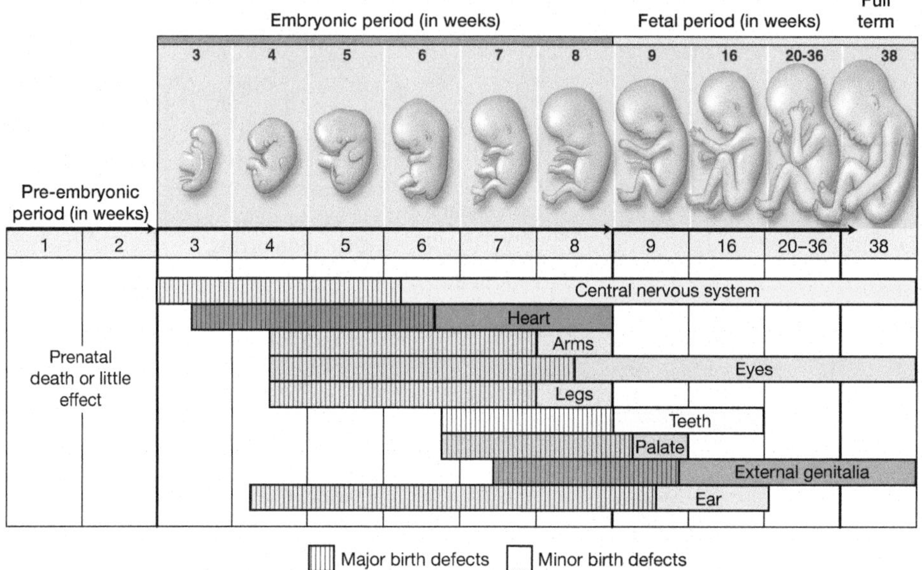

FIGURE 10.2 Timeline of fetal development.

Source: National Institutes of Health.

By the end of pregnancy, a woman will typically have gained 25–35 lbs (11–16 kg) over her prepregnancy weight (see Table 10.1). The mother carrying twins or triplets will, of course, gain considerably more weight—about 50 lbs (23 kg) for triplets.

Low-Birthweight Newborns

An undernourished mother is likely to give birth to a smaller baby. An infant that weighs less than 5.5 lb. is considered **low birthweight**. Low-birthweight babies are at risk for several problems such as infection, lung problems, learning disabilities, insufficient physical growth, and death. Of course, other factors can cause a baby to be low in birthweight besides nutrition, but the impact of nutrition cannot be ignored.

low birthweight
A birth weight of less than 5.5 lb.

BEFORE YOU GO ON...

1. Why is it important to start a healthy diet before pregnancy?
2. Describe the development of the fetus during the three stages of pregnancy.
3. Define *low birthweight* and list four potential health implications from this condition.

NUTRITIONAL NEEDS DURING PREGNANCY

Weight Gain

Pregnant women are frequently concerned about gaining too much weight. Keep in mind that the mother's diet is the main source of energy for the baby and that weight gain is necessary for the development of a healthy baby. Also, not all weight gain during pregnancy is fat (see Table 10.1). How much weight a woman gains during pregnancy is typically based on prepregnancy weight. Expected weight gains should be individualized. Current recommendations suggest that a woman who is of a healthy weight before pregnancy as defined by BMI should gain 25–35 lb. If a woman is overweight, she should gain less, but some weight gain is normal. If she is underweight, she should gain more. Despite these guidelines, only 10–40 percent of women in the United States gain the recommended amount of weight (see Table 10.2).

Table 10.1 Where Does the Weight Come From?

Baby	7½ lb.
Amniotic fluid	2 lb.
Placenta	1½ lb.
Uterus	2 lb.
Breasts	2 lb.
Body fluids	4 lb.
Blood	4 lb.
Maternal stores of fat, protein, and other nutrients	7 lb.

Source: American College of Obstetricians and Gynecologists. *Your Pregnancy and Birth*, 5th ed. Washington, DC: ACOG, 2010.

Table 10.2 Recommended Weight Gain for Pregnant Women by Prepregnancy Body Mass Index (BMI)*

Prepregnancy BMI	BMI + (kg/m^2) (WHO)	Total Weight Gain Range (lbs)	Rates of Weight Gain* 2nd and 3rd Trimester (Mean Range in lbs/wk)
Underweight	<18.5	28–40	1 (1–1.3)
Normal weight	18.5-24.9	25–35	1 (0.8–1)
Overweight	25.0-29.9	15–25	0.6 (0.5–0.7)
Obese	≥30.0	11–20	0.5 (0.4–0.6)

+ To calculate BMI go to www.nhlbisupport.com/bmi/

* Calculations assume a 0.5–2 kg (1.1–4.4 lbs) weight gain in the first trimester (based on Siega-Riz et al., 1994; Abrams et al., 1995; Carmichael et al., 1997)

Source: http://iom.edu/~/media/Files/Report%20Files/2009/Weight-Gain-During-Pregnancy-Reexamining-the-Guidelines/Report%20Brief%20-%20Weight%20Gain%20During%20Pregnancy.pdf

Meeting Increased Nutrient Needs

The need for some nutrients increases significantly, making nutrient density the main focus of nutrition goals during pregnancy (see Chapter 2 for more on nutrient density). This is also not a time to diet or to restrict any one food group, because it is important to gain weight during pregnancy. No specif-

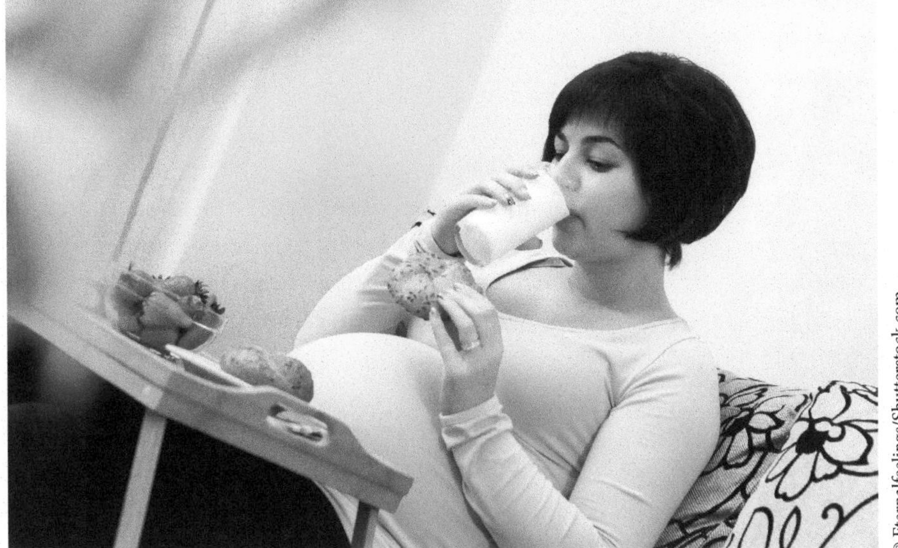

© Eternalfeelings/Shutterstock.com

In order to meet the increased nutrient needs during pregnancy, it is important to consume nutrient-dense foods rather than a lot of extra Calories.

ic diet needs to be followed. In fact, eating a nutrient-dense, balanced diet during pregnancy is a good way to establish healthy eating habits for life. It is a good idea to limit intake of "empty Calories" or "junk" foods and instead eat lots of nutrient-dense vegetables, whole grains, and lean proteins. During the first trimester, a pregnant woman does not need any additional Calories.

Calorie needs increase by 340 kcals per day during the second trimester and 450 kcals per day during the third trimester. The Academy of Nutrition and Dietetics states that according to the 2015 *Dietary Guidelines for Americans*, women should consume a variety of foods (with cultural food practices considered) to meet energy and nutrient needs and gain the recommended amount of weight. An example of a nutrient dense snack that would meet the extra kcals required during the second trimester would be a cup of 1% milk, 1 slice of whole grain bread, 1 tbsp peanut butter and 2 tsp jam.

Protein

As discussed in Chapter 5, protein is important for building body tissues—exactly what pregnancy is all about. Protein needs during pregnancy increase by 25 g per day. Many American women already consume this amount of protein. However, women who are vegetarians may need to pay close attention to their protein intake. Some vegetarian women may opt to add meat, eggs, and/or dairy to their diet during pregnancy and return to a vegetarian diet later. They can, however, attain adequate protein intake without animal products by adding protein sources such as tofu, legumes, nuts, and grains. Women who follow a strict vegan diet (no meat, eggs, or dairy) may need to consider supplemental vitamin B_{12} because animal food sources are the primary source of B_{12}.

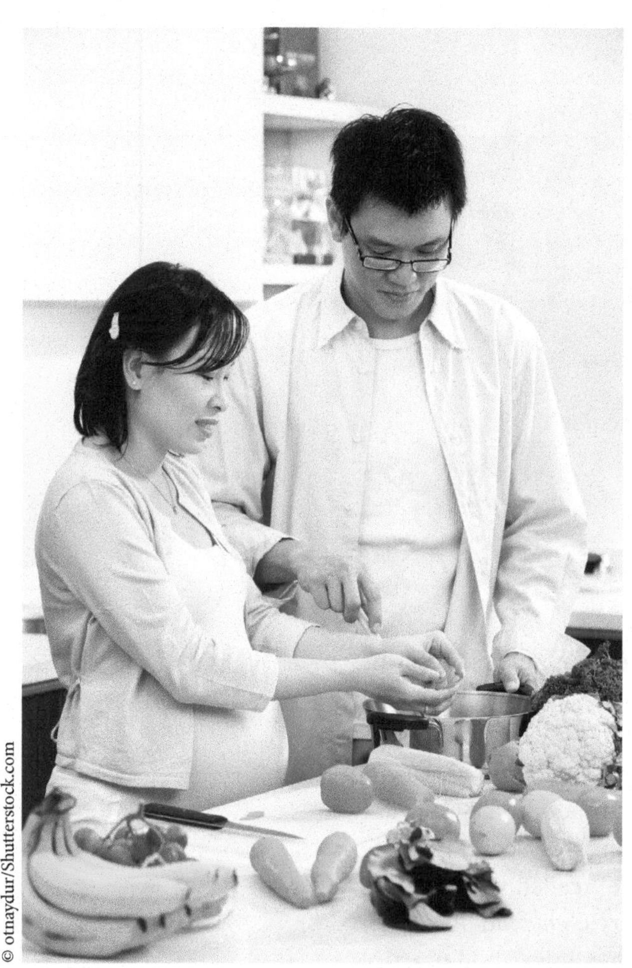
© otnaydur/Shutterstock.com

A well-planned vegetarian diet can supply the nutrient needs of pregnancy.

Carbohydrates

The main source of extra energy for a pregnant woman is carbohydrates. Fiber is also very important, as it helps prevent constipation and hemorrhoids which are often a problem during pregnancy. In addition, it is helpful to decrease intake of simple sugars or empty Calories in order to meet the increased nutrient needs (see Chapter 3 for more information on carbohydrates).

Fats

Although the recommended fat intake does not change during pregnancy, fats are an important source of energy, and during the third trimester, the fetus will store fat for energy use as a newborn. Therefore, the mother should consume adequate fat for her own health and for the health of the fetus. To ensure an adequate supply of essential fatty acids, intake should focus on the polyunsaturated and monounsaturated fats found in nuts, oils, fish and whole grains (see Chapter 4 for more on fats).

Vitamins and Minerals

Generally, a woman's need for vitamins and minerals increases by about 30 percent during pregnancy. Folate and iron requirements increase by about 50 percent and vitamin B_6 needs by almost as much.

Folate

Folate, naturally occurring in many dark green leafy vegetables, beans, citrus fruits, whole grains, poultry, pork, and shellfish, may not be adequately available in modern Western diets. In the 1970s, a deficiency in dietary folate became clearly linked to *neural tube defects* (see Chapter 8). The neural tube develops into the brain and spinal cord during the first 28 days after conception. Without adequate folate, the tube may not close completely, resulting in the condition known as *spina bifida*. Another form of neural tube defect, *anencephaly*, occurs when the spinal cord fails to close at the top. Fortification of cereals and grains with folic acid, the synthetic form of folate, became mandatory in the United States and Canada in 1998. It has been estimated that this fortification increases daily folate intake by 100 μg.

The U.S. Public Health Service and the March of Dimes recommend that all women of childbearing age consume 400 μg of folate per day. This recommendation is made for all women because adequate intake is so crucial in the

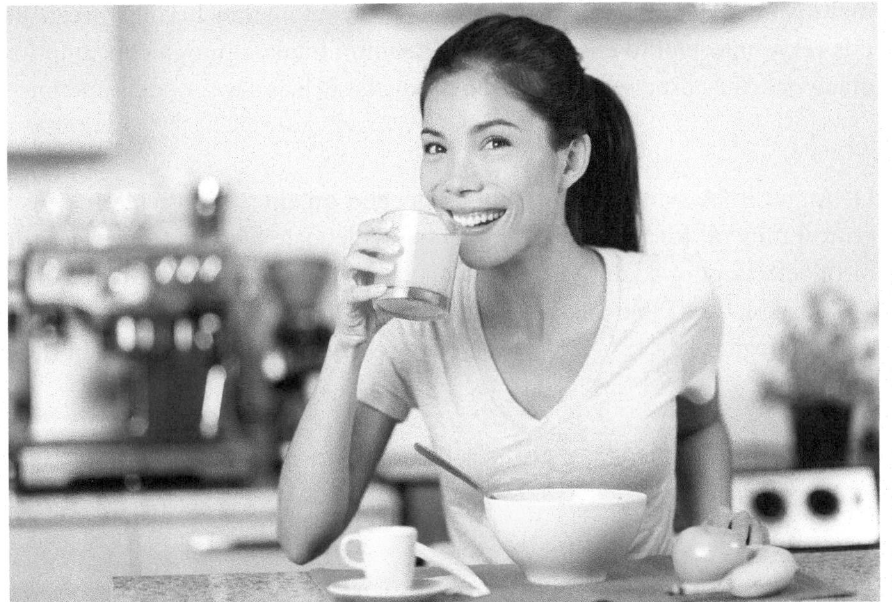

© Shutterstock.com

It is important to consume adequate folate even before you become pregnant.

first 28 days of pregnancy, which typically passes before most women know they are pregnant. Once pregnant, the recommended intake increases to 600 μg a day. Low folate levels in the mother increase the risk of a preterm delivery, a low-birthweight baby, and slow fetal growth rate.

Iron

The DRI for iron increases from 18 to 27 mg per day during pregnancy. Because a pregnant woman is no longer losing blood and iron through menstruation, more iron is available for fetal use. However, an increased iron intake helps ensure that the mother's own iron status does not suffer while she provides for her fetus. Many physicians recommend iron supplements for their pregnant patients because it is difficult for women to get adequate amounts from the diet alone. Iron is important for building red blood cells in the fetus and for the oxygen-carrying capacity of blood in both the mother and fetus. In addition, maternal iron-deficiency anemia is associated with an increased risk of giving birth prematurely, as well as low birthweight and low iron stores in the infant. It is important that the newborn have adequate iron stores because breast milk is a poor source of iron, and the infant will need those stores to last until iron-rich foods can be provided at 4–6 months of age.

Calcium

Calcium is needed during pregnancy to promote proper development of bones and teeth in the fetus and to maintain strength in the bones of the mother. Calcium needs increase by as much as 30 mg a day during the last trimester. However, since the body increases absorption of calcium during pregnancy, the RDA for calcium does not increase above prepregnancy needs. Since many women do not get enough calcium even before they become pregnant, it is very important to ensure adequate calcium intake through consumption of low-fat dairy products or fortified products such as soy products and juice.

Zinc

DNA and RNA synthesis in the body depend on zinc, and therefore, it is a critical mineral for the developing fetus. Inadequate zinc intake can lead to birth defects, poor cognitive development after birth, premature delivery, and prolonged labor. Table 10.3 lists the DRI for various vitamins and minerals during pregnancy. See Chapters 7–8 for a review of the food sources of these nutrients.

Table 10.3 Changes in Nutrient Recommendations with Pregnancy for Adult Women

Micronutrient	Prepregnancy	Pregnancy	% Increase
Folate	400 μg/day	600 μg/day	50
Vitamin B6	1.3 mg/day	1.9 mg/day	46
Vitamin B12	2.4 μg/day	2.6 μg/day	8
Vitamin C	75 mg/day	85 mg/day	13
Vitamin A	700 μg/day	770 μg/day	10
Vitamin D	5 μg/day	5 μg/day	0
Calcium	1000 mg/day	1000 mg/day	0
Iron	18 mg/day	27 mg/day	50
Zinc	8 mg/day	11 mg/day	38
Sodium	1500 mg/day	1500 mg/day	0
Iodine	150 μg/day	220 μg/day	47

Source: Adapted from Germann W., and Stanfield, C., *Principles of Human Physiology,* 2/e, Fig. 22–21, Pearson Benjamin Cummings.

Prenatal Vitamin and Mineral Supplements

Eating a nutrient-dense diet combined with the naturally increased absorption of nutrients that occurs during pregnancy is usually adequate to meet most nutrient needs. It is always best to meet increased nutrient needs by consuming nutrient-dense foods. That being said, supplements are often prescribed for pregnant women and women who wish to become pregnant as a precautionary measure.

A woman should always check with her health care provider before taking any supplements, whether over-the-counter or prescribed. Supplements should provide no more than 100 percent of the DRI for pregnant women and include 30 mg of iron and 600 μg of folic acid daily. Folic acid supplementation should begin 1 month before conception if at all possible.

Vitamin/mineral supplements are also recommended for women who may be at a nutritional risk. This includes women who are vegans, are breastfeeding, follow restrictive diets, smoke cigarettes, abuse alcohol, or are carrying twins or triplets.

To Supplement OR NOT

SHOULD PREGNANT WOMEN TAKE HERBAL AND BOTANICAL SUPPLEMENTS?

Because most medication cannot be taken during pregnancy, many women consider taking herbal and botanical products to treat various symptoms, thinking they are a natural and healthy alternative to medications. For example, many women take ginger to treat the symptoms of nausea often experienced during the first trimester. One study reported no adverse effects, but there is concern that it could increase bleeding. The American College of Obstetricians and Gynecologists recommends taking three 250 mg capsules of ginger daily with one taken before bedtime to alleviate nausea. No formal studies have reported on other supplements commonly taken for nausea, such as red raspberry and wild yam. The same caution should be applied to herbal and botanical supplements as to medications and other supplements. Before taking any herbal or botanical supplement pregnant women should always check with their health care provider first. There is very little research regarding the safe use of most herbal and botanical supplements during pregnancy. Table 10.4 provides a list of some that may *not* be safe for consumption during pregnancy.

Table 10.4 Herbal and Botanical Supplements That May Not Be Safe During Pregnancy

Herb	Why You Should Avoid It
Aloe (taken internally)	Causes severe diarrhea
Black cohosh	Can cause premature contractions
Chamomile oil	A uterine stimulant
Cinnamon	A uterine stimulant in high doses; safe as a culinary herb; avoid the essential oil completely
Fennel	Uterine stimulant in high doses, but OK as a culinary herb
Korean ginseng	High doses may lead to the development of an androgynous baby
Lavender	High doses can be a uterine stimulant
Licorice	High doses can exacerbate high blood pressure
Peppermint oil	Avoid completely; it can be a uterine stimulant
Tea, black	Limit to 2 cups a day, as excess can lead to palpitations and increased heart rate

Source: Courtesy of the U.S. Department of Agriculture.

Hydration

General fluid needs increase during pregnancy in order to support fetal circulation, amniotic fluid, and a higher blood volume. Adequate fluid intake can also help prevent constipation by keeping food wastes moving through the intestines. Individuals generally need 8 to 10 cups of fluid per day to meet their needs.

BEFORE YOU GO ON...

1. What is the best way to meet the increased nutritional needs of pregnancy?
2. How many additional Calories per day are needed and how many pounds should a woman of healthy weight gain during pregnancy?
3. Why is it so important to make sure all women of child-bearing age consume adequate folate?

FACTORS THAT CAN AFFECT NUTRITIONAL INTAKE AND PREGNANCY OUTCOME

Many factors can influence whether a pregnancy is successful with nutrition being one of the greatest. Let's begin by first discussing some of the factors that can affect nutritional intake and pregnancy outcome.

Exercise and Pregnancy

Current research, although limited, consistently shows that women who exercised before pregnancy can continue to do so once pregnant. Moderate-intensity aerobic exercise has been shown to be safe in pregnancy. Many studies indicate that trained athletes may be able to exercise at a higher level than is currently recommended by the American College of Obstetricians and Gynecologists, but pregnant women in this category should consult their health care professional before doing so.

Compared to women who are inactive, those who exercise during pregnancy are reported to have an approximately 50 percent reduction in the risk for gestational diabetes and an approximately 40 percent reduction in the risk of developing high blood pressure. In addition, moderate exercise is associated with a reduced risk for back pain, excessive weight gain during pregnancy, and blood clots. Because overheating does occur in humans, extra care should be taken to maintain adequate hydration during exercise and to avoid extreme temperatures. Experiencing a body temperature of 102 °F or higher during the first 6 weeks of pregnancy has been shown to cause an increased risk of neu-

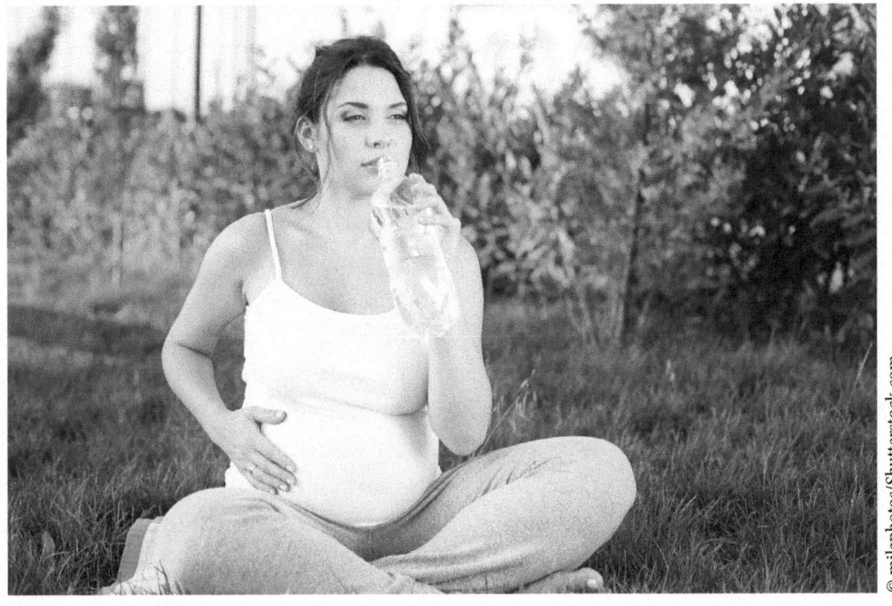

© milaphotos/Shutterstock.com

It is important for pregnant women to remain hydrated by drinking eight to ten cups of fluids a day.

Women who exercised before pregnancy can continue during pregnancy.

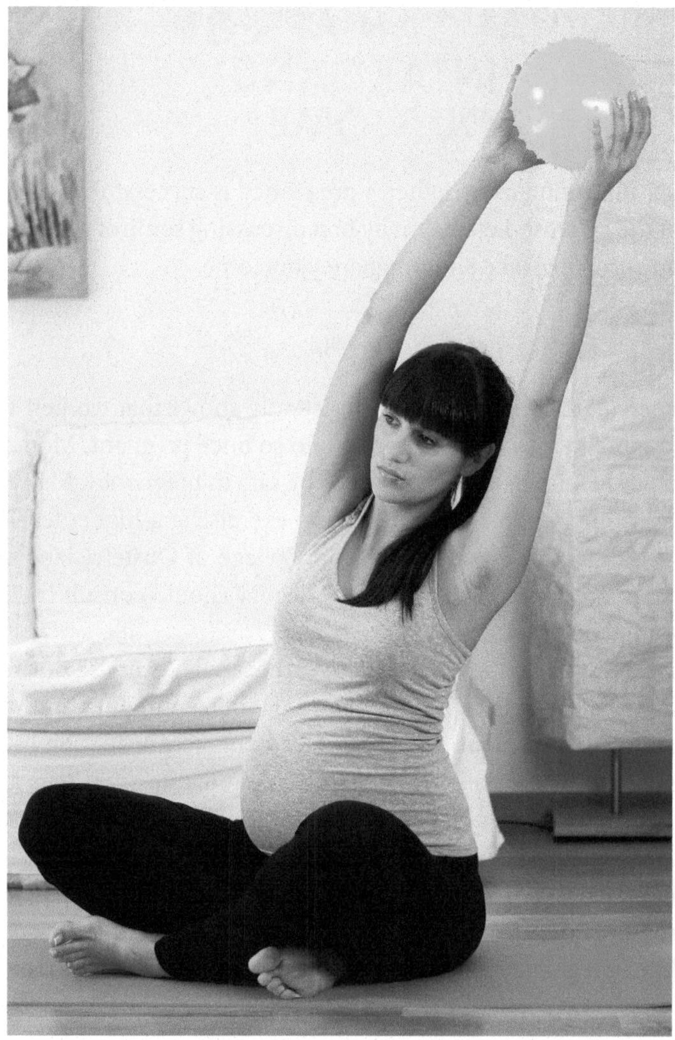

© Photographee.eu/Shutterstock.com

What about exercise and weight training during pregnancy?

ral tube defects. Studies of pregnant women engaging in moderate resistance training while avoiding maximal lifts have reported no negative outcomes. Exercise is not recommended for women with complications during pregnancy or with a history of complications.

Morning Sickness

Although not usually a big threat to pregnancy outcome, morning sickness can make it difficult to consume all of the needed nutrients at the outset of pregnancy (first trimester) when it is so crucial. For most women, morning sickness occurs between weeks 5 and 12 of pregnancy. "*Morning*" *sickness* is perhaps not the best term for this condition, as many pregnant women experience nausea at various times of day. It is most commonly experienced in the morning because long periods without food can trigger it. To help alleviate this feeling on wakening, many women keep crackers or dry cereal at their bedside so they can eat something before getting out of bed. Smaller, more frequent meals can also help, along with avoiding strong smells that appear to trigger the nausea.

I've heard that women often crave weird foods during pregnancy. Is that true?

Food Cravings

Some women do experience specific food cravings during pregnancy. Typically, these preferences are for sweet or salty foods. These cravings are harmless and can easily be fulfilled. They are, however, typically not associated with the body's need for a certain nutrient, as was once thought.

Occasionally, cravings can be harmful, particularly when they involve something other than food—clay, chalk, or even dirt. This behavior is called **pica** and generally refers to the compulsive eating of nonfood substances. Pica can lead to a variety of negative health issues for the mom and the baby.

pica
Compulsive eating of nonfood substances such as clay, chalk, or dirt.

Nutrition & DISEASE

GESTATIONAL DIABETES

Gestational diabetes refers to any form of glucose intolerance that is diagnosed during pregnancy in a woman who did not have the condition before becoming pregnant. A pregnant woman whose blood glucose is above normal is considered to have gestational diabetes. This occurs in about 9 percent of all pregnant women in the United States, and it usually goes away once the baby is born. Most women can control the condition through diet and exercise, but some need insulin. If controlled, gestational diabetes does not harm either the baby or the mother. If uncontrolled, the mother may experience high blood pressure. It can also result in a baby that is very large because of all the excess glucose it received during fetal development. Women diagnosed with gestational diabetes may be at higher risk for diabetes later in life as is the child. Testing for gestational diabetes is performed between 24 and 28 weeks' gestation.

Health Precautions During Pregnancy

To decrease the risk of complications during pregnancy and to minimize occurrence of some of the issues discussed previously, certain things should be avoided or limited.

Extremes in Weight

As previously mentioned, the weight of the mother is a critical factor in terms of the outcome of pregnancy. Being overweight or underweight carries risks for both the mother and the fetus. Thirty-eight percent of pregnancies in the United States occur in women who are overweight. An obese woman is more likely to experience gestational diabetes, hypertension, and other complications during pregnancy and labor. An infant born to an overweight mother is more likely to be large at birth and is at increased risk for birth defects. Despite these risks, pregnancy is not the time to lose weight or to diet, and women attempting to do so can put their baby at risk. It is best to lose the weight in a healthy way before becoming pregnant. This will ensure a healthier pregnancy for both the mother and the baby.

Of course, being underweight is not healthy either. An underweight woman increases her risk of having a premature birth and a low-birthweight baby, which in turn can increase the child's susceptibility to cardiovascular disease, diabetes, and stroke as an adult.

FIGURE 10.3 A pregnant woman should limit her daily caffeine intake to no more than 300 mg per day

Caffeine

Some studies have suggested that drinking more than two or three cups of coffee daily (the equivalent of approximately eight cups of tea or nine cans of caffeinated soft drinks) when pregnant increases the chances of miscarriage or having a low-birthweight baby. Other studies have disagreed. However, caffeine can travel through the placenta and affect the heart rate and breathing of the fetus. Therefore, it is wise to consume caffeine in moderation and to discuss it with your health care provider. A woman planning a pregnancy or who is pregnant should either avoid caffeine or limit her daily caffeine intake to no more than 300 mg per day.

Alcohol

Even moderate alcohol intake of one drink per day or one episode of binge drinking has been linked to impaired fetal growth and lower health outcomes of the baby at birth. The first trimester is a particularly vulnerable time; however, during any part of pregnancy, periods of heavy drinking are especially harmful. In fact, no truly safe level has ever been determined, and because damage can occur before a woman even realizes that she is pregnant, it is strongly recommended that pregnant women and women who believe that they might become pregnant avoid alcohol altogether. **Fetal alcohol syndrome (FAS)** is a disorder characterized by growth retardation, facial abnormalities, and central nervous system (CNS) dysfunction caused by alcohol intake during pregnancy. Other abnormalities include reduced birth weight, heart defects, irritability and a short attention span, mental retardation, hyperactivity, and vision and hearing deficits. These reflect some degree of permanent brain damage that could have been avoided. Alcohol can impair cell division in an embryo and fetus and can reduce the flow of oxygen and nutrients across the placenta.

fetal alcohol syndrome (FAS)

A disorder in infants caused by alcohol intake during pregnancy and characterized by growth retardation, facial abnormalities, and central nervous system (CNS) dysfunction.

Drugs

It is important to make sure that any medicine or supplement you take during pregnancy is safe for the developing fetus as many of them can cross the placental barrier. Any drug, even herbal supplements, no matter how insignificant they may seem, can have a negative impact. Even a drug that may have minimal effects on the mother can alter how her baby develops. In fact, many drugs approved by the FDA for adults have never been tested on pregnant women or developing fetuses. So be aware that adequate scientifically based information may not be available on many medications.

Smoking

One of the worst things people can do to their health is to smoke, as smoking has many negative health implications beyond the scope of this chapter. Therefore, one can assume that when a pregnant mother smokes, it will have a severe negative impact on her developing baby. In fact, smoking is associated with increased risks for many complications, including miscarriages, below-average fetal growth, and preterm delivery. Mothers who smoke have smaller placentas, thereby limiting nutrient delivery and removal of wastes produced. During development, smoking may impair blood flow to the fetus and therefore decrease nutrient and oxygen delivery. Infants born to women who smoke during pregnancy have a lower average birthweight when compared to infants born to women who do not smoke. Once they are born, children of mothers who smoke are more likely to have asthma and upper respiratory conditions than children of nonsmoking mothers.

What if people around a pregnant woman are smoking, like her partner or the people she works with?

Foodborne Illness and Toxins

Pregnant women are at an increased risk for foodborne illness. During pregnancy, a woman's immune system is weakened and the fetus' is not fully developed, which makes it harder for their bodies to fight off harmful foodborne microorganisms. Two foodborne microorganisms are of greatest concern: listeria and toxoplasmosis. Listeria is a bacteria that can be found in uncooked meats and vegetables, unpasteurized milk, and ready to eat foods such as hot dogs and deli meats. Toxoplasmosis is caused by a parasite found in undercooked meat, eating from utensils contaminated by the meat or from cat litter.

According to the March of Dimes, our everyday environment contains more than 400 million toxins. These toxins include lead, usually found in the paint of old buildings, and mercury, which is mostly found in fish. Mercury is most concentrated in large fish at the top of the food chain—those that eat other fish, such as swordfish, shark, king mackerel, and tilefish. Accordingly, pregnant women should not eat these fish. In addition, consumption of tuna, especially albacore, should be limited. Fish such as salmon and crustaceans (lobster, crab, and shrimp) have lower levels of mercury depending on the area where they were caught or farmed.

BEFORE YOU GO ON...

1. What are the exercise limitations for pregnant women?
2. What are some things that women should avoid or limit during pregnancy to prevent potential health problems for themselves and their baby?
3. What are the risks of being overweight during pregnancy?
4. Name two foodborne illnesses pregnant women are at an increased risk for and explain why.

BREASTFEEDING

Health professionals and organizations recommend breastfeeding as the preferred method of feeding for newborns and infants. The Academy of Nutrition and Dietetics states, "Exclusive breastfeeding provides optimal nutrition and health protection for the first 6 months of life, and breastfeeding with complementary foods is the ideal feeding pattern for infants." Although exclusive breastfeeding is ideal, even some breastfeeding appears to be beneficial.

Benefits of Breastfeeding

Breast milk is recommended for the infant as it has all the necessary nutrients for the baby and some added benefits as well (see Table 10.5). According to the American Academy of Pediatrics and the Academy of Nutrition and Dietetics, newborns who are breastfed are less likely to experience the following:

- Allergies and intolerances
- Ear infections (otitis media)
- Vomiting
- Diarrhea
- Pneumonia, wheezing, and other respiratory diseases
- Meningitis
- Sudden infant death syndrome (SIDS)

Other reasons why human milk is good for the infant:

- It provides optimal nutrition for the infant.
- It enhances the baby's immune system.
- It improves cognitive function (the longer the duration of breastfeeding, the greater the benefit).
- It may decrease the baby's chance of becoming obese as a child.
- Decreased risk of autoimmune disease.
- It is easier for babies to digest.
- It does not need to be prepared.
- It is good for the environment because there are no bottles, cans, or boxes to put in the garbage.
- It provides physical contact, warmth, and closeness, which help create a special bond between a mother and her baby.

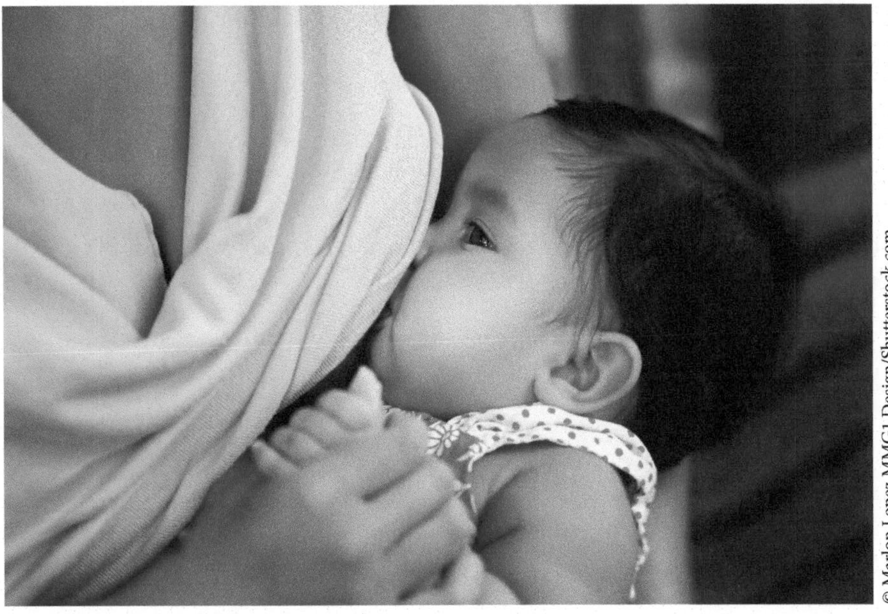

Breastfeeding offers many benefits for the mother and the baby. Initiatives to support and encourage it are available throughout the world.

Breastfeeding also provides many health benefits for the mother:

- It burns more Calories and in some cases helps the mother get back to her prepregnancy weight more quickly.
- It reduces the risk of ovarian cancer and breast cancer.
- It builds bone strength to protect against bone fractures in older age.
- It helps the uterus return to its normal size more quickly.
- Cost savings.

At first glance, it may appear that formula provides more nutrients than human milk and is therefore superior. However, many of the nutrients in breastmilk are easier for the baby to absorb and the benefits to the immune system of the infant cannot be underestimated. Furthermore, human milk is designed to meet the nutrient needs of the infant; exceeding these needs is not necessarily beneficial. In addition, unlike formula, breast milk composition changes over time, both over the course of a single feeding and as the infant ages, to provide optimal nutrition for the child.

Table 10.5 Comparison of Nutrient Content of Human Milk to Infant Formula

Nutrient (per 100 mL or 3.4 oz.)	Human Milk	Infant Formula
Kcal	70	67
Protein (g)	0.9	1.5
Total fat (g)	4.2	3.5
Iron (µg)	40	1,000–1,200
Vitamin A (µg)	47	60
Vitamin D (µg)	0.04	1.0
Folic acid (µg)	5.2	10
Alpha-lactalbumin (mg)*	161	None
Lactoferrin (mg)*	167	None
IgA (mg)*	142	None

*Provides important immune functions.

Source: Adapted from American Academy of Pediatrics, *Pediatric Nutrition Handbook,* 5th ed. Elk Grove, IL: American Academy of Pediatrics, 2004, Appendix E.

What's HOT

ARE BREASTFED INFANTS LESS LIKELY TO BECOME OVERWEIGHT?

Recent studies have suggested that infants who are breastfed have less risk of becoming obese as adults compared to their formula-fed counterparts. Although the research is not conclusive, in one study children who had been breastfed were 21–34 percent less likely to be overweight than formula-fed babies. Some, but not all, of the studies suggest that the benefits increase the longer the child is exclusively breastfed. Several factors may contribute to this difference. One possibility is that breastfed infants may learn to self-regulate their food intake better than formula-fed infants. In other words, the mother is not as aware of how much a breastfed baby is consuming and may be less likely to force or encourage consumption. Conversely, parents may be more likely to force a bottle-fed baby to finish the bottle even though the baby is full. Signs the baby is full include spitting out the nipple, turning the head away, or paying more attention to other things. More research is needed to determine whether these differences in self-regulation really exist between breast and formula-fed infants and, if they do, what influence they exert on self-regulation later in life.

Another possible explanation for this difference in adult weight is that early methods of feeding may affect hormone levels and therefore have implications for appetite, fat deposition, and weight gain later in life. Much more research is needed in this area. The causes of obesity are complex and are most likely due to the interactions of many factors. However, breastfeeding does appear to influence the risk of being overweight later in life, and therefore the role of breastfeeding is important to consider in efforts to prevent overweight and obesity.

FIGURE 10.4
Percent of women in the U.S. who are breastfeeding at various stages of infant development.

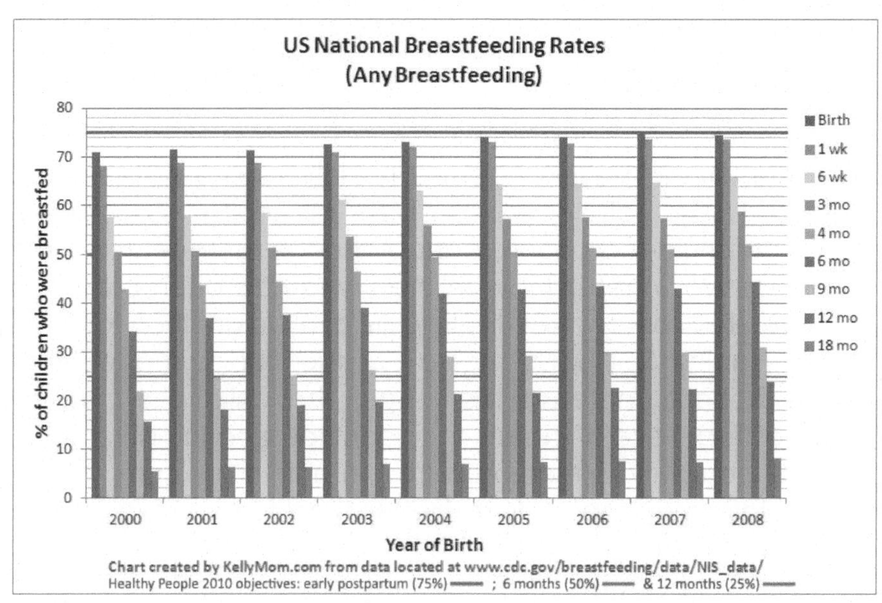

Despite the known health benefits to infants and mothers, only about 71 percent of U.S. women ever start breastfeeding (see Figure 10.4). Less than one third continue breastfeeding until the baby is 6 months old, and even fewer breastfeed throughout the first year. African Americans and socioeconomically disadvantaged groups have even lower breastfeeding rates. This is not the case worldwide. Although breastfeeding rates vary by country, around the world breastfeeding is much more common than in the United States.

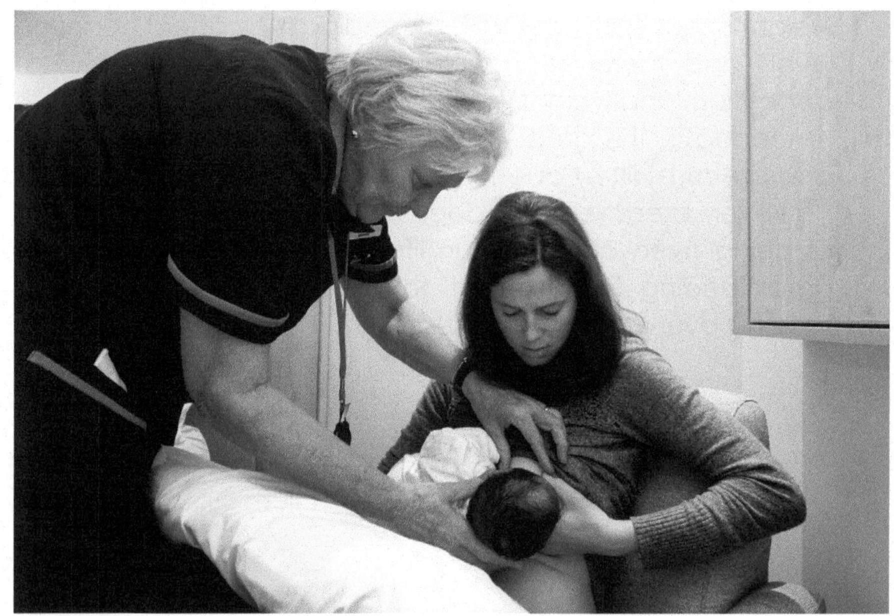

© ChameleonsEye/Shutterstock.com

Although it is a very natural phenomenon, new mothers should be taught how to breastfeed properly. Lactation failure, which can harm the infant and even prove fatal in severe cases, is frequently the result of incorrect feeding techniques.

Breastfeeding in the First Days Following Birth

A baby's stomach is tiny at the start so most of his or her early meals from the breast are no more than 2–20 mL (½ tsp. to slightly over a tablespoon). **Colostrum** is the first milk produced after birth. It is high in antibodies and is of a thinner consistency and has a slightly yellowish color. Frequent, small meals of colostrum in the first few days coat the baby's digestive tract and help prevent invasion by pathogens and foreign substances.

colostrum
The breast milk produced by mothers in the first few days following birth. It has a thinner consistency than subsequent breast milk, has a slightly yellowish color, and is rich in antibodies.

Breastfeeding After 6 Months

Babies should be exclusively breastfed for the first 6 months, with continued supplemental breastfeeding for up to a year. Breastfeeding is still a baby's main source of Calories, even after introducing solid foods at about 4-6 months. Slowly, at a rate that varies greatly from child to child depending on their development, solids become the main food source and the contribution of breast milk to the daily Calorie intake gradually diminishes.

APPLICATION TIP

The type of fat a mother consumes during breastfeeding may affect the baby's immunity. Consuming adequate amounts of omega-3 fatty acids while breastfeeding accelerates the development of the baby's immune system, which leads to benefits that can last even after breastfeeding is discontinued.

Nutritional Needs of the Breastfeeding Mother

Women who exclusively breastfeed their infants will typically need additional Calories above their prepregnancy Calorie requirement. Because some of these extra Calories can come from fat stores established during pregnancy, the National Academy of Sciences suggest an extra 330 kcals/day for the first 6 months and an extra 400 Calories per day during the second 6 months. If no weight loss is needed, an extra 500 Calories per can be consumed.

A mother's need for complex carbohydrates during breastfeeding increases from prepregnancy requirements. Good sources of dietary fiber—both soluble and insoluble—should also be emphasized in the mother's diet. Protein needs increase by 15–20 g above prepregnancy requirements. Both the types and amounts of fat in breast milk vary according to the kinds of fat that the mother consumes. It is recommended that Omega-3 fats be emphasized to support the infant's brain and eye development. Intake of vitamins A, C, E, and B_{12} and many B vitamins should increase during lactation. Iron needs actually decrease during lactation due to the fact that the mother's menstrual cycle is suppressed by the hormones that promote milk production.

Foods to Avoid

Lactating mothers should avoid both caffeine and alcohol, especially in the early stages of breastfeeding. Small amounts may be tolerated as the baby grows, but daily intake beyond a cup of coffee or one drink containing alcohol are not recommended. About 20 percent of all newborns experience **colic**. Colic is extended crying or fussiness in babies that are otherwise healthy and well nourished. It occurs in infants that are between 2 weeks and 4 months of age. In the past, it was thought to be caused by digestive system symptoms such as painful gas. It is now believed to have more to do with an immature nervous system.

colic
A condition with unknown causes that is characterized by extended crying in babies that are otherwise healthy and well nourished.

Barriers to Breastfeeding

There are several reasons why women in the United States may choose not to breastfeed. While some women may have medical reasons for not breastfeeding, such as being diagnosed with HIV or taking certain medications, the majority of women do not breastfeed due to other reasons. For instance, lack of knowledge is a large contributor. While most women in the United States have probably heard that breastfeeding is the best option for the infant, they may not be informed of what to expect during breastfeeding or how to successfully do so. Breastfeeding techniques such as how to properly position the infant

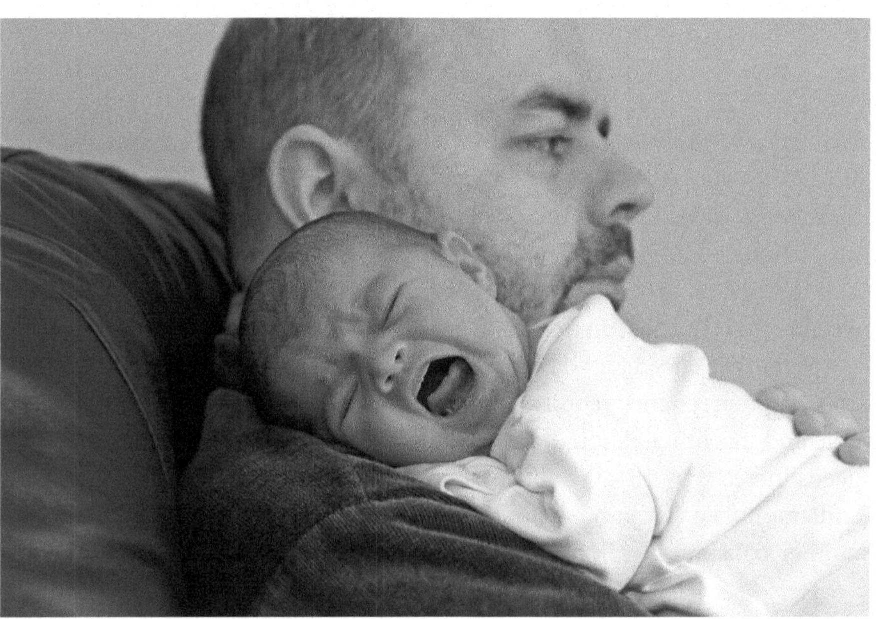

© Jo Tunney/Shutterstock.com

Babies who cry excessively may be suffering from colic.

and how to achieve a good latch on are not inherent skills and are some of the many issues a lactation consultant can help mothers overcome.

Social norms may also come into play. Within the United States alone, the percentage of women who report they breastfeed has a wide range from state to state. In 2013, Mississippi had the lowest percentage of women breastfeeding at 6 months, 19.7 percent, while Idaho had the largest at 74.5 percent. For exclusive breastfeeding for 6 months, the range is from 4.1 percent (Tennessee) to 27.4 percent (California.)

Breastfeeding is a time-consuming endeavor and this may cause a mother to decide against breastfeeding, particularly if she has a job outside the home. It is possible to pump breast milk while at work to feed to the child at a later time. In fact, the Affordable Care Act supports nursing mothers returning to the work force by requiring employers to provide reasonable break time and a suitable, private, non-bathroom location for mothers to express breast milk during their workday until the child reaches a year in age.

Additional barriers to breastfeeding may include embarrassment over breastfeeding or the feeling that the child is not satisfied. In some cases, it is physically impossible for a mother to breastfeed, whether due to lack of milk production or other factors.

Is Infant Formula Acceptable?

What is wrong with using infant formula?

The simple answer is—nothing is wrong with infant formula. When human milk is not available, commercial formulas support acceptable growth and development. In addition, many mothers choose to feed their babies a combination of bottle and breast milk. Regardless of the circumstance, infant formulas can provide a healthy alternative.

Commercial infant formulas are designed to support the baby's growth and development. Formulas come in both powder and liquid forms.

APPLICATION TIP

Infants under 1 year should never be given cow's milk, goat's milk, soy milk, or any product not specially formulated to match the nutrient needs of an infant.

More specialized infant formulas are available for premature infants and babies who have specific medical conditions.

Feeding a baby formula or breast milk through a bottle offers an opportunity for the father and other family members to participate in feeding and bonding with the baby.

© Paul Hakimata Photography/Shutterstock.com

BEFORE YOU GO ON...

1. What are the benefits of breastfeeding?
2. Describe the nutritional needs of the breastfeeding mother.

THE NUTRITIONAL NEEDS OF INFANTS BEYOND MILK

Infants need about 40–50 Calories per pound of body weight per day. They need more in the first month of life and less as they approach 12 months of age, when the rapid growth of infancy begins to slow (see Figure 10.5).

Infants younger than age 2 need more fat than children beyond that age. Breastmilk provides approximately 55% of its energy from fat so it is assumed that this is the amount appropriate for infants. The high amount of fat is necessary to support the rapid growth and development experienced during these first years.

Protein is also important for growth, but the immature kidneys of infants are unable to process too much of it. Accordingly, no more than 20 percent of their Calories should come from this source. Carbohydrates provide the remaining Calories to meet energy needs. As infants begin to consume solid foods, whole-grain sources of carbohydrates should become an important part of their daily intake.

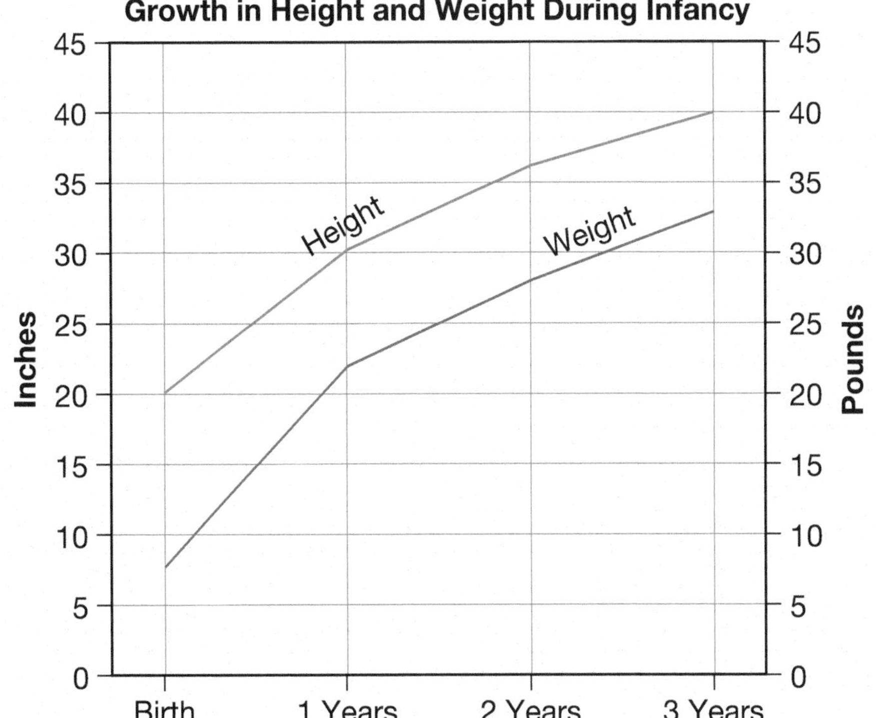

FIGURE 10.5
Note the rapid growth that occurs in the first year of life.

APPLICATION TIP

Children ages 1–2 should be given whole milk to provide the extra fat they need. Once they reach age 2, they can be switched to low fat or skim milk and should begin eating the same balanced diet the rest of the family is eating.

Hydration

Infants are at an increased risk for dehydration. Because of their size, they lose more water via evaporation and their kidneys are not completely developed. Breast milk or formula will meet the fluid needs of an infant unless the infant is vomiting, has diarrhea, or is exposed to extreme heat. It is not advisable to dilute formula with water, as too much water dilutes the sodium in their blood, causing water intoxication, which can lead to seizures, coma, and death.

Once complementary foods have been introduced at around 6 months of age, many parents also start to incorporate juice in their child's diet. The American Academy of Pediatrics recommends that juice not be given to a child until they are able to hold a cup and that it be used as part of a meal or a snack and not sipped throughout the day. Constant exposure of the teeth to the sugars in juice promotes cavity formation. If given, juice should be limited to 4-6 fl oz per day.

Vitamins and Minerals

In general, breast milk and commercial formulas contain adequate amounts of vitamins and minerals. It is recommended that exclusively breastfed infants receive a vitamin D supplement to prevent the development of rickets. At 4-6 months of age the infant will need an outside source of iron. Iron can be provided in a fortified cereal. Babies who are breastfed by mothers who follow a vegan diet may need B_{12} supplements. Formula-fed infants who are healthy do not require supplementation.

Giving the baby extra vitamins and minerals is probably unnecessary under normal conditions and can be dangerous if excessive amounts are given.

Starting Solid Foods

When it comes to starting solid foods, the single most important word is *wait*. Both the American Academy of Pediatrics and the World Health Organization recommend waiting until 6 months of age before introducing anything but breast milk (or, if necessary, commercial formula) to a baby's diet. This is because the iron and zinc content of human milk decreases rapidly after about 3 months, and the baby's stores from birth will typically be used within the first 6 months.

complementary foods
Solids and liquid foods that join breastfeeding in the normal progression toward adult eating patterns.

Complementary foods are the solids and liquids that supplement breastfeeding in the normal progression toward adult eating patterns. There is no evidence that a healthy, thriving baby benefits from complementary foods before 4-6 months of age. In fact, feeding solids to infants too early can lead to serious health problems. Iron-fortified cereal, our culture's traditional first food, is a starch that requires an enzyme for digestion that many babies do not produce in sufficient amounts until about 4-6 months of age. Chunky foods offered to a baby who can't yet use his or her tongue and jaws well can result in choking. In addition, research indicates that introducing solids early can increase the risk of obesity in later life.

Breastfed babies must be given complementary foods that are high in iron and zinc at 6 months of age. This is the time when they will have depleted most of the mineral stores they were born with and, as noted previously, human breast milk does not provide the baby with adequate amounts of zinc and iron, especially by the time he or she reaches 6 months of age. Therefore, improving the quality of complementary foods may be one of the most cost-effective strategies for improving health and reducing illness and death in young children. Iron-fortified cereals are often the first foods introduced. Nutrients that have been identified as problematic for breastfed infants after 6 months of age are iron, zinc, vitamin A, and vitamin B_6. These nutrients are not as great a concern for formula-fed babies because formulas will be fortified with them.

© Igor Stepovik/Shutterstock.com

Solids may be introduced to babies at 4-6 months of age in the form of iron-fortified cereals in addition to breast milk.

Physical signs that the baby is ready for solid foods are perhaps the best indicator that it is time to start introducing them. By 4-6 months of age, most babies have lost the tongue-thrusting reflex, or **extrusion reflex**. They are capable of sitting on their own or with minor support and have probably become intrigued with the sight of a spoon, fork, or cup going to their parents' mouths. Most important, a 6-month-old is generally capable of bringing an interesting item to his or her mouth.

extrusion reflex
The tongue-thrusting reflex that exists at birth but is usually gone by 6 months of age.

Even after solids are started, human milk or infant formula remains the cornerstone of a baby's diet until about 12 months of age. No single food or combination of foods equals breast milk in its comprehensive nutritional value.

APPLICATION TIP

Do not give a baby cereal or any food in the bottle. It can cause allergies, choking, and diarrhea in infants under 4 months of age. If given to older infants, it may impede the development of the motor reflexes needed for chewing and swallowing. Furthermore, babies who are given cereal in a bottle are more likely to be obese as children, teens, and adults. You can mix the cereal with breast milk or formula in a bowl and feed it to the baby on a spoon.

It is important to allow the baby to progress to solid foods at his own pace. Part of the exploration of new foods includes touching, smelling, and tasting new foods.

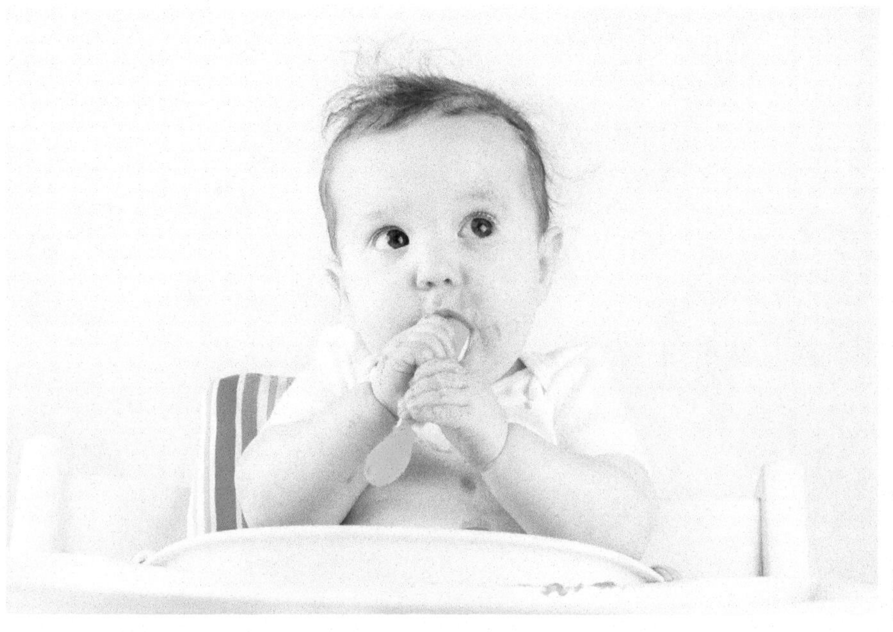

Sequencing Solid Foods

The traditional recommendations regarding the order for introducing foods are based on preventing allergies. Introducing one food at a time and then waiting 2 to 3 days to introduce another makes it easier to identify whether the infant has a food allergy as well as which food is causing the allergic reaction. The typical order of introduction of foods in the United States is iron-fortified cereal, then vegetables and fruits, and finally meats.

Iron-fortified rice cereals are recommended as a first food because rice is less likely to cause allergic reactions. Other easy early foods are listed here, along with some to be avoided. A tablespoon once or twice a day makes a fine start for a first food, gradually increasing the volume according to the baby's pace and growth.

Some Starting Foods

- Iron-fortified rice cereal and other single-grain cereals
- Ripe banana
- Avocado
- Cooked yam or sweet potato
- Grated or cooked apple or pear
- Chopped cooked prune
- Chopped or ground beef (in the form of baby food or puréed)
- Small slivers of chicken (moistened if needed)
- Whole-grain breads (toasted or stale)

By Nine Months of Age, Most Babies Can Enjoy:

- Peas, perhaps cooked and squeezed from their skins to improve digestibility
- Easy-to-handle pasta
- Soft-cooked vegetable pieces
- Soft-cooked fruits except citrus and pineapple
- Cubed soft foods
- Fish (Note: allergic families may want to avoid during the first year)
- Tofu (Note: allergic families may want to avoid during the first year)
- Products from cow's milk such as cheese and yogurt in small amounts (Note: allergic families may want to avoid during the first year or more)
- Bread and toast

Foods That May Cause Choking in the Early Years:

- Nuts
- Whole grapes
- Popcorn
- Hot dog pieces
- Any large chunks of raw foods that must be thoroughly chewed (carrots, celery, and apple)
- Small candies (be careful of dishes that contain small candies such as M&Ms and mints—these are tempting to infants and are choking hazards)
- Cherries and some dried fruits

APPLICATION TIP

What is the best way to make sure that your toddler doesn't become overweight? Be a good role model. Studies show that this is more what you do than what you say. Model healthy eating and exercise habits without ever saying a word!

Bottle-Mouth Syndrome

Infants or toddlers who go to bed with a bottle or sippy cup of milk or juice are at risk for developing **bottle-mouth syndrome**. The fluid tends to pool around the front teeth and provides a breeding ground for decay-causing bacteria. However, some children have teeth that are more susceptible to damage than others, and some strains of mouth bacteria are more likely to cause decay. All small children should have their teeth wiped carefully at least once a day and practicing with a damp washcloth should be part of the nighttime routine even before the first tooth emerges.

bottle-mouth syndrome
Tooth decay in infants caused by bacteria-producing fluids (milk, fruit juice, etc.) that pool around the front teeth.

Putting babies to bed with a bottle can lead to bottlemouth syndrome or decaying teeth.

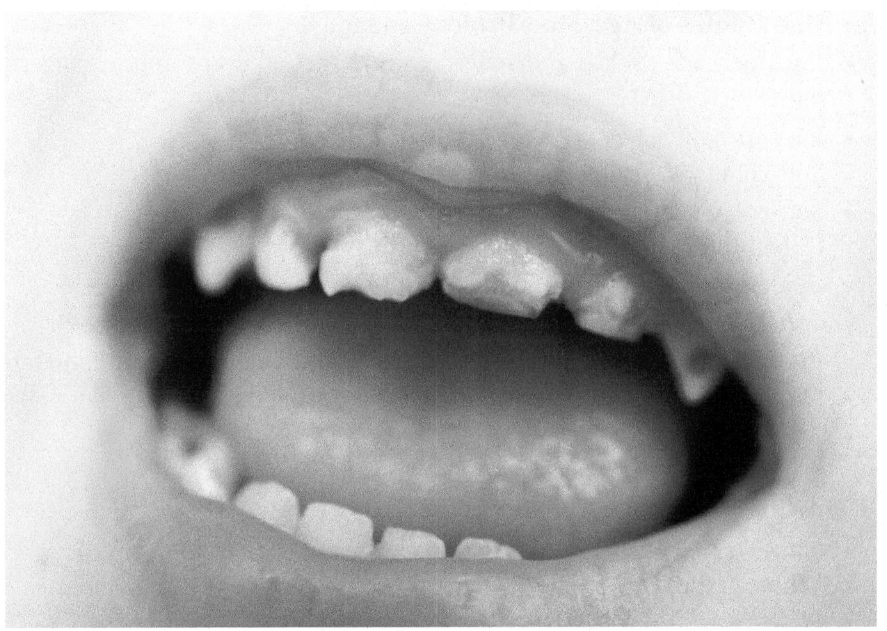

©NRT/Shutterstock.com

BEFORE YOU GO ON...

1. Identify the first four foods that are recommended for infants.
2. When should solid foods be introduced to an infant and why?
3. Why should you introduce solid foods gradually?

NUTRITION DURING CHILDHOOD

Parents and relatives often become frustrated with the eating habits of children and teenagers. A young child going through a growth spurt may have a huge appetite and then suddenly reduce the volume of his or her food consumption as growth slows. Young children and teenagers also continue to have high nutrient requirements because of growth.

The time between being a toddler and becoming a child is a period of tremendous change, both physically and emotionally. *Toddlers* are ages 12–24 months, and most people define *childhood* as the time that spans from the second birthday until prepuberty. The rate of growth from infancy through the end of childhood drops and levels off (Figure 10.6). The rate increases during the growth spurt as puberty begins. The childhood years with their steady and gradual growth are a great time to store nutrients for the adolescent years, when growth is so rapid that nutrient needs cannot always be met with diet.

Rapid Development Change in Childhood

Early and middle childhood is characterized by slow and steady growth. The child's growth rate after age one is slow relative to what it was during the first year of life. Appetite and food preferences vary as children go though a period of *food jags,* in which they may eat only one type of food for a while and then switch to another food preference. As noted earlier, children normally consume more food when they are in a growth phase and then decrease their food intake when the growth phase slows or ceases.

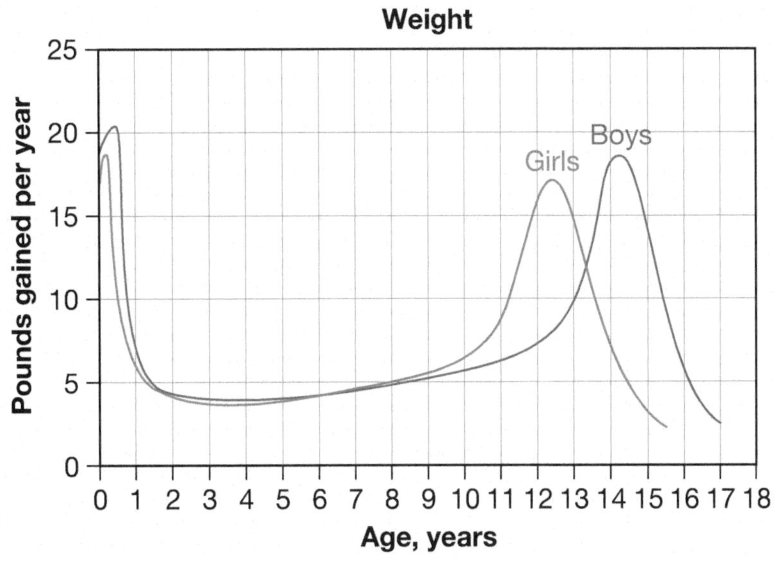

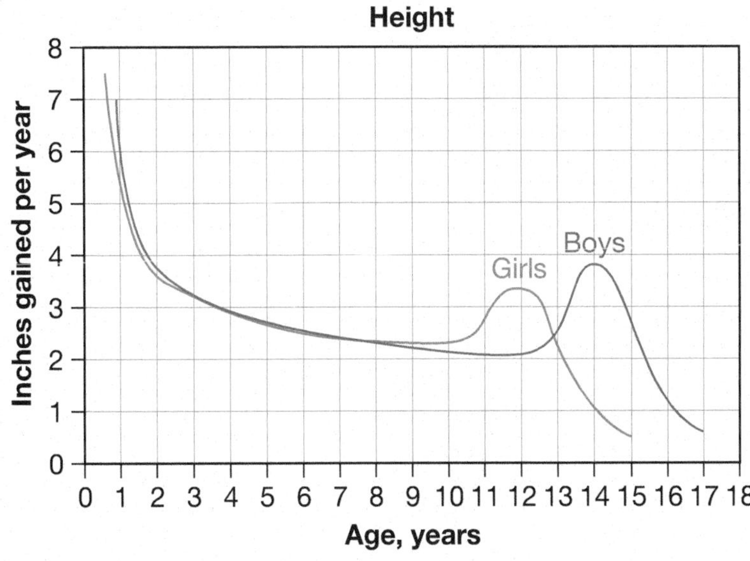

FIGURE 10.6
A comparison of the rate of growth in both height and weight. The rate for both slows down at about 2 years of age. Note that the growth spurt begins earlier for girls than for boys.

The Nutritional Needs and Eating Habits of Children

A child's need for Calories depends on body size, activity, and growth rate. A lack of Calories will slow the growth of a child. The number of Calories needed per kilogram of weight is greater in childhood, but it decreases as we go through adolescence, leveling off as we become adults. As growth occurs, the total amount of Calories required increases because the energy must support a greater body weight.

You may find it interesting that young children have the innate ability to monitor their own caloric intake. Studies in pre-school aged children have shown that children given a sugared beverage prior to a meal will consume fewer Calories during the meal compared to children who received a low-Calorie beverage. It is only as we grow older that we lose this ability and choose to ignore our body's satiety signals.

What Children Like to Eat and Why

As children become older, their diet should become more varied to help ensure adequate nutritional intake. Ellyn Satter is a registered dietitian and authority on childhood eating and feeding. She states that "the parent is responsible for the what, when, and where of feeding. The child is responsible for how much." See www.ellynsatter.com for more information.

It is advisable to allow children to play a more active role in meal planning and perhaps even in meal preparation. Allow older children to make more choices while maintaining guidance. For example, ask the child what kind of cereal he or she would like for breakfast. You have made the guiding choice that he or she will eat cereal, and you have purchased the different types to guide the choice, but the child will ultimately feel that he or she has decided what to eat for breakfast.

Children are more receptive to trying new foods if they are able to help with the meal preparation.

What causes a child to accept certain foods? Children may be afraid to try something new, and some foods may need to be offered to them as many as 15 times before they will accept them. Children react to such things as color, flavor, texture, temperature, serving size, and even the attitude of the server/preparer and the atmosphere in which the food is presented.

Most children like foods that are soft. Typically, they do not like dry, tough parts, or foods that are too thick. Children also respond to what others in their family unit consume. This may be the most significant factor. If they observe a parent or sibling eating a food item, children are more likely to try it. Likewise, if they hear a negative comment about a food, they will be less likely to try that food item.

Children have the greatest number of taste buds during the preschool period. as a consequence, preschoolers tend to dislike strongly flavored food, such as cooked vegetables, spicy foods, and temperature extremes. As taste buds are lost throughout life, they are not replaced. Therefore, adults can usually tolerate a broader array of flavors in foods than younger people, who taste more acutely.

The serving size presented to a child normally affects what they will eat. The quantity of food should be less than what the parent expects the child will eat. It is preferred that they ask for seconds. A good rule of thumb for serving size is a tablespoon of each item for each year of age up to age 5. For instance, 2 tbsp. of corn for a 2-year-old would be an appropriate serving size. Table 10.6 presents serving sizes by food groups for children of different ages.

TABLE 10.6 Serving Sizes per day of Foods within Food Groups by a Child's Age and Assuming Less Than 30 Minutes of Activity per Day

Age (years)	Milk, Cheese Yogurt	Meat, Fish, Poultry, Beans, Nuts, and Eggs	Vegetables	Fruit	Pasta, Cereal, Rice, and Bread
			Girls		
2–3	2 c.	2 oz.	1 c.	1 c.	3 oz.
			Boys		
	2 c.	3 oz.	1–½ c.	1 c.	4 oz.
			Girls		
4–8	2 c.	3 oz.	1 c.	1–½ c.	4 oz.
			Boys		
	2 c.	4 oz.	1–½ c.	1–½ c.	5 oz.

Source: United States Department of Agriculture.

Snacking

Snacks are okay if well chosen, because frequent eating at these ages is essential for proper growth and development. Fruit juice should be limited to no more than 4-6 fluid ounces per day and only 100% fruit juice should be given. See the brief list below for some nutritionally healthy snacks that offer positive alternatives to the fat-laden products many children are given.

- Apples and cheese
- Graham crackers and low-fat milk

- Crackers and cheese
- Oatmeal cookies and low-fat milk
- Fresh fruit
- Raisins
- Celery sticks with peanut butter
- Cauliflower, broccoli, celery, cucumber, and carrot sticks with low-fat dip
- Fruit and yogurt
- Unsalted nuts
- Low-sugar cereal and low-fat milk
- Baked chips with cheddar cheese and boiled/drained whole beans

Is it okay for kids to snack?

Health Concerns of Childhood

Throughout childhood and adolescence, numerous nutritional-related conditions can affect growth, development, and general health. Some of the more common ones are listed here.

Iron-Deficiency Anemia

Iron-deficiency anemia is often a problem among children. In fact, it remains the number one problem in terms of nutrient deficiency in the United States today. Iron deficiency may influence one's mood and attention span because less oxygen is being carried to tissues, including the brain. In addition to these physical limitations, children with anemia score lower on standardized exams. It is important that children be screened for anemia. Good sources of iron for children include more than just meat, although iron from meat sources is more absorbable. Peanut butter, which many children love, is also a good source of iron. Flour tortillas, fortified cereals, beans, sunflower seeds, rice noodles, green peas, dried peaches and apricots, chicken, eggs, nuts, and potato skins are some of the other iron containing foods that kids may enjoy.

Although iron deficiency is a problem in children, iron toxicity can also be an issue. Iron toxicity is a leading cause of poisoning among children under age 6. This frequently occurs when children accidentally consume iron tablets meant for an adult. Because of this and the potential for other toxic reactions, supplements should always be locked away from children.

Obesity and Overweight

One of the most significant problems among children is that of obesity. The incidence in the United States has more than tripled since the early 1960s, when only 5 percent of children were considered overweight or obese, to nearly a third of American kids and teens (Figure 10.7). Physical inactivity, video games, television, excessive snacking on empty Calorie foods, large portion sizes, overconsumption of Calories, saturation of food advertising directed to children, vending machines in the school system, widespread availability

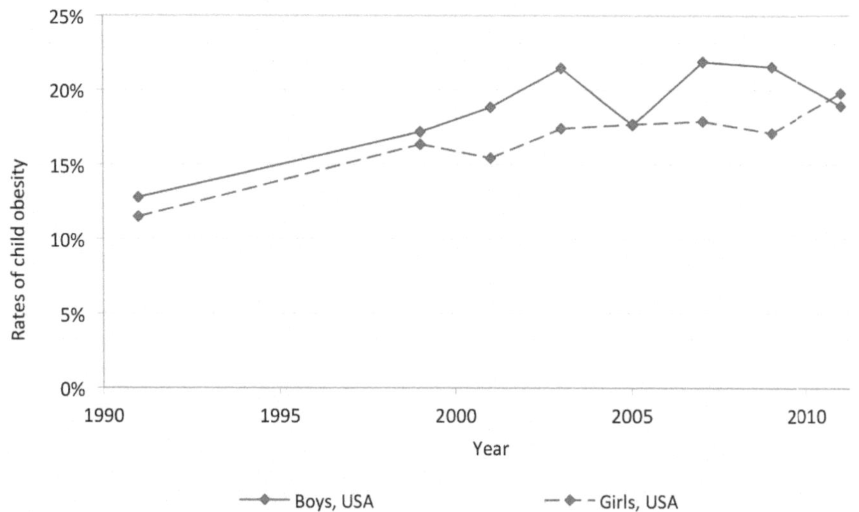

FIGURE 10.7 Obesity in children and adolescents has grown at an alarming rate since the mid-1970s.

Source: Reprinted from the Centers for Disease Control

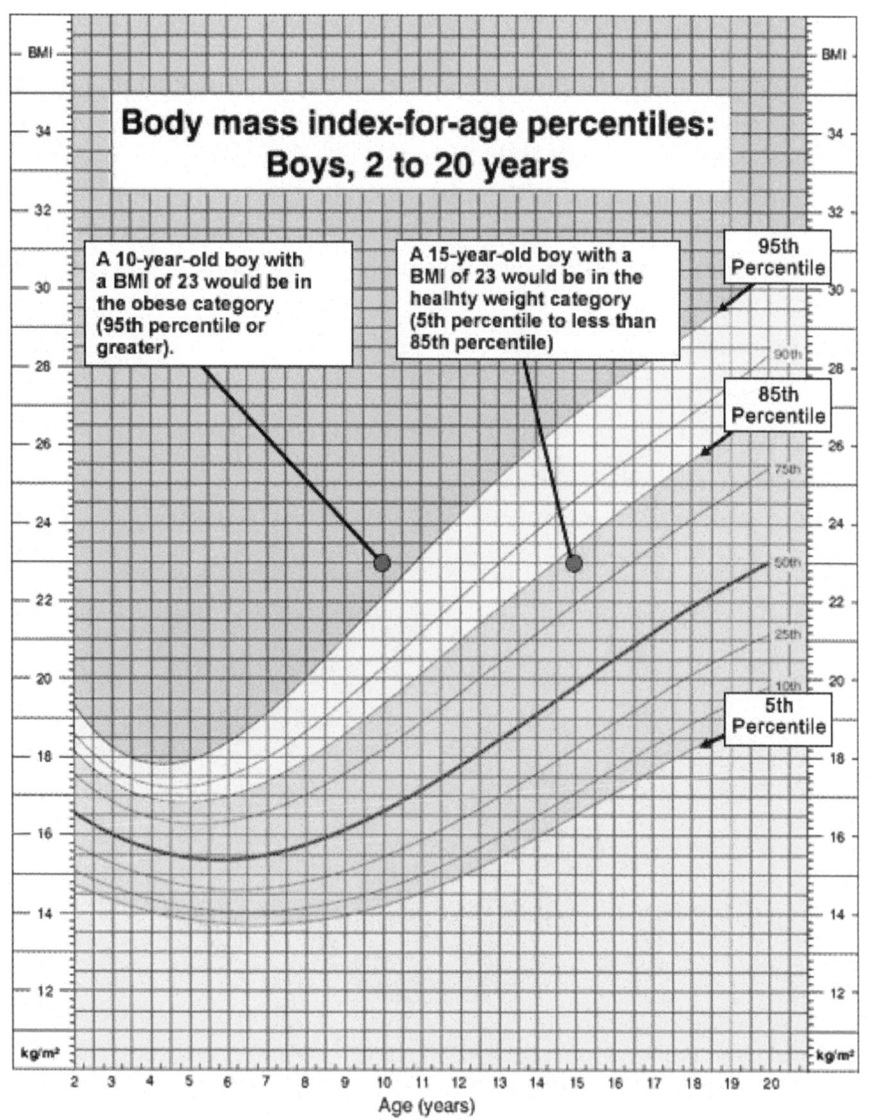

FIGURE 10.8 Interpreting a BMI chart. This is an example of a hypothetical 10-year-old boy with different BMI values. Above the 95th percentile for the BMI, he is considered obese; between the 85th and 95th percentile, he is overweight. On the other extreme, a BMI below the 5th percentile is considered underweight. BMIs between the 5th and 85th percentiles are considered healthy.

Source: Reprinted from the Centers for Disease Control and Prevention.

of food, and the use of food as a reward to motivate positive behaviors are all reasons proposed as causes.

How do you know whether a child or even a teenager is overweight or obese? The body mass index (BMI), discussed in Chapter 9, is needed. The Centers for Disease Control and Prevention has developed BMI charts for children through teens of each sex from age 2 to 20 in which percentile growth curves can be used (Figure 10.8). If a child or teen's BMI is at the 85th percentile or greater, the individual is "overweight." If the BMI for age and sex is at the 95th percentile or above, the individual is "obese."

Since children are still growing, weight loss is only recommended under certain conditions since restricting Calories may impede growth. In general, it is advised that the child try to maintain their weight and grow into it as they gain height. When it is deemed that weight loss is necessary, it should only be done under the supervision of a pediatrician to ensure their development is not being negatively impacted.

Dental Decay

The water in many communities in the United States has naturally occurring or added fluoride, which has decreased the incidence of tooth decay by increasing the strength of the enamel on teeth. Fluoridation of water has remained a controversial issue in some locales due to the fact that fluoride toxicity can weaken bones and can lead to fluorosis as discussed in Chapter 7. Besides fluoridation, avoiding sweet, sticky foods (e.g., caramel and

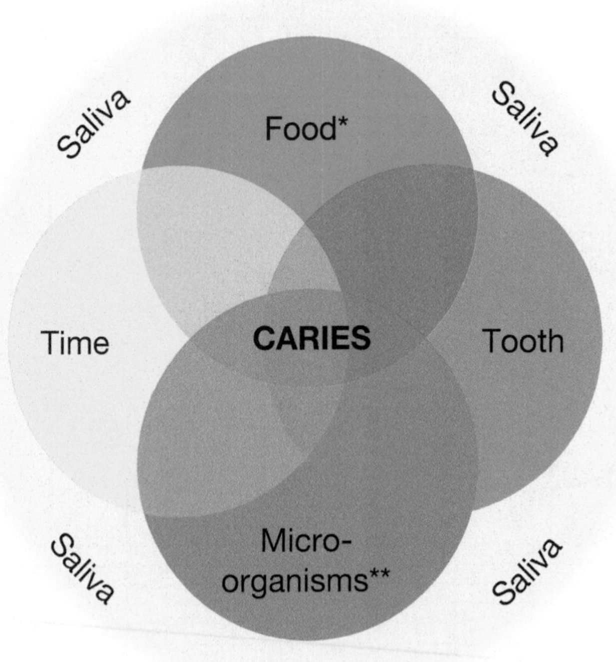

FIGURE 10.9 Various factors in the microenvironment of the mouth interact and lead to the production of dental cavities.

taffy) and practicing good oral hygiene are important. Sticky foods, such as candies, allow bacteria to attach to the tooth. Acid is secreted by bacteria feeding on the sugar of the sticky surface, thereby eating away at the tooth's enamel (Figure 10.9). As previously discussed, a poor practice that can contribute to severe dental decay in toddlers is giving a bottle of juice and milk, especially at bedtime. Bedtime bottle feeding allows the sugar in the juice or milk to react longer with the bacteria and dissolve the enamel on the teeth to produce cavities.

Food Allergies and Food Intolerance

food allergy

A condition in which the body produces antibodies against particular food molecules and physical symptoms result.

anaphylactic shock

A condition in which blood pressure is very low and breathing is shallow. If medical attention is not sought immediately, death can result.

Food allergies in children are a major concern of parents. It is estimated that they effect 1 in 13 children. A food allergy is an immune response in which the body produces antibodies against particular proteins in food and physical symptoms result. *Mild reactions can include hives, eczema, sneezing and gastrointestinal issues such as nausea, vomiting and diarrhea. Severe symptoms may include trouble swallowing, shortness of breath, and swelling of the tongue. Most severe allergic reactions happen within seconds or minutes after ingestion of the suspected item. Some reactions may occur after several hours.*

One can avoid a specific allergic reaction by completely removing the offending food item from the diet. Ninety percent of all food allergies are caused by wheat, eggs, soy, fish, shellfish, tree nuts, peanuts, and milk. Many food allergies, except peanuts, are outgrown. Peanuts are especially notorious for causing allergic reactions, not only in children but in people of all ages. People who are allergic to peanuts can experience **anaphylactic shock**, a condition in which blood pressure is very low

The seven major allergens.

© Tong J/Shutterstock.com

© eAlisa/Shutterstock.com

© Evgeniya Uvarova/Shutterstock.com

and breathing is shallow. Signs and symptoms of anaphylaxis include a rapid, weak pulse, a skin rash, and nausea and vomiting. If medical attention is not sought immediately, death can result. Occasionally, the allergy is so severe that even breathing the food particles can trigger the allergic response.

food intolerance

An adverse reaction to a food or a food additive without producing antibodies.

A food allergy is different from **food intolerance**. Food intolerance is an adverse reaction, often involving the GI tract, to a food or a food additive. Since the immune system is not triggered, not antibodies are produced. A good example is lactose intolerance, as discussed in Chapter 3 or the headaches some people get following consumption of sulfites.

Food and Behavior in Children

Do certain foods cause hyperactivity in children?

Parents often ask whether certain foods cause hyperactivity in children. Is there any evidence to support this? The basic answer is no. However, it is not uncommon for people to believe that sugar and food additives can lead to behavior problems in children. Despite these suspicions, carefully controlled studies do not support this notion. The cause of attention deficit disorder and behavioral problems is an issue of brain chemistry. In order for food to have an impact, it would have to alter brain chemistry. Drug therapy can sometimes control hyperactivity in children. Any effect that the elimination of certain foods appears to have on hyperactivity is most likely a placebo effect. Although eating breakfast can improve the attention span in children, no evidence exists that specific food items such as sugar cause hyperactivity.

Stimulants such as caffeine and products that contain caffeine can be a problem in children just as in adults. Sodas and chocolate contain caffeine, and parents should be aware of this. Caffeine content is often found on the ingredients part of the food label, not on the Nutrition Facts Panel. Caffeine can cause sleeplessness and irritability. Children are less able to break down caffeine compared to adults, and thus its stimulating effect is much greater. It may actually be the caffeine in the soda and candy that increases a child's activity and not the sugar content.

BEFORE YOU GO ON...

1. What are some important factors in determining what a child will eat?
2. What is the number one nutritional deficiency among children in the United States?
3. How do health professionals define a child who is at risk for being overweight? An overweight child?
4. What is the basic difference between food intolerance and a food allergy?

NUTRITION DURING THE ADOLESCENT YEARS

As in childhood, significant bodily changes continue to occur throughout the teen years. Some of these changes are as dramatic as in the first year of life, and many hormone changes contribute to overall body growth and development during this period. Figure 10.10 shows how the proportions of our bodies change from birth to young adulthood. Note that the head is relatively larger in infancy and decreases thereafter, whereas the relative size of the legs increases.

Let's explore these changes and how nutrition can affect them.

Rapid Growth

The growth spurt for girls occurs before that for boys. In girls it occurs around age 10–11, and in boys around 12–13. The timing of the growth spurt depends on the child's attaining a certain critical weight. This can vary by parts of the world. In the United States, it is generally about 30 kg or 66 pounds and when body fat is 10 percent. The rate of growth is an interaction between heredity and the environment, with nutrition playing a big role in achieving genetic potential.

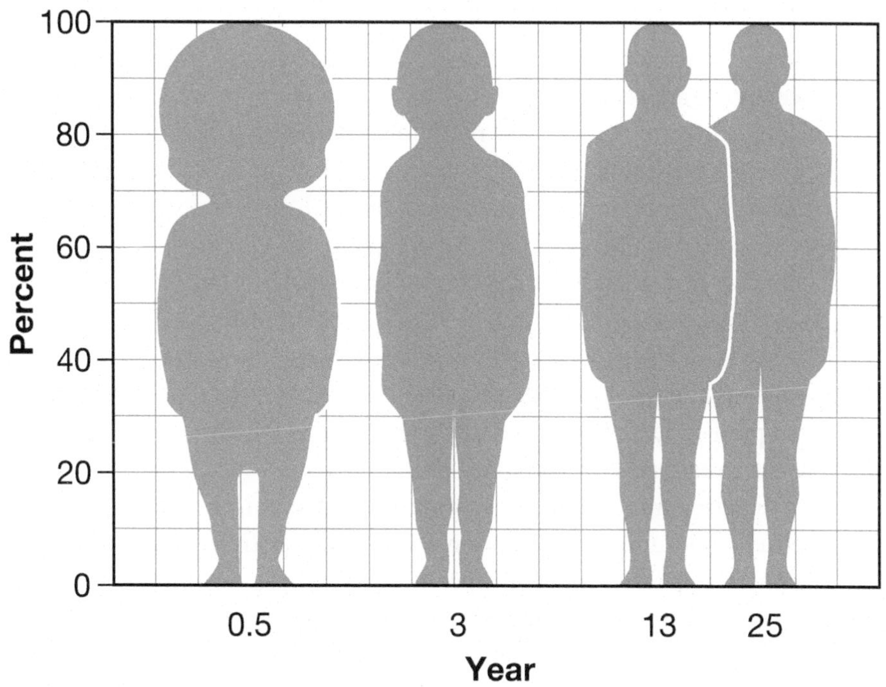

FIGURE 10.10
Human development from infancy to young adult.

Nutrient Needs of Adolescents

In general, adolescents need more energy. However, these Calories are useful only if the vitamins, minerals, and protein needed for growth are available. If an adolescent consumes Calories, but not other nutrients at appropriate levels for growth, any excess Calories will be stored as fat and result in teen-onset obesity.

Most surveys report that the levels of iron, calcium, and vitamin A consumed in these age groups are not adequate. Iron is one of the most critical needs of teenage girls. Table 10.7 shows the RDA for iron. However, because boys have more muscle tissue, their iron needs are also important.

TABLE 10.7 Iron RDAs for Teenage Boys and Girls by Age and Adults

Age (years)	Boys	Girls
9–13	8 mg/day	8 mg/day
14–18	11 mg/day	15 mg/day
Adult	8 mg/day	18 mg/day

Calcium deposits into bone mass during the teenage years, and calcium needs are higher during this period than at any time in the entire lifespan. For boys and girls ages 9–18, the DRI is 1,300 mg per day. For an adult, it is 1,000 mg per day. During adolescence, it is important to obtain the greatest level of bone mass because bone loss increases as one ages.

Food Habits of Adolescents

Adolescents normally become more independent as they age. Many adolescent girls are sensitive to criticism about their appearance, and weight comments can result in skipped meals or other eating disorders. Anorexia and bulimia have a high incidence among teenage girls, and perhaps more boys than once thought. Many of these individuals have a distorted image of themselves, believing that they are overweight or fat. Parents should continue to encourage their adolescent children to participate in family meals for the purposes of promoting better nutrition and communication.

The more meals teens consume away from home, the more likely they are to eat foods that do not provide adequate nutrient content. Some of the most common poor food habits picked up by teens are as follows:

- Failure to eat breakfast or some other meal
- Not drinking milk or not consuming other calcium-rich foods
- Nutrient-poor food selection in meals eaten away from home
- An overriding fear of obesity, especially among girls, which leads to dieting
- Use of bodybuilding supplements among boys to increase muscle mass
- Excessive intake of convenience foods and fast foods

Adolescents tend to skip breakfast at a higher rate than any other age group. Having a healthy breakfast has two major advantages:

1. It generally provides nutrients, especially vitamin C, calcium, and riboflavin (vitamin B2). These particular nutrients are best supplied by breakfast foods such as milk, cereals, juices, and fresh fruit.
2. The availability of a readily usable carbohydrate results in a rapid increase in blood glucose levels. This improves or maintains performance level, reduces accidents, and enhances attention span.

Breakfast need not be the usual fruit, cereal, toast, and beverage pattern. It can be a combination of foods, either liquid or solid, that provides at least 300 kcal and sufficient protein and fat and a sense of satiety (satisfaction) with a reasonable contribution of nutrients. Examples include a sandwich, a fruit-and-yogurt smoothie, yogurt with granola, whole-wheat toast with peanut butter, cereal with milk and fruit, low-fat granola, a whole-grain bagel with low-fat cream cheese, and leftovers from the night before.

Adolescent Eating Patterns and Disease Risks

During adolescence, we see a transition from dependence on adults to independence, and this includes eating behavior and patterns. Teenagers often eat alone and frequently prepare their own food. Because the incidence of overweight and obesity has increased in this age group and the rate of increase has been accelerating, numerous intervention programs have been developed to help both children and teenagers eat more nutritiously and to improve their nutrition knowledge and practices. With obesity, we begin to note increased levels of cholesterol, which can lead to an early onset of heart disease such as atherosclerosis. In addition, we are witnessing a rapid increase in type 2 diabetes among children and adolescents, and this is also linked to obesity. High blood pressure is becoming more common among adolescents. Those who have abnormally high blood pressure during their teen years are more likely to be hypertensive as adults, and there is a strong relationship between being overweight at this early age and developing hypertension. Losing weight is a good step in the direction of correcting this problem. In summary, good food habits at this age are critical to ensuring continued healthy food habits during adulthood.

Physical Activity Guidelines

*The Physical Activity Guidelines for Americans, issued by the U.S. Department of Health and Human Services, recommend that children and adolescents aged 6-17 years should have 60 minutes (1 hour) or more of physical activity each day.

Myths & LEGENDS

DO CERTAIN FOODS CAUSE OR CONTRIBUTE TO ACNE?

Acne is an inflammation of the sebaceous glands of the skin and is normally caused by physiological changes that accompany becoming an adult. When these glands become blocked by sloughed skin cells, the sebum produced by the sebaceous glands gets trapped and bacteria populate the blocked pore. This is what causes a pimple. Testosterone stimulates the secretion of sebum from the glands, and estrogen can reduce it. Mechanical irritation of the skin from clothing friction and the use of oil-based cosmetics can also aggravate or cause an eruption of acne.

It is not uncommon to see a story about how the foods you eat during adolescence can cause acne. Foods such as potato chips, soda, chocolate, sugar-filled, and greasy food items have been blamed for causing acne in teenagers. Emerging evidence suggests that diet does indeed influence the development of acne.

Several nutrients play a role in maintaining the health of the skin. For instance, vitamins A, E, and C along with the trace element zinc have a role in skin health. The drug Accutane is a vitamin A derivative that can improve the skin with respect to cystic acne, but it should not be taken for more than 6 months at a time and must not be taken during pregnancy because it has been shown to cause birth defects. However, young people need to be aware that taking massive doses of vitamin A will not have a beneficial effect on acne, as it differs from the drug Accutane. Good hygiene is far more important than diet in preventing acne.

Youth Physical Activity Guidelines

- Children and adolescents should have 60 minutes (1 hour) or more of physical activity daily.
    - **Aerobic:** Most of the 60 or more minutes a day should be either moderate- or vigorous-intensity aerobic physical activity and should include vigorous-intensity physical activity at least 3 days a week.

- **Muscle-strengthening:** As part of their 60 or more minutes of daily physical activity, children and adolescents should include muscle-strengthening physical activity on at least 3 days of the week.
- **Bone-strengthening:** As part of their 60 or more minutes of daily physical activity, children and adolescents should include bone-strengthening physical activity on at least 3 days of the week.

- It is important to encourage young people to participate in physical activities that are appropriate for their age, that are enjoyable, and that offer variety.*

NUTRITION FOR OLDER ADULTS

The average age of Americans is becoming much older, with more than one-fifth of the population over age 65. This is double the number in 1950. We are living much longer, healthier lives today. A 70-year-old today is much more youthful physiologically than 70-year-olds several generations ago. An increasing number of people are *octogenarians* (living to age 80 or older), and it's no longer rare for someone to live past age 100. In fact, the number of people living past age 100 has doubled in the past decade. Clearly, better medical care, better methods of treating infectious diseases, and better nutrition have all contributed to our increased longevity. Much of our emphasis in nutrition is devoted to enhancing the quality of the remaining years of the older adult. The baby boomers are retiring, and as a generation, they are very health conscious.

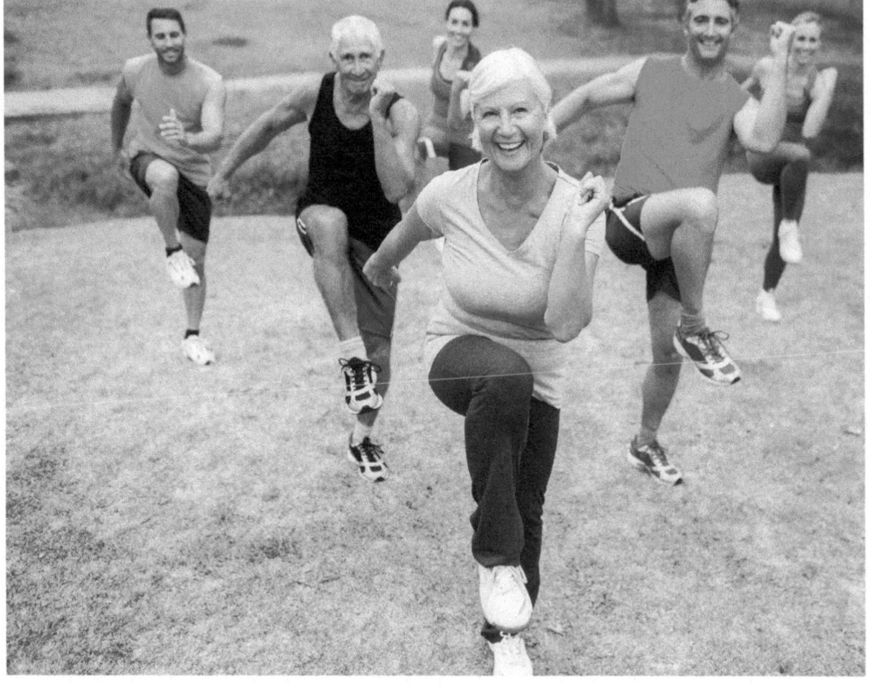

© Paul Vasarhelyi/Shutterstock.com

It is important for older adults to stay active in order to maintain quality of life and promote health.

What age are we referring to when we discuss the "older adult"? Surprisingly, given our increased life expectancy, the National Research Council defines anyone age 50 or older as an older adult. In setting nutrition requirements and DRIs, a separate category for people over age 50 is listed. However, there is no distinction in the recommendations for those who are age 55 versus age 75, although there are separate recommendations by sex. This does not mean that there are no differences in these age groups beyond age 50 with respect to several nutrient requirements. It is likely that a consensus among the scientific community has yet to emerge and a separate category for those age 70 or older may be appropriate.

Social and Psychological Aspects of Aging

The psychological and social aspects of aging have as profound an impact on nutrition as do the biological aspects. These are generalities and may not apply to all older adults.

Living Alone

People who live alone frequently lack the motivation to cook regular meals, which may lead to the consumption of less-healthy snack foods at irregular times. Normally people eat better when they have companionship. Community eating centers are usually helpful in getting older adults to socialize and eat healthier as a result of the food served to them in a social environment.

Depression is common among older adults, and it can affect food intake, resulting in malnutrition.

Depression

Older adults may be more vulnerable because of sociological and biological changes. This condition frequently affects food intake, as either overeating or undereating.

Anxiety

People who are anxious or concerned frequently report a loss of appetite. Anxious people often have changes in hormones and other nervous system chemicals. These changes affect how much digestive secretions the body releases. Many times the anxious person releases less digestive secretions. This results in a decreased ability to digest and absorb nutrients from the food consumed.

Long-Standing Food Habits

Food preferences and patterns among older people are often the result of life-long food habits. The grocery store today is much different than that of the 1950s and 1960s, when there was much less variety. People who are 70 and 80 years old may have established their food habits 50 or 60 years ago. They may regard fruits and vegetables as seasonal items, consuming them only when they are "in season" as they did when they were younger.

Older adults may consume foods they associate with pleasant memories, often referred to as "comfort foods." Some of these foods may be high in fat, Calories, and sodium. They also may harbor misconceptions about certain foods, such as that cheese is constipating, or that milk is only for younger people or infants.

Economic Considerations

Most times, the first thing that people cut back on when money is tight is food. Older adults living on fixed incomes typically cannot purchase more costly food items. High-carbohydrate foods, such as breads and grain products, which are relatively inexpensive, tend to be purchased more often. Expensive products such as meat, fish, and fresh fruits and vegetables are more likely to be avoided.

Many older adults on fixed incomes live in inexpensive housing. This cheaper housing frequently lacks adequate cooking and refrigeration facilities, which in many cases contributes to the poor nutrition habits of its senior occupants.

In the United States, health care and medication costs are high. As a result, many older adults do not seek needed care or fill prescriptions. Older adults may resort to other modes of therapy in an attempt to save money, making them more vulnerable to fad diets or products designed as anti-aging

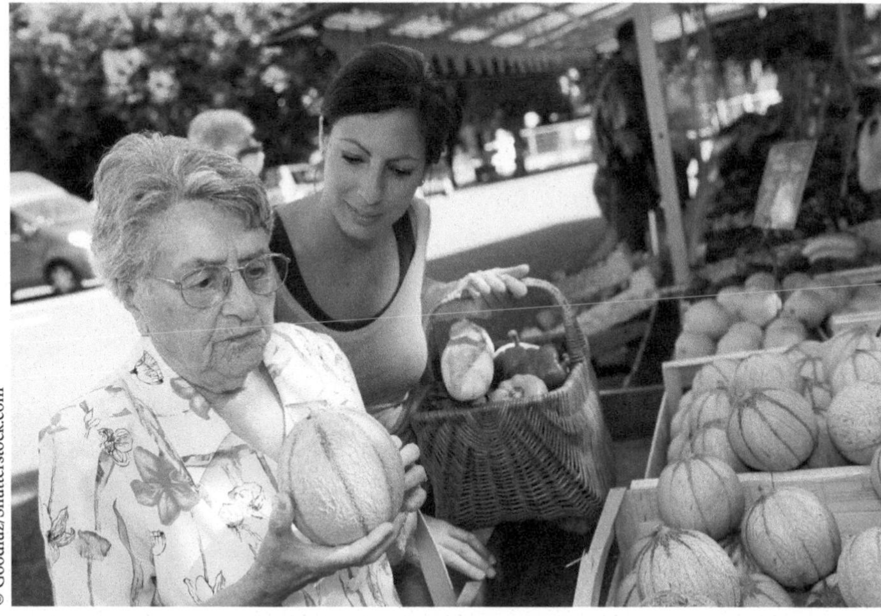

Older adults may have learned to consume fruits and vegetables only during certain times of the year, when in season. Today, fresh fruits and vegetables are made available year-round in many places.

Make it a **PRACTICE**

COMMUNITY FOOD PROGRAMS

Community food programs are very important to the nutritional well-being of many older adults. Not only do adults benefit from having a balanced meal, they benefit from companionship. It is often difficult to cook for one person, and many older adults prefer not to cook for themselves. This causes them to snack instead of consuming nutritious meals. The *Elderly Nutrition Program* is an initiative of the federal government designed to improve the nutritional well-being of older adults, prevent medical problems, and help them stay in their community rather than being institutionalized. Low-cost, nutritious meals are offered. Meals served at senior citizen sites are available in many communities. Home delivered meals, such as the *Meals on Wheels* program, offer nutritious meals but lack the social interaction older adults often need.

Shopping assistance, counseling and referral to social services, and help with transportation are also available. By law, the Elderly Nutrition Program must provide at least one-third of the RDA for nutrients. All adults older than age 60 are eligible to receive meals from these programs regardless of how much money they have, although priority is given to those who are economically disadvantaged.

Many older adults benefit from the federally sponsored Supplemental Nutrition Assistance Program (SNAP), formerly known as food stamps. Some choose not to use them out of pride, whereas others simply lack the knowledge regarding eligibility. Today, use of a debit card has helped minimize the negative stereotype or embarrassment in the checkout line. Throughout the country, the county extension agent can be contacted to provide information regarding these programs.

Many communities offer meals at senior citizen centers. The availability of companionship, as well as having someone else prepare meals, helps to assure better nutrition.

products. They also may be tempted to consume large quantities of supplements or buy those that are unproven and sometimes dangerous. Although supplements within the DRI recommendations are generally considered safe, they are not a substitute for good food selection and balanced nutrition. Worse, the expense of supplements may contribute to a lack of funds for purchasing adequate, nutrient-dense foods.

Physical and Physiological Factors

As we reach older adulthood, many organs of the body decline in function. All parts of the body are eventually affected.

Loss of Teeth

Many older adults did not have the benefits of good dental care during their life. Fifty percent of adults over age 65 and 65 percent of adults over age 75 have experienced tooth loss to varying degrees. Almost 80 percent of these individuals either fail to replace their teeth with dentures or use poorly fitting ones. Some of the dental problems older adults experience may also be due to the loss of the supporting bone from periodontal disease. Loss of teeth can be caused by low dietary calcium and vitamin D intake as well as poor dental hygiene and/or lack of dental care.

Because of their susceptibility to health claims, many older adults are more likely to consume supplements. Unfortunately, many of these claims are not supported by science.

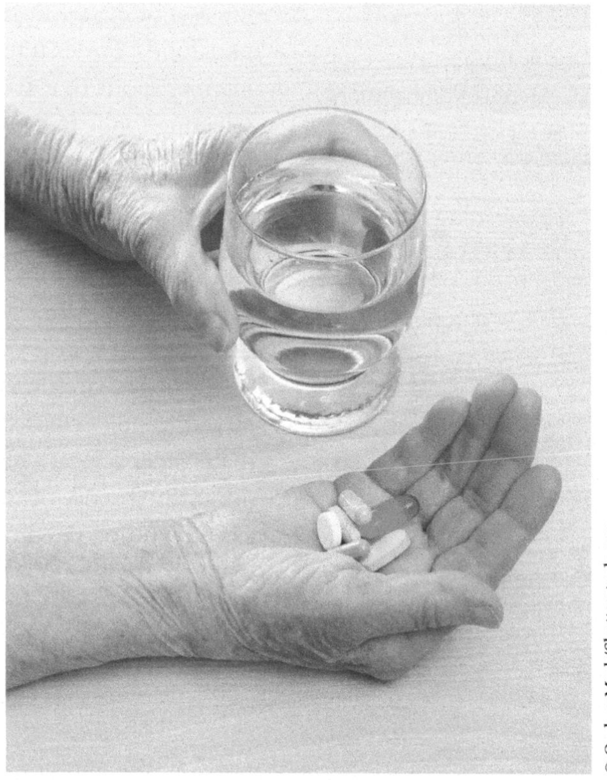

Because of these dental problems, chewing food is much more difficult and often results in swallowing difficulties. Accordingly, many older people replace nutritious foods with too many "less" nutritious choices that are easier to chew. Plant foods are tougher to chew, and therefore fruits and vegetables may be limited or omitted from the diet, or softened by prolonged cooking. This reduction in the consumption of fruits and vegetables or excessive cooking can result in decreased nutrients and fiber that leads to lower *motility* (the ability to move food along) in the gastrointestinal tract and constipation. However, canned fruits and vegetables are much easier to eat and can be consumed by people with poor dentition because they are easier to chew. Meat is difficult to chew, but omitting it from the diet can lead to low intakes of protein, iron and zinc. Even foods such as seeds, nuts, salads, and popcorn, all good sources of nutrients, are difficult to eat if there are dental problems. Eggs, tofu, milk, cheese and soft cooked meats can be used in place of hard-to-chew protein sources.

Loss of Neuromuscular Coordination

Older adults may develop tremors from a wide variety of disorders, including Parkinson's disease. This makes handling food items and utensils more difficult. Rather than risk the embarrassment that would come with spilled food or the inability to cut meat or eat soup, older people are likely to avoid such food items. They may fear working with boiling water on stoves and thus may choose foods that do not need to be cooked. In the grocery store, they may not wish to reach for food items on the upper or lower shelves because of lack of strength or flexibility or increased back pain. Overall, these restrictions result in a decrease in the variety of foods selected.

APPLICATION TIP

If you or others in your family have trouble chewing, try the following: cooking vegetables instead of eating them raw, choosing more tender cuts of meat, grinding nuts and seeds before adding them to recipes, removing the skin from fruits and vegetables, and drinking lots of water or fluids with meals.

Impaired Vision

age-related macular degeneration
A condition that affects a specific region of the retina known as the macular region and is a cause of blindness in older adults.

cataracts
Cloudiness of the lens of the eye that can lead to blindness.

Impaired vision caused by conditions, such as **age-related macular degeneration** or **cataracts**, may impact an individual's ability to purchase and prepare foods. For example, an individual who cannot read labels or who cannot identify foods that are not directly at eye level has a greatly reduced basis for selecting foods in a grocery store. An inability to see clearly makes it difficult for older adults to remain independent.

Diminished Sense of Taste and Smell

Our senses of taste and smell decrease as we age. By the time we are 70 years old, we have lost 36 percent of our taste buds compared to when we were 30. Smell is connected to taste. Ever notice that you cannot taste something when you have nasal congestion from a cold? Loss of taste normally results in decreased eating pleasure and decreased intake. Loss of salt and sweet tastes are most notable for many older adults, who then add a lot of extra salt and sugar to compensate. The diminished sense of taste and smell can increase the risk of foodborne illness. Compounding the problem is the fact that older adults may also have a greater intake of medications that can affect their senses, particularly taste. Not only is there a decrease in taste, but the sense of taste may be negatively altered. Some drugs can cause high-protein foods, such as meat, to taste bitter.

Physical Discomfort

Older adults may experience discomfort after consuming certain foods. This happens in almost all age groups but is more of an issue in older adults. Some

© Robert Kneschke/Shutterstock.com

foods may be more likely to cause heartburn, indigestion, and gastric discomfort. People may again refrain from eating particular food items, reducing their variety, in order to avoid the discomfort.

High-fat foods may lead to heartburn. Carbonated beverages, caffeinated beverages, spices, green peppers, onions, and garlic are food items that may not be tolerated in some older adults.

Loss of Muscle Mass

The loss of muscle mass in older adults is a major problem. This is often referred to as **sarcopenia**. With less muscle mass, strength is diminished and limited. Remember, muscle requires more Calories to maintain. Consequently, the basal metabolism is lower in older adults because they have less muscle. Muscle mass can be better maintained if some type of strength training exercises are included regularly. Daily walks, hiking, yoga, and low-impact aerobics should also be part of the older adult's daily activities.

Sarcopenia
The loss of muscle mass, strength, and function in older adults.

BEFORE YOU GO ON...

1. List the social and psychological factors that may influence nutrition habits in older adults.
2. How do age-related macular degeneration and cataracts impact nutrition?
3. How would loss of neuromuscular coordination affect food selection in older adults?

Nutrient Requirements of Older Adults

Older adults especially need a nutrient-dense diet. This means that they should consume foods high in vitamins, minerals, and high-quality protein but with limited Calories. Meats, vegetables, fruits, milk, eggs, and even cheese are good examples of nutrient-dense foods. At the same time, sweets and fats need to be limited.

Energy recommendations decrease for men and women over age 50. Further reductions are recommended for those older than age 75 because people in this age group normally engage in less physical activity and have less lean body mass.

The needed high-quality protein should be obtained from lean meats, fish, poultry, eggs, low-fat or skim milk, and legumes. If the older adult is underweight or malnourished, then snacking between meals or the use of nutritional liquid supplements may be necessary to meet the body's needs.

Proper water intake is another nutrition issue about which older adults should be aware. As we age, we do not recognize thirst as easily or quickly as we do when we were younger, and as a result dehydration is frequently a problem. In some cases, those who have lost some bladder control may be reluctant to consume liquids, thereby worsening the risk for dehydration. Water is also important to help older adults better tolerate fevers. Older adults should consume at least 6 cups of fluids each day in order to stay properly hydrated.

Inadequate intake of certain other nutrients is common among older adults. Specifically, many older adults fail to consume adequate quantities of vitamin D, folate, vitamins B_6 and B_{12}, calcium, zinc, magnesium, and iron. In order to address this issue, they must exercise extra care to select foods that provide these nutrients. Calcium requirements increase from 1,000 to 1,200 mg per day for women after age 50. For both men and women greater than 70 years of age, the DRI is 1,200 mg per day. In order to minimize or reduce the rate of bone loss, especially among postmenopausal women, daily requirements of calcium, and vitamin D need to be met. The DRI for vitamin D increases from 15 to 20 µg per day for both men and women greater than 70 years of age. Inadequate levels of vitamin B_6 are of concern in older adults because of the body's inability to maintain sufficient stores as we age. And because older adults have difficulty absorbing vitamin B_{12}, they need to consciously increase their intake.

Factors Affecting Nutrient Use

As we age, our physiological functions change. Often, our gastrointestinal system and other vital organs are less efficient in performing the jobs required. This circumstance has a significant impact on our ability to use nutrients. What are some of these changes?

- Decreased digestive secretions and inability to break down foods
- Lower gastric motility, leading to constipation and swallowing disorders
- Deterioration in kidney function
- Nutrient malabsorption due to changes in the digestive tract

MAJOR NUTRITION-RELATED ISSUES AND OLDER ADULTS

Some nutrition issues are common to all age groups—for example, obesity and anemia. However, as we will discuss, many age-related changes alter nutrient requirements. For example, the use of certain prescription drugs, which can interfere with nutrient absorption and utilization, to treat many conditions and diseases is just one of many issues that can have a significant nutritional impact on older adults. Some other issues include the following:

- Obesity
- Anemia
- Constipation
- Osteoporosis
- Drug-nutrient interaction

The Most Common Issues

Obesity

In the United States, one out of four individuals over age 50 is obese, and this percentage is increasing. Of those who are older than 50 and obese, 75 percent of them are age 50–69. After age 70, the ratio drops to 17 percent. Rates are higher for those with lower incomes and with less education, and obesity is also more common in older women than men. BMI, one indicator of obesity, starts to decrease at age 60. However, this statistic may be misleading because many of those who were extremely obese may have died. Also, sarcopenia may partly explain this observation.

One of the reasons for obesity in older adults is lowered metabolism due to decreased muscle mass. Older adults are less physically active, and lack of activity leads to muscle atrophy (wasting). The combination of a lower basal metabolism and less physical activity means less energy required. Another factor that can lead to decreased basal metabolism may be less thyroid hormone secretion. Hormones produced in the thyroid gland normally increase basal metabolism. However, as the body reaches an advanced age, fewer hormones are secreted, including thyroxin, which results in a lower metabolism.

Anemia

Anemia observed in older adults is more likely due to other causes rather than failing to consume enough dietary iron. Many times, issues such as gastric ulcers and other related ailments lead to blood loss over time, which results in iron deficiency anemia. Vitamin B_{12} deficiency causes large-cell anemia, which can happen if there is insufficient stomach acid or not enough intrinsic factor needed for absorption. The DRI committee recommends cereals that are fortified with vitamin B_{12} or supplements for older adults.

Constipation

Twenty-six percent of women and 16 percent of men over 65 years of age report suffering from constipation in Westernized countries. These numbers increase even more with age. Oftentimes, constipation is a side effect of one or more of the medications the elderly person may be taking. Other factors increasing the risk for constipation include low fiber diets, reduced fluid intake, and reduced activity. The easiest way for elderly persons to relieve constipation is through increasing fiber intake. However, be mindful of the need for adequate fluid intake, which is a common problem in this age group. If fiber is added to the diet without adequate fluid intake, a worsening of constipation can occur.

Osteoporosis

We discussed this disease in Chapter 7. Osteoporosis is typically apparent in older adulthood. Although it is more of a problem in women, more attention is being directed to older men, who also have a higher incidence than men of a younger age. Osteoporosis is not simply lack of calcium. Taking more calcium at this stage will not reverse it, but having sufficient nutrients, including calcium and vitamin D, along with doing weight-bearing exercise, can slow the process. Older adults are at risk for low vitamin D because the ability to synthesize it through ultraviolet light exposure decreases by up to 75 percent. Also, they may not have as much sun exposure compared to younger people.

Older adults can fall and break a hip, or they can first break a hip with the slightest of force and then fall. When someone breaks a hip, it is much more serious than just bone healing. Nearly 15 percent of older adults who fall and break a hip die within a year from complications: loss of lean body mass, limited mobility, pneumonia, and general malnutrition. Collapse of the spinal column (which can occur in osteoporosis) causes severe and chronic pain. The best way to treat osteoporosis is to prevent it from occurring in the first place. As we've noted, the best means to accomplish this is by maximizing peak bone mass in the adolescent and early adult years.

Drug-Nutrient Interaction

Extensive use of prescription drugs by older adults, known as polypharmacy, has significant nutritional implications. Some drugs cause a lack of appetite. Others interfere with absorption of some nutrients. This may lead to weight loss and/or inadequate intake of many nutrients. Oral diuretics to control blood pressure and other ailments can cause the excretion of water-soluble vitamins and minerals. Some drugs lead to depletion of zinc stores, which can result in a loss of appetite and taste. Others taken to neutralize stomach acidity can interfere with calcium, iron and vitamin B_{12} absorption.

The rate of drug metabolism and detoxification in the liver is much slower in older individuals. Consequently, drugs remain in the body longer and have a longer time to affect nutrients. In some cases, nutrients may interfere with drugs.

SHOULD OLDER ADULTS USE VITAMIN AND MINERAL SUPPLEMENTS?

You DECIDE

In order to maintain a healthy weight, older people need to make sure that they consume a diet that is nutrient dense, meaning that it provides adequate vitamins and minerals without supplying excess Calories. However, what about the use of supplements to get your vitamins and minerals? As we become older, many will turn to supplements to obtain the needed vitamins and minerals. In fact, older adults tend to be big users of supplements of various types. Is there a chance that older adults who supplement may get too much of a good thing? The answer could be "yes." A study has suggested that some who supplement may exceed the upper tolerable limit for the DRIs for calcium, vitamin C, and magnesium. On the other hand, this is not the case for potassium, where those who were users and non-users of supplements continued to have diets low in potassium. (Remember that fruits are good sources of potassium.) Another study suggested that older adults who supplemented exceeded the Upper Tolerable Limit for niacin, folic acid, and vitamin A. Consistent with the new USDA Dietary Guidelines for Americans, the use of supplements may not be the best solution to obtain these micronutrients as we age. Consuming nutrient-dense foods may be the best advice for middle aged and older adults. What do you think of older adults using supplements?

BEFORE YOU GO ON ...

1. List at least three nutrition issues/diseases older adults may experience and explain their causes.
2. List the primary reasons for lower energy requirements in older adults.
3. Besides iron-deficiency anemia, what other nutrient factor can most likely cause anemia in older adults?

CHAPTER SUMMARY

- The rate of mortality in newborns is higher in the United States than in almost all other developed countries, most likely because of socioeconomic disparities in health care for pregnant women.
- The best approach to meeting the nutritional needs of pregnancy is to maintain a healthy diet and a healthy weight before, during, and after pregnancy.
- Pregnancy lasts for 38–42 weeks and is divided into three phases of about 13 weeks called trimesters.
- The first trimester is the time when the fetus is most vulnerable to inadequate nutrition and harmful substances such as drugs and alcohol in the mother. That is why it is critical to ensure adequate nutrient intake and to consider any medications or supplements if there is even a chance you could get pregnant.
- An infant who weighs less than 5.5 lb. is considered low-birthweight. Low-birthweight babies are at risk for illness, infection, lung problems, learning disabilities, insufficient physical growth, and death.
- Current recommendations suggest that a woman who is of normal weight before pregnancy should gain 25–35 lb. If a woman is overweight, she should gain less, but some weight gain is normal. If she is underweight, she should gain more and obese women should gain less.
- Pregnancy is a time when the nutritional needs are increased and must be met by eating many nutrient-dense foods.
- All women of childbearing age should consume 400 μg of folate per day. The recommendation is made for all women because adequate intake is crucial in the first 28 days of pregnancy, before many women even know that they are pregnant.
- Pregnancy-induced hypertension is diagnosed when there is a rapid rise in blood pressure above 140/90; it is related to pre-eclampsia and eclampsia, which can lead to death.
- Obese and overweight mothers and their babies are at higher risk for complications.
- Alcohol, drugs, and smoking should be avoided during pregnancy.
- Because fish may be contaminated with industrial pollutants such as PCBs, pregnant women or women who could become pregnant should not consume any fish without checking with their state or local health department or the EPA.
- Health professionals and organizations recommend exclusive breastfeeding for newborns and infants for the first 6 months.
- Breastfeeding can help protect babies against a number of childhood illnesses, including diarrhea, respiratory infections, autoimmune diseases, and obesity.
- A mother may choose not to breastfeed for many reasons. These reasons could be cultural, personal, or medical, or the mother may simply not be able to physically do so. Regardless of the reason, if a mother does not breastfeed, she should not feel shamed or inadequate for not doing so.
- Formulas offer an adequate substitute to breast milk.
- After an infant reaches 6 months of age, most experts agree that solids should be offered while breastfeeding continues.
- The World Health Organization recognizes four acceptable liquid foods for consumption by infants less than 6 months old: breastfeeding, mother's milk given via a bottle, milk from another human mother, and commercial formula.
- Infant formulas are made from cow's-milk, soy-based, or protein hydrolysate formula.
- Infants need about 40–50 Calories per pound of body weight per day. They need more in the first months and less as they approach 12 months of age as the rapid growth of infancy slows down. Infants younger than age 2 need more fat than children over age 2.

- Infants are at risk for dehydration but can meet fluid needs through breast milk or formula unless there are medical complications such as diarrhea contributing to fluid loss.
- Complementary foods can be given at 6 months of age.
- Iron-fortified cereals or similar foods should be given to breastfed infants at 4-6 months of age to avoid anemia.
- Foods should be introduced gradually and one at a time to avoid allergies.
- Throughout the stages of the life cycle, nutrient requirements change. Children and teenagers are growing rapidly and therefore need high levels of nutrients.
- Children adjust their food intake in accordance with their rate of growth. At the same time, they are developing food preferences and go through "food jags" during which they may change their preferences.
- Iron-deficiency anemia and obesity are the top health concerns of children. However, other health issues such as dental decay, food intolerance, and allergies are common, and steps can be taken to prevent them.
- Food preferences of children can be due to factors such as food temperature, textures, flavors, and serving sizes. A major factor in getting a child to accept new food is seeing the parents consume it.
- Compared to children, adolescents have both similar and different health concerns. Changes in hormonal secretions by sex result in large differences in body composition and nutrient requirements. Another major health concern for adolescents is the lack of parental supervision in food selection as the teen becomes more independent and eats away from home more frequently. Poor food habits such as skipping breakfast and not drinking milk become apparent.
- Older adults are less active, are not growing, and use nutrients less efficiently. This means that they require less energy but still need a balanced and adequate supply of other nutrients.
- Older adults have many nutrition concerns that are affected by sociological, psychological, and economic factors. Living alone, depression, anxiety, long-standing food habits, and financial considerations may negatively affect their nutrition.
- Drug-nutrient interactions are common in older adults. The practice of polypharmacy can affect nutrient utilization, absorption, and excretion and may negatively impact appetite. Polypharmacy can result in a malnourished older adult.
- Physical and physiological changes in older adults occur and must be taken into account in order to provide them with adequate nutrition. Difficulty in chewing, loss of neuromuscular coordination, impaired hearing and taste, and the physical discomfort generated by certain foods can all negatively affect their eating choices.
- Older adults should consume foods that are nutrient-dense and contain adequate levels of protein, vitamins, and minerals, while monitoring caloric intake so as to avoid obesity.

KEY TERMS

AGE-RELATED MACULAR DEGENERATION A condition that affects a specific region of the retina known as the *macular region* and is a cause of blindness in older adults.

ANAPHYLACTIC SHOCK A condition in which blood pressure is very low and breathing is shallow. If medical attention is not sought immediately, death can result.

BOTTLE-MOUTH SYNDROME Tooth decay in infants caused by bacteria-producing fluids (milk, fruit juice, etc.) that pool around the front teeth.

CATARACTS Cloudiness of the lens of the eye that can lead to blindness.

COLIC A condition with unknown causes that is characterized by extended crying in babies that are otherwise healthy and well nourished.

COLOSTRUM The breast milk produced by mothers in the first few days following birth. It has a thinner consistency than subsequent breast milk, has a slightly yellowish color, and is rich in antibodies.

COMPLEMENTARY FOODS Solids and liquid foods that join breastfeeding in the normal progression toward adult eating patterns.

EXTRUSION REFLEX The tongue-thrusting reflex that exists at birth but is usually gone by 6 months of age.

FETAL ALCOHOL SYNDROME (FAS) A disorder in infants caused by alcohol intake during pregnancy and characterized by growth retardation, facial abnormalities, and central nervous system (CNS) dysfunction.

FOOD ALLERGY A condition in which the body produces antibodies against particular food molecules and physical symptoms result.

FOOD INTOLERANCE An adverse reaction to a food or a food additive without producing antibodies.

LOW BIRTHWEIGHT A birth weight of less than 5.5 lb.

SARCOPENIA The loss of muscle mass, strength, and function in older adults.

PICA Compulsive eating of nonfood substances such as clay, chalk, or dirt.

PLACENTA The organ formed in the uterus and that provides for nourishment of the fetus and elimination of waste products.

UMBILICAL CORD A cord full of arteries and veins that connects the baby to the mother through the placenta.

REFERENCES

https://www.cia.gov/library/publications/the-world-factbook/rankorder/2091rank.html
https://www.cia.gov/library/publications/the-world-factbook/rankorder/2223rank.html
http://www.acog.org/~/media/For%20Patients/faq126.pdf?dmc=1&ts=20140521T1753123440
http://www.nal.usda.gov/fnic/DRI/Essential_Guide/DRIEssentialGuideNutReq.pdf
http://www.cdc.gov/breastfeeding/pdf/2013breastfeedingreportcard.pdf
http://www.ncbi.nlm.nih.gov/pubmed/23836309
http://www.aaaai.org/Aaaai/media/MediaLibrary/PDF%20Documents/Practice%20and%20Parameters/Primary-prevention-allergic-disease-through-nutrition.pdf
Birch et al 1997. Ann N Y Acad Sci. 1997 May 23;819:194-220
http://www.cdc.gov/healthyweight/assessing/bmi/childrens_bmi/about_childrens_bmi.html
J Drugs Dermatol. 2014 Apr;13(4):428-35
Clin Dermatol. 2010 Nov-Dec;28(6):598-604
Robertson et al. *Am Fam Physician.* 2004 Jul 15;70(2):343-350

Dietary Reference Intakes (DRIs): Estimated Average Requirements
Food and Nutrition Board, Institute of Medicine, National Academies

Life Stage Group	Calcium (mg/d)	CHO (g/d)	Protein (g/kg/d)	Vit A (μg/d)[a]	Vit C (mg/d)	Vit D (μg/d)	Vit E (mg/d)[b]	Thiamin (mg/d)	Ribo-flavin (mg/d)	Niacin (mg/d)[c]	Vit B_6 (mg/d)	Folate (μg/d)[d]	Vit B_{12} (μg/d)	Copper (μg/d)	Iodine (μg/d)	Iron (mg/d)	Magnes-ium (mg/d)	Molyb-denum (μg/d)	Phos-phorus (mg/d)	Sele-nium (μg/d)	Zinc (mg/d)
Infants																					
0 to 6 mo																					
6 to 12 mo			1.0													6.9					2.5
Children																					
1–3 y	500	100	0.87	210	13	10	5	0.4	0.4	5	0.4	120	0.7	260	65	3.0	65	13	380	17	2.5
4–8 y	800	100	0.76	275	22	10	6	0.5	0.5	6	0.5	160	1.0	340	65	4.1	110	17	405	23	4.0
Males																					
9–13 y	1,100	100	0.76	445	39	10	9	0.7	0.8	9	0.8	250	1.5	540	73	5.9	200	26	1,055	35	7.0
14–18 y	1,100	100	0.73	630	63	10	12	1.0	1.1	12	1.1	330	2.0	685	95	7.7	340	33	1,055	45	8.5
19–30 y	800	100	0.66	625	75	10	12	1.0	1.1	12	1.1	320	2.0	700	95	6	330	34	580	45	9.4
31–50 y	800	100	0.66	625	75	10	12	1.0	1.1	12	1.1	320	2.0	700	95	6	350	34	580	45	9.4
51–70 y	800	100	0.66	625	75	10	12	1.0	1.1	12	1.4	320	2.0	700	95	6	350	34	580	45	9.4
> 70 y	1,000	100	0.66	625	75	10	12	1.0	1.1	12	1.4	320	2.0	700	95	6	350	34	580	45	9.4
Females																					
9–13 y	1,100	100	0.76	420	39	10	9	0.7	0.8	9	0.8	250	1.5	540	73	5.7	200	26	1,055	35	7.0
14–18 y	1,100	100	0.71	485	56	10	12	0.9	0.9	11	1.0	330	2.0	685	95	7.9	300	33	1,055	45	7.3
19–30 y	800	100	0.66	500	60	10	12	0.9	0.9	11	1.1	320	2.0	700	95	8.1	255	34	580	45	6.8
31–50 y	800	100	0.66	500	60	10	12	0.9	0.9	11	1.1	320	2.0	700	95	8.1	265	34	580	45	6.8
51–70 y	1,000	100	0.66	500	60	10	12	0.9	0.9	11	1.3	320	2.0	700	95	5	265	34	580	45	6.8
> 70 y	1,000	100	0.66	500	60	10	12	0.9	0.9	11	1.3	320	2.0	700	95	5	265	34	580	45	6.8
Pregnancy																					
14–18 y	1,000	135	0.88	530	66	10	12	1.2	1.2	14	1.6	520	2.2	785	160	23	335	40	1,055	49	10.5
19–30 y	800	135	0.88	550	70	10	12	1.2	1.2	14	1.6	520	2.2	800	160	22	290	40	580	49	9.5
31–50 y	800	135	0.88	550	70	10	12	1.2	1.2	14	1.6	520	2.2	800	160	22	300	40	580	49	9.5
Lactation																					
14–18 y	1,000	160	1.05	885	96	10	16	1.2	1.3	13	1.7	450	2.4	985	209	7	300	35	1,055	59	10.9
19–30 y	800	160	1.05	900	100	10	16	1.2	1.3	13	1.7	450	2.4	1,000	209	6.5	255	36	580	59	10.4
31–50 y	800	160	1.05	900	100	10	16	1.2	1.3	13	1.7	450	2.4	1,000	209	6.5	265	36	580	59	10.4

NOTE: An Estimated Average Requirement (EAR) is the average daily nutrient intake level estimated to meet the requirements of half of the healthy individuals in a group. EARs have not been established for vitamin K, pantothenic acid, biotin, choline, chromium, fluoride, manganese, or other nutrients not yet evaluated via the DRI process.

[a] As retinol activity equivalents (RAEs). 1 RAE = 1 μg retinol, 12 μg β-carotene, 24 μg α-carotene, or 24 μg β-cryptoxanthin. The RAE for dietary provitamin A carotenoids is two-fold greater than retinol equivalents (RE), whereas the RAE for preformed vitamin A is the same as RE.

[b] As α-tocopherol. α-Tocopherol includes *RRR*-α-tocopherol, the only form of α-tocopherol that occurs naturally in foods, and the *2R*-stereoisomeric forms of α-tocopherol (*RRR-*, *RSR-*, *RRS-*, and *RSS*-α-tocopherol) that occur in fortified foods and supplements. It does not include the *2S*-stereoisomeric forms of α-tocopherol (*SRR-*, *SSR-*, *SRS-*, and *SSS*-α-tocopherol), also found in fortified foods and supplements.

[c] As niacin equivalents (NE). 1 mg of niacin = 60 mg of tryptophan.

[d] As dietary folate equivalents (DFE). 1 DFE = 1 μg food folate = 0.6 μg of folic acid from fortified food or as a supplement consumed with food = 0.5 μg of a supplement taken on an empty stomach.

SOURCES: *Dietary Reference Intakes for Calcium, Phosphorous, Magnesium, Vitamin D, and Fluoride* (1997); *Dietary Reference Intakes for Thiamin, Riboflavin, Niacin, Vitamin B_6, Folate, Vitamin B_{12}, Pantothenic Acid, Biotin, and Choline* (1998); *Dietary Reference Intakes for Vitamin C, Vitamin E, Selenium, and Carotenoids* (2000); *Dietary Reference Intakes for Vitamin A, Vitamin K, Arsenic, Boron, Chromium, Copper, Iodine, Iron, Manganese, Molybdenum, Nickel, Silicon, Vanadium, and Zinc* (2001); *Dietary Reference Intakes for Energy, Carbohydrate, Fiber, Fat, Fatty Acids, Cholesterol, Protein, and Amino Acids* (2002/2005); and *Dietary Reference Intakes for Calcium and Vitamin D* (2011). These reports may be accessed via www.nap.edu.

Dietary Reference Intakes (DRIs): Recommended Dietary Allowances and Adequate Intakes, Vitamins

Food and Nutrition Board, Institute of Medicine, National Academies

Life Stage Group	Vitamin A (μg/d)[a]	Vitamin C (mg/d)	Vitamin D (μg/d)[b,c]	Vitamin E (mg/d)[d]	Vitamin K (μg/d)	Thiamin (mg/d)	Riboflavin (mg/d)	Niacin (mg/d)[e]	Vitamin B_6 (mg/d)	Folate (μg/d)[f]	Vitamin B_{12} (μg/d)	Pantothenic Acid (mg/d)	Biotin (μg/d)	Choline (mg/d)[g]
Infants														
0 to 6 mo	400*	40*	10	4*	2.0*	0.2*	0.3*	2*	0.1*	65*	0.4*	1.7*	5*	125*
6 to 12 mo	500*	50*	10	5*	2.5*	0.3*	0.4*	4*	0.3*	80*	0.5*	1.8*	6*	150*
Children														
1–3 y	**300**	**15**	**15**	**6**	30*	**0.5**	**0.5**	**6**	**0.5**	**150**	**0.9**	2*	8*	200*
4–8 y	**400**	**25**	**15**	**7**	55*	**0.6**	**0.6**	**8**	**0.6**	**200**	**1.2**	3*	12*	250*
Males														
9–13 y	**600**	**45**	**15**	**11**	60*	**0.9**	**0.9**	**12**	**1.0**	**300**	**1.8**	4*	20*	375*
14–18 y	**900**	**75**	**15**	**15**	75*	**1.2**	**1.3**	**16**	**1.3**	**400**	**2.4**	5*	25*	550*
19–30 y	**900**	**90**	**15**	**15**	120*	**1.2**	**1.3**	**16**	**1.3**	**400**	**2.4**	5*	30*	550*
31–50 y	**900**	**90**	**15**	**15**	120*	**1.2**	**1.3**	**16**	**1.3**	**400**	**2.4**	5*	30*	550*
51–70 y	**900**	**90**	**15**	**15**	120*	**1.2**	**1.3**	**16**	**1.7**	**400**	**2.4**[h]	5*	30*	550*
> 70 y	**900**	**90**	**20**	**15**	120*	**1.2**	**1.3**	**16**	**1.7**	**400**	**2.4**[h]	5*	30*	550*
Females														
9–13 y	**600**	**45**	**15**	**11**	60*	**0.9**	**0.9**	**12**	**1.0**	**300**	**1.8**	4*	20*	375*
14–18 y	**700**	**65**	**15**	**15**	75*	**1.0**	**1.0**	**14**	**1.2**	**400**[i]	**2.4**	5*	25*	400*
19–30 y	**700**	**75**	**15**	**15**	90*	**1.1**	**1.1**	**14**	**1.3**	**400**[i]	**2.4**	5*	30*	425*
31–50 y	**700**	**75**	**15**	**15**	90*	**1.1**	**1.1**	**14**	**1.3**	**400**[i]	**2.4**	5*	30*	425*
51–70 y	**700**	**75**	**15**	**15**	90*	**1.1**	**1.1**	**14**	**1.5**	**400**	**2.4**[h]	5*	30*	425*
> 70 y	**700**	**75**	**20**	**15**	90*	**1.1**	**1.1**	**14**	**1.5**	**400**	**2.4**[h]	5*	30*	425*
Pregnancy														
14–18 y	**750**	**80**	**15**	**15**	75*	**1.4**	**1.4**	**18**	**1.9**	**600**[j]	**2.6**	6*	30*	450*
19–30 y	**770**	**85**	**15**	**15**	90*	**1.4**	**1.4**	**18**	**1.9**	**600**[j]	**2.6**	6*	30*	450*
31–50 y	**770**	**85**	**15**	**15**	90*	**1.4**	**1.4**	**18**	**1.9**	**600**[j]	**2.6**	6*	30*	450*
Lactation														
14–18 y	**1,200**	**115**	**15**	**19**	75*	**1.4**	**1.6**	**17**	**2.0**	**500**	**2.8**	7*	35*	550*
19–30 y	**1,300**	**120**	**15**	**19**	90*	**1.4**	**1.6**	**17**	**2.0**	**500**	**2.8**	7*	35*	550*
31–50 y	**1,300**	**120**	**15**	**19**	90*	**1.4**	**1.6**	**17**	**2.0**	**500**	**2.8**	7*	35*	550*

NOTE: This table (taken from the DRI reports, see www.nap.edu) presents Recommended Dietary Allowances (RDAs) in **bold type** and Adequate Intakes (AIs) in ordinary type followed by an asterisk (*). An RDA is the average daily dietary intake level; sufficient to meet the nutrient requirements of nearly all (97-98 percent) healthy individuals in a group. It is calculated from an Estimated Average Requirement (EAR). If sufficient scientific evidence is not available to establish an EAR, and thus calculate an RDA, an AI is usually developed. For healthy breastfed infants, an AI is the mean intake. The AI for other life stage and gender groups is believed to cover the needs of all healthy individuals in the groups, but lack of data or uncertainty in the data prevent being able to specify with confidence the percentage of individuals covered by this intake.

[a] As retinol activity equivalents (RAEs). 1 RAE = 1 μg retinol, 12 μg β-carotene, 24 μg α-carotene, or 24 μg β-cryptoxanthin. The RAE for dietary provitamin A carotenoids is two-fold greater than retinol equivalents (RE), whereas the RAE for preformed vitamin A is the same as RE.

[b] As cholecalciferol. 1 μg cholecalciferol = 40 IU vitamin D.

[c] Under the assumption of minimal sunlight.

[d] As α-tocopherol. α-Tocopherol includes *RRR*-α-tocopherol, the only form of α-tocopherol that occurs naturally in foods, and the *2R*-stereoisomeric forms of α-tocopherol (*RRR-*, *RSR-*, *RRS-*, and *RSS*-α-tocopherol) that occur in fortified foods and supplements. It does not include the *2S*-stereoisomeric forms of α-tocopherol (*SRR-*, *SSR-*, *SRS-*, and *SSS*-α-tocopherol), also found in fortified foods and supplements.

[e] As niacin equivalents (NE). 1 mg of niacin = 60 mg of tryptophan; 0–6 months = preformed niacin (not NE).

[f] As dietary folate equivalents (DFE). 1 DFE = 1 μg food folate = 0.6 μg of folic acid from fortified food or as a supplement consumed with food = 0.5 μg of a supplement taken on an empty stomach.

[g] Although AIs have been set for choline, there are few data to assess whether a dietary supply of choline is needed at all stages of the life cycle, and it may be that the choline requirement can be met by endogenous synthesis at some of these stages.

[h] Because 10 to 30 percent of older people may malabsorb food-bound B_{12}, it is advisable for those older than 50 years to meet their RDA mainly by consuming foods fortified with B_{12} or a supplement containing B_{12}.

[i] In view of evidence linking folate intake with neural tube defects in the fetus, it is recommended that all women capable of becoming pregnant consume 400 μg from supplements or fortified foods in addition to intake of food folate from a varied diet.

[j] It is assumed that women will continue consuming 400 μg from supplements or fortified food until their pregnancy is confirmed and they enter prenatal care, which ordinarily occurs after the end of the periconceptional period—the critical time for formation of the neural tube.

SOURCES: *Dietary Reference Intakes for Calcium, Phosphorous, Magnesium, Vitamin D, and Fluoride* (1997); *Dietary Reference Intakes for Thiamin, Riboflavin, Niacin, Vitamin B₆, Folate, Vitamin B₁₂, Pantothenic Acid, Biotin, and Choline* (1998); *Dietary Reference Intakes for Vitamin C, Vitamin E, Selenium, and Carotenoids* (2000); *Dietary Reference Intakes for Vitamin A, Vitamin K, Arsenic, Boron, Chromium, Copper, Iodine, Iron, Manganese, Molybdenum, Nickel, Silicon, Vanadium, and Zinc* (2001); *Dietary Reference Intakes for Water, Potassium, Sodium, Chloride, and* Sulfate (2005); and *Dietary Reference Intakes for Calcium and Vitamin D* (2011). These reports may be accessed via www.nap.edu.

Dietary Reference Intakes (DRIs): Recommended Dietary Allowances and Adequate Intakes, Elements
Food and Nutrition Board, Institute of Medicine, National Academies

Life Stage Group	Calcium (mg/d)	Chromium (μg/d)	Copper (μg/d)	Fluoride (mg/d)	Iodine (μg/d)	Iron (mg/d)	Magnesium (mg/d)	Manganese (mg/d)	Molybdenum (μg/d)	Phosphorus (mg/d)	Selenium (μg/d)	Zinc (mg/d)	Potassium (g/d)	Sodium (g/d)	Chloride (g/d)
Infants															
0 to 6 mo	200*	0.2*	200*	0.01*	110*	0.27*	30*	0.003*	2*	100*	15*	2*	0.4*	0.12*	0.18*
6 to 12 mo	260*	5.5*	220*	0.5*	130*	**11**	75*	0.6*	3*	275*	20*	**3**	0.7*	0.37*	0.57*
Children															
1–3 y	**700**	11*	**340**	0.7*	**90**	**7**	**80**	1.2*	**17**	**460**	**20**	**3**	3.0*	1.0*	1.5*
4–8 y	**1,000**	15*	**440**	1*	**90**	**10**	**130**	1.5*	**22**	**500**	**30**	**5**	3.8*	1.2*	1.9*
Males															
9–13 y	**1,300**	25*	**700**	2*	**120**	**8**	**240**	1.9*	**34**	**1,250**	**40**	**8**	4.5*	1.5*	2.3*
14–18 y	**1,300**	35*	**890**	3*	**150**	**11**	**410**	2.2*	**43**	**1,250**	**55**	**11**	4.7*	1.5*	2.3*
19–30 y	**1,000**	35*	**900**	4*	**150**	**8**	**400**	2.3*	**45**	**700**	**55**	**11**	4.7*	1.5*	2.3*
31–50 y	**1,000**	35*	**900**	4*	**150**	**8**	**420**	2.3*	**45**	**700**	**55**	**11**	4.7*	1.5*	2.3*
51–70 y	**1,000**	30*	**900**	4*	**150**	**8**	**420**	2.3*	**45**	**700**	**55**	**11**	4.7*	1.3*	2.0*
> 70 y	**1,200**	30*	**900**	4*	**150**	**8**	**420**	2.3*	**45**	**700**	**55**	**11**	4.7*	1.2*	1.8*
Females															
9–13 y	**1,300**	21*	**700**	2*	**120**	**8**	**240**	1.6*	**34**	**1,250**	**40**	**8**	4.5*	1.5*	2.3*
14–18 y	**1,300**	24*	**890**	3*	**150**	**15**	**360**	1.6*	**43**	**1,250**	**55**	**9**	4.7*	1.5*	2.3*
19–30 y	**1,000**	25*	**900**	3*	**150**	**18**	**310**	1.8*	**45**	**700**	**55**	**8**	4.7*	1.5*	2.3*
31–50 y	**1,000**	25*	**900**	3*	**150**	**18**	**320**	1.8*	**45**	**700**	**55**	**8**	4.7*	1.5*	2.3*
51–70 y	**1,200**	20*	**900**	3*	**150**	**8**	**320**	1.8*	**45**	**700**	**55**	**8**	4.7*	1.3*	2.0*
> 70 y	**1,200**	20*	**900**	3*	**150**	**8**	**320**	1.8*	**45**	**700**	**55**	**8**	4.7*	1.2*	1.8*
Pregnancy															
14–18 y	**1,300**	29*	**1,000**	3*	**220**	**27**	**400**	2.0*	**50**	**1,250**	**60**	**12**	4.7*	1.5*	2.3*
19–30 y	**1,000**	30*	**1,000**	3*	**220**	**27**	**350**	2.0*	**50**	**700**	**60**	**11**	4.7*	1.5*	2.3*
31–50 y	**1,000**	30*	**1,000**	3*	**220**	**27**	**360**	2.0*	**50**	**700**	**60**	**11**	4.7*	1.5*	2.3*
Lactation															
14–18 y	**1,300**	44*	**1,300**	3*	**290**	**10**	**360**	2.6*	**50**	**1,250**	**70**	**13**	5.1*	1.5*	2.3*
19–30 y	**1,000**	45*	**1,300**	3*	**290**	**9**	**310**	2.6*	**50**	**700**	**70**	**12**	5.1*	1.5*	2.3*
31–50 y	**1,000**	45*	**1,300**	3*	**290**	**9**	**320**	2.6*	**50**	**700**	**70**	**12**	5.1*	1.5*	2.3*

NOTE: This table (taken from the DRI reports, see www.nap.edu) presents Recommended Dietary Allowances (RDAs) in **bold type** and Adequate Intakes (AIs) in ordinary type followed by an asterisk (*). An RDA is the average daily dietary intake level; sufficient to meet the nutrient requirements of nearly all (97-98 percent) healthy individuals in a group. It is calculated from an Estimated Average Requirement (EAR). If sufficient scientific evidence is not available to establish an EAR, and thus calculate an RDA, an AI is usually developed. For healthy breastfed infants, an AI is the mean intake. The AI for other life stage and gender groups is believed to cover the needs of all healthy individuals in the groups, but lack of data or uncertainty in the data prevent being able to specify with confidence the percentage of individuals covered by this intake.

SOURCES: *Dietary Reference Intakes for Calcium, Phosphorous, Magnesium, Vitamin D, and Fluoride* (1997); *Dietary Reference Intakes for Thiamin, Riboflavin, Niacin, Vitamin B_6, Folate, Vitamin B_{12}, Pantothenic Acid, Biotin, and Choline* (1998); *Dietary Reference Intakes for Vitamin C, Vitamin E, Selenium, and Carotenoids* (2000); and *Dietary Reference Intakes for Vitamin A, Vitamin K, Arsenic, Boron, Chromium, Copper, Iodine, Iron, Manganese, Molybdenum, Nickel, Silicon, Vanadium, and Zinc* (2001); *Dietary Reference Intakes for Water, Potassium, Sodium, Chloride, and* Sulfate (2005); and *Dietary Reference Intakes for Calcium and Vitamin D* (2011). These reports may be accessed via www.nap.edu.

Dietary Reference Intakes (DRIs): Recommended Dietary Allowances and Adequate Intakes, Total Water and Macronutrients

Food and Nutrition Board, Institute of Medicine, National Academies

Life Stage Group	*Total* Water[a] (L/d)	Carbohydrate (g/d)	Total Fiber (g/d)	Fat (g/d)	Linoleic Acid (g/d)	α-Linolenic Acid (g/d)	Protein[b] (g/d)
Infants							
0 to 6 mo	0.7*	60*	ND	31*	4.4*	0.5*	9.1*
6 to 12 mo	0.8*	95*	ND	30*	4.6*	0.5*	**11.0**
Children							
1–3 y	1.3*	**130**	19*	ND[c]	7*	0.7*	**13**
4–8 y	1.7*	**130**	25*	ND	10*	0.9*	**19**
Males							
9–13 y	2.4*	**130**	31*	ND	12*	1.2*	**34**
14–18 y	3.3*	**130**	38*	ND	16*	1.6*	**52**
19–30 y	3.7*	**130**	38*	ND	17*	1.6*	**56**
31–50 y	3.7*	**130**	38*	ND	17*	1.6*	**56**
51–70 y	3.7*	**130**	30*	ND	14*	1.6*	**56**
> 70 y	3.7*	**130**	30*	ND	14*	1.6*	**56**
Females							
9–13 y	2.1*	**130**	26*	ND	10*	1.0*	**34**
14–18 y	2.3*	**130**	26*	ND	11*	1.1*	**46**
19–30 y	2.7*	**130**	25*	ND	12*	1.1*	**46**
31–50 y	2.7*	**130**	25*	ND	12*	1.1*	**46**
51–70 y	2.7*	**130**	21*	ND	11*	1.1*	**46**
> 70 y	2.7*	**130**	21*	ND	11*	1.1*	**46**
Pregnancy							
14–18 y	3.0*	**175**	28*	ND	13*	1.4*	**71**
19–30 y	3.0*	**175**	28*	ND	13*	1.4*	**71**
31–50 y	3.0*	**175**	28*	ND	13*	1.4*	**71**
Lactation							
14–18	3.8*	**210**	29*	ND	13*	1.3*	**71**
19–30 y	3.8*	**210**	29*	ND	13*	1.3*	**71**
31–50 y	3.8*	**210**	29*	ND	13*	1.3*	**71**

NOTE: This table (take from the DRI reports, see www.nap.edu) presents Recommended Dietary Allowances (RDA) in **bold type** and Adequate Intakes (AI) in ordinary type followed by an asterisk (*). An RDA is the average daily dietary intake level; sufficient to meet the nutrient requirements of nearly all (97-98 percent) healthy individuals in a group. It is calculated from an Estimated Average Requirement (EAR). If sufficient scientific evidence is not available to establish an EAR, and thus calculate an RDA, an AI is usually developed. For healthy breastfed infants, an AI is the mean intake. The AI for other life stage and gender groups is believed to cover the needs of all healthy individuals in the groups, but lack of data or uncertainty in the data prevent being able to specify with confidence the percentage of individuals covered by this intake.

[a] *Total* water includes all water contained in food, beverages, and drinking water.

[b] Based on g protein per kg of body weight for the reference body weight, e.g., for adults 0.8 g/kg body weight for the reference body weight.

[c] Not determined.

SOURCE: *Dietary Reference Intakes for Energy, Carbohydrate, Fiber, Fat, Fatty Acids, Cholesterol, Protein, and Amino Acids* (2002/2005) and *Dietary Reference Intakes for Water, Potassium, Sodium, Chloride, and Sulfate* (2005). The report may be accessed via www.nap.edu.

Dietary Reference Intakes (DRIs): Acceptable Macronutrient Distribution Ranges

Food and Nutrition Board, Institute of Medicine, National Academies

Macronutrient	Range (percent of energy)		
	Children, 1–3 y	Children, 4–18 y	Adults
Fat	30–40	25–35	20–35
n-6 polyunsaturated fatty acids[a] (linoleic acid)	5–10	5–10	5–10
n-3 polyunsaturated fatty acids[a] (α-linolenic acid)	0.6–1.2	0.6–1.2	0.6–1.2
Carbohydrate	45–65	45–65	45–65
Protein	5–20	10–30	10–35

[a] Approximately 10 percent of the total can come from longer-chain *n*-3 or *n*-6 fatty acids.

SOURCE: *Dietary Reference Intakes for Energy, Carbohydrate, Fiber, Fat, Fatty Acids, Cholesterol, Protein, and Amino Acids* (2002/2005). The report may be accessed via www.nap.edu.

Dietary Reference Intakes (DRIs): Acceptable Macronutrient Distribution Ranges

Food and Nutrition Board, Institute of Medicine, National Academies

Macronutrient	Recommendation
Dietary cholesterol	As low as possible while consuming a nutritionally adequate diet
Trans fatty Acids	As low as possible while consuming a nutritionally adequate diet
Saturated fatty acids	As low as possible while consuming a nutritionally adequate diet
Added sugars[a]	Limit to no more than 25 % of total energy

[a]Not a recommended intake. A daily intake of added sugars that individuals should aim for to achieve a healthful diet was not set.

SOURCE: *Dietary Reference Intakes for Energy, Carbohydrate, Fiber, Fat, Fatty Acids, Cholesterol, Protein, and Amino Acids* (2002/2005). The report may be accessed via www.nap.edu.

Dietary Reference Intakes (DRIs): Tolerable Upper Intake Levels, Vitamins

Food and Nutrition Board, Institute of Medicine, National Academies

Life Stage Group	Vitamin A (µg/d)[a]	Vitamin C (mg/d)	Vitamin D (µg/d)	Vitamin E (mg/d)[b,c]	Vitamin K	Thiamin	Riboflavin	Niacin (mg/d)[c]	Vitamin B_6 (mg/d)	Folate (µg/d)[c]	Vitamin B_{12}	Pantothenic Acid	Biotin	Choline (g/d)	Carotenoids[d]
Infants															
0 to 6 mo	600	ND[e]	25	ND	ND	ND	ND	ND	ND	ND	ND	ND	ND	ND	ND
6 to 12 mo	600	ND	38	ND	ND	ND	ND	ND	ND	ND	ND	ND	ND	ND	ND
Children															
1–3 y	600	400	63	200	ND	ND	ND	10	30	300	ND	ND	ND	1.0	ND
4–8 y	900	650	75	300	ND	ND	ND	15	40	400	ND	ND	ND	1.0	ND
Males															
9–13 y	1,700	1,200	100	600	ND	ND	ND	20	60	600	ND	ND	ND	2.0	ND
14–18 y	2,800	1,800	100	800	ND	ND	ND	30	80	800	ND	ND	ND	3.0	ND
19–30 y	3,000	2,000	100	1,000	ND	ND	ND	35	100	1,000	ND	ND	ND	3.5	ND
31–50 y	3,000	2,000	100	1,000	ND	ND	ND	35	100	1,000	ND	ND	ND	3.5	ND
51–70 y	3,000	2,000	100	1,000	ND	ND	ND	35	100	1,000	ND	ND	ND	3.5	ND
> 70 y	3,000	2,000	100	1,000	ND	ND	ND	35	100	1,000	ND	ND	ND	3.5	ND
Females															
9–13 y	1,700	1,200	100	600	ND	ND	ND	20	60	600	ND	ND	ND	2.0	ND
14–18 y	2,800	1,800	100	800	ND	ND	ND	30	80	800	ND	ND	ND	3.0	ND
19–30 y	3,000	2,000	100	1,000	ND	ND	ND	35	100	1,000	ND	ND	ND	3.5	ND
31–50 y	3,000	2,000	100	1,000	ND	ND	ND	35	100	1,000	ND	ND	ND	3.5	ND
51–70 y	3,000	2,000	100	1,000	ND	ND	ND	35	100	1,000	ND	ND	ND	3.5	ND
> 70 y	3,000	2,000	100	1,000	ND	ND	ND	35	100	1,000	ND	ND	ND	3.5	ND
Pregnancy															
14–18 y	2,800	1,800	100	800	ND	ND	ND	30	80	800	ND	ND	ND	3.0	ND
19–30 y	3,000	2,000	100	1,000	ND	ND	ND	35	100	1,000	ND	ND	ND	3.5	ND
31–50 y	3,000	2,000	100	1,000	ND	ND	ND	35	100	1,000	ND	ND	ND	3.5	ND
Lactation															
14–18 y	2,800	1,800	100	800	ND	ND	ND	30	80	800	ND	ND	ND	3.0	ND
19–30 y	3,000	2,000	100	1,000	ND	ND	ND	35	100	1,000	ND	ND	ND	3.5	ND
31–50 y	3,000	2,000	100	1,000	ND	ND	ND	35	100	1,000	ND	ND	ND	3.5	ND

NOTE: A Tolerable Upper Intake Level (UL) is the highest level of daily nutrient intake that is likely to pose no risk of adverse health effects to almost all individuals in the general population. Unless otherwise specified, the UL represents total intake from food, water, and supplements. Due to a lack of suitable data, ULs could not be established for vitamin K, thiamin, riboflavin, vitamin B_{12}, pantothenic acid, biotin, and carotenoids. In the absence of a UL, extra caution may be warranted in consuming levels above recommended intakes. Members of the general population should be advised not to routinely exceed the UL. The UL is not meant to apply to individuals who are treated with the nutrient under medical supervision or to individuals with predisposing conditions that modify their sensitivity to the nutrient.

[a] As preformed vitamin A only.

[b] As α-tocopherol; applies to any form of supplemental α-tocopherol.

[c] The ULs for vitamin E, niacin, and folate apply to synthetic forms obtained from supplements, fortified foods, or a combination of the two.

[d] β-Carotene supplements are advised only to serve as a provitamin A source for individuals at risk of vitamin A deficiency.

[e] ND = Not determinable due to lack of data of adverse effects in this age group and concern with regard to lack of ability to handle excess amounts. Source of intake should be from food only to prevent high levels of intake.

SOURCES: *Dietary Reference Intakes for Calcium, Phosphorous, Magnesium, Vitamin D, and Fluoride* (1997); *Dietary Reference Intakes for Thiamin, Riboflavin, Niacin, Vitamin B_6, Folate, Vitamin B_{12}, Pantothenic Acid, Biotin, and Choline* (1998); *Dietary Reference Intakes for Vitamin C, Vitamine E, Selenium, and Carotenoids* (2000); *Dietary Reference Intakes for Vitamin A, Vitamin K, Arsenic, Boron, Chromium, Copper, Iodine, Iron, Manganese, Molybdenum, Nickel, Silicon, Vanadium, and Zinc* (2001); and *Dietary Reference Intakes for Calcium and Vitamin D* (2011). These reports may be accessed via www.nap.edu.

Dietary Reference Intakes (DRIs): Tolerable Upper Intake Levels, Elements

Food and Nutrition Board, Institute of Medicine, National Academies

Life Stage Group	Arsenic[a]	Boron (mg/d)	Calcium (mg/d)	Chromium	Copper (μg/d)	Fluoride (mg/d)	Iodine (μg/d)	Iron (mg/d)	Magnesium (mg/d)[b]	Manganese (mg/d)	Molybdenum (μg/d)	Nickel (mg/d)	Phosphorus (g/d)	Selenium (μg/d)	Silicon[c]	Vanadium (mg/d)[d]	Zinc (mg/d)	Sodium (g/d)	Chloride (g/d)
Infants																			
0 to 6 mo	ND[e]	ND	1,000	ND	ND	0.7	ND	40	ND	ND	ND	ND	ND	45	ND	ND	4	ND	ND
6 to 12 mo	ND	ND	1,500	ND	ND	0.9	ND	40	ND	ND	ND	ND	ND	60	ND	ND	5	ND	ND
Children																			
1–3 y	ND	3	2,500	ND	1,000	1.3	200	40	65	2	300	0.2	3	90	ND	ND	7	1.5	2.3
4–8 y	ND	6	2,500	ND	3,000	2.2	300	40	110	3	600	0.3	3	150	ND	ND	12	1.9	2.9
Males																			
9–13 y	ND	11	3,000	ND	5,000	10	600	40	350	6	1,100	0.6	4	280	ND	ND	23	2.2	3.4
14–18 y	ND	17	3,000	ND	8,000	10	900	45	350	9	1,700	1.0	4	400	ND	ND	34	2.3	3.6
19–30 y	ND	20	2,500	ND	10,000	10	1,100	45	350	11	2,000	1.0	4	400	ND	1.8	40	2.3	3.6
31–50 y	ND	20	2,500	ND	10,000	10	1,100	45	350	11	2,000	1.0	4	400	ND	1.8	40	2.3	3.6
51–70 y	ND	20	2,000	ND	10,000	10	1,100	45	350	11	2,000	1.0	4	400	ND	1.8	40	2.3	3.6
> 70 y	ND	20	2,000	ND	10,000	10	1,100	45	350	11	2,000	1.0	3	400	ND	1.8	40	2.3	3.6
Females																			
9–13 y	ND	11	3,000	ND	5,000	10	600	40	350	6	1,100	0.6	4	280	ND	ND	23	2.2	3.4
14–18 y	ND	17	3,000	ND	8,000	10	900	45	350	9	1,700	1.0	4	400	ND	ND	34	2.3	3.6
19–30 y	ND	20	2,500	ND	10,000	10	1,100	45	350	11	2,000	1.0	4	400	ND	1.8	40	2.3	3.6
31–50 y	ND	20	2,500	ND	10,000	10	1,100	45	350	11	2,000	1.0	4	400	ND	1.8	40	2.3	3.6
51–70 y	ND	20	2,000	ND	10,000	10	1,100	45	350	11	2,000	1.0	4	400	ND	1.8	40	2.3	3.6
> 70 y	ND	20	2,000	ND	10,000	10	1,100	45	350	11	2,000	1.0	3	400	ND	1.8	40	2.3	3.6
Pregnancy																			
14–18 y	ND	17	3,000	ND	8,000	10	900	45	350	9	1,700	1.0	3.5	400	ND	ND	34	2.3	3.6
19–30 y	ND	20	2,500	ND	10,000	10	1,100	45	350	11	2,000	1.0	3.5	400	ND	ND	40	2.3	3.6
31–50 y	ND	20	2,500	ND	10,000	10	1,100	45	350	11	2,000	1.0	3.5	400	ND	ND	40	2.3	3.6
Lactation																			
14–18 y	ND	17	3,000	ND	8,000	10	900	45	350	9	1,700	1.0	4	400	ND	ND	34	2.3	3.6
19–30 y	ND	20	2,500	ND	10,000	10	1,100	45	350	11	2,000	1.0	4	400	ND	ND	40	2.3	3.6
31–50 y	ND	20	2,500	ND	10,000	10	1,100	45	350	11	2,000	1.0	4	400	ND	ND	40	2.3	3.6

NOTE: A Tolerable Upper Intake Level (UL) is the highest level of daily nutrient intake that is likely to pose no risk of adverse health effects to almost all individuals in the general population. Unless otherwise specified, the UL represents total intake from food, water, and supplements. Due to a lack of suitable data, ULs could not be established for vitamin K, thiamin, riboflavin, vitamin B_{12}, pantothenic acid, biotin, and carotenoids. In the absence of a UL, extra caution may be warranted in consuming levels above recommended intakes. Members of the general population should be advised not to routinely exceed the UL. The UL is not meant to apply to individuals who are treated with the nutrient under medical supervision or to individuals with predisposing conditions that modify their sensitivity to the nutrient.

[a] Although the UL was not determined for arsenic, there is no justification for adding arsenic to food or supplements.

[b] The ULs for magnesium represent intake from a pharmacological agent only and do not include intake from food and water.

[c] Although silicon has not been shown to cause adverse effects in humans, there is no justification for adding silicon to supplements.

[d] Although vanadium in food has not been shown to cause adverse effects in humans, there is no justification for adding vanadium to food and vanadium supplements should be used with caution. The UL is based on adverse effects in laboratory animals and this data could be used to set a UL for adults but not children and adolescents.

[e] ND = Not determinable due to lack of data of adverse effects in this age group and concern with regard to lack of ability to handle excess amounts. Source of intake should be from food only to prevent high levels of intake.

SOURCES: *Dietary Reference Intakes for Calcium, Phosphorous, Magnesium, Vitamin D, and Fluoride* (1997); *Dietary Reference Intakes for Thiamin, Riboflavin, Niacin, Vitamin B_6, Folate, Vitamin B_{12}, Pantothenic Acid, Biotin, and Choline* (1998); *Dietary Reference Intakes for Vitamin C, Vitamin E, Selenium, and Carotenoids* (2000); *Dietary Reference Intakes for Vitamin A, Vitamin K, Arsenic, Boron, Chromium, Copper, Iodine, Iron, Manganese, Molybdenum, Nickel, Silicon, Vanadium, and Zinc* (2001); *Dietary Reference Intakes for Water, Potassium, Sodium, Chloride, and Sulfate* (2005); and *Dietary Reference Intakes for Calcium and Vitamin D* (2011). These reports may be accessed via www.nap.edu.

Index

A

B

C

D

E

F

G

H

I

J

K

L

M

N

O

P

Q

R

S

T

U

V

W

Z